AF742547

Mae'r eitem yma ar gael i chi hyd y dyddiad neu'r amser a nodir isod, oni bai fod darllenydd arall yn ei alw'n ôl ynghynt.

This item is on loan to you until the date or time shown below, unless it is recalled sooner by another borrower.

10/4/14

16/4/14.

15.05.14

GATS AND THE REGULATION OF INTERNATIONAL TRADE IN SERVICES

This collection of essays takes stock of the key challenges that have arisen since the entry into force of the General Agreement on Trade in Services in the mid-1990s and situates them in the context of the WTO's Doha Development Agenda and the proliferation of preferential agreements addressing services today. The multidisciplinary approach provides an opportunity for many of the world's leading experts and a number of new analytical voices to exchange ideas on the future of services trade and regulation. Cosmopolitan approaches to the treatment of labour mobility, the shape of services trade disciplines in the digital age and pro-competitive regulation in air transport are explored with a view to helping readers gain a better understanding of the forces shaping the changes. An essential read for all those concerned with the evolution of the rules-based trading system and its impact on the service economy.

MARION PANIZZON is Senior Research Fellow at the World Trade Institute, Berne. She specialises in international economic law, a field in which she publishes on subjects as diverse as intellectual property law, human rights and trade, services and sources of law.

NICOLE POHL held the position of Director of Studies at the World Trade Institute until October 2007. Since November 2007, she has been working with the School of Management at Zurich University of Applied Sciences to prepare the launch of several new Master programmes.

PIERRE SAUVÉ is a faculty member and senior research fellow at the World Trade Institute in Berne where he directs a Swiss National Science Foundation project on the regulation of trade in services. He holds visiting professor appointments at the London School of Economics and Political Science, the College of Europe in Bruges and at the University of Barcelona.

GATS AND THE REGULATION OF INTERNATIONAL TRADE IN SERVICES

Edited by

MARION PANIZZON,

NICOLE POHL

and

PIERRE SAUVÉ

CAMBRIDGE
UNIVERSITY PRESS

LLYFRGELL PRIFYSGOL BANGOR UNIVERSITY LIBRARY

CAMBRIDGE UNIVERSITY PRESS
Cambridge, New York, Melbourne, Madrid, Cape Town, Singapore, São Paulo, Delhi

Cambridge University Press
The Edinburgh Building, Cambridge CB2 8RU, UK

Published in the United States of America by Cambridge University Press, New York

www.cambridge.org
Information on this title: www.cambridge.org/9780521896887

© Cambridge University Press 2008

This publication is in copyright. Subject to statutory exception
and to the provisions of relevant collective licensing agreements,
no reproduction of any part may take place without
the written permission of Cambridge University Press.

First published 2008

Printed in the United Kingdom at the University Press, Cambridge

A catalogue record for this publication is available from the British Library

ISBN 978-0-521-89688-7 hardback

Cambridge University Press has no responsibility for the persistence or
accuracy of URLs for external or third-party internet websites referred to
in this book, and does not guarantee that any content on such
websites is, or will remain, accurate or appropriate.

BU Law Library
K3973 .G38 2008
30110008230568

GATS and the regulation of international
trade in services

CONTENTS

CONTRIBUTORS

RUDOLF ADLUNG, Senior Economist, World Trade Organization, Trade in Services Division, Geneva

MIREILLE COSSY, Counsellor, World Trade Organization, Trade in Services Division, Geneva

WILLIAM DAVEY, Guy Raymond Jones Chair, University of Illinois College of Law

PANAGIOTIS DELIMATSIS, Senior Research Fellow, World Trade Institute, University of Berne

NORA DIHEL, Economist, Chief Economist Unit, European Commission – DG Trade

FELIX ESCHENBACH, Post-Doctoral Researcher, Groupe d'Economie Mondiale, Sciences Po, Paris

CARSTEN FINK, Senior Economist, World Bank Institute, Geneva

HENRY GAO, Assistant Professor, Faculty of Law, University of Hong Kong

MARK GLYNN, Doctoral Candidate, Institute of Air and Space Law, McGill University, Montreal

RICHARD JANDA, Associate Professor, Faculty of Law, Institute of Air and Space Law, McGill University, Montreal

MARION JANSEN, Counsellor, World Trade Organization, Geneva

CLARE KELLY, Counsellor, Permanent Mission of New Zealand to the World Trade Organization, Geneva

MARKUS KRAJEWSKI, Professor, University of Potsdam

KANITHA KUNGSAWANICH, Counsellor, Thailand Permanent Mission to the World Trade Organization, Geneva

ERIC LEROUX, Senior Counsel, Trade Law Bureau, Government of Canada

AIK HOE LIM, Counsellor, World Trade Organization, Trade in Services Division, Geneva

JUAN MARCHETTI, Counsellor, World Trade Organization, Trade in Services Division, WTO Secretariat, Geneva

MARTIN MOLINUEVO, Research Fellow, World Trade Institute, University of Berne

DEUNDEN NIKOMBORIRAK, Research Director for Economic Governance, Sectoral Economics Program, Thailand Development Research Institute, Bangkok

MARION PANIZZON, Senior Research Fellow, World Trade Institute, and Lecturer, University of Berne

CHRISTIAN PAULETTO, Head, Swiss State Secretariat for Economic Affairs, Berne

JOOST PAUWELYN, Professor, Duke University School of Law, Durham, NC

FERNANDO PIEROLA, Counsel, Advisory Centre on WTO Law, Geneva

NICOLE POHL, Director of Studies, World Trade Institute, University of Berne

PIETRO PORETTI, Visiting Fellow, Georgetown University Law Center, Washington, DC and PhD Candidate, University of Berne

MARTIN ROY, Counsellor, World Trade Organization, Trade in Services Division, Geneva

PIERRE SAUVÉ, Visiting Professor, London School of Economics and Senior Research Fellow, World Trade Institute, University of Berne

BEN SHEPHERD, Consultant, Development Economics Research Group, The World Bank

ANDREW W. SHOYER, Partner, Sidley Austin LLP, Washington, DC

ELISABETH TÜRK, Economic Affairs Officer, United Nations Conference on Trade and Development, Division on International Trade in Goods, Services and Commodities, Geneva

SIMON WALKER, Advisor on Human Rights and Disability, Office of the United Nations High Commissioner for Human Rights, UNOG–OHCHR, Geneva

SACHA WUNSCH-VINCENT, Counsellor, Organisation for Economic Co-operation and Development (OECD), Paris and Institute for International Economics, Washington, DC

FIGURES

TABLES

ABBREVIATIONS

ACP	African, Caribbean and Pacific Group
AIMS	American Institute of Merchant Shipping
AFAS	ASEAN Framework on Services
AIA	ASEAN Investment Area
AIMS	American Institute of Merchant Shipping
ANZCERTA	Australia New Zealand Closer Economic Relations Trade Agreement
AoA	Agreement on Agriculture
ASCM	Agreement on Subsidies and Countervailing Measures
APEC	Asia-Pacific Economic Cooperation
APT	Asia Pacific Telecommunity
ASEAN	Association of Southeast Asian Nations
BIT	bilateral investment treaty
BOP	balance of payments
CAFTA	Central American Free Trade Agreement
CENSA	Council of European and Japanese National Shipowners' Associations
CEPA	Closer Economic Partnership Arrangement
CEPII	Centre d'études prospectives et d'informations internationales
CISG	Convention on Contracts for the International Sale of Goods
CPC	Central Product Classification
CRNM	Caribbean Regional Negotiating Machinery
CTG	Council for Trade in Goods
CTS	Council for Trade in Services
DDA	Doha Development Agenda
DSB	Dispute Settlement Body
DWP	Doha Work Programme
DSM	(WTO) dispute settlement mechanism

DSU	Understanding on Rules and Proceedings Governing the Settlement of Disputes
ECAA	European Common Aviation Area
ECLAC	Economic Commission for Latin America and the Caribbean
EFTA	European Free Trade Association
EIA	economic integration agreement
ESM	emergency safeguard mechanism
FATS	Foreign Affiliates Trade in Services
FDI	foreign direct investment
FTA	free trade agreement
FTAP	fair and transparent arbitration process
GATS	General Agreement on Trade in Services
GATT	General Agreement on Tariffs and Trade
GDP	gross domestic product
GPA	Agreement on Government Procurement
GTAP	Global Trade Analysis Project
HS	harmonised system
IATA	International Air Transport Association
ICAO	International Civil Aviation Organization
ICSE	International Classification of Status in Employment
ICSID Convention	Washington Convention on the Settlement of Investment Disputes between States and Nationals of Other States
ICT	information communication technologies
ICTSD	International Centre for Trade and Sustainable Development
IBD	Inter-American Development Bank
IIA	international investment agreement
ILC	International Law Commission
ILO	International Labour Organization
ISCO	International Standard Classification of Occupations
ITU	International Telecommunications Union
LDC	least-developed country
LRP	licensing requirements and procedures
M&A	mergers and acquisitions
MAI	Multilateral Agreement on Investment
MALIAT	Multilateral Agreement on the Liberalisation of International Air Transportation (Kona open skies agreement)

MAT	marine, aviation and transport
MENA	Middle East and North Africa
MFN	most-favoured nation
MRA	mutual recognition agreement
NAFTA	North American Free Trade Agreement
NAMA	non-agricultural market access
NGBT	Negotiating Group on Basic Telecommunications
NGMTS	Decision establishing the Negotiating Group on Maritime Transport Services
NTB	non-tariff barriers
OECD	Organisation for Economic Co-operation and Development
PTA	preferential trade agareement
QRP	qualification requirements and procedures
RIA	regional integration agreement
RTA	regional trade agreement
SPS	(Agreement on) Sanitary and Phytosanitary Measures
SSCL	Services Sectoral Classification List
TBT	(Agreement on) Technical Barriers to Trade
TDB	Trade and Development Board
TRI	trade restrictiveness index
TRIPS	trade-related aspects of intellectual property rights
TS	technical standards
UNCITRAL	United Nations Commission on International Trade Law
UNCTAD	UN Conference on Trade and Development
VCLT	Vienna Convention on the Law of Treaties
WIPO	World Intellectual Property Organization
WPDR	Working Party on Domestic Regulation
WPGR	Working Party on GATS Rules
WPPS	Working Party on Professional Services
WTO	World Trade Organization

PREFACE

The World Trade Forum series was established to help spread the conviction that a multidisciplinary approach to international trade is warranted. The 10th World Trade Forum was held from 20–22 September 2006 at the World Trade Institute of the University of Berne on the theme of the General Agreement on Trade in Services (GATS). The participants were in broad agreement that, in its present shape and form, GATS insufficiently promotes further liberalisation of services. But, during the conference, it became apparent that scholars, practitioners and government officials were committed to improving the way services trade is conducted. Valuable proposals for progress were tabled and researched and have led to this collection of essays viewing trade in services from a variety of perspectives, domestic and international, economic and legal, past and future. Thus, the 10th World Trade Forum could not have successfully taken place without the active involvement of the participants, many of whom contributed to the articles collected in this volume now entitled 'GATS and the Regulation of International Trade in Services'.

Thus, we wish to thank the authors of the chapters in this collection who have worked beyond the call of duty to accommodate the guidelines and suggestions of the editors. We are also grateful for the support of the Ecoscientia Foundation, which helped to make the conference a truly engaging event for everyone involved and facilitated the in-house editing process at the World Trade Institute. Organising the conference required true teamwork from all those involved and their efforts were much appreciated. Thanks are also due to the in-house scientific editor, Susan Kaplan and her assistant, Jane Müller, for preparing the manuscript. Moreover, we wish to express our gratitude to the administrative staff of the World Trade Institute, especially Margrit Vetter and Stephan Deutsch for their capable organisation of the event. This book would not have been possible without the funding of the Swiss National Science Foundation in support of the National Centre for Competence in

Research (NCCR) Trade Regulation. The editors are indebted to NCCR Trade Regulation's Director, Professor Thomas Cottier, for establishing the contact with Cambridge University Press and selecting GATS as the topic of the 10th World Trade Forum. Thanks also go to the scientific coordinator of NCCR Trade Regulation, Susan Brown, whose foresight enabled this 10th World Trade Forum conference, and this volume, to mark the beginning of a tradition of joint effort between the World Trade Institute and the NCCR Trade Regulation. Such a high-level exchange of expertise on services trade would not have been possible without the guidance of Pierre Sauvé, the leader of the NCCR Trade Regulation's project on services. The co-editors of this volume, Marion Panizzon, the alternate leader of NCCR's project on services and Nicole Pohl, the World Trade Institute's Director of Studies, are indebted to Pierre Sauvé for his significant role in encouraging high-level participation in the 10th World Trade Forum conference and making the event an interesting one for all those who attended.

Last, but not least, we wish to thank Finola O'Sullivan from Cambridge University Press for her commitment to the book project. Conceptualised as a reference volume, we hope that this book will complement and update other publications on international trade in services and find an interested, yet critical readership, ready to shape the future of a cosmopolitan regime for services trade.

PART 1

Beyond regulatory control and multilateral flexibility: Gains from a cosmopolitan GATS

1

Testing regulatory autonomy, disciplining trade relief and regulating variable peripheries: Can a cosmopolitan GATS do it all?

MARION PANIZZON AND NICOLE POHL

The Doha Round seeks to fulfil the mandate of progressive liberalisation inscribed in the General Agreement on Trade in Services (GATS). Members of the World Trade Organization (WTO) agreed to progressively negotiate market access and equal conditions of competition in more services sectors to achieve both a deepening and widening of services trade liberalisation beyond the actual status quo of commitments laid down in GATS during the Uruguay Round. Yet the main benchmark of progress against which a services trade regime will be measured post-Doha lies in formulating behind-the-border disciplines on domestic regulation, agreeing on comprehensive multilateral trade exits, such as trade remedies and temporary import relief, as well as in fostering mutually supportive relationships with services-related agreements, such as in the field of air transport, labour migration, energy and health.

This collection of essays entitled 'GATS and the Regulation of International Trade in Services' analyses two periods of cross-border service supply – the post-Uruguay Round era of multilateral and plurilateral liberalisation, with the associated standardisation of services regulation worldwide and development of a services-specific case law on GATS disputes, and the process, postulates and progress of the current Doha Round negotiations – and speculates on the post-Doha GATS regime.

Services trade is an insufficiently studied field in academia, yet services constitute the complex, higher-value work that affords many countries a competitive advantage on the global labour market. The value of services exports worldwide has increased substantially from US$ 17,439.9 million in 2001 to US$ 26,319.3 million in 2004.[1] Services have become engines of growth for many economies and the added value of services as a share of GDP has reached levels higher than 70 per cent in high-income countries and nearly 50 per cent in low-income countries.[2] At the same time, the share of services in international trade has remained below 20 per cent.[3] The continuing technological revolution has significantly enhanced the tradability of many services, emphasising the gap between the potential benefits from services liberalisation, not least because of the trickle-down effects for other sectors, and actual gains from such trade. Therefore, rules conducive to international trade in services and a framework that permits and promotes the gradual liberalisation of the sector were and are important elements of the trade agenda.

Nearly half a century of negotiations in goods markets has taught negotiators that a decade is not a long time when the output has to be assessed in terms of trade liberalisation measures requiring consent from all WTO Members. Looking at services liberalisation ten years after the conclusion of the Uruguay Round, one sees that a decade is a very short time indeed for negotiating free trade in a sector:

- for which there is no international agreement on the state-of-the-art for regulatory standards or on the objectives of regulation;
- which permits trade in several modes, not all of which are yet well understood and for each of which the range of imaginable measures to limit competition seems limitless;
- in which the needs of developing and developed countries differ significantly; and
- for which reliable data are difficult to come by.

Although progress in services liberalisation has sometimes been perceived as difficult and too slow, the GATS provides quite a comprehensive and complex framework of multilateral disciplines. Nonetheless, opinions regarding the best path to liberalisation differ, creating uncertainty as to whether a regime of multilateral disciplines for services paralleling those that already exist for goods would be the best option. While disciplines for goods are complex and controversial, as arguments

[1] Figures from OECD Manual on Statistics of International Trade in Services; the data concern trade between residents and non-residents of countries and are presented in millions of US dollars.

[2] Figures from WTO Secretariat, Measuring Trade in Services, March 2006, for 2005.

[3] Figures from WTO Secretariat, International Trade Statistics 2005, for 2004.

over safeguards and trade remedies demonstrate, the services sector reveals even more idiosyncrasies to force negotiators to revisit relatively basic questions such as how to measure trade or how to define like products.

The Doha Development Agenda seeks to advance the built-in agenda for services of the Uruguay Round, which Members failed to finalise. Thus, the Doha Declaration did not introduce any new negotiating mandate for services. Instead, the General Council incorporated the pre-existing negotiating mandates of GATS relating to domestic regulation, subsidies, emergency safeguards and government procurement into the Doha Round negotiations. Nevertheless, much has changed for global trade in services in between the Uruguay Round and the Doha Round.

To most authors, the basis for the challenges facing the post-Doha services regime lies within the GATS itself: the flexibility in rule-making and regulation hampers advances in recognition of services disciplines, the divide between deepening horizontal or increasing sector-specific commitments together with the asymmetry between modes of supply, such as the scarcity of mode 4 commitments relative to other modes,[4] threatens meaningful progressive liberalisation. The timing and manner of tackling the unfinished rule-making mandates deepens the divide between developing and industrialised countries.[5]

While the content of discussions, the negotiating positions and the level of commitment relating to the treaty's working programme have remained the same since the establishment of GATS, the political economy and the legal questions of services trade have matured during the first ten years of existence of the multilateral legal framework for services trade. For example, cosmopolitan concerns about expanding the scope of GATS to labour mobility under mode 4, to include air transport services, e-commerce and energy trading into GATS, characterise the debate about the scope of GATS today. Proponents of distributive fairness of GATS relating to the universality of access to services in essential sectors, such as education, health and water, seek a clarification of the underlying policy goals of the GATS. On the issue of sovereignty, governments are faced with a trade-off between committing more sectors to liberalisation

[4] See WTO CTS, Communication from Argentina, Bolivia, Brazil, Chile, Colombia, India, Mexico, Pakistan, Peru, Philippines, Thailand and Uruguay, Categories of Natural Persons for Commitments under Mode 4 of GATS, TN/S/W/31, 18 February 2005.

[5] See WTO CTS, Communication from Switzerland, Temporary Admission of Installers and Maintainers under the GATS: A Case for Mode 4 Commitments, TN/S/W/61, 2 April 2007, as an example for broadening its horizontal commitments on mode 4 by the category of 'installers and maintainers'.

and offering deeper commitments in existing sectors while retaining a degree of regulatory autonomy over quality control of services supplied.[6] This introduction seeks to set the stage for the following debates in the various chapters by questioning whether a cosmopolitan GATS can do it all: testing regulatory autonomy, disciplining trade relief and regulating variable peripheries. The notion of cosmopolitanism stands for a two-tiered regulatory direction of GATS. In a horizontal dimension, cosmopolitanism establishes a coherent and open relationship to other services-related public international norms and private standards. In a vertical dimension, cosmopolitan services regulation expresses the multi-levelled regulatory jurisdiction linking multilateral disciplines with regional and domestic regulatory autonomy. A third and normative value qualifies the cosmopolitan services supply as one which respects basic human rights, including core labour standards, as well as one which realises a measure of distributive equity of supply and universality of access to essential services.

The choice is one between regulatory competition and transnational regulatory approximation or one between more cosmopolitan content of rules (such as temporary import relief, subsidies, government procurement) or regulatory autonomy for technical standards and licensing requirements. Should GATS seek to define a standard of harmonisation and, if so, how much would such standards reduce the policy space of domestic regulators? Or, should WTO Members agree instead on introducing regulatory competition among WTO Members and how could developing countries keep up in such a situation? To what extent could disciplines in services be set up by drawing on lessons learnt from the goods sector or does the sound regulation of trade in services require an approach distinct from that of the goods regime? To what extent does the GATS model of liberalisation spill over to other services fields governed up to now by non-WTO international norms, such as air transport services, labour migration, accounting and prudential disciplines in finance?

Yet more mundane questions than those relating to unfinished rule-making and the degree of regulatory impact must be asked: how could WTO Members be lured into increasing what some consider to be the disappointingly low liberalisation gains of commitments? How could the emergence of plurilateral and regional free trade agreements be

[6] See Panagiotis Delimatsis, 'Due Process and "Good" Regulation Embedded in the GATS – Disciplining Regulatory Behaviour in Services through Article VI of the GATS', *Journal of International Economic Law* 10(1) (2006), pp. 13–50.

monitored for their compatibility with GATS? What issues or which GATS provisions characterised the first decade of GATS jurisprudence from its beginnings in *EC – Bananas* in 1997, when GATS was only dealt with as an accessory to goods to the first two self-standing GATS cases, *Mexico – Telecoms* in 2004 and *US – Gambling* in 2005?

Since only a pluridisciplinary approach to services trade can capture the complex interconnectedness of regulation, liberalisation and negotiation or compare the cosmopolitan nature of multilateral liberalisation with the effectiveness of regionalism, the organisers of the Forum on International Trade in Services – New Perspectives on Liberalisation, Regulation and Development, held in September 2006 at the World Trade Institute of the University of Berne, Switzerland – brought together trade lawyers and economists, as well as political scientists to debate the open issues of GATS and pre-empt new challenges. The resulting collection of essays thus captures the shift in the impact of the GATS from being a classic beacon of trade liberalisation to a behind-the-border promoter of constitutional change.

Participants were asked to take a cross-cutting approach as opposed to making a sector-specific analysis of trade in services. Most contributions use modes of liberalisation and sectoral themes to illustrate specific legal, economic or political challenges to GATS as opposed to discussing a mode of service supply or market access in a sector as an issue in itself. The two exceptions are a chapter on investment in services disputes dealing with mode 3 and a chapter dealing with the air transport services sector.

Drawing on the expertise of the participants from the academic, trade negotiating, regulatory and private sectors, following the introduction, the second part of the book is devoted to economic issues and commercial interests in GATS and the final part covers the political and economic implications of liberalisation of trade in services. Most authors however, discuss legal issues of services trade. The book aims to serve as a reference guide on international trade in services in the context of the GATS, its negotiating methods as well as its emerging jurisprudence. Structurally, the book's eight parts mirror the GATS' identity set around the three pillars of liberalisation, regulation and negotiations.

The book examines the experiences and challenges coming out of a decade of negotiations that are not specific to particular services sectors. Thus, the chapters reflect the challenge of removing distortions that impede the ability of foreign service suppliers to be placed on an equal footing with domestic ones. Another cross-cutting issue dealt with is the benefits of GATS for developing countries, for example, how GATS induces reform of domestic law, the increased level of efficiency resulting from more competition and how the dismantling of barriers to foreign services could produce the much needed inflows of capital, investment and skilled labour. On the other hand, many contributions also deal with the overall obstruction of the capacity for openness towards foreign service providers. Such obstructions result from the reluctance to take commitments beyond those locking in the status quo, either because of strategic motivations, such as membership of preferential trade agreements, or because of the 'regulatory weakness' of the GATS, the lack of economic infrastructure and the scarcity of information about relevant services markets.

While the main aim of this book is to evaluate and rethink strategies for liberalising services, taking into account the experience of the last decade, it also examines new avenues for services liberalisation. They show that, in some areas of services liberalisation, although the work agenda is relatively clear, a lot of work needs to be done. At the same time, there are other areas where the agenda has not yet even been defined.

The rest of the book is divided into seven parts. Part 2 deals with 'unexplored economic dimensions', in which trade economists consider the main points of the debate on trade in services and the GATS from an economic viewpoint. It examines the desirability and effects of preferential, often GATS-plus services trade agreements, as opposed to multilateral liberalisation, the relevance of services trade for developing countries, the lack of appropriate data, as well as the emergence of services-specific rules of origin. Using the South–South services trade agreements to demonstrate the fragmentation of services trade into regional and sectoral GATS-plus agreements, Roy, Marchetti and Lim (chapter 3) impressively illustrate how bilateral and regional agreements with levels of commitments higher than those in GATS are being negotiated among developing countries. These authors provide for a qualitative assessment of GATS-plus commitments in preferential trade agreements finding a mixture of new and improved bindings combined with levels of openness that exceed Doha Round offers, in particular in agreements with the US, but with differences across modes of supply. They use evidence from the South–South agreements to demonstrate how the relevance of services trade for developing countries has a bearing on the perceived interests and trade-offs in trade negotiations at both the bilateral and multilateral levels. While they find problems of compliance with Article V GATS in services sectors the fact that in contrast to GATT, which does not provide for non-reciprocal treatment in MFN exceptions, the GATS is equipped in Article V:3 with a specific exception for allowing special and differential treatment in South–South trade agreements, suggests that the flexibility in GATS may at times also work in favour of developing country members.[7] Given such new trading opportunities for developing countries, it is suggested that perhaps trade in services is not exclusive to the agendas of developed countries, although some commentators maintain that the virtual absence of commitments in modes 3 and 4 renders GATS irrelevant for developing countries and reflects the fundamental imbalance or bias of GATS towards industrialised countries.

Sufficient data on trade in services for an economic assessment of the effects of barriers to trade in services are as yet unavailable, as the chapter by Dihel, Eschenbach and Shepherd makes clear (chapter 2). Dihel and her co-authors, however, suggest two ways to compensate for the lack of data: first, by suggesting a gravity model approach using foreign direct investment stocks as proxies for trade in services in mode 3; second, by providing figures on South–South services trade which, according to their analysis, takes place predominantly at the regional level. The relevance of bilateral and preferential agreements and the different modes of service supply combined with the diverse nature of trade barriers to services liberalisation add complexity to the topic. Rules of origin have often been seen as potentially protectionist sources of complexity for the goods sector. The research on the effects of different rules of origin in the goods sector is still in its early stages and for the services sector, the level of understanding is still lower. This is the starting point for the research done by Fink and Nikomborirak (chapter 4), who assess the implications of different rules of origin for five Association of Southeast Asian Nations (ASEAN) countries. Their work points to domestic ownership and control as well as incorporation as the most important rule of origin criteria and they note a number of implementation issues related to these criteria. Fink and Nikomborirak lead the way for further research on rules of origin, but also show that rapid liberalisation is not always conducive to the efficient functioning of services trade, since areas

[7] See Cosmas M. Ochieng, 'The EU-ACP Economic Partnership Agreements and the "Development Question": Constraints and Opportunities Posed by Article XXIV and Special and Differential Treatment Provisions of the WTO', *Journal of International Economic Law* 10(2) (2007), pp. 374–377.

characterised by a high level of technical complexity may not get the attention necessary to ensure sound implementation of rules of origin.

Part 3 entitled 'the limits of request–offer negotiations: plurilateral and alternative approaches to services liberalisation' explores the different strategies for conducting services negotiations. The ability to find effective and efficient strategies to negotiate new packages depends as much on the ability of negotiators to design appropriate rules as on their speed of liberalisation. Three chapters in this volume contribute to the analysis of the experience with negotiating approaches adopted so far and make suggestions for alternative approaches. Türk (chapter 6) discusses plurilateral negotiations and finds that they have contributed to enhancing transparency on negotiating positions and shedding light on technical issues, but have failed to produce concrete outcomes. Plurilateral negotiations in services replace the traditional request-and-offer mode and have further-reaching potential for unblocking other areas of trade negotiations.[8] Türk points to the value of 'narrowing down' and 'zooming in' processes as procedural outcomes of plurilateral negotiations. In addition, she suggests a number of criteria against which negotiation approaches can be judged, thus bringing more structure to the discussion about negotiation strategies.

Kelly (chapter 7) examines New Zealand's experience with bilateral and plurilateral negotiations focusing on their impact on the country's negotiating positions and the decisions on resource allocation. She concludes that, despite being time-consuming and costly, the bilateral request–offer is a vital element in negotiations because of the contribution it makes in terms of generating information and building relationships with key interlocutors. She describes plurilateral negotiations as complements to bilateral negotiations because they build on shared interests and draw on the strengths of other parties. Gao (chapter 8) adds to these findings by looking at sectoral and modal approaches which, he argues, are inherently plurilateral in their approach and become feasible alternatives as the complexity of the negotiations increases. Overall, all three papers agree that the formation of plurilateral perspectives is a constructive process per se. Although the negotiation process yields information

[8] Alejandro Jara, Speaking Notes, Annual Conference NCCR-Trade, World Trade Institute, Berne, Switzerland, 3 July 2007, observes that plurilateral negotiations in services have been compared to sectoral negotiations in non-agricultural market access (NAMA) and could supposedly be used in agriculture, when a group of members agrees to a level of ambition for one sector that is higher than the result of a formula cut, given that obviously that result is applied on a MFN basis.

about objectives, issues and political realities, it can also prove extremely burdensome. It is, however, a process that helps negotiators to understand the shape of a possible services package.

The jurisprudence of GATS forms Part 4 of the book. In 'GATS case law: a first assessment', four authors describe the transition of GATS from being an ancillary item of disputes over goods, to services issues becoming the subject of contentious claims in their own right. While Andrew Shoyer (chapter 10) puts the emphasis on the *Mexico – Telecoms* case, which has not been appealed, both Eric Leroux (chapter 11) and William Davey (chapter 12) investigate the systemic issues of GATS adjudication. While Leroux points out the relationship between the GATS guidelines for domestic regulation, adjudication of domestic law and interpretation of scheduled commitments, Davey unravels services specificities that have challenged the trade-in-goods bias of the WTO judiciary. Finally, Martín Molinuevo (chapter 13) asks whether foreign investors can benefit from the WTO dispute settlement systems when their investment abroad qualifies as commercial presence as defined by mode 3 of the GATS. Given that WTO adjudication, unlike investor–state arbitration under International Centre for the Settlement of Investment Disputes (ICSID) and other arbitral tribunals is closed to claims from private parties, there is a need to examine what private investors in services stand to gain if their governments launch a dispute against the host government before the WTO, but also whether elements of WTO law have shaped the content and scope of investor–state arbitration.

Part 5 comprises four chapters on 'market access, national treatment and domestic regulation'. The papers revolve around the common theme of non-discrimination in services liberalisation and regulation. Firstly, national treatment is preconditioned on the likeness of services and service suppliers. Thus, Mireille Cossy (chapter 14) discusses the concept of likeness in services by comparison to that in relation to goods and suggests 'something different' in the form of an improved aims-and-effects test according to which elements related to the regulatory context 'of the service and/or of the supplier should play a role in relation to GATS national treatment'. Such a bona fide regulatory distinction that operates without creating disproportionate burdens on foreign services providers comes close to the necessity test as suggested by Panagiotis Delimatsis. Joost Pauwelyn (chapter 15) finds Cossy to follow a 'misguided' approach to national treatment as the GATS 'core' principle of non-discrimination. In his view, the prevailing focus on the 'likeness' test should be replaced by defining what constitutes less favourable treatment, including examining the criteria for de facto discrimination. By studying which modifications of the conditions of competition in favour of domestic services or service suppliers should be prohibited, one could, argues Pauwelyn, escape the pitfall of comparing the non-existent aims-and-effects test in GATT jurisprudence with the improved aims-and-effects test as suggested by Cossy. Panagiotis Delimatsis' paper (chapter 16) discusses different proposals and cautions against the 'necessary evil' of a GATS necessity test. According to Delimatsis, a horizontal necessity test would best bring about the completion of the still open GATS Article VI:4 mandate on non-discriminatory domestic regulation. The necessity test functions as a 'benchmark against which the WTO judiciary would judge the measures' that WTO Members may use when applying national qualification and licensing requirements, as well as technical standards indiscriminately to foreign and domestic service suppliers. Markus Krajweski (chapter 17) puts the debate started by Delimatsis on which type of necessity test is necessary for completing the GATS Article VI:4 mandate into the context of the necessity tests that already exist in the WTO legal system and identifies two different types of tests outside of GATS: the necessity tests, which 'can be part of requirements of an exception clause', such as Art. XX GATT and the necessity tests, which are 'integrated in positive obligations', such as in the agreement on technical barriers to trade (TBT) and the one in the agreement on sanitary and phytosanitary (SPS) measures. Krajewski argues that the difficulty of including a necessity test for assessing the trade-limiting effects of domestic regulatory measures will be a procedural one of knowing whether it has been fulfilled or violated rather than the material question of defining the exact scope and requirements of such a test. The WTO dispute settlement system, says Krajewski, is not equipped to 'adequately adjudicate a necessity test in light of domestic regulatory interests', because cases brought before the WTO have, in contrast to cases brought before the European Court of Justice, not been tested at the national court level. This missing judicial dialogue between the WTO judiciary and the national courts, according to Krajewski, is likely to be the thorny issue in completing the GATS Article VI:4 mandate.

Part 6 of the book deals with the time and costs of delaying the as yet uncompleted rule-making of the GATS: safeguard and subsidy disciplines for services. Markus Krajewski in chapter 18 offers a taxonomy of the WTO liberalisation instruments and considers that recognition, standardisation or harmonisation are the most advanced tools for reducing the trade-distorting effect of diverging domestic regulations, priming the necessity tests. Given their strong impact on domestic regulatory autonomy,

Krajewski questions the degree of bindingness such tools would have under WTO law, should they be based, for GATS, under Articles VI and VII. Krajweski's instrument of choice would be regulatory competition, because it allows for more policy space and offers more flexibility to WTO Members to choose a regulatory services regime appropriate to their needs than a mode of standardisation or harmonisation would. Fernando Piérola (chapter 19) discusses the feasibility and desirability of introducing an emergency safeguards regime. While introducing a safeguard regime for GATS is mandated by the treaty itself, the issue divides industrialised and developing countries, given that a WTO Member today can make use of flexibilities in the GATS to avoid the necessity of imposing a safeguard. Along those lines, but on a different subject, Pietro Poretti (chapter 20) debates the advantages and disadvantages of completing the rule-making on a subsidies discipline of GATS. Drawing from the Trade Policy Review data suggesting that certain services sectors such as transport, financial, audiovisual and tourism services regularly receive domestic support, Poretti finds that introducing a possibility for ad hoc sector-specific instruments may be a more appropriate means to address the subsidies in GATS than establishing a single horizontally applicable discipline. Kanitha Kungsawanich (chapter 21) gives additional reasons why the prospects for including a horizontal subsidies discipline in GATS are bleak. In addition to noting the lack of any sense of urgency from WTO Members to complete the negotiating mandate of Article XV, Kungsawanich points to the carve-out of the audiovisual sector from GATS subsidy disciplines by the UNESCO Convention on the Protection of the Diversity of Cultural Expressions of 2005 as one of the developments undermining the establishment of sound subsidy disciplines in services. Kungsawanich gives reasons for the lack of data on the degree of distortion of services trade through subsidies, including the fact that in GATS subsidies are indicated in the Schedules only as limitations to commitments, thus revealing little additional information as to their policy purposes and consequently illuminating only the import side of services trade. Drawing a useful and innovative connection between the two open negotiating mandates, emergency safeguard mechanism (ESM) and subsidies, Kungsawanich suggests that as long as disciplines on unfair trade practices are lacking in GATS, at least the ESM, as an instrument of temporary import relief, could temporarily fill the gap left by the absence of a discipline for unfair trade practices, such as subsidies.

The five papers in part seven appear under the heading of the 'Challenges to the scope of GATS and cosmopolitan governance in services trade'. The recurring theme of this section is an assessment of the desirability and feasibility of expanding the GATS liberalisation coverage by providing the framework within which WTO Members can introduce commitments on e-commerce, human rights and air transport services. Whereas the first question of completing the GATS mandate–introducing disciplines to prevent the circumvention of liberalisation was discussed in Part 6, Part 7 challenges the scope of GATS coverage by asking whether expanding the liberalisation obligations by removing barriers to trade in more services sectors will enhance the governance of GATS if it is thus established as the lead treaty in services trade. Spill-over effects of GATS on both domestic services regulation and on international norms relating to services are discussed in all five contributions to Part 7, and the chapter by Richard Janda and Mark Glynn (chapter 26) names this phenomenon 'cosmopolitan vocation' for trade in services. The first chapter in this section, by Sacha Wunsch-Vincent (chapter 22), diagnoses a disparity in the degree to which regional trade agreements have started to liberalise the digital cross-border trade flows in data, services and digital products, while the GATS has lagged behind in including commitments on e-commerce. The question of GATS scope relating to e-commerce then only becomes relevant if WTO Members find that the principle of technological neutrality does not apply to GATS. Drawing from the *US – Gambling* case, Wunsch-Vincent (chapter 22) confirms for instance the view that electronic delivery of services is an integral part of any mode 1 commitment, unless a Member excludes electronic delivery from other forms of mode 1 services supply. Wunsch-Vincent systematically identifies areas of divergence faced by WTO Members when dealing with electronically provided services. The principle of technological neutrality has been governing the debate on whether e-commerce is to be understood as an expansion of the scope of GATS liberalisation with the subsequent call for added regulatory disciplines or whether e-commerce has always been an integral part of GATS jurisdiction including the WTO Members' specific commitments. Wunsch-Vincent discusses the main challenges facing GATS through the lens of e-commerce or digital trade and poses the following questions: does technological neutrality render a digital service 'like' a non-electronically delivered service? Is a differentiation between electronically and non-electronically supplied services warranted given the disagreement among Members as to whether a *lex specialis* to GATS Article VI (in addition to GATS Article XIV) is necessary to protect consumers, public morals and privacy from the greater vulnerability assumed to be associated with electronic delivery? How should electronically delivered services be classified? How could new digital trade barriers be best anticipated? In sum, Wunsch-Vincent finds that these open issues are more likely to be effectively resolved through adjudication than through negotiations. Christian Pauletto (chapter 23) places Wunsch-Vincent's paper into a broader historical context by depicting the electronic technologies as the factors for 'eroding the distance barrier in trade'. However, Pauletto calls upon domestic regulators to address and remedy within the multilateral framework of GATS the lack of confidence which characterises consumers' and legislators' safety concerns relating to the intrusiveness of technological innovation. The second paper by Marion Panizzon (chapter 24) establishes the link between GATS and human rights by pointing out the close affinity GATS has with natural persons supplying services. Panizzon suggests that a WTO Member violating the human rights of a foreign service supplier may actually be diminishing the value of its specific commitments, if the violation of human rights leads to less services trade between the two countries. The economic effects of violations of human rights are discussed by Simon Walker (chapter 25), who distinguishes the 'altruistic' protection of human rights falling into the realm of non-WTO international jurisdiction from the 'instrumental' role of trade in protecting human rights. Citing the example of remittances as the 'positive link' between the movement of natural persons providing services under GATS, human rights and development, Walker also cautions against seeing GATS mode 4 as the panacea for realising development, and thus human rights, through trade. Using the example of how the brain drain of health professionals, exacerbated by GATS mode 4, decreases the enjoyment of the right to health in many poorer countries, Walker makes the point that since the enjoyment of a human right to migrate may come at the cost of other human rights, it is important to carefully balance these. The cosmopolitan argument for services, as introduced by Janda and Glynn in chapter 26, connects the advocates for completing the GATS negotiating mandates (Delimatsis, Krajweski, Pierola and Poretti) with the proponents of more aggressive market opening, whether multilaterally through GATS or plurilaterally through regional trade agreements (Sauvé). The cosmopolitan argument judges by the global gains in economic welfare whether or not to extend market opening by progressive liberalisation or to introduce more regulatory disciplines into GATS. The cosmopolitan argument for services trade as introduced by Janda and Glynn would say that trade is beneficial if it leads to a gain for consumers coupled with a decrease in production costs and this effect is generated through movements of capital and labour. However, the cosmopolitan approach to trade in services may justify regulatory disciplines, such as the introduction of competition safeguards in GATS, in order to offset the costs of welfare losses to citizen-consumers due to monopolistic structures. In addition to calling for liberalisation in principle and requiring regulation when needed, the cosmopolitan argument is aligned with protection and respect of non-economic values, such as the environment, labour standards and human rights. As such it draws from John Stuart Mill's writings on distributing the gains of trade liberalisation among many instead of keeping them in the hands of a few and was propagated by Ulrich Beck in 2006. Janda and Glynn transpose the cosmopolitan argument to trade in aviation rights to demonstrate how GATS could break down barriers to cross-border aviation rights and integrate air transport rights into its scope. Using the Chicago Convention's failed Transport Agreement of 1944 with its 'multilateral exchange of air traffic rights' Janda and Glynn illustrate how bilateral agreements, restricted to reciprocal economic advantages, fail to increase the cosmopolitan benefits of trade, because such agreements do not 'develop an ethos of cooperation between governments'. Today, the bilateral regulation of air traffic agreements is characterised by an asymmetrical allocation of bargaining power and an absence of special and differential treatment which goes against the cosmopolitan argument for trade. Accordingly, the authors advocate an MFN approach to create a cosmopolitan, and thus multilateral, aviation regime, which would reduce the spaghetti bowl of bilateral open skies agreements, regional and plurilateral open aviation areas. A GATS reference paper on aviation transport services and on lifting the exclusion of air traffic rights in GATS commitments laid down in paragraph 2 of the Annex on Aviation Services is suggested to prevent 'the anti-cosmopolitan tendency of asserting national sovereignty over airspace'.

The seven substantive parts of the book are evidence of the diversity of issues already contained within and being continually brought into the scope of GATS today. Part 8 by Pierre Sauvé (chapter 27) concludes the book with the observation that much has been done, but more remains to be undertaken for GATS to become a reference treaty on services trade for the twenty-first century. Most of the challenges facing GATS are specific to its rules and disciplines (or lack thereof) so that solutions for GATS cannot be replicated from GATT, TRIPS (Agreement on Trade-Related Aspects of International Property Rights) or any other WTO legal tool.

Combined with the high degree of flexibility which distinguishes services liberalisation from GATT rules or harmonisation of intellectual property laws in the Agreement on TRIPS, the complexity of GATS proves that as a treaty it is more comprehensive than the sum of its parts. Such vastness of scope in both the horizontal and vertical dimensions, the unfinished regulatory agenda, the unrefined underlying policy goals (universality of supply or cosmopolitan welfare gains) also leave legislators with a general feeling of uncertainty as to the limits of the scope of jurisdiction of the GATS, as well as identifying its regulatory object and purpose and aligning its future direction.

The fear of the capitals resulting in the indecision of Geneva's WTO missions about investing in resources for negotiating additional commitments and new rules (subsidies, safeguards and government procurement) reflects a lack of confidence by governments in the purpose of GATS as well their reluctance to sell the GATS to the citizens, consumers and taxpayers. The complexity of services causes paralysis in 'risk-averse bureaucracies' leading to a standstill in GATS rule-making, and putting at risk the gains from GATS for developing countries and the overall distributive fairness of GATS. It seems to be the reigning attitude of our times that WTO Members prefer to refer to the GATS' intrusion into national regulatory autonomy, its potential to hamper equal distribution and access to public services rather than to embrace the task of repairing the flaws of GATS. Accordingly, many WTO Members increasingly move services regulation to the 'periphery of preferential trade agreements',[9] because it is an easier solution than to render GATS not only fit for the future, but also more fairly balanced for all.

On the other hand, the more serious grounds for this impasse in services liberalisation lie in the rift between developing and industrialised countries over the creation of trade remedy disciplines and over regulating access to public services. This conflict was already apparent at the adoption of the GATS in 1994, but it remains unresolved and has been exacerbated as it embeds the additional conflict between more rule-making and the use of existing flexibilities. Industrialised countries are deterred from moving forward the negotiations on the unfinished regulatory agenda for trade remedies because they fear having GATS-consistent temporary import relief imposed on them by developing countries. Since industrialised countries feel that safeguards can be

[9] Pierre Sauvé, 'Adding Value at the Periphery: Aiming for GATS+ Advances in Regional Agreements on Services', NCCR Working Paper, 2 June 2006, available at: www.nccr-trade.org/ip-8/adding-value-at-the-periphery-2.html, last accessed 23 July 2007.

included in an additional commitment under Article XVIII, or the need for such a safeguard circumvented by not committing a sensitive sector to GATS market access, they see no reason for institutionalising a safeguard clause or disciplines for subsidies. At the same time however, they ask developing countries to commit more sectors to GATS liberalisation rules while refusing to give them the chance to protect infant service industries by such safeguard actions. The situation is unlike that for trade in goods, where flexibility in the terms of preferential access for products from developing countries through the Special and Differential (S&D) Treatment provisions or the General System of Preferences may have provided developing countries with more market access opportunities. Except for the regionalism exception allowing for S&D treatment, flexibility in the GATS works against developing WTO Members, since it discourages Members from agreeing on stronger disciplines for temporary import relief, which, if installed, would actually generate more commitments by developing countries and consequently spur growth of their services trade.[10] If the possibility of imposing import relief were to be codified as an ESM under GATS, it would actually increase the preparedness of developing countries to submit more services sectors and to commit to deeper levels of services liberalisation. The fear of losing policy space through transfer of regulatory power from WTO Members to the WTO/GATS exacerbates a tendency for WTO Members to pack all sorts of issues into the GATS commitments, such as safeguards, labour conditions and wage parity. Thus, the scope and legal authority of GATS commitments is becoming the focal point of GATS research and practice today. This leads to two challenges: first, the question of how to interpret GATS commitments must be clarified and, second, the question of how to monitor the WTO Members' compliance with the commitments must be addressed. Three scenarios could resolve this uncertainty: first, the existing legal basis could be used to resolve unfinished GATS business including transferring open issues to GATS commitments, second, one could outsource to plurilateral agreements; and third, one could reform GATS and continue to use the multilateral system of trade liberalisation for services. The concept of flexibility underlies the GATS potential for uncertainty: the varying peripheries of GATS in the face of plurilateral choice, the variable degree of regulatory

[10] See Ochieng, note 7 above, pp. 374–377 on flexibility favouring S&D treatment in GATS regionalism exception; see for flexibility in GATS generally, Sauvé, Pierre, 'Been There, Not Yet Done That', chapter 27 in this volume).

autonomy, the variety of negotiating methods. The challenge of flexibility may also hold the key to a GATS cosmopolitanism of the future understood as a regulatory jurisdiction for services embedded in coherence-seeking regime choice. In contrast to the challenge of consistency facing the single undertaking of pre-Doha WTO law, the challenge of cosmopolitanism required of a post-Doha WTO *acquis* does not just tolerate variance, but has developed models for the regulation of coordinated, mutually supportive variety.[11]

The initial question introducing this collection of essays was whether a cosmopolitan GATS can do it all. One possible answer to how GATS cosmopolitanism can address the open challenges of services trade lies in the notion of flexibility as openness or variance as to rule-consistency to integrate new areas of services activity into the scope of GATS while respecting the need for sensitive rules in other areas. This tenth World Trade Forum opened the door to an interesting and informed debate which demonstrated that services not only have an existence ancillary to improving the competitiveness of the goods sector, but that they have a legitimacy of their own as in lowering transaction costs, educating the labour force, spreading risk and improving the distribution of returns.

[11] See Craig VanGrasstek and Pierre Sauvé, 'The Consistency of WTO Rules: Can the Single Undertaking Be Squared with Variable Geometry?', *JIEL* 9(4) (2006), pp. 837–864, who portray the rules of the GATS and other WTO Agreements as being challenged by the notion of consistency, which the WTO single undertaking never quite achieves given the various dichotomies, such as the one between federal and centralised forms of government, monist and dualist traditions, GATS/GATT commitments and rules. Conquest of consistency increases the WTO legal system's potential for variance.

PART 2

Unexplored economic, political and judicial dimensions of GATS

2

South–South services trade

NORA DIHEL, FELIX ESCHENBACH AND BEN SHEPHERD*

This chapter contributes to the debate on the development potential of South–South trade in services. It represents the first attempt to identify key features governing the South–South dimension of services. Services trade between developing countries is predominantly regional and may reflect an increasing tendency to incorporate disciplines to liberalise services trade in regional agreements. It is estimated that cross-border South–South exports currently represent around 10 per cent of services exports worldwide. The bulk of exports from developing countries is destined for the markets of developed countries, save in the case of developing Asian countries whose services export markets are predominantly regional.

The chapter also shows that the gravity model can successfully be applied to trade in services using foreign direct investment stocks in services sectors as a proxy for trade in services through mode 3. The analysis points to the importance of policy barriers in hindering trade, and implies that countries could increase mode 3-related trade in services across all sectors by relaxing restrictions on foreign establishment. Finally, one important finding is that the impact of lifting restrictions on performance may increase more than proportionally with the scale of the liberalisation measure. Our results suggest that if services sectors are closed to foreign competition, the improvement of their performance requires a major rather than a minor or moderate

* The views expressed in this paper are those of the authors and do not necessarily reflect the positions or policies of the OECD or the World Bank. The authors wish to thank Raed Safadi, Head of the Trade Policy Dialogue Division for supervising the writing of this paper. Our work has also benefited from research and statistical assistance provided by Alena Brin, Rafael Espinoza, Jane Korinek, Karinne Logez and Rebecca Ygberg. The paper has benefited from helpful comments by Bill Cave and Bettina Wistrom (both OECD Statistics Directorate), Andreas Maurer, Joscelyn Magdeleine, Yann Marcus (all WTO Statistics Department) as well as participants at the 10th World Trade Forum, 2006.

LLYFRGELL PRIFYSGOL BANGOR UNIVERSITY LIBRARY

liberalisation effort. More research is needed to further assess whether a courageous liberalisation effort is required to achieve notable improvements in outcomes, which may particularly benefit goods exports of less developed countries.

Introduction

This study on South–South[1] services trade aims at combining theoretical analyses with exploratory empirical exercises to investigate the scale, potential and the opportunities for South–South trade in services through various modes of supply as well as its impact on the direction and volume of trade in services and goods. It aims at informing the debate on the development potential associated with South–South services liberalisation by examining key questions, including:

- What is the impact of removing services barriers to South–South services flows?
- What is the role of South–South trade in services as a potential driver of increased exports from developing countries?

Theoretical analyses and policy discussions on the development potential of South–South cooperation have focused almost exclusively on the potential for promoting South–South trade in goods. This has been the case even though services in many developing countries account for about 50 per cent of their aggregate gross domestic product (GDP) and employment opportunities, and contribute almost 15 per cent to their total exports. Among the most important reasons behind this neglect are the theoretical challenges related to the applicability of goods theories to services trade, lack of data on trade in services between developing countries and difficulties related to identifying and quantifying services barriers. More recently, discussions on South–South trade in services have begun to emerge as a way of exploring new and dynamic ways of realising the potentials of developing countries.

This report presents the results of a study on the South–South dimension of services trade. The analysis here is the first attempt to investigate

[1] The study has attempted to use the categorisation described in the paper on South–South goods trade (see OECD Working Paper No. 40), including the countries in Eastern Europe and Central Asia with per capita GNI not exceeding US$ 9,075 in 2003; however, some adjustments taking into account the availability of statistical information were made in certain cases. Whenever necessary, departures from this definition are noted.

the nature and scale of South–South services trade. The report is structured as follows. Section 1 contains statistical investigations and exploratory empirical analyses concerning estimates of South–South services trade. Section 2 presents empirical explorations that aim at quantifying the impact of services barriers on South–South FDI stocks in services and goods export performance in general. Section 3 presents the conclusions and identifies areas for further research.[2]

1. South–South services trade – stylised facts

There are few systematic analyses of trends in the structure of services trade among developing countries because of the numerous difficulties related to the measurement of trade in services. Chief among them are:

- The current practice of gathering data on international services transactions (in both developed and developing countries) is not consistent with the four-type classification of trade in services adopted in the GATS,[3] as it does not recognise that much of the trade in services takes place in ways that are different from trade in goods (owing to the special characteristics of services such as the proximity requirement for services provision).
- Lack of partner-country data on trade in services between developing countries hinders meaningful quantitative analysis of South–South services trade.

Therefore, to shed some light on the nature and scale of South–South services trade, it is necessary to identify and analyse all possible sources

[2] Information on the theoretical challenges associated with a better understanding of analyses related to services measurement issues and the determinants and potential for South–South services trade as well as details on the gravity model employed in the paper are available upon request from the authors (contact nora.dihel@oecd.org).

[3] The four-part typology of international services transactions adopted in the GATS encompasses: *Cross-border supply* (mode 1) of a service from one jurisdiction to another; *Consumption abroad* (mode 2), which requires the presence of consumers in the supplier's country of residence; (3) *Commercial presence* (mode 3), where a service supplier establishes a foreign-based corporation, joint venture, partnership or other establishment in the consumer's country of residence, to supply services to persons in the host country; and (4) *Presence of natural persons* (mode 4), which involves an individual, functioning alone or in the employ of a service provider, temporarily travelling abroad to deliver a service in the consumer's country of residence. Individuals seeking access to the employment market of another country on a permanent basis or for citizenship or residency purposes are not included in this category.

of information and apply exploratory techniques to estimate the magnitude of services trade between developing countries.

Box 1 summarises the various sources of information needed to provide statistics for the various modes of services supply.[4] The proposed allocation by modes of supply in Box 1 is based on the scheme presented in the Manual on Statistics of International Trade in Services (2002). However, given the limited direct information on the GATS modes of supply in balance of payment (BOP) statistics and other data sources, it should only be considered as an approximate estimate and treated with caution.

In addition, the following sources of partner-country data are useful in studying South–South trade in services:

- the OECD database on trade in services by partner country (BOP statistics);
- the UNCTAD database on FDI statistics;
- World Tourism Organisation statistics on number of visitors;
- International Air Transport Association (IATA) statistics that provide some information on flows of international passengers by region; and
- migration statistics.

The above sources of information have been used to determine the essential features of the South–South dimension of services trade via the various modes of supply, which are briefly described in the next section.

1.1 Cross-border trade and consumption abroad

Estimates based on BOP statistics

Table 1 presents the estimated patterns of world and South–South[5] cross-border (total) services trade in 2002 based on reported data on exports of services available to OECD countries and regions and mirror statistics (see explanation below). It shows that South–South exports represent around 10 per cent of world exports, while South–North exports seem to have a larger share of approximately 13 per cent of total exports. In terms of South–South and South–North differentiation, it is worth noting that exports from Asian developing countries to other developing countries represent around 8 per cent of world

[4] A detailed description of the measurement issues by modes of supply and partner-country data related to trade in services is presented in OECD (2006c).

[5] South covers all non-OECD countries for the purpose of these estimations.

Box 1: Statistical coverage of modes of supply

Mode	Statistical coverage
Mode 1 Cross-border supply	**BPM5**: transportation (most of), communications services, insurance services, financial services, royalties and licence fees Part of: *computer and information services, other business services* and *personal, cultural and recreational services* **Sectoral statistics**: telecommunications, air transport
Mode 2 Consumption abroad	**BPM5**: travel (excluding goods bought by travellers); repairs to carriers in foreign ports (goods); part of *transportation* (supporting and auxiliary services to carriers in foreign ports) **Sectoral statistics**: tourism
Mode 3 Commercial presence	**Foreign Affiliates Trade in Services**: FATS statistics **BPM5**: part of *construction services* **FDI statistics**: as a complement to FATS statistics
Mode 4 Presence of natural persons	**BPM5**: part of: *computer and information services; other business services; personal, cultural and recreational services* and *construction services* **FATS** (supplementary information): foreign employment in foreign affiliates **BPM5** (supplementary information): labour-related flows **Other sources**: ILO International Standard Classification of Occupations (ISCO 88); International Classification of Status in Employment (ICSE-93): classifications according to status of employment; migration statistics; tourism statistics (business visitors); statistics on number of work permits issued

Source: Adapted from the Manual on Statistics of International Trade in Services (2002).

exports, accounting for more than half of their total exports (see Table 2). In contrast, for developing countries in all other regions, exports to developed countries appear to be more important: for non-OECD European countries they represented over 70 per cent of their total exports

Table 1 *Estimated patterns of world and OECD trade in services, percentage of total world exports, 2002*

Exporter \ Importer	World	Total OECD	NAFTA	OECD Asia and Oceania	EU	OECD Europe other	Total non OECD	Africa	America non OECD	Asia and Oceania non OECD	Europe non OECD
World	100.0	73.8	19.6	9.0	40.5	4.7	24.9	2.3	4.0	16.2	2.4
Total OECD	76.3	61.1	15.4	5.9	35.3	4.4	14.0	1.6	3.3	7.4	1.7
NAFTA	20.9	15.1	4.7	3.0	6.7	0.7	5.6	0.4	2.3	2.6	0.3
OECD Asia and Oceania	*7.2*	*4.7*	*2.3*	*1.0*	*1.3*	*0.1*	*2.5*	*0.1*	*0.2*	*2.1*	*0.1*
EU total	*42.7*	*36.4*	*7.5*	*1.7*	*23.8*	*3.4*	*5.2*	*1.1*	*0.8*	*2.5*	*0.9*
OECD Europe other	*5.5*	*4.9*	*0.9*	*0.1*	*3.5*	*0.2*	*0.7*	*0.0*	*0.0*	*0.2*	*0.4*
Total non OECD	23.6	12.7	4.2	3.1	5.1	0.3	10.9	0.8	0.7	8.8	0.7
Africa	*2.1*	*1.5*	*0.2*	*0.2*	*1.1*	*0.0*	*0.6*	*0.4*	*0.0*	*0.2*	*0.0*
America non OECD	*3.4*	*2.9*	*1.7*	*0.4*	*0.7*	*0.0*	*0.6*	*0.0*	*0.4*	*0.1*	*0.0*
Asia and Oceania non OECD	*15.4*	*6.6*	*2.0*	*2.4*	*2.1*	*0.1*	*8.7*	*0.3*	*0.2*	*8.0*	*0.2*
Europe non OECD	*2.7*	*1.7*	*0.2*	*0.1*	*1.2*	*0.2*	*1.0*	*0.0*	*0.0*	*0.5*	*0.5*

Derived from source: OECD (2004), Statistics on International Trade in Services.

Table 2 *Estimated patterns of world and OECD trade in services, million USD and percentage, 2002*

Exporter \ Importer	World	Total OECD	NAFTA	OECD Asia and Oceania	EU	OECD Europe other	Total non OECD	Africa	America non OECD	Asia and Oceania non OECD	Europe non OECD
World	1,641,291	73.8%	19.6%	9.0%	40.5%	4.7%	24.9%	2.3%	4.0%	16.2%	2.4%
Total OECD	1,251,939	80.0%	20.2%	7.7%	46.3%	5.8%	18.3%	2.1%	4.3%	9.7%	2.2%
NAFTA	342,775	72.5%	22.3%	14.6%	32.0%	3.5%	26.6%	1.7%	11.0%	12.7%	1.3%
OECD Asia and Oceania	118,316	65.0%	31.4%	14.1%	18.0%	1.4%	35.0%	1.6%	3.1%	29.6%	0.7%
EU total	700,318	85.2%	17.7%	3.9%	55.8%	7.9%	12.3%	2.6%	1.8%	5.8%	2.2%
OECD Europe other	90,531	88.2%	17.2%	2.7%	63.9%	4.3%	11.8%	0.4%	0.7%	2.8%	7.9%
Total non OECD	387,533	53.8%	17.7%	13.1%	21.7%	1.3%	46.2%	3.2%	2.8%	37.2%	3.0%
Africa	34,048	70.8%	8.3%	9.2%	52.7%	0.5%	29.2%	18.5%	0.6%	9.0%	1.1%
America non OECD	56,486	83.2%	50.8%	11.6%	20.4%	0.3%	16.8%	0.2%	12.4%	3.9%	0.2%
Asia and Oceania non OECD	252,000	43.3%	13.3%	15.8%	13.6%	0.6%	56.7%	2.2%	1.2%	52.2%	1.3%
Europe non OECD	44,998	63.0%	8.2%	2.9%	45.1%	6.9%	37.0%	1.3%	1.2%	16.7%	17.8%

Derived from source: OECD (2004), Statistics on International Trade in Services.

and for developing countries in Africa and Latin America, over 80 per cent of their total exports (in 2002). Intra-regional exports account for the largest share of developing countries' total South–South exports.

Combining IMF BOP data with OECD figures on mirror imports produces more refined estimates for South–South transport, other commercial services and travel exports. These are presented in Tables 3–5. The figures reveal that in 2002, South–South transport exports represented around 8.5 per cent of world transport exports, South–South other commercial services exports almost 15 per cent of other commercial services exports worldwide, while South–South travel exports accounted for approximately 16 per cent of world travel exports.

Estimates based on sectoral statistics

The following sources cover separately cross-border trade in air transport and consumption abroad (tourism) and provide information on the volume of such trade.

Cross-border trade The International Air Transport Statistics produced by IATA provide some information on flows of international passengers and freight tonnes by region. The data in Table 6 show that, except for flows between Asia and other developing regions, flows of international passengers between developing countries are extremely low – very often under 1 per cent of reported passenger flows. (The reported IATA data represent 90 per cent of total passenger flows.)

Consumption abroad While the estimates based on BOP statistics for travel services (presented above) suggest that almost 30 per cent of world travel exports come from developing (non-OECD) countries, with South–South travel exports representing around 16 per cent of the world total, data compiled from the statistics of the World Tourism Organization presents additional information on visitor arrivals by region in 2002 on a partner-country basis for 208 countries (see Table 7). South–South movements account for approximately 20 per cent of total visitors, South–North arrivals 14 per cent, North–South arrivals 9 per cent and North–North arrivals 57 per cent of total visitor flows. Around 70 per cent of visitors from non-OECD or developing countries go to other developing countries.

Table 3 *Estimated patterns of world and OECD trade in transport services, percentage of world transport exports, 2002*

Exporter \ Importer	WORLD	OECD TOTAL	NAFTA	OECD ASIA AND OCEANIA	OECD EUROPE	EU15	OECD EUROPE OTHER	NON-OECD TOTAL
WORLD	100.0	76.5	20.2	11.8	43.5	39.8	4.1	25.2
OECD TOTAL	74.6	55.8	14.4	6.3	35.1	31.5	4.0	16.8
NAFTA	15.2	11.1	3.4	2.5	5.2	4.7	0.5	4.6
OECD ASIA AND OCEANIA	11.9	6.6	2.9	1.4	2.4	2.2	0.1	4.4
OECD EUROPE	47.6	38.0	8.1	2.4	27.5	24.6	3.4	7.8
EU15	41.0	32.2	6.6	2.2	23.4	20.4	3.0	7.1
OECD EUROPE OTHER	6.6	5.8	1.5	0.2	4.1	4.2	0.3	0.7
NON-OECD TOTAL	29.1	20.7	5.9	5.5	8.5	8.3	0.2	8.4

Note: Non-OECD total credits to OECD countries refer to mirror data for OECD debits from non-OECD countries.
Source: OECD data are taken from OECD (2004); Statistics on International Trade in Services, non-OECD country data are from IMF Balance of Payments Current Account statistics.

Table 4 *Estimated patterns of world and OECD trade in other services, percentage of world other services exports, 2002*

Exporter / Importer	WORLD	OECD TOTAL	NAFTA	OECD ASIA AND OCEANIA	OECD EUROPE	EU15	OECD EUROPE OTHER	NON-OECD TOTAL
WORLD	100.0	77.1	22.6	7.0	47.6	41.8	5.9	27.1
OECD TOTAL	80.7	67.4	18.7	5.3	43.4	37.8	5.8	13.2
NAFTA	22.6	18.0	4.9	3.0	10.1	8.8	1.2	5.5
OECD ASIA AND OCEANIA	6.9	4.6	2.8	0.5	1.3	1.2	0.1	2.1
OECD EUROPE	51.3	44.8	11.0	1.8	32.1	27.8	4.4	5.7
EU15	46.6	39.8	9.7	1.7	28.4	24.1	4.2	5.5
OECD EUROPE OTHER	4.7	5.1	1.2	0.2	3.7	3.7	0.2	0.2
NON-OECD TOTAL	23.5	9.6	3.8	1.7	4.1	4.0	0.2	13.8

Note: Non-OECD total credits to OECD countries refer to mirror data for OECD debits from non-OECD countries.
Source: OECD data are taken from OECD (2004), Statistics on International Trade in Services, non-OECD country data are from IMF Balance of Payments Current Account statistics.

Table 5 *Estimated patterns of world and OECD trade in travel services, percentage of world travel exports, 2002*

Exporter \ Importer	WORLD	OECD TOTAL	NAFTA	OECD ASIA AND OCEANIA	OECD EUROPE	EU15	OECD EUROPE OTHER	NON-OECD TOTAL
WORLD	100.0	69.8	16.3	8.2	45.3	41.0	4.5	27.6
OECD TOTAL	72.7	56.0	11.4	5.6	39.0	35.0	4.3	11.7
NAFTA	22.1	14.3	5.8	3.2	5.3	4.7	0.5	6.6
OECD ASIA AND OCEANIA	4.4	2.2	0.5	1.1	0.6	0.6	0.0	1.4
OECD EUROPE	46.2	39.6	5.2	1.3	33.1	29.7	3.7	3.7
EU15	39.9	35.9	4.8	1.2	30.0	26.4	3.5	3.3
OECD EUROPE OTHER	6.3	3.6	0.3	0.1	3.1	3.2	0.2	0.4
NON-OECD TOTAL	29.6	13.7	4.9	2.6	6.3	6.1	0.2	15.9

Note: Non-OECD total credits to OECD countries refer to mirror data for OECD debits from non-OECD countries.
Source: OECD data are taken from OECD (2004), Statistics on International Trade in Services, non-OECD country data are from IMF Balance of Payments Current Account statistics.

Table 6 *International scheduled passenger flows by region as percentage of total thousands of passengers (2000)*

	North America	Central America	South America	Europe	Middle East	Africa	Asia	South West Pacific
North America	0.03	0.05	0.02	0.11	0.00	0.00	0.05	0.01
Central America		0.01	0.00	0.01			0.00	
South America			0.01	0.01		0.00	0.00	0.00
Europe	0.37				0.02		0.05	0.01
Middle East					0.01		0.02	
Africa				0.04	0.01	0.01	0.00	0.00
Asia	0.09							0.03
South West Pacific	0.00							

Source: IATA (2004).

7.2 Commercial Presence

Estimates based on FDI statistics

Information on non-OECD countries' FDI in services or FATS flows on a partner-country basis is scarce. Using data from sources such as the World Bank, the IMF, the OECD and UNCTAD, Aykut and Ratha (2004) estimate South–South FDI flows in the 1990s indirectly (Table 8).[6] They posit that in 2000, more than one-third of FDI in developing countries originated in other developing countries, with India, China, Brazil and South Africa among the main sources. They also indicate that South–South FDI is driven by similar 'push' and 'pull' factors as well as similar structural, cyclical and policy factors as drive North–South flows. They note, however, that these figures should be interpreted with great care given the quality of data, the round-tripping problems (as in

[6] South is here defined as a group of 31 developing countries for which reasonably detailed FDI data are available. FDI data cover not only services, but also agriculture and manufacturing. Notwithstanding these limitations, these general indications on FDI flows among developing countries could be used for further sectoral and/or country-specific disaggregations.

Table 7 *Visitor arrivals by region, percentage of total visitor arrivals*

Importer \ Exporter	OECD Total	NAFTA	OECD Asia and Oceania	EU	OECD Europe other	NON OECD total	America non OECD	Asia and Oceania non OECD	MENA	Europe non OECD	AFRICA	Total
OECD total	56.7%	10.9%	1.6%	38.3%	5.9%	13.8%	2.7%	4.9%	1.0%	3.7%	1.5%	70.4%
NAFTA	11.5%	8.6%	0.3%	2.3%	0.3%	3.0%	1.8%	0.9%	0.2%	0.1%	0.1%	14.5%
OECD Asia and Oceania	2.7%	0.8%	0.9%	0.9%	0.1%	2.7%	0.0%	2.6%	0.0%	0.1%	0.0%	5.5%
EU	38.3%	1.4%	0.3%	32.3%	4.2%	6.6%	0.8%	1.3%	0.7%	2.5%	1.2%	44.9%
OECD Europe other	4.2%	0.2%	0.0%	2.8%	1.2%	1.4%	0.1%	0.1%	0.1%	1.0%	0.1%	5.6%
NON OECD Total	8.8%	1.0%	0.9%	3.5%	3.4%	20.7%	2.0%	6.8%	3.4%	6.0%	2.6%	29.6%
NON OECD nec	0.4%	0.0%	0.1%	0.3%	0.0%	1.9%	0.3%	0.4%	0.1%	0.6%	0.5%	2.3%
America non OECD	1.2%	0.6%	0.0%	0.5%	0.0%	1.7%	1.6%	0.1%	0.0%	0.0%	0.0%	2.9%
Asia and Oceania non OECD	1.9%	0.3%	0.8%	0.7%	0.2%	6.8%	0.0%	5.8%	0.7%	0.2%	0.1%	8.7%
MENA	0.4%	0.1%	0.0%	0.2%	0.1%	2.5%	0.0%	0.1%	2.0%	0.1%	0.2%	2.9%
Europe non OECD	4.5%	0.0%	0.0%	1.5%	3.0%	5.7%	0.0%	0.3%	0.2%	5.1%	0.1%	10.2%
AFRICA	0.4%	0.0%	0.0%	0.3%	0.0%	2.1%	0.0%	0.1%	0.3%	0.0%	1.7%	2.5%
TOTAL	65.5%	12.0%	2.5%	41.8%	9.2%	34.5%	4.7%	11.7%	4.3%	9.7%	4.1%	100.0%

Notes: OECD Europe other may include non-OECD countries recorded under a general category 'ALL C/E EUR' or 'ALL EUROPE'.
Source: 206 countries from World Tourism Organisation (2004).

Table 8 *Estimation of South–South FDI flows 1994–2000 (billion dollars)*

	1994	1995	1996	1997	1998	1999	2000
South–South flows	4.6	15.3	25	57.4	56.6	49.7	53.9
Share of total South–South FDI flows	6	16.2	22.3	38.7	36.8	31	36.4

Source: D.Aykut, D. Ratha, 'Transnational Corporations, South–South FDI flows: How big are they?' UNCTAD 2003.

the case of China) and the impossibility of clearly distinguishing between North–South flows routed through locations in the South (e.g. a Mexican affiliate of a United States company investing in Brazil) and genuine South–South flows.

Finally, UNCTAD (2004a, 2004b) provides some information on mergers and acquisitions (M&A) between developing countries and non-equity arrangements: M&A sales/purchases in services among developing countries represented around 40 per cent of the world total during the periods 1991–1994, 1995–1997 and 2001–2003, and 17 per cent during 1998–2000. More variation is observable with respect to transition economies among which M&A sales/purchases in services accounted for around 6 per cent of the world total during the periods 1991–1994 and 1998–2000 and for 13 per cent during 2001–2003.

1.3 Movement of natural persons for services provisions

While migration statistics are very imperfect proxies for trade in services via the temporary movement of people, they could be helpful in providing a broad picture of migratory trends.

Estimates based on migration statistics

Building on existing migration statistics, Parsons *et al.* (2005) constructed a database on the international bilateral migration stock for 226 countries. The database represents a first attempt to provide a general overview of current migration trends in terms of the overall magnitude of migrant stocks and regional migration patterns. Primary data sources are national population censuses and migration statistics from the United Nations and the Economic Commission for Latin America and the Caribbean (ECLAC). Databases produced by

Eurostat, the OECD, the Migration Policy Institute, the ILO and the Middle East Central Asia Databook constitute secondary sources.

Table 9 gives information on the proportion of all world migrants recorded bilaterally across selected subcontinental regions, on the percentages of immigrants living in other subcontinental regions and on the percentages of emigrants sent from these states. The table shows that Europe is home to a third of the world's immigrants, while Asia and North America are each home to approximately a quarter. Europe and Asia are the most significant senders of migrants abroad. The table is also useful in terms of analysing the importance of regional migration: overall it would be fair to assume that migration does occur at the regional level. As already indicated, the figures should be interpreted with care in the context of mode 4 trade in services.

1.4 Participation of developing countries in world services trade

This is the first attempt to rigorously identify the share of South–South services trade in world trade according to the four modes of supply. As opposed to goods trade, for which the evolutionary process is more easily documented, the empirical evidence presented here should be seen as a starting point for future analysis and should be treated with caution in light of the quality of the data and the potential underreporting. It can be further refined as more data become available. New information can also enable trends to be analysed. At this stage, the most important conclusion to emerge is that services trade between developing countries takes place predominantly at the regional level for all modes of supply; this might be due to the increasing tendency to incorporate disciplines to liberalise services trade within regional trade agreements.

Where then does South–South services trade stand in relation to world services trade? It is difficult to find benchmarks against which to compare the figures derived here. However, given the dynamism of developing countries in world services trade, there appears to be a certain potential for developing South–South services trade.

As far as cross-border trade is concerned, the role of developing countries in international trade in services has increased on both the export and import sides. As a group, the share of low- and middle-income countries in world services trade rose from 26 per cent in 1994 (284 billion US dollars) to 28 per cent in 2004 (648 billion US dollars), representing an average growth of 9 per cent per year. The comparable

Table 9 *Migrants recorded by origin and destination, by continent, percentage of total migrants*

Host region \ Sending region	Oceania	Asia	North America	South America	Europe	Africa	Total
Oceania	0.4	0.2	0.2	0.0	0.2	0.1	1.0
Asia	0.8	14.9	6.2	0.1	9.5	2.5	34.1
North America	0.1	1.7	10.8	0.1	1.5	1.0	15.1
South America	0.0	0.7	1.3	1.3	1.0	0.3	4.6
Europe	1.4	9.2	4.8	0.7	17.1	2.9	36.0
Africa	0.1	2.2	0.7	0.0	3.7	2.3	9.1
Total	2.9	28.7	24.1	2.2	33.0	9.1	100.0

Source: GTAP Migration Database (2005).

figure for growth in services in industrialised countries is 7 per cent per annum. The share of developing countries in world services exports rose from 26 per cent to 29 per cent between 1994 and 2004. Developing countries now account for 33 per cent of exports in transportation, 35 per cent of global travel services and 23 per cent of world exports in other commercial services.

As far as consumption abroad is concerned, travel and tourism appear to be dynamic sectors for most developing countries and are the top currency earners for 40 developing countries. From a regional perspective, between 1990 and 2000, exports from low- and middle-income areas of Asia, Central and Eastern Europe and Latin America and the Caribbean grew at higher average annual rates than world services exports.

Commercial presence through FDI in services has expanded, with the world's inward stock of FDI in services quadrupling between 1990 and 2002, and the share of services in world FDI stock rising from 25 per cent in the 1970s to about 60 per cent in 2002. Developed countries remain the main source of outward FDI, but the share of developing countries grew from 1 per cent in 1990 to 10 per cent of global outward FDI services stock in 2002. On the inward side, developing countries' FDI has increased (to 25 per cent of inward FDI stock in services), although developed countries remain the main recipients. In 2002, services accounted for about 55 per cent of the total stock of inward FDI in developing countries and some 85 per cent of the inward FDI stock of developing countries (UNCTAD, 2004b).

Finally, there are at present no reliable global figures on the size of mode 4 trade. Very rough estimates suggest that mode 4, valued at USD 30 billion in 1997, is the smallest of all modes of services supply defined in the GATS. This is likely to be a significant underestimate, however. Also, this should not be seen as a reflection of the potential for mode 4 but rather as an indication of the existing limits and restrictions imposed on the movement of people.

Some studies highlight that while permanent migration is mainly a South–North phenomenon, triggered by wage differentials and the expectation of better living standards, temporary flows (which come closer to mode 4) are mainly a result of bilateral agreements between governments wishing to foster cooperation. Additional demographic complementarities between different developing countries could provide a strong argument for utilising some countries' human resources without having to consider longer term immigration. Therefore, contrary to the general belief, mode 4 is not only a developed versus developing country issue. Developing countries seem to be important exporters of services via mode 4 and there appears to be scope for further expansion of South–South mode 4 trade.

2. Empirical investigations

This Section explores in more detail the general findings about the determinants and the potential for South–South trade. The analysis considers the impact of services barriers on South–South FDI in services (as a proxy for trade in services through mode 3) using a gravity model. Given the important role of services as intermediate inputs, this part also seeks to analyse the impact of services barriers on goods trade by developing countries.

2.1 Barriers to trade in services: differences between developing and developed countries

Although GATS schedules of commitments do not necessarily involve liberalisation, it could be useful to examine them as they provide an indication of countries' past intentions, and the prospects and challenges for the current round of negotiations. There is considerable diversity across groups of WTO Members in terms of sectoral and modal coverage and levels of commitment. In terms of sectoral coverage, of a total of 160 sub-sectors, least-developed countries (LDCs) have on average made commitments in twenty-four sub-sectors and developing economies in forty-two sub-sectors (with wide variations between countries: some LDCs or developing countries have committed in one sector only, whereas a few have included over 100). By contrast, transition economies have made commitments in more sectors than even developed countries. Overall, least-developed and developing countries have made commitments in fewer sectors than developed and transition countries.[7]

From a modal perspective, the level of unrestricted commitments for modes 1 and 2 does not differ significantly between developed and developing countries, whereas countries in transition and LDCs have tended to undertake more open commitments. The situation is different for mode 3 where developing countries have more restrictions than all other groups.[8] However, in terms of the various types of market access

[7] Adlung and Roy (2005) and Marchetti (2004). [8] Marchetti (2004).

and national treatment restrictions affecting mode 3, commitments do not seem to differ significantly between groups except in cases where developing countries more often include limitations on the admissible types of legal entity and foreign equity participation (for market access restrictions) and land-related restrictions (for national treatment restrictions), and where they rely more heavily on discriminatory subsidies and nationality and residency requirements (for national treatment restrictions).[9] Finally, with respect to mode 4, it is worthwhile noting that all country groupings have restrictive commitments.

Recent work on sectoral restrictiveness indices undertaken by the OECD Trade Directorate[10] shows that many non-OECD countries record restrictiveness indices well above the OECD average in banking, insurance, telecommunications, distribution and engineering. Figures 1–6 reproduce in graphical form the aggregate trade-restrictiveness index (TRI) results for selected countries; the horizontal line represents the OECD sample average (i.e. the selected OECD countries included in our sample).

It is worth noting that Asian non-OECD countries such as Malaysia, China, India and Thailand are the most restrictive in banking, insurance, mobile telecom, engineering and distribution. The Middle-East and North Africa (MENA) countries analysed represent the most restrictive group in fixed telecom services. The analysis confirms that among the selected non-OECD countries, transition economies are leading the process of liberalisation in almost all sectors. Russia, however, is in general the most restrictive of the transition economies analysed. In most of the sectors analysed, Latin American countries record rather moderate restrictiveness indices as compared to the Asian countries analysed or to Russia. The impact of these barriers on services trade is analysed below using a gravity model; this is followed by an analysis of their impact on goods export on the basis of an export supply function.

2.2 South–South trade in services: A gravity model approach

The 'gravity model' has been used in hundreds of papers modelling international trade in goods since it was first proposed by Jan Tinbergen

9 Adlung and Roy (2005).

10 OECD (2005), 'Modal Estimates of Services Barriers', TD/TC/WP(2005)36. In the first stage, the qualitative information on GATS commitments and sectoral regulatory reform is translated into quantitative scores using a system of weights and scores. In the second stage, the tax equivalent corresponding to these restrictions is calculated using econometric techniques.

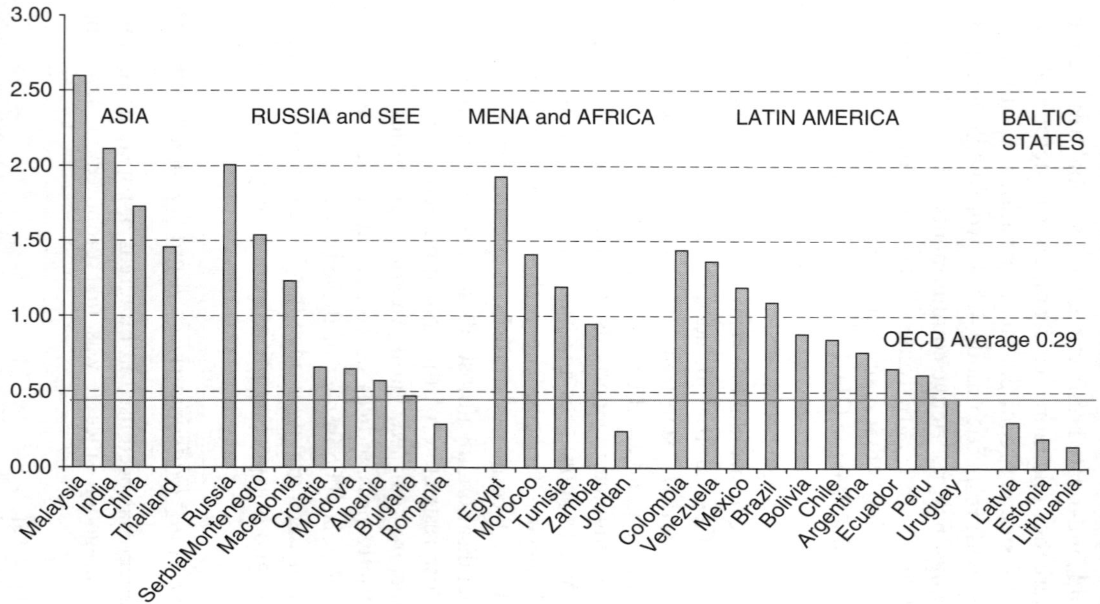

Source: OECD (2005).

Figure 1 Aggregate trade restrictiveness index – Banking

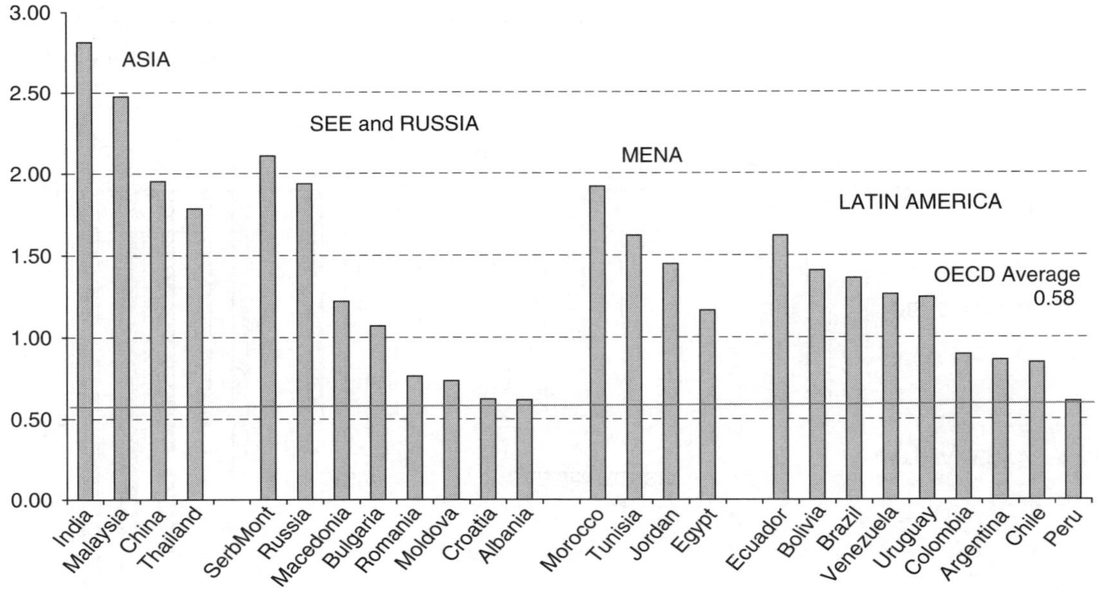

Source: OECD (2005).

Figure 2 Aggregate trade restrictiveness index – Insurance

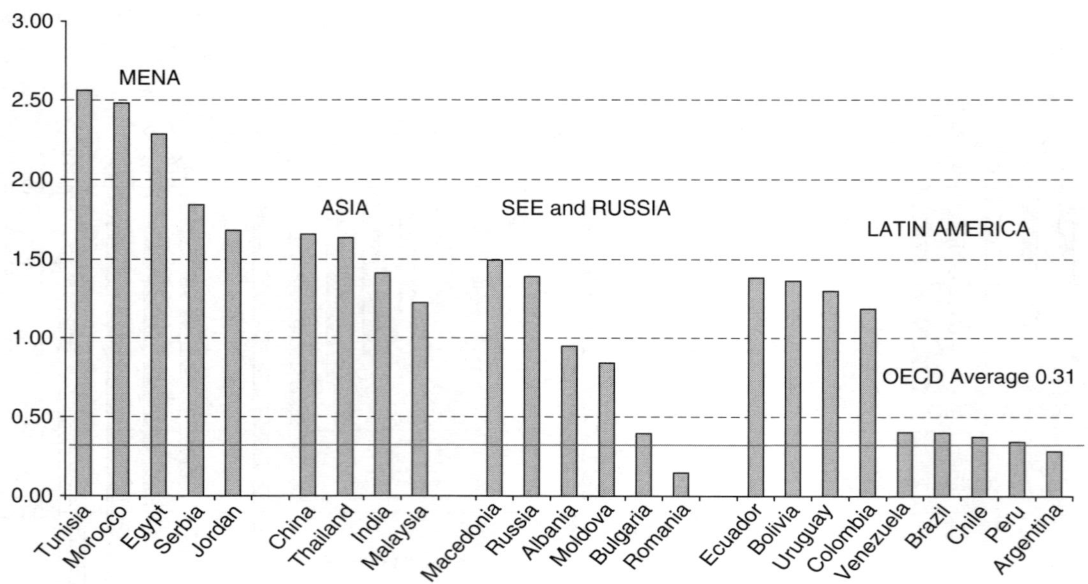

Source: OECD (2005).

Figure 3 Aggregate trade restrictiveness index – Fixed telecommunication

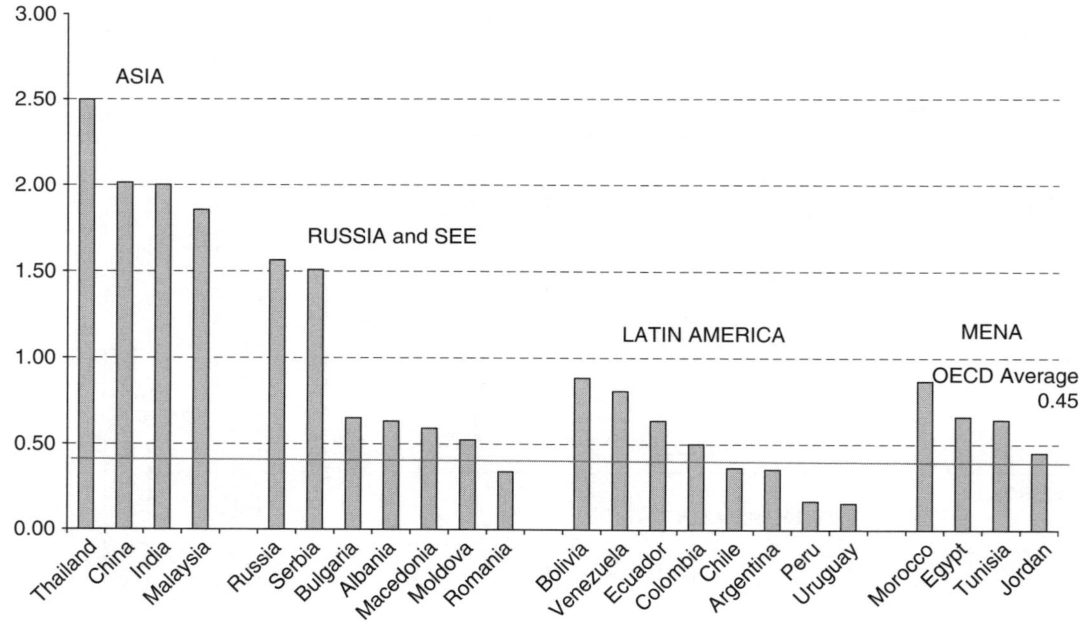

Source: OECD (2005).

Figure 4 Aggregate trade restrictiveness index – Mobile telecommunication services

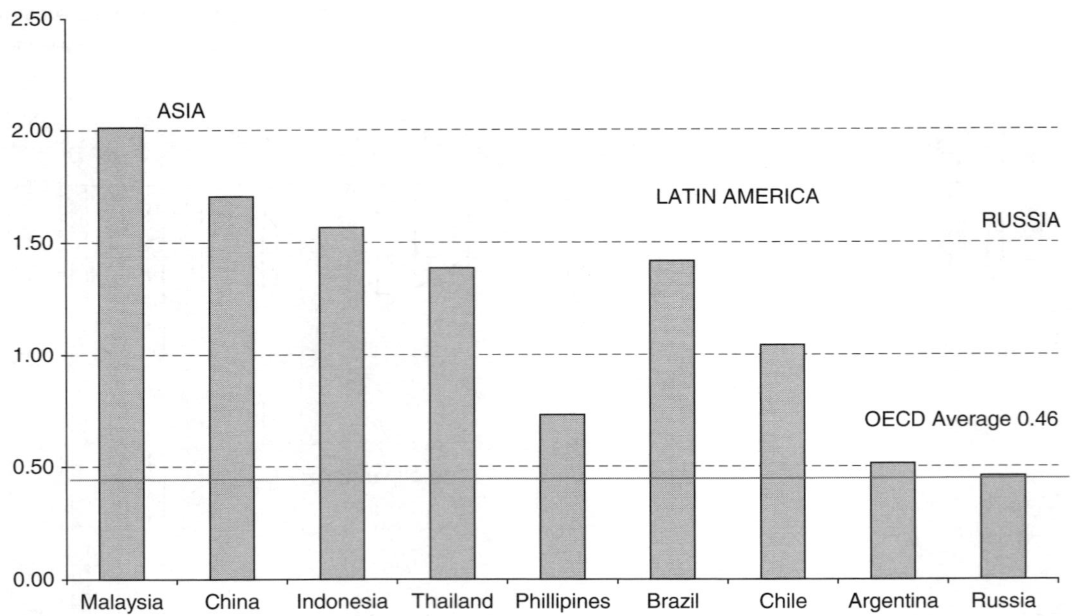

Source: OECD (2005).

Figure 5 Aggregate trade restrictiveness index – Engineering services

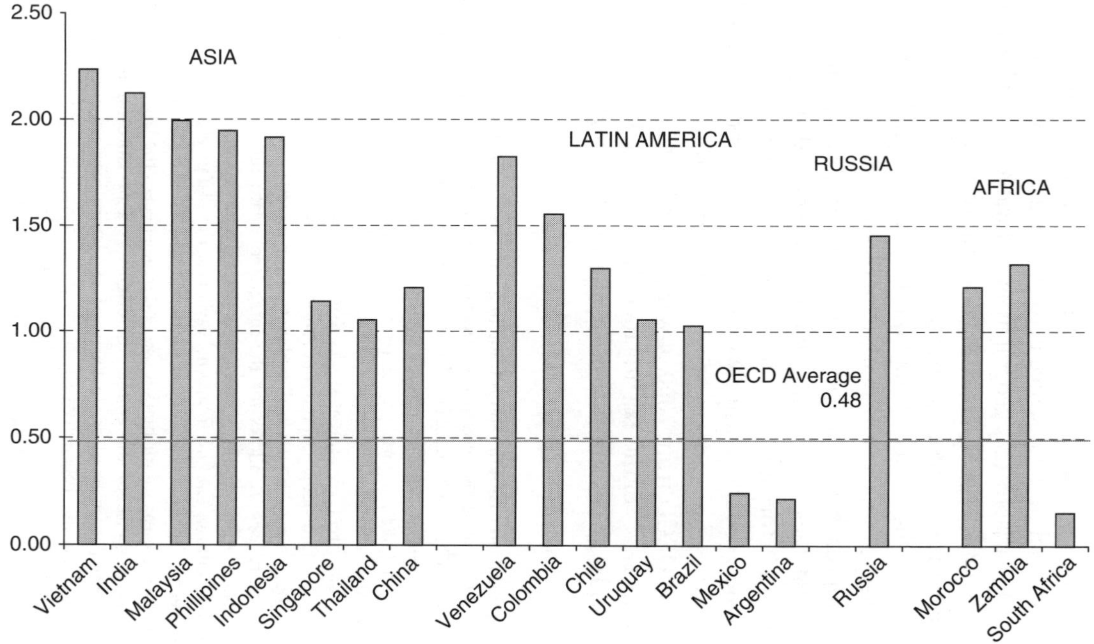

Source: OECD (2005).

Figure 6 Aggregate trade restrictiveness index – Distribution services

in 1962.[11] However, it is only much more recently that its application to international trade in services has been made feasible by the compilation of extensive new datasets, including by the OECD. When applied to services, the basic idea behind the model remains the same, namely that trade between two countries is directly proportional to their economic size and inversely proportional to the distance between them. Indeed, many of the customary gravity variables (e.g. geography or cultural historical links) tend to find their way into services models, making for relatively easy comparability between studies in these two areas.

For guidance on the choice of methods to be employed in this study, Table 10 provides summary information on recent papers that have used gravity-based approaches to analyse international trade in services.[12] It is worth noting that these are recent working papers and the results are sometimes contradictory and should therefore be interpreted with care. Also, these models cover exclusively OECD countries and are based on the recent statistics on trade in services available from partner data published by the OECD from 2000 onwards. Finally, it is interesting to observe that only two[13] of the existing models analyse FDI in the context of services (mode 3) despite this being the most important mode of services supply.

[11] For a recent application to South–South trade in goods, see OECD (2006b).

[12] Buch (2005) and Guerin (2006) also deserve mention, since they use the gravity model to analyse the related questions of international asset and liability positions of banks, and capital flows respectively. Neither, however, directly deals with international trade in services. In addition, Hoekman (2000) reports partial results for a gravity-based exercise covering business/construction and financial services; however, full details are not provided.

[13] To explain bilateral direct investment stocks Kox *et al.* (2002) adapt the gravity model with elements of the knowledge-capital model developed by Markusen *et al.* (2000). The latter model is becoming the standard explanation for direct investment decisions by multinational enterprises. It allows for the integrated treatment of trade and direct investment decisions in international services markets. To explain bilateral direct investment stocks, the authors use the following variables: the distance and differences in languages between countries (as a measure for trade costs), GDP in the country of origin and destination (as a measure for market size and scale effects), the labour productivity level in the service sector of the country of origin (as a measure for technological advantage) and regulatory barriers. In terms of regulatory barriers, they investigate both the level and the heterogeneity of national product market regulations and FDI restrictions, correcting for unobserved variables in the country of origin and the destination. Grünfeld and Moxes (2003) base their gravity model on the theory developed by Markusen and Venables (1995) that explains activity of national and foreign affiliates as a function of country income and transport costs. Some of their results are in line with the predictions of the gravity model. For example, the theory predicts that affiliate sales increase with income in both the foreign and domestic markets, which is also a feature of the gravity model.

Table 10 *Previous gravity models of international trade in services*

Paper	Countries	Years	Modes	Sectors	Explanatory Variables
Freund and Weinhold (2002)	US + 31 partners	1996–1999	BOP data (mainly modes 1 and 2)	Education, financial, telecom, advertising, data processing, information, R&D, consulting and PR, legal, construction and engineering, maintenance, other business and other services	GDP, population, distance, language, common border, financial depth, Internet penetration.
Grünfeld and Moxnes (2003)	22 OECD exporters/ importers + non-OECD importers	1999–2000	BOP data (mainly modes 1 and 2) and FDI stocks in services for OECD (mode 3)	Aggregate services trade	GDPs and GDPs per capita (raw, total and 'similar-ity'), distance, TRI, corruption, RTA
Jansen and Piermartini (2004)	US and UK (exporters) + up to 50 importers	1999–2001 (ave.)	BOP data (mainly modes 1 and 2)	Aggregate services trade	GDP, GDP per capita, distance, language, mode 4 trade, corruption, common border
Kimura and Lee (2006)	10 OECD exporters + 47 OECD and non-OECD importers	1999–2000	BOP data (mainly modes 1 and 2)	Aggregate services trade	GDPs, distance, remote-ness, common border, RTA, economic freedom, common language

Table 10 (*cont.*)

Paper	Countries	Years	Modes	Sectors	Explanatory Variables
Kox *et al.* (2005)	EU-15	1999–2001	BOP data (mainly modes 1 and 2)	Other commercial services	GDPs, distance, language, product market regulation, barriers to entrepreneurship, regulatory heterogeneity
Lejour and Verheijden (2004)	EU-15, Canadian provinces	1997–1999 (Canada) 1999–2001 (EU)	BOP data (mainly modes 1 and 2)	*Canada*: transport & storage, wholesale & retail distribution, hotels & restaurants, business, finance, communication, education, health, other *EU*: other commercial, transport, travel, government	GDPs, distance, language, common border, product market regulation
Nicoletti *et al.* (2003)	20 OECD exporters and 27 OECD importers	1999–2000	BOP data (mainly modes 1 and 2)	Aggregate services trade	Total GDP, size similarity, factor dissimilarity, human capital dissimilarity, distance, product market regulations

Building on the work presented in Table 10, the present paper employs the gravity model to assess the impact of services barriers on FDI flows (as a proxy for services trade through mode 3). The paper seeks to extend the analysis in four ways.

(i) South–South dimension

Country coverage is expanded to include up to eighteen non-OECD countries, both as importers and exporters (FDI receivers and senders). Our dataset includes flows among non-OECD countries, not just between OECD and non-OECD countries, making it possible to look for differences in behaviour affecting South–South trade.

(ii) Expanded sectoral and country coverage for FDI stock in service sectors (as a proxy for trade in services through mode 3)

Sectoral coverage and country coverage are widened by using service sector FDI stocks as a proxy for foreign affiliate sales (mode 3). The dependent variable used in this paper is a bilateral measure of FDI stock by service sector, taken from a bilateral capital stock matrix for 2001 that was developed in-house. Bilateral FDI stocks covering 57 sectors and 92 countries/regions were estimated from the new OECD FDI database, UNCTAD World Investment Directory, local government sources for China, Hong Kong, Russia, Singapore, Chile, Peru and Brazil, and ASEAN (2004) for Malaysia, the Philippines, Thailand and Vietnam. This information allowed the construction of a consistent database of bilateral FDI stocks by region and sector following the methodology employed for the construction of previous FTAP databases.[14]

It is important to emphasise that the FTAP data do not directly measure international trade in services via mode 3, which involves sales by foreign affiliates rather than the act of investing itself (i.e. establishing a foreign affiliate). However, it is reasonable to expect that FDI stock will be correlated with sales by foreign affiliates, and that it may therefore constitute an acceptable proxy variable. It would obviously be preferable to use data that measure sales by foreign affiliates directly, but a gravity analysis on that basis is not currently possible. In particular, it would be impossible to use gravity to look at South–South trade under mode 3. The approach taken here is therefore a pragmatic one, designed to give some indicative results in relation to mode 3 trade, which is relatively under-researched in the literature. Assuming that more

[14] See Phamduc (2000) and Verikios and Zhang (2001b).

complete data on sales by foreign affiliates become available in the future, it would be important to reassess the results presented here in light of that new information.

(iii) Inclusion of direct measures affecting policies in service sectors

In an important addition to previous work, the present paper also includes direct measures of trade policy affecting services in the form of OECD trade restrictiveness indices (TRIs) for individual services sectors (OECD 2005) and an index of 'FDI friendliness' of regional trade agreements (RTAs) taken from OECD (2006a). OECD (2005) presents TRIs for five services sectors (banking, insurance, telecom, engineering[15] and distribution), disaggregated by mode of supply. In addition to the sectors dealt with in that paper, this one also covers air and maritime transport, using data on trade restrictions in those sectors taken from Doove *et al.* (2001) and Fink *et al.* (2001), respectively.[16]

Combining TRIs with data on 'investment friendliness' of RTAs from OECD (2006a) allows us to create an approximate measure of bilateral trade policy, in the form of MFN restrictiveness weighted by RTA liberalisation. To our knowledge, this paper is the first to include such detailed measures of trade policy as it applies to services.[17] The papers listed in Table 10 that take account of the potential impact of RTAs do so using only a binary dummy variable that provides nothing like the level of detail in the OECD (2006) measure. Moreover, only Grünfeld and Moxnes (2003) include a TRI, but their measure is a simple average of six

[15] The TRI for engineering services is used here as a proxy for restrictions relating to 'other business services' in terms of the FTAP sectoral classification. While engineering has previously been used as one example of trade restrictiveness in professional services (Nguyen-Hong, 2000), its appropriateness as a proxy in the present context is doubtful. Future work could usefully concentrate on producing a more broad-based TRI covering the other business services sector.

[16] The TRI used here is the simple average of the index numbers for cargo handling restrictions and mandatory services calculated by Fink *et al.* (2002).

[17] In addition, models for the finance and insurance sectors contain a 0/1/2 dummy variable to take account of one or both countries in a given exporter–importer pair signing on to the WTO Understanding on Commitments in Financial Services. This is included on the basis that it is relevant both to the degree of liberalisation of both parties and to the certainty of their trade policy, since it represents a binding WTO commitment. General indicators of sectoral regulatory practice are not included, since they do not carry such an interpretation and indeed would take the research in quite a different direction, namely the general impact of regulation and regulatory heterogeneity on trade flows in services (cf. Kox *et al.*, 2005).

sectoral TRIs applied to total (aggregate) services trade, which does not allow for possible differences in cross-sectoral impacts.

The availability of information on policy determinants determines the aggregation used in the paper. The aggregation used here covers seven sectors and up to forty-one countries for the year 2001. (For more details on coverage by individual sector, see Table 11.)

(iv) Model specification

On a technical level, this paper sticks closely to the 'theoretical' gravity model of Anderson and Van Wincoop (2003, 2004).[18] The right-hand side of the gravity equation[19] includes geographical, historical and cultural data from the Centre d'Etudes Prospectives et d'Informations Internationales (CEPII) (Mayer and Zignago, 2006).[20] In addition, dummy variables are included to take account of the impact of common language (on an ethnographic basis, not limited to official languages), common border, common coloniser and existence at any time of a colonial link between the exporting and importing countries.

The main results of this exercise (see Tables 12–14) are summarised below:

The distance effect on trade is less strong (−0.65 to −0.89) than is usually found in work with goods trade (around −1; see OECD (2006b)). The inclusion of distance as a measure of trade costs is more problematic for services than for goods. In the latter context, inclusion of distance between trading partners has at least two appealing interpretations: as an indicator of the cost of shipping goods from the exporter to the importer, and as an indicator of the difficulty of accessing market information (e.g. Buch, 2005). Generally, the first interpretation will not apply in relation to services trade (except potentially in relation to modes 2 and 4, in which

[18] None of the papers listed in Table 10 explicitly takes account of the resistance (relative price) terms predicted by the model developed by Anderson and Van Wincoop (2003, 2004), although some of them employ empirical specifications that are robust to the presence of those terms since they include appropriate fixed effects. However, some of the estimates in Table 14 remain potentially subject to significant mis-specification bias in this regard.

[19] See OECD (2006c) for a theoretical description of the gravity model employed in this paper.

[20] Specifically, the distance measure used is the simple great circle distance between each country's largest city. In the sensitivity analysis (not reported, available on request), it was found that the choice of CEPII distance measure (standard, weighted, capital cities) made little difference to results.

Table 11 *Gravity model – Breakdown of country coverage by sector*

Sector	No. of Exporting Countries	No. of Importing Countries	South–South Pairs (% of Total)
Finance	36	36	12.4
Insurance	35	35	11.1
Telecom	35	34	10.1
Other Business	33	33	3.7
Distribution	41	41	11
Air Transport	38	38	7.3
Maritime Transport	41	41	9.7

consumers and producers, respectively, have to be transported). Applied work therefore relies, at least implicitly, on the second interpretation only. Future work could usefully challenge that assumption, in particular by extending the work of Freund and Weinhold (2002, 2004) to look more broadly at the interplay between distance and communication technology in determining information costs. However, such an exercise is beyond the scope of the present study, and we rely on the straightforward interpretation of distance as a proxy for information costs – in line with the approach taken in all of the papers listed in Table 10.

Our finding fits well with the interpretation of the role of distance in services trade discussed above, namely that it reflects only information costs and not transport costs; in a gravity equation for goods, it reflects both effects and therefore should be correspondingly stronger. This finding is in accordance with most of the results presented in the papers listed in Table 10.

The TRI always has an estimated negative impact on trade, but only in three out of seven cases is that impact statistically significant. While the possible causes of such a result are many and varied, it should be stressed that one likely problem relates to measurement error in the TRIs themselves, as well as in the dependent variable. In the former case, measurement error is due to the inherent complexity of transforming qualitative information on services barriers into a quantitative measure (OECD, 2005), while in the latter it is because the variable is used as a proxy for data that, at this stage, cannot be observed directly. Moreover, the sectoral correspondence between the TRIs and the FTAP data is not always exact, which introduces a further dimension of error. While the

Table 12 *Regression results for finance, insurance, telecom and professional services*

Variable	Finance	Insurance	Telecom	Other Business
Log(Distance)	−0.654679***	−0.554004***	−0.709075***	−0.890904***
	0.138768	*0.098672*	*0.107074*	*0.084565*
Log(TRI_RTA)	−0.141548	−0.796146	−0.471211	−0.469127
	0.272779	*1.023085*	*1.029979*	*0.519283*
Colony	1.647908***	1.068628***	1.484965***	0.653636**
	0.334579	*0.293324*	*0.371881*	*0.316587*
Common Colonizer	0.623869	0.700443	0.99204	0.952352*
	0.850413	*1.470533*	*1.535444*	*0.542011*
Common Language	0.217934	0.221513	0.358205*	0.625243***
	0.200148	0.188822	0.209694	0.199779
Common Border	0.433204	0.002959	0.176964	−0.494147*
	0.307953	0.301107	0.31581	*0.262754*
UCFS	0.427629	0.536658**	NA	NA
	0.26218	0.239182		
R2	0.755106	0.795228	0.718478	0.813505
Adj. R2	0.735766	0.778498	0.696188	0.797735
Jarque-Ber	32.291***	84.631***	39.089***	99.818***
RESET(2)	0.497	10.412***	0.421	0.166
Observations	1053	994	996	886

Notes: (1) level of significance (***= 1%, **= 5%, *= 10%)
(2) Dependent variable = log(FDI), estimation by OLS with White robust standard errors. Estimated standard errors are in italics (estimated fixed effects suppressed)

estimated signs for the TRI coefficients (negative) are likely to prove robust, additional work with new and more detailed data will be required before more precise conclusions can be drawn as to magnitude.

A final aspect of the estimated coefficients that deserves mention relates to the so-called 'border effect'. In the goods market context, it is usually expected that countries with a common (land) border trade

Table 13 *Regression results for distribution, air transport and maritime transport services*

Variable	Distribution	Air Transport[21]	Maritime Transport
Log(Distance)	−0.845555*** *0.105669*	−0.671851*** *0.099608*	−0.777034*** *0.077352*
Log(TRI_RTA)	−0.580986** *0.226676*	−0.703199* *0.380886*	−2.811131** *1.234122*
Colony	1.103263*** *0.291238*	0.417227 *0.272673*	0.762626*** *0.266244*
Common Colonizer	0.204804 *0.341964*	0.548726 *0.600443*	−0.524178 *0.334446*
Common Language	0.251467 *0.164004*	0.792015*** *0.194461*	0.498164*** *0.170493*
Common Border	−0.155138 *0.264395*	−0.417876 *0.285525*	−0.074168 *0.332644*
R2	0.754927	0.779000	0.724221
Adj. R2	0.738754	0.751375	0.703474
Jarque-Bera	63.869***	27.845***	84.909***
RESET(2)	1.105	0.589	0.053
Observations	1374	712	1173

Notes: (1) level of significance (***= 1%, **= 5%,*= 10%)
(2) Dependent variable = log(FDI), estimation by OLS with White robust standard errors. Estimated standard errors are in italics (estimated fixed effects suppressed)

relatively more than do countries without such a connection.[22] However, Tables 12 and 13 suggest that this effect is only in evidence in three out of the seven cases. For the two transport sectors, this finding accords well with the fact that adjacent countries are likely to trade with each other through

[21] In the case of air transport services, the TRI is already bilaterally disaggregated and therefore is not interacted with the RTA index.

[22] A similar result is reported by Lejour and Verheijden (2004) using data for Canadian provinces, as well as for one sector (other commercial services) within the EU.

Table 14 *South–South regression results for finance, insurance, telecom and professional services*

Variable	Finance	Insurance	Telecom	Distribution	Maritime Transport
Log(Distance)	−0.70292***	−0.584729***	−0.798192***	−0.817704***	−0.727266***
	0.138641	*0.098443*	*0.105893*	*0.120094*	*0.11434*
Log(Distance)*South–South	0.21453	0.055572	0.473039	0.224417	−0.204411
	0.311131	*0.282904*	*0.309019*	*0.3158*	*0.244956*
Log(TRI_RTA)	−0.072736	−0.769688	−0.545049	−0.387594	−1.449345
	0.279331	*1.050688*	*1.058795*	*0.248809*	*1.796201*
Log(TRI_RTA)*South–South	0.349261	1.295091**	0.643945	0.140558	1.056474
	0.886002	*0.611234*	*0.75848*	*0.136379*	*1.783434*
Colony	1.639944***	1.05847***	1.313171***	1.541379***	0.992633***
	0.333335	*0.291156*	*0.369739*	*0.30586*	*0.320143*
Common Colonizer	0.35997	−0.117541	0.751108	0.337043	0.481435
	0.886765	*1.526873*	*1.682151*	*0.846017*	*1.375696*
Common Language	0.238171	0.262723	0.419312**	0.13884	0.458791**
	0.201899	*0.189907*	*0.206846*	*0.183601*	*0.215846*
Common Border	0.417374	−0.050919	0.091805	−0.026402	−0.178491
	0.307513	*0.304766*	*0.301568*	*0.281901*	*0.371763*
UCFS	−0.029139	0.082764	NA	NA	NA
	0.304026	*0.26803*			

Table 14 (*cont.*)

Variable	Finance	Insurance	Telecom	Distribution	Maritime Transport
South–South	−1.070094	−0.662587	−3.959273	−1.396361	2.502948
	2.821878	2.495337	2.742423	2.861081	2.137515
R2	0.757214	0.797980	0.736268	0.768353	0.729725
Adj. R2	0.737232	0.780759	0.713938	0.750077	0.702376
Jarque-Bera	33.657***	88.648***	45.118***	39.150***	51.881***
RESET(2)	1.278	9.331***	3.667*	2.983*	0.003
Observations	1053	994	949	1054	741
F-Statistic[23]	2.350732*	4.258314***	3.364923**	1.372669	3.052228**

Notes: (1) level of significance (***= 1%, **= 5%,*= 10%)

(2) Dependent variable = log(FDI), estimation by OLS with White robust standard errors. Estimated standard errors are in italics (estimated fixed effects suppressed)

[23] Wald test of the null hypothesis that the South–South coefficients in an equation are jointly zero.

road and rail links, and therefore mode 3 trade in air and maritime transport might tend to be relatively less. In the case of distribution and other business services, one possible explanation is that adjacent countries favour trade in these sectors through modes 1, 2 and 4, and trade relatively less through mode 3. However, this remains conjecture, and could usefully be tested in future work using more detailed data.

In order to use the above framework to investigate the particularities of South–South trade in services, we adopted the simple expedient of including a set of dummy variables to take account of possible differences in the impact of policy variables and selected geographical variables on trade flows according to the income groups involved. (The definition of 'South' used here includes all countries that are not members of the OECD.) The results of these regressions appear in Table 14, together with tests of the null hypothesis that the South–South coefficients are equal to zero. It is necessary to be cautious in interpreting these regressions, as the number of observations on South–South trade is relatively limited (see Table 11); indeed, for two sectors (air transport and professional services) it was impossible to run regressions with South–South dummies due (effectively) to the small number of observations involved.

It can be seen from Table 14 that, in all but one case, the South–South coefficients are jointly statistically significant at the 10 per cent level; however, in only one case are they significant at the 1 per cent level. In four out of five cases, the South–South intercept dummy is negative, suggesting that for given characteristics of the importer and exporter, such trade flows tend to be systematically smaller than is the case for other flows (North–North and North–South); however, the effect is never statistically significant. The positive estimated coefficient for maritime transport services is puzzling, but also statistically insignificant. The remaining South–South interaction coefficients are statistically significant only in one case, and should be interpreted with care since they suggest results that are generally counter-intuitive, namely: i) that the distance effect is less strong for South–South trade than for other forms of trade; and ii) that the effect of trade policy is less for South–South trade than for other forms of trade.

In the context of this model, there is little statistical evidence of systematic differences between South–South and other types of FDI in services, because the individual coefficient estimates are generally not statistically significant. This means that the usual determinants of services trade intensity, including policy factors, apply to South–South trade in much the same way that they do to other forms of trade. In order to obtain more precise indications on this question, future work will need to be based on a more detailed and wide-ranging dataset on services trade than is currently available.

2.3 Impact of services liberalisation on goods exports

Given the important role of services as intermediate inputs, the central question of this analysis relates to the impact of backbone producer services on the production and export of goods, and the extent to which this impact is different for developing and developed economies. We want to explore if and to what extent openness and performance of important producer service sectors affects the performance of goods-exporting sectors. Therefore, we first discuss the general two-stage link between service sector openness and performance on the one hand, and service sector performance and goods exports on the other hand. We then exemplify the second stage of the link by examining the impact of the performance of three crucial sectors (finance, telecoms, transport) on goods exports. The analysis is conducted in two steps.

First, we assume that liberalisation of services improves the performance of the respective sectors. Liberalisation and privatisation of services induces entry of new domestic and foreign providers. This may (i) improve the quality and reliability of existing services due to new investment and stronger competition (e.g. infrastructure investment, more efficient credit allocation by banks). It may (ii) make new types of services (e.g. digital value-added services in telecommunications) accessible and (iii) make formerly user-specific services generally available (e.g. business consulting services for small firms instead of only large ones). Foreign entrants in particular are likely to bring not only physical investment, but also know-how and management techniques to the country in which they set up business. This has a direct impact on the performance of their own firms which may spill over to domestic firms.

Second, we explore the two channels through which service sector performance is linked with the volume of goods exports. Services such as transport, communication and finance reduce trade costs and allow for greater specialisation. In addition, many services are direct inputs into the production process of manufacturing firms. Improved performance of these activities may therefore lead to productivity gains in the goods exporting sectors that improve the international competitiveness of relevant firms.[24]

[24] Arnold, Javorcik, and Mattoo (2007) find evidence for a positive relationship between service sector reform and the performance of domestic firms in downstream manufacturing sectors in the Czech Republic over the period 1998–2003.

The arguments presented here should be interpreted with caution, however. There is reason to believe that the mechanisms explained here play a more important role in developing than in developed countries. More specifically, the relationship between service sector performance and goods exports is likely to be U-shaped. The reason for this assumption, which will be tested econometrically, is that in the long run (i.e. as economies mature) service sector performance is positively correlated with the share of services and negatively with the share of manufacturing in GDP. This fact may weaken the causal chain to a considerable extent, at least as long as we consider a sample of countries that includes the richest and most developed economies in the world. This highlights the particular policy relevance of service sector liberalisation with respect to the goods-exporting sectors in developing countries as opposed to more advanced economies.

The econometric exercise conducted in this section involves a standard cross-country analysis for the period from 1995 to 2003 where the supply of export goods is a function of various macroeconomic variables. In addition, we use a set of indicators reflecting performance of specific service sectors. Table 15 gives an overview of the first set of regressions based on the entire sample of developed and developing countries as well as some transition economies (see Table 20) for an overview of the sample countries). Table 21 provides information on data and their sources.

The dependent variable for the models presented in Table 15 is the share of goods exports in GDP. Model (1) is the reduced form or standard export supply function in which national absorption, the price ratio between exports and GDP, net FDI inflows and the size of the economy are explanatory factors. In models (2) to (8) we use various alternative indicators of service sector performance. The following services sectors are covered: telecoms, finance and transport. In models (2) and (3) we measure the performance of the telecoms sector in terms of the number of Internet users and (fixed and mobile) telephone subscriptions per 1000 people. In models (4) to (6) we use three different indicators that directly or indirectly measure transport sector performance: port efficiency, air passengers (per capita of the population), and the size of the road network[25] (per square kilometre). Port efficiency is rated on a one-to-seven index which measures

[25] The road network is strictly speaking an indicator of the quality of infrastructure, not a service performance index. Limao and Venables (2000), however, show that infrastructure is an important determinant of transport costs and thus of service sector performance. Clark *et al.* (2004) show that port efficiency is an important determinant of shipping costs.

Table 15 *Export supply functions with service sector performance indicators as explanatory factors (full sample)*

Dependent variable	EXGDP	EXGDP	EXGDP	EXGDP	EXGDP	EXGDP	EXGDP	EXGDP
Model No.	(1)	(2)	(3)	(4)	(5)	(6)	(7)	(8)
Independent variables								
A	−1.00	−0.85	−0.96	−1.83	−0.89	−1.00	−0.51	−0.73
	(−2.37)**	(−1.92)*	(−2.12)**	(−2.51)**	(−2.03)**	(−2.32)**	(−1.05)	(−1.46)
PxPd	31.99	27.71	30.15	25.08	29.62	31.48	26.11	27.73
	(2.13)**	(1.81)*	(1.91)*	(1.14)	(1.95)*	(2.07)**	(1.69)*	(1.79)*
FDI	2.06	1.91	2.02	1.72	1.90	1.87	1.95	2.07
	(4.27)***	(3.91)***	(4.06)***	(3.11)***	(3.81)***	(2.72)***	(4.11)***	(4.28)***
SIZE	−0.79	−1.03	−0.85	−0.87	−0.97	−1.06	−1.45	−1.02
	(−2.00)**	(−2.38)**	(−2.01)**	(−1.79)*	(−2.28)**	(−1.32)	(−2.84)***	(−2.19)***
INT		0.027						
		(1.34)						
TELE			0.002					
			(0.41)					
PORT				1.66				
				(0.75)				
AIR					0.03			
					(1.17)			
ROAD						0.01		
						(0.38)		
BANK							0.10	
							(1.96)*	
STOCKS								0.05
								(0.88)
No. of observations	53	53	53	37	53	53	52	52
R-squared	0.44	0.46	0.44	0.52	0.46	0.44	0.48	0.44

Note: reported are coefficients, t-values in brackets, and the level of significance (***= 1%, **= 5%,*= 10%), constant term included but not reported.

whether port facilities and inland waterways are extensive and efficient (based on survey answers). Financial service sector performance (models (7) and (8)) is measured by the share of credit allocated to the private sector (in percentage of GDP) and by the value of stocks traded on the country's exchanges (also scaled by GDP). It is clear that the link between goods exports and these indicators is weak at best.

The general result is robust in the sense that all indicators have the expected positive sign, but are not significant explanatory factors of the dependent variable (except for a weakly significant effect of the banking variable in model (7)). Given that there are two different channels through which service sector performance may affect the supply of export goods in opposite ways, the result is not surprising. Services improve the logistical framework required to export and induce higher productivity in manufacturing firms, but their increasing sophistication also reflects the shift towards a service-oriented economy in developed countries. This finding is in line with our hypothesis. In order to test for the policy relevance in developing countries we use a small sample that excludes developed economies (see Table 16).

The sample we use is documented in Table 16 and the countries we omit are italicised in Table 20. The main results are summarised below.

As far as the service sector variables are concerned, the results all point in the same direction. In models (2) to (8) all previously insignificant variables now become significant at the 5 or 1 per cent level. This gives additional backing to the hypothesised non-linear relationship between service sector development and goods export performance.

Internet connectivity seems to be an important factor in this respect. Holding all other factors constant, the coefficient in model (2) suggests that an increase by 100 users per 1000 people is associated with an increase in the goods export ratio of 14 percentage points. This finding is underlined by an impressive improvement in the fit of the model relative to model (1). The result for telephone connections is similar, but weaker.

All three transport indicators are significant at the 5 per cent level. One more passenger carried per capita of the population is associated with a 43.3 percentage point increase in the dependent variable (the coefficient 0.43 must be multiplied by 100 because the variable is measured as a percentage). One more kilometre of road per square kilometre implies a 17 percentage point increase in the goods exports ratio. The port efficiency index is more difficult to interpret, but the relationship is also highly significant.

Both coefficients for banks and stock markets are highly significant. If credit to the private sector doubled from 25 per cent to 50 per cent of

Table 16 *Export supply functions with service sector performance indicators as explanatory factors (small sample)*

Dependent variable	EXGDP	EXGDP	EXGDP	EXGDP	EXGDP	EXGDP	EXGDP	EXGDP
Model No.	(1)	(2)	(3)	(4)	(5)	(6)	(7)	(8)
Independent variables								
A	−2.21	−1.91	−2.16	−2.65	−1.18	−2.93	−1.04	−1.38
	(−3.04)***	(−2.99)***	(−3.16)***	(−2.34)**	(−1.49)	(−3.94)***	(−1.21)	(−2.12)**
PxPd	44.03	33.39	35.64	30.85	31.58	39.15	36.48	33.18
	(2.50)**	(2.14)**	(2.09)**	(1.28)	(1.85)*	(2.36)**	(2.09)**	(2.22)**
FDI	3.80	2.51	3.23	4.85	3.06	3.95	2.32	4.16
	(2.46)**	(1.79)*	(2.19)**	(2.89)**	(2.11)**	(2.75)**	(1.43)	(3.16)***
SIZE	−7.89	−7.37	−7.75	−6.78	−6.42	−8.50	−8.64	−11.36
	(−2.11)**	(−2.28)**	(−2.21)**	(−1.71)	(−1.83)*	(−2.44)**	(−2.42)**	(−3.47)***
INT		0.14						
		(3.19)***						
TELE			0.027					
			(2.16)**					
PORT				13.64				
				(2.59)**				
AIR					0.43			
					(2.43)**			
ROAD						0.17		
						(2.30)**		
BANK							0.20	
							(2.21)**	
STOCKS								0.39
								(3.52)***
No. of observations	33	33	33	19	33	33	32	32
R-squared	0.37	0.54	0.46	0.71	0.48	0.47	0.47	0.57

Note: reported are coefficients, t-values in brackets, and the level of significance (***= 1%, **= 5%,*= 10%), constant term included but not reported.

GDP, the coefficient implies that goods exports increase by 5 percentage points of GDP. An identical increase in the ratio of value traded on stock exchanges would imply an export performance that is almost doubled.

In terms of other variables, absorption generally has a stronger explanatory power than in the full sample. This is not surprising as in developed countries the services sector is expanding faster than goods production. Therefore domestic demand pressure exerts a greater impact on the supply of export goods in the small sample. In less developed economies, an increase in national absorption squeezes the supply of goods for export markets more than it does in rich countries. A second interesting observation can be made with respect to FDI. Relative to the large sample it loses some explanatory power which is a signal that FDI inflows tend to shift towards export-related activities as countries become richer.

We expand this exercise by analysing the performance of exports of selected sectoral goods. Table 17 focuses on certain sectors in which the impact of service sector performance is expected to be particularly strong. The dependent variable is the sum of the exports of textiles, motor vehicles, machinery and equipment and manufacturing not classified elsewhere, measured as a share of GDP. The sectors we look at require large-scale investment and specialised labour inputs. Financial services play a key role because they are intermediate between small-scale savings and large-scale investment. Transport and telecoms services are also important because the manufacturing activities in question require intermediate inputs or raw materials from many geographically dispersed small-scale suppliers. In line with Francois (1990) we therefore expect scale and specialisation of production to be heavily dependent on appropriate logistical services.

We use the same specifications as before even though the dependent variable is a subset of the one in Tables 15 and 16. The macroeconomic indicators remain good proxies for factors determining the supply of the relevant goods, however. While most of the macroeconomic variables (with the exception of the price ratio) turn out to be less robustly related to the dependent variable, the opposite holds for the services indices. In general the coefficients are only slightly smaller than in the previous set of regressions. The financial sector variables are particularly significant and the coefficient of the banking variable is higher than in Table 16. This finding is interesting and suggests that the impact of service sector liberalisation and performance on goods exports is stronger in relative terms (for banking even in absolute terms) than for the sample with total goods exports as the dependent variable. On average the selected sectors account for less than 40 per cent of total goods exports in the sample

Table 17 *Export supply functions with service sector performance indicators as explanatory factors (small sample and selected sectors)*

Dependent variable	SELEXGDP	SELEXGDP	SELEXGDP	SELEXGDP	SELEXGDP	SELEXGDP	SELEXGDP	SELEXGDP
Model No.	(1)	(2)	(3)	(4)	(5)	(6)	(7)	(8)
Independent variables								
A	−1.28	−1.05	−1.24	−1.00	−0.28	−1.88	0.04	−0.62
	(−2.10)**	(−2.00)*	(−2.13)**	(−0.93)	(−0.44)	(−2.99)***	(0.08)	(−1.17)
PxPd	28.03	28.03	31.83	27.98	26.19	33.64	27.46	28.23
	(2.18)**	(2.18)**	(2.19)**	(1.21)	(1.92)*	(2.40)**	(2.18)**	(2.31)**
FDI	1.72	0.68	1.28	2.67	0.97	1.89	0.14	2.24
	(1.31)	(0.59)	(1.00)	(1.65)	(0.82)	(1.53)	(0.12)	(2.07)**
SIZE	−2.69	−2.18	−2.59	−1.56	−1.30	−3.13	−3.41	−5.66
	(−0.87)	(−0.82)	(−0.87)	(−0.41)	(−0.47)	(−1.08)	(−1.32)	(−2.17)**
INT		0.12						
		(3.35)***						
TELE			0.02					
			(1.90)*					
PORT				12.19				
				(2.39)**				
AIR					0.42			
					(2.96)**			
ROAD						0.14		
						(2.22)**		
BANK							0.23	
							(3.66)***	
STOCKS								0.36
								(4.04)***
No. of observations	32	32	32	19	32	32	32	32
R-squared	0.27	0.49	0.36	0.56	0.45	0.38	0.52	0.55

Note: reported are coefficients, t-values in brackets, and the level of significance (***= 1%, **= 5%,*= 10%), constant term included but not reported.

countries. If the variation in the explanatory variable suggests an identical (e.g. one percentage point) increase in export performance, this is considerably greater in relative terms than if the dependent variable comprises only a selection of sectors rather than total exports. These regression results therefore point to the particular relevance of service sector liberalisation with respect to the manufacturing sectors in question. They also emphasise the role of financial services as a driving force of manufacturing sector development as hypothesised earlier on.

Finally, Tables 18 and 19 present evidence about the relationship between restrictiveness and performance in the financial and telecoms[26] sectors. The regressions are reduced form models and deliberately exclude other factors determining service sector performance as the causal relationship is complex and would require a lot of additional information. Financial sector performance, for instance, is highly correlated with economic performance in a broad sense. But this unclear causal relationship implies the existence of a simultaneity bias so that measures of the level or growth rate of GDP may be inappropriate explanatory factors.

Tables 18 and 19 indicate that the predicted negative relationship between restrictiveness and performance can be confirmed for both the financial and the telecom sectors and for two different performance indicators, respectively. The tables also show that the relationship is non-linear. Interpreting the coefficients of the non-linear specifications correctly (which is a priori difficult to see) implies that the impact of lifting restrictions on performance may increase more than proportionally with the scale of the liberalisation measure. This may mean that moderate liberalisation is not enough to achieve an impact on performance if the initial degree of restrictiveness is high.[27] More research is needed to further assess whether a courageous liberalisation effort is required to obtain notable improvement in outcomes, which may particularly benefit goods exports of less developed countries.

[26] See OECD (2005) for a description of the data. Restrictiveness is measured by mode of supply (1–4) and as separate indices for banking, insurance, fixed line and mobile telecoms respectively. To obtain the broadest possible coverage, the variables used here are the averages of the indices for fixed and mobile telecoms, and for banking and insurance so that there is only one measure for finance and telecoms each averaged over all four modes.

[27] This conclusion remains valid when indirect measures of services restrictiveness such as banking concentration index, port efficiency and cargo handling restrictiveness are employed.

Table 18 *Telecom sector performance and the OECD restrictiveness index*

Dependent variable Model No. Independent variables	INT (1)	INT (2)	TELE (3)	TELE (4)
OECDTEL	−187.14 (9.52)***	−274.63 (−3.38)***	−445.58 (−6.71)***	−1163.74 (−4.81)***
OECDTEL^2		92.69 (2.15)**		394.43 (3.07)***
No. of observations	47	47	47	47
R-squared	0.36	0.42	0.50	0.59

Note: reported are coefficients, t-values in brackets, and the level of significance (***= 1%, **= 5%,*= 10%), constant term included but not reported.

Table 19 *Financial sector performance and the OECD restrictiveness index*

Dependent variable Model No. Independent variables	BANK (1)	BANK (2)	STOCKS (3)	STOCKS (4)
OECDFIN	−33.74 (−2.92)***	−118.63 (−3.10)***	−28.33 (−2.64)**	−125.87 (−3.53)***
OECDFIN^2		40.47 (2.32)**		46.27 (2.85)***
No. of observations	46	46	46	46
R-squared	0.16	0.26	0.14	0.27

Note: reported are coefficients, t-values in brackets, and the level of significance (***= 1%, **= 5%,*= 10%), constant term included but not reported.

The results of our econometric analysis generate four main observations. First, there is no significantly positive association between performance of backbone (financial, telecoms and transport) service sectors with goods exports (as a share of GDP) as long as a broad sample of developed and developing countries is analysed. We assume that these effects are weaker for developed countries because on average the share

Table 20 *The sample countries*

Albania	*Finland*	*New Zealand*
Argentina	*France*	Peru
Australia	*Germany*	*Portugal*
Austria	*Greece*	Romania
Belgium	India	Russia
Bolivia	*Ireland*	Serbia/Montenegro
Brazil	*Italy*	*Spain*
Bulgaria	*Japan*	*Sweden*
Canada	Jordan	*Switzerland*
Chile	Korea	Thailand
China	Latvia	Tunisia
Colombia	Lithuania	Turkey
Croatia	Macedonia	*UK*
Czech Republic	Malaysia	Uruguay
Denmark	Mexico	*USA*
Ecuador	Moldova	Venezuela
Egypt	Morocco	Zambia
Estonia	*Netherlands*	

Note: Industrialised countries excluded in the small sample are printed in italics.

of manufacturing in GDP and the supply of goods relative to services decreases as economies mature. Second, eliminating the most advanced economies from the sample and considering only developing countries and transition economies yields a different result. Service sector performance becomes significant at explaining goods exports in developing countries. Third, services matter in particular where manufacturing activities are on a large scale and require specialised labour, many intermediate inputs and raw materials from geographically dispersed small-scale suppliers. Finally, if services sectors are closed to foreign competitors, a major, rather than a small or intermediate, liberalisation effort is required to improve the performance of the service activities.

3. Conclusions and directions for future research

This paper reports on the results of an attempt to identify the key features governing the South–South dimension of services trade via the various

Table 21 *The variables and their sources*

EXGDP	Goods exports in % of GDP	Calculated from IMF BoP and GDP data
SELEXGDP	Selected categories of goods exports in % of GDP (textiles, motor vehicles, machinery and equipment nec, manufactures nec)	Comtrade and IMF GDP data
A	Domestic absorption in % of GDP	Calculated from World Bank World development indicators
PxPd	Ratio of export vs. GDP price indices	Calculated from World Bank World development indicators
FDI	Net FDI inflows as a share of GDP	World Bank World development indicators
SIZE	Share of domestic GDP in World GDP in %	Calculated from World Bank World development indicators
INT	Internet users (per 1000 people)	International Telecommunication Union
TELE	Fixed and mobile phone subscribers (per 1000 people)	International Telecommunication Union
PORT	Scale and efficiency of port facilities and inland waterways from 1 (worst) to 7 (best)	Global Competitiveness Report
AIR	Air transport, passengers carried (per capita of population, in %)	International Civil Aviation Organization
ROAD	Roads, total network (km per sq km expressed in %)	International Road Federation, World Road Statistics
BANK	Credit to private sector in % of GDP	IMF International Financial Statistics (line 32 d scaled by GDP)

Table 21 (*cont.*)

STOCKS	Value traded on stock exchange in percentage of GDP	Emerging Stock Markets Factbook S&P, formerly published by IFC
OECDFIN	Financial sector restrictiveness index (banking and insurance)	OECD Trade Directorate estimates
OECDTEL	Telecom sector restrictiveness Index (fixed and mobile)	OECD Trade Directorate estimates
CONC	Concentration of the banking sector (share of 3 largest banks assets in total commercial bank assets)	Bankscope database, Bureau van Dijk and Fitch IBCA
CARGO	Cargo handling restrictiveness from 0 (no restrictions on foreign suppliers) to 1 (foreign suppliers forbidden to provide services)	Fink, Mattoo, and Neagu (2002a)

Note: the data are averaged over the period 1995–2003, the OECD restriction indices refer to the periods 2001–2003.

modes of supply. The most important conclusion that can be drawn from the analysis is that services trade among developing countries takes place predominantly at the regional level for all modes of supply; this may be due to the increasing tendency to incorporate disciplines for liberalising services trade within regional trade agreements. In terms of the magnitude of South–South services trade via different modes of supply, the estimates based on BOP statistics suggest that South–South exports via modes 1 and 2 represent around 10 per cent of world exports. While exports from developing countries to developed countries seem to be more important for the majority of non-OECD regions, the opposite is true for Asian developing countries: their exports to developing regions represent more than half of their total services exports. Except in Asia, air transport exchanges between developing countries seem to be negligible. In terms of mode 3, indirect estimates suggest that in 2000 more than one-third of FDI in developing countries originated in other developing countries.

This paper has shown that the gravity model can be applied successfully to trade in services using FDI stock in services sectors as proxies for trade in services through mode 3. The gravity model of international trade in services presented here builds on previous work in a number of ways. Firstly, use of the latest version of the FTAP database has allowed us to consider additional country groups (particularly developing countries) and sectors. Secondly, we have included a measure of trade restrictiveness based on detailed information compiled at the sectoral level for individual modes of supply (mode 3 in this case). Finally, we have taken care to use an empirical specification that accords with recent theoretical work.

In line with much previous work, we find that the effect of distance on services trade appears to be less strong than for goods trade, which is consistent with an interpretation in terms of information rather than transport costs. Our results also highlight the importance of policy barriers, and imply that countries have the ability to increase trade in services across all sectors by relaxing restrictions on foreign establishment. There is little statistical evidence of systematic differences between South–South and other types of trade in services as the individual coefficient estimates are generally not statistically significant. This means that the usual determinants of services trade intensity, including policy factors, apply to South–South trade in much the same way as they do to other forms of trade.

However, there remain many areas for future research. As emphasised in the text, the main difficulty confronting modelling work in this area is the lack of data. The expedient adopted here, i.e. using service sector FDI stocks as a proxy for foreign affiliate sales, has given useful empirical results, but involves numerous approximations. Once sales data on foreign affiliates become available for a wider range of countries, it should be possible to obtain much more precise indications as to the determinants of services trade. Moreover, gains in estimating efficiency (i.e. precision) may result if trade in services across the four different modes of supply could be modelled simultaneously. As detailed data become available, future work could usefully move in that direction.

Given the important role of services as intermediate inputs, services liberalisation has a positive impact on goods exports through the resulting improvements in the performance of the relevant services. These improvements potentially foster the export performance of goods-producing sectors through better transport, communication and financial infrastructure which reduces trade costs and facilitates the international division of labour. In addition, producer services are direct inputs to the production of manufactured export goods so that related productivity gains can increase the competitiveness of firms. As opposed to developed countries where these effects are weaker because the share of manufacturing and supply of exported goods in GDP decreases as economies mature, in the case of developing countries service sector performance becomes significant at explaining goods exports. Services matter in particular where manufacturing activities are large-scale and require specialised labour, many intermediate inputs and raw materials from geographically dispersed small-scale suppliers.

Preliminary results suggest that if services sectors are closed to foreign competition, improving their performance requires a major rather than a minor or moderate liberalisation effort. The impact of lifting restrictions on performance may increase more than proportionally with the scale of the liberalisation measure. This may mean that moderate liberalisation is not enough to achieve an impact on performance if the initial degree of restrictiveness is high. More research is needed to further assess whether a courageous liberalisation effort is required for notable improvement in outcome, which may particularly benefit goods exports of less developed countries.

Bibliography

Adlung, R. and M. Roy (2005), 'Turning Hills Into Mountains? Current Commitments under the GATS and Prospects for Change', WTO, Geneva, March.

Anderson, J. E. and E. Van Wincoop, 'Gravity with Gravitas: A Solution to the Border Puzzle', *The American Economic Review* 93(1) (2003), pp. 170–192.

——'Trade Costs', *Journal of Economic Literature* 42(3) (2004), pp. 691–751.

APEC (Asia-Pacific Economic Cooperation) (1995), 'Foreign Direct Investment and APEC Economic Integration', APEC Economic Committee, Singapore.

Arnold, J. M., B. S. Jovorcik and A. Mattoo (2007), World Bank Policy Research Working Paper Series, No. 4109.

ASEAN (2004), 'Statistics of Foreign Direct Investment in ASEAN', Sixth Edition, Investment & Enterprise Unit Bureau for Economic Integration, ASEAN Secretariat 2004.

Asher, M. and R. Sen (2005), 'India: An Integral Part of New Asia', National University of Singapore, Working Paper 63.

Aykut, D. and D. Ratha (2003), 'Transnational Corporations, South–South FDI Flows: How Big are They?', United Nations Conference on Trade and Development, UNCTAD/ITE/IIT/2004/3.

Buch, C. M., 'Distance and International Banking', *Review of International Economics* 13(4) (2005), pp. 787–804.

Clark, X., D. Dollar and A. Micco (2004), 'Port Efficiency, Maritime Transport Costs, and Bilateral Trade', NBER Working Paper 10353.

Doove, S., O. Gabbitas, D. Nguyen-Hong and J. Owen (2001), 'Price Effects of Regulation: International Air Passenger Transport, Telecommunications and Electricity Supply', Staff Research Paper, Australian Productivity Commission.

Fink, C., A. Mattoo and C. Neagu, 'Trade in International Maritime Services: How much Does Policy Matter?', *The World Bank Economic Review* 16(1) (2002), pp. 81–108.

Francois, J. F., 'Producer Services, Scale, and the Division of Labour', *Oxford Economic Papers* 42(4) (1990), pp. 715–729.

Francois, J. F. and I. Wooton, 'Trade in International Transport Services: The Role of Competition', *Review of International Economics* 9(2) (2001), pp. 249–261.

Freund, C. L. and D. Weinhold, 'The Internet and International Trade in Services', *American Economic Review* 92(2) (2002), pp. 236–240.

——'The Effect of the Internet on International Trade', *Journal of International Economics* 62 (2004), pp. 171–189.

Global Trade Analysis Project (GTAP), www.gtap.org

Greenwood, J. and B. D. Smith, 'Financial Markets in Development, and the Development of Financial Markets', *Journal of Economic Dynamics and Control* 21(1) (1997), pp. 145–181.

Grünfeld, L. A. and A. Moxnes (2003), 'The Intangible Globalisation: Explaining the Patterns of International Trade in Services', Paper No. 657–2003, Norwegian Institute of International Affairs, Oslo.

Guerin, S. S., 'The Role of Geography in Financial and Economic Integration: A Comparative Analysis of Foreign Direct Investment, Trade and Portfolio Investment Flows', *The World Economy* 29(2) (2006), pp. 189–209.

Hanslow, K., T. Phamduc and G. Verikos, (2000), 'The Structure of the FTAP Model', Research Memorandum No. MC-58, Australian Productivity Commission.

Hoekman, B. (2000), 'The Next Round of Services Negotiations: Identifying Priorities and Options', *Review of the Federal Reserve Bank of St. Louis* (July–August 2000), pp. 31–47.

IATA (2004), 'World Air Transport Statistics', International Air Transport Association.

IMF (2006), Balance of Payment Statistics, online database.

ITC (2001), 'Statistical Indicators for Regional Trade Potential', Working Paper prepared by the South–South Trade Promotion Programme (SSTP) in close cooperation with the Market Analysis Section (MAS).

Jansen, M. and R. Piermartini (2004), 'The Impact of Mode 4 on Trade in Goods and Services', Staff Working Paper No. ERSD-2004-07, World Trade Organization, Geneva.

Kimura, F. and H. H. Lee, 'The Gravity Equation in International Trade in Services', *Review of World Economics* 142(1) (2006), pp. 92–121.

Krugman, P., 'Increasing Returns and Economic Geography', *Journal of Political Economy* 99(3) (1991), pp. 483–499.

Kox, H. L. M., A. M. Lejour and R. Montizaan (2005), 'The Free Movement of Services Within the EU', Document No. 69, CPB Netherlands Bureau for Economic Policy Analysis.

Lejour, A. M. and J. W. De P. Verheijden (2004), 'Services Trade Within Canada and the European Union: What do They Have in Common?', Discussion Paper No. 42, CPB Netherlands Bureau for Economic Policy Analysis.

Limão, N. and A. J. Venables, 'Infrastructure, Geographical Disadvantage, Transport Costs, and Trade', *World Bank Economic Review* 15 (2000), pp. 451–479.

Marchetti, J. A. (2004), 'Developing Countries in the WTO Services Negotiations', WTO, Geneva, September.

Markusen, J., T. Rutherford and D. Tarr (2000), 'Foreign Direct Investment in Services and the Domestic Market for Expertise', Policy Research Paper No. 2413, World Bank, Washington DC.

Markusen, J. R. and A. J. Venables (1995), 'Multinational Firms and the New Trade Theory', Working Paper No. 5036, NBER Working Paper Series, University of Colorado, London School of Economics, February.

Mayer, T. and S. Zignago (2006), 'Notes on CEPII's Distance Measures', Working Paper, 3 May 2006, CEPII.

Mirza, D. and G. Nicoletti (2004), 'What is so Special About Trade in Services?', (February 2004), University of Nottingham, Research Paper No.2004/02.

Nguyen-Hong, D. (2000), 'Restrictions on Trade in Professional Services', Staff Research Paper, Australian Productivity Commission.

OECD (2004), 'OECD Statistics on International Trade in Services – Detailed Tables by Partner Country', OECD.

OECD (2005), 'Modal Estimates of Services Barriers', forthcoming as OECD Working Paper, TD/TC/WP(2005)36, OECD.

OECD (2006a), 'Analysis of the Investment Provisions in Regional Trade Agreements', Working Paper No. 36, TD/TC/WP(2005)40/REV1, OECD.

OECD (2006b), 'South–South Trade in Goods', OECD Trade Policy Working Paper No. 40, OECD.

OECD (2006c), 'South-South Trade in Services', OECD Trade Policy Working Paper No. 39, OECD.

Parson, C., R. Skeldon, T. Whalsmsley and A. Winters (2005), 'Quantifying the International Bilateral Movements of Migrants', Working Paper 13, Development Research Centre on Migration, Globalisation and Poverty.

Phamduc, T. (2000), 'The Construction of a Bilateral Capital Stocks Matrix for GTAP Industries', FTAP Working Paper.

Sharma, K. (2000), 'Export Growth in India: Has FDI Played a Role ?', Economic Growth Center Discussion Paper 816, Yale University.

UN (2002) Manual on Statistics of International Trade in Services Statistics, ESA/STAT/Ser.M/86, New York.

UNCTAD (2003), Trade in Services and Development Implications, TD/B/COM, Geneva, December.

UNCTAD (2004a), 'International Trade Negotiations, Regional Integration and South–South Trade, Especially in Commodities', UNCTAD/DITC/TNCD/MISC/2004/3, Geneva, March.

UNCTAD (2004b), 'The Shift Towards Services', World Investment Report, United Nations New York and Geneva, July.

UNCTAD (2005a), 'Some Key Issues in South–South Trade and Economic Cooperation: Outcome and Papers Presented to the Work Shop on Trade', Doha High-Level Forum on Trade and Investment, UNCTAD/DITC/TNCD/2005/6, Doha, Qatar, 5–6 December.

UNCTAD (2005b), 'Transnational Corporations and the Internationalization of R&D', World Investment Report, United Nations New York and Geneva, July.

Verikios, G. and X-G. Zhang (2001a), 'Global Gains from Liberalising Trade in Telecommunications and Financial Services', Productivity Commission Staff Research Paper, Ausinfo, Canberra, October.

——(2001b), 'The FTAP 2 Model: Theory and Data', Productivity Commission Research Memorandum, Ausinfo, Canberra, October.

World Tourism Organisation (2004), 'Yearbook of Tourism Statistics', Data 1998–2002, WTO, Madrid, April.

3

The race towards preferential trade agreements in services: How much market access is really achieved?

MARTIN ROY, JUAN MARCHETTI AND AIK HOE LIM*

Economists recognise that multilateral liberalisation is superior to preferential trade deals, which can distort trade and create costs, especially for non-parties. Despite the different characteristics of trade in goods and trade in services, the same basic conclusion applies.[1] Nevertheless, the view that preferential agreements carry no or limited downsides is often expressed – even for those preferential agreements that are not part of a broader regional integration effort. It is sometimes pointed out that preferential liberalisation, especially as regards newer areas such as services, is better than no liberalisation at all[2] and that the process of preferential liberalisation would largely 'multilateralise' itself: first, those not party to these preferential arrangements (especially with larger markets such as the US) would want to take part so as not be left behind; second, those countries having made reforms as part of preferential deals would find it easier to undertake liberalisation commitments at the

* Trade in Services Division, WTO Secretariat. The views expressed are those of the authors alone. They do not necessarily represent the views of the WTO Secretariat and cannot be attributed to it. The authors are grateful for Delphine Naville's assistance, as well as for comments by Rolf Adlung, Lee Tuthill and participants at the World Trade Forum 2006, in particular Americo Beviglia-Zampetti.

1 See Jagdish and Arvind Panagariya Bhagwati, 'Preferential Trading Areas and Multilateralism; Strangers, Friends, or Foes?' in J. Bhagwati and A. Panagariya (eds.), *The Economics of Preferential Trade Agreements* (Washington, DC: American Enterprise Institute Press, 1996); Arvind Panagariya, 'Preferential Trade Liberalization: The Traditional Theory and New Developments', *Journal of Economic Literature* 38(2) (2000), pp. 287–331; Carsten Fink, and Aaditya Mattoo, 'Regional Agreements and Trade in Services: Policy Issues', *Journal of Economic Integration* 19(4) (2004), pp. 742–779.

2 Sherry Stephenson, 'Regional Versus Multilateral Liberalisation of Services', *World Trade Review* 1(2) (2002), pp. 187–209.

WTO. Such views often find echo in the US, where the expression 'competitive liberalisation' has been coined to describe the recent turn of the US towards bilateral free trade agreements.[3]

The number of preferential trade agreements (PTAs) signed by the US in the last few years, together with the number of countries that have engaged in PTA discussions with the US or expressed interest in doing so, suggest that the competition aspect seems at play. Also apparently at play, however, is competition from other big economies to get similar access conditions as the ones the US is ensuring for its own suppliers through its bilateral agreements. Only recently did Japan, China and India sign some services PTAs and become involved in the negotiation of other potential agreements. The European Union (EU) has shifted course recently by adopting, on 4 October 2006, a new strategy proposing among other things the negotiation of a 'new generation' of bilateral free trade agreements with key partners which would give a sharper focus to new areas of growth such as services (along with such other topics as investment, procurement or competition).[4] While the EU strategy, as in the case of the US, indicates that such agreements would be stepping stones for liberalisation in the WTO, it is likely that concerns about losing ground in comparison to the access that the United States obtains through its bilateral trade agreements appear to have played a significant role in this reversal. The European Commission's documents indeed noted, in laying ground for the new strategy, that several priority target markets (e.g., ASEAN members, Korea) had been negotiating PTAs with the EU's competitors (e.g., the US and Japan) and expressed concerns about the risks of trade diversion detrimental to the EU.[5]

[3] On this topic, see: C. Fred Bergsten, (1996), 'Competitive Liberalization and Global Free Trade: A Vision for the Early 21st Century', Working Paper 96–15, Institute for International Economics; C. Fred Bergsten, 'Globalizing Free Trade', *Foreign Affairs* 75 (3) (2002), pp. 105–120; Evenett, Simon, 'The Sequencing of Regional Integration', *Aussenwirtschaft* IV (December, 2004); Simon Evenett, and Michael Meier (2006), 'An Interim Assessment of the US Trade Policy of "Competitive Liberalization"', mimeo, 24 July 2006; Jeffrey J. Schott, 'Assessing US FTA Policy', in *Free Trade Agreements: US Strategies and Policies*, J. Schott (ed.), (Washington, DC: Institute for International Economics,. 2004).

[4] Incidentally, these are Singapore issues that were pulled out of the Doha work programme.

[5] European Commission (2006), 'Global Europe: Competing in the World; A Contribution to the EU's Growth and Jobs Strategy', Commission Staff Working Document, Brussels, 4 October 2006.

This chapter aims at shedding light on the phenomenon of regionalism in services trade, which is a relatively recent but intensifying phenomenon. Notifications to the WTO, which are mandatory by virtue of Article V of the GATS, help illustrate the change in pace in the negotiations of services PTAs. Indeed, 43 economic integration agreements have been notified to the WTO since the start of the services negotiations in 2000, compared to 12 before this date.[6] It is interesting to note that most of the pre-Doha Round notifications (8 out of 12) involved agreements relating to the process of European integration, e.g., Europe Agreements with candidates for EU accession in Eastern Europe. In contrast, most of the agreements notified since 2000 were not part of a regional integration effort and, in fact, often linked countries from different continents.

The focus of this chapter is not to examine whether liberalisation achieved in PTAs is likely to soon be multilateralised or not. The main objective is rather to provide a qualitative assessment of the GATS+ commitments made in the recent wave of preferential trade agreements. A clearer picture of the actual content of the new and improved commitments in PTAs (when compared to GATS commitments and offers) may help explain why key trading partners feel compelled to jump on the PTA bandwagon so as not to lose ground. It may also shed additional light on services liberalisation processes and the perspectives for achieving binding international commitments, e.g., priorities in terms of types of measures maintained or withdrawn and modes liberalised per sector. Such qualitative analysis of the content of commitments should, at the same time, also allow us to answer some questions and to highlight patterns that a more quantitative analysis was not meant to assess, e.g. the extent to which countries undertake different services commitments for the same sectors in their different preferential agreements and, in such cases, which trading partners tend to get the better commitments.[7]

[6] Notifications under Article V, as of 15 October 2006.

[7] This contribution is therefore intended to complement the study by Martin Roy, Juan Marchetti and Hoe Lim, 'Services Liberalization in the New Generation of Preferential Trade Agreements (PTAs): How Much Further than the GATS?', *World Trade Review* 6(2) (2007), pp. 155–192, which, through a cross-sectoral computation of the proportion of new and improved market access commitments on services established that PTA commitments, overall, go significantly beyond multilateral commitments under GATS and Doha Round services offers.

The next section provides a brief overview of advances made in PTAs in terms of liberalisation commitments in services. Section II, which is the core of this contribution, analyses the GATS+ commitments in PTAs in a sample of sectors. The conclusion summarises findings, discusses Article V implications and identifies some avenues for further research.

I. An overview of liberalisation commitments in PTAs

A key characteristic of services commitments in the GATS is that the 'liberalisation obligations' (market access in Article XVI and national treatment in Article XVII) only apply to the sectors that each Member chooses to include in its schedule of commitments, and in line with limitations or conditions attached. As a result, unlike for goods, many services sectors are not subject to any market access commitments and remain unbound, meaning that no guarantee of access whatsoever is provided to trading partners. As a matter of fact, the majority of WTO Members have no market access commitments in the majority of sectors.[8] The number of services sub-sectors where a given level of openness has been guaranteed, known in the GATS jargon as the sectoral coverage of schedules, is therefore an important indicator of the quality of commitments. The other such quality indicator is the depth of commitments, i.e., the actual level of access granted in light of the existence – or not – of specific restrictions.

Accordingly, to what extent have PTAs made progress compared to existing GATS commitments and offers submitted in the Doha Round in terms of sector coverage of commitments?[9] Based on the commitments undertaken by 29 countries in 28 recent PTAs, Figure 7 presents the average proportion of sub-sectors committed in the GATS, in Doha offers and in PTAs for mode 1 and mode 3.[10] The Figure shows that, in

[8] Rolf Adlung and Martin Roy, 'Turning Hills into Mountains? Current Commitments under the GATS and Prospects for Change', *Journal of World Trade* 39(6) (2005), pp. 1161–1194.

[9] In the ongoing services negotiations in the context of the Doha Development Agenda, WTO Members negotiate the improvement of each Members' existing GATS commitments (i.e. those already in force) through bilateral requests and offers. The proposed improvements (i.e. either new bindings and/or improvements to existing ones) are contained in offers. The offers are revised periodically to reflect the evolution of negotiations. Up to 1 November 2006, 69 WTO Members (counting EC-25 as one) have submitted services offers. The submission of offers started in March 2003.

[10] The PTAs reviewed are the following: New Zealand–Singapore; EFTA–Mexico; EC–Mexico; Chile–Costa Rica; Japan–Singapore; Singapore–Australia; US–Chile;

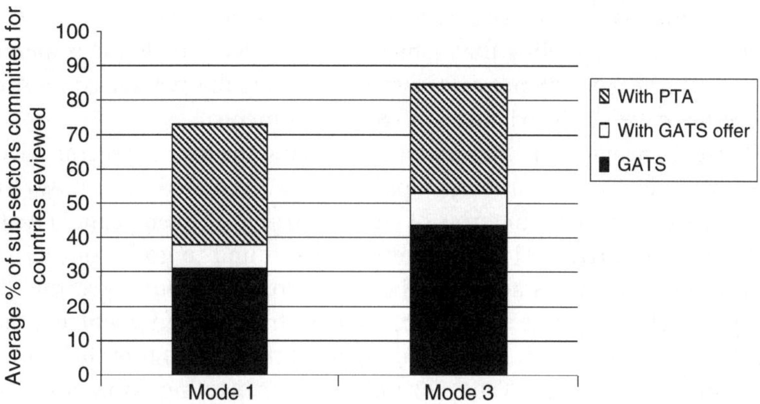

Figure 7 Sector coverage of PTAs in comparison with GATS offers and GATS schedules

terms of breadth of commitments, the PTAs have provided for spectacular advances overall for both modes of supply. Even for the 29 countries reviewed here, which include many of those with most GATS commitments and that participate most actively in the multilateral negotiations, the average level of sub-sectors bound in the prevailing GATS schedules is low (31 per cent for mode 1 and 44 per cent for mode 3). Moreover, for these 29 countries offers had not significantly modified this picture (moving up 7 percentage points to 38 per cent for mode 1 and up 9 points to 53 per cent for mode 3). On the other hand, the value-added of PTAs in terms of sector coverage, i.e. new sub-sectors bound under PTAs, which is illustrated by the striped part of the bar, is

US–Singapore; Chile–El Salvador; Korea (Rep.)–Chile; EC–Chile; EFTA–Singapore; China–Hong Kong, China; China–Macao, China; EFTA–Chile; US–Australia; Thailand–Australia; Panama–El Salvador; Japan–Mexico; US–Bahrain; US–Oman; US–Central America and Dominican Republic; US–Morocco; US–Peru; Japan–Malaysia; Korea (Rep.)–Singapore; US–Colombia; Singapore–India. This sample includes agreements signed but not yet implemented or notified to the WTO. In computing sector coverage, we have looked at the best commitments undertaken by each country across any of its agreements. The EU-15 is counted as one. Macao and Hong Kong's commitments are not computed. We only focus here on modes 1 and 3, which represent more than 80 per cent of world services trade; mode 4 liberalisation commitments represent high stakes for many countries, but they are typically crafted along somewhat different parameters. This aspect merits a paper of its own. For further details on data issues, as well as country-specific results, see Martin Roy, Juan Marchetti and Hoe Lim, 'Services Liberalization in the New Generation of Preferential Trade Agreements (PTAs): How Much Further than the GATS?', *World Trade Review*, 6(2) (2007), pp. 155–192.

quite impressive. For mode 1, sector coverage reaches 73 per cent on average, almost doubling that achieved by GATS offers. For commercial presence, it reaches 85 per cent, almost doubling the average proportion of sectors covered by existing GATS commitments.

Table 22 provides further detail by showing the average sector coverage for mode 3 for different groups of reviewed countries. It shows that while there is diversity in terms of additional sector coverage in PTAs for individual countries, PTAs are nevertheless found to go beyond GATS existing commitments and GATS offers across all country groups. The jump in sector coverage for developing countries is naturally bigger than for developed countries, which had higher sector coverage in their GATS schedule to start with. Table 22 highlights interesting contrasts when comparing the sector coverage of positive-list and negative-list type agreements, and that of countries that have signed a PTA with the US and those that have not. It suggests that agreements signed by the US, as well as other agreements based on a negative-list approach to scheduling, account for a good share of the overall value-added of PTAs, at least in terms of sector coverage. Positive-list type agreements notably include all those signed by the EC and EFTA.

The value-added of PTAs over GATS commitments and GATS offers can also be highlighted by looking at the proportion of the 29 Members that, in their PTAs, either improve upon their GATS offer or undertake commitments for this first time in selected sector groupings. In Figures 8 and 9, the bars labelled 'PTA' show the proportion of the countries reviewed that have, for each sector grouping, either (1) undertaken certain commitments in the

Table 22 *Average percentage of sub-sectors subject to market access commitments (mode 3), by groups of countries reviewed.*[a]

	GATS	With GATS offer	With PTA
ALL	44	53	85
Developing Countries	36	46	86
Developed Countries	67	74	82
Positive List	57	66	69
Negative List	37	47	93
US PTA partner	30	39	93
Not US PTA Partner	56	66	76

[a] Countries falling under the 'negative list' category are those that have signed at least one such agreement.

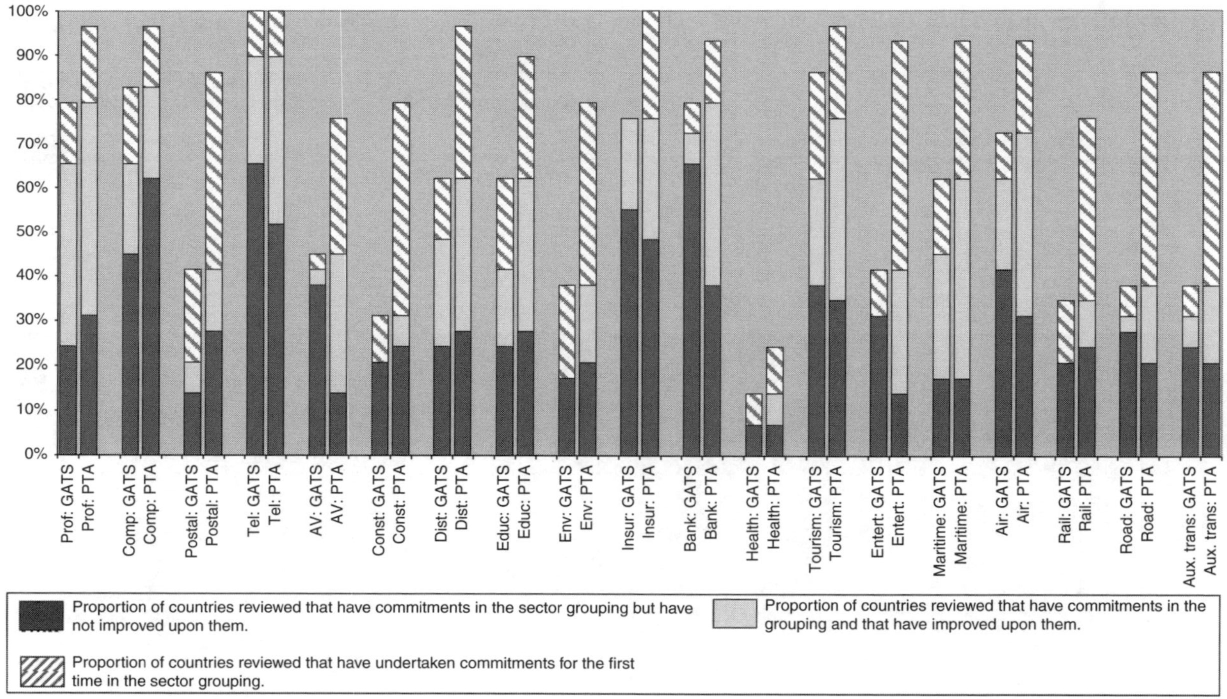

Figure 8 Proportion of countries reviewed that improve their commitments or commit for the first time in selected sector groups (mode 1)

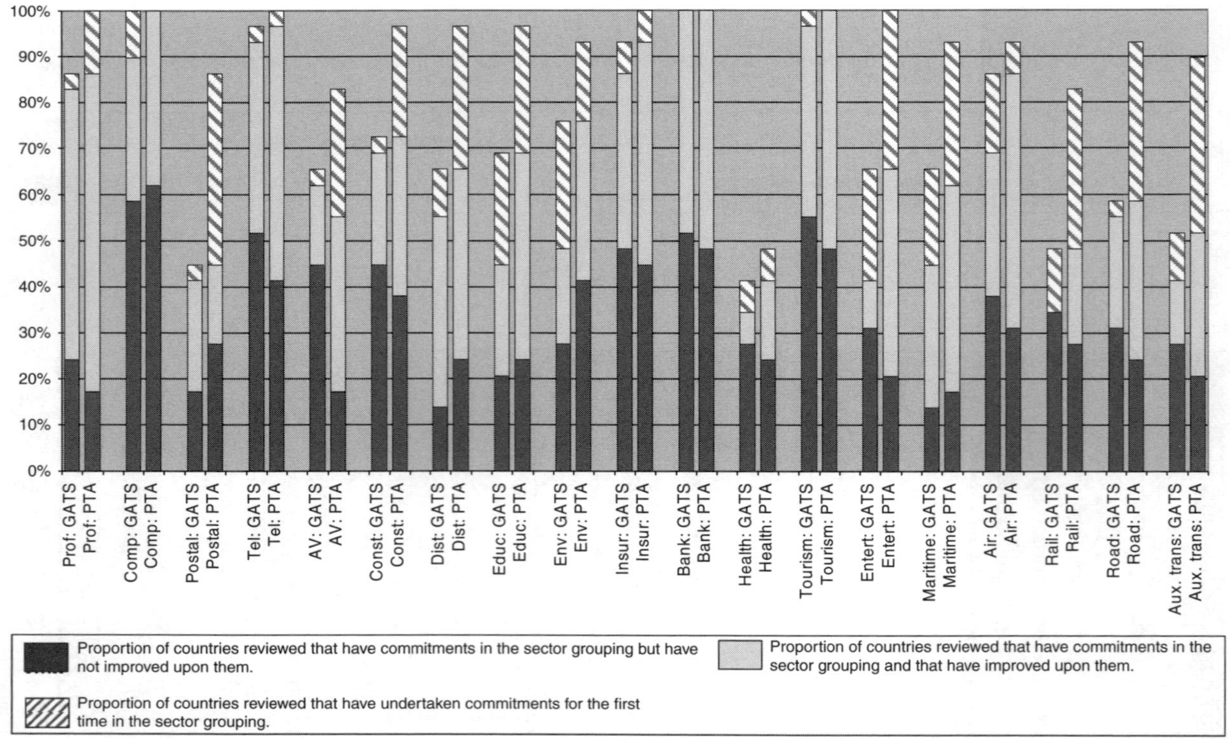

Figure 9 Proportion of countries reviewed that improve their commitments or commit for the first time in selected sector groups (mode 3)

GATS offer for the sector grouping and did not improve upon them in the PTA (bottom part of the bars); (2) undertaken certain commitments in the GATS offer for the sector and improved upon them in the PTA (lighter part of the bar above); (3) undertaken, through PTAs, commitments for the first time in a given sector grouping (striped part of the bar further above); (4) taken no commitment, either in the PTA or in the GATS offer. The bars labelled 'GATS' do the same by comparing commitments proposed in the GATS offers to those contained in GATS schedules.

These Figures highlight that overall, PTAs have provided for important advances over GATS offers across sectors. These advances over GATS offers have taken not only the form of new bindings, but also improvements to the level of access granted in sectors already committed (or offered). In many sectors (e.g. audiovisual, postal-courier, distribution, maritime transport and auxiliary transport), a good number of the countries reviewed undertook commitments for the first time through PTAs. In other sectors, such as financial services, telecommunications or professional services, where most countries reviewed had at least some commitments in their GATS schedules/offers, the PTAs nevertheless made advances through improvements to existing commitments/offers within these sector groupings.

For example, under mode 3, Figure 9 shows that GATS offers had not yet dented the relatively low level of bindings in the postal-courier services sector: 16 of the 29 Members reviewed remained unbound despite the rounds of offers. Taking PTA commitments into account, only 4 of these remained without any commitments in this sector, as PTAs have induced 12 Members to take market access commitments in the sector for the first time, in addition to seeing 5 others improve upon their commitments in GATS schedules/offers. This is largely due to the PTAs involving the US, for which this sector is a priority: 10 of these 12 Members which took commitments for the first time in the sector were US PTA partners. Three other countries that have signed a PTA with the US have improved upon the level of access foreseen in their GATS offer.[11]

By presenting information on sector groupings where GATS offers improved upon GATS schedules, Figures 8 and 9 also highlight that PTAs provide for advances both for sectors that had tended to attract fewer offers in the GATS (e.g. audiovisual, road, rail, postal-courier), as

[11] In addition, it should be noted that US PTAs typically include, within the services chapter, additional obligations on express delivery services, e.g. disciplines on cross-subsidisation.

well as for those that attracted more (e.g. professional, financial services). One exception is health services, where PTA commitments do not appear to go very significantly beyond what is contained in GATS offers.

II. Assessing the content of GATS+ commitments in selected sectors

This section attempts to go beyond an overview of PTA advances in terms of sector coverage or of the number of new and improved commitments by looking in greater detail at the content of the PTA commitments that go beyond GATS schedules/offers. It does so by focusing on advances in a sample of sectors: financial services, distribution, audiovisual, telecommunications, education and professional services.[12] The sectors selected include some infrastructure services that have already attracted many GATS commitments/offers (e.g. telecom, financial), as well as some others that have proved more difficult in multilateral negotiations (e.g. education, audiovisual). The section will identify not only commitments going beyond GATS, but also those more easily detectable instances of PTA commitments providing for real liberalisation, i.e. commitments providing for the phasing out of restrictions in place.

A. Financial services

When it comes to trade negotiations, financial services has always been considered a special and controversial sector because of its strategic importance for economic development and its political sensitivity. Despite these characteristics, finance is one of the sectors where WTO

[12] We sometimes make reference in our analysis to plurilateral requests, which were envisaged in the Hong Kong Ministerial Declaration. Plurilateral requests are requests prepared by groups of WTO Members with interest in the liberalisation of a given sector or mode of supply that are addressed to other individual target Members. The plurilateral requests represent the joint aspirations of the *demandeurs* in various areas of the services negotiations. Plurilateral requests are meant to complement and not to replace the traditional bilateral request-offer process. It is worth clarifying that while negotiations may be conducted bilaterally or plurilaterally, the outcome of such market access negotiations, i.e. the offers and eventually the final set of specific commitments, remain multilateral in nature. While plurilateral requests have not been notified to the WTO Secretariat or circulated to the whole WTO membership, various internet sites from NGOs or business associations provide copies of such requests. See, for example, www.uscsi.org/wto/crequests.htm.

Members have made more commitments than in any other sector grouping except tourism. The 29 WTO Members whose PTA commitments were reviewed for this paper had already made some commitments on financial services at the WTO before negotiating these preferential trade agreements. The sectoral coverage was however variable: while all developed countries had made commitments in all sub-sectors of financial services; developing countries had tended to take commitments on insurance and core banking services[13] rather than in capital-market related services.[14] Stronger commitments were in general made under mode 3 (establishment) than under mode 1 (cross-border trade). With few exceptions, multilateral commitments on financial services did not involve real liberalisation when they were undertaken.[15] In the best of the cases, they represented bindings of existing levels of access. Significant restrictions remained, particularly with regard to types of legal entity through which services can be supplied (the branch vs. subsidiary debate), foreign equity limitations and limitations on the number of suppliers, including monopolies. This picture has not changed significantly with the submission of offers in the Doha Round. Among the countries analysed in this paper, only a handful introduced significant changes in their offers on financial services. Among these, Norway's offer is particularly interesting, since it is the only developed country that has made a concrete offer to expand its commitments on cross-border trade for some financial services where the consumer is supposed to be sophisticated enough, i.e. cruise vessels, fishing vessels, offshore exploration or insurance contracts regarding domestic companies with an activity of at least 10-man-years or annual sales above a certain threshold. The other countries having made offers on financial services proposed to eliminate or reduce foreign equity limitations on different financial activities, although sometimes not even matching the actual practice (e.g. India on banking services).

[13] Deposit taking, lending, payment and money transmission services, financial leasing and guarantees and commitments.

[14] Trading in securities, underwriting and asset management.

[15] Excluding the most recent accessions to the WTO (e.g. China), current commitments on financial services date back, for most WTO Members, to 1997 (end of the so-called extended negotiations). In some cases, however, commitments date back to 1993 (end of the Uruguay Round) or to 1995 (end of the first extended negotiation on financial services).

(i) A diversity of liberalisation modalities

Unlike other sectors, the sensitivities surrounding financial services have translated into different liberalisation modalities for financial services in different agreements. One modality has been to explicitly exclude the sector from the PTA (e.g. Chile–El Salvador; Chile–Costa Rica; Chile–Korea). Sometimes, this exclusion is accompanied by a commitment to review the situation after the entry into force of the PTA (e.g. Chile–EFTA). A variation of the latter modality is to avoid sectoral exclusions from the scope of the agreement, but to exclude the sector from the initial schedules of market access commitments, with the promise to include it in future rounds of negotiation (e.g. Thailand–Australia).

Another modality is to develop an additional chapter or annex that clarifies or elaborates upon more general provisions in the PTA for the sake of trade in financial services (e.g. Japan–Singapore; Australia–Singapore; EFTA–Singapore; Japan–Malaysia; Singapore–India). Still another modality is to develop a separate, self-contained, chapter on financial services that governs all aspects of trade in financial services. Such chapters become therefore a sort of agreement within the agreement. This modality has been followed by the US in all its PTAs, and also by EFTA–Mexico; EC–Mexico; EC–Chile; Panama–El Salvador; Japan–Mexico; and Korea–Singapore.

PTAs also differ as to the liberalisation approach adopted: positive list, negative list and a combination of the two. Negative list approaches have been followed in the Panama–El Salvador, and Australia–Singapore PTAs. Positive list approaches *à la* GATS have been followed in a number of agreements, e.g. by Japan–Singapore, EC–Chile, EC–Mexico, EFTA–Mexico, EFTA–Singapore, China–Hong Kong, China–Macao, Japan–Malaysia, Korea–Singapore, and India–Singapore.

In all its PTAs, the US has used a combination of these approaches, with variations depending on the mode of supply. These PTAs contain a provision on market access for financial services modelled on GATS Article XVI, but which only apply to mode 3, and whose liberalisation is subject to the traditional negative list approach (establishment is allowed in all financial service activities unless a reservation is made). Cross-border trade, however, is subject to a different approach, similar to the one adopted in the WTO Understanding on Commitments in Financial Services – i.e. the listing of non-conforming measures for a specified (positive) list of financial services sub-sectors.

(ii) How much further than GATS?

PTAs provide, overall, for significant improvements over GATS commitments, sometimes even leading to real liberalisation of the market. The advances in PTAs have, in general, well exceeded the offers made in the context of the Doha Round, and in some cases – particularly in the US PTAs – have matched the proposals in the plurilateral requests made pursuant to the WTO Hong Kong Ministerial Declaration.[16]

Agreements following a GATS-type approach to liberalisation have tended to produce more limited results, either in terms of new bindings or in terms of further liberalisation. PTAs following a negative list (Panama–El Salvador) or a hybrid approach (the US PTAs) have tended to produce more significant results. A second general feature is that commercial presence has clearly been favoured as a mode of supply over cross-border trade. With only few exceptions (basically the agreements signed by the US and Panama–El Salvador), PTAs have not led to very significant improvements in bindings for cross-border trade in financial services.

When it comes to cross-border trade in financial services, countries having signed agreements with the US have all coalesced around an implicit model which improves – albeit timidly – on the level of liberalisation embedded in the WTO Understanding on Commitments in Financial Services. As a rule, these countries have accepted commitments vis-à-vis the US on the cross-border supply of: marine, aviation and transport (MAT) insurance services; reinsurance services; services auxiliary to insurance; provision and transfer of financial information and financial data processing; and advisory and other auxiliary financial services relating to banking. In addition, most of them (including the US itself) have accepted to go even further by assuming commitments on insurance intermediation (broking and agency) and on the cross-border

[16] The plurilateral request on financial services was sponsored by Australia, Canada, Chinese Taipei, Ecuador, EC, Hong Kong China, Japan, Korea, Norway and the US. The market access objectives for mode 1 are the following: undertake commitments for MAT insurance (marine, aviation and transport insurance); reinsurance; insurance intermediation; insurance auxiliary services; financial advisory services and financial information and data processing services; and provide for additional liberalisation, especially where the consuming agent is sophisticated, for example, an institutional consumer of securities services. The objectives for mode 3 include undertaking commitments for all financial services sectors, encompassing rights to establish new and acquire existing companies, in the form of wholly-owned subsidiaries, joint ventures and branches; and removing limitations such as monopolies, numerical quotas or economic needs tests and mandatory cessions.

provision of portfolio management services by asset management firms to mutual funds located in any of these countries. This template of commitments on mode 1 matches the plurilateral request made at the WTO by the US and other Members, as explained earlier. For some of the US trading partners, these cross-border commitments will require further liberalisation. For example, Bahrain and Chile will allow the cross-border supply of MAT insurance services (including brokerage of those services) one year after the entry into force of the PTA; while Morocco will allow cross-border supply of MAT insurance services (including brokerage of those services) two years after entry into force. Moreover, as part of its commitments with the US, Morocco will eliminate mandatory cession requirements in no more than 8 years. Moreover, for some of them (e.g. Dominican Republic, El Salvador, Guatemala, Nicaragua) the commitments on the cross-border supply of portfolio management services by US asset management firms will require the introduction of regulatory frameworks on collective investment schemes, which are currently not regulated in these countries.

Foreign equity limitations have been generally barred from these agreements, with the exceptions of India, Malaysia, Morocco and Thailand.[17] Some progress has been made with regard to restrictions on the form of legal entity through which foreign financial institutions can access local markets, although subsidiaries continued to be preferred over branches by some developing countries participating in these PTAs. The US is the only trading partner that has made significant progress in this area by prompting important commitments to allow branching in Chile (life and non-life insurance), Australia (non-life insurance), El Salvador (all insurance services), Colombia (insurance and banking), Costa Rica (insurance), Dominican Republic (direct insurance and reinsurance), Guatemala (insurance and banking), Morocco (life and non-life insurance) and Nicaragua (insurance). All these commitments to allow branching will require real liberalisation, evidenced by the fact that most of them have been undertaken as pre-commitments, with specific timeframes for the phasing out of restrictions in place.[18]

Apart from the examples of real liberalisation brought about by these PTAs that have been highlighted in previous paragraphs, the cases of

[17] Thailand has no commitments on financial services in its agreements with Australia.

[18] Australia did not take a phase-in commitment in this area, but the regulation allowing for branching operations of foreign non-life insurance was introduced right after the signature of the PTA with the US.

Costa Rica and Singapore deserve particular attention. Indeed, as a result of its PTA with the US, Costa Rica will fully liberalise the insurance sector and eliminate the existing monopoly in several phases. Upon entry into force of the agreement, foreign insurance companies will have access to the insurance sector on a cross-border basis. After 2008, establishment in Costa Rica, including through branching, will be permitted, but restrictions on third party auto liability and on workers compensation will continue until 2011, after which the sector will be fully liberalised. On the other hand, in its PTA with the US, Singapore committed to: (i) eliminating the ban on new licences for full-service banks within 18 months of signing the PTA with the US, and the ban on 'wholesale' banks serving large transactions within 3 years of signature; (ii) allowing US licenced full-service banks to offer all their services at up to 30 locations in the first year, and at an unlimited number of locations within 2 years after signature; and (iii) allowing locally incorporated subsidiaries of US banks to apply for access to the local ATM network within two and a half years of signature, and branches of US banks to get access to the ATM network in 4 years.

B. *Distribution services*

While distribution is a key infrastructure service, with significant impact on goods trade and consumer welfare, it is one of the services sectors where WTO Members have fewest commitments (52 schedules). Only 39 developing country Members (about a third of WTO Members from that group) have commitments in this sector. Offers submitted as part of the Doha Round did not significantly change that state of affairs. The PTAs reviewed have, in contrast, brought about a number of advances over GATS schedules/offers, most notably through the undertaking of commitments from some developing country Members that had none or only limited ones. In PTAs at least, the gap between the economic importance of the sector and its treatment under liberalisation obligations is not as large as in the GATS. Apart from China, the countries that have undertaken significant GATS+ commitments in PTAs have all been involved in preferential agreements with the US.

Bahrain, Chile, Colombia, Costa Rica, Dominican Republic, El Salvador, Guatemala, Honduras, Morocco and Nicaragua, which had no GATS commitments in the sector – and had not made offers except for one – all undertook PTA commitments across all aspects of distribution services (retailing, wholesale trade, franchising, commission agents' services). These commitments provide either for full openness (Guatemala, Chile, Nicaragua) or for a few circumscribed limitations, e.g. restrictions on articrafts for Colombia, monopolies for such products as sugar for the Dominican Republic and restrictions on oil and derivatives for Costa Rica. Bahrain also took commitments across the board, with local presence requirements for wholesale trade and retailing with respect to cross-border trade. These new commitments largely meet the expectations of those WTO Members with export interest in distribution, as they are exempt from the barriers felt to be most important for this sector, such as limitations to foreign equity participation, economic needs tests and broad and numerous product exclusions.

In addition, a number of developing countries which already had some GATS commitments in the sector significantly improved their bindings. In its PTA with the US, Oman permitted foreign nationals to own up to 100 per cent of equity in any established retail enterprise valued at greater than US$5 million. In contrast, Oman's prevailing multilateral commitments limit foreign ownership of any enterprise to 49 per cent. In addition, this PTA explicitly provides for future liberalisation by specifying that, starting in 2011, full foreign ownership will be permitted for enterprises of more than US$1 million.

China, whose openness of the distribution market was a key issue in its accession negotiations, provided, in its PTAs with Hong Kong and Macao, a number of improvements over GATS in relation to commission agents' services, wholesale trade and retailing under mode 3. China's PTAs provide for certain product exclusions to be phased out more quickly than under multilateral commitments. Furthermore, restrictions, listed in GATS, that prevent foreign wholly-owned operations of multi-product chain stores with more than 30 outlets, have been waived.

Thailand, an important emerging market in this sector, only has GATS distribution commitments in commission agents' services along with a 49 per cent foreign equity limitation applying to all sectors. In its PTA with Australia, it permitted up to 100 per cent foreign equity participation for wholesale and retail trade of products manufactured by Australian companies in Thailand. Singapore proposes new commitments on retailing, which are generally liberal despite some restrictions on pharmacies and certain products such as medical goods. Singapore's PTAs with the US, Australia and Korea provide for greater product coverage than in its PTAs with other countries.

Improvements over GATS for other countries involved in PTAs are smaller in nature. For example, Australia withdrew restrictions on the sale of pharmaceutical goods in its PTA with the US (but not in its PTA with Singapore); Korea removed restrictions under mode 1 for pharmaceutical and medical goods in its PTA with Chile (but not in its PTA with Singapore); New Zealand and Mexico offer new commitments on franchising; Peru binds full openness under mode 1 (which was unbound in GATS) and undertakes new commitments on commission agents' services, except for articrafts; Japan reduces the number of product exclusions compared to GATS (e.g. rice under mode 3).

Despite PTA advances, important target countries in the GATS negotiations on distribution – because of their market size and the existence of significant restrictions – such as Malaysia and India, have not provided for improvements over either their GATS offer or over their lack of offer or commitments in this sector, as in the case of Malaysia. Panama, where retailing is essentially reserved to nationals, has maintained such restrictions in its PTA with El Salvador.

The US already had full commitments on distribution in the GATS. PTA commitments undertaken by the EC, Norway and Switzerland do not very significantly go beyond their GATS schedules/offers.

C. *Audiovisual services*

As is well known, audiovisual services have been a sensitive issue in the WTO, where key Members have traditionally held very divergent views. Not surprisingly, and given the political sensitivities underlying these views, audiovisual services have not attracted commitments or offers from a significant share of the membership (26 Members have commitments, 6 have made offers).[19] In comparison, PTAs appear to have provided for much more significant advances.

(i) PTAs involving the US

The PTAs reviewed highlight that the United States, the main *demandeur* and home to leading international suppliers, has made significant headway in terms of obtaining certain guarantees of access in the audiovisual sector. Indeed, each of the US's PTA partners, all of which had no audiovisual commitments at the WTO (nor offers, except one), have undertaken commitments in the various areas of audiovisual services, i.e. movie-related,

[19] For more information on issues relevant to negotiations in this sector, see: Martin Roy, 'Audiovisual Services in the Doha Round: *Dialogue de Sourds, the Sequel?*', *Journal of World Investment & Trade* 6(6) (December 2005), pp. 923–952.

TV and radio-related, and sound recording, although often with many limitations: Australia, Bahrain, Chile, Colombia, Costa Rica, Dominican Republic, El Salvador, Guatemala, Honduras, Morocco, Nicaragua, Oman, Peru and Singapore. Taking into account these countries' commitments vis-à-vis the US, the number of WTO Members with commitments on audiovisual in either PTAs or the WTO goes up by more than 50 per cent! Clearly, for the US, progress on the audiovisual front appears easier than in the WTO, where the undertaking of commitments by the membership might prove more difficult given the stance taken by certain other Members in relation to politically sensitive issues of culture.

In general, the commitments taken by the US's PTA partners tend to have fewer restrictions attached to their commitments in movie-related services (production, distribution and projection) as well as in sound recording, as opposed to services related to TV and radio. Commitments on sound recordings are typically without limitations. Only Morocco, Colombia, Peru, Dominican Republic and Costa Rica have maintained market access restrictions in relation to movie-related services (apart from discriminatory subsidies, which are typically permitted in US-type agreements). Nevertheless, none of these PTAs allow for the imposition of restrictions on the number of cinema theatres or their level of foreign equity participation.

Regarding commitments on services relating to television and radio, the situation is quite different; the maintenance of a number of restrictions – including content quotas – is the norm rather than the exception, although, at the same time, a level of predictable access is granted. Although the approaches taken by individual US PTA partners differ, restrictions listed tend to be more numerous for free-to-air television, e.g. content quotas and foreign equity limitations (including by the US for the latter). In contrast, more liberal access is often granted where the US likely has more interests, e.g. satellite TV, foreign programming for cable TV and interactive audio/video services. These are indeed areas where regulatory regimes are often less restrictive, where local capacity is sometimes lacking, and where content quotas carry different policy implications in the light of technological developments permitting increasing consumer control over content and expanding shelf space. From the US perspective, there is value in locking in the current open access in these areas and ensuring significant openness for future developments in digitally delivered content.

PTAs signed by the US also prompted real liberalisation in a few cases. As part of its commitments with the US, Colombia undertook to eliminate restrictions on the number of subscription television concessions at the zonal, municipal and district level once the current concessions at those levels expire and in no case beyond 31 October 2011. Additionally, quotas for broadcasting of locally produced programming on free-to-air national television services on weekends/holidays will be reduced from 50 per cent to 30 per cent from 1 February 2009.

Overall, the audiovisual commitments undertaken by the US's PTA partners, even if not free of restrictions, appear to provide significant value-added for the US since discussions on this topic in the WTO face some strong resistance. Even if the target countries are of course not all the same, the commitments secured by the US in these PTAs appear to generally exceed the objectives sought by the group of WTO *demandeurs* on audiovisual services in their plurilateral request, which does not even touch upon television/radio-related services.

(ii) PTAs not involving the US

Certain commitments undertaken by Members not party to PTAs with the US also include notable improvements over those undertaken or offered in the GATS. China has offered improvements in all sub-sectors of audiovisual services in its PTAs with Hong Kong China and Macao. For movie projection and sound recording, it raises the foreign equity limit from 49 per cent in its GATS commitment to 100 per cent in the PTAs. Concerning movie distribution, it permits foreign equity participation up to 70 per cent; the commitment also covers the distribution of certain movies, while China's GATS commitment is in contrast limited to the distribution of audiovisual products other than movies. China also undertakes some limited commitments on services relating to TV transmission and production, where it had no GATS commitments, e.g. regarding jointly-produced TV dramas.

Panama, Korea and Mexico also provide for certain significant GATS+ commitments. For example, Mexico goes beyond its GATS schedule/offer by not maintaining any of the restrictions for movie-related services that it had listed at the WTO, e.g. screen quotas for domestic films and foreign equity limit for motion picture projection services.

Other WTO Members have not gone beyond their GATS commitments in the PTAs. This is the case for Japan, India, Malaysia, New Zealand and Thailand, which already have GATS commitments in the sector – although of much varying depth – as well as those that had abstained from taking commitments in the sector at the WTO, i.e. the European Communities and EFTA Members. In the case of the European Communities, the sector is even excluded from the services chapter's scope. It can also be noted that a number of countries (e.g. Australia, Singapore, El Salvador, Chile, Korea) appear to have provided different guarantees of access in their various PTAs. When the US is involved as a PTA partner (e.g. of Australia), it always gets the better treatment.

D. Education services

Education services in the GATS has always been the subject of much heated public debate. For example, some interest groups consider that the GATS exclusion of services 'supplied in the exercise of governmental authority' lacks clarity in view of the range of public-private institutions that exist in most education systems around the world today. Given the sensitivity of the sector, it is thus not surprising that education is one of the sectors that has attracted fewest commitments in the GATS. Only 47 WTO members (counting EC15 as 1) have taken a commitment in at least one of the five education sub-sectors (primary education, secondary education, higher education, adult education and other education services). The offers submitted so far in the Doha Round have not significantly changed that state of affairs.

In terms of GATS+ commitments in PTAs, there is a stark difference between those countries which negotiated with the United States and those that did not. In the case of the former, the PTAs have resulted in significant liberalisation commitments. The results are often dramatic, as most of the countries which negotiated with the US previously either had no, or only very limited, GATS commitments in education services.

(i) PTAs involving the US

All of the countries that signed PTAs with the US undertook better education commitments than in their GATS schedules/offer. In terms of countries with no or only very limited GATS bindings, they tend to fall into three main groups. The first includes those countries (El Salvador, Guatemala and Oman) which took PTA commitments across all five education sub-sectors without limitations.[20] Of these countries, only Oman had GATS commitments in education. The second are those which took PTA commitments across all education sub-sectors but subjected them to a reservation allowing them to maintain existing or

[20] Services chapters of US-type agreements also include an exclusion for 'services provided in the exercise of governmental authority'.

undertake new restrictions in relation to public education.[21] Countries falling within this group include Bahrain, Colombia, Dominican Republic, Morocco, Nicaragua and Peru. Among them, only Colombia and Peru had included education services in their offers. In the third group, all sub-sectors are committed, but additional restrictions not relating to public education are imposed. Costa Rica and Honduras, for instance, committed all sub-sectors, but adopted nationality requirements for faculty and administrative staff.

Other PTAs involving the US provide for relatively fewer improvements. Chile, for example, only took commitments under mode 3 and kept the right to impose any measures relating to natural persons supplying education. Singapore took new commitments in primary, secondary and higher education, and improved the sector coverage of other education services, but reserved the right to impose any measures in relation to the provision of primary and secondary education to Singaporean citizens. Mexico took new commitments on adult education with 49 per cent foreign equity limitation. Australia took a new commitment in adult education and improved the GATS bindings in 'other education services' by not limiting it solely to 'English language'. The US's PTA commitments do not add significantly to its GATS schedule/offer. While there are new commitments on primary and secondary education, these are accompanied by a public education carve-out that most likely diminishes their practical relevance.

Notwithstanding the 'public education' reservation, commitments taken by US PTA partners would, overall, still have value.[22] There is after all a growing private sector market for higher and adult education supplied through cross-border trade (mode 1) and commercial presence (mode 3). The 'public education' reservation certainly has more implications for primary and secondary education, although the private sector share for this part of the education sector tends to be smaller. Moreover, while cross-border education is assuming greater importance for higher and adult education, it is unlikely to be as commercially relevant for primary and secondary education. This would appear to be supported by the plurilateral request on education services, which targets only private higher education and private other education services. Although target countries are not always the same, PTA commitments on private

[21] Such Annex II-type reservation typically covers public education services to the extent that these are social services maintained or established for a public purpose/interest.

[22] The formulation in most PTAs involving the US is to exclude 'public education' to the extent that they are social services established or maintained for a public purpose.

education for the majority of the countries reviewed also tend to meet the objectives of the plurilateral request, namely, full commitments for cross-border trade and commercial presence.

(ii) PTAs not involving the US

PTA commitments taken by countries that have not negotiated with the US provide for some improvements, although their commitments are much lower than the above group of countries, both in terms of the number of countries going beyond GATS and the depth of the new/improved commitments.

For example, Thailand improved upon its GATS schedule/offer by allowing up to 60 per cent (compared with 49 per cent) foreign equity participation for higher education services. Panama added to its GATS schedule/offer on education by taking commitments on private education for all sub-sectors, with only a reservation preserving the teaching of civic history and national history to Panamanians. Japan expanded the sector coverage for primary education under mode 3. Korea provided certain improvements to its education bindings in its GATS schedule/offer, for both modes of supply. Malaysia made a small improvement by adding some criteria to its economic needs test for higher education. Other countries such as China, EC, EFTA Member States, India and New Zealand provide for more limited or no GATS+ commitments in their PTAs.

It can be noted that a number of countries (e.g. Australia, Chile, Japan, Korea and Singapore) appear to have undertaken different commitments in their various agreements. For instance, Australia did not give Singapore the same improvements as it did to the US for adult and other education. Chile gave the same GATS+ commitments to all PTA partners, except to the EC and EFTA. Singapore gave the same GATS+ commitments to the US, Australia and Korea, but did not extend them to New Zealand, Japan, India and EFTA. Despite the variations, as a general rule, the US always gets the best treatment as compared to that given by the same country to other PTA partners. Apart from Thailand, which took a commitment to phase-in a 60 per cent equity limitation as from January 2005, this is not a sector where there have been commitments providing for the phasing-in of liberalisation.

E. Telecommunication services

Unlike for other sectors (e.g. distribution, education), PTA negotiations on telecommunication services have benefited from the sound starting point provided by the far-reaching commitments already made by many WTO Members, including most of the countries examined in this chapter. Indeed, as a result of the extended negotiations concluded in February 1997 at the WTO, an important number of WTO Members committed to opening their national markets to international competition, thus removing the more important market access barriers.

For example, in the case of fixed public voice telephony, among the countries examined in this chapter, most of them had made GATS commitments in all market segments (local services, domestic long distance, and international long distance), at least on a facilities-basis, but sometimes also on a resale basis: Australia (with foreign equity limitations for Telstra); China (with foreign equity limitations); Dominican Republic; El Salvador; EC (with foreign equity limitations in France, for radio licences, and Portugal); Iceland; Japan (with foreign equity limitations for NTT/KDD); Korea (with foreign equity limitations for both KT and other suppliers); Malaysia (with foreign equity limitations, and confined to the existing number of suppliers); Mexico (with foreign equity limitations); New Zealand (with limits for single foreign investors in NZT); Norway; Oman (with foreign equity limitations until 2005); Peru; Singapore (with foreign equity limitations); and the US (with foreign equity limitations for radio licences).

Others had left one or more market segments unbound or subject to a monopoly, such as Chile for local services, Colombia for national and international long distance services; Guatemala for domestic long distance services, India for international long distance services; and Morocco and Nicaragua (for all of them). Bahrain, Costa Rica and Honduras, the three of them with monopolistic regimes at the time, had not made any commitments at the WTO, while Liechtenstein and Panama did not have commitments on basic telecommunication services.[23] Among the countries that did make commitments on basic telecommunications, sectoral coverage could still be improved (e.g. China, India, Mexico, Morocco, Nicaragua, Singapore and Thailand). In the case of value-added services, some of these countries reviewed had not made any GATS commitments (Dominican Republic, El Salvador, Guatemala) or had only made limited GATS commitments in terms of sectoral coverage (Chile, Morocco, Singapore, Thailand).

PTA negotiations have certainly contributed to closing the gap between the GATS commitments and the actual, more liberal practice,

[23] Panama had a monopoly on basic telecommunication services at the time.

which had continued to evolve towards further liberalisation after the 1997 multilateral negotiations. Most of the countries examined made commitments in their respective PTAs, covering all telecommunications services (both basic and value-added services), and with fewer limitations than those listed at the WTO. In some cases, these more 'liberal' commitments were simply a reflection of previous autonomous liberalisation, while in other cases countries made phase-in commitments to open up their markets partially or completely, thus using the commitments as a lock-in mechanism for reforms that were already underway.

The cross-border supply of basic telecommunication services has been generally bound with no limitations in the PTAs examined, with only few exceptions (e.g. China, Costa Rica, India). In the case of basic telecommunication services supplied under mode 3, countries can be divided into: (i) those that made commitments similar to those in the GATS (e.g. China, EFTA countries, El Salvador, Guatemala, Japan, Mexico, New Zealand, Oman and Thailand); (ii) those that made their bilateral commitments match their WTO offers in the Doha Round (e.g. Australia, India, Korea, Malaysia and the US); (iii) those that improved on their GATS schedules/offers (e.g. Chile, Colombia, Dominican Republic, EC, Morocco, Peru and Singapore); and, finally, (iv) those that made new commitments in their PTAs without making or offering any commitment at the WTO (e.g. Costa Rica, Nicaragua and Panama).

In some of these cases, improvements on the multilateral commitments appear quite significant. For example, Chile allowed US suppliers access to its market for local basic services; in Colombia, resale of international telecommunication traffic will be permitted as of 2007; Nicaragua and Honduras committed to completely eliminating the exclusivity for their respective incumbents by the end of 2005; and Bahrain committed to eliminating the two-operator limit on the number of mobile telecommunication suppliers by the end of 2005. Costa Rica, which had a monopoly on telecommunication services, committed to allowing US telecommunications services providers, on a non-discriminatory basis, to supply direct private network services and Internet services no later than January 2006, and mobile wireless services no later than January 2007. Such types of commitments did not only appear in the US PTAs. Other interesting commitments may be found in bilateral agreements between developing countries. In its agreement with El Salvador, Panama committed to eliminating its monopoly on basic telecommunication services by January 2003.

It is clear that the value added for telecommunication services of many such PTAs can also be found elsewhere – in the regulatory disciplines. The US PTAs, for example, combine elements of the NAFTA, the GATS Annex on Telecommunications and the WTO Reference Paper to form a comprehensive set of regulatory disciplines, which are GATS+ in some areas (in areas such as co-location of interconnection equipment, resale, number portability and leased circuits services), but whose study goes further than the scope of this chapter.

F. Professional services

Most trade in professional services takes place via the temporary presence of natural persons, which – as a mode of supply – is outside the scope of this chapter. The importance of mode 4 for professional services sometimes makes it difficult to assess the real value of the commitments made in PTAs with regard to modes 1 and 3 (the focus of this study). For example, while establishment rights are valuable for companies, they lose importance when the capacity to transfer professionals from the home country is limited. Another difficulty in providing an overview of GATS+ commitments for professional services is the sheer diversity of professional services, which groups together a variety of professions, each facing different impediments to trade.

Overall, countries with GATS+ commitments have tended to maintain greater restrictions on legal, medical and dental services, and provide for a relatively more liberal treatment of architecture, engineering and accountancy services. This is particularly true for those developing countries that either had none or only a few existing GATS commitments and which concluded a PTA with the US. Countries falling within this category often took new commitments across all the professions with few limitations – except for legal, medical and dental services, which tend to be more restricted. For legal services in particular, in many of these PTAs, the practice of host country law or representation before a court remains reserved to nationals. With few exceptions, commitments on medical and dental services are often qualified by a reservation allowing future restrictions on health to the extent that these are social services maintained or established for a public purpose/interest. For accounting, architectural and engineering services, the trend has been towards further liberalisation with full commitments with no or few limitations, although there are exceptions (e.g. Morocco which has nationality requirements; El Salvador and Costa Rica have residency requirements;

Nicaragua requires to supply accounting services through a local firm). It should be pointed out that Central American countries have subjected their PTA commitments on professional services with respect to the US to a reciprocity provision, likely to limit the access granted only to those US states that provide for similar access.

For other developing countries, the improvements are more limited but again the tendency – with a few exceptions (China, Singapore) – is towards greater liberalisation of the sector while retaining more restrictions on legal, medical and dental services. For example, Oman improved upon its GATS bindings for all professional services except legal services, where foreign equity is still limited to 70 per cent. India improved upon its GATS schedule/offer in various sub-sectors, although it left legal services uncommitted. Chile improved on its offer by taking full commitments in architecture and engineering, as well as in other professions, but only Chilean nationals are allowed to practise as lawyers. Panama took new and improved commitments under mode 3 across all professions, but left mode 1 uncommitted. China relaxed various limitations under mode 3, including for legal, and medical and dental services. Singapore took a new commitment in legal services and improved other sub-sectors.

For developed countries, there are fewer improvements overall as they often start from a higher level of bindings in the GATS. Australia, for instance, improved on the sector coverage for legal, as well as medical and dental services, but excluded health services for a public purpose. New Zealand improved the sector coverage for legal services, which rather exceptionally already permitted foreign lawyers to practise domestic law, and committed dental services with nationality limitations. Korea took a new commitment in medical and dental services but took a public health services exclusion. For the EC, commitments do not vary significantly from their GATS offer.

Another group of countries have provided no or limited GATS+ commitments (e.g. Thailand, Malaysia, Japan, EFTA and the US).

It can be noted that a number of countries (e.g. Australia, Chile, Japan, Korea and Singapore) appear to have provided different treatment in their various agreements. Overall, as with other sectors, the US tends to always get the best treatment as compared to that given by the same country to other PTA partners. It can also be noted that a few countries have commitments suggesting explicit liberalisation: Bahrain, for instance, will phase out some local presence requirements within 3 years of the date of entry into force of the agreement and others within 7 years of the date of signature; China will permit wholly owned operations in architectural and engineering as from December 2006; and Singapore committed to modifying its existing laws so as to relax conditions under which US law firms are permitted to provide legal services.

III. Conclusion

The recent wave of preferential trade agreements has led some observers and decision-makers to speak about 'competitive liberalisation', a process that would force other countries to join in the race, spur global trade and facilitate subsequent multilateral liberalisation. Others have argued that these bilateral agreements would rather make multilateral liberalisation more difficult and create trade distortions.[24] Whether recent preferential liberalisation will be 'multilateralised' or not remains to be seen, but the phenomenon is worth analysing. Indeed, regionalism or 'preferentialism' is not new, the escalation of cross-regional preferential agreements between developed and developing countries, the considerable variation and innovation in the design and content of such agreements, and the speed at which they are being concluded are certainly giving rise to what seems to be a new, yet largely not well understood, phase in international trade relations.

On the face of it, the proliferation of PTAs since 2000 might not appear to be too different from that of the preceding two decades. As in the wake of failed ministerial meetings during the Uruguay Round, the suspension of the Doha Round in July 2006 would seem to have hastened the recourse to preferential deals. However, this logic can be turned on its head. It is worth bearing in mind that the process leading to many of the PTAs that have recently come into fruition predates not only the suspension, but also the launch of the Doha Round. Indeed, it may well be that the current proliferation of PTAs may have led rather than followed the slowdown in the Doha Round as big *demandeurs* divert their resources and attention away from multilateral negotiations.[25]

[24] A number of risks for the multilateral trading system in services are discussed in Martin Roy, Juan Marchetti and Hoe Lim, 'Services Liberalization in the New Generation of Preferential Trade Agreements (PTAs): How Much Further than the GATS?', *World Trade Review* 6(2) (2007), pp. 155–192.

[25] For further views on implications of the proliferation of services PTAs for the multilateral trading system, see *Ibid.*

More bindings, but what about quality?

The main objective of this chapter has been to help shed light on the quality of GATS+ commitments made in the recent wave of PTAs. A clearer picture of the actual content of the new and improved commitments in PTAs (when compared to GATS offers) is vital to assessing the economic consequences and policy impacts of such agreements. Our closer look at the GATS+ commitments of 29 countries taking part in 28 recent PTAs suggests that these agreements, overall, provide not only for many new and improved bindings, but also for significant levels of openness that well exceed the offers made in the context of the Doha Round in terms of the depth of commitments. This is supported by an assessment of the content of PTA commitments in a number of sectors (i.e. financial services, distribution, audiovisual, telecommunications, education and professional services). Although there is diversity in terms of the commitments taken by different Members within each sector, the depth or quality of commitments is reflected by the fact that they generally match or even exceed the objectives sought by WTO Members in their plurilateral requests for these sectors, and that they often induce 'real' liberalisation, as exemplified by a number of commitments providing for the phasing-out of restrictions in place.

We would consider that these results, especially the GATS+ market access achieved by the US and some other important economies, help explain the proliferation of services agreements and, in particular, why other services exporter countries, e.g. the EC, might feel compelled – or pushed by part of their private sector – to join the PTA 'race' so as to get similar access to what is being reaped by their competitor service suppliers in, for example, the US. Indeed, the assessment of the level of access provided through the GATS+ commitments also underscores the stark difference between the commitments adopted by countries that signed agreements with the US – where the depth of commitments secured appears greater – and those that did not. Furthermore, the analysis also highlighted that countries always make better commitments in the agreements that they sign with the United States than in agreements they sign with other trading partners.

The review of the content of PTA commitments also highlighted that the treatment of modes 1 and 3 was quite different in some sectors. For financial services, commitments under PTAs have prioritised the liberalisation of supply through commercial presence. With some exceptions (notably the US PTAs), the agreements reviewed have not led to very significant improvements in bindings for cross-border trade in financial services. On the other hand, the cross-border supply of basic telecommunication services has been generally bound with no limitations in the PTAs examined, with only few exceptions (e.g. China, Costa Rica, India). For professional services, it is worth bearing in mind that an important part of trade in this sector takes place via the temporary presence of natural persons (mode 4), which as a mode of supply is outside the scope of this chapter. The assessment of the commitments made with regard to modes 1 and 3 may thus not give the full picture.

The value-added, as reflected in the types of limitations removed, also differs quite considerably between the various sectors. While difficult to summarise, a few salient points are worth highlighting. In financial services, unlike other sectors, the sensitivities surrounding the sector have translated into different liberalisation modalities in different agreements. The overall effects though are significant improvements over GATS commitments with many instances of actual liberalisation. The value-added for telecommunication services of many of these PTAs can also be found in the form of GATS+ regulatory disciplines often contained in a separate chapter. In distribution services, many new commitments are exempt from the barriers felt to be most important for this sector, such as limitations to foreign equity participation, economic needs tests and broad and numerous product exclusions. What is interesting in audiovisual and education services, which are traditionally difficult sectors in multilateral negotiations, is the extent to which countries that have neither commitments nor offers for these sectors at the WTO were able to make far-reaching commitments under a PTA. Not surprisingly, most advances are found in the agreements signed with the US, which is the main *demandeur* and home to leading international suppliers in both sectors. In professional services, most progress is made in architecture, engineering and accountancy services while relatively more restrictions remain in place for legal, medical and dental services.

How does the recent wave of services PTAs square with Article V of GATS?

Even if our research suggests that a number of PTAs provide for significant GATS+ commitments, the review of the content of the PTAs nevertheless raises some questions as regards compliance with Article V of the GATS. The Article provides a derogation from the obligation of most-favoured-nation treatment in Article II of the GATS for services

PTAs, subject to these agreements meeting some requirements, the aim of which is to help ensure that preferential agreements complement more than hinder multilateral liberalisation. Assessing whether compliance with Article V is secured is made difficult by the lack of clarity of some of the key conditions, such as the requirements of ensuring 'substantial sector coverage', the 'absence or elimination of substantially all discrimination', and of not raising the overall level of barriers for non-parties, as well as by the provisions providing additional flexibility for developing countries in meeting these criteria.[26] Crucial questions arising for example are: do agreements that exclude completely certain important sectors from the PTA or from its liberalisation obligations comply with the Article V requirement of 'substantial sector coverage'? Do PTAs that leave 40 or 50 per cent of all services sub-sectors unbound comply with this same requirement? To what extent does the flexibility for developing countries (Article V: 3(a)) make a difference in that regard?

Further questions can be raised not only as regards the requirement of sector coverage, but also the level of liberalisation granted in PTAs. Paragraph 1(b) of Article V states that PTAs have to provide for 'the absence of substantially all discrimination, in the sense of Article XVII … through: (i) elimination of existing discriminatory measures, and/or (ii) prohibition of new or more discriminatory measures'. Members had expressed very divergent views on the benchmark implied by this provision, although these tended to be voiced before the more recent wave of PTAs involving many of them. Some Members, like the US, interpreted the 'and/or' language to mean that a Member could comply by choosing to eliminate the possibility of adding new discriminatory measures, rather than to eliminate the existing discriminatory measures. Others had expressed the view that the requirement was that of the absence of substantially all discrimination in the *chapeau* and that the language in (i) and (ii) was only meant to offer flexibility in meeting such a test. Although the term 'absence of substantially all' leaves some room for

[26] Sherry Stephenson, 'GATS and Regional Integration', in P. Sauvé and R. Stern (eds.), *GATS 2000: New Directions in Services Trade Liberalization*, (Washington, DC: The Brookings Institution Press, 2000); Sherry Stephenson, 'Regional Agreements on Services in Multilateral Disciplines: Interpreting and Applying GATS Article V', in Sherry Stephenson (ed.), *Services Trade in the Western Hemisphere: Liberalization, Integration and Reform* (Washington, DC: Brookings Institution Press, 2000); see also: WTO (2000), Synopsis of 'Systemic' Issues Related to Regional Trade Agreements, Note by the Secretariat, Committee on Regional Trade Agreements, 2 March 2000.

interpretation, it is unclear, under the latter interpretation, how many services PTAs, apart from true integration arrangements, would actually meet such a test.

Many other issues of interpretation or operationalisation have been raised by Members with respect to Article V requirements. These complexities in interpretation might flow from the lack of precision of the legal text, although the deeper cause might be the sheer complexity of the relationship between the preferential and multilateral liberalisation in the field of services. In any event, the issue would deserve further attention and, ideally, additional guidance on Article V criteria would be useful, given that the provision should play a key role in ensuring that PTAs do not undermine the multilateral trading system. Clarification would prove difficult, given WTO Members' wariness in tinkering with existing legal provisions and in the light of the political reality that many WTO Members are involved in PTAs. However, lack of legal clarity may further argue in favour of developing stronger surveillance of PTA implementation.

An agenda for further research

Research into the new generation of PTAs, especially the services component of these agreements, remains very much in its infancy. Many fundamental questions concerning the implications of such agreements and the costs and benefits that they engender remain to be answered.

For one, further empirical research would seem warranted so as to better assess the economic consequences flowing from the implementation of PTA commitments. The characteristics of trade in services are such that many services restrictions, embedded in regulatory regimes, may prove difficult to remove on a preferential basis. Nevertheless, other types of measures that can be applied on a preferential basis are likely to be at point of establishment and mainly focus on mode 3 (or mode 4), e.g. foreign equity limitations, quotas or discretionary authority in the granting of licences. Fink and Mattoo[27] have pointed out that preferential access in services could engender important costs for non-parties by providing lasting advantages to first movers that might be hard to reverse through subsequent extension of access to other countries. In that context, further information on the extent to which countries actually

[27] Carsten Fink and Aaditya Mattoo, 'Regional Agreements and Trade in Services: Policy Issues', *Journal of Economic Integration* 19(4) (2004), pp. 742–779.

implement preferences, based on case studies, would prove helpful. The way some of the commitments reviewed are crafted can lead observers to wonder whether preferential treatment might be granted in practice. For example, India's commitments on banking services in its PTA with Singapore allowed three specifically mentioned Singaporean banks (DBS Group Holdings Limited, United Overseas Bank Limited and Overseas-Chinese Banking Corporation Limited) to establish joint ventures with Indian investors, and to establish 15 branches over four years. One also wonders whether the examples of real liberalisation mentioned earlier (i.e., commitments to phase out over time restrictions in place), which typically involved entry-barriers as opposed to restrictions embedded into regulatory regimes, are extended to non-parties from the onset.

To ascertain the economic implications of PTAs, one would, however, need to dig deeper. Firstly, one would need to ascertain that preferences are applied and determined, on the basis of country and sector-specific case studies. Secondly, one would need to examine how the agreements were implemented in practice. Indeed, the level of discretion in entry procedures, e.g. the granting of licences, makes it hard to detect, from the text of the law, whether preferences are applied. One could more meaningfully ascertain trade distortion by examining, for example, over a number of years following the entry into force of an agreement, which suppliers applied for a licence, which were denied entry and which were not. In a similar light, one could examine whether preferences are eroded over time through the conclusion of other trade agreements or not.

A second avenue for further research would aim at providing a more holistic assessment of PTAs. Further insights might be gleaned by looking at additional services sectors and modes of supply. For example, Australia's mode 4 commitments in its PTA with Thailand went beyond its GATS offer. PTAs might also exert further impacts on services trade flows through any GATS+ provisions on government procurement in services or recognition issues. Similar research could also be done regarding market access on the goods side. This could allow one to assess the extent to which improvements in services commitments in PTAs are being exchanged for preferential goods access (which might erode with time). To what extent have governments used support from domestic coalitions benefiting from preferential access to overseas goods markets to overcome resistance to liberalising domestic service sectors? Since the findings of our research beg the question as to why countries undertook such commitments in PTAs and not in the GATS, one could further investigate, through country-specific case studies, why similar coalitions could not be put together at the multilateral level? Once additional trade agreements are negotiated and notified, one could also compare the level of liberalisation achieved between genuine regional integration efforts and other types of bilateral trade agreements.

Few research fields are as pertinent as this one in the current context of stalled multilateral trade negotiations. Yet, few fields in trade policy research are currently as open. We have tried to contribute to that research by shedding light on the ever-growing phenomenon of PTAs in services. The issues just highlighted in this last section are, in our view, some of the most important ones that might shape an agenda for further research.

Bibliography

Adlung, Rolf and Martin Roy, 'Turning Hills into Mountains? Current Commitments under the GATS and Prospects for Change', *Journal of World Trade* 39(6) (2005), 1161–1194.

Antkiewicz, Agata and John Whalley, 'China's New Regional Trade Agreements', *World Economy* 28(10) (2005).

Baldwin, Richard (2006), 'Managing the Noodle Bowl: The Fragility of East Asian Regionalism', CEPR Discussion Paper No. 5561, March.

——(2006), 'Multilateralising Regionalism: Spaghetti Bowls as Building Blocs on the Path to Global Free Trade', CEPR Discussion Paper No. 5775, August.

Bergsten, C. Fred (1996), 'Competitive Liberalization and Global Free Trade: A Vision for the Early 21st Century', Working Paper 96–15, Institute for International Economics.

Bergsten, C. Fred, 'Globalizing Free Trade', *Foreign Affairs* 75(3) (2002), 105–120.

Bhagwati, Jagdish and Arvind Panagariya, 'Preferential Trading Areas and Multilateralism – Strangers, Friends, or Foes?' in J. Bhagwati and A. Panagariya, (eds.), *The Economics of Preferential Trade Agreements* (Washington, DC: American Enterprise Institute Press, 1996).

Crawford, Jo-Ann and Roberto V. Fiorentino (2005), 'The Changing Landscape of Regional Trade Agreements', WTO Discussion Paper No. 8.

European Commission (2006), 'Global Europe: Competing in the World; A Contribution to the EU's Growth and Jobs Strategy', Commission Staff Working Document, Brussels, 4 October 2006.

Evenett, Simon, 'The Sequencing of Regional Integration', *Aussenwirtschaft* IV (December 2004).

Evenett, Simon and Michael Meier, 'An Interim Assessment of the US Trade Policy of "Competitive Liberalization"', mimeo, 24 July 2006.

Feinberg, Richard E., 'The Political Economy of the United States' Free Trade Arrangements', *World Economy* 26(7) (2003), 1019–1040.

Fink, Carsten and Aaditya Mattoo, 'Regional Agreements and Trade in Services: Policy Issues', *Journal of Economic Integration* 19(4) (2004), 742–779.

Jansen, Marion (2006), 'Services Trade Liberalization at the Regional Level: Does Southern and Eastern Africa Stand to Gain from EPA Negotiations?', WTO Staff Working Paper, May 2006.

Marchetti, Juan (2004), 'Developing Countries in the WTO Services Negotiations' WTO Staff Working Paper, September 2004.

Mattoo, Aaditya and Sacha Wunsch-Vincent, 'Pre-Empting Protectionism in Services: The WTO and Outsourcing', *Journal of International Economic Law* 7 (2004), 765–800.

Messerlin, Patrick, 'Three Variations on "the Future of the WTO"', *Journal of International Economic Law* 8(2) (2005), 299–309.

OECD (2002), 'The Relationship Between Regional Trade Agreements and the Multilateral Trading System: Services', Paris.

Panagariya, Arvind, 'Preferential Trade Liberalization: The Traditional Theory and New Developments', *Journal of Economic Literature* 38(2) (2000), 287–331.

Roy, Martin, Audiovisual Services in the Doha Round: 'Dialogue de Sourds, the Sequel?', *Journal of World Investment & Trade* 6(6) (December 2005), 923–952.

Roy, Martin, Juan Marchetti and Hoe Lim, 'Services Liberalization in the New Generation of Preferential Trade Agreements (PTAs): How Much Further than the GATS?', *World Trade Review*, 6(2) (2007), 155–192.

Sauvé, Pierre (2005), 'Adding Value at the Periphery: Elements of GATS+ Regional Agreements on Services', paper prepared for a public seminar at the IDRC, Ottawa, Canada, 17 February 2005.

Schott, Jeffrey J. 'Assessing US FTA Policy', in J. Schott (ed.), *Free Trade Agreements: US Strategies and Policies*, (Washington, DC: Institute for International Economics, 2004).

Stephenson, Sherry, 'GATS and Regional Integration', in P. Sauvé and R. Stern (eds.), *GATS 2000: New Directions in Services Trade Liberalization* (Washington, DC: The Brookings Institution Press, 2000).

——'Regional Agreements on Services in Multilateral Disciplines: Interpreting and Applying GATS Article V', in Sherry Stephenson (ed.), *Services Trade in the Western Hemisphere: Liberalization, Integration and Reform* (Washington, DC: Brookings Institution Press, 2000).

——'Regional Versus Multilateral Liberalisation of Services', *World Trade Review* 1(2) (2002), 187–209.

Thangavelu, S. M. and Mun-Heng Toh, 'Bilateral "WTO-Plus" Free Trade Agreements: The WTO Trade Policy Review of Singapore 2004', *World Economy* 28 (2005).

WTO (2000), Synopsis of 'Systemic' Issues Related to Regional Trade Agreements, Note by the Secretariat, Committee on Regional Trade Agreements, 2 March 2000.

4

Rules of origin in services: A case study of five ASEAN countries

CARSTEN FINK AND DEUNDEN NIKOMBORIRAK*

Abstract

An important question in the design of bilateral and regional free trade agreements covering services is to what extent non-members benefit from the trade preferences that are negotiated among members. This question is resolved through services rules of origin. Even though the number of FTAs in services has increased rapidly in recent years, hardly any research is available that can guide policy-makers on the economic implications of different rules of origin. The chapter summarises the main findings of a research project that has assessed these implications for five countries in the ASEAN region, focusing on selected service sub-sectors.

1. Introduction

The number of bilateral and regional free trade agreements (FTAs) involving members of the Association of South East Asian Nations (ASEAN) is increasing at a mind-boggling pace. Table 23 offers an overview of agreements in which at least one ASEAN country participates. All of these agreements seek the liberalisation of trade in services, at a faster pace than what is foreseen under the WTO's General Agreement on Trade in Services (GATS).

* This chapter is based on a research project on rules of origin in services undertaken by the ASEAN Economic Forum research network and supported by the World Bank Institute. The authors are grateful to George Manzano, Pierre Sauvé and participants at the World Trade Forum for helpful comments and suggestions. The views expressed in this chapter are the authors' own and do not necessarily represent those of their respective institutions.

Table 23 *Free trade agreements of ASEAN countries*

Signed agreements	*Status*
ASEAN Framework Agreement on Services	Signed in 1995, subsequently ratified in all countries except Malaysia
Singapore–Australia	Entered into force in 2003
Singapore–Brunei–Chile–New Zealand	Signed in 2005
Singapore–EFTA	Entered into force in 2003
Singapore–India	Signed in 2005
Singapore–Japan	Entered into force in 2002
Singapore–Jordan	Entered into force in 2005
Singapore–Korea	Entered into force in 2006
Singapore–New Zealand	Entered into force in 2001
Singapore–Panama	Signed in 2006
Singapore–United States	Entered into force in 2004
Malaysia–Japan	Entered into force in 2006
Thailand–Australia	Entered into force in 2005
Vietnam–United States*	Entered into force in 2001
Laos–United States*	Entered into force in 2005
Under preparation/negotiation	*Partner countries*
Singapore	Bahrain, Canada, Egypt, Kuwait, Mexico, Pakistan, Peru, Qatar, Sri Lanka, United Arab Emirates
Indonesia	Australia, Japan
Malaysia	Australia, United Status
Thailand	India, Japan, United States, Peru, Mexico, South Africa
Philippines	Japan
ASEAN	Australia, China, Japan, Korea, New Zealand, India

* Only FTAs with a substantial services component are included. Technically, the Vietnam–US and Laos–US agreements are not free trade agreements, but bilateral trade agreements.

An important question in the design of FTAs covering services is to what extent non-members benefit from the trade preferences that are negotiated among members. This question is resolved through so-called rules of origin (sometimes also referred to as denial of benefit). The restrictiveness of rules of origin determines the degree of preferences entailed in market-opening commitments, shaping the bargaining incentives of FTAs and their eventual economic effects.

Notwithstanding the conclusion of many new FTAs, hardly any research is available that can guide policy-makers on the economic implications of different rules of origin. This chapter summarises the main findings of a research project that investigated some of these implications for five ASEAN countries: Laos, Malaysia, the Philippines, Thailand and Vietnam. In particular, for selected service sub-sectors and a number of criteria for rules of origin, national research studies in these countries simulated which service providers would or would not be eligible for preferences negotiated under an FTA.

The chapter is structured as follows. We first describe the rules of origin question in greater detail, explain why it is important, what different options for rules of origin exist and what factors determine the relevance and restrictiveness of rules of origin. Based on this discussion, we then summarise the main findings of the national research studies. The final section offers concluding remarks.

2. Rules of origin in services: Conceptual issues

What are rules of origin in services?

Rules of origin have long been a prominent issue in the case of goods trade. In the goods case, they seek to prevent the transshipment of goods for the sole purpose of obtaining preferential tariff treatment under an FTA. This case is illustrated in Figure 10. Suppose countries A and B sign a trade agreement that eliminates tariffs on all trade between the two countries. Suppose also that country A's remaining tariff for imports from the rest of the world – its most favoured nation (MFN) tariff – is lower than country B's MFN tariff. Ignoring transport costs, exporters from the rest of the world would have an incentive to transship their exports to country B through country A and thereby avoid paying country B's higher tariff. If this were possible, an FTA would de facto reduce member countries' external tariffs to the lowest MFN rate in the FTA area. To allow varying MFN tariff rates among FTA members, FTAs need to establish rules of origin that define the level of transformation imported goods need to undergo in order for the transformed product to be exported to the FTA partner at the preferential tariff.

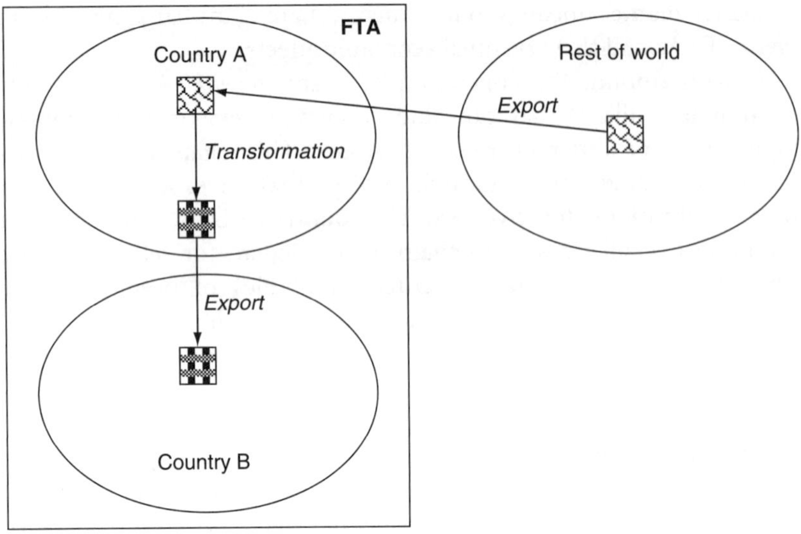

Figure 10 Rules of origin for cross-border trade

What is different about trade in services? One important difference is that protection in services does not take the form of tariffs, but is exercised through a class of non-tariff measures, ranging from quantitative limitations to regulatory restrictions. Nonetheless, for some forms of services trade, the issue is broadly similar. Consider the supply of cross-border call centre services. Suppose two countries form an FTA that eliminates a ban on the cross-border provision of these services. Would a supplier in one member country be allowed to offer call centre services to the other member, if the supplier sub-contracted these services further to a company located in a third country, not party to the FTA? What level of 'service transformation' would need to take place for a call centre service imported into an FTA member to qualify for trade preferences?

Interestingly, this question is only beginning to receive attention in trade agreements. This may be partly because the notions of imported intermediated inputs and domestic value-added are not as well developed in services as they are in the goods context. It may also be because this form of trade has, so far, been largely unrestricted. However, in view of the rapid growth of cross-border trade in services, the imposition of trade barriers may well be conceivable in future (see Mattoo and

Wunsch, 2004).[1] Indeed, the recent bilateral trade agreement of Singapore with Japan contains language that could be construed as a restrictive rule of origin for cross-border trade in services.[2]

Notwithstanding these more recent developments, the focus of rules of origin in services trade agreements has, so far, been a different one. Rather than defining the origin of a service, they have sought to delineate the origin of a service supplier. This is largely due to the inherent characteristics of services. Most services require physical proximity between the supplier and consumer of the service and therefore cannot be traded cross-border. For example, a haircut service cannot be supplied remotely and can therefore also not be 'transshipped' through a third country. For precisely this reason, trade agreements typically adopt a wide definition of trade in services to include the purchase of services by consumers moving to the country of the producer (mode 2 trade) and the sale of services by producers moving to the country of the consumer. The latter case includes the establishment of a commercial presence by services firms (mode 3 trade) and the movement of individual service suppliers (mode 4 trade).

The rule of origin question for service suppliers is illustrated in Figure 11 – both for the case of companies (juridical persons) and individuals (natural persons). In the case of juridical persons, suppose a company from the rest of the world establishes a commercial presence in country A. Under what circumstances would the subsidiary or branch established in country A benefit from trade preferences under the FTA, if it wishes to supply services to country B? Note that this question is relevant for service exports supplied through modes 1, 2 and 3. In the case of natural persons, suppose an individual from the rest of the world relocates to country A. Under what circumstances would this individual benefit from the trade preferences on mode 4 negotiated under the FTA?

[1] The question of rules of origin for cross-border trade is far from theoretical. Suppose the US imposed restrictions on outsourcing business services to India – as has been considered by a number of US states. The US would be free to do so for every sub-sector not currently scheduled as unrestricted under the GATS. Would it be possible for Indian companies to supply these services through an affiliated or unaffiliated company in Mexico, taking advantage of the liberal market access conditions provided for under NAFTA's negative list in services?

[2] Following GATS Article XXVII, Article 70(a) of the Singapore–Japan FTA enables a party to deny the benefits of the services chapter 'to the supply of any service, if it establishes that the service is supplied from or in the territory of a non-Party'.

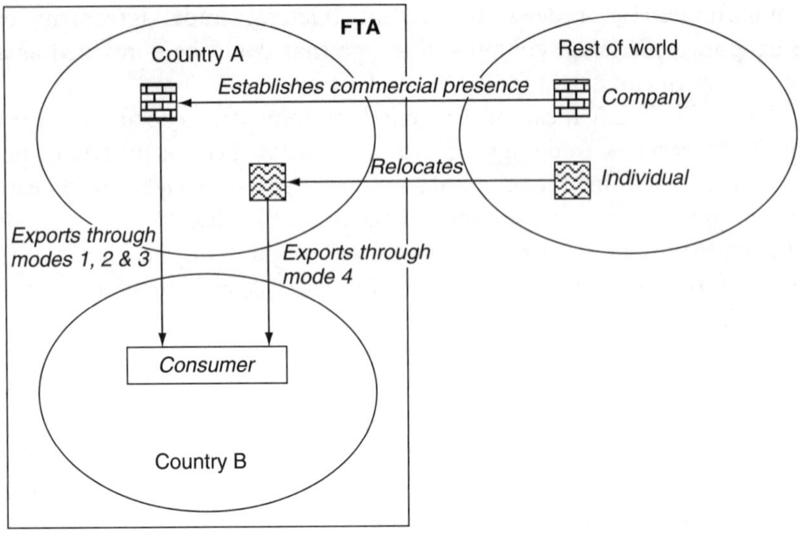

Figure 11 Rules of origin for service suppliers

Why is the rules of origin question important?

Rules of origin in services determine the extent of preferences entailed in market opening commitments that countries undertake in FTAs. A liberal rule of origin enables service providers from non-member countries to benefit from improved market access negotiated under an FTA. Such a rule still falls short of MFN treatment, because service providers from non-members need to be established in at least one FTA member country first. But if entry conditions in at least one member country are liberal, a non-restrictive rule of origin will de facto afford broad market access within the FTA territory to service providers from non-FTA countries. By contrast, if a restrictive rule of origin is chosen, only a subset of service providers established in an FTA area benefits from liberalisation commitments undertaken by member countries. This difference in treatment has both economic and bargaining implications, which will be discussed in turn.

Economic implications

Mattoo and Fink (2004) analyse the economic effects of preferential versus MFN liberalisation in services. They draw the following main conclusions, from the viewpoint of the importing FTA member (country B in Figure 11):

- First, relative to the status quo, preferential liberalisation in services brings about static welfare gains. This finding differs from the more ambiguous conclusion drawn in the goods case. The key difference is that protection in services does not generate fiscal revenue, as do tariffs on imported goods. Thus, trade diversion effects associated with preferential liberalisation in services do not lead to any loss in government revenue that can lead to negative welfare effects in the case of goods.
- Second, MFN liberalisation yields greater welfare gains than preferential liberalisation. Non-discriminatory market opening does not bias competition from abroad and therefore promotes entry of the most efficient service providers. Additional gains from trade, associated with greater economies of scale and knowledge spillovers, are also likely to be greater if liberalisation proceeds on an MFN basis. There is one exception to this conclusion. If 'learning by doing' effects are important, preferential liberalisation may enable domestic service suppliers from member countries to become more efficient, as they face some competition from within the FTA territory, but are not yet exposed to global competition. In theory, preferential liberalisation can thus prepare infant domestic suppliers for competition at the global level.
- Third, there is a special long-term trade diversion effect to worry about. Preferential liberalisation may offer a first-mover advantage to potentially second-best service providers from within the FTA territory. Since many service industries are characterised by high location-specific sunk costs, first-best providers from outside the FTA territory may be deterred from entering the market when trade is eventually liberalised on an MFN basis. Thus, even if preferences are temporary, they may have long-term implications for a country's ability to attract the world's most efficient service providers.

What do these conclusions imply for the choice of rule of origin? Unless preferential FTAs are specifically designed to promote learning-by-doing, a liberal rule of origin is in economic terms more desirable. Even though a liberal rule of origin does not fully eliminate discrimination against non-member countries, it does away with some discrimination and therefore enlarges the pool of foreign suppliers competing for access to the domestic market. By contrast, if policy-makers believe that their domestic service industries are at an infant stage and cannot be immediately exposed to global competition, a restrictive rule of origin may be a prerequisite for governments to commit to market opening in an FTA. This consideration is relevant for the ASEAN region, where policy-makers have frequently advanced learning-by-doing externalities as a motivation for regional integration.

From the viewpoint of the exporting FTA member (country A in Figure 11), additional considerations apply. The choice of rule of origin determines who will benefit from an FTA. One can broadly distinguish between three groups of beneficiaries: national service suppliers, foreign suppliers already established and foreign suppliers not yet established (more on how these suppliers are defined below). This raises the following issues:

- If service suppliers take the form of firms (juridical persons), a restrictive rule of origin would limit export and associated employment gains to national suppliers (or, more broadly, already established suppliers). This outcome may be sought for non-economic reasons, such as the promotion of certain ethnic groups. In addition, a restrictive rule of origin could also underpin possible 'learning-by-doing' effects mentioned above.

  By contrast, a liberal rule of origin may attract new FDI from outside the FTA territory. Indeed, a country with liberal entry conditions for suppliers from outside the free trade area may specifically seek to become a hub for companies to access markets within the free trade area. The benefits from this form of FDI would depend on the modes through which services are exported to other FTA members. In the case of modes 1 and 2, there may be significant employment gains in the exporting country. In the case of mode 3, employment gains may be small, but governments may still benefit from higher tax revenues. Depending on the nature and purpose of FDI, there may also be important spillover externalities for the host economy.
- If service suppliers take the form of individuals (natural persons), a restrictive rule of origin again limits export gains to nationals, which may be sought for non-economic reasons (see above). However, the effects of a liberal rule of origin are trickier. Hypothetically, if service workers from outside the FTA territory merely used the exporting FTA member as a transit point to other FTA markets, a liberal rule of origin would yield little benefit to this member (unless this type of transit were taxed). Benefits would only arise if service providers from outside the FTA territory had an economic interest in the exporting member – that is, if they spent at least part of their income in the

exporting FTA member. From an economic perspective, the centre of an individual's economic interest thus seems a more important criterion for a rule of origin than the individual's nationality.

In sum, from an economic perspective, the choice of rule of origin depends on the objectives attached to an FTA. A liberal rule of origin promotes greater economic efficiency by reducing discrimination and can attract FDI from outside the FTA territory, but it can undermine learning-by-doing externalities sought after in an FTA.

Bargaining implications

There are various reasons why countries engage in bilateral or regional trade negotiations, rather than pursuing liberalisation on an MFN basis at the WTO. One is that bargaining may be more productive among a smaller set of countries. The WTO now has 149 members at all levels of development and the multilateral trade agenda has much expanded since the GATT days. Trade negotiations at the multilateral level therefore tend to be complex and time-consuming. For countries ready to commit to market opening in services, a bilateral or regional forum may deliver quicker results.

Another handicap of multilateral negotiations is that countries can free-ride on the bargaining efforts of others. Multilateral services negotiations proceed on a bilateral request and offer basis, but eventual commitments are made on an MFN basis. Thus, even though one WTO Member may be interested in improved market access in another member, it may be reluctant to engage in reciprocal bargaining if there are third members interested in the same market access. The end result is a less ambitious negotiating outcome. In principle, FTAs offer a way out, as the smaller number of players reduces the scope for free-riding on the bargaining efforts of others.[3] However, this assumes that countries not party to an FTA do not benefit from deeper market access negotiated under the FTA. In other words, for free-rider problems to be less severe in a bilateral or regional context, FTAs need to adopt a restrictive rule of origin.

This argument has an important upshot, which is of current relevance to the bargaining situation of several ASEAN countries. Suppose a country negotiates sequentially two or more bilateral FTAs. If it commits to liberal market access in the first FTA and this FTA adopts a liberal rule of origin, the trading partner for the second FTA may be unwilling to 'pay' for making the same commitment in the second FTA. In other

[3] This point is more fully elaborated in Mattoo and Fink (2005).

words, with a liberal rule of origin, it may not be possible to 'sell' the same market access commitment twice.[4]

In sum, a liberal rule of origin may undermine the bargaining advantages that FTAs offer relative to multilateral trade negotiations.

What are the options for rules of origin in services?

Rules of origin for service suppliers can be defined along a number of criteria. Some guidance is available from existing trade agreements in services – in particular, the 2003 China–Hong Kong Closer Economic Partnership Agreement (CEPA), which arguably has the most detailed rule of origin seen so far (see Box 1).[5] For companies (juridical persons), key criteria for rules of origin include:

- Incorporation. A first requirement may simply be for a service supplier to be incorporated under the laws of the exporting FTA member.
- Substantive business operations. This could be defined by the possession of a business or service licence in the exporting FTA member, although this would say little about the scale of a service supplier's activities. Additional options include the payment of local profit taxes, the owning or renting of premises, a minimum sales requirement, a minimum number of years of establishment and a requirement that the export of services within the FTA territory be of the same nature as the services supplied in the exporting FTA member.
- Domestic ownership and control. Eligibility for preferences may be confined to firms that are owned and/or controlled by persons of the exporting FTA member. This is usually defined through the equity share in a company or the voting rights controlled by domestic shareholders. In FTAs involving more than two countries, it is also possible to introduce a more liberal cumulated ownership and control criterion. In other words, eligibility for preferences would be widened to service providers that are majority owned or effectively controlled by persons from FTA member countries.

[4] There may still be a benefit for the second FTA partner from replicating the commitment made under the first FTA. It would make the commitment subject to the disciplines of the second FTA's rules – in particular, possible provisions for the settlement of disputes.

[5] Beviglia Zampetti and Sauvé (2004) offer a detailed overview of rules of origin in services encountered in existing investment and trade agreements.

Box 1: Rules of origin in the China–Hong Kong Closer Economic Partnership Agreement

The China–Hong Kong Closer Economic Partnership Agreement (CEPA) is in many ways a special trade agreement. It grants Hong Kong-based service providers preferential access to China's market, in advance of the liberalisation schedule to which China committed as part of its accession package to the WTO. China's offer to Hong Kong under CEPA had little to do with classical arguments of trade bargaining. Hong Kong, being one of the most open economies in the world, had little to give in terms of improved market access for Chinese suppliers. Rather, the Agreement was intended to promote deeper integration between the Mainland and Hong Kong and has to be understood in the context of the 'one country, two systems' formula.

If CEPA had adopted a liberal rule of origin and given Hong Kong's liberal entry policies, service suppliers from outside of Hong Kong would have had a way to enter the Chinese market in advance of the WTO schedule. This was not the intention of the Chinese and Hong Kong governments. Thus, CEPA has an annex on the definition of service suppliers, which translates into one of the most detailed rules of origin so far seen in a trade agreement. In particular, for Hong Kong companies to enjoy preferential treatment under CEPA, they must have had substantive business operations for 3–5 years in Hong Kong for the services they intend to provide in the Mainland; they must have paid profit tax in Hong Kong; they must own or rent premises for business operations in Hong Kong; and more than 50 per cent of employees must be Hong Kong residents (or Chinese people staying in Hong Kong on a one-way permit). Additional rules exist for law firms, which require the sole proprietor and all partners of a firm to be registered as practising lawyers. In the case of individuals (natural persons), eligibility for preferential treatment is confined to Hong Kong permanent residents.

In order to be certified as Hong Kong Service Suppliers under CEPA, interested service suppliers must submit an application to Hong Kong's Department of Trade and Industry, along with documentation which verifies that suppliers meet the above criteria. The Agreement came into force on 1 January 2004. As of May 2005, 788 certificates for Hong Kong Service Suppliers were issued.

Source: Information provided on the website of Hong Kong's Department of Trade and Industry (www.tid.gov.hk/english/cepa/fulltext.html)

- Domestic employment. Trade preferences under an FTA may be confined to firms in which a minimum share of employees consists of nationals or local residents.

For individual service suppliers (natural persons), key criteria for rules of origin include:

- Nationality. This can be determined straightforwardly by the passport of an interested service supplier.
- Residency. A residency approach would be broader than a nationality approach, as it would include some foreign nationals present in the exporting FTA member. Options would depend on the forms of residency available in that member. For example, a rule of origin could include permanent residents, but exclude temporary residents.
- Centre of economic interest. This would be akin to the concept of substantive business operations in the case of firms. An individual's centre of economic interest can be defined by a minimum number of years of residency, the payment of local income taxes or the owning or renting of a dwelling. In practice, to the extent that a country's residency requirements are rooted in the centre of economic interest principle, the two approaches would yield similar outcomes.

As a final note, the GATS imposes certain disciplines on rules of origin that WTO Members entering into FTAs may adopt. In particular, WTO Members are required to extend trade preferences to commercially established service suppliers from third countries that engage in substantive business operations within an FTA territory (Article V:6). However, in the case of FTAs involving only developing countries, preferential treatment may, in addition, be limited to companies 'owned or controlled by natural persons of the parties' to an FTA (Article V:3b). Interestingly, the GATS does not create any discipline on the rule of origin FTA members may adopt for individual service providers.

What factors determine the relevance and restrictiveness of rules of origin?

As already indicated, the relevance of a rule of origin for service suppliers depends critically on the pattern of remaining market access restrictions that FTA members maintain against non-members. Suppose that these restrictions are identical for all FTA members – the equivalent of a customs union in the case of goods trade. If services can only be delivered through the establishment of a commercial presence (mode 3), rules of origin would lose their relevance. This is because service providers from outside the FTA territory would not need to establish an intermediate presence in one of the FTA members for the purpose of obtaining better access to other FTA markets. However, they would still be relevant if services can be delivered on a cross-border basis (mode 1) or through consumption abroad (mode 2). Because of economies of scale and scope, a service provider from outside the FTA may prefer to serve the whole FTA territory from one location, rather than establish a commercial presence in every FTA member. For example, such a scenario would apply to the creation of hub-and-spoke networks for the provision of transport services.

Rules of origin would also not be binding when service suppliers from outside the region would voluntarily establish a presence in the intermediate country and voluntarily access other FTA markets from this presence. But in many circumstances, this will not be the preferred route. Assuming that rules of origin are indeed binding, their de facto restrictiveness is determined by the costs they impose on service suppliers from non-member countries. In general, one can distinguish among the following two types of costs:

- Tax obligations. Exporting services from a subsidiary within the FTA territory rather than from the parent firm outside the FTA territory may lead to different tax obligations. Depending on the tax rules and tax rates prevailing in different jurisdictions, exports from a subsidiary may lead to lower or higher tax payments.
- Business transaction costs. Establishing and maintaining a commercial presence in the intermediate country can create non-trivial transaction costs. For example, a strict definition of 'substantial business operations' may imply greater investments into the local market than a foreign service supplier would undertake voluntarily – especially if the local market is small. A 'domestic ownership and control' requirement would force the foreign service supplier to enter into a (minority) joint venture arrangement with a local partner, which can entail significant transaction costs. Similarly, domestic employment requirements could drive up operational costs, if the service supplier preferred hiring expatriate workers.

Similar considerations apply, in theory, also to individual service providers. But in practice, they seem less relevant for mode 4 trade, because immigration and residency requirements typically pose a sufficiently high barrier against using an FTA member as a transit point to other FTA markets.

3. Simulation of different rules of origin in five ASEAN countries

In order to assess more fully the economic and bargaining implications of alternative rules of origin that may be adopted in FTAs, it is necessary to obtain a better empirical understanding of the issues outlined in the preceding discussion. A research project of the ASEAN Economic Forum research network has taken a first step at providing some empirical guidance, focusing on the rules of origin for juridical persons in selected service sub-sectors. National research studies were conducted in the following five ASEAN countries: Lao PDR, Malaysia, the Philippines, Thailand and Vietnam.[6] A core element of these studies is a simulation exercise assessing which service providers would or would not be eligible for preferences negotiated under a region-wide FTA.

To motivate the analysis, we first provide some background information on ASEAN economic integration. We then review the different rules of origin that have been adopted in FTAs negotiated by ASEAN countries. The final part of this section describes the simulation set-up and summarises the studies' main findings.

ASEAN trade and investment policy

ASEAN is one of the most successful regional groupings among developing countries to date. Its combined GDP totalled US$ 2.53 trillion, roughly 4.5 per cent of the World GDP, while its exports totalled US$ 500 billion, approximately 6 per cent of total world exports.[7] ASEAN has made a remarkable achievement in liberalising trade in goods within the region under the ASEAN Free Trade Agreement (AFTA). In January 2003, tariffs between member countries were reduced to 0–5 per cent for all products, except those on the general exception and sensitive product lists of each member country. By contrast, the region's record on service sector and investment liberalisation is much less impressive. Countries' commitments under the ASEAN Free Trade Agreement in Services (AFAS) improve only marginally on those made in the GATS.[8] The ASEAN Investment Area (AIA), in principle, became effective in

[6] See, respectively, Douangboupha, Thiengthepvongsa and Vilavong (2006), Tham and Zainal Abidin (2006), Avila and Manzano (2006), Arunanondchai and Nikomborirak (2006), Nhu-Van, Chien-Thang and Hoang-Dat (2006).

[7] CIA World Fact Book 2005. [8] See Stephenson and Nikomborirak (2002).

January 2003, but its liberalisation content is substantially undermined by extensive lists of exemptions.[9]

Starting in 2001, several of the more ambitious ASEAN members – particularly Singapore – have entered into a series of bilateral free trade agreements with countries outside the ASEAN region, including the United States and Japan (see Table 23). Thailand also signed FTAs with a number of developing countries and is negotiating an FTA with the United States and Japan as well. The trade agreements with the most far-reaching implications for ASEAN service sector liberalisation have arguably been those with the United States. For example, the bilateral trade agreements that Laos and Vietnam signed with the US require market access to telecommunications, financial, healthcare, tourism and distribution services. Similarly, the Singapore–US FTA requires across-the-board service market liberalisation with only few reservations listed.

What rules of origin have been adopted in existing services agreements?

As in trade in goods, the rule of origin for services trade in each bilateral or regional free trade agreement may differ, depending on the particular interests of the signatories or their relative bargaining power if interests are divergent. At the same time, in crafting rules of origin in an FTA, members of the WTO are bound by the disciplines of GATS Article V – as discussed above.

The narrowest rule of origin with respect to investment is that which defines origin of a service supplier by the nationality of the person(s) who own or control the service supplier. The Thailand–Australia Free Trade Agreement (TAFTA) stipulates that either Party may deny the benefits of pre-establishment national treatment to 'an investor of the other Party that is a juridical person of such Party and to investments of such an investor where the Party establishes that the juridical person is owned or controlled by persons of a non-Party'. That is, foreign owned or controlled companies incorporated under Australian Law may be denied benefits under the TAFTA. A similar rule of origin is embedded in the India–Singapore Economic Cooperation Agreement, but only for services supplied through

[9] For Lao PDR, Vietnam, and Myanmar, the AIA will only become effective in 2010. See Nikomborirak (2004).

commercial presence.[10] Domestic ownership and control is also required in the Treaty of Amity signed between Thailand and the United States in 1966. The Treaty grants benefits only to American or Thai owned or controlled companies engaging in substantial business operations in either country. Consequently, American companies applying for benefits under the Treaty to invest in businesses restricted to foreigners would have to prove that the majority of their 'ultimate beneficial owners' are indeed American citizens.[11]

Aside from these two agreements, all other services agreements involving ASEAN countries have adopted a rule requiring only substantial business operations in the territory of a Party. In other words, a non-party service supplier which engages in substantial business operations may also benefit from the bilateral free trade agreement. Most FTAs, including the AFAS and FTAs involving the United States and Japan, adopt this rule of origin with only small deviations. It should be noted, however, that even though this broader rule of origin extends trade preferences to third-Party service suppliers, it still discriminates between Party and non-Party suppliers in that the latter can be denied benefits in the absence of proof of substantial business operation, while the former is entitled to the benefit regardless of the size of its business operation in the territory of the Party. For example, a subsidiary of an American company operating in a third country, say Citibank operating in Brazil, may also benefit from the Singapore–US Free Trade Agreement (SUSFTA), while a German company, say Siemens, can take advantage of the agreement only through its subsidiary operating in the United States.[12]

[10] As mentioned in the previous section, Article V:6 of the GATS Agreement requires WTO Members to extend the benefits of preferential agreements to foreign owned and controlled service suppliers that engage in substantial business operations in the territory of a member. Preferential agreements involving only developing countries can restrict the benefits to domestically owned and controlled service suppliers. Since Australia would likely be considered a developed country in the WTO, it is not immediately clear how the TAFTA rule of origin complies with the requirements under GATS Article V:6. Compatibility of the rule of origin of the India–Singapore agreement with GATS requirements seems to depend on whether Singapore would be considered a developing country under WTO law (see also footnote 18).

[11] Thailand has scheduled an MFN exemption under the GATS for the preferences granted to the United States under the Treat of Amity. See WTO document GATS/EL/85. However, the 'intended' duration of this exemption was 10 years, which expired on January 1, 2005.

[12] Some FTAs of ASEAN countries also allow the denial of benefits to service suppliers that are owned or controlled by persons from countries with which a party does not maintain diplomatic relations.

None of the FTAs in the ASEAN region defines the term 'substantial business operations' more closely – for example, along the lines of the China–Hong Kong CEPA discussed earlier. Implementation is left to FTA parties and, so far, there has not been any jurisprudence on this question. The term 'owned and controlled' is also not clearly defined in FTAs. In the Japan–Singapore Economic Partnership Agreement (JSEPA), a company is 'owned' by persons of a party if more than 50 per cent of the equity interest in it is '*ultimately owned* by the persons of that party'. As for the issue of control, JSEPA stipulates that a company is 'controlled' by persons of a Party if such persons have the power to name the majority of its directors or otherwise legally direct its actions. Presumably, this refers to the nationality of the person who can legally represent the company or who is the designated official whose signature must accompany the company's seal on all legal documents.

Finally, most agreements extend benefits to incorporated and non-incorporated legal entities, as long as the substantial business criterion is met. In other words, branches and representative offices of enterprises incorporated in non-parties are typically eligible for FTA preferences.[13]

Simulations of different rules of origin

The five country case studies undertook a simulation, seeking to investigate the following question: which of the currently established non-ASEAN service providers would (or would not) benefit from FTA preferences if progressively more restrictive rules of origin were adopted? This is a hypothetical exercise, though it has practical relevance. The ASEAN group is currently negotiating the liberalisation of trade in services under the ASEAN-China Comprehensive Economic Cooperation Agreement and the question of which rule of origin to adopt has not been resolved. Additional 'ASEAN-plus' FTAs have been initiated or are envisaged with Australia, India, Japan, Korea and New Zealand. Moreover, even though the AFAS currently maintains a liberal rule of origin, this rule could be changed in the course of future negotiating rounds.

The five country case studies focused on selected service sub-sectors. The choice of sectors was determined by data availability and the need to have at least some non-ASEAN service providers already present in the market.

[13] In particular, most agreements define an enterprise or a juridical person of another party as any legal entity which is constituted or otherwise organised under the law of that other party. One exception is the investment chapter of the Malaysia–Japan Economic Partnership Agreement, which expressly excludes 'branches of an enterprise of a third State'.

Table 24 presents the sectors that were analysed in the five countries as well as the level of openness as measured by the extent of foreign equity ownership allowed. In the end, all five case studies chose banking services for the simulation. Insurance services were analysed in four countries. Several other sectors – distribution services, maritime shipping services, port and freight forwarding services, health services and telecommunications services – were covered by at least two studies.

The level of openness varies across countries and sectors. While certain sectors in some countries are open to full foreign ownership, others are restricted to minority equity participation. However, certain caveats to the level of openness described in Table 24 apply. First, foreign investment in services may be restricted by other barriers, notably limits to the number of service suppliers allowed or economic needs tests. Second, Malaysia and Thailand appear to be most restrictive in the participation of foreign equity – especially in banking and insurance services. At the same time, foreign investors in Thailand are able to secure corporate control despite a 49 per cent foreign ownership ceiling through either indirect equity holding involving layers of holding companies up the ownership chain, or through Thai nominees (see also the discussion below). In Malaysia, for historical reasons, several established foreign service suppliers hold majority or full equity ownership and their larger foreign equity holdings have been grandfathered. Finally, Vietnam currently does not permit majority foreign ownership in the three sectors shown in Table 27. However, Vietnam is in the final stages of negotiating accession to the WTO and, if past accession agreements are any guide, it may well commit to majority or full foreign ownership in at least some of these sectors.

The criteria for rules of origin simulated are based on those found in the Hong Kong-Mainland CEPA (see previous section), plus an ownership and control criterion. In particular, the simulations adopted the following criteria:[14]

(A) Incorporation under domestic laws
(B) Substantial business operations, as measured by:
  (B1) Possession of an operating licence
  (B2) Minimum capitalisation requirement (for financial services)
  (B3) Minimum number of years of establishment (3–5 years)
  (B4) Owning or renting of premises

[14] Depending on data availability and the characteristics of the different sectors, the studies sometimes had to adopt the 'substantial business operations' criterion.

Table 24 *Foreign equity participation allowed in selected service sectors (percentage)*

	Financial services			Maritime transport			
Country	Banking	Insurance	Distribution services	Shipping services	Port and freight Forwarding services	Health services	Telecoms
Laos	50	49	na	na	Na	100	49(a)
Malaysia	30(b)	30(b)	70(b)	na	Na	30(b)	na
Philippines	100	100	100	40	40	na	na
Thailand	25	25	100(c)	49	49	49	49
Vietnam	50	na	na	49	49	na	na

Notes:

(a) Higher foreign equity participation is in principle allowed, but subject to government approval.

(b) For historical reasons, higher foreign equity participation and even full foreign ownership may exist for already established foreign service suppliers.

(c) Wholly owned foreign distributors are allowed only when registered capital exceeds 100 million baht (roughly US$ 2.5 million).

Sources: Douangboupha, Thiengthepvongsa and Vilavong (2006), Tham and Zainal Abidin (2006). Avila and Manzano (2006), Arunanondchai and Nikomborirak (2006), Nhu-Van, Chien-Thang and Hoang-Dat (2006).

(C) Domestic ownership and control, as measured by more than 50 per cent of equity holdings
(D) Share of domestic employees greater than 50 per cent

As an illustration, Table 25 presents the simulation results for the Philippines' banking sector. The results in this case are relatively straightforward. All but two of the non-ASEAN banks in the Philippines are branches of foreign-incorporated banks. Thus, only two foreign banks would meet the domestic incorporation criterion. The substantial business operations criteria are all met, as they mirror operational requirements under domestic laws and all banks have been operational for at least 5 years. None of the non-ASEAN banks would meet the domestic ownership and control requirement, but all of them employ 50 per cent or more Filipino residents.

Overall, three main findings emerge from the five country case studies.

First, the single most relevant rule of origin criterion is domestic ownership and control. In other words, when allowed, non-ASEAN service providers prefer to enter foreign markets through majority or fully owned affiliates, rather than entering into minority joint ventures with local companies. Thus, if a company entered an ASEAN country for the sole purpose of obtaining preferential access to another market and was forced into a minority joint venture, it would most likely depart from its preferred way of doing business and incur certain transaction costs.

In the case of financial services, incorporation is also a relevant criterion, because foreign service suppliers often enter the domestic market by means of establishing a branch rather than a subsidiary. An exception is Malaysia, because the establishment of branches by foreign-incorporated financial institutions is restricted by law. In the case of Laos, the Philippines, Thailand and Vietnam, a rule of origin that expressly excludes branches leads to a marked reduction in the number of service providers eligible for FTA benefits.

To illustrate the importance of these two criteria, Table 26 presents the number of non-ASEAN service providers that are domestically owned and controlled, foreign owned and controlled and branches of foreign-incorporated enterprises.

Most other criteria are relatively easily met – partly because they are already operational requirements under domestic laws. The number of years of establishment is generally not restrictive if kept at a minimum of five years because most foreign companies operating in the selected sectors have had commercial presence over a longer period of time.

Table 25 *Simulation of rules of origin for non-ASEAN foreign banks in the Philippines*

Bank	Country of origin	Criteria for rules of origin						
		A	B1	B2	B3	B4	C	D
ANZ Banking Group, Ltd.	Australia		Q	Q	Q	Q		Q
Bank of America, N.A.	USA		Q	Q	Q	Q		Q
Bank of China – Manila Branch	China		Q	Q	Q	Q		Q
Bank of Tokyo-Mitsubishi, Ltd. – Manila Branch	Japan		Q	Q	Q	Q		Q
Citibank, N.A. (Phils.)	USA		Q	Q	Q	Q		Q
Deutsche Bank AG	Germany		Q	Q	Q	Q		Q
International Commercial Bank of China	Taipei		Q	Q	Q	Q		Q
JP Morgan Chase Bank	USA		Q	Q	Q	Q		Q
Korea Exchange Bank	S Korea		Q	Q	Q	Q		Q
Mizuho Corporate Bank, Limited – Manila Branch (Fuji Bank)	Japan		Q	Q	Q	Q		Q
ING Bank N.V. – Manila Branch	Netherlands		Q	Q	Q	Q		Q
Standard Chartered Bank	United Kingdom		Q	Q	Q	Q		Q
The Hongkong and Shanghai Banking Corporation, Ltd.	Hongkong		Q	Q	Q	Q		Q
ABN-AMRO Bank, Inc.	Netherlands		Q	Q	Q	Q		Q
Chinatrust (Phils.) Commercial Bank Corporation	Taipei	Q	Q	Q	Q	Q		Q
HSBC Savings Bank (Phils.)	Hong Kong	Q	Q	Q	Q	Q		Q

Notes:
'Q' means qualified under the particular criterion heading. The different criteria for rules of origin are described in the text. For criterion B3, the minimum capital requirements are those set by prudential banking regulations in the Philippines.
Source: Avila and Manzano (2006).

Table 26 *Type of ownership and legal entity of non-ASEAN service providers*

	Domestically owned and controlled	Foreign owned and controlled	Branches of foreign-incorporated enterprises
Banking			
Laos	6	0	5
Malaysia	5	13	0
Philippines	na	7	15
Thailand	9	2	18
Vietnam	2	7	25
Insurance			
Thailand	23	7 (a)	1
Philippines	120	14	6
Laos	0	1	0
Malaysia	15	10	2
Distribution services			
Thailand	9	10 (a)	0
Malaysia	6	7	0
Telecommunications services			
Thailand	4	2	0
Laos	2	2	
Freight forwarding services			
Malaysia	1	3	2
Thailand	120	5 (a)	0
Health services			
Laos	24 (public)	5	0
Malaysia	33	2	0

Notes:
(a) Service providers are controlled by a foreign person but legally a Thai company since foreign equity share is less than 49%. This occurs because Thai laws prohibit majority foreign equity holdings in all service sectors. Therefore, MNCs must invest through indirect equity holding using holding companies (legal in Thailand) or nominees (technically illegal).
Sources: Douangboupha, Thiengthepvongsa and Vilavong, (2006), Tham and Zainal Abidin (2006). Avila and Manzano (2006), Arunanondchai and Nikomborirak (2006), Nhu-Van, Chien-Thang, Hoang-Dat (2006).

This reflects the fact that most ASEAN countries partially opened up their service markets in the 1990s or even earlier. At the same time, the simulation studies applied the different rules of origin criteria to established service providers only. A substantive business operations requirement would still be relevant in restricting the entry of shell companies that merely seek to exploit the trade preferences available under an FTA.

Second, a rule of origin that incorporates a domestic ownership and control criterion raises non-trivial implementation questions. In classifying service providers as domestically owned and controlled, the five country case studies mostly relied on information on direct (or immediate) equity holdings. Data on indirect equity holdings and ultimate shareholders are typically not available to the public. Thus, companies that may appear to be domestically owned and controlled may ultimately be foreign owned and controlled. The deviation between the origins of the immediate shareholders versus ultimate shareholders is likely to be prominent where restrictions on foreign equity participation prevail. Through multi-level equity holdings, foreign investors can manage to exercise corporate control of service providers, in the absence of a direct majority equity ownership.

Thailand is a prominent example of this phenomenon. In principle, foreign equity participation in most service sectors in Thailand is limited to a minority stake (see Table 24). However, foreign companies have managed to exercise control over companies that are directly majority owned by Thai natural or juridical persons. According to Nikomborirak and Tawannakul (2006), foreign controlled public companies – as revealed by the composition of the board of directors and the nationality of the director(s) whose signatures must accompany all legal documents binding a company – accounted for 17.48 per cent of the market capitalisation of the Stock Exchange of Thailand. However, only 2.39 percentage points of the 17.48 per cent figure represent direct foreign equity holdings. Interestingly, the circumvention of statutory ownership restrictions does not only involve multi-level equity holdings, but also share ownership by Thai 'nominees' who act on behalf of foreign persons.[15]

If an FTA adopts a rule of origin that uses an immediate domestic ownership and control criterion, service suppliers that are ultimately foreign owned and controlled may still benefit. The same issue arises under a cumulated ownership and control criterion at the regional level:

[15] Even though such nominee arrangements are against Thai laws, they appear to have been common practice in Thailand.

service suppliers that are ultimately owned and controlled by persons from outside the region may still benefit. The concept of ownership and control is not well developed in ASEAN countries' legal and statistical frameworks. As revealed by the case studies, information on the ultimate ownership of companies is typically not published.[16] The same is true for information on the details governing corporate control – such as the composition of the board of directors or the nationality of the director(s) whose signature(s) must accompany all legal contracts binding a company. A related problem is posed by service suppliers whose equity is publicly traded. Share ownership may be diffused across a large number of countries, may change hands frequently, and no single shareholder may exercise control over the company.

Nonetheless, one way to effectively implement an ultimate domestic (or regional) ownership and control criterion is to place the burden of proof on the service providers that seek to benefit from an FTA. For example, under the Treaty of Amity between Thailand and the United States, it is up to companies to prove that they are ultimately owned and controlled by residents of either party. Similarly, the certification system under the Mainland and Hong Kong CEPA puts the onus on companies to prove that they meet the rules of origin of the agreement (see Box 1).[17]

Third, there is some evidence that non-ASEAN service providers may find it costly to use one ASEAN country as a hub to obtain preferential access to another ASEAN country. The case study for the Philippines analysed to what extent the non-ASEAN foreign banks present in the Philippines are also present in other ASEAN countries (Avila and Manzano, 2006). As shown in Table 27, most of the banks in question already have a presence in the other markets – at least in the commercially significant ones. The investments in these countries were not effectuated by the Filipino affiliates of the banks. In other words, if non-ASEAN banks were to use their Filipino affiliates to obtain preferential access to other markets, they would likely depart from their preferred global corporate structure.

[16] In Thailand, the Government's database of registered companies assigns the nationality of a legal entity only by the place of incorporation. See Arunanondchai and Nikomborirak (2006).

[17] Note that an ultimate ownership and control test may also be necessary for a rule of origin that merely requires that non-party service suppliers engage in substantial business operations. As discussed in the text, there may be domestically owned and controlled service suppliers that do not engage in substantial business operations in the domestic territory, but that may wish to exploit the preferences available under an FTA.

Table 27 *ASEAN presence of non-ASEAN banks established in the Philippines*

Bank	Brunei	Indonesia	Malaysia	Singapore	Thailand	Myanmar	Vietnam
ANZ Banking Group, Ltd.	yes	yes	yes	yes	yes		yes
Bank of America, N.A.		yes	yes	yes	yes		
Bank of China – Manila Branch		yes	yes	yes	yes		yes
Bank of Tokyo-Mitsubishi, Ltd. – Manila Branch		yes	yes	yes	yes	yes	yes
Citibank, N.A. (Phils.)	yes	yes	yes	yes	yes		yes
Deutsche Bank AG		yes	yes	yes	yes		yes
International Commercial Bank of China			yes	yes	yes		yes
JP Morgan Chase Bank		yes	yes	yes	yes		yes
Korea Exchange Bank		yes		yes			yes
Mizuho Corporate Bank, Limited – Manila Branch (Fuji Bank)		yes	yes	yes	yes		yes
ING Bank N.V. – Manila Branch			yes	yes	yes		
Standard Chartered Bank	yes	yes	yes	yes	yes		yes
The Hongkong and Shanghai Banking Corporation, Ltd.	yes	yes	yes	yes	yes		yes
ABN-AMRO Bank, Inc.		yes	yes	yes	yes		yes
Chinatrust (Phils.) Commercial Bank Corporation		yes					yes

Source: Avila and Manzano (2006).

This point is reinforced by evidence on the tax treatment of corporate income in Thailand and the United States. Suppose a US service provider considers investing in, say, Indonesia, either from its parent in the US or from its subsidiary in Thailand. The United States government collects corporate income tax on a global basis. But US subsidiaries in Thailand also pay income tax to the Thai government as they are considered a Thai legal entity. Hence, there is double taxation of income generated by US subsidiaries in Thailand. Although a bilateral tax treaty allows US companies to claim credits for taxes paid to the Thai government, the procedures can be costly and any tax dues exceeding the applicable US rate would not be reimbursed. In addition, Thailand imposes a 10 per cent withholding tax on profits repatriated overseas. This represents additional costs that the company would have to bear if returns from a particular investment had to be transferred to the parent company in the future (see Arunanondchai and Nikomborirak, 2006).

4. Conclusions

As governments enter into negotiations to establish bilateral or regional FTAs covering trade in services, they need to decide to what degree non-parties should benefit from the preferential treatment established by these agreements. For countries in the ASEAN region, this question applies at two levels. First, as reaffirmed by ASEAN Economic Ministers in August 2006, ASEAN countries are committed to establishing free regional trade in services by 2015. Second, ASEAN as a whole has entered into services negotiations with China, and additional negotiations with Australia, Japan, Korea, India and New Zealand may well be launched.

Progress towards integrating regional service markets has so far been marginal. Would a more restrictive rule of origin make any difference in this context? Two arguments can be made. First, some countries in the region such as Singapore are already open to foreign participation in services and host to many of the world's most efficient service suppliers. Vietnam will likely commit to open service markets upon acceding to the WTO. Other countries are more reluctant to open up, fearing the displacement of domestic service providers. A restrictive rule of origin may assuage the concerns of the latter countries, as liberalisation would be partial in terms of the set of service suppliers allowed to enter. Second, a more restrictive rule of origin may limit the scope for free-riding by countries outside the ASEAN region, which are negotiating with ASEAN countries at the WTO or in the context of bilateral FTAs.

Having said this, the five case studies discussed in this paper suggest that the most restrictive criterion for a rule of origin is domestic ownership and control. Ignoring implementation challenges, it is not clear whether a domestic ownership and control criterion would satisfy the disciplines of GATS Article V. This will depend on whether the FTA in question would be an agreement involving developing countries only.[18] In addition, a restrictive rule of origin would come with certain economic costs: it may promote the entry of second-best service providers or force first-best service providers to depart from their most efficient global corporate structures. These outcomes would diminish the gains from market opening in services.

While the studies reviewed in this chapter present insightful evidence on an understudied topic, more research is needed to provide better guidance to policy-makers on the benefits and costs of different rules of origin in services trade. From an economic perspective, the choice of rule of origin is closely linked to the broader question of the dynamic effects of trade policies in services. The limited evidence available suggests a higher overall growth potential for economies with open service markets (Mattoo *et al.*, 2001). But little is known about the relevance of learning-by-doing effects in specific service sectors and their potential size in relation to the efficiency costs of trade protection. Equally, little is known about the relevance and size of trade diversion costs from preferential treatment in services. Surveys of multinational companies could shed greater light on the tax implications and business transaction costs associated with different geographical structures of corporations. In addition, case studies of past preferential treatment in services could shed light on whether a first-mover advantage has affected the performance of service markets even after entry was liberalised on an MFN basis.

[18] A critical question in this respect is whether Singapore could be considered a developing country under the GATS. The WTO has a formal list only of least-developed countries (LDCs), based on United Nations criteria. In principle, non-LDC WTO Members can decide for themselves whether they are to be considered 'developed' or 'developing' countries. In this context, it is interesting to note that Singapore has already entered into one FTA that has incorporated an ownership and control criterion (see footnote 10). However, a member's decision on developing country status may be challenged by other members. So far, there has been no jurisprudence that could give guidance on what criteria would be used to resolve a disagreement on this question.

Bibliography

Arunanondchai, Jutamas and Deunden Nikomborirak (2006), 'Thailand's Rules of Origin in Services in Regional and Bilateral Trade Agreements'. Mimeo.

Avila, John Lawrence and George Manzano (2006), 'Rules of Origin in Services: A Philippine Perspective'. Mimeo.

Beviglia Zampetti, Americo and Pierre Sauvé, 'Rules of Origin for Services: A Review of Current Practice', in Estevadeordal, Antoni, *et al.* (eds.), *The Origin of Goods* (London: Oxford University Press and CEPR, 2006), pp. 114–145.

Douangboupha, Latthana, Thavichanh Thiengthepvongsa, and Buavanh Vilavong (2006), 'Rules of Origin in Services Regional Trade Agreements: The Practices in Laos'. Mimeo.

Mattoo, Aaditya, Randeep Rathindran and Arvind Subramanian (2001), 'Measuring Services Liberalization and Its Impact on Economic Growth'. *Policy Research Working Paper*, No. 2655 (The World Bank).

Mattoo, Aaditya and Carsten Fink, 'Regional Agreements and Trade in Services: Policy Issues', *Journal of Economic Integration* 19(4) (2004), pp. 742–779.

Mattoo, Aaditya and Sacha Wunsch-Vincent, 'Pre-Empting Protectionism in Services: The GATS and Outsourcing', *Journal of International Economic Law* 7(4) (2004), pp. 765–800.

Nhu-Van, Dang, Nguyen Chien-Thang and Vu Hoang-Dat (2006), 'Rule of Origin in Services: Selected Sectors in Vietnam's Case'. Mimeo.

Nikomborirak, Deunden (2004), 'An Assessment of the Investment Regime: Thailand Country Report'. Available at www.iisd.org/pdf/2004/investment_country_report_thailand.pdf.

Nikomborirak, Deunden and Suneeporn Tawannakul (2006), 'The Face of Foreign Companies in the Thai Economy'. Paper presented at the Mid-year Conference of the Thailand Development Research Institute, August 25, 2006 (in Thai only).

Stephenson, Sherry and Deunden Nikomborirak, 'Regional Liberalization in Services', in Stephenson, Sherry, Christopher Findlay and Soonhwa Yi (eds.), *Services Trade Liberalisation and Facilitation* (Asia Pacific Press at Australian National University, 2002).

Tham, Siew Yean and Mahani Zainal Abidin (2006), 'Rules of Origin in Services: Case of Malaysia'. Mimeo.

5

Comment: Is services trade like or unlike manufacturing trade?

MARION JANSEN

Carsten Fink and Deunden Nikomborirak in chapter 4 in this volume bring us one step further in understanding the sometimes blurry but at the same time complex concept of services trade. Services trade currently represents around one fifth of total trade at the global level and it thus appears to be crucial for economists and policy-makers to get a better understanding of its intricacies. In this respect, their chapter provides very useful insights, in particular by emphasising the differences in the design of rules of origin for services and for manufacturing trade.

In the case of manufacturing trade, rules of origin tend to be based on a value-added criterion. Only goods that have been transformed sufficiently on the territory covered by the regional trade agreement, i.e. only goods to which sufficient value has been added within the relevant territory, are eligible for preferential treatment. The design of rules of origin for services trade differs significantly from this approach. In particular, instead of targeting the traded services and their level of transformation within the relevant territory, they tend to make reference to characteristics of services suppliers. In the case of companies, they, for instance, make reference to their incorporation under domestic law, their level of domestic employment or to domestic ownership and control, where 'domestic' refers to one of the members of the regional agreement. They also make reference to the level of business operations within the relevant territory. One reason for this difference in designing rules of origin may lie in the fact that the nature of services trade differs significantly from goods trade which makes a value-added rule inappropriate or difficult to apply in the case of services. Indeed, it is only under mode 1 trade that services cross borders. In the case of mode 3 and mode 4 trade, suppliers cross borders rather than the actual services, and in the case of mode 2 it is consumers who cross borders. Targeting suppliers rather than the services they supply may thus be an appropriate thing to do from a 'technical' point of view.

But the description of rules of origin given in this chapter also hints at another reason for the difference between rules of origins in manufacturing and in services: they may not always serve the same purpose. In the case of manufacturing trade, rules of origin quite explicitly serve the purpose of delimiting the extent to which non-members benefit from the trade preferences that are negotiated among members. Trade negotiators may have had a similar purpose in mind when basing services rules of origin on criteria like the level of business operations or the level of domestic employment in the case of companies or on criteria related to individuals' centre of interest in the case of individual service providers.

But other criteria used in the case of rules of origin in services may pursue goals that are more related to regulatory questions than to pecuniary interests. Criteria like incorporation under domestic law in the case of companies or residency in the case of individual services suppliers refer to the legal relationship between service suppliers and the relevant territory. This could be the case because trade negotiators intended to clarify the relationship between services suppliers and regional regulators. At this stage this is only a conjecture, but there are certainly instances where such an approach could make economic sense. Indeed, in a number of services sectors, like the financial sector or telecommunications, regulation plays a crucial rule in order to guarantee the efficient functioning of markets.[1] In these cases policy-makers need to ensure that trade liberalisation does not jeopardise the regulation of relevant markets. It would be interesting to analyse whether these were the motives treaty drafters had in mind when deciding to use criteria based on incorporation or residency, or whether the choice of these criteria was driven by other motives. If regulatory considerations played a role and were appropriately taken into account, one would expect the design of rules of origin to differ significantly across services sectors and to reflect the differences in the importance and the nature of regulation across sectors.

A related question is to analyse how other criteria like 'domestic ownership and control', in the case of companies, and 'nationality', in the case of individual services suppliers, fit into the picture depicted so far. The condition that owners or managers are domestic may reflect the intention to ensure that decisions taken in regional establishments reflect the interest of those establishments and not those of holding companies situated outside the region's territory. Such concerns have, for instance,

[1] See Stephenson (2002) for a discussion of the role of regulation in services sectors and resulting implications for regional or multilateral trade liberalisation.

been raised by New Zealand's and Australia's bank regulators, although the solutions they opted for are not linked to the nationality of managers or owners. Instead, in both countries banks must include directors that are independent from the holding company of the bank on their boards in order to make sure that management acts in the best interest of the local institution.[2] New Zealand authorities also require banks to have constitutions that explicitly prevent directors from damaging the subsidiary established in New Zealand and its creditors while pursuing benefits for the holding company. How do such considerations fit into our common thinking on the political economy forces that drive regional liberalisation? Do such considerations play a more important role in specific services sectors, like the financial sector that is crucial for economic stability? Or are, in the case of services trade, criteria based on nationality or domestic ownership simply a suitable way to ensure that the benefits of preferential trade arrangements are not spread to non-members?

The distinctly different role of suppliers and, to a lesser extent, consumers in the case of services trade may not only have implications for the design of rules of origin. One important question that arises is, whether it has also implications for the political economy mechanisms that are driving trade liberalisation in general and regional liberalisation in particular. From the point of view of the multilateral trading system it would be particularly interesting to analyse to what extent political economy aspects that are specific to services trade affect the potential for regional services agreements to serve as building blocks towards multilateral liberalisation. Baldwin's (2006) recent contribution to this literature argues that changes in the political equilibrium resulting from the creation of FTAs combined with the phenomenon of unbundling manufacturing processes may have strengthened the building block characteristics of regional trade agreements. It would be interesting to analyse whether similar processes have or will be observed in services trade. In this regard, the question arises whether production processes in services are sufficiently 'like' those in manufacturing in order for unbundling to play an important role.

To summarise, the chapter by Fink and Nikomborirak does not only bring us a step further in understanding the similarities and differences between manufacturing and services trade, it also opens interesting and important avenues for further research – research that would hopefully help us to better understand the implications of differences between manufacturing and services trade.

[2] See Cárdenas *et al.* (2003) for a more detailed discussion.

Bibliography

Baldwin, Richard E. 'Multilateralising Regionalism: Spaghetti Bowls as Building Blocs on the Path to Global Free Trade', *The World Economy* 29(11) (2006), pp. 1451–1518.

Cárdenas, Juan, Juan Pablo Graf and Pascual O'Dogherty (2003) 'Foreign Banks Entry in Emerging Market Economies: a Host Country Perspective', Banco de México Paper prepared for the CGFS Working Group on FDI in the financial sector, Basel: Bank for International Settlements.

Stephenson, Sherry M. 'Regional versus Multilateral Liberalization of Services', *World Trade Review* 1(2) (2002), pp. 187–209.

PART 3

The limits of request–offer negotiations: Plurilateral and alternative approaches to services liberalisation

6

Services post-Hong Kong – initial experiences with plurilaterals

ELISABETH TÜRK[1]

1. Introduction

During the first half of 2006 WTO Members held three rounds of plurilateral negotiations on services based on more than twenty plurilateral requests. Despite some talk about refocusing on bilaterals, the process has been considered useful for shedding light on technical issues and on specific negotiating positions, outlining the contours of what could be a possible package in the Doha Work Programme's (DWP) services area.[2] In the words of Ambassador Fernando de Mateo, Chair of the Council for Trade in Services, Special Session (CTS-SS), '[t]he level of engagement in the plurilateral negotiations has been better than expected … The overall assessment was that the meetings were useful … [the process of] preparing and discussing collective requests has been positive.'[3]

This chapter discusses the DWP's plurilateral services negotiations. It first looks at the Hong Kong (HK) Ministerial text on plurilaterals; secondly, it discusses the origins of services plurilaterals, including the broader context of benchmarking and the so-called failure of bilateral negotiating methods; thirdly, the paper looks at initial experiences and patterns emerging in three rounds of plurilateral meetings. The paper

[1] Economic Affairs Officer, UNCTAD, DITC, TNCDB. The views expressed are those of the author and do not reflect the views of the UNCTAD secretariat or its member states. I am grateful for the valuable comments by Luis Abugattas, Rolf Adlung, Phillipe Borell, Joy Kategekwa, Christina Leb, Mina Mashayekhi, Marion Panizzon, Nicole Pohl, Scott Sinclair and Sabrina Varma. Special thanks to Anna-Emilia Autio and Eva Hendriks for their assistance.

[2] For a discussion of the way forward on services, post-HK, see Mina Mashayekhi and Elisabeth Türk, 'WTO Services Negotiations & Development: A Post-Hong Kong Review', *Bridges Monthly*, Year 10, No. 1, 2006, pp. 3–5.

[3] Ambassador Fernando de Mateo, Chair of the CTS-SS, 'Statement for Item F: Organization of Future Work', CTS-SS, July 2006 Services Cluster.

concludes by asking whether plurilaterals met the expectations and objectives envisaged.

2. The Hong Kong language on plurilaterals

WTO Members conducted plurilateral negotiations according to the HK Ministerial Declaration.[4] Annex C of the HK text sets forth various methods for negotiating specific commitments.[5] Before HK, no other Ministerial Declaration had resulted in a 'services text' with a comparable level of detail. The Declaration's services language (paragraphs 25 to 27 of the main text and Annex C) was interpreted as showing Ministers' commitment to moving the DWP's services agenda further, with some considering the reference to plurilaterals the most significant outcome of the Ministerial.[6] However, the HK services language was intensively negotiated, proving controversial until the closing of the Conference.[7]

The text relevant for plurilaterals is in paragraph 7 of Annex C:

> (7). In addition to bilateral negotiations, we agree that the request-offer negotiations should also be pursued on a plurilateral basis in accordance with the principles of the GATS and the Guidelines and Procedures for the Negotiations on Trade in Services. The results of such negotiations shall be extended on an MFN basis. These negotiations would be organized in the following manner:
>
> a) Any Member or group of Members may present requests or collective requests to other Members in any specific sector or mode of supply, identifying their objectives for the negotiations in that sector or mode of supply.

[4] WT/MIN(05)/DEC.

[5] Specific commitments are set out in Members' schedules and form an integral part of the GATS Agreement, and are legally binding for the particular Member in question (Article XX GATS).

[6] Scott Sinclair, 'Crunch Time in Geneva: Benchmarks, Plurilaterals, Domestic Regulation and other Pressure Tactics in the GATS Negotiations', CCPA (Canadian Centre for Policy Alternatives), June 2006, p. 14.

[7] The HK services language and particularly Annex C was highly contested, including by LDCs, the African Group, Caribbean countries and individual developing country governments. Disagreement was reflected by 'bracketing' the reference to Annex C in the draft Declaration which negotiators sent to the Ministerial. Ultimately, however, only a few changes were made to the text and – apart from Venezuela and Cuba, who lodged reservations against Annex C – Ministers endorsed the services annex in the HK meeting's concluding session. Sinclair (2006) – footnote 3, p. 25.

b) Members to whom such requests have been made shall consider such requests in accordance with paragraphs 2 and 4 of Article XIX of the GATS and paragraph 11 of the Guidelines and Procedures for the Negotiations on Trade in Services.
c) Plurilateral negotiations should be organized with a view to facilitating the participation of all Members, taking into account the limited capacity of developing countries and smaller delegations to participate in such negotiations.

Ministers also gave specific guidance on the timelines for pursuing plurilaterals, in paragraph 11 Annex C:

b) Groups of Members presenting plurilateral requests to other Members should submit such requests by 28 February 2006 or as soon as possible thereafter.
c) A second round of revised offers shall be submitted by 31 July 2006.
d) Final draft schedules of commitments shall be submitted by 31 October 2006.

While novel in its specific formulation, the idea of plurilateral negotiations had already been part of the WTO's post Uruguay Round (UR) services negotiations. Most importantly, paragraph 4 of Article XIX, the provision mandating current GATS negotiations, states: '[t]he process of progressive liberalization shall be advanced ... through bilateral, plurilateral or multilateral negotiations directed towards increasing the general level of specific commitments undertaken by Members under this Agreement'. Subsequently, the March 2001 Negotiating Guidelines[8] also refer to plurilateral negotiations. Paragraph 11 states that '[l]iberalization shall be advanced through bilateral, plurilateral or multilateral negotiations', followed by the statement that '[t]he main method of negotiation shall be the request-offer approach'.

Moreover, while not strictly speaking plurilateral, some of the post-UR 'sector focused' negotiations and Members' practice to act in so-called 'friends' groups exhibited certain features relevant for current plurilateral services talks. However, both post-UR sectoral negotiations and 'friends groups' differ from the spring 2006 plurilaterals: the extended post-UR negotiations were conducted by formal negotiating bodies (e.g. Group on Basic Telecom), different from the informal nature of the spring 2006 plurilaterals, without institutionalised structure; the 'friends' are informal,

[8] As mandated by Article XIX GATS, Members adopted the Guidelines and Procedures for the Negotiations on Trade in Services, S/L/93, 29 March 2001.

technical gatherings, allowing Members to benefit from a close and intensive working relationship, but not strictly speaking negotiating groups.

Regardless of the closeness between plurilaterals and earlier initiatives, the respective HK language was subject to intense negotiations. Members (and other affected stakeholders) had diverging views about the

Box 1: Negotiating methods and initiatives

Friends groups: 'Friends' are informal sectoral or modal groups of like-minded Members, intensively working together (e.g. on classification, levels of ambition) through, e.g., model schedules and checklists. While membership in 'friends' varies, it usually comprises those Members committed to liberalisation of a particular sector or mode. In 2005/2006 there were approximately 14 such groups.[9]

Bilateral request/offer (R/O) negotiations: building on the method of negotiating tariffs for trade in goods, R/O was the main method for negotiating services liberalisation in the UR, and according to the Negotiating Guidelines (and the GATS) also in the DWP. While bargaining is done on a bilateral basis and according to the requests and offers submitted by the two parties, the results of such bilateral negotiations are multilateralised, i.e. extended on an MFN basis to other WTO Members.

Formulas: They can be quantitative or qualitative and are considered a method for securing a core level of liberalisation (overall and by individual parties), avoiding the free-rider problem and facilitating the negotiating process among a high number of parties.[10]

Model schedules: Sometimes considered a form of formula, they were used during the post–UR negotiations on maritime transport and telecom services. They are seen as providing greater clarity, standardisation and user-friendliness. Several current plurilateral requests contain model schedules (e.g. legal, computer etc.).

[9] 'Friends' focused on e.g. logistics, air transport, maritime, audiovisual, legal, computer-related services, environmental, construction, express delivery, energy, telecom, financial, mode 4: Alejandro Jara and M. del. Carmen Dominguez, 'Liberalization of Trade in Services and Trade Negotiations', *JWT* 40(1) (2006), p. 122.

[10] Rachel Thompson; 'Formula Approaches to Improving GATS Commitments', in Sauvé /Stern, *GATS 2000 – New Directions in Services Trade Liberalization* (2000), pp. 487 ff.

Sectoral services negotiations: sectoral services negotiations were conducted post-UR, e.g. for telecom, maritime and financial, with results in market access and rule-making (e.g. Telecom Reference Paper, Understanding on Financial Services). While originally envisaged to bind only selected Members (e.g. those negotiating the documents), their application is being broadened (e.g. regarding the Reference Paper accession countries are asked to subscribe and it is a central feature of the plurilateral request on telecom).

Plurilateral agreements in WTO: the WTO legal framework contained four plurilateral agreements: Trade in Civil Aircraft, Government Procurement, the International Dairy Agreement and the International Bovine Meat Agreement. The latter two phased out. Unlike in the case of multilateral agreements, only a sub-set of WTO Members are party to a plurilateral agreement.

Plurilateral services negotiations in the DWP: services plurilaterals include many but not all WTO Members. However, it is envisaged that the benefits resulting from plurilateral negotiations (the results of which are binding only for a sub-set of Members), will be generalised among all Members on an MFN basis.

desirability of such negotiations; the most appropriate manner of conducting them and the manner in which the Ministerial Declaration should refer to them. Aside from the overall concern that the Ministerial text was too prescriptive, some feared that plurilateral negotiations might result in – or possibly enforce – higher levels of liberalisation commitments in specific sectors; that they would allow the 'friends' to reach out more formally to other Members (possibly leading to a formalisation of sectoral negotiating initiatives); that they would limit the use of the GATS' flexibilities (which are central to GATS principles and architecture); that Annex C would supplant GATS Negotiating Guidelines; or that plurilaterals would require an amount of time and resources which Members would be unable to devote, thereby having repercussions on the work in other services negotiating bodies.[11]

At the same time, aspects raised as concerns by some (e.g. giving a formal platform to the 'friends groups'; allowing them to draw in a critical mass of

[11] Aileen Kwa, 'Plurilateral Request-Offer Approaches in GATS Draft Text: Entry Point for Dangerous Sectoral Negotiations', Focus on the Global South, November 2005.

Members; setting the stage for subsequent sectoral negotiations post-DWP) were considered as positive and desirable by others. These differences in views on specificities of the negotiating process reflect broader differences in opinion and approach: on the one hand, there are those who view the DWP's services negotiations as useful to facilitate much needed and beneficial services liberalisation – both in export markets and at home; on the other hand, there are those who consider the negotiations as a mechanism to 'force' services markets open – against the express will of affected stakeholders at the national level.

Amongst others, these differences arise from deeper differences regarding what would be a balanced outcome of this Round. For some an overall balanced deal would mean meaningful liberalisation by all Members (apart from LDCs). For others, including many developing countries, a balanced outcome of the DWP would imply meaningful commitments for developing countries (e.g., in mode 4) with a true positive development impact, in effect 'compensating' for the 'imbalances' arising from the UR. Such meaningful commitments would be accompanied by appropriate policy space and flexibilities regarding the commitments undertaken by developing countries.

Accordingly, the language on plurilaterals saw numerous variations. Three of the changes particularly relevant to the plurilateral negotiations are: (1) shifting from a legally binding, mandatory mandate to engage in plurilaterals to a 'best endeavour' formulation; (2) adding a reference to GATS Article XIX paragraphs 2 and 4 (flexibilities and increasing the level of specific commitments); and (3) certain changes regarding nature and formalisation of plurilateral meetings.

On the first of these changes, the original mandatory instruction to *enter* into plurilateral negotiations was turned into a somewhat softer instruction to *consider* plurilateral requests. In line with the overall perception that (in theory) one central feature of plurilateralism is voluntary participation, some had been reluctant to embrace the original, mandatory language. Accordingly, the final Annex C paragraph 7 c states that 'Members to whom such requests have been made *shall consider* such requests' (emphasis added). In contrast, an earlier version of the text had read '[a]ny Member or group of Members who have made such requests in a specific sector or mode of supply, together with Members to whom such requests have been made, and any other interested Member, *shall enter into plurilateral negotiations to consider such requests*' (emphasis added).[12]

[12] Similar changes had taken place in the *chapeau* language to para 7.

While one could debate the practicability of a mandatory, legally binding mandate to enter into plurilateral negotiations, the change in language nevertheless reflects concerns that the original text would have obliged Members to engage in plurilaterals. According to some, entering into a negotiation implied willingness to reach an agreement, and the institutional structure created through the plurilateral negotiations would create effective drivers for such an agreement. This might not have been desirable for weaker Members, who would have preferred resorting to GATS flexibilities.[13] Others, in turn, suggested that the linguistic changes in the final text would make little difference as the text still secured the main objective of the *demandeurs*, namely the launching of plurilateral negotiations.[14]

Second, the final language on plurilaterals contains references to paragraphs 2 and 4 of GATS Article XIX. These references could be seen as an attempt to respond to two sets of concerns: on the one hand, the fear that plurilaterals would restrict flexibility (thus the reference to Article XIX paragraph 2, a provision central for GATS flexibilities); and on the other hand, the fear that a real softening of the language would possibly take the 'teeth' out of the Ministerial services text (hence the reference to Article XIX paragraph 4, a provision emphasising that negotiations be directed towards increasing specific commitments undertaken). Similar references, undertaken in an effort to assuage concerns voiced about the possible stringency of plurilaterals can also be found in the services language of the Ministerial Declaration's main text.[15]

A third change in language refers to the degree of formalisation and institutionalisation of the plurilateral negotiations. Earlier language[16] had included a paragraph 10 c, asking the CTS-SS to 'review progress' in the plurilateral negotiations and a paragraph 15 c, requiring Members to notify the CTS-SS on the sectors in which they intend to engage in plurilateral negotiations. The absence of such language in subsequent texts could be seen as a success for those who wanted to avoid formalisation and institutionalisation which would have facilitated 'finger pointing' and 'blaming' about any lack of progress in the negotiations. While

[13] See also, South Centre, 'Comments on Chairman Draft Ministerial Text on Services JOB (05)/262/Rev.1', November 2005, South Centre.

[14] Sinclair (2006), p. 14.

[15] E.g. paras. 25 and 26 containing references to flexibility (for individual developing countries) and to objectives and principles of GATS (e.g. right to regulate, respect for national policy objectives).

[16] Job(05)/262/Rev.1, 3 November 2005.

Annex C, last paragraph, indeed refers to a review of progress, its focus is much broader than merely plurilaterals.

In sum, these modifications appear to lean in favour of those reluctant to embrace plurilateral negotiations. However, these changes also have to be seen in the broader context of agreeing to Annex C – with plurilaterals as one of the main elements: while DCs managed to soften the language in various instances, they nevertheless ended up with a clear and specific mandate to pursue plurilateral negotiations. Here it might be important to also consider broader negotiating dynamics. Having used much energy and negotiating clout in their struggle to resist proposals on benchmarking, many developing country negotiators might have felt somewhat uncomfortable to continue opposing new proposals – such as those on plurilaterals. Obviously, there was a strong call for showing constructive engagement, rather than continuing opposition. This was supported, not least by a possible trade off with the agricultural side of the DWP negotiations.

3. Plurilaterals and their broader context: Benchmarking and the bilateral request-offer negotiations

An appraisal of the HK language on plurilaterals must also look at the broader context surrounding the evolution of paragraph 7, including developments during and before the HK Ministerial.

This chapter investigates two main factors, which might lie behind Members' agreement to the language on plurilaterals in the HK Ministerial Declaration. It first looks at the trade-offs and negotiating dynamics which had arisen between suggestions for benchmarking and suggestions for plurilaterals. It then looks at the argument (put forward by the *demandeurs* of plurilaterals) that plurilateral negotiating methods would help overcome the deficiencies of bilateral negotiating methods. For a better comprehension of the latter argument, the discussion is preceded by an outline of what are seen as the possible reasons for the so-called failure of the bilateral request-offer (R/O) negotiating method. The chapter concludes by highlighting some of the concerns which had been voiced with respect to plurilaterals.

Controversies about benchmarking – setting the scene for plurilaterals

Central to the developments preceding the HK Ministerial were the perceptions that bilateral R/O negotiations had failed to generate sufficient momentum and ambitious results, leading to what some viewed as a crisis in the negotiations. The bottom-up approach of scheduling together with the bilateral R/O method cannot, it was argued, ensure sufficiently ambitious results. Debate about a crisis emerged in May 2005, when the date for submitting revised offers passed and some voiced concern about the 'unsatisfactory quality of offers'. According to the Chair of the CTS-SS, '[m]ost Members feel that the negotiations are not progressing as they should'.[17] Others however, felt that the so-called 'crisis scenario' was mainly 'fabricated'. Setting aside the 'quality' of offers, the numbers of offers submitted in services compares favourably to respective developments in agriculture and NAMA.

This debate about a 'crisis' in the DWP's services negotiations spurred a series of initiatives – mostly by developed countries – to establish quantitative and qualitative benchmarks.[18] While some proposals aimed to use benchmarks merely for the (voluntary) self-assessment of individual offers/commitments; others clearly aimed at the establishment of joint 'benchmarks', 'baselines' or 'criteria' for further liberalisation. Some quantitative criteria indicated – in percentages – the number of sectors/sub-sectors (from an agreed list) for taking commitments; others suggested making commitments of no less than the existing level of openness. Despite differences in details, most proposals concurred in using simple and artificially set cross-sectoral, formula-type approaches, establishing 'quantitative' and 'qualitative' criteria to which individual offers should correspond.[19] Flexibility would be granted by according specific liberalisation percentages to different groups of countries, a means perceived to account for different levels of development. Sometimes however, this flexibility was subject to negotiation rather than automatically granted. Moreover, not all proposals excluded LDCs.

According to the proponents, combining a collectively agreed level of ambition with certain flexibilities would ensure a successful outcome for DWP's services negotiations for all WTO Members, including LDCs.

[17] CTS-SS Chair report to the TNC, 11 July 2005.

[18] Australia, Canada, EC, India, Japan, Korea, New Zealand, Switzerland and Chinese Taipei, available at www.ourworldisnotforsale.org/showarticle.asp?search=741.

[19] According to some calculations, the EU suggestion on benchmarking would have demanded from developed countries an increase in the number of sub-sectors committed to GATS to 139 out of 163 (from an average of 106), and from developing countries an increase in the number of committed sub-sectors to 93 out of 163 (from an average of 50). This proposal would not apply to LDCs and some, at that point in time unspecified, 'vulnerable developing countries': Peter Hardstaff: 'Benchmarking in GATS: Exposing the EU Aggressive Service Agenda', World Development Movement, November 2005, www.ourworldisnotforsale.org/showarticle.asp?search=943.

However, as stated by many developing countries, this was a problematic combination – a view also shared by numerous civil society groups. Many developing countries voiced their concerns in the WTO's September 2005 Services Cluster and in UNCTAD's October 2005 Trade and Development Board (TDB). At the TDB it was emphasised that the complementary approaches would reverse the logic and spirit of the GATS and the Negotiating Guidelines, leading to a substantial loss of flexibilities.[20] In sum, many made clear that they did not support the use of benchmarks. Moreover, by placing services on the same 'product based' formula framework as NAMA and agriculture, complementary approaches would ignore the complexity of services sectors and their regulatory frameworks.[21]

Some of these concerns about the benchmarking were not only voiced by those aiming to preserve the GATS flexibilities, but also by those in favour of deeper liberalisation. Richard Self (previously deputy USTR and closely associated with putting services on OECD/GATT agendas) states that 'unlike industrial tariffs and agriculture supports, services do not lend themselves to negotiations by formula'.[22] Robert Vastine (President of the US Coalition of Services Industries) highlights the 'fatal flaw' in the quantitative proposals, in so far as they would not 'assure quality of offers'.[23] Thus, while benchmarks were suggested as a response to the so-called 'crisis', the deficiencies of this response – both political and practical – were also obvious.

In the broader context, however, the controversy surrounding benchmarks might have facilitated agreement on the language on plurilateral negotiations. Ultimately the adoption of the plurilateral language had been rather smooth and one could possibly argue that benchmarks were proposed to deviate attention away from the proposal on plurilaterals[24] while already having in mind the possibility to ultimately agree on a

[20] See item 6 of UNCTAD's 2005 TDB, statements of Mauritius on behalf of the ACP Group, China and Jamaica; see also President's Summary TD/B/52/L.6.

[21] Importantly, GATS had been hailed a development-friendly agreement, mainly because of the flexibility it grants in terms of allowing Members to choose which sub-sectors to commit to and which conditions/limitations to attach to such commitments.

[22] Richard Self, 'Energizing the Negotiations on Services in the Doha Round', *Trade Policy Analyses*, Cordell Hull Institute, 8(10) (April 2006).

[23] Robert Vastine, 'Services Negotiations in the Doha Round: Promise and Reality', October 2005, Gerald R. Ford School of Public Policy, University of Michigan, p. 4.

[24] While recognising the dynamics between the negotiating proposals, it is important to note that both proposals emerged in response to the call by the then CTS-SS Chairman Ambassador Jara, suggesting delegations to come forward with ideas that might help unblock the negotiations. At some point, Canada put forward a first suggestion for plurilateral negotiations.

fall-back option. With most of the controversies in the run-up to HK focusing on benchmarking,[25] other initiatives had been left languishing and plurilaterals were agreed upon with comparably little scrutiny.[26] No reasonable trade negotiator could have realistically expected that WTO Members would, within a few months – not to say weeks – of negotiations, agree on negotiations modalities that were as complex, controversial – and possibly infeasible – as suggested by the benchmarking proponents. The argument to view benchmarks as some sort of 'fake battleground' for plurilaterals gains even more ground, when recognising that quantitative benchmarks and formulas had been discussed earlier, without however, gaining much traction amongst policy-makers.[27]

Ultimately, the Annex C language as it was agreed upon omitted explicit references to benchmarking, and therefore appealed to all those whose objective was to avoid Ministerial agreement on mandatory benchmarks. Moreover, in its amended and softened form it appeared to alleviate some of the concerns which developing countries had voiced regarding a possible shift to plurilateral negotiations. At the same time, detailed language on plurilateral services negotiations (including timelines) not only ensured that Members would seize the previously granted possibility for plurilateral negotiations, but also showed a strong step forward in terms of responding – at the ministerial level – to what was perceived a major crisis in the DWP services negotiations. In sum, plurilaterals were an expected move away from the sort of rigid, numerical targets, which had attracted criticism (from both industry and developmental interests) for being arbitrary, possibly even irrelevant. Instead, under plurilaterals, the *demandeurs* would support goals and targets which they themselves felt willing to adopt.

Plurilaterals: A Tool to put the DWP's services agenda back on track?

Proponents of plurilaterals suggested that this negotiating method could be helpful for remedying the deficiencies of the bilateral R/O approach – and the WTO's services negotiations more broadly. The following will first look at the possible reasons for the so-called crisis in the DWP's services negotiations, including R/O-related problems (a); and then highlight how plurilaterals could possibly help remedy such deficiencies (b).

25 This is also true for most of the work of civil society groups and NGOs, who were monitoring the preparations for the HK Ministerial.

26 Kwa (2005). 27 Thompson (2000), pp. 473–487.

(a) Difficulties in the WTO's services negotiations

The reasons for the so-called crisis of the market access area of the DWP's services talks appear to be many and diverse. Some relate more broadly to the services negotiations, and others, more specifically to the bilateral R/O method.[28]

Most important are the close linkages between different areas of WTO negotiations. The opportunity for cross-issue trade-offs, resulting in the so-called 'single undertaking' covering agriculture, NAMA, rules, services and many other issues, is one of the greatest potentials of the WTO negotiating setting. It is, however, also a source of its greatest challenges. In essence, during much of the DWP, the services portfolio appeared to be 'hijacked' by lack of progress in agriculture and NAMA. Several countries argued that the DWP's services agenda should proceed in parallel with appropriate progress across other negotiating areas – notably agriculture.[29] Lack of progress in agriculture was seen as a reason for reluctance to move on services.

Setting aside these broader dynamics, one could see the reason for failure lying in the practicalities of the negotiations, particularly the bilateral R/O method. The inadequacies of the negotiating process itself lead to a 'low level equilibrium trap, where little is expected and less is offered'.[30] In a process where bargaining proceeded bilaterally[31] the bilaterally submitted requests tended to be highly ambitious, sometimes calling for free trade and requiring countries to remove practically all conditions/limitations. Sometimes requests essentially appeared a 'copy and paste exercise', without clear linkages to the target country's services regime. Conversely, responses (conditional offers) were minimalistic – sometimes called the 'bare minimum'. Besides the effect of overwhelming requests, the desire to protect negotiating leverage, clout and bargaining chips for subsequent phases of the negotiations might have been behind this tendency.

An additional reason for failure could be detected in the highly resource intensive nature of the bilateral process. Sector by sector and country by country negotiation of commitments requires significant

[28] Vastine (2005), pp. 5–6.

[29] Note that similar arguments for parallelism were also made within the services agenda, notably between GATS rules and market access.

[30] Aaditya Mattoo, 'Regulatory Authorities and WTO Negotiations on Services', *Trade Policy Analyses*, Cordell Hull Institute, 8(9) (April 2006).

[31] Note, however, that offers – unlike requests – were circulated on a multilateral basis.

transaction costs and coordination at the national and international levels, straining human and other resources, both in Geneva and national capitals, and particularly in developing countries.[32] Linked to that is what some call the logistical nightmare of organising bilateral meetings so that individual capital-based officials meet their respective, sector-specific counterparts from another country. The need for feedback and linkages between Geneva and national capitals also requires the sort of coordination mechanisms for keeping domestic actors involved and informed – a procedural and institutional aspect which is frequently missing in developing countries.[33]

The resource intensive nature of the services negotiations emanates, amongst others, from the need to involve domestic stakeholders, most importantly regulators of different services sectors. However, regulators to be involved are not only many (leading to the above challenge of organising meetings), but sometimes also come with mindsets different from those of trade negotiators. While trade negotiators tend to focus on eliminating barriers to services trade, for many regulators the objective is to preserve their scope, right and prerogative for designing, implementing and enforcing domestic regulations. More broadly, this is complemented by the sensitive political nature of some services sectors (e.g. health, education, financial), the attendant scrutiny from civil society groups and disagreement (some would call it 'misunderstanding') about the nature and implications of services liberalisation. Frequently, the political will to liberalise services markets is missing at the national level.[34] Once this domestic resistance to change is overcome – one could argue – it should not be too difficult to solve logistical problems related to the technicalities of the negotiations.

Another, possibly related reason for failure is seen in the lack of high-level attention for services negotiations. While Ministerial Meetings before HK had given high-level attention to NAMA and agriculture, efforts to promote and accelerate services liberalisation had been of a

[32] Pierre Sauvé and Mary Irace, 'The Doha Development Agenda and GATS, the Benefits of Open Services Markets', A Report for the National Foreign Trade Council, July 2006, p. 12.

[33] For a discussion of the difficulties developing countries face in bilateral R/O negotiations, see Mina Mashayekhi and Elisabeth Tuerk, 'The WTO Services Negotiations: Some Strategic Considerations', Working Paper No. 14, South Centre, T.R.A.D.E., January 2003.

[34] While for some, this is a sign of preserving democratic choices in a globalised world, for others this amounts to buying into resistance to change at the domestic level.

LLYFRGELL PRIFYSGOL BANGOR UNIVERSITY LIBRARY

much lower scale. For some, the tendency that 'services portfolios' are handled by junior officials is also as a factor contributing to the failure of the DWP's services negotiations.[35]

Others focus on developing countries' resistance to proactively engaging in services market access work as a reason for failure: reluctance to open services markets through bilateral R/O negotiations equates to lack of engagement, leadership and political will. At the same time, developing countries lack many of the preconditions for active and meaningful participation in such negotiations. Amongst others, they lack human and institutional resources to effectively determine their negotiating interests,[36] as well as the bargaining clout required for effective bilateral negotiations. Moreover, it is widely acknowledged that the proper pacing and sequencing of regulation and liberalisation is a crucial factor when striving to harness services trade for development.

In sum, while some of these reasons for failure cut across the DWP or the services negotiations more broadly, others are specifically related to the bilateral R/O process. Difficulties with the bilateral R/O process, however, were not unexpected. In fact, already prior to the launching of the GATS 2000 negotiations there were calls and suggestions for negotiating commitments in methods different from the bilateral R/O process. This included calls for plurilateral negotiations.[37]

(b) Plurilaterals and their potential to address deficiencies of the bilateral R/O approach

How then could plurilateral negotiations help remedy the aforementioned deficiencies? A first, major advantage of plurilateral negotiations was that they avoided the need to barter commitment country by country and that they could substantially reduce transaction costs. Plurilaterals were perceived as an option to economise on 'the scarcest of commodities' – time and human resources – an issue of particular importance in the final stretch of the DWP.[38] Moreover, to the extent that they are combined with some sort of formula approaches (e.g. model schedule), plurilaterals were seen as an option to avoid the free-rider problem.

A second advantage cited for plurilaterals was that they could offer developing countries significant economies of scale in negotiating efforts.

[35] Vastine (2005), p. 6.

[36] See statement of South Africa, when submitting its offer in the WTO's 2006 summer cluster.

[37] Thompson (2000), pp. 473–487. [38] Sauvé/Irace (2006), p. 12.

While some developing countries voiced concerns about the level of resource allocation required for the plurilateral processes, some commentators argued that plurilaterals would be beneficial for developing countries, in light of the GATS experience that the bilateral R/O process was 'significantly more taxing' for developing countries than for developed ones.[39] Moreover, one could argue that plurilaterals could help developing countries remedy the deficiencies they experience in bilaterals, including their lack in political and negotiating clout. In fact, some suggested that plurilaterals would help address some of the specific challenges for developing countries. Having limited negotiating powers individually, it was argued that 'developing countries should seriously consider acting collectively with other developing countries, sharing common interests and thereby enhancing their position in the negotiations'.[40]

Thirdly, plurilateral negotiations could also be seen as the logical consequence of the 'friends groups', which had emerged as an initial and informal response to the difficulties of the bilateral R/O process (see box). Plurilateral negotiations were seen as an opportunity to give these groupings some higher standing; to provide them with some sort of institutional backing and format; and to make it easier for them to draw in a higher number of countries, with the view to – ultimately – arrive at the type of 'critical mass' needed for successfully concluding a services package.

In fact, before the HK Ministerial, when talking about scheduling and other tools provided by the 'friends', some expressed hope that 'an ever-increasing number of Members understand and incorporate these tools in their negotiating strategy… leading to a "critical mass" of Members willing to adopt, for example, a new classification approach that will allow for deeper commitments in a sector'.[41] Similarly it was suggested that for 'friends' to be effective, they must 'energetically recruit a larger circle of Members in order to reach a critical mass, which will allow them to go public with their proposals and secure wide acceptance of them'.[42] Some also referred to the dynamics required for a critical mass of results, suggesting that '[r]esults will only be acceptable to a particular group of Friends provided that they feel satisfied that the relevant actors in a sector will undertake the commitments'.[43] Similarly, it was suggested that one way for these groups to 'intervene in the negotiations is through the tracking of advances in the R/O process in their area of interest and by collectively setting targets for the

[39] *Ibid.* [40] Jara and Dominguez (2006), p. 123.
[41] Jara and Dominguez (2006), p. 122. [42] Vastine (2005), p. 9.
[43] Jara and Dominguez (2006), p. 122.

Friends and others to meet by the end of the Round'.[44] Thus, even pre-Hong Kong, the 'friends' were directly associated with the idea of a minimum package of commitments for each sector with such a minimum package then turning into a central component of the plurilateral negotiating method.

Some also viewed plurilaterals as an opportunity for setting the stage to carry over sectoral work beyond the conclusion of the DWP. 'The experience of this plurilateral approach', it was suggested, 'could well pave the way to formally organize future negotiations on a sectoral or modal basis'.[45] Moreover, flagging plurilateral negotiations in the Ministerial text was also considered to have broader benefits. Devoting significant space in the Ministerial Declaration to services was also seen as positive, in so far as it showed some high-level Ministerial commitment. This provided the sort of engagement which some had claimed was lacking in the services context (vis-à-vis NAMA and agriculture).

Some of the concerns raised with respect to plurilaterals

As mentioned before, what some perceived as positive and desirable, others perceived as a challenge, threat or inherently dangerous trend. While this difference in views largely originates from different beliefs about the goals of the DWP (and its services negotiations), several of the concerns voiced regarding plurilateral negotiations merit attention.

Most importantly, plurilaterals would have initiated a negotiating dynamic, creating expectations about a certain 'level of ambition' to be achieved. Developing countries feared that such expectations would be hard to resist and that they would effectively be pressured into going along with them. Further, they feared that in case they refrained from going along with highly ambitious objectives, they would be identified as the prime reasons for failure, possibly being taken as a reason for downgrading results in agriculture. Along these lines, some also feared that plurilateral negotiations could operate as a tool to shift the focus of blame away from the EC – onto the developing world.[46]

Some concerns were linked to the role of the 'friends groups' which notably include those countries in favour of liberalisation. It was feared that these groups would first broker an agreement amongst themselves, and then put this forward to other WTO Members – in practice

[44] *Ibid.* [45] *Ibid.*

[46] Having numerical targets for services, in parallel to numerical targets in agriculture would also have well served this purpose.

operating on a 'take it or leave it basis'. By allowing the friends to reach out more formally to other Members, and to speak with the authority of the group, plurilaterals would effectively set the stage for such dynamics.

There were also concerns related to the formalisation of sectoral negotiating initiatives. Formalised sectoral negotiating groups were viewed with suspicion, as they could pave the way for carrying over negotiations beyond the conclusion of the DWP with some considering plurilateral R/O negotiations as 'entry points for dangerous sectoral negotiations'.[47] In light of the UR experiences, carry-over negotiations tend to be successful in sectors of export interest to developed countries (financial and telecom) and less so in sectors of export interest to developing countries (maritime services and mode 4).

Similarly, a request-offer process that is sector based, rather than country based, would possibly put higher pressure on certain sectors – most likely those of export interest to developed countries. Moreover, during the negotiations, any agreements reached in the plurilateral context could end up serving as a 'floor' for the expected commitments in each sector. When working in tandem with bilateral negotiations, this could lead to a particularly high level of liberalisation. Finally, any outcomes of sectoral negotiations – even if not being 'enforced' upon other Members – could become 'de facto' global standards for future services regimes. Again, the experience with the Telecom Reference Paper and the respective texts for financial services offer instructive examples.

As mentioned above, a series of other arguments suggest that plurilaterals would limit the use of the GATS' flexibilities (questioning the principles and architecture of GATS); that the Annex C language would expand, and arguably supplant the GATS Negotiating Guidelines;[48] and that plurilaterals would require an amount of time and resources which Members – particularly developing ones – would be unable to devote.

In sum, many of these concerns fell on fruitful ground, partly because some Members and their constituencies at home feel reluctant about making far-reaching GATS commitments. Lack of understanding about the proper pacing and sequencing of regulation and liberalisation, together with the experiences in the *US – Gambling* and the *Mexico – Telecoms* cases, have supported perceptions that GATS commitments should be

47 Kwa (2005).

48 The Guidelines constitute a central document guiding the DWP's services negotiations with important developmental references. They have since been reaffirmed in the Doha and HK Ministerial Declarations.

undertaken in a careful manner, and based on thorough and prudent evaluation of domestic circumstances. The potential of being pressured into legally binding market openness commitments does not fit well with such an approach.

4. Post-HK: State of play and practicalities of plurilateral services negotiations

After HK, Members engaged in three rounds of plurilateral negotiations. During the first half of 2006, they submitted more than twenty plurilateral requests and conducted numerous plurilateral meetings. The following reviews Members' initial experiences with plurilaterals.

Emerging patterns – format, countries and content of plurilateral requests

While the HK Ministerial text provides an unprecedented level of detail in terms of instructions and guidance for the plurilateral services negotiations, in their endeavour to implement the mandate, Members nevertheless faced a series of novel questions.

For example, the Ministerial text does not give any guidance about the format of plurilateral requests, nor were there any subsequent CTS decisions on the implementation of the mandate. Members also stopped short of requesting any guiding notes by the WTO Secretariat's Services Division.[49] Despite this lack of guidance, plurilateral requests tend to have a typical format: they identify the requesting Members; they state the number of Members receiving the request (sometimes identifying them); they highlight the importance of the sector/mode in question and refer to the economic benefits which liberalisation in these sectors/modes would bring about; and they typically seek enhanced commitments, including through the removal or substantial reduction of limitations and conditions to market access/national treatment commitments[50] in the various sectors or issue areas concerned. Sometimes (e.g. for maritime transport, computer and related, or legal services) they contain a model schedule of commitments.

[49] See previous guiding notes on e.g. editorial conventions for the submission of offers.

[50] Note that sometimes, plurilateral requests go beyond typical market access and national treatment issues, also covering issues related to transparency or, in the case of telecom, the adoption of the Reference Paper.

Importantly, most plurilateral requests specifically state that the *demandeurs* are also considered recipients of the request. Usually, one delegation is mentioned as the group coordinator, giving contact details of the Geneva and capital based officials.

In line with previous practice for most of the bilateral requests, the intention was to keep plurilateral requests confidential, communicating them only to the receiving Members, without officially circulating them through (and to) the WTO Secretariat or other affected stakeholders. Unlike some earlier bilateral requests, however, the plurilateral requests do not contain a specific instruction to keep them confidential. Most of the requests, once circulated to the receiving Members, leaked to the public, and are now available on the World Wide Web.

Plurilateral requests covered about Seventeen sectors: legal; architectural/engineering/integrated engineering; computer-related services; postal/courier, including express delivery; telecom; audiovisual; construction and related engineering; distribution; education; environmental; financial; online entertainment; maritime transport; air transport; logistics; energy; services related to agriculture; and several cross-cutting modal issues, such as cross-border services trade, mode 3, mode 4 and MFN exemptions.

Plurilateral requests were mainly submitted by developed countries and targeted mostly large developing country markets.[51] Amongst the developed country *demandeurs*, Australia, Canada, EC, Japan, New Zealand, Norway, Switzerland and the US were particularly active. Several plurilateral requests even originate from developed countries only, with express delivery, air transport and mode 3 serving as examples. Frequently, the groups of plurilateral requestors overlap with earlier 'friends groups'.

Developing countries only selectively acted as *demandeurs*, with the main examples being middle-income countries, such as Taiwan Province of China (energy, environmental, construction, telecom, financial, maritime, education, logistics, maritime); Mexico (construction, architectural and engineering, audiovisual); Turkey (construction); Chile (architectural and engineering, legal, logistics); Republic of Korea (architectural and engineering, maritime, financial); Panama (maritime); or Saudi Arabia (energy).

[51] Note that this refers to the target countries other than those who are also requesting countries.

There are three requests involving broader developing country participation, namely cross-border supply (modes 1 and 2, supported by India, Chile, Mexico, Pakistan, Singapore and Taiwan, Province of China); mode 4 (supported by Argentina, Brazil, Chile, China, Colombia, Dominican Republic, Egypt, Guatemala, India, Mexico, Morocco, Pakistan, Peru, Thailand and Uruguay); and computer-related services (supported by Chile, India, Republic of Korea, Mexico, Pakistan, Peru, Singapore and Taiwan, Province of China).

Two major requests of developing countries were only submitted to developed countries. These were a request in mode 4 with the target countries being US, EC, Australia, Canada, Japan, New Zealand, Switzerland, Norway and Iceland and services related to agriculture (submitted by Brazil and Argentina) with the target countries being Australia, Canada, EC, Iceland, Japan, New Zealand, Norway, Switzerland, and the US.

No LDC was amongst the requestors[52] and many – notably African countries – remained absent from the list of *demandeurs*. Amongst others, this could be because many smaller developing countries are still grappling with essential services issues and – apart from mode 4 – do not yet view services exports as a possible trade and development strategy. In fact, the pattern of requests reflects Members' potential for services exports and comparative advantages in the services sector; their ability to clearly identify their sectors and mode of export interest; and their capacity to formulate their respective proposals. All of this builds upon a process requiring human capital, information/data and institutional coordination and cooperation processes, which many of the developing countries are lacking. Institutional constraints are maybe most obvious amongst the LDCs, who have struggled to identify sectors and modes of export interest.[53]

Interestingly, there are examples of developing countries which originally co-sponsored a request, and then withdrew from it, arguably, because of difficulties when assessing the development impact of the negotiating proposal and their role as co-*demandeur*.

On the other hand, developing countries figure prominently as 'demandees/requestees', with the main target countries being developing countries with large markets, such as Argentina, Brazil, Chile, China, Colombia, Egypt, India, Indonesia Malaysia, Mexico, Philippines,

[52] Some suggested that this absence was due to the fact that LDCs have their own modalities, the so-called LDC modalities (Modalities for the Special Treatment for Least-Developed Country Members in the Negotiations on Trade in Services (TN/S/13).

[53] Note the respective reference in Annex C para. 9 (d).

Singapore, South Africa and Thailand. A few smaller developing countries have also not been spared requests: Bolivia (architectural); Fiji (air transport); Jamaica (architectural and engineering); Mauritius (logistics); Peru (cross-border, energy, logistics, architectural and engineering, audiovisual, construction and related engineering, environmental, and maritime transport); and Namibia (environmental). Several African countries received a series of plurilateral requests, including Nigeria (logistics, energy, telecom, construction, engineering, financial and maritime transport services), South Africa, Egypt and Morocco. Arguably, the human capital, data and institutional coordination processes required for making a request would arise when needing to respond to a request, thereby giving rise to a series of questions regarding developing countries' abilities to properly respond to these requests.

Perceptions about the content of the plurilateral requests differ. According to one commentator[54] the 'content of proposals is generally strong, full of the level of detail necessary to provide countries with a clear idea of the precision of industry coverage as well as the level of obligations peculiar to each industry'. According to another commentator, '[t]he plurilateral requests are less extensive', also because '[t]he demandeurs had to scale back the ambitions of the requests, because not all of them were willing to abide by full commitments'.[55] In essence, the content of the plurilateral requests is less far-reaching than what had been demanded previously in bilateral requests. Some trace this back to the so-called lowest common denominator effect, by which Members stop short of requesting what they themselves would not be willing to give.[56] While less far-reaching, this could also be perceived as a move towards realism. Maybe this would even be considered positive, in that Members formulated targets which they actually perceived as possible to achieve.

The amount of attention put into the development of the plurilateral requests is also evident when looking at how the requests deal with political sensitivities surrounding particular services sectors. In essence, for some of the highly sensitive sectors, no plurilateral request was made (e.g. health services); and certain sensitive sub-sectors were explicitly excluded from the request (e.g. water for human use). Sometimes, the request refers to the sector's particular sensitivities, recognising the

[54] Self (2006), p. 8. [55] Sinclair (2006), p. 16.

[56] One example is the plurilateral request in telecom services, a sector where the US and the EC have different approaches to liberalisation commitments.

essential role it plays for achieving universal access goals and the attendant need for an appropriate regulatory and institutional framework.

In sum, the plurilateral requests appear to be the result of intense technical work, reflecting the specificities of the sector/mode in question.

Plurilateral negotiations: Initial experiences with the meetings

During the first half of 2006, Members held three rounds of plurilateral negotiations.[57] In so doing, Members had to break new ground in terms of the format and practicalities of these talks. Despite the detail and guidance provided in the Ministerial Declaration (e.g. a request or collective request may be presented by any Member or group of Members, in any specific sector or mode; the receiving Members shall consider such requests; plurilateral negotiations should be organised with a view to facilitating the participation of all Members, taking into account the limited capacity of developing countries and smaller delegations to participate), Members still confronted a series of unique issues. Many of these were addressed in the CTS-SS as well as in informal meetings where Members discussed the pros and cons of the various options.

These included procedural and practical questions about, for example, the role of the CTS-SS and the WTO Secretariat; whether there would be chairs for the various negotiating groups and who would coordinate the groups; how to avoid overlap (time-tables) and satisfy the need for logistical support; how to ensure inclusiveness and the greatest possible amount of transparency and information sharing (including for the public).

While Members stopped short of making formal decisions on the conduct of the negotiations (there were, for example, no additional Negotiating Guidelines or other 'modalities'), some specific patterns emerged.

Most importantly, the negotiations were conducted in an informal spirit, without a formal chair and without formal minutes. At the same time, some countries emerged as the coordinators of the specific plurilateral requests and of the respective group meetings. Usually they are designated in the request. Frequently, these were the ones sending out the letters to the recipients and coordinating the meetings. Often, these were

[57] A total of 21 plurilateral request are said to have been circulated on or briefly following the February 28 deadline set out in Annex C. During the May 2006 services cluster, 15 plurilateral requests appeared active. For a further description see, Sinclair (2006), pp. 14–15.

also the Members who had already been active on this particular sector/mode in the respective 'friends group'. Examples of coordinators include the EC for environmental services, India for mode 4 and HK for logistics services and for MFN exemptions.

As regards timing and scheduling of negotiations, Members took the opportunity offered by the services clusters (the periodic negotiations held in Geneva),[58] folding together the meetings of some of the subsidiary bodies and using the freed-up time (as well as some of the time scheduled for bilaterals) for plurilateral meetings. Most plurilaterals were scheduled to last between two and three hours and usually they were held in the premises of the WTO Secretariat. Resources and time permitting, Members were free to hold bilateral talks in addition to, before, after and in parallel to the plurilateral meetings.

Important questions also arose regarding the role the WTO Secretariat should play in this context. The presence of the Secretariat could facilitate note-taking, ensure some institutional memory of the issues discussed and provide the technical expertise of sectoral experts. However, the presence of the Secretariat was also perceived as a first step towards institutionalising the plurilateral meetings, a trend which some Members anxiously wanted to avoid.

Moreover, there were important questions about transparency and information sharing with the public, other WTO Members and amongst the groups. Would groups report back to the CTS-SS? How would the public be informed? How would one deal with Members who were neither requestors nor requestees, and nevertheless would like to attend the plurilateral meetings? The tendency was to grant Members the opportunity to attend the meetings, and for group coordinators to report back (to the CTS-SS) on their plurilateral work.

5. Evaluating the success of plurilaterals

As shown above, the expectations for the outcomes of plurilateral negotiations were high – among both proponents and opponents of this particular negotiating method. How then do plurilaterals fare in terms of fulfilling expectations – be they 'hopes' or 'fears'? After three rounds of

[58] Subsequent to the Doha Ministerial, the CTS-SS held periodic negotiations in the form of so-called 'services clusters'. Initially, such clusters lasted for two weeks, with the first week devoted to the meetings of the subsidiary bodies, followed by time for bilateral meetings, concluded by meetings of the CTS-SS.

plurilaterals, many WTO Members considered the process as useful for having shed light on technical issues (through direct interaction between capital-based experts/regulators of various countries). Plurilateral meetings also served to increase transparency about negotiating positions (including bottom lines) of various parties. However, those seeking higher levels of liberalisation commitments found that the process had failed to produce concrete outcomes. Moreover, there was talk about returning back to bilateral and other methods, with some recalling that the plurilateral process was always envisaged as a complement to and not a replacement of the bilateral process.

The 'somewhat limited' outcome of plurilaterals: Selected reasons

This 'somewhat limited' outcome could be traced back to numerous reasons, some of which are discussed here.[59] First, there is the so-called 'lowest common-denominator effect'. As one commentator put it: 'while far-reaching in intent, the plurilateral request-offer process has set off certain countervailing forces that may limit its ultimate effect. The plurilateral requests are less extensive than some *demandeurs* would like because their formulation required pre-negotiation among the sponsors'.[60] In essence, *demandeurs* had to scale back the ambitions of their requests, for several reasons, one being that not all of them were willing to abide by far-reaching commitments themselves.

A second – albeit not insurmountable – reason for the difficulties in the pursuit of deeper liberalisation through plurilateral negotiations could be in the nature of group negotiations. The anticipated time of three hours per plurilateral would hardly allow a group of thirty or more negotiators to get into the depth of bargaining and negotiations. Much time might be spent on introductory remarks and technical clarifications, without getting to the essence of bargaining. Moreover, the fact that requestees were high in number also allowed them to deflect attention from the particular concession each of them was sought to give: through strength in numbers, requestees gained clout and negotiating leverage.[61]

[59] This does not address broader issues, like those linked to the overall suspension of the DWP.

[60] Sinclair (2006), p. 16.

[61] For a discussion of 'groupings' as a manner to address lack in bargaining and negotiating clout faced by individual developing countries, see Mashayekhi and Tuerk (2003), pp. 37 ff.

Also, timing could be a source of difficulties. With the end of July 2006 as the date envisaged for the submission of revised offers and the first plurilaterals having been held in early spring of that same year, there had remained little time for running through inter-ministerial coordination processes or coordinating and double-checking possible moves towards liberalisation with the relevant line-ministries in capitals.

Another possible reason for difficulties could be transparency. Given that plurilateral requests were freely available to the interested public – a situation that was maybe not intended by those engineering the process – such transparency could be seen as inviting greater scrutiny and analysis, particularly by those reluctant to embrace further far-reaching services liberalisation.

Moreover, the broader linkages between services and agriculture, as well as Members' reluctance to embrace services trade liberalisation through the negotiation of internationally binding commitments could have played a role.

The 'somewhat limited outcome' – truly limited or better than expected?

Obviously, the success of a process depends on the expectations that were set in it. If the expectation was for initial rounds of plurilaterals to directly translate into highly ambitious offers, then – clearly – the plurilateral process was a failure. If, however, the expectation was that the plurilateral process would be one important component – a supporting step in – in a larger process, then it could be considered a success.

Under the latter assumptions, some of the above deficiencies of the plurilaterals could also be viewed as highly beneficial. For example, the 'lowest common denominator effect' required Members to 'narrow down' and 'zoom in' on what they perceive as the crucial/minimum content of plurilateral requests. Compared to earlier requests, this was an important step in the process. Thus, already the process of formulating the requests required *demandeurs* to: a) prioritise market opening on specific sectors and barriers; b) indicate what they were willing to give; c) identify the Members forming a 'critical mass'. Together with the focus on technical discussions, this revealed what could be a 'possible landing zone' for the services market access negotiations.

Accordingly, when viewing plurilateral negotiations as a step in the process, they could well be considered successful. In the words of Fernando de Mateo, the Chair of the CTS-SS, '[w]hat is emerging, in effect, is the first approximation of what, for lack of a better name, may be called the "critical mass" of commitments to be expected at the end of the negotiations. The plurilaterals offered an opportunity for delegations to engage in detailed, substantive exchanges … However, we must be candid about the problems that lie ahead. The real test of substance will be the submission of the revised offers.'[62]

Viewing plurilateral negotiations as a step in a process also fits well with the imperative that international commitments (in services trade liberalisation) reflect good economic policy rather than the mandates of domestic political economy or of international negotiating pressures. Negotiating tactics alone cannot be expected to generate optimal outcomes, and the experiences of accession countries serve as an example. Therefore, pushing liberalisation through negotiating tactics, methods, formulas/targets etc. might not be the ideal approach.

How then, could such an optional outcome be achieved? Several elements appear important, each of which complements the others: an efficiently working services sector with the proper regulatory and institutional framework in place; sufficient knowledge and information about the economics and regulatory aspects of the domestic services regime; negotiating methods which allow for the proper pacing and sequencing of regulation and liberalisation. However, several of these elements remain missing today – particularly in developing countries.

Bibliography

Hardstaff, Peter, 'Benchmarking in GATS: Exposing the EU Aggressive Service Agenda', World Development Movement, November 2005, www.ourworldisnotforsale.org/showarticle.asp?search=943.

Jara, Alejandro and M. del Carmen Dominguez, 'Liberalization of Trade in Services and Trade Negotiations', *Journal of World Trade* 40(1) (2006).

Kwa, Aileen, 'Plurilateral Request-Offer Approaches in GATS Draft Text: Entry Point for Dangerous Sectoral Negotiations', Focus on the Global South, November 2005.

Mashayekhi, Mina and Elisabeth Türk, 'WTO Services Negotiations & Development: A Post-Hong Kong Review', *Bridges Monthly*, Year 10, No. 1, pp. 3–5.

——'The WTO Services Negotiations: Some Strategic Considerations', Working Paper No. 14, South Centre, T.R.A.D.E., January 2003.

[62] Ambassador Fernando de Mateo, Chair of the CTS-SS, 'Statement for Item F: Organization of Future Work', CTS-SS, July 2006 Services Cluster.

Mattoo, Aaditya, 'Regulatory Authorities and WTO Negotiations on Services', *Trade Policy Analyses* 8(9), Cordell Hull Institute (April 2006).

Sauvé, Pierre and Mary Irace, 'The Doha Development Agenda and GATS, the Benefits of Open Services Markets', A Report for the National Foreign Trade Council, July 2006.

Self, Richard, 'Energizing the Negotiations on Services in the Doha Round', *Trade Policy Analyses* 8(10), Cordell Hull Institute (April 2006).

Sinclair, Scott, 'Crunch Time in Geneva: Benchmarks, Plurilaterals, Domestic Regulation and other Pressure Tactics in the GATS Negotiations', Canadian Centre for Policy Alternatives, June 2006.

South Centre, 'Comments on Chairman Draft Ministerial Text on Services', JOB (05)/262/Rev.1, November 2005, South Centre.

Thompson, Rachel, 'Formula Approaches to Improving GATS Commitments', in Pierre Sauvé and Robert M. Stern (eds.), *GATS 2000 – New Directions in Services Trade Liberalization* (Brookings Institution Press, 2000).

UNCTAD, Meeting of the Trade And Development Board, October 2005, President's Summary TD/B/52/L.6.

Vastine, Robert, 'Services Negotiations in the Doha Round: Promise and Reality', October 2005.

7

Negotiating approaches from a Member's perspective

CLARE KELLY*

Introduction

This chapter looks at practical aspects of managing the WTO services negotiation, and how different negotiating approaches can affect these. It makes some observations about the experience of New Zealand, a small but active WTO Member managing a complex negotiation from a long distance and with modest resources, in relation to the two main negotiating approaches it has encountered to date during the Doha Round negotiations on trade in services. It examines, from an individual negotiator's viewpoint, the costs and benefits arising from the bilateral and plurilateral approaches and their impact on the negotiating positions and resourcing decisions New Zealand has taken during the negotiation to date. It also looks very briefly at New Zealand's reaction to the attempt to establish numerical targeting as a core negotiating approach. Finally, it moves to some tentative conclusions about the merits of the various approaches and their effect on the ability of delegations like New Zealand to achieve their negotiating objectives.

New Zealand's approach to the WTO services negotiations: Objectives and resourcing

While principally known as an exporter of agricultural products, trade in services is an increasingly important component of New Zealand's overall export profile. Approximately 66 per cent of GDP is generated by the services sector, and exports of services have expanded in recent years to

* This chapter represents the author's personal view, and does not represent an official position of either the New Zealand Permanent Mission in Geneva, or the New Zealand Ministry of Foreign Affairs and Trade.

28 per cent of total exports.[1] Tourism is New Zealand's biggest services export (and indeed most significant export overall), followed by audiovisual services, education, professional services, business services and environmental services. Tourism and education aside, the exporting services sector is dominated by small and medium enterprises, who typically access their key markets in Asia, Europe and the Americas via modes 1 (cross-border supply) and 4 (movement of natural persons). Tourism and education services rely heavily on mode 2 (consumption abroad) delivery. As a major goods exporter distant from its key markets, New Zealand has a strong consumer interest in effective and reliable global networks in air and maritime transportation, distribution and freight logistics services.

An extensive programme of economic regulatory reform and deregulation during the 1980s and early 1990s transformed the services sector into one of the most liberal amongst the WTO membership, and allowed New Zealand to undertake comprehensive commitments during the Uruguay Round. Early in the Doha Round, a services negotiation resulting in a higher overall level of liberalisation in commitments on trade in services, where New Zealand's trading partners matched its own level of commitment in key exporting sectors, was identified as a key objective to the WTO membership[2] and the domestic audience.[3]

New Zealand's participation in the negotiation is resourced principally through the Ministry of Foreign Affairs and Trade (MFAT), reporting to the Minister for Trade Negotiations, which has primary carriage within the New Zealand government of policy development, implementation and negotiation associated with multilateral trade. Other government agencies play a significant role in various aspects of the WTO negotiations (most notably, the Ministry of Agriculture and Forestry in respect of the agriculture negotiations), but MFAT's Trade Negotiations Division has the lead role in formulating and implementing the government's WTO policy. The Services Unit of the Trade Negotiations Division consists of one senior negotiator, and three policy analysts/negotiators.

[1] New Zealand Ministry of Foreign Affairs and Trade website paper 'Overview and Summary of New Zealand's Revised Conditional Offer', p. 1 www.mfat.govt.nz/foreign/tnd/marketaccess/services.html.

[2] Communication from New Zealand – Objectives for the Resumed Services Negotiations (S/CSS/W/90).

[3] New Zealand Ministry of Foreign Affairs and Trade website paper 'Ten Guiding Principles for Preparing New Zealand's Initial Services Offer', www.mfat.govt.nz/foreign/tnd/marketaccess/10guideprinciples.html.

The primary responsibility for the day-to-day management of New Zealand's relationship with the WTO and its Members, and for participation in the negotiating bodies, lies with the Permanent Mission in Geneva. Each of the Permanent Representative's five officials has responsibility for several negotiating areas. One counsellor-level officer covers, inter alia, the GATS negotiations. As each of the Wellington and Geneva-based services officials have additional responsibilities in relation to other negotiations (within the WTO, APEC and OECD, and also Free Trade Agreements), the proportion of their collective time allotted to the WTO services negotiations amounts to the equivalent of three full-time policy analysts/negotiators.

With a small team, and a wide-ranging and complex negotiation to manage, resourcing is a key issue for the New Zealand delegation. Domestically, consultation with other government agencies and other domestic stakeholders including exporters and civil society is an ongoing and time-consuming responsibility. In Geneva, the services delegate of the New Zealand Permanent Mission (NZPM) attends the formal and informal meetings of the Council for Trade in Services in the regular session, and its subsidiary bodies. For the special negotiating session, and accompanying bilateral and plurilateral meetings, the delegation normally expands to include Wellington-based officials, from MFAT and other agencies, such as the Ministries of Transport and Education, who typically spend a week or sometimes two attending formal and informal negotiating meetings – bilateral, plurilateral and 'Friends' meetings. The cost of sending an official to Geneva from New Zealand is considerable, not only in terms of airfares, accommodation and *per diem* allowances, but also in terms of time spent out of the office and away from other work.

These elements – a significant level of ambition for the negotiation, a sense of obligation towards the negotiation and a desire to assume an active and supportive role in it, and the need to make best use of relatively modest resources by developed country standards – have required careful balancing, and constant review of the alignment of the negotiation with New Zealand's objectives. The structure of the two key negotiating approaches encountered by the delegation during the course of the negotiation to date have been a major factor in shaping the conduct of New Zealand's negotiations.

The bilateral approach

The core negotiating approach in the services negotiation was and remains the bilateral request-offer approach, and it is via this approach that New Zealand has undertaken the bulk of its negotiating effort since the first exchange of initial requests in 2002.

By their nature, services negotiations of any kind involve an extraordinary amount of preparatory work. The structure of the WTO bilateral request-offer negotiations and consequent resourcing implications had a significant impact on how New Zealand identified the best way to proceed in the initial request phase of the negotiation. The logistics of managing multiple bilateral negotiations meant a strong degree of realism had to be exercised in determining where best to direct New Zealand's efforts, whereas some other delegations identified broader objectives for the scope of their requests, such as emphasising the development benefits of trade in services in strong infrastructural services sectors.

For New Zealand, identifying those trade partners to whom requests should be directed was a reasonably straightforward process of looking at what statistical information was available on overall export flows, with a bias toward the Asia-Pacific region. LDC Members were not amongst New Zealand's key markets and accordingly, no need was seen to make requests to them. The result was that requests were directed to other APEC members, plus the European Union and some important non-APEC Latin American and Pacific markets, and one key African trade partner.

With the pool of trade partners identified, the next step was to decide which sectors should be targeted. The primary considerations in this respect were to actively pursue commitments only in key active exporting sectors and modes, particularly where New Zealand exports were niche interests which would not necessarily be the focus of other delegations. For example, education services are a major export for New Zealand, the second largest services export, and seventh-most important export overall. A greater degree of commitment on trade in education services as an outcome of the Doha Round is one of New Zealand's most important objectives for the negotiation. However, it is a sector about which there is a considerable level of civil-society concern in respect of trade and the exchange of commitments, given that education services are delivered by the public as well as the private sector. This has meant that even some of the WTO's most important education exporters have shied away from engaging in request-offer negotiations on this sector. It was clear to New Zealand negotiators that their efforts could be most usefully directed at this and other such sectors of niche export interest, whereas the major infrastructural sectors such as telecommunications and financial services were of widespread interest, and other delegations could be relied upon to pursue a high-quality outcome. Requests were therefore strictly confined to the exporting sectors, and those supporting goods exports. This filtering process delivered 25 requests – a fairly modest number of requests by the standards of the major WTO delegations – with a particular emphasis on modes 1 and 4, professional and other business services, communications (postal services), distribution, education, environmental services, air and maritime transport and tourism.

As the negotiation got underway and the pattern evolved of two-week services 'clusters', the second week of which would be largely devoted to bilateral meetings, the New Zealand delegation initially prioritised its efforts, as did most other delegations, on meeting as many 'requestees' as possible (and indeed delegations which had made their own requests to New Zealand), to explain the requests and gauge likely responses to them. The process was at first very useful as an information exchange, yielding considerable amounts of material about other delegations' objectives and their reasoning and motivation for their individual negotiating positions. This continued to be the case when initial offers began to be tabled in 2003, and considerable amounts of Members' collective time were devoted to introducing and defending their offers.

The bilateral approach format has been less burdensome when responding to requests. With one offer to deliver in response to all requests, the most challenging aspect of the process has been keeping track of the 30-odd requests received, and assessing the extent to which the specific improvements requested could be considered and incorporated into offers. This situation improved as 'Friends' groups of Members with similar interests and objectives for the negotiations formed around specific sectors, modes of supply and negotiating processes. The pooling of efforts amongst Friends to produce collective negotiating materials such as issues papers, model schedules and scheduling approaches was an important development, and New Zealand benefited considerably from working with like-minded colleagues in key sectors of interest. In line with the objectives of achieving a high-quality outcome, and being an active participant, New Zealand has involved itself in some eleven Friends groups.

Bilateral work has been constant and ongoing since early 2002. However, by the time offers and requests had been in circulation for almost two years, and several rounds of meetings held, it became increasingly difficult for the New Zealand delegation to sustain a sense that there was much new to extract via the bilateral process, and in particular, to take the step beyond exchanging information and into actual negotiation. There seemed to be several reasons for this perception.

The first and most fundamental reason was the political realities of the overall negotiation and, specifically, the progress of the agriculture negotiation. Given the priority accorded to the agriculture negotiation by most Members, the services negotiation has inevitably been held hostage to the latter's progress or lack thereof. This has permitted the services negotiation to progress only in incremental steps, despite the relative ease with which services negotiators have been able to agree on their internal deadlines and modalities. To a significant extent, therefore, slow progress via the bilateral track was an inevitable phase of the negotiating process.

Another factor is the format of the bilateral approach itself. From the perspective of a delegation such as New Zealand, it has been a cumbersome process to manage. While it yields an enormous amount of information, many man-hours are required to process that information and make effective use of it in future negotiating meetings. The long hiatus between offers makes it difficult for delegations to assess what actual progress is being made in negotiations. There are positive aspects to the measured pace of the bilateral negotiations that should certainly be acknowledged. It does offer a certain degree of comfort to delegations, as it is not simple to stampede each other into making commitments. Furthermore, a bilateral exchange permits a high degree of confidentiality, and can encourage genuine frankness between negotiators. It also permits time for key relationships to develop between delegations. These characteristics could be argued to suit delegations with a predominantly defensive approach to the negotiations.

The other side of the coin is that smaller delegations with very specific interests in a sector or sub-sector with limited appeal find it difficult to apply the pressure necessary to achieve a higher level of liberalisation in that area. Notwithstanding the sense of obligation towards active participation in the negotiation, this has led to a sense at points in the negotiation that further bilaterals were not the best use of resources for the New Zealand team – as they would only go back over ground already well traversed – with the result that the Wellington team has on occasion not travelled to Geneva. It has further been a challenge to persuade other government agencies with expertise in the regulation of individual services sectors to involve themselves in the negotiation when they do not perceive visible signs of momentum.

From New Zealand's perspective, one of the most positive outcomes of the bilateral approach has been the emergence of the Friends Groups.

In the absence of more frequent exchanges of offers, these have proved an effective way of gauging the extent to which delegations' views were evolving, and have encouraged the forming of crucial strategic alliances. Papers produced by Friends Groups proved a very useful indicator of what would be most valued in the 2005 revised offers, and laid the foundations for much of the work to emerge from the plurilateral process.

The plurilateral approach

When the idea of supplementing the bilateral negotiations with a parallel plurilateral process emerged in the lead-up to the Hong Kong Ministerial Meeting, New Zealand gave the proposal its strong support, seeing such a process as a logical next step in the negotiation, which by harnessing collective effects and interests could deliver some much-needed momentum. The emergence of this process also appeared to present a rare opportunity to put two of New Zealand's sectoral interests which did not enjoy widespread support – education and air transport services – on the same footing as more mainstream services exports, and to expose arguments in favour of a greater level of commitment in these sectors to a wider audience than had been possible via the bilateral process. Accordingly, the decision was taken to engage actively in the process and to invest resources, including those of specialist agencies, in establishing and leading plurilateral negotiations on these two sectors. Once the existing mandate for plurilateral negotiations contained in the Negotiating Guidelines and Procedures (S/L/93) was reiterated by Ministers in Hong Kong, New Zealand acted quickly to register its interest in coordinating collective requests on each of these two sectors. It co-sponsored another nine requests, and was a recipient of a further four.

From New Zealand's perspective, the actual mechanics of the process worked very smoothly, given that it was a new development. The groundwork already done in Friends Groups meant that in most cases, the likely composition of the group of requesting Members was already known, and the drafting of the collective requests could be based on previous work and completed within a few months. This drafting was also largely to be done by e-mail, which meant that Wellington-based officials could be fully involved in this work. Much of the actual planning of the negotiating sessions was spent on deciding to which Members requests would be made, and how meetings could be designed in order to ensure they were inclusive, transparent and non-threatening, but also to extract something valuable for the requesting Members – specifically, a much clearer idea of the likely level of future offers in a sector, and a better understanding of particular regulatory or political concerns limiting future offers.

Education has been one sector where the coalition of support, and the collective request itself, has had to be developed largely from scratch. Unlike most of the other areas of plurilateral negotiation groups, there was no preceeding Friends Group which focused on market access issues in trade in education services. Throughout much of the negotiation an education contact group with a diverse membership existed, but as a reflection of the sensitivity of the sector and the level of civil society concern in many domestic constituencies about trade in education, it focused on quality issues rather than specific market access and national treatment concerns. The plurilateral process offered New Zealand and co-sponsors the opportunity to tackle these concerns directly, with a significant cross-section of the WTO membership.

The concerns which had kept education out of active discussion during much of the Doha Round stem from the role of government in the funding, delivery and quality control of education in WTO Member countries, and perceptions amongst teacher groups in particular that an exchange of commitments on commercially provided education could somehow hinder the ability of governments to sustain their traditional role in education. The plurilateral process allowed several ways to address these. First, the collective request was designed to be narrowly and specifically focused on actual market interests in private education only. Secondly, the request suggested an example of the scheduling of private education, but left definitions of private education up to individual Members. Third, plurilateral meetings lent themselves well to a forthright discussion of the most difficult questions about the sector, and the co-sponsors encouraged requested delegations to bring their education experts to ensure that these issues had a proper airing.

The ensuing discussion went into considerable detail about issues such as the role of government in the provision and funding of education services; how Members could schedule commitments on education services provided on a commercial basis so as to clearly exclude public education, and what regulatory requirements would be regarded as market access and national treatment limitations; the role of domestic regulation in quality assurance, particularly in relation to mode 1 supply, and recognition of qualifications. This frank and detailed discussion of regulatory and political questions in an open forum was of considerable benefit to New Zealand, and allowed it to make some genuine headway in addressing perceptions of risk in scheduling education commitments.

New Zealand's experience of the plurilateral negotiating approach to date has therefore been positive. From the point of view of resourcing, the cooperative aspects of the process have been a boon, spreading the negotiating load, and allowing New Zealand to benefit from the interaction of many delegations' ideas and opinions. It has also provided a sense of impetus and momentum that was missing from the bilateral process, and which was especially useful for New Zealand in facilitating expert engagement from other government agencies. There has further been an important degree of engagement by a broad range of developing countries in the plurilateral negotiations, including as *demandeurs*, which New Zealand has found to be a significant and welcome development. The constructive and cooperative spirit with all delegations involved in the process was an unanticipated benefit, and the degree of frankness with which Members were prepared to discuss their intentions allowed a clearer picture to emerge of the likely future package of commitments. In terms of negotiating objectives, the process has permitted New Zealand to benefit from the collective negotiating weight of other delegations in key sectors, improving the prospects of an eventual outcome which focuses also on New Zealand's interests. For the drafting of revised offers, the circulation of the collective requests has made extremely clear what value delegations place on particular commitments.

Numerical targeting

For the sake of completeness it is worth making a brief reference to New Zealand's reaction to the proposals which also emerged in advance of the Hong Kong Ministerial to develop numerical targets as a core negotiating approach. The questions of the political viability of such proposals aside, New Zealand could see the appeal in an approach that sought to mimic the formula approach of the goods negotiation. The delegation agreed with proponents that this type of approach could complement bilateral negotiations, deliver some immediate prospect of concrete outcomes and so generate a greater sense of momentum in the negotiation. The potential drawbacks and disparities of this type of approach were also clear, looking at various tables produced by Members and the Secretariat[4] which counted commitments. A simple counting method yielded a total for New Zealand's Uruguay Round commitments that was lower than for most other developed countries, yet the content of these

[4] Pg 121, Trade Profiles 2005, WTO Publications, World Trade Organisation.

commitments was often of a high actual value, as they were not limited by sectoral reservations or significant horizontal limitation. Accordingly, New Zealand sought to add value to the discussion with the tabling of a sectoral scoring model, which was designed to support targets by permitting a qualitative assessment of commitments and their value in meeting targets.

Some conclusions

Some conclusions can be drawn from New Zealand's experience. The first is that the bilateral request-offer approach, even if it is not the default negotiating option, is a necessary stage in the negotiation, and one that has distinct benefits in terms of generating information on political and regulatory issues confronting trade partners, and allowing negotiators to build up important relationships with key interlocutors through their repeated contacts. Its drawbacks for a small active delegation like New Zealand are that it is time-consuming and costly to manage, especially from a distance and, over long periods of time, may not be the most effective way for these delegations to make best use of shared negotiating positions and objectives in order to apply pressure in key areas of interests.

For delegations which take a largely defensive approach to the services negotiations, there may be benefits from the measured pace of the bilateral track. For delegations with offensive interests to advance, there are difficulties to overcome, unless the delegation in question has the requisite negotiating clout by virtue of its market size. New Zealand's experience may be shared by other Members. New Zealand's export profile is in many ways very like that of some developing countries – in terms of reliance on mode 1 and 4 delivery, the dominance of very small enterprises in the exporting sector and niche exporting interests. If New Zealand finds the bilateral process a challenge to manage, even with a long history of WTO membership, and a developed country's infrastructure and regulatory regime, then many other Members must struggle. These resourcing issues can be alleviated to an extent by working collectively, in Friends Groups or regional alliances. Such groups are crucial in building alliances, having a hand in directing processes, and keeping track of sectoral developments.

The logical extension of Friends Groups, the plurilateral request-offer negotiations, has offered New Zealand a useful, timely and necessary complement to the bilateral process that has enabled it to build on shared interests, to draw on the strengths of other delegations, to mainstream niche interests and to have a clearer sense of where real trade-offs lie. This is not to say that the plurilateral approach is the better approach, because the two – bilateral and plurilateral – seem interconnected and should the negotiations resume, the bilateral process will be integral to the work of finalising schedules of commitments. But for New Zealand, it is worth noting that the plurilateral request-offer process has been one of the more important recent developments in the services negotiation, and points to the virtue for a small delegation of remaining receptive to proposals to alternative negotiating approaches.

8

Evaluating alternative approaches to GATS negotiations: Sectoral, formulae and others

HENRY GAO*

In addition to the request–offer approach, which predominates in the current round of negotiations under the General Agreement on Trade in Services (GATS), the WTO Members have experimented with some alternative approaches over the years. These include negotiations along sectoral and modal lines, as well as those based on certain formulae or quantitative benchmarks. This article will discuss the lessons learnt from the negotiating experiences relating to these alternative approaches, and offer some suggestions on how the current and future GATS negotiations could benefit from the use of these approaches.

I. Alternative approaches in services negotiations: Experiences from the Uruguay Round

As noted by many commentators, the United States was instrumental in bringing services on to the agenda of the multilateral trading system.[1] In early 1980, the US successfully persuaded the Trade Committee of the Organisation for Economic Co-operation and Development (OECD) to conduct a study on trade in services, which laid the groundwork for including this area of trade in multilateral trade negotiations. This did

* This chapter has benefited from the generous support provided by the Seed Funding for Basic Research at The University of Hong Kong. Almost all of the substantive work on this chapter was completed while the author was on leave as a Visiting Professor at Bond University in Gold Coast, Australia. The author wishes to note his deep appreciation to Dean Duncan Bentley, Professors Ross Buckley, Vai Io Lo and Winne Ma for their most generous help at Bond. The author is also grateful to Rolf Adlung for his helpful comments. Of course, all errors remain the author's own.

1 See Howse and Trebilcock, at p. 356; Stewart, at pp. 2345–2358. For a general background on the services negotiations before and during the Uruguay Round, see also Drake and Nicolaidis, Croome.

not lead to automatic inclusion of services in the trade agenda, however, as the contracting parties became engaged in a heated debate over the next few years on the desirability of regulating services trade under the framework of the GATT.

On the one hand, the enthusiasm of the US for opening services markets stems from two basic premises: first, as services are a contributing factor in many goods, liberalisation of trade in services could reduce the overall costs for the economy and is important for an 'effective operation of the global economy'.[2] Second, while many manufacturing sectors of the US have lost their competitive edge over the years, services have risen to become the main strength of the US, especially in sectors with high knowledge or technology contents, such as financial services, telecommunications and professional services.[3]

On the other hand, many developing countries were reluctant to agree to the inclusion of services in the trade agenda for the following reasons: first, even though services liberalisation could improve the efficiency of the whole economy, most developing countries feared that their services providers would be out-competed by firms from the US and other developed countries in both their home markets and the markets of other countries.[4] Thus, they might well end up with a smaller slice of the pie even if the pie had grown larger. Moreover, developing countries perceived the comparative advantage enjoyed by developed countries with respect to services as being a result of their overall higher level of economic and technological development, and thus they would lose their domestic market before they had even had a chance to nurture their own services providers.[5] Second, the developing countries were taken aback by the aggressive 'market access' approach taken by the US with regard to the services agreement.[6] It appeared that the US was interested not only in the extension of the national treatment obligation to services, but also in demanding changes in the domestic regulatory regimes of the other countries in order to prise open the markets for US firms.[7] For developing countries that have yet to adopt regulatory reforms, this means that they would be forced to embark upon regulatory reforms dictated by a foreign power, which certainly would not be well received by the domestic constituencies with its undertone of surrender of sovereignty. For those developing countries that have started or are about to start the reform process, this could severely limit their leeway in dealing with unexpected challenges that might arise during the

[2] Stewart, at p. 2356. [3] Howse and Trebilcock, at p. 356.
[4] *Ibid.* [5] *Ibid.* [6] *Ibid.* at p. 357. [7] *Ibid.*

transition to deregulation and privatisation.[8] Third, as services trade is complicated and notoriously difficult to measure, until the middle of 1986, several contracting parties, including the UK, regarded it as premature to consider whether services should be included in multilateral action before the process of exchange of information had been completed.[9] Fourth, during the early discussions on services negotiations, the US explored the idea of using the GATT as the legal instrument for regulating services trade. Some contracting parties expressed doubts as to whether the GATT has legal competence over trade in services issues and whether it should be the proper venue for regulating trade in services.[10]

In response to these concerns, the contracting parties came up with the following compromises. First, although services would be negotiated under the 'umbrella' of the Uruguay Round, the results of such negotiations would be embodied in an agreement that is legally separate from the GATT, i.e., the GATS.[11] This should ensure that the sensitivities and peculiarities of services trade are fully taken into account. Second, in terms of the coverage of the agreement, the contracting parties were split as to whether the 'universal' or 'sectoral' approach should be adopted.[12] Under the universal approach, all services sectors would be covered.[13] Under the sectoral approach, the contracting parties can choose to liberalise only some sectors, while excluding others from coverage.[14] Drawing on lessons learnt from the unpleasant experiences with the effective exclusions of agricultural and textile and clothing products from the coverage of the GATT, most contracting parties embraced the former approach as one that could help to maintain a balance of interests by avoiding the exclusion of sectors of primary interest to some contracting parties.[15] On the other hand, the sectoral approach is most attractive to contracting parties that wish to exclude certain sectors, as well as to those that wish to single out some sectors that are particularly important to be treated in stand-alone agreements separate from a general framework agreement.[16] Even though the US initially preferred the universal approach, it decided to move towards the sectoral approach as negotiations progressed, in response to domestic pressures to exclude sectors such as maritime and airline transport services while giving sectors such as telecommunication and financial services special treatment in sectoral negotiations.[17]

[8] *Ibid.* [9] Stewart, at pp. 2355–2356. [10] *Ibid.* at p. 2356.
[11] Howse and Trebilcock, at p. 358. [12] Stewart, at pp. 2363. [13] *Ibid.*
[14] *Ibid.* at p. 2364. [15] *Ibid.* at pp. 2363–2364. [16] *Ibid.* at p. 2364.
[17] *Ibid.* at p. 2364–2365.

Thus, in the end, a hybrid of universal and sectoral approaches was adopted. In principle, all services sectors are included although several of them are subject to sector-specific negotiations. This led to the fourth issue, i.e. whether services liberalisation should proceed on the basis of a 'negative list' or a 'positive list' approach.[18] Under the former, all services sectors are covered by default except those which are specifically excluded in negative lists. Under the latter approach, the contracting parties can pick and choose the sectors they wish to liberalise with the result that only those sectors that are included in the schedules would be subject to market access commitments whereas those that are not included would not entail any liberalisation obligations. The adoption of the universal approach in general seems to suggest that the negative list approach should be followed, and this is indeed what the US and EC tried to push for at first.[19] Many contracting parties, especially the developing countries, however, feared that the negative list approach could force them to make concessions in every sector and preferred the positive list approach.[20] Owing to the strong resistance of these parties, the US backed off in the end and the positive list approach was adopted. As the positive list approach prevailed, it became natural for the contracting parties to adopt the request–offer process as the primary method of negotiation.[21] In the Uruguay Round, however, there were no pre-existing schedules of commitments. Thus, the participants started the process with the submission of offers.[22] In this approach, each contracting party identifies those service sectors in the markets of another party in which it has interests, and decides what it would like the other party to do. Four types of requests may be made, i.e. addition of sectors which were not previously included, removal or relaxation of existing limitations, undertaking additional commitments, or removal of most-favoured nation (MFN) exemptions.[23] Such a request is then presented in the form of a letter addressed to the other party. For a variety of reasons, many contracting parties kept their requests confidential and even the

[18] For a general discussion on the two different approaches, see Stephenson.

[19] Stewart, at p. 2371.

[20] *Ibid.* As noted by Hoekman and Messerlin (1999), however, the experience of the Multilateral Agreement on Investment (MAI) negotiations, conducted under the auspices of the OECD, revealed that a 'negative' list approach to scheduling commitments is not necessarily a much better way of dealing with complex barriers to competition as negotiators can simply get around the basic disciplines by tabling long exception lists.

[21] See Feketekuty (1988), at pp. 279–280.

[22] Technical Aspects of Requests and Offers, WTO Seminar on the GATS, 20 February 2002.

[23] *Ibid.*

Secretariat was not always aware of the content or even the existence of particular requests.[24] Although offers would typically include the same contents as the requests, they were normally presented in the form of draft schedules of commitments, which were in turn circulated to all parties rather than only to certain parties.[25]

A. *Why the sectoral negotiations and agreements?*

With the adoption of the request–offer approach as the main negotiating method, one might wonder why the contracting parties still conducted negotiations and reached agreements along sectoral lines. There are several likely explanations for this. First, as the Uruguay Round negotiation was mainly a rule-setting exercise in services trade, sectoral negotiations might be undesirable as their narrow focus could make it more difficult to highlight the broader economic reasons why a liberalisation of policies would further the general public interest, which provided a major justification for the services negotiation as it had been subject to strong resistance from a majority of the contracting parties from the beginning.[26] Second, because the individual services sectors in most countries are typically regulated by ministries other than the ministry of trade, negotiations conducted purely along sectoral lines would be dominated by the regulatory agenda of the sector in question. This could make the negotiations more difficult as such an agenda is not necessarily in line with the overall objective of trade liberalisation but tends to focus on the major philosophical differences among countries with regard to the proper role of government and the optimal regime for achieving regulatory objectives.[27] Third, as the requests and offers would be made on sectoral bases anyway, there might be little need to single out particular sectors for negotiations. Indeed, the trade ministers were keenly aware of these concerns when they declared at Punta del Este that '[n]egotiations [on trade in services] shall aim to establish a multilateral framework of principles and rules for trade in services, including elaboration of possible disciplines for individual sectors'.[28] As noted by Feketekuty, on the one hand, the Declaration supports the traditional trade policy view that general, across-the-board rules are needed to advance the liberalisation of trade barriers; on the other hand, it also recognises that sectoral differences are more fundamental in services

[24] *Ibid.* [25] *Ibid.* [26] Feketekuty (1988), at p. 195.
[27] *Ibid.* at p. 241. [28] Uruguay Round Declarations.

than in goods and that effective negotiations have to be conducted on a sector-by-sector level.[29]

In the view of the author, the sectoral focus could be the result of a combination of several factors. First, until the Uruguay Round, the contracting parties had no experience of a multilateral agreement regulating trade in services. Moreover, an analysis of the general nature of services trade and the universal rules and disciplines governing trade in services could hardly be conducted at the abstract level without 'reality checks' associated with the real-world operations of one or more services sectors. Thus, it was no wonder that the contracting parties conducted sector-specific discussions (or 'sector testing') at the very start of the GATS negotiations.[30] The sectoral examinations involved the following sectors: telecommunications and construction, transport and tourism, professional services and financial services.[31] In addition to the sector-specific issues, these exercises also highlighted several issues of a more general nature, such as transparency, domestic regulations and national treatment.[32] Second, as service sectors are more diverse than those of goods, each service sector has inherent peculiarities and problems which would merit individual treatment. The more complicated a sector, the fewer people will be able to understand that sector, thus the sector will be subject to the control of a small number of specialists. Although the number of users affected by such service sectors might be quite large, the Collective Action Theory holds that they would not be able to get together to effectively prevent the capture of the sector by the specialists.[33] In the end, it would be natural for the specialists to structure the negotiations along sectoral lines to maintain the exclusive club-like feel of that sector. This is particularly true with regard to the two sectors that are the subjects of sectoral agreements, i.e. the telecommunication and financial services sectors, which are widely regarded as complicated sectors. Third, as has been revealed following the experience of trade liberalisation for goods, trade negotiators, like all human beings, have a tendency to try to leave the most difficult issues until last, in this case by starting with those products that have lower tariffs to begin with. In the

[29] Feketekuty (1988), at p. 195. [30] Stewart, at p. 2372.

[31] *Ibid.* [32] *Ibid.* at pp. 2372–2373.

[33] According to the Collective Action Theory, the larger a group, the higher the cost of organising the members and the smaller the gains for each member of the group. Thus, it is more difficult for larger groups to act in their common interest than smaller ones, even though the collective gains for the larger group might be bigger than those for the smaller group. For a general background on the Collective Action problem, see Mancur Olson.

years leading to the conclusion of the negotiations on financial services and telecommunications, both sectors were marked by rapid and significant trade-liberalising changes, which included the global integration of markets, increased competition, deregulations and the mergers and acquisitions activities which led to the consolidation among the services providers.[34] As noted by Hoekman and Messerlin, '[transparency] *alone* is not sufficient to move a liberalization agenda forward. It needs to be supported by domestic political forces that favor moving forward in the pursuit of liberalization. The existence of such a domestic consensus was a major factor behind the successful conclusion of the GATS basic telecom talks'[35] (emphasis in the original). Thus, it was not surprising that these two sectors, rather than any of the others, were picked for sectoral initiatives as the contracting parties wanted to use the GATS negotiation as a way to lock in the achievements of the trade liberalisation efforts. As most of the GATT commitments lock in the status quo, it is no surprise that the commitments in financial services and telecommunications are among the most popular among WTO Members.[36] Fourth, both financial services and telecommunications are important infrastructural services. They are crucial in maintaining the overall well-being of the economy, as well as attracting the inflow of foreign direct investment (FDI).[37] In the case of financial services, for example, as the WTO Secretariat noted in one study, 'the financial services sector is far more important than its direct share in the economy implies. Financial services are the backbone of modern economies. It is difficult to think of any economic activity, except perhaps those that remain largely outside the money economy in less well-off countries, that does not depend in a significant way (either directly or indirectly) upon services provided by the financial sector.'[38] Thus, both the developed and developing countries perceived a need to start with liberalisation in these sectors in order to capture the full benefit of trade liberalisation.[39]

[34] See e.g., statements made by many contracting parties on their telecom reform programmes at the ninth meeting of the Negotiating Group on Basic Telecommunications held on 6 October 1995, S/NGBT/9.

[35] Hoekman and Messerlin (1999).

[36] See e.g., Hoekman, Mattoo, and English, at pp. 263–264.

[37] See e.g., Eschenbach and Hoekman. See also, WTO 1997, 17–22.

[38] WTO, 1997, 7.

[39] See e.g., statements made by many contracting parties on the benefits of liberalisations in the telecom sector at the ninth meeting of the Negotiating Group on Basic Telecommunications held on 6 October 1995, S/NGBT/9.

B. Issues arising from sectoral negotiations

The experiences of the sectoral negotiations on telecommunications, financial services and maritime services highlighted several issues that would have to be dealt with in any future sectoral negotiations in order to facilitate the proper functioning of the negotiations. These include the following:

i. Observer status

The Decision establishing the Negotiating Group on Basic Telecommunications (NGBT) and the Decision establishing the Negotiating Group on Maritime Transport Services (NGMTS) stated that these two groups shall be open to all contracting parties that announce their intention to participate in the negotiations on basic telecommunications. Presumably, this meant that participation in the first meeting would be open to all, but it was unclear whether those who had not indicated their intention to participate fully in the negotiations, or observers, should also be allowed to participate in future meetings. The NGBT and NGMTS discussed this issue during their first few meetings and agreed on the following:[40]

First, there shall be an open door policy on observers, which means that observer status in the two Negotiating Groups will be granted upon request to members of the Sub-Committee on Services who have not yet notified their intention to participate in the negotiations. There are two reasons for this decision: first, as a matter of principle, because these negotiations represented an extension of the Uruguay Round and would lead eventually to multilateral commitments, there was a need to avoid being overly rigid with respect to observer status as long as observers did not obstruct the negotiations. Second, from a practical point of view, as the markets for these services are becoming increasingly globalised, the participants should encourage the widest possible participation in these negotiations in order to gain maximum benefits from such negotiations. Indeed, at least at the beginning of the telecom negotiations, some important countries did not participate in the negotiations due to various concerns. In order to ensure a commercially meaningful outcome, many participants viewed the granting of observer status as a good way to allow countries to get a taste of the negotiations by participating initially as observers until a decision to participate could be taken. During the course of the negotiations, nineteen

[40] TS/NGBT/1. PC/SCS/1.

observers decided to become full participants after observing the negotiations for some time.

Second, observers are entitled to attend formal meetings of the negotiating groups and to receive documents prepared for the groups by the Secretariat. Presumably, the discussions at the formal meetings would focus on issues of a general nature and the participation of the observers in the formal meetings could enable them to keep up to date with the progress of the negotiations. As an example, it was suggested that the telecom negotiations could lead to major changes in regimes, i.e. the provision of basic telecommunications on a competitive basis. As this represented for many a radical departure from current regimes, not all countries would be able to participate. Nevertheless, it would be beneficial for countries that could not make radical changes to participate as observers in order to understand what was entailed. As to the informal meetings and bilateral negotiations, they are generally confidential and are not open to observers.

Third, the observers generally do not take part in decisions taken by the groups and are entitled to speak only upon invitation by the Chairman, normally at the conclusion of interventions by participants. One concern raised during the negotiations on telecommunications was that the commitments being exchanged could have implications for the framework and the Annex on Telecommunications, which are applicable to all Members. Thus, it was suggested that the observers should be given the right to speak with respect to such issues. This suggestion was dismissed on the basis that, first, it was not the intention of the negotiations to alter the framework or the Annex, second, even if either were to be amended at any time, this would have to be done according to the correct procedures, and third, issues related to competition in basic telecommunications were different from the issues addressed by the Annex.

In addition to the observer status of WTO Members, the negotiating groups discussed the possibility of international organisations participating as observers. As the negotiations aimed to promote trade liberalisations in the telecom sector on a global level, it was felt that it would be of great benefit to allow those international organisations with an interest in telecommunications to participate as observers so that the negotiations could benefit from the expertise of these organisations on technical issues and the WTO could coordinate its liberalisation efforts with the agendas of these international organisations more closely. On this basis, international organisations with universal memberships, such as the International Telecommunications Union (ITU), UNCTAD and the World

Bank were readily admitted as observers. Difficult issues arose, however, when international organisations with limited or regional membership, such as the Asia Pacific Telecommunity (APT) and the OECD, sought observer status in the groups. Some representatives expressed reservations regarding the admissibility of such organisations by referring to a precedent established during the Uruguay Round in the Group of Negotiations on Services whereby organisations with limited or regional membership, rather than universal membership, were not normally granted observer status. In the end, it was decided that the Group should not be bound by precedents and the primary consideration in making a decision in this regard should be the relevance of the work of the organisation in question to the subject matter being discussed by the Group. On this basis, both the APT and OECD were granted observer status.

A related issue, which surfaced in the negotiations on maritime services, was whether private-sector organisations, such as the Council of European and Japanese National Shipowners' Associations (CENSA) and the American Institute of Merchant Shipping (AIMS), could be granted observer status. Several delegations preferred to limit observer status to inter-governmental organisations. One potential risk of granting observer status to private-sector organisations was that the WTO negotiations might then be perceived as catering to private interests. For this reason, the group decided not to grant observer status to these organisations.

ii. Exchange of information

As noted by many scholars, barriers to trade in services are heterogeneous and difficult to quantify.[41] Thus, an information-collecting exercise aimed at identifying the relevant barriers in a specific sector is a necessary first step before any sectoral negotiations can take place. To facilitate the information exchange, the negotiating groups issued questionnaires that asked participants to provide details of their regulatory regimes in particular sectors. The one for telecommunications covered definitions and market structure, competition and regulatory issues, whereas the one for maritime services addressed market structure and regulatory issues. Both the full participants and observers were encouraged to respond to the questionnaire. In response to the concerns expressed by some delegations, the Chairman stressed that the questionnaire should in no way be intended to prejudice the position of

[41] Howse and Trebilcock, at p. 352.

any participant regarding the final outcome of negotiations on commitments. Once the participants had submitted their responses, the groups undertook reviews of the responses. During the reviews, participants were invited to briefly introduce their documents and to answer questions aimed at eliciting further details or clarification of the responses. Many governments participated actively in this exercise. In the telecommunications group, for example, 37 of the 53 full participants and two of the 24 observer governments submitted completed questionnaires. Similarly, in the maritime services group, 35 of the 56 full participants and two of the 16 observer governments submitted completed questionnaires.

iii. Examination of outstanding technical and conceptual issues

As the sectoral negotiations involved highly technical issues which had never before been subject to the regulatory framework of the GATT/WTO multilateral trading system, it was important that the participants first had discussions on technical and conceptual issues so that they could reach a common understanding on these issues and were not comparing apples with oranges when making specific commitments. In the telecom group, the issues discussed included technical matters relating to the scheduling of commitments and regulatory issues such as licencing, interconnection, competition safeguards, transparency, independent regulatory bodies, frequency and numbering, standards and type approval, tariffs and accounting rates, termination services, rights of way and planning and universal service. In the maritime services group, the issues discussed were technical matters relating to the scheduling of commitments on international shipping, auxiliary services, access to and use of port facilities and multimodal transport services.

In the telecom negotiations, one achievement of these discussions was an informal Reference Paper on regulatory disciplines. Originally described as a tool to help participants arrive at an understanding of the kinds of commitments they might undertake on regulatory matters, the participants were later encouraged to use it as a guideline for the scheduling of additional commitments. Formally speaking, there is no binding commitment arising from the paper per se; it is only when a Member explicitly incorporates the reference paper in its schedule of commitments that a legally binding commitment will be undertaken.

iv. The bilateral request-offer negotiations

Even though the sectoral negotiations started out as an exception to the general bilateral request-offer approach and as a plurilateral or multilateral initiative, in the real world, such negotiations could not be conducted without being supplemented by a bilateral request-offer process. As countries are at different stages of liberalisation, the adoption of a minimum regulatory standard such as the reference paper would simply mean that some countries would have to give more than they would receive in return and this would not be conducive for trade negotiations which are generally based on quid pro quo. Even though during the discussions on the reference paper, there had been calls to adopt a flexible and gradual approach to take account of the varied nature of the regulatory systems and structures of each country, such an approach was against the very nature of a benchmark instrument such as the reference paper and thus could not be adopted. The only way to ensure the acceptability of the general principles in the reference paper would be to allow some countries to be able to request more concessions in the bilateral request-offer process in order to 'compensate' them for the 'losses' they have incurred by subscribing to the reference paper. Moreover, although participants needed discussions on the general disciplines to gain an idea of the rules that would apply once commitments were in place, some of the specific problems and the appropriate rules for addressing them could only be identified and formulated as a result of bilateral negotiations. Thus, the discussions on general technical and conceptual issues were held concomitantly with the bilateral negotiations and drafting of schedules. As with the bilateral negotiations, which were conducted under the auspices of the GATS, these offers were explicitly made conditional upon the quality and extent of the commitments made by others. Moreover, as the negotiations on the general regulatory disciplines such as the reference paper continued until the very end of the telecom negotiations, some offers were also implicitly conditional upon the acceptance of these regulatory principles by a sufficient number of participants.

v. The roles of the formal meetings

While informal negotiations and meetings were instrumental in hammering out the details of the individual schedules and regulatory principles, the formal meetings, generally held monthly throughout the negotiations, also played an important role. First, the formal meetings provided an opportunity for the Members to get together and take stock on the progress of the negotiations. During the two-year period from April 1994 to April 1996, the two negotiating groups held 16 meetings each. At almost every meeting, especially the later meetings, the groups would conduct reviews on the number of full participants, new or revised offers made and the progress of bilateral negotiations, as well as the results of the discussions on outstanding technical and conceptual issues. During such reviews, appeals were frequently made to observers to become full participants, to participants who had not submitted draft offers to do so, to participants who had submitted initial offers to revise their offers and to participants having second thoughts over their offers to refrain from withdrawing or diluting their offers.

The formal meetings can be a way for the more active participants to apply peer pressure on their less active trade partners. In this sense, the formal meetings are similar to half-time breaks during football matches to revive the spirits of the players. Second, the formal meetings were the forum of choice to deal with issues of a general nature. As noted above, this includes, for example, the discussions on the granting of observer status and the technical and conceptual issues. Third, especially during the earlier meetings, these formal meetings were used to lay out the schedule for the organisation of future work and to ensure that the negotiations were conducted according to the original timetable.

vi. Choice of instruments

Both the financial services negotiations and the telecom negotiations resulted in a number of different instruments. Rather than reflecting the deliberate choices made by WTO Members, these complex webs of instruments were the results of the incompleteness of these negotiations at the closure of the Uruguay Round in December 1993 and the compromises between different views as to how the negotiations should be completed.[42]

In the financial services sector, for example, there are two Annexes on financial services, an Understanding on Commitments in Financial Services and one Decision on Financial Services. The Annex on Financial Services was included as an integral part of the original GATS to spell out the application of several GATS provisions to the financial services sector. As such it does not contain any specific liberalisation commitments. When the Uruguay Round drew to a close in 1993, the negotiations on financial services were unfinished.[43] Even though Members made specific commitments on both market access and national treatment, some, in particular the US, did not consider them to be sufficient to conclude the negotiations.[44] The US threatened to schedule broad MFN exemptions based on reciprocity and proceed with bilateral and regional negotiations in the

[42] Howse and Trebilcock, at p. 379. [43] Hoekman, Mattoo and English, at p. 265.
[44] *Ibid.* See also, Howse and Trebilcock, at p. 379.

sector instead. As any agreement on financial services would be rendered useless without the participation of the US, home to some of the biggest financial services providers and the largest financial services market in the world, the Members came up with a compromise to extend the negotiations for a six-month period following the entry into force of the GATS in 1995, while the US would suspend its MFN exemptions for the same period pending the result of the negotiations. This compromise was recorded in the Second Annex on Financial Services and the Decision on Financial Services, both of which were adopted at the end of the Uruguay Round. The Second Annex provides that a Member may, during a period of sixty days beginning four months after the date of entry into force of the WTO Agreement, schedule new MFN exemptions, or 'improve, modify or withdraw' all or some of the specific commitments on financial services inscribed in its Schedule. The Decision on Financial Services includes similar language, while also providing that Article II Exemptions which are conditional upon the level of commitments undertaken by other participants or upon exemptions by other participants will not be applied during this period. As a result of the 1995 negotiations, 29 WTO Members (counting the EU as one) improved their schedules of specific commitments and/or removed, suspended or reduced the scope of their MFN exemption in financial services. This outcome, however, was still deemed insufficient by the US, which continued with very broad MFN exemptions. This led to the Members deciding to temporally lock in the liberalisation results in an 'interim agreement' while agreeing to commence further negotiations within two years to improve the commitments. The new negotiations resulted in significant improvements in commitments and considerable expansion of the Membership. Satisfied with the results, the US, together with India and Thailand, withdrew their broad MFN exemptions based on reciprocity.

Similarly, the telecom sector negotiations were also a leftover from the Uruguay Round negotiations. Pursuant to the Decision on Negotiations on Basic Telecommunications, the Members continued the negotiations, which were originally scheduled to conclude by 30 April 1996. At the eleventh hour, however, the US walked out of the talks in dissatisfaction over the liberalisation offers made by other Members. The WTO Secretariat intervened and successfully proposed that the negotiations be extended until early 1997.[45] At the conclusion of the extended negotiations, the Members made substantial commitments and all but two

[45] Howse and Trebilcock, at p. 392.

countries subscribed to the reference paper. Finally satisfied with the results, the US agreed to make MFN commitments in most areas.

At one point during the negotiations on telecommunications, suggestions were made that instead of using the reference paper, the GATS could be amended to incorporate the regulatory principles contained in the proposed reference paper.[46] In the end, however, the Members decided to proceed with the reference paper. In the view of the author, this was a sensible decision as the matters dealt with under the reference paper were probably too sector-specific to be included in a framework agreement like the GATS. Moreover, as the GATS obligations are to be met universally by all the Members, or at least those Members that have undertaken specific or additional commitments, a GATS amendment would have to face an uphill battle with those Members that were reluctant to participate in the NGBT negotiations in the first place and might even endanger the successful conclusion of the whole process of negotiation. In this regard, the Members are well advised to follow the wisdom embodied in the old saying 'if it ain't broke, don't fix it'.

II. Issues in the current round

Article XIX of the GATS establishes a built-in agenda for new negotiations on trade in services by requiring Members to 'enter into successive rounds of negotiations, beginning not later than five years from the date of entry into force of the WTO Agreement and periodically thereafter'. In order to assist the Members in this effort, on 28 March 2001, the Special Session of the Council for Trade in Services adopted the Guidelines and Procedures for the Negotiations on Trade in Services. According to Paragraph 11 of the Guidelines, '[t]he *main* method of negotiation shall be the request-offer approach' (emphasis added). This does not necessarily mean, however, that the bilateral request-offer approach should be the *sole* method of negotiation. Indeed, the same paragraph also envisages the possibility of advancing the liberalisation through other approaches, such as bilateral, plurilateral or multilateral negotiations. The plurilateral negotiations could include sectoral and formula approaches. In the following section the author discusses some of the pros and cons of these two approaches.

[46] S/NGBT/12.

A. *Sectoral approach*

As noted by the former WTO Deputy Director-General Andrew Stoler in a recent article, the Doha Round is very different from the Uruguay Round in the sense that the latter 'is a market access round, not a round involving the introduction and elaboration of complex new rules like the last round'.[47] This is especially true for trade in services, which was only brought under the regulation of the multilateral trading system in the Uruguay Round. Thus, during the last round, 'a considerable percentage of the effort went into writing the rules to govern services trade', while after the Uruguay Round most of the specific commitments in WTO Members' schedules only reflected the status quo of market access in the mid-1990s rather than offering any real opportunities. Even though there are still some issues relating to unfinished rules, such as those on safeguards, subsidies, government procurement and domestic regulation,[48] it is most likely that the current round will focus on market access negotiations. Generally, it is much easier to negotiate general rules or principles, as people have yet to fully grasp the real implications of such rules, whereas a much harder battle has to be fought when people try to bring the trade policies in individual sectors into conformity with these principles as it is only then that the real interests of service suppliers will be affected and political costs be incurred. This also explains the general paucity of substantial offers so far.

With its focus on market access and the heterogeneous nature of service sectors, the current Round will be more directed towards sectoral negotiations. Moreover, as many developing Members were reluctant to join the services negotiations in the Uruguay Round, the priority then was to persuade them to accept the framework agreement of the GATS rather than undertaking substantial market access commitments. Now that the general rules in the GATS have been firmly established as a cornerstone of the multilateral trading system, the major services exporters will shift their priority towards addressing what they perceive as imbalances in the level of commitments. In this regard, the observation made by Sauvé on the difference between the financial services negotiations in the Uruguay Round and the Doha Round is equally applicable to most services sectors: there will be challenges arising from differences between countries at different levels of development, between different

[47] Stoler, at p. 1. [48] For a discussion on these issues, see Sauvé (2002).

modes of supply and competing business models and between different market segments.[49]

The advantage of the sectoral approach is that it could take into account the institutional and market realities of the individual services sectors, which include many differences such as 'differences in market structure and the scope for competition, differences in regulatory objectives and the nature of government regulation, and differences in the historical development of domestic and international institutions'.[50] As each sector involves highly technical aspects, a sectoral approach could ensure that the discussions would be mainly held among the technical experts in the field, who would be presumed to have a better appreciation of the issues and challenges facing the particular sector and thus would be more capable of formulating the policy appropriate for addressing these problems so as to achieve greater market liberalisation.

A sectoral approach is also more manageable, as it is much easier to compare the values of concessions given in one sector rather than to compare the gains that would arise from the liberalisation of sectors which are totally independent of one another, such as the education and health sectors. In some circumstances, for example when the technological and regulatory landscapes in a particular sector have undergone fundamental shifts, it might be useful to push for negotiations in this sector without waiting for movements in other sectors in order to guarantee an 'early harvest' by locking in the gains from unilateral liberalisation. In this regard, the experience from the telecommunication negotiations is especially enlightening. As noted by Adlung, telecommunications is an example of a services liberalisation that was 'virtually irresistible' and driven by several factors. First, technological progress has created new alternatives to long entrenched regimes and/or rendered them unenforceable. Second, when the users learned about the liberalisation policies abroad, they became impatient with the slow reform process (or its absence) at the domestic level and held the telecom ministries accountable for performance deficits (higher charges, lower penetration, non-availability of advanced services, etc.).[51] It was against this background that many governments recognised and adjusted to what was happening in reality.[52]

To some extent, the flourishing of the so-called 'Friends Groups' in the current services negotiations attests to the popularity of the sectoral approach. Currently there are about twenty such groups, covering sectors ranging from those that had been the subjects of sectoral negotiations in the

[49] Sauvé, at p. 133. [50] Feketekuty, at p. 241. [51] Adlung (2004), at p. 21. [52] *Ibid.*

Uruguay Round, i.e. financial services, telecommunications, maritime services and mode 4, to sectors with newly-discovered interests, such as audiovisuals, computer services, environmental services, distribution services, postal services, construction services, tourism services, logistics services, energy services and legal services. These groups are largely driven by export interests. These 'Friends Groups' have done a lot of work to advance the negotiations by taking stock of the main barriers to trade in the particular sectors, identifying the major traders of these services, and even drafting some model schedules in which the Members can inscribe their market access commitments.

On the other hand, the sectoral approach is not without its pitfalls. First, as sectoral approaches are normally driven by export interests or the interests of the service providers, they can easily be influenced by private interest groups and be biased towards reflecting and protecting the interests of the service suppliers. While most service suppliers are on a constant look-out for opportunities to expand the markets for their services, this is not always the case. Indeed, in markets that are subject to the control of monopolistic or oligopolistic firms, there might be no incentive to push for liberalisation at all, as these firms are likely to be comfortable with their positions. This seemed to be confirmed by a recent study by Fink *et al.* on the possible causes of the high prices in international maritime services. The study shows that private anticompetitive practices apparently have a greater effect on prices than public trade restrictive practices. In the author's view, this is probably one of the reasons why the post-Uruguay Round sectoral negotiations on maritime services did not succeed. There have been calls to adopt a user-oriented approach to some sectoral negotiations,[53] but such initiatives are unlikely to work for most sectors due to collective action problems. Second, it has been widely held that the success of the Uruguay Round owes a lot to the fact that negotiations on industrial products were held together with those on agricultural products, services and TRIPS in a 'single undertaking'. It would have been almost impossible to conclude negotiations on each of these different sectors had they been negotiated separately. Similarly, a purely sectoral approach in services could deprive the trade negotiators of the invaluable policy space that they would need to find trade-offs across sectors in order to justify making concessions in one sector. Still worse, almost every services sector would be subject to

[53] Feketekuty, for example suggested such an approach in the sectoral negotiations on transportation services. See Feketekuty (1998), at p. 11.

the regulation of at least one and sometimes several government ministries or bureaux within a single country. With each side-payment or issue linkage there will invariably be a bureaucratic loser within each government.[54] This might not be a serious problem in a cross-sectoral undertaking, but it would be much harder to justify if a strict sectoral approach were to be institutionalised. Indeed, as observed by Feketekuty, as bureaucrats rush to defend their own turf, '[a]ny purely sectoral discussion is likely to turn into an effort to justify and reinforce sectoral regulations that tend to be restrictive and interventionist'. Third, as not all Members are interested in the same sectors, any sectoral approach would have to be a plurilateral rather than multilateral initiative. Thus, the sectoral approach could further exacerbate the imbalance of the commitments by Members across sectors. Moreover, for sectors which are the subjects of international rule-making, the sectoral approach would carry the risk of subjecting the Members to different sets of rules, which could lead to the 'Balkanisation' of the multilateral trading system as happened on the basis of the Tokyo Round's Codes.

B. Formula approach

In addition to the sectoral approach, various formula approaches have been proposed in recent years. There is no uniform definition of a formula approach. In terms of coverage, they could encompass both sectoral and cross-sectoral initiatives. In terms of content, they could include rule-making exercises as well as ways to increase the number of commitments. One general observation about formula approaches is that they provide a much more efficient means of negotiation than the traditional request–offer process by reducing transaction costs,[55] and this largely explains their popularity. However, each formula approach has to be dealt with on its own merits. Adlung (2004) provides a good summary of the formula approaches,[56] and the author will use this summary as a starting point for discussion.

The first formula approach relates to common definitions of terms frequently used in schedules. This includes, for example, the definition of what constitutes 'temporary' presence of natural persons, a clear definition of the categories of skilled workers such as managers, executives and specialists. As noted by Low and Mattoo, such an approach is also useful in delineating the boundaries of different sub-sectors, as well as defining

[54] Levy, at pp. 5–6. [55] Mattoo (2005), at p. 16. [56] Adlung (2004) at p. 16.

areas where differing degrees of liberalisation were feasible.[57] For example, in the post-Uruguay Round maritime negotiations, the Members agreed to exclude cabotage from the scope of the negotiations. They also reached consensus to separate bulk and liner shipping services, which enabled them to offer more in the former area than they would have been willing to do without such separation. Similarly, in telecoms negotiations, the differentiation between international, domestic long-distance and local loop telephony services was instrumental in ensuring the success of the negotiations.

The second formula approach is standard policy instruments or concepts for adoption. The best known example in this regard is the telecom reference paper, while the latest proposals along this line include the creation of a 'GATS visa' for movements under mode 4, one-stop information or contact points for interested groups and a proposed reference paper for economic needs tests. This approach usually involves a high degree of international rule-making and is most useful in addressing problems in heavily regulated sectors on issues such as the allowable forms and extent of competition and the minimum performance standards that should be met.[58]

The third approach is framework undertakings, whereby Members refrain from implementing and/or scheduling measures considered to be particularly restrictive or distortive. Examples include the moratorium on duties on electronic transmissions, as embodied in the Ministerial Declaration on Global Electronic Commerce of 25 May 1998, and the proposals to exclude specified transactions from economic needs tests.

The fourth approach is the model schedule, which gives Members options to undertake standardised commitments in individual sectors, technology areas or modes. Examples from the last round include the Understanding on Commitments in Financial Services,[59] the Model Schedule for Basic Telecommunications and the Draft Schedule for Maritime Transport Services, while the current round has also seen proposals relating to model schedules of mode 4 and information technology and business process outsourcing. Of these, the Understanding on Commitments in Financial Services is particularly interesting. It essentially

[57] Low and Mattoo (1999), at p. 19. [58] Feketekuty (1998), at p. 4.

[59] Low and Mattoo (1999) deem the Understanding on Commitments in Financial Services to be a formula rather than a model schedule. As this chapter uses the word 'formula' as a broad term that includes all cross-cutting approaches, the Understanding is classified as a model schedule here.

provides an alternative method of scheduling by specifying the content of market-access commitments.

All four of the approaches discussed above involve some degree of international rule-making. This is a cause of concern among developing countries, which fear that such regulatory obligations would 'put liberalisation and "pro-competitive" objectives and the rights of foreign firms ahead of national objectives such as universal provision'.[60] In their view, such international regulatory frameworks are usually drafted by the developed countries and fail to address the particular needs of most developing countries, such as the need to allow for the development of strong local service industries. This is illustrated by the recent ruling in the *Mexico – Telecoms* case, where the Panel refused to allow Mexico to include in its interconnection charges the costs incurred for the development of the telecoms infrastructure of Mexico, which was allegedly essential to enable Mexico to achieve its aim of providing universal telecoms services in its domestic market.[61]

Another concern for the developing countries is that their lack of experience, or the non-existence of adequate national regulation, would put them at a great disadvantage when negotiating with their developed partners on the international regulatory framework.[62] One way to solve this problem would be to adopt, along the lines suggested by Mattoo, a credible international assistance mechanism to help the developing countries diagnose and remedy regulatory inadequacies so that they could be better prepared for making liberalisation commitments.[63] Another way would be to accord more flexibility to developing countries in implementing their commitments, possibly through policy instruments such as emergency safeguard mechanisms.

The developing countries also expressed concern about the potential loss of flexibility caused by the international rule-making exercises effectively pressurising them into making commitments that they would otherwise be unwilling to make.[64] Such anxiety is probably more imagined than real, however, as developing countries usually do not have sufficient bargaining power in the bilateral request-offer process to take advantage of any flexibility they might have on paper. Instead, as Mattoo has suggested, in a world of unequal bargaining power, multilaterally

[60] Kwa (2005).

[61] Panel Report, *Mexico – Measures Affecting Telecommunications Services*, WT/DS204/R, adopted 1 June 2004.

[62] Kwa (2005). [63] Mattoo (2005). [64] Kwa (2005).

agreed approaches that must be seen to be equitable and efficient are more likely to produce a desirable outcome than bilateral negotiations.[65]

The fifth approach is scheduling 'standstill' obligations, whereby Members agree to bind the currently applied regime in scheduled sectors. This is a useful way for the Members to lock in their existing liberalisation efforts and guard against backsliding that might be brought about by the changes in regulatory philosophy or administration, as international obligations, once signed, generally cannot be reversed. The Understanding on Commitments in Financial Services, for example, contains a standstill provision, and this is probably why most developing countries have not accepted the Understanding, as financial matters, if handled inappropriately, could have serious consequences for the economy.

The sixth approach is the cluster approach, whereby complementary commitments are assumed for clusters of interlinking sectors. Currently, proposals exist for the following clusters: courier and related transport services (e.g. road freight transport); various environmentally significant services; health care and health insurance services; and multimodal transport services (maritime transport and related road and waterways transport).

The last approach is numerical targets, or minimum sector coverage. This again includes two slightly different sub-approaches. The first is a 'qualitative' approach, whereas the second is the pure 'quantitative' approach. The first sub-approach aims at improving the quality of the commitments and would require Members to include certain core sectors in all schedules. There are proposals, for example, on achieving more comprehensive coverage of strategically and/or economically important services (e.g. business process outsourcing, telecommunications and financial services) and/or to liberalise services that are transmitted electronically. The second sub-approach focuses on increasing the quantity of the commitments and would require Members to include a minimum number of sectors in all schedules. The major developed countries are the main proponents of such an approach, with the EU as the chief advocate. According to the EU proposal, there are mandatory numerical targets for each individual country; developed countries are required to make commitments in 139 of the 163 services sub-sectors and developing countries are required to make commitments in 93 sub-sectors. Developing countries are generally opposed to the introduction of mandatory numerical

[65] Mattoo (2005), at p. 16.

targets. They argue that, since developing countries have different abilities to make commitments, such an approach would effectively require the larger ones to 'take up the slack' for smaller ones that are unable to make the commitments necessary to achieve the average target.[66] For example, if developing countries were required to have commitments in an average of 80 sub-sectors, and smaller developing countries could only make commitments in 30 sub-sectors, larger developing countries would have to make commitments in more than 140 sub-sectors in order to meet the average target.[67] The US tried to bridge the difference by offering an alternative proposal to allow Members flexibility in choosing the sectors in which they make commitments.[68] Although the developing countries acknowledged that the US proposal would give Members more flexibility, they pointed out that this could also mean that developed countries could choose to open their markets only in sectors that are not of particular interest to developing countries, which is against the mandate in the Doha Declaration to promote 'the development of developing and least-developed countries' and the requirement in the Negotiating Guidelines to give special consideration to 'sectors and modes of supply of export interest to developing countries'. Another concern of the developing countries is that, when developing country markets are prised open, the services markets will be even more concentrated.[69] As most developing countries lack significant export capacities in services, it would be extremely difficult for them to nurture their local service industries.[70] This, however, is not necessarily always the case. Indeed, in recent years, service providers from several developing countries in sectors such as financial, telecom and engineering services have become very competitive. In this regard, the development of the Internet holds special promise for developing countries to close the gap in their service sectors by enabling them to catch up in a technological leap.

Putting aside the question of the desirability of the quantitative approach, the author also has reservations with regard to the effectiveness of this approach as a negotiating mechanism. Indeed, as several studies that have analysed the patterns of commitments across sectors have illustrated, some of the sectors, such as tourism, financial services, business services and communications services have already attracted numerous commitments.[71] Thus, even in the absence of the explicit

[66] Inside US Trade, *U.S. Fights For Numerical Targets In Services Talks*, 11 November 2005.
[67] *Ibid.* [68] *Ibid.* [69] Kwa (2005). [70] *Ibid.*
[71] Hoekman, Mattoo, English, at pp. 263–264. Adlung, at pp. 8–9.

requirement of a mandatory numerical target, most Members have already made commitments in several sectors. Adding such a requirement could probably only achieve the same results as would be seen without such a requirement: the Members will just pick the ones that they would schedule anyway. It is probably more meaningful to discuss the quality of the commitments.

III. Concluding observations

In conclusion, the author would like to make the following observations with regard to the choice of negotiating approaches:

First, during the GATT era, the tariff negotiations gradually shifted from bilateral to sectoral and formula approaches. Even though the nature of services is quite different from that of goods, we are likely to observe a similar shift in negotiating approaches as the increased membership and the complexity of the multilateral trading system mean that sectoral and formula approaches are probably the most efficient (or feasible) ways to negotiate. With goods, as the rules framework for services is finalised, there is probably more need to negotiate along sectoral and formula lines.

Second, even though sectoral negotiations (and formula negotiations along sectoral lines) are inherently plurilateral in nature, it is nevertheless important that they include a critical mass of countries in that particular sector to ensure their success. As the experiences during the negotiations on telecoms, financial services and maritime services have illustrated, unless countries representing 90 per cent of the markets in a particular sector sign up to a sectoral agreement, there is no hope of achieving real results. Thus, when the US, home to the largest financial services market, threatened to walk out of the financial services negotiations in 1993, the negotiations almost collapsed. It was only when the US later returned to the negotiating table that a deal could be struck. Thus, contrary to the statement made by Hong Kong when the maritime services negotiations were about to fall apart due to the lack of offers from the US, 'absence of one or two participants' would actually 'spell doom for the negotiations or the GATS'[72] and 'a multilateral agreement' could well 'depend on … one country'.[73]

Third, although the experience on dispute settlement cases related to services is limited, these cases have clearly revealed the 'inherent

[72] S/NGMTS/13. [73] S/NGMTS/14.

incomprehensibility and unpredictability' of the GATS rules and commitments: even the WTO Members with the largest numbers of trade experts and negotiators claimed to have been surprised by the full implications of the GATS as spelt out in panel rulings in cases in which they were named respondents.[74] Thus, whatever the negotiating approach taken, the Members should always keep in mind the interpretive difficulties that might arise in future dispute settlement cases. Otherwise, even when equipped with the best possible negotiating approach, the Members might be reluctant to make commitments because they could never be fully aware of exactly what they are getting themselves into.[75]

Bibliography

Adlung, Rudolf, 'The GATS Turns Ten: A Preliminary Stocktaking', WTO Staff Working Paper ERSD-2004-05, August, 2004.

——'Services Negotiations in the Doha Round: Lost in Flexibility?', *Journal of International Economic Law* 9(4) (2006).

Croome, John, *Reshaping the World Trading System: A History of Uruguay Round*, (Kluwer Law International, 1999).

Drake, William J. and Kalypso Nicolaïdes, 'Ideas, Interests and Institutionalization: "Trade in Services" and the Uruguay Round', in Peter Haas (ed.), *Knowledge, Power and International Policy Coordination,* a special issue of *International Organization*, vol. 45 (Winter 1992), pp. 37–100.

Eschenbach, Felix and Bernard Hoekman, 'Services Policy Reform and Economic Growth in Transition Economies, 1990–2004' (June 2005). World Bank Policy Research Working Paper No. 3663. Available at SSRN: http://ssrn.com/abstract=770950.

Feketekuty, Geza, *International Trade in Services: An Overview and Blueprint for Negotiations* (Ballinger, 1988).

——'Setting the Agenda for the Next Round of Negotiations on Trade in Services', 1998, available at www.commercialdiplomacy.org/articles_news/trade_services.htm.

Fink, Carsten, Aaditya Mattoo and Ileana Cristina Neagu, 'Trade in International Maritime Services: How Much Does Policy Matter?', *World Bank Economic Review* 16(1) (2002), pp. 81–108.

Gao, Henry, 'Reflections On The Relationship Between WTO Negotiations And Dispute Settlement – Lessons From The GATS', in Yasuhei Taniguchi, Alan Yanovich and Jan Bohanes (eds.), *The WTO In The*

[74] Mattoo (2005), at p. 10. [75] Gao.

Twenty-First Century: Dispute Settlement, Negotiations and Regionalism in Asia (Cambridge University Press, 2007).

Hoekman, Bernard, 'Assessing the General Agreement on Trade in Services', in W. Martin and L. A. Winters (eds.), *The Uruguay Round and the Developing Countries* (Cambridge University Press, 1996).

Hoekman, Bernard, Aaditya Mattoo, and Philip English (eds.), *Development, Trade, and the WTO: A. Handbook* (World Bank, 2002).

Hoekman, Bernard and Patrick A. Messerlin, *Liberalizing Trade in Services: Reciprocal Negotiations and Regulatory Reform* (World Bank, 1999).

Howse, Robert and Michael J. Trebilcock, *The Regulation of International Trade*, 3rd edition (Routledge, October 2005).

Kwa, Aileen, '*Plurilateral Request-Offer Approach in GATS Draft Text: Entry Point for Dangerous Sectoral Negotiation*, 18 November 2005.

Levy, Philip I., 'Do We Need an Undertaker for the Single Undertaking? Considering the Angles of Variable Geometry', 2004, available at www.yale.edu/ycias/globalization/levy_paper.pdf.

Low, Patrick and Aaditya Mattoo, 'Is there a Better Way? Alternative Approaches to Liberalization Under the GATS', presented at the Services 2000: New Directions in Services Trade Liberalization Conference, Washington DC, 1–2 June 1999.

Mattoo, Aaditya, 'Services in a Development Round: Three Goals and Three Proposals', World Bank Policy Research Working Paper No. 3718, September 2005.

Olson, Mancur, *The Logic of Collective Action : Public Goods and the Theory of Groups* (Harvard University Press, 1995).

Sauvé, Pierre, 'Completing the GATS Framework: Addressing Uruguay Round Leftovers', *The Swiss Review of International Economic Relations (Aussenwirtschaft)* 57(3) (2002), Zurich: Rüegger, pp. 301–341.

Stephenson, Sherry M., 'Approaches to Liberalizing Services' (May 1999), World Bank Policy Research Working Paper No. 2107. Available at SSRN: ssrn.com/abstract=604916.

Stewart, Terence P. (ed.), *The GATT- Uruguay Round: A Negotiating History*, (Kluwer Law and Taxation Publishers, 1995).

Stoler, Andrew L., 'Major Issues in the DDA Negotiations: The Central Place of Market Access for the WTO's Development Round', in Yasuhei Taniguchi, Alan Yanovich and Jan Bohanes (eds.), *The WTO In The Twenty-First Century: Dispute Settlement, Negotiations and Regionalism in Asia* (Cambridge University Press, 2007).

WTO Secretariat, *Study on Financial Services: Opening Markets in Financial Services and the Role of the GATS* (1997).

9

Trade liberalisation under the GATS: An odyssey?

RUDOLF ADLUNG*

In over seven years, the services negotiations under the GATS have produced little, if any, progress in terms of commercially meaningful offers. A number of Members elected to remain on the sidelines, sometimes despite significant autonomous liberalisation, while others confined their offers to predominantly cosmetic improvements of existing commitments. The absence of momentum stands in remarkable contrast to what has happened in other fora. It looks as if governments are reluctant to 'squander' negotiating coinage at the multilateral level, which they are pleased to use in a bilateral or regional context. Against this background, this chapter discusses why the momentum that has driven past trade rounds under the GATT has not, or not yet, been discernible. While the Hong Kong Ministerial Declaration may be viewed as an encouraging response to the deplorable state of play, the services negotiations have since fallen victim to (non-)events in other areas, notably agriculture and non-agricultural market access. The litmus test on Members' readiness to promote multilateral services liberalisation or, as a minimum, to bring their offers more closely into line with applied regimes, is thus still outstanding. Also, doubts linger whether the explicit exemption of LDCs, in paragraph 26 of the Hong Kong Declaration, from the expectation to undertake new commitments is in these countries' best economic interest. There is little reason to assume that they would not benefit as well from binding ongoing reform projects or at least past reforms that have been tested successfully in practice. The concluding section discusses briefly how governments' reticence in these negotiations might be addressed.

* All views expressed are those of the author and cannot be attributed to the WTO Secretariat or WTO Members.

1. *Reciprocity: Why old tricks might not work in services*

> The function of the GATT [WTO] as a negotiating forum is to enable countries to defend the national economic interest not against the national interest of other countries but against sectional interests within their own and other countries.[1]
>
> If economists ruled the world, there would be no need for a World Trade Organization … The implicit mercantilist theory that underlies trade negotiations does not make sense on any level … but it nonetheless governs actual policy.[2]

The core rationale of 'classical' trade rounds consists of allowing governments, beleaguered by vested interests, to do the right things for the wrong reasons. The expansionist interests of more dynamic industries are mobilised to counterbalance the retarding influence of long-entrenched 'stakeholders', i.e. hitherto protected domestic producers.[3] Shifts towards less distortive and more economically efficient regimes, though unilaterally achievable, are thus presented domestically as 'concessions' that need to be made in exchange for better access opportunities abroad. Moreover, since the outcome is secured in the form of tariff bindings, governments find it easier to ignore 'the songs of (protection-seeking) sirens' once these swell around election day.[4]

The situation in services is more complicated. Given the diversity of the sectors concerned and the broad modal application of the Agreement, which extends to consumer and factor movements (capital and labour) as well, cross-country trade-offs are not only more difficult to conceive of, but also more politically challenging to organise. (Why would a transport ministry expose its constituency, e.g. road freight carriers, to more competition for the sake of the country's banks being able to branch cross-border?) The wide array of permissible trade

[1] Frieder Roessler, 'The Scope, Limits and Function of the GATT Legal System', *World Economy* 8 (1985), pp. 287–298 at 297.

[2] Paul Krugman, 'What Should Trade Negotiators Negotiate About?', *Journal of Economic Literature* 35 (1997), pp. 113–120 at 114.

[3] Typically, the chances of policy influence are closely related to the economic size of a sector (in terms of GDP, employment, etc.), its age, regional concentration and initial level of protection. The higher the rents at stake, the larger the entities involved and the stronger their presence in a country's political and commercial centres, the stronger the producers' weight in the policy-making process. See, for example, Rudolf Adlung, 'GATS and Democratic Legitimacy', *Aussenwirtschaft* 59 (2004), pp. 127–149.

[4] Roessler (above n. 1) likened GATT tariff bindings to Odysseus' decision to have himself lashed to the mast in order to be able to resist the songs of the sirens.

restrictions, from numerical quotas to discriminatory taxation or regulation, adds a further element of complexity. There is simply no single indicator, comparable to ad valorem tariffs, that could be used to measure levels of protection across sectors or modes of supply and to negotiate their reduction, as mandated in the GATS, 'with a view to promoting the interests of all participants on a mutually advantageous basis and to securing an overall balance of rights and obligations' (Article XIX:1). Governments' wider scope for regulatory intervention, compared to the GATT, proves an additional source of uncertainty. Similar levels of 'formal' access barriers, as reflected in the schedules of services commitments that Members were held to submit under the GATS, thus do not guarantee similar competitive opportunities.

At the same time, given the infrastructural role of service sectors such as telecommunications, construction, finance or transport, it is obvious that the protection of 'stakeholders' may take a high toll on many user industries. Since price-based protection is rare in services, as compared to merchandise trade, the ensuing losses are not even partially counterbalanced by tariff revenue. Thus, while the disparate nature of individual regimes makes it easier for incumbents to coalesce with 'their' Ministries, normally organised along sector lines and keenly interested in defending competencies, the perpetuation of traditional arrangements may prove particularly costly.[5]

2. *Services liberalisation under the GATS: No more than wishful thinking?*

> In virtually every economy, the performance of the services sector can make the difference between rapid and sluggish growth … The income gains from a reduction to protection in services are estimated to be multiples of those from trade liberalization in goods.[6]

[5] For example, the costs of one day in transit have been estimated to amount roughly to 0.8 per cent of product value. In the case of Sub-Saharan Africa, where the delivery time in merchandise trade averages about 50 days for exports and 60 days for imports, this is tantamount to operating a tax on trade – and, thus, on international economic integration – of some 40 and 50 per cent, respectively. (The equivalent estimate for high-income OECD countries is in the order of 10 per cent for both exports and imports.) Services reforms, which would reduce these periods by, say, 20 per cent, could thus be compared to tariff reductions of some 8 and 10 percentage points, respectively. See OECD Trade Directorate, 'Logistics and Time as a Trade Barrier' (2006) Trade Policy Working Paper No. 35 (TD/TC/WP(2006)3/Final), at pp. 9–13.

[6] World Bank, Global Economic Prospects (Washington, DC: The World Bank, 2002), at p. 69.

There is no shortage of empirical studies documenting the economic benefits of – well-conceived – services liberalisation.[7] Nevertheless, the GATS has not served as a catalyst for reform in 'mainstream' WTO Member economies to date. The vast majority of current commitments has not gone beyond the access conditions, in a limited number of sub-sectors, that existed in the early 1990s. Many Uruguay Round schedules have since been overtaken by autonomous liberalisation moves.[8] Exceptions remained confined to essentially two sectors, telecommunications and financial services, where negotiations among some 70 governments continued until 1997, and the schedules of countries that have since acceded.

Some recently acceded Members, not least Eastern European and Central Asian transition economies (Georgia, Kyrgyz Republic, Moldova), have undertaken more numerous and ambitious commitments than any developed country.[9] China's accession schedule of 2001 is considered to represent the most radical services reforms ever negotiated in the WTO.[10] And while the Uruguay Round schedules submitted by the then 30 LDC Members contained 24 sub-sectors on average, which is about 15 per cent of the services universe covered by the relevant classification list, two recently acceded LDCs, Cambodia and Nepal, were ready to commit 94 and 77 sectors, respectively, at significant levels of access. The high share of phase-in commitments that are to be implemented within specified timeframes, applying to 50 per cent and more of all scheduled sectors in the cases of Vietnam, China and Nepal, also suggests that the obligations assumed were more liberal than pre-existing market conditions.[11]

3. *A force of change: The interests of user industries*

> The growing use of services had a significant favourable effect on growth of output in Indian manufacturing in the 1990s, when major trade and

[7] See, for example, Bernard Hoekman, 'Liberalizing Trade in Services: A Survey', World Bank Policy Research Working Paper (WPS 4030, 2006).

[8] For a more detailed discussion of these issues, see Rudolf Adlung and Martin Roy, 'Turning Hills into Mountains? Current Commitments under the General Agreement on Trade in Services and Prospects for Change', *Journal of World Trade* 6 (2005), pp. 1161–1194, and Rudolf Adlung, 'Services Negotiations in the Doha Round: Lost in Flexibility?', *Journal of International Economic Law* 9 (2006), pp. 865–893.

[9] See Adlung and Roy, (2005).

[10] Aaditya Mattoo, 'China's Accession to the WTO: The Services Dimension' *Journal of International Economic Law*, 6 (2003), pp. 299–339 at 333–334.

[11] Rudolf Adlung, 'The Contribution of Services Liberalization to Poverty Reduction: What Role for the GATS?', *Journal of World Investment & Trade* 8 (2007) 4 (forthcoming).

> industrial reforms were carried out. The contribution of services input to output growth in Indian manufacturing (organised) was about one per cent in the 1980s, and it increased to about 25 per cent in the 1990s.[12]

The absence of commercially meaningful offers from 'old' Members in the Doha Round must not be confused with the absence of reform, however. Quite to the contrary, many governments have made significant strides in opening and upgrading infrastructural services with a view to promoting the country's attractiveness for internationally mobile resources. The most prominent example is the proliferation of telecom reforms since about the early 1990s.

A push factor may have played a role as well. Private consumers tend to have little influence on the domestic political process, while industrial users not only have better policy access, but also stronger incentives to use it. This is the case, in particular, if they are unable in their markets to pass on the cost of inefficient services inputs. Increasing international economic integration, due to tariff liberalisation, new communication technologies and so on, could thus stimulate the liberalisation of infrastructural sectors as well. However, this may presuppose an initial level of openness in the economies concerned. An autarkic system is less likely to self-generate the internal pressure operating in favour of (further) liberalisation and may thus depend even more heavily on some sort of external prodding. Yet, where could this be coming from?

4. *The benefits of external policy bindings: Increasing the reform premium*

> Controlling for geographical region and income level, countries that have made GATS commitments in basic telecommunications tend to outperform those countries that have not made commitments in basic telecommunications with respect to fixed and mobile penetration as well as sector revenues (as a percentage of GDP).[13]
>
> Bilateral investment agreements that focus on the non-discrimination in the treatment of foreign firms, lay specific standards of investment

[12] Rashmi Banga and Bishwanath Goldar, 'Contribution of Services to Output Growth and Productivity in Indian Manufacturing: Pre and Post Reforms', Indian Council for Research on International Economic Relations (ICRIER, 2004), Working Paper No. 139.

[13] Kent Bressie, Michael Kende and Howard Williams, 'Telecommunications Trade Liberalization and the WTO' (2005) 7 info 3–24, at 20.

protection and contain provisions for the settlement of disputes, have an important impact on FDI inflows.[14]

Proponents of the concept of 'policy space' tend to emphasise the need for a reforming government to retain scope for subsequent policy corrections. Empirical evidence suggests, however, that the stability and predictability of an ensuing regime, whether achieved under the GATS or elsewhere, are economically relevant. In turn, this implies that 'policy space' comes at a notional cost. This may be fully justified in the event of sweeping changes. However, is it equally important for arrangements that are modelled on widely-used templates or, in the event of innovative moves that have already proven their effectiveness over an extended period of time?

A number of governments were able in such instances to overcome old-fashioned reciprocity considerations and volunteer new commitments. For example, Egypt and Honduras autonomously improved their telecom entries in the wake of domestic reforms in 2002 and 2005, respectively.[15] Yet there are no comparable cases in other sectors, despite ample evidence of successful (autonomous) liberalisation moves in many WTO Member economies.[16]

While possibly anathema for the advocates of 'policy space', recent accession schedules are further evidence that broad and deep services commitments are not inconsistent with development objectives. Of course, it may be mere coincidence that one the of world's most vibrant economies, China, is also among the most ambitious services liberalisers under the GATS. Nevertheless, there can be little doubt that – well-conceived and carefully prepared – commitments are as much a boon for development as a 'concession' vis-à-vis trading partners.

5. *The risk of inertia: GATS commitments of secondary importance?*

What has been termed the 'spaghetti bowl' of customs unions, common markets, regional and bilateral free trade areas, preferences and an endless

[14] Rashmi Banga, 'Do Investment Agreements Matter?', *Journal of Economic Integration* 21 (2006), pp. 40–63 at 55. Other authors, however, could not corroborate the existence of a significant positive relationship between BITs and investment flows. For an overview see Rudolf Adlung in above n. 11.

[15] The relevant schedules are contained in WTO documents GATS/SC/30/Suppl.3, 5 June 2002, and GATS/SC/38/Suppl.2, 16 September 2005.

[16] See, for example, the services chapters of WTO Trade Policy Reviews.

> assortment of miscellaneous trade deals has almost reached the point where MFN treatment is exceptional treatment. Certainly the term might now be better defined as LFN, least-favoured nation treatment. Does it matter? We believe it matters profoundly to the future of the WTO.[17]

The absence of tangible progress in the current round, even after seven years of negotiations, stands in striking contrast with the obligations assumed in other contexts. Questions abound.

Why does an increasing number of Members, including developing countries, assume obligations under Preferential Trade Agreements (PTAs) that go way beyond not only their GATS schedules, but also their initial or revised offers?[18] Why are they easily available for bilateral negotiations with major trading partners although imbalances in political strength are certainly more taxing than in a multilateral setting? Are there 'side-payments' in non-services or even non-trade areas? Are the Doha negotiations perceived to lack pace and ambition? Or are governments simply keen not to miss the boat and be subjected to 'LFN' treatment?

Equally puzzling is the proliferation of Bilateral Investment Treaties (BITs). Some 1,900 such Treaties are currently in force, while an additional 600 reportedly await ratification.[19] Germany and Switzerland alone have each concluded over 100 BITs, most of which guarantee full national treatment, post-establishment, to foreign investors in foreign-majority owned or controlled companies.[20] Note that, barring some specified exceptions, the commitments under these Treaties apply across all sectors, including manufacturing and non-scheduled services under the GATS, and that the services-related obligations may need to be extended on an MFN basis, barring few exceptions, to all WTO

[17] Report by the Consultative Board, chaired by Peter Sutherland, to the Director-General Supachai Panitchpakdi, 'The Future of the WTO' (Geneva: WTO, 2004), at p. 19.

[18] See the contribution by Roy, Marchetti and Lim in this volume as well as Malcolm Bosworth and Dionisius A. Narjoko, 'Desirability, Feasibility and Options for Establishing ESM within the AFAS' (2006), REPSF Project No. 05/007, Final Report, at pp. 6–7.

[19] The status is not clear in all cases. See UNCTAD, The Entry into Force of Bilateral Investment Treaties (BITs), IIA Monitor No. 3 (2006) 3 (UNCTAD/WEB/ITE/IIA/2006/9).

[20] Switzerland's partner countries include Albania, Argentina, Bangladesh, Botswana, Chile, Egypt, India, Jamaica, Malaysia, Mexico, Pakistan, South Africa, Sri Lanka, Thailand, Tunisia and Venezuela. See also Rudolf Adlung, 'Negotiations on Safeguards and Subsidies in Services: A Never-Ending Story?', *Journal of International Economic Law* 10 (2007), pp. 235–265 at 252.

Members. Less than a dozen Members have listed Article II (MFN) exemptions that would allow them to deny the benefits conceded under BITs to non-signatory WTO Members.[21] (In the case of German- or Swiss-type BITs, which merely provide for post-establishment national treatment, MFN application presupposes that the country concerned allows for foreign-majority ownership or control.) Observers tend to argue that these Treaties are instrumental in securing markets and attracting resources in an increasingly globalised economy.[22] However, why don't governments use the GATS instead?

Ongoing liberalisation moves at bilateral or regional level may have significant implications for those 'old' WTO Members that elect to sit on the fence. Abstaining from meaningful offers in the round, whether out of inertia or reciprocity-related concerns, is not tantamount to preserving the status quo, but falling back in competition for capital and know-how. The race for ever more PTAs may prove no viable option either, given *inter alia* the resources required for negotiating and administering such agreements and, more importantly, the systemic implications for the WTO system;[23] and BITs are simply too narrow in focus.

6. *Who defines a country's 'economic interest', 'need for flexibility', etc.?*

Two souls, alas, are dwelling in my breast ...'[24]

As indicated before, there are obvious inconsistencies in governments' approach to services liberalisation in different contexts. Despite the rapid proliferation of BITs, involving WTO Members at virtually all levels of development, the proposed negotiations on trade and investment in the WTO, one of the so-called Singapore issues, were given a first-class funeral by the General Council in July 2004.[25] Despite their fierce

[21] BITs do not qualify as preferential agreements since their scope is essentially confined to one mode of supply (mode 3). A footnote to GATS Article V (Economic Integration) provides that, in order to qualify for cover, agreements must not provide for the a priori exclusion of any mode.

[22] UNCTAD, Systemic Issues in International Investment Agreements (IIAS), IIA Monitor No. 1 (2006) 2 (UNCTAD/WEB/ITE/IIA/2006/2), and Zachary Elkins, Andrew T. Guzman and Beth A. Simmons, 'Competing for Capital: The Diffusion of Bilateral Investment Treaties, 1960–2000', *International Organization* 60 (2006), pp. 811–846 at 814.

[23] See, for example, the discussion in above n. 17.

[24] 'Zwei Seelen wohnen, ach!, in meiner Brust ...' (Johann Wolfgang von Goethe, *Faust I*).

[25] WTO document WT/L/579 of 2 August 2004.

resistance against formula-based negotiations in the Doha Round, some of the same governments have been ready to sign, with minor modifications, the template BITs proposed by large developed countries. And despite LDCs' insistence on being exempt from expectations to liberalise under the GATS in the current round (see below), four of them have undertaken significant obligations, concerning national treatment on a pre- *and* post-establishment basis, in investment treaties with the United States. (The obligations assumed are comparable to commitments under mode 3 of the GATS that guarantee the absence of discriminatory quotas, foreign equity ceilings, joint venture requirements and any other departures from national treatment.)[26] In turn, while GATS negotiators from developed countries continuously emphasise the benefits of open investment regimes, they tend to fall silent when it comes to the movement of natural persons under Mode 4.

It has been suggested that PTAs may prove more attractive than a WTO deal not only because they can be negotiated within a shorter timeframe and come with more positive publicity, but also because the relevant dispute settlement mechanisms tend to offer more political leeway. However, while the publicity factor cannot easily be dismissed, in particular from the viewpoint of small country governments, the question arises whether flexible enforcement provisions are really in the interest of smaller and economically weaker participants. Moreover, while such considerations may prove relevant for PTAs, they do not necessarily apply to BITs. Compared to the WTO mechanism, BITs offer an additional, potentially powerful avenue for dispute resolution: the possibility of investor-state challenges before independent international commissions (ICSID or UNCITRAL).

Why these contradictions? They certainly beg the question whether governments speak with one voice, regardless of the negotiating context, or whether it is more reasonable to hypothesise the existence of different decision-making centres that are activated on different occasions. For example, ministers of finance may take the initiative, possibly without

[26] While the US has included some 110 sub-sectors under these BITs, roughly commensurate with the number of its GATS bindings, the corresponding average for the LDCs involved (Bangladesh, Democratic Republic of Congo, Mozambique and Senegal) exceeds 130, which is more than seven times the average number of sub-sectors they bound under the GATS. (These estimates are subject to an element of an uncertainty, however, since the sector definitions in BITs cannot easily be converted into the classification generally used for scheduling purposes under the GATS.) The Treaties are available at www.unctadxi.org/templates/DocSearch__779.aspx.

much coordination, when it comes to BITs; the prime ministers' offices are likely to initiate and oversee the WTO accession process or negotiations on high-profile PTAs; while the ministers of trade, not necessarily heavyweights in Cabinet, seek to persuade their colleagues responsible for finance, transport, migration, and so on to contribute something to a Doha deal.[27] Thus, though WTO negotiations offer an ideal opportunity, more than possibly any other context, for inter-ministerial coordination and coherent policy-making across sectors and modes, they might receive no commensurate political backing. Too many souls dwelling in governments' breasts?

7. *It is not yet too late, but …*

If your time to you
Is worth savin'
Then you better start swimmin'
Or you'll sink like a stone
For the times they are a-changin'.[28]

There have been variations over time in Members' perception of the most suitable negotiating approach (bilateral, plurilateral or multilateral). While Article XIX:4 of the GATS is neutral in this regard, the 2001 Negotiating Guidelines prioritise the (bilateral) request-offer process. Given the number of Members, sectors, modes and restrictions involved (see above), this was certainly the most cumbersome option available. It might be asked, therefore, whether the lack of progress to date is an unintended side-effect or, rather, the initially intended corollary of a low-ambition agenda. Yet, the Hong Kong Ministerial Declaration introduced some novel elements. The rediscovery of a plurilateral option, combined with an outline of desirable outcomes (Annex C, para. 1), might be indicative of fresh political resolve or, at least, a tacit understanding among participants that a fiasco as at the 2003 Meeting in Cancun must be avoided. At the time of writing, however, Annex C still remained to be tested – in the form of meaningful revised offers.

As noted before, the discussions surrounding the negotiating approach are difficult to understand from a purely economic perspective in any event (section 1). Why would governments request concessions

[27] See also Patrick Messerlin, 'Three Variations on the "The Future of the WTO"', *Journal of International Economic Law* 8 (2005), pp. 299–309 at 304–305.

[28] Bob Dylan, 'The Times They Are A-Changin'', 1964.

for the termination of inherited arrangements, often more the result of historical accidents than deliberate design, that are likely to operate as a drag on national economic performance? Why don't they simply enable their economies to capitalise on the opportunities ensuing from rapid regulatory and technical innovation (e-commerce, etc.), regardless of the response of trading partners?

In the same vein, it is difficult to find an economic rationale for exempting least-developed countries from the expectation to undertake new commitments. Referring to their 'particular economic situation', the Hong Kong Declaration (para. 26) suggests that LDCs may remain on the sidelines, thus implying that policy bindings are no good for poor countries.[29] Why this invitation to complacency? The consequences may prove particularly serious since, as has been argued before, the countries concerned are less likely than more economically advanced Members to mobilise the internal forces operating in favour of more open services regimes.

8. *How to encourage more active engagement*

> Removing even minimal obligations will not hasten the day that policy changes are made to promote development and secure integration into the global economy. Such a move would also deny what little negotiating leverage least-developed countries currently wield in WTO negotiations.[30]

Market-oriented reforms in poor countries are subject to particular technical and institutional challenges, however. Assistance is certainly needed to develop a services infrastructure that promotes integration in international markets, stimulates domestic structural adjustment, and helps attract – and regulate – internationally mobile investors. It would be irresponsible to talk the governments concerned into obligations they are unable, for lack of appropriate regulation, supervision and experience, to implement. On the other hand, however, there is no reason to assume that they are less vulnerable to 'sectional interests' – the songs of the sirens – than their counterparts in other parts of the world.[31] What might be expected in their situation is generous technical support,

[29] As noted before, however, two recently acceded LDCs were expected to bind three times as many sectors, at ambitious levels, than had been scheduled on average by LDCs in the Uruguay Round.

[30] See above n. 17, at p. 68.

[31] See above n. 1 and 4. In the words of Arthur Okun: 'Indeed, across the spectrum of primitive, ancient, medieval and modern societies, the market has been restricted more often to preserve unequal power and distinction for the few than to guarantee equal

offered in legally binding terms, and the possibility, via suitable templates, to condition access commitments on appropriate funding for, and progress in, domestic institution-building.[32]

Moreover, when considering the pros and cons of binding ambitious multi-annual reforms under the GATS, it might be reassuring for the authorities concerned if there was a possibility to suspend implementation in the event of non-anticipated disturbances. Some of the phase-in commitments undertaken in the context of the negotiations on basic telecommunications extend over ten years and more, and the occurrence of serious political or economic disruptions cannot simply be precluded during such long periods. In 2003/2004, when Albania experienced implementation problems in telecommunications, the authorities sought and were granted a one-year waiver, without counter-concessions, under Article IX:3 of the WTO Agreement. However, doubts remain whether higher-profile cases could be solved as easily and smoothly as that. The possibility to suspend ambitious multi-annual reform projects in critical circumstances might thus help to encourage more meaningful commitments under the GATS.[33]

It would certainly be time for such issues to be raised in GATS fora in order to assist Members in safely ending their Odyssey.

Bibliography

Adlung, Rudolf, 'GATS and Democratic Legitimacy', *Aussenwirtschaft* 59 (2004), pp. 127–149.

——'Services Negotiations in the Doha Round: Lost in Flexibility?', *Journal of International Economic Law* 9 (2006), pp. 865–893.

——'Negotiations on Safeguards and Subsidies in Services: A Never-Ending Story?', *Journal of International Economic Law* 10 (2007), pp. 235–265.

——'The Contribution of Services Liberalization to Poverty Reduction: What Role for the GATS?', *Journal of World Investment & Trade* 8 (2007) 4 (forthcoming).

Adlung, Rudolf and Martin Roy, 'Turning Hills into Mountains? Current Commitments under the General Agreement on Trade in Services and Prospects for Change', *Journal of World Trade* 6 (2005), pp. 1161–1194.

rights for the many.' Arthur M. Okun, *Equality and Efficiency – The Big Tradeoff* (Washington, DC: The Brookings Institution), at p. 21.

32 Similar thoughts have been expressed by Aaditya Mattoo. See, for example, 'Services in a Development Round: Proposals for Overcoming Inertia', in Richard Newfarmer (ed.), *Trade, Doha, and Development* (Washington, DC: The World Bank, 2006), pp. 161–174.

33 See Adlung in above n. 20, at p. 254–255.

Banga, Rashmi, 'Do Investment Agreements Matter?', *Journal of Economic Integration* 21 (2006), pp. 40–63.

Banga, Rashmi Bishwanath Goldar, 'Contribution of Services to Output Growth and Productivity in Indian Manufacturing: Pre and Post Reforms', Indian Council for Research on International Economic Relations (ICRIER, 2004), Working Paper No.139.

Bosworth, Malcolm and Dionisius A. Narjoko, 'Desirability, Feasibility and Options for Establishing ESM within the AFAS' (2006) REPSF Project No. 05/007, Final Report.

Bressie, Kent, Michael Kende and Howard Williams, 'Telecommunications Trade Liberalization and the WTO', (2005) 7 info 3–24 at 20.

Elkins, Zachary, Andrew T. Guzman and Beth A. Simmons, 'Competing for Capital: The Diffusion of Bilateral Investment Treaties, 1960–2000', *International Organization* 60 (2006), pp. 811–846.

Hoekman, Bernard, 'Liberalizing Trade in Services: A Survey', World Bank Policy Research Working Paper (WPS 4030, 2006).

Krugman, Paul, 'What Should Trade Negotiators Negotiate About?', *Journal of Economic Literature* 35 (1997), pp. 113–120.

Mattoo, Aaditya, 'China's Accession to the WTO: The Services Dimension', *Journal of International Economic Law* 6 (2003), pp. 299–339.

——'Services in a Development Round: Proposals for Overcoming Inertia', in Richard Newfarmer (ed.), *Trade, Doha, and Development* (Washington, DC: The World Bank, 2006), pp. 161–174.

Messerlin, Patrick, 'Three Variations on "The Future of the WTO"', *Journal of International Economic Law* 8 (2005), pp. 299–309.

OECD Trade Directorate, 'Logistics and Time as a Trade Barrier' (2006) Trade Policy Working Paper No. 35 (TD/TC/WP(2006)3/Final).

Okun, Arthur M., *Equality and Efficiency – The Big Tradeoff* (Washington, DC: The Brookings Institution).

Roessler, Frieder, 'The Scope, Limits and Function of the GATT Legal System', *World Economy* 8 (1985), 287–298.

UNCTAD, Systemic Issues in International Investment Agreements (IIAS), IIA Monitor No. 1 (2006) 2 (UNCTAD/WEB/ITE/IIA/2006/2).

UNCTAD, The Entry into Force of Bilateral Investment Treaties (BITs), IIA Monitor No. 3 (2006) 3 (UNCTAD/WEB/ITE/IIA/2006/9).

World Bank, Global Economic Prospects (Washington, DC: The World Bank, 2002).

WTO, Report by the Consultative Board, chaired by Peter Sutherland, to the Director-General Supachai Panitchpakdi, 'The Future of the WTO' (Geneva: WTO, 2004).

PART 4

GATS case law: A first assessment

10

Lessons learned from litigating GATS disputes: *Mexico – Telecoms*

ANDREW W. SHOYER*

The use by the United States of World Trade Organization (WTO) dispute settlement procedures to address Mexico's restrictions on international long distance telecommunications services[1] was, in my view, a nearly unalloyed success. The United States took on Mexico's most powerful private stakeholder (Teléfonos de México), protected by a complex regulatory scheme in a technically complicated services sector, and showed that the WTO dispute settlement mechanism was up to the task. The parties were not able to resolve the matter through negotiation, and a panel proceeding ensued. But no appeal was deemed necessary, nor was Mexico's compliance challenged. The US Federal Communications Commission's international traffic statistics published in March 2006 indicated that the call volume from the United States to Mexico doubled between 2003 and 2004.[2] It appears that much of that growth may have been driven by lower prices coming as a direct result of regulatory reform generated by the WTO case.

* The author is grateful to his partner, Todd Friedbacher, who played a prominent role in the *Mexico – Telecoms* dispute, for his comments on this chapter. Note well: The author is, at this stage in his unheralded career, a paid advocate. As such, it is the legal interpretation that serves the interests of the client of the moment, and not the author's own notions of jurisprudence, that clothes and feeds his family. It is with this in mind that the author offers the following, very personal musings on his experience as part of the litigation team in *Mexico – Telecoms*. Nothing in this chapter is intended as a prediction of, or prescription for, how legal or factual issues in future GATS disputes will or should be addressed. Should you, the reader, find something in this chapter that you feel serves to support a position that you seek to advocate in an academic setting or adversarial proceeding, be assured, dear reader, that the credit for such insight is entirely your own, and none should be attributed to the author or his clients.

1 *Mexico – Telecoms*, Mexico – Measures Affecting Telecommunications Services, Panel Report, WT/DS204/R, adopted 1 June 2004.

2 US Federal Communications Commission, 2004 International Telecommunications Data (March 2006), reprinted at www.fcc.gov/ib/sand/mniab/traffic/files/CREPOR04.pdf.

It was a great privilege to be one of the lawyers involved in the development and prosecution of the claims brought in that dispute. The case represents many 'firsts'[3] – the first pure services dispute litigated in the WTO; the first dispute involving the interpretation of the 'Reference Paper' on basic telecommunications services; the first WTO dispute in which a panel applied WTO competition law.[4] I describe below some of the lessons that I learned in the process that are not specific to the telecommunications sector.[5]

1. Panel selection

I have already treated elsewhere the general subject of Panel selection in WTO dispute settlement proceedings.[6] The challenge in this particular case was the selection of a technical expert in telecommunications services.[7] There were several considerations in this regard. It was generally understood that the technical aspects of telecommunications services would play an important role in the Panel's interpretation of Mexico's treaty obligations. WTO dispute settlement Panels are composed more often than not by WTO generalists – trade policy diplomats who serve or have served in Geneva. From where would such a Panel secure the insights into these technical points?

- The Panel might rely on the assistance of the WTO Secretariat and its Trade in Services Division; and yet, the WTO Secretariat is not generally staffed by electrical engineers or other technical experts in each of the myriad services sub-sectors covered by Members' GATS schedules – with the possible exception of consultancy and legal services!

[3] *Mexico – Telecoms*, at para. 7.2.

[4] *Ibid.* at paras. 7.222 *et seq.* and pp. 236–238 (reprinting Mexico's reference paper additional commitments).

[5] Subscribers of www.worldtradelaw.net will find a useful list of more thoughtful articles on the dispute. For a decidedly different and negative view of the dispute from the perspective of non-trade economists, see J. G. Sidak and H. Singer, 'Überregulation Without Economics: The World Trade Organization's Decision in the US–Mexico Arbitration on Telecommunications Services', *Federal Communications Law Journal* 57 (2004), 1, reprinted at www.law.indiana.edu/fclj/pubs/v57no1.html.

[6] A. Shoyer, 'Panel Selection in WTO Dispute Settlement Proceedings', *Journal of International Economic Law* 6 (2003), p. 203.

[7] The Uruguay Round Ministerial Decision on Certain Dispute Settlement Procedures for the General Agreement on Trade in Services provides in paragraph 4 that '[p]anels for disputes regarding sectoral matters shall have the necessary expertise relevant to the specific services sectors which the dispute concerns'.

- The Panel has the right under Article 13.1 of the Dispute Settlement Understanding to secure the assistance of technical experts, such as has the been the practice in disputes under the Agreement on the Application of Sanitary and Phytosanitary Measures.[8] Panels have generally consulted with the parties to a dispute on the criteria for selection of technical experts in those cases. But nothing requires a panel to do so. Would the Panel turn to technical experts from an international organisation such as the International Telecommunications Union? If the ITU was perceived to have an agenda regarding international disciplines on the regulation of basic telecommunications services (and in particular, on the regulation of settlement rates), and that agenda was somehow at odds with the disciplines set forth in GATS schedules, would that have an impact on the outcome of the analysis?

In the end, the Director-General composed the Panel. One of the panellists, Mr Bjorn Wellenius,[9] had technical expertise in telecommunications services. Indeed, the Panel itself commented on this aspect of its composition in the introduction to its report.[10]

2. Use of language

One of the great challenges in litigating a case based on a services schedule is unique words and phrases. On the one hand, the services schedule is treaty text and therefore subject to interpretation under Articles 31 and 32 of the Vienna Convention on the Law of Treaties.[11] On the other hand, Members can employ terms and phrases in their services schedules that have no antecedent in the United Nations Central Product Classification or other international lexicon. These terms might be derived from municipal law. But a Member might need to describe a situation in its services schedule that has not yet occurred in its municipal law – for example, 'the establishment and operation of *comercializadoras* [commercial agencies]' in Mexico subject to 'relevant regulations'

[8] See, e.g., *European Communities – Measures Concerning Meat and Meat Products (Hormones)*, Panel Report, WT/DS26/R, adopted 13 February 1998, as modified by the Appellate Body Report, WT/DS26/AB/R, DSR 1998:I, 135.

[9] *Mexico – Telecoms*, at para. 1.5. [10] *Mexico – Telecoms*, at para. 7.2.

[11] *Mexico – Telecoms*, at para. 7.15 ('Since the commitments provided for in Mexico's Schedule are part of the terms of the treaty, the only rules which may be applied in interpreting the meaning of a commitment are the general rules of interpretation as set out in the Vienna Convention.')

not yet issued. In the case of *comercializadoras*, Mexico provided a definition in a footnote to its schedule, but it might not have done so. Although goods schedules may include unique terms and phrases in tariff commitments below the six-digit Harmonized System level, the phenomenon is just as likely to occur in services schedules.

The other aspect of language that could have played a significant role in the dispute was translation from Spanish to English. One term in particular, *basadas en costos*, played an important role in the case because it described the standard for interconnection under Mexico's Reference Paper obligations.[12] There was no question that the term was only binding in Spanish, as the schedule was authentic only in Spanish. The question was rather one of knowing how the panel would understand that term, particularly in light of the English-language term 'cost-oriented' that had appeared in the English translation of the Mexican schedule prepared and circulated by the WTO Secretariat (and attached to the panel report).

The question of translation was also critical in Japan – Measures Affecting Consumer Photographic Film and Paper,[13] in which a Japanese term *taisaku* that was translated by the United States as 'countermeasures' was significant in evaluating the overall case. The panel drew up 'Procedures for Resolution of Possible Translation Issues' and reached out to translation experts to review and comment on those issues. The comments of experts are attached to the Panel report.[14]

There are two clear differences between the translation issues in *Mexico – Telecoms* and *Japan – Film*. First, the translation issues in *Japan – Film* related to the interpretation of a language that is not one of the three working languages of the WTO, and which does not lie within the core competence of the WTO Secretariat's Translation Division. Second, the issues in *Japan – Film* involved the interpretation of Japanese law, regulations and 'guidelines'; in contrast, the translation issues of concern in *Mexico – Telecoms* related to the interpretation of WTO treaty text (i.e. Mexico's Reference Paper commitments).

The panel in *Mexico – Telecoms* confronted the question whether *basadas en costos* was best understood in English as 'cost-oriented', as

[12] *Mexico – Telecoms* at pp. 236–238 (reprinting Mexico's Reference Paper additional commitments).

[13] *Japan – Measures Affecting Consumer Photographic Film and Paper*, Panel Report, WT/DS44/R, adopted 22 April 1998, DSR 1998:IV, 1179.

[14] *Ibid.* at pp. 527 *et seq.*

the phrase in English read, or as 'cost-based', which would be a more literal translation from the English and might have suggested (helping the United States and hurting Mexico) a closer relationship between rates and costs. The discrepancy was pointed out to the Panel – ironically, by Japan.

> With respect to the term `cost-oriented', we note that Japan, a third party to these proceedings, drew the Panel's attention to a discrepancy between the original Spanish term `*basadas en costos*' and its translation into English `cost-oriented'. It was said that the correct translation of `*basadas en costos*' should have been `based on costs' and that there was a difference in the meaning between those two terms. Although the Panel agreed with this second translation as being the closer to the original Spanish, both parties indicated to the Panel that they did not see any substantive difference in meaning between `*basadas en costos*' and `cost-oriented'. Therefore, in the absence of disagreement between the parties on this point, the Panel considers that `*basadas en costos*' and `cost-oriented' are interchangeable.[15]

In the end, the Panel dealt with the translation questions without difficulty, quoting long passages of the original Spanish text whenever it was necessary to clarify points in the English version of the report.

3. Extraterritorial application

One of the most vexing aspects of the case was the interpretation of the scope of the sub-sectors subject to Mexico's commitments. In its schedule, Mexico had stated in the left-hand column that the commitments covered 'telecommunications services supplied by a facilities-based public telecommunications network'. Mexico made commitments in mode 1 as well as mode 3, which on its face, seemed to suggest that the right to market access in Mexico depended on whether the service supplier in the United States (for example) owned its own lines or instead leased them from another supplier.

The lawyers involved in developing the claims in the dispute were greatly troubled by this reading. What would be the regulatory interest of Mexico in limiting services delivered into the territory of Mexico based on the nature of the business model of the service provider in the territory of another Member? We were concerned that a panel would

[15] *Mexico – Telecoms*, at para. 7.167.

not accept an extraterritorial reading of Mexico's schedule, and we sought another, more plausible explanation.

Ironically, Mexico did not claim before the Panel that the schedule should be read to have extraterritorial application. Instead, it said that the introductory heading in the sectoral column had little or no effect.[16]

The Panel resolved the issue differently from what was argued by either of the parties. In effect, the Panel accepted an 'extraterritorial' interpretation of this aspect of Mexico's schedule, reading the term 'facilities-based' literally to provide that 'Mexico has undertaken commitments for the services at issue supplied only on a facilities basis' on either side of the Mexican border.[17] However, the Panel softened this interpretation somewhat, finding separately that Mexico had written an exception to the facilities-based rule into its schedule – through the sub-sector heading for *comercializadoras* – for services supplied through leased capacity.[18]

4. Modes of supply

It was surprisingly difficult to apply the modes of supply, as set forth in Article I of the GATS, to the patterns of service presented in the dispute. Even though the delivery of services by means of telecommunications is the most common example of cross-border service used by the WTO,[19] it was not easy to fit telecommunications services themselves into the boxes provided by the GATS.

Mode 3 is defined by GATS Article I as delivery 'by a service supplier of one Member, through commercial presence in the territory of any other Member'. One of the first questions that the legal team confronted was whether a leased line would fit the definition of mode 3.

Assume a service provider of one Member wished to provide long distance voice telephony services in the territory of another Member via international simple resale (ISR) by leasing a line from an existing facility and reselling capacity to commercial customers. At the outset, it did not appear that this means of supply would fit into mode 1, as there was no service moving from the territory of one Member into the territory of another Member.

[16] *Mexico – Telecoms*, at para. 7.53.
[17] *Mexico – Telecoms*, at para. 7.71.
[18] *Mexico – Telecoms*, at para. 7.72.
[19] *Mexico – Telecoms*, at para. 7.43.

But was it mode 3? The definition of 'commercial presence' set forth in GATS Article XXVIII defined the term to mean:

> any type of business or professional establishment, including through
> (i) the constitution, acquisition or maintenance of a juridical person, or
> (ii) the creation or maintenance of a branch or a representative office,
> within the territory of a Member for the purpose of supplying a service.

Here again, assume that the service supplier of one Member had no branch or subsidiary in the territory of the other Member – just the lease agreement. Did this constitute a 'business or professional establishment'? We were concerned that a Panel might find that it did not. The GATS does not define the term 'services'. GATS Article I:1 defines the scope of the GATS in terms of 'measures by Members affecting trade in services', and defines 'trade in services' in Article I:2 solely in terms of the four modes of supply. Thus, if ISR fell outside the scope of the four modes of supply, then it appeared that measures restricting ISR would not be covered by any GATS disciplines – not even the most-favoured-nation treatment obligation.

In the end, the practical significance in this particular situation was not as great as had been feared. It seemed likely that a service supplier of another Member that had secured a lease would establish a subsidiary or joint venture or some type of commercial entity in the territory of the other Member to send invoices and receive payments from customers.

Exactly what constitutes the cross-border provision of telecommunications services was not nearly as clear, however. Recall that mode 1 requires a service from the territory of one Member into the territory of another Member. The traditional legal arrangement in international long distance telephony carried through a cable is that the service supplier of one Member carries the signal to the border, and the service supplier on the other side carries the signal from the border to the next relevant switch. In those circumstances, did the service supplier of one Member provide a service up to but not into the territory of another Member? The implications for those of us developing the claims seemed huge – if there were no mode 1 service provided, then there might be no basis for a claim under Section 2 of the Reference Paper, since for that provision to apply, Mexico had to have made a market access commitment in the first place.

Thankfully, the Panel thought through the question more clearly than we did, even if the answer proved to be no easier to support. The Panel decided that international long distance voice telephony is delivered via mode 1. The Panel relied, at least in part, on its interpretation of the CPC code inscribed in Mexico's schedule, which the Panel said envisioned a 'high degree of interaction between … networks' to deliver a 'seamless' service. In essence, then, the Panel read out of the schedule the relevance of the 'hand off' at the border.[20] The Panel also found comfort in a statement in a GATT Secretariat document prepared as an 'Explanatory Note' for the Group of Negotiations on Services in the Uruguay Round. In that document, the Secretariat had stated that the supply of a service through telecommunications is an example of cross-border supply 'since the service supplier is not present within the territory of the Member where the service is delivered'.[21] In the end, however, it is not clear that this support was critical to its interpretation – as the Panel said, it simply found 'absurd' the notion that international telecommunications would fall completely outside the scope of the GATS.[22]

The most lasting insight from this section of the Panel report is found in the statement that

> a supplier of services under the GATS is no less a supplier solely because elements of the service are subcontracted to another firm, or are carried out with assets owned by another firm. *What counts is the services that the supplier offers and has agreed to supply to a customer.*[23]

In other words, whatever the commercial arrangements made by the supplier to facilitate supply of a service, what matters is the supplier's commitment to its customer to deliver that service. As the panel noted, the customer pays a single service supplier to connect a call 'end-to-end', and does not care whether that supplier subcontracts with others to complete the call from the point of origination to the point of termination.[24]

5. Zero quotas

The Panel addressed for the first time in any WTO dispute the meaning of 'limitations' as used in GATS Article XVI:2(a) and, in particular, whether a prohibition on the provision of services that is not stated in

[20] *Mexico – Telecoms*, at para. 7.39. [21] *Mexico – Telecoms*, at para. 7.43.
[22] *Mexico – Telecoms*, at para. 7.41. [23] *Mexico – Telecoms*, at para. 7.42. [24] *Ibid.*

quantitative terms qualifies effectively as a 'limitation on the number of service suppliers', or a 'zero quota'.[25]

At the outset, the need to rely on a 'zero quota' theory was one of the most daunting aspects of the case. Lawyers involved in developing the claims were not at all enthusiastic about the prospects that a WTO Panel would interpret GATS Article XVI:2(a) in a manner that would cover such a restriction. First, Mexico's routing restriction[26] was not set in quantitative terms. Second, the routing restriction prohibited some, but not all services described in that portion of the schedule.

The Panel did not appear to be troubled by these concerns, finding that the routing restriction in Mexico's schedule prohibited end-to-end international simple resale, and thus, that it was a zero quota that is required to be scheduled under GATS Article XVI:2(a).[27]

The 'zero quota' question was raised again in the *US – Gambling* dispute, where the panel and the Appellate Body focused not on language of the schedule, but rather on the wording in the US measures themselves. The Appellate Body in *US – Gambling* accepted the notion of a zero quota and clarified that GATS Article XVI:2(a) is concerned not with the form of a measure, but with its numerical, or quantitative, nature.[28] The Appellate Body quoted approvingly the following passage from the panel report: 'If a Member wants to maintain a full prohibition, it is assumed that such a Member would not have scheduled such a sector or subsector and, therefore, would not need to schedule any limitation or measures pursuant to Article XVI:2.'[29]

It is telling that neither the Panel nor the Appellate Body in *US – Gambling* referred to *Mexico – Telecoms*, in which the Panel appeared to have no difficulty accepting the notion that a Member might schedule a full prohibition in its schedule.

[25] *Mexico – Telecoms*, at para. 7.85.

[26] *Ibid.*, at para. 7.84 ('the phrase "through the facilities of", placed in the context of the categories of the Chairman's Note, refers not to a requirement simply to use the equipment or physical assets of a Mexican concessionaire, but to supply the service on a facilities-basis, and not through capacity leased to the cross-border supplier'.)

[27] *Ibid.*, at para. 7.85.

[28] *US – Gambling*, United States – Measures Affecting the Cross-Border Supply of Gambling and Betting Services, Appellate Body Report, WT/DS285/AB/R, adopted 20 April 2005, at para. 232.

[29] Appellate Body Report in *US – Gambling* at para. 234, quoting *US – Gambling*, Panel Report, WT/DS285/R, adopted 20 April 2005, at para. 6.331.

6. Additional commitments

Finally, the Panel in *Mexico – Telecoms* had the first experience adjudicating additional commitments of Members made pursuant to GATS Article XVIII. The Panel rejected the argument of the United States that a limitation inscribed in either the market access or the national treatment column cannot limit the applicability of an additional commitment under Article XVIII.[30] In the Panel's view, the text of the additional commitments was dispositive, and the Reference Paper provision was linked directly to what the schedule said about a particular sub-sector and mode of supply.[31]

The Panel also had no difficulty interpreting the terms of the Reference Paper as obligations taken on by Mexico, notwithstanding that the *chapeau* of the Reference Paper provides that '[t]he following are principles and definitions on the regulatory framework for the basic telecommunications services'. Section 2 of the Reference Paper utilises 'will' rather than 'shall', the term that the WTO Agreement normally uses to denote an obligation. Yet the Panel referred throughout to the 'interconnection obligation'.[32] The interpretation as a binding obligation is fully consistent with Mexico's characterisation in the additional commitments column of its schedule: 'Mexico undertakes the obligations contained in the Reference Paper attached hereto.'

7. Conclusion

The *Mexico – Telecoms* dispute demonstrates the power and broad scope of WTO disciplines on the regulation of trade in services. It shows that the WTO dispute settlement system can successfully address highly technical aspects of services trade, just as it has done so in the context of food safety and patent rights. Although GATS negotiators have not yet employed a 'Reference Paper' for any other service sector, the *Mexico – Telecom* panel's interpretation of Mexico's additional commitments might be helpful in future cases involving additional commitments, such as those in China's schedule of specific commitments on services.

30 *Mexico – Telecoms*, at para. 7.94.

31 *Ibid.* ('It would seem reasonable to conclude, therefore, that the right to interconnect accorded by Section 2.2 should apply where, *with respect to a particular subsector and mode of supply*, a Member's market access and national treatment commitments specifically accords the right to supply that service.')

32 *Ibid.*

Bibliography

Shoyer, A., 'Panel Selection in WTO Dispute Settlement Proceedings', *Journal of International Economic Law* 6 (2003), 203.

Sidak J. G. and H. Singer, 'Überregulation without Economics: The World Trade Organization's Decision in the US–Mexico Arbitration on Telecommunications Services', *Federal Communications Law Journal* 57 (2004), 1, reprinted at www.law.indiana.edu/fclj/pubs/v57no1.html.

US Federal Communications Commission, 2004 International Telecommunications Data (March 2006), reprinted at www.fcc.gov/ib/sand/mniab/traffic/files/CREPOR04.pdf.

11

From *Periodicals* to *Gambling*: A review of systemic issues addressed by WTO adjudicatory bodies under the GATS

ERIC H. LEROUX*

1. Introduction

The General Agreement on Trade in Services (GATS) broke new ground when it entered into force on 1 January 1995 as part of the Marrakesh Agreement Establishing the World Trade Organization (WTO Agreement). It put in place a set of disciplines that now regulates trade in services among close to 150 countries. GATS negotiators faced a significant challenge when having to craft a comprehensive set of disciplines in this area. Trade in services is complex, in particular due to the various forms of delivery that are involved and the extensive nature of regulation in many sectors, for instance, financial services and professional services. Disciplines also often had to be developed anew.

The result is somewhat complex. Some obligations, in particular the most-favoured-nation treatment (MFN) obligation, apply to any measure affecting trade in services.[1] Others, like the market access and national treatment obligations, apply only in respect of service sectors or sub-sectors (hereinafter 'sectors') of a Member's choosing. There is overlap between the market access and national treatment obligations,[2] and the relationship between these two disciplines and those on domestic regulation is not clearly established.[3] Additional obligations have been

* The views expressed in this paper do not necessarily reflect those of the Government of Canada and may not be attributed to it. The author thanks, without implicating, Pierre Sauvé, Rodney Neufeld, Valerie Hughes, Don McRae, Martin Roy, Mireille Cossy, Nicole Pohl and Marion Panizzon for comments on a previous draft of this chapter.

[1] Subject only to limited exemptions listed in the Annex on Article II Exemptions. GATS Article II.

[2] This is reflected in Article XX:2.

[3] That is, the relation between Articles XVI and XVII, on the one hand, and Article VI:4 and 5, on the other.

adhered to on a voluntary basis, in particular those contained in the Reference Paper on basic telecommunications services and the Understanding on Commitments in Financial Services. In general, the interpretation and understanding of Members' Schedules of Specific Commitments ('Schedules') proves to be a laborious exercise.

This provides fertile ground for difficult and often sensitive interpretive issues to arise. However, Members have thus far not made extensive use of dispute settlement procedures to resolve them. There have been only five cases that touched upon the GATS. Only two of them were exclusively related to trade in services – *Mexico – Telecoms*[4] and *US – Gambling*.[5] While still limited, the case law has nevertheless shown the reach of GATS disciplines and their potential impact on Members' policies and regulations. A measure primarily relating to trade in goods can be reviewed under, and found inconsistent with, the GATS. Competition-type disciplines related to the behaviour of a private actor have contributed to forcing a Member to open up its market on telecommunications services. A Member's measures prohibiting the remote supply of gambling services have been scrutinised and found inconsistent with that Member's market access commitments. That last case – *US – Gambling* – has, in particular, contributed to bringing the GATS to the fore. It has sparked a debate as to what should be the right balance between trade constraints, on the one hand, and the autonomy of Members' service regulators, on the other.

This chapter reviews the GATS case law with a view to offering a critical assessment of the main systemic issues that have been addressed by WTO adjudicatory bodies. Those issues that are common to all service sectors and are addressed successively in this chapter concern: (i) the scope of application of the GATS, (ii) the interpretation of specific commitments in Members' Schedules, (iii) market access and (iv) the general exceptions.

2. Broad scope of application and overlap with the GATT

The scope of the GATS is defined in its first Article, which provides that the GATS 'applies to measures by Members affecting trade in services'.[6]

[4] *Mexico – Telecoms*, Mexico – Measures Affecting Telecommunications Services, Panel Report, WT/DS204/R, 2 April 2004. The decision of the Panel was not appealed before the Appellate Body. As a result, the law as decided by the Panel cannot be said to have 'crystallised' yet.

[5] *US – Gambling*, United States – Measures Affecting the Cross-Border Supply of Gambling and Betting Services, Appellate Body Report, WT/DS285/AB/R, 7 April 2005; Panel Report, WT/DS285/R, 10 November 2004.

[6] GATS Article I:1.

The measures of all levels of governments are covered, as well as those of non-governmental bodies taken in the exercise of powers delegated to them by such governments.[7] 'Trade in services' refers to four modes of supply of services, that is: (i) from the territory of one Member into the territory of another Member (cross-border trade); (ii) in the territory of one Member to the service consumer of another Member (consumption abroad); (iii) by the service supplier of one Member through commercial presence in the territory of another Member (commercial presence); (iv) by the service supplier of one Member through presence of natural persons of that Member in the territory of another Member (movement of natural persons).[8] All services fall within the scope of the GATS, with the exception of services supplied in the exercise of governmental authority[9] and certain air transport services.[10]

The first issue relating to the application of the GATS arose in the context of the *Canada – Periodicals* case. Canada argued in that case that a tax equal to 80 per cent of the value of all the advertisements contained

7 GATS Article I:3(a). 'Measure' is broadly defined. It means any measure by a Member, whether in the form of a law, regulation, rule, procedure, decision, administrative action, or any other form. GATS Article XXVIII(a).

8 GATS Article I:2.

9 A service supplied in the exercise of governmental authority means any service which is supplied neither on a commercial basis, nor in competition with one or more service suppliers. This concept has yet to be interpreted by WTO adjudicatory bodies. For a discussion on the meaning to be ascribed to that concept, see: E. H. Leroux, 'What Is a "Service Supplied in the Exercise of Governmental Authority" under Article I:3(b) and (c) of the GATS?'*Journal of World Trade* 3 (2006), 345–385; R. Adlung, *Public Services and the GATS*, World Trade Organization, Economic Research and Statistics Division, Working Paper ERSD-2005–03, July 2005.

10 Paragraphs 2 and 3 of the Annex on Air Transport Services specify that:

> 2. The [GATS], including its dispute settlement procedures, shall not apply to measures affecting:
>   (a) traffic rights, however granted; or
>   (b) services directly related to the exercise of traffic rights, except as provided in paragraph 3 of this Annex.
> 3. The [GATS] shall apply to measures affecting:
>   (a) aircraft repair and maintenance services;
>   (b) the selling and marketing of air transport services;
>   (c) computer reservation system (CRS) services.

Further to the Convention on International Civil Aviation of 1944, which recognises States' sovereignty over their air space, traffic rights are governed under bilateral agreements negotiated on the basis of reciprocity. That system has essentially been left out of the GATS. See E. H. Leroux, 'L'Accord général sur les services (AGCS): règles propres à des secteurs particuliers', *Cahiers de Droit* 43 (2002), p. 379, at 419–424.

in so-called split-run periodicals[11] was a measure affecting trade in services and thus only subject to the disciplines of the GATS. In other words, Canada argued that the measure could only be reviewed under the national treatment obligation of the GATS (not under Article III of the GATT) in respect of which no commitments on advertising services were undertaken. Both the Panel and the Appellate Body rejected Canada's argument, determining that the obligations of both agreements are cumulative and coexist, rather than that the obligations of one agreement (GATS) override those of the other (GATT).[12] This put in place the seeds for a later determination that the GATT and the GATS are not mutually exclusive and may overlap. That determination was made in *EC – Bananas* and later affirmed in *Canada – Autos*.

The *EC – Bananas* case concerned the European Community's banana import licencing regime, that is, measures dealing with the importation, sale and distribution of bananas. The Panel, and then the Appellate Body, gave a very broad scope to the GATS, relying in particular on the use of the term 'affecting' in Article I:1. The Appellate Body stated as follows:

> In our view, the use of the term 'affecting' reflects the intent of the drafters to give a broad reach to the GATS. The ordinary meaning of the word 'affecting' implies a measure that has 'an effect on', which indicates a broad scope of application. This interpretation is further reinforced by the conclusions of previous panels that the term 'affecting' in the context of Article III of the GATT is wider in scope than such terms as 'regulating' or 'governing'. We also note that Article I:3(b) of the GATS provides that '"services" includes *any service* in *any sector* except services supplied in the exercise of governmental authority', and that Article XXVIII(b) of the GATS provides that the '"supply of a service" includes the production, distribution, marketing, sale and delivery of a service'. There is nothing at all in these provisions to suggest a limited scope of application of the GATS. We also agree that Article XXVIII(c) of the GATS does not narrow 'the meaning of the term 'affecting' to 'in respect of'.[13] (italics in text; underline added; footnote omitted)

[11] Split-run periodicals are Canadian issues of foreign periodicals that contain the same editorial content as that appearing in the foreign issues, but advertisements directed to the Canadian market (different advertisements from those appearing in the foreign issues).

[12] *Canada – Periodicals*, Canada – Certain Measures Concerning Periodicals, Appellate Body Report, WT/DS31/AB/R, 30 June 1997, pp. 18–22.

[13] *EC – Bananas*, European Communities – Regime for the Importation, Sale and Distribution of Bananas, Appellate Body Report, WT/DS27/AB/R, 9 September 1997, para. 220.

The Appellate Body agreed with the Panel that no measure is a priori excluded from the scope of the GATS.

Further to its determination in *Canada – Periodicals*, the Appellate Body also specified that the GATT and the GATS can overlap, depending on the nature of the measures at issue. It clarified as follows, identifying two situations when a measure can be reviewed under the GATS:

> Certain measures could be found to fall exclusively within the scope of the GATT 1994, when they affect trade in goods as goods. Certain measures could be found to fall exclusively within the scope of the GATS, when they affect the supply of services as services. There is yet a third category of measures that could be found to fall within the scope of both the GATT 1994 and the GATS. These are measures that involve a service relating to a particular good or a service supplied in conjunction with a particular good. In all such cases in this third category, the measure in question could be scrutinized under both the GATT 1994 and the GATS. However, while the same measure could be scrutinized under both agreements, the specific aspects of that measure examined under each agreement could be different. Under the GATT 1994, the focus is on how the measure affects the goods involved. Under the GATS, the focus is on how the measure affects the supply of the service or the service suppliers involved. Whether a certain measure affecting the supply of a service related to a particular good is scrutinized under the GATT 1994 or the GATS, or both, is a matter that can only be determined on a case-by-case basis.[14]

Unlike what the negotiators of the GATS may have expected, the same measure can thus be reviewed under both the GATT and the GATS, although separate aspects of the same measure will be scrutinised under each agreement.[15] In *EC – Bananas*, that meant that the European Communities' banana import licencing regime could be reviewed not only under the GATT, but also under the GATS. The same operators (enterprises) that bought and imported bananas were also engaged in other activities involving the wholesale distribution of bananas. While the

[14] *EC – Bananas*, Appellate Body Report, para. 221.

[15] The goods and services Uruguay Round negotiators may not have foreseen the possibility of overlap between the GATT and the GATS. Otherwise, one would think that a provision dealing with potential conflicts would have been included, as it was for conflicts between the *WTO Agreement* and the Multilateral Trade Agreements. See *WTO Agreement*, Article XVI:3. The absence, in the GATS, of a general exception similar to that in Article XX(g) of the GATT concerning the conservation of natural resources also suggests that GATS negotiators did not expect or intend overlap between goods and services disciplines.

measures of the European Communities related primarily to the goods activities of the operators, they also affected the latter in their capacity as service suppliers, thereby justifying the application of the GATS.[16]

These principles were reaffirmed in *Canada – Autos*, a dispute concerning Canada's measures on the duty free importation of vehicles. Both the Panel and the Appellate Body reiterated the broad scope of the GATS as determined in *EC – Bananas*. Fortunately, however, the Appellate Body reversed and corrected the Panel's finding on the application of the GATS because it was based on an assumption that the import duty exemption enjoyed by certain manufacturers in Canada also affected wholesale trade services of motor vehicles. Rather than basing its finding on evidence relating to the provision of wholesale trade services of motor vehicles within the Canadian market, including who supplied those services and how they were supplied, the Panel relied on the assumption that the import duty exemption granted only to some manufacturers bore upon the conditions of competition in the supply of distribution services. In effect, the Panel determined that the import duty exemption constituted a measure affecting trade in services within the meaning of Article I:1 of the GATS by looking at whether the measure was consistent with the Agreement's substantive obligations on MFN and national treatment.[17] Such reasoning proved circular.

The Appellate Body recalled that the structure and logic of the GATS requires that for its substantive obligations to apply, a complainant must first demonstrate that a particular measure 'affects trade in services' within the meaning of Article I:1.[18] In other words, a demonstration must be made that a particular measure affects the supply of a service under one of the four modes of supply described in Article I:2 – cross-border trade, consumption abroad, commercial presence and movement of natural persons. A determination that the GATS applies cannot be based on mere assumptions, but rather on an examination of relevant facts, including who supplies the service at issue and how that service is supplied.[19] This should not require the existence of trade flows, as they may be prevented by the challenged measure, such as in the case, for instance, of a ban.

[16] *EC – Bananas*, Appellate Body Report, paras. 223–228.

[17] *Canada – Autos*, Panel Report, WT/DS139/R, WT/DS142/R, 11 February 2000, para. 10.234.

[18] *Canada – Autos*, Appellate Body Report, WT/DS139/AB/R, WT/DS142/AB/R, 31 May 2000, para. 151.

[19] *Canada – Autos*, Appellate Body Report, paras. 155–167.

It is worth noting, in this regard, that the Panel in *US – Gambling* initiated its analysis with a determination of whether the United States included specific commitments on gambling services in its Schedule.[20] One can understand the practical reasons for doing so: in the absence of specific commitments, Antigua and Barbuda's ('Antigua') claims must fail.[21] From a legal standpoint, however, and notably for due process reasons and ensuring that a complainant's initial burden of proof regarding the application of the GATS is not circumvented, it would appear better for adjudicatory bodies to always conduct their analysis in accordance with the sequencing indicated by the Appellate Body in *Canada – Autos*.[22] Otherwise, there may exist, in some cases, the risk that an initial determination of the existence of specific commitments will have the inadvertent effect of relieving the complainant, in whole or in part, from its (separate) duty to clearly demonstrate that specific and identified measures taken by the respondent 'affect' the supply of services by suppliers of the complainant.

3. Interpretation of specific commitments in a Member's Schedule

3.1 Interpretation in accordance with the rules of the Vienna Convention, and identification of the common intention of WTO Members

Pursuant to Article XX:3 of the GATS, the Schedule of a Member forms an integral part of the GATS. Hence, the rules of interpretation that apply with respect to a Schedule are the same as those applicable to the rest of the Agreement. This means that the Schedule of a Member, and the specific commitments contained therein, must be interpreted in accordance with Articles 31 and 32 of the Vienna Convention on the Law of

[20] *US – Gambling*, Panel Report, sections VI(A) and (B). In *US – Gambling*, Antigua brought a claim against the United States alleging that its restrictions on cross-border gambling services violated its obligations under the GATS. More specifically, Antigua argued that the United States was in violation of: (i) its market access and national treatment commitments under Articles XVI and XVII, (ii) its transparency and due process obligations and its obligation to administer its domestic service regulations in an objective manner under Articles VI:1 and VI:3, and (iii) its obligation to avoid restrictions on international transfers and payments under Article XI:1. The Panel and the Appellate Body only made findings in respect of the claim of breach of Article XVI.

[21] This is explained by the Panel, at paras. 6.4–6.7 of its report.

[22] This point is made for systemic reasons, not to suggest that in *US – Gambling* the Panel did not carry out its mandate under Article I:1 of the GATS.

Treaties (Vienna Convention).[23] This position was firmly adopted in *US – Gambling*[24] and followed in the footsteps of prior decisions concerning the interpretation of GATT Schedules.[25] Accordingly, the specific commitments of a Member, like any other treaty term, must be interpreted in good faith, in accordance with the ordinary meaning of the Member's scheduled entries taken in their context and understood in the light of the object and purpose of the GATS and the WTO Agreement more generally.[26] Recourse may also be had to supplementary means of interpretation as appropriate.[27]

Also following in the footsteps of GATT case law is the determination in *US – Gambling* that while a Member's Schedule only binds that Member, it represents a common agreement among all WTO Members. Hence, the task of ascertaining the meaning of a commitment in a Schedule involves identifying the common intention of Members.[28] The Appellate Body had previously decided along those lines in *EC – Computer Equipment*, where the interpretation of tariff concessions under the GATT was at issue.[29] This is a reflection of the fact that specific commitments contained in a Member's GATS Schedule are, like tariff commitments, reciprocal and result from a mutually advantageous negotiation between importing and exporting Members.[30]

In the end, this simply emphasises the fact – obvious some might say – that the interpreter must stay away from subjective and unilateral interpretation of the terms of a Member's Schedule. The interpreter must focus on finding an objective meaning that can best be said to represent the common intention of both *demandeurs* and *offreurs*, that is, the deal struck at the negotiating table. In the GATT context, this was further reflected in *EC – Chicken Cuts*, where the Appellate Body, agreeing with the Panel and referring to *EC – Computer Equipment*, emphasised that

[23] Vienna Convention on the Law of Treaties of 23 May 1969, 1155 U.N.T.S. 331; 8 ILM 679.

[24] *US – Gambling*, Appellate Body Report, para. 160.

[25] See *EC – Computer Equipment*, European Communities – Customs Classification of Certain Computer Equipment, Appellate Body Report, WT/DS62/AB/R, WT/DS67/AB/R, WT/DS68/AB/R, 5 June 1998, para. 84.

[26] Vienna Convention, Article 31.

[27] Vienna Convention, Article 32.

[28] *US – Gambling*, Appellate Body Report, para. 159.

[29] *EC – Computer Equipment*, para. 109.

[30] See Preamble of the GATS, third paragraph. See also GATS Article XIX:1, which provides that the process of negotiating further liberalisation shall take place with a view to promoting the interests of all participants on a mutually advantageous basis and to securing an overall balance of rights and obligations.

one Member's unilateral object and purpose for the conclusion of a tariff commitment cannot form the sole basis for an interpretation of that commitment.[31]

The *EC – Chicken Cuts* decision also contains additional developments and clarifications that could prove beneficial in the context of the interpretation of GATS Schedules. More specifically, the Appellate Body clarified that interpretation pursuant to the rules of the Vienna Convention is ultimately a holistic exercise that should not be mechanically subdivided into rigid components.[32] In order to ascertain the meaning of tariff commitments under the GATT, recourse was broadly had to a range of interpretive elements, including context, the object and purpose of the treaty, the subsequent practice of Members and supplementary means of interpretation. The latter category was given a broad scope in that one can look at any circumstance connected to the conclusion of a treaty and the taking of a particular commitment that may help in ascertaining the common intention of Members. The relevance and weight to be ascribed to any particular element depends on such factors as objectivity, timing, the type of events, acts or instruments at issue and their source or origin.[33]

In the context of the GATS, this could prove beneficial, especially when interpreting market access and national treatment reservations that are more often than not drafted very succinctly and in a way that does not truly reflect the legal regime and domestic measures that underpin them and that are meant to be protected. In order to ascertain the true and accurate meaning of many reservations, and therefore avoid serious interpretive mistakes, one will often need to refer to and consider the whole range of (objective) circumstances connected to them, including the relevant domestic legal regime at the time the reservations were taken.

3.2 Relevance and interpretive value of the W/120, the Scheduling Guidelines and the scheduling practice of other Members

The Service Sectoral Classification List[34] – the so-called 'W/120' – was prepared by the then GATT Secretariat at the request of Uruguay Round

[31] *EC – Chicken Cuts*, European Communities – Customs Classification of Frozen Boneless Chicken Cuts, Appellate Body Report, WT/DS269/AB/R, WT/DS286/AB/R, 12 September 2005, para. 239.

[32] *EC – Chicken Cuts*, para. 176. [33] *EC – Chicken Cuts*, paras. 277–309.

[34] Uruguay Round, Group of Negotiations on Services, *Services Sectoral Classification List*, MTN.GNS/W/120, 10 July 1991.

participants. In particular, the Montreal Ministerial Declaration called for the preparation of such a list by the Secretariat.[35] The revised version of the W/120, dated 10 July 1991, which is the version that was, and still is, used by Members, is based on comments from Uruguay Round participants.[36] In elaborating upon how Members may suspend concessions with respect to service sectors, the DSU relies on the W/120 to define these sectors.[37]

The 1993 Scheduling Guidelines, also prepared by the then GATT Secretariat at the request of Uruguay Round participants, called for the general use of the W/120 in order to achieve the greatest possible degree of clarity in the description of each sector scheduled.[38] They state, in relevant part:

> The legal nature of a schedule as well as the need to evaluate commitments, require the greatest possible degree of clarity in the description of each sector or sub-sector scheduled. In general the classification of sectors and sub-sectors should be based on the Secretariat's revised Services Sectoral Classification List. Each sector contained in the Secretariat list is identified by the corresponding Central Product Classification (CPC) number. Where it is necessary to refine further a sectoral classification, this should be done on the basis of the CPC or other internationally recognised classification (e.g. Financial Services Annex). The most recent breakdown of the CPC, including explanatory notes for each sub-sector, is contained in the UN Provisional Central Product Classification.
>
>> Example: A Member wishes to indicate an offer or commitment in the sub-sector of map-making services. In the Secretariat list, this service would fall under the general heading 'Other Business Services' under 'Related scientific and technical consulting services' (see item l.F.m). By consulting the CPC, map-making can be found under the corresponding CPC classification number 86754. In its offer/schedule, the Member would then enter the sub-sector under the 'Other Business Services' section of its schedule as follows:
>
> Map-making services (86754)
>
> If a Member wishes to use its own sub-sectoral classification or definitions it should provide concordance with the CPC in the manner indicated in the above example. If this is not possible, it should give a sufficiently

35 MTN.TCN/7 (MIN), 9 December 1988, Part II, para. 10. See also Note by the Secretariat: Reference List of Sectors, MTN.GNS/W/50, 13 April 1989.

36 See cover Note by the Secretariat on the W/120.

37 DSU Article 22(3)(f)(ii).

38 Scheduling of Initial Commitments in Trade in Services: Explanatory Note, MTN.GNS/W/164, 3 September 1993 ('1993 Scheduling Guidelines').

> detailed definition to avoid any ambiguity as to the scope of the commitment.[39] (footnotes omitted)

There is no question that the 1993 Scheduling Guidelines are not an authoritative legal interpretation of the GATS. Indeed, they specifically state that they are not. There is also no question that, in accordance with their stated purpose, they assisted all Members in the preparation of their Schedules and the listing of their specific commitments.[40] For instance, the GATS does not prescribe any particular format for the Schedules of Members, apart from what is specified in Article XX. The 1993 Scheduling Guidelines provided a standard format for the Schedules of Members, which was used and followed by all Members. Following consultations, a revised version of the 1993 Scheduling Guidelines was adopted by the Council for Trade in Services on 23 March 2001 for the purpose of the current round of negotiations.[41]

In *US – Gambling*, the Appellate Body determined that both the W/120 and the 1993 Scheduling Guidelines constitute supplementary means of interpretation within the meaning of Article 32 of the Vienna Convention. This means that they can be referred to in order to confirm the meaning of specific commitments resulting from the application of Article 31, or to determine the meaning of such commitments when the interpretation according to Article 31 leaves the meaning ambiguous or obscure (as was found to be the case in *US – Gambling*) or leads to a result which is manifestly absurd or unreasonable.[42] This was a reversal of the

[39] 1993 Scheduling Guidelines, para. 16.

[40] 1993 Scheduling Guidelines, para. 1. This paragraph reads as follows:

> This note is intended to assist in the preparation of offers, requests and national schedules of initial commitments. Its objective is to explain, in a concise manner, how commitments should be set out in schedules in order to achieve precision and clarity. It is based on the view that a common format for schedules as well as standardisation of the terms used in schedules are necessary to ensure comparable and unambiguous commitments. The note cannot answer every question that might occur to persons responsible for scheduling commitments; it does attempt to answer those questions which are most likely to arise. The answers should not be considered as an authoritative legal interpretation of the GATS.

[41] Guidelines for the Scheduling of Specific Commitments under the General Agreement on Trade in Services (GATS), adopted by the Council for Trade in Services on 23 March 2001, S/L/92 ('2001 Scheduling Guidelines').

[42] As indicated above, in the more recent *EC – Chicken Cuts* decision the Appellate Body gave a broad interpretation to the concept of 'supplementary means of interpretation' and expressed the view that adjudicatory bodies have wide flexibility to have recourse to them.

Panel's determination that both instruments qualify as 'context' under Article 31(2) of the Vienna Convention, that is, they constitute an agreement made between all the parties or an instrument made between some parties and accepted by the others as such.[43] In the previous *Mexico – Telecoms* decision, the Panel had been inclined to consider the 1993 Scheduling Guidelines as supplementary means of interpretation, although the possibility that they could qualify as 'context' was not ruled out.[44]

One could take issue with the Appellate Body's conclusion in *US – Gambling* that the W/120 does not qualify as 'context' within the meaning of Article 31(2) of the Vienna Convention, based, in particular, on the fact that the reference to it in the DSU (for the purpose of the suspension of concessions)[45] evidences formal and official acceptance of that instrument as being 'related to' the WTO Agreement, including the GATS. It is worth recalling Article 31(2) of the Vienna Convention:

> The context for the purpose of the interpretation of a treaty shall comprise, in addition to the text, including its preamble and annexes:
> (a) any agreement relating to the treaty which was made between all the parties in connection with the conclusion of the treaty;
> (b) any instrument which was made by one or more parties in connection with the conclusion of the treaty and accepted by the other parties as an instrument related to the treaty.

Having accepted that authorship by a delegated body (the GATT Secretariat) does not necessarily preclude specific documents from

[43] See *US – Gambling*, Panel Report, para. 6.77.

[44] *Mexico – Telecoms*, paras. 7.43–7.44. The qualification of an instrument as 'context' rather than 'supplementary means of interpretation' gives that instrument a higher legal status for interpretive purposes. 'Context' must be taken into account pursuant to Article 31 of the Vienna Convention, whereas supplementary means of interpretation under Article 32 of the Vienna Convention only have to be used as needed and as appropriate. Such distinction will be of minimal practical significance where, as in the case of the W/120 and the Scheduling Guidelines, it will more often than not prove necessary to have recourse to those instruments to shed light on the meaning of commitments that would otherwise remain obscure.

[45] Article 22(3) of the DSU provides, in relevant part:

> 3. In considering what concessions or other obligations to suspend, the complaining party shall apply the following principles and procedures: …
> (f) for purposes of this paragraph, 'sector' means: …
> (ii) with respect to services, a principal sector as identified in the current 'Services Sectoral Classification List' which identifies such sectors;[14] [footnote 14: The list in document MTN.GNS/W/120 identifies 11 sectors.]

constituting at least an 'instrument' within the meaning of Article 31(2)(b),[46] it is not clear why the Appellate Body considered that the second leg of the test under that provision was not met, given that the reference to the W/120 in the DSU must necessarily reflect acceptance of the relationship between that document (instrument) and the WTO Agreement, including the GATS.[47] Unfortunately, this point is not specifically addressed by the Appellate Body when reversing the Panel's finding on the status of the W/120.[48]

The Appellate Body's conclusion is all the more surprising considering the later determination in *EC – Chicken Cuts* that the Harmonized System constitutes 'context' for the purpose of interpreting WTO agreements. Having emphasised that while the Harmonized System is not formally incorporated into the WTO Agreement, it is referred to in certain

[46] *US – Gambling*, Appellate Body Report, para. 175.

[47] In *United States – Section 110 (5) of the US Copyright Act*, Panel Report, WT/DS160/R, 15 June 2000, para. 6.45, the following remarks were made concerning the requirements for an 'agreement' or 'instrument' to exist within the meaning of Article 31(2) of the Vienna Convention:

> The International Law Commission explains in its commentary on the final set of draft articles on the law of treaties that this provision is based on the principle that a unilateral document cannot be regarded as forming part of the context unless not only was it made in connection with the conclusion of the treaty, but its relation to the treaty was accepted by the other parties. 'On the other hand, the fact that these two classes of documents are recognized in paragraph 2 as forming part of the 'context' does not mean that they are necessarily to be considered as an integral part of the treaty. Whether they are an actual part of the treaty depends on the intention of the parties in each case'. *It is essential that the agreement or instrument should be related to the treaty. It must be concerned with the substance of the treaty and clarify certain concepts in the treaty or limit its field of application. It must equally be drawn up on the occasion of the conclusion of the treaty. Any agreement or instrument fulfilling these criteria will form part of the 'context' of the treaty and will thus not be treated as part of the preparatory works but rather as an element in the general rule of interpretation.* (quotation marks in text; emphasis added; footnotes omitted)

[48] The Appellate Body later refers, at para. 181, to Article 22(3)(f)(ii) of the DSU, when 'looking beyond the GATS to other covered agreements'. While the DSU is a WTO agreement separate from the GATS, the provision at issue – Article 22(3)(f)(ii) – specifically relates to services and thus to the application and implementation of the GATS. Article XXIII mandates the use of the rules of the DSU for the settlement of disputes and the enforcement of rights and obligations under the GATS. In that context, it remains unclear why Article 22(3)(f)(ii) does not constitute evidence of WTO Members' acceptance that the W/120 is related to the GATS.

agreements and was used as a basis for the preparation of the Uruguay Round GATT Schedules, the Appellate Body concludes as follows:

> The above circumstances confirm that, prior to, during, as well as after the Uruguay Round negotiations, there was broad consensus among the GATT Contracting Parties to *use* the Harmonized System as the basis for their WTO Schedules, notably with respect to agricultural products. In our view, this consensus constitutes an 'agreement' between WTO Members 'relating to' the WTO Agreement that was 'made in connection with the conclusion of' that Agreement, within the meaning of Article 31 (2)(a) of the Vienna Convention. As such, this agreement is 'context' under Article 31(2)(a) for the purpose of interpreting the WTO agreements, of which the EC Schedule is an integral part. In this light, we consider that the Harmonized System is relevant for purposes of interpreting tariff commitments in the WTO Members' Schedules.[49] (emphasis in text; footnote omitted)

This corresponds to the criticism expressed by Ortino with respect to the Appellate Body's conclusion in *US – Gambling* that the W/120 and 1993 Scheduling Guidelines do not constitute 'context' under Article 31 (2) of the Vienna Convention. Ortino has argued that these two documents constitute evidence of an underlying consensus, that is, agreement, among Uruguay Round negotiators to use the W/120 and the corresponding CPC codes as a general benchmark or default model.[50] The W/120 and the corresponding CPC codes have essentially been to services what the Harmonized System has been to goods. Based on *EC – Chicken Cuts*, one would conclude that the W/120 and the corresponding CPC codes constitute 'context' for the purpose of interpreting Members'

[49] *EC – Chicken Cuts*, paras. 195–199.

[50] F. Ortino, 'Treaty Interpretation and the WTO Appellate Body Report in *US – Gambling*: A Critique', *JIEL* 1 (2006), p. 117, at 128–129. The author argues as follows:

> [I]t is not clear why the Appellate Body did not go beyond the mere formal features of W/120 and the 1993 Scheduling Guidelines and inquire whether the two documents constitute *evidence* of an underlying, albeit more limited in scope, consensus among parties that had emerged during the negotiations ... Thus, the underlying agreement may be said to have been to employ the CPC list (as translated into the GATS context by W/120) as a sort of 'default model'. If a Member wished to deviate from such a model it had to be clear about the meaning of its entries. (emphasis in text)

It may be noted that the Schedule of a Member cannot be understood without recourse to the 1993 Scheduling Guidelines used during the Uruguay Round. The format and structure of Schedules as well as terms such as 'None' and 'Unbound' are not addressed in the GATS itself.

specific commitments under the GATS. This is an issue that might need to be revisited in future cases.

In any event, it is clear from *Mexico – Telecoms* and *US – Gambling* that, given the often difficult task of interpreting a Member's GATS specific commitments, WTO adjudicatory bodies will have recourse to and will consider carefully the W/120 and the scheduling guidelines relevant to a specific round in order to shed additional interpretive light on the meaning of those commitments.[51] This is in accordance with a holistic approach to interpretation, referred to by the Appellate Body in the recent *EC – Chicken Cuts* decision.[52] As Sinclair put it:

> It is clear that no would-be interpreter of a treaty, whatever his doctrinal point of departure, will deliberately ignore any material which can usefully serve as a guide towards establishing the meaning of the text with which he is confronted.[53]

In *US – Gambling*, this led the Panel, and then the Appellate Body, to conclude that the United States has included specific commitments on gambling services in its Schedule. It was essentially determined that the W/120, including the CPC codes referred to in it, constitutes the general benchmark used by Uruguay Round participants to negotiate and schedule their commitments.

Any country was free to depart from that benchmark, provided this was clearly indicated and expressed. Most Members specifically refer to CPC codes, which means that they are bound by the CPC definitions. In other words, those CPC definitions form an integral part of the text of those Members' Schedules. The United States' Schedule follows the

[51] In *Mexico – Telecoms*, para. 7.43, the Panel accorded substantial interpretive value to the 1993 Scheduling Guidelines. It stated:

> [W]e find that the source, content, and use by negotiators of the Explanatory Note [1993 Scheduling Guidelines], together with its later adoption by Members as the Scheduling Guidelines [2001 Revised Scheduling Guidelines], provides an important element with which to interpret the provisions of the GATS.

[52] Ortino (2006), at pp. 117 *et seq.*, argues that the decision of the Appellate Body in *US – Gambling*, e.g. the finding that the W/120 does not constitute 'context' for interpretive purposes, shows that a holistic approach to interpretation has not been truly embraced by the Appellate Body. The *EC – Chicken Cuts* decision certainly reflects a significant move towards the adoption of such an approach, whereby the interpreter looks thoroughly at all the relevant elements under Section 3 of the Vienna Convention (Articles 31 – 33).

[53] I. Sinclair, *The Vienna Convention on the Law of Treaties*, Second Edition, (Manchester University Press, 1984), p. 116.

W/120, but does not explicitly refer to CPC codes. In the view of the Appellate Body, this does not mean that the CPC definitions are irrelevant. Rather, they can be referred to in the event that the text of the commitments, interpreted in context and in the light of the object and purpose of the GATS, leaves the meaning of such commitments ambiguous or unclear. This was found to be the case with the entry for 'Other Recreational Services (except sporting)', thereby justifying recourse to CPC codes (definitions) to shed additional light on the meaning of that entry (commitment).

It should be noted that the conclusion of the Panel and the Appellate Body with respect to the meaning of the United States' commitments is also based on a number of other interpretive elements that were considered relevant and informative, in particular: (i) a cover note in draft United States' schedules indicating that specific commitments were scheduled in accordance with the W/120's nomenclature[54]; and (ii) a United States International Trade Commission's 1997 concordance indicating that while the United States' Schedule makes no explicit references to CPC codes, it corresponds closely with the W/120's nomenclature.[55] These elements no doubt greatly influenced the decision of the Panel and the Appellate Body as to whether, notwithstanding the absence of explicit references to CPC codes in the United States' Schedule, the W/120's nomenclature was used as the general basis for that Member's specific commitments.

In the end, what this all means is that the W/120 and the corresponding CPC codes constitute the general benchmark against which Members' GATS-specific commitments are interpreted. Hence, unless a Member has clearly indicated in its Schedule that its commitments, or parts of

[54] See *US – Gambling*, Appellate Body Report, para. 206. The note on the United States' draft schedules read:

> Except where specifically noted, the scope of the sectoral commitments of the United States corresponds to the sectoral coverage in the Secretariat's Service sectoral Classification List (MTN.GNS/W/120, dated 10 July 1991) [W/120].

This indicates that except where specifically noted in its Schedule, the scope of the United States' specific commitments corresponds to the sectoral coverage in the W/120. Since the W/120 defines sectoral coverage by referring to relevant CPC codes, this means that, except where specifically noted in the United States' Schedule, the scope of that Member's specific commitments corresponds to the scope of relevant CPC codes (setting out the scope of particular service sectors) referred to in the W/120.

[55] See *US – Gambling*, Appellate Body Report, paras. 209–211.

them, are not scheduled in accordance with the W/120 and the corresponding CPC codes, and subject to such commitments having a clear scope on their face (a remote possibility in most instances, given the generic and vague nature of service sectors included in Schedules), the W/120's nomenclature will likely weigh heavily on the meaning to be ultimately ascribed to those commitments.[56]

This obviously constitutes a call for greater clarity, consistency and precision in the scheduling of commitments under the GATS, objectives that would ideally be achieved through negotiations rather than through dispute settlement. Members have been lukewarm about any clarification exercise, however, often due to the perceived threat that this could lead, in certain circumstances, to a reduction in the level of commitments ('roll-back'). For the foreseeable future, it therefore seems likely that clarification will come mostly through dispute settlement.

A related issue, as WTO Members go through successive rounds of negotiations under the GATS, is the extent to which other Members' Schedules, in particular the scheduling practice reflected therein, will be relevant when interpreting one's own Schedule.

In *Chile – Price Band*, the Appellate Body indicated, in the context of GATT Schedules, that the Schedule of one Member, and even the scheduling practice of a number of Members, is not relevant in interpreting the meaning of a treaty provision, unless that practice amounts to 'subsequent practice in the application of the treaty' within the meaning of Article 31(3)(b) of the Vienna Convention.[57] In *US – Gambling*, the Appellate Body specified that for a 'practice' within the meaning of Article 31(3)(b) to be established, there must be a common, consistent, discernible pattern of acts or pronouncements, and those acts or pronouncements must imply agreement on the interpretation of the relevant provision.[58] This was reaffirmed in *EC – Chicken Cuts*, which dealt with GATT Schedules.[59] In that case, the Appellate Body recalled that while it

[56] See M. Krajewski, 'Playing by the Rules of the Game?', *Legal Issues of Economic Integration* 4 (2005), p. 417, at 428, where a similar conclusion is reached. It is worth noting that in the event of a conflict between a heading and a CPC code included in a Member's Schedule, the CPC code will prevail. *Canada – Autos*, Panel Report, para. 10.281.

[57] *Chile – Price Band*, Chile – Price Band System and Safeguard Measures Relating to Certain Agricultural Products, Appellate Body Report, WT/DS207/AB/R, 23 September 2002, para. 272. Article 31(3)(b) of the Vienna Convention provides that the interpreter shall take into account, together with the context, any subsequent practice in the application of the treaty that establishes the agreement of the parties regarding its interpretation.

[58] *US – Gambling*, Appellate Body Report, paras. 191–192.

[59] *EC – Chicken Cuts*, Appellate Body Report, paras. 251–276.

is not necessary that each and every Member has engaged in a particular practice, practice by only a few will normally prove irrelevant and unhelpful.[60]

In the light of this, any scheduling 'practice' followed by a majority of Members in the Doha Round and subsequent rounds of service negotiations will become an important tool for the interpretation of GATS Schedules.[61] Any Member that does not follow a particular scheduling convention would be well-advised to clearly say so in its Schedule.

4. Market access

4.1 Introductory remarks

Article XVI of the GATS, entitled 'Market Access', is included in Part III of the GATS on 'Specific Commitments'.[62] In addition to an obligation on market access, this Part comprises a national treatment obligation

[60] *EC – Chicken Cuts*, Appellate Body Report, para. 259.
[61] Pursuant to Article 31(3)(b) of the Vienna Convention.
[62] Article XVI reads as follows:

> 1. With respect to market access through the modes of supply identified in Article I, each Member shall accord services and service suppliers of any other Member treatment no less favourable than that provided for under the terms, limitations and conditions agreed and specified in its Schedule.
> 2. In sectors where market-access commitments are undertaken, the measures which a Member shall not maintain or adopt either on the basis of a regional subdivision or on the basis of its entire territory, unless otherwise specified in its Schedule, are defined as:
>   (a) limitations on the number of service suppliers whether in the form of numerical quotas, monopolies, exclusive service suppliers or the requirements of an economic needs test;
>   (b) limitations on the total value of service transactions or assets in the form of numerical quotas or the requirement of an economic needs test;
>   (c) limitations on the total number of service operations or on the total quantity of service output expressed in terms of designated numerical units in the form of quotas or the requirement of an economic needs test;
>   (d) limitations on the total number of natural persons that may be employed in a particular service sector or that a service supplier may employ and who are necessary for, and directly related to, the supply of a specific service in the form of numerical quotas or the requirement of an economic needs test;
>   (e) measures which restrict or require specific types of legal entity or joint venture through which a service supplier may supply a service; and
>   (f) limitations on the participation of foreign capital in terms of maximum percentage limit on foreign shareholding or the total value of individual or aggregate foreign investment. (footnote omitted)

(Article XVII) and a provision on additional commitments (Article XVIII). The latter allows Members to undertake obligations that go beyond those on market access and national treatment.[63] A specific characteristic of the obligations in Part III is that they do not automatically apply to all measures on trade in services falling within the scope of the GATS. Rather, they apply only to specific service sectors that a Member has included in its GATS Schedule. For instance, a Member is subject to the market access and national treatment obligations of Articles XVI and XVII in the financial services sector only if it has included that sector in its Schedule. In connection with a listed service sector, a Member may have inscribed limitations for measures that are inconsistent with the market access and/or national treatment obligations.

While the national treatment obligation prohibits de jure and de facto discrimination against services and service suppliers of another Member, the market access obligation in Article XVI is meant to capture measures that restrict trade and competition – and therefore access to a market – through the application of quantitative-type limitations that are often non-discriminatory in nature.[64] The national treatment and market access disciplines complement each other in ensuring real and effective access to the market of a Member in a committed service sector.

The inclusion of a service sector, minus any market access and national treatment reservations, plus any additional commitments, reflects a Member's 'specific commitments'. In accordance with the 1993 Scheduling Guidelines, which clarified and elaborated upon Members' obligations under Article XX, each Member has scheduled its market access and national treatment specific commitments on a mode-of-supply basis, that is, commitments have been undertaken (or not) for each one of the four modes of supply covered by the GATS.[65]

The obligations in Part III of the GATS are to be contrasted with other obligations, most notably the MFN obligation in Article II, that apply across-the-board.[66] This means that unlike the GATT, the GATS has a

[63] For instance, those Members that have adhered to the additional obligations of the Reference Paper on basic telecommunications have done so pursuant to Article XVIII of the GATS.

[64] See on the subject: J. Pauwelyn, '*Rien Ne Va Plus*? Distinguishing Domestic Regulation from Market Access in GATT and GATS', *World Trade Review* 2 (2005), p. 131, at 153–155; Ortino (2006), at p. 142; Krajewski (2005), p. 417, at 430–431.

[65] Cross-border trade in services (mode 1), consumption abroad (mode 2), commercial presence (mode 3), movement of natural persons (mode 4). See 1993 Scheduling Guidelines, Part II.

[66] The MFN obligation in Article II is only subject to specific and limited exemptions listed in the Annex on Article II Exemptions. GATS Article II:2.

hybrid nature. Some obligations apply to any measure by a Member that affects trade in services (e.g. MFN obligation), while the application of others is, in addition, subject to specific commitments having been taken by a Member (e.g. market access and national treatment). This reflects a middle ground between countries that wanted an agreement with the broadest scope of application possible and others that were reluctant to adhere to service disciplines.[67]

At the outset, one must acknowledge the difficulty faced by WTO adjudicatory bodies when they first had to interpret the obligations in Part III of the GATS, in particular Article XVI. There is no precedent, as there is no real corresponding provision in the GATT. The relationship between Articles XVI, XVII and VI:4–5 is also not clearly set out in the GATS. To complicate matters further, Article XVI overlaps with Article XVII on national treatment. This is suggested by Article XX:2 and the 1993 Scheduling Guidelines, which specifically state that the limitations prohibited under Article XVI can be discriminatory or not.[68] In that context, the introductory remark by the Panel in *Mexico – Telecoms* is especially apt:

> WTO negotiators sometimes praise the political wisdom of resorting to 'constructive ambiguity' as a diplomatic means of enabling consensus on WTO rules. The limited legal task of dispute settlement findings is very different. It is to decide on the legal claims, in a particular dispute, based on the 'ordinary meaning' of the WTO provisions concerned 'in their context' and in light of the 'object and purpose' of the agreement.[69] (footnote omitted)

This can be seen as a caveat whereby the Panel indicated that while it understood the reality of trade negotiations, where trade-offs and

[67] See A. Ahnlid, 'Comparing GATT and GATS: Regime Creation under and after Hegemony', *Review of International Political Economy* 3 (1996), at pp. 65–94, where the author explains the negotiating dynamic that led to the possibility to take MFN exemptions and to subject the application of national treatment to the taking of specific commitments. See also E. H. Leroux, 'Trade in Financial Services under the World Trade Organization', *Journal of World Trade* 3 (2002), p. 413, at 415–417 and 422–424.

[68] 1993 Scheduling Guidelines, para. 4. The 2001 Scheduling Guidelines, at para. 8, go farther by specifically stating that 'all measures falling under any of the categories listed in Article XVI:2 must be scheduled, whether or not such measures are discriminatory according to the national treatment standard of Article XVII'. This is manifestly incorrect with respect to Article XVI:2(f), which, on its face, only captures limitations on foreign ownership, that is, discriminatory limitations. That statement does not correspond to the earlier statement in those Guidelines describing Article XVI:2(f) as a restriction on 'foreign equity participation'.

[69] *Mexico – Telecoms*, para. 7.3.

compromises often need to be made at the expense of clarity and precision, negotiators may only have themselves to blame if adjudicatory bodies, doing their best to give, in accordance with applicable rules of treaty interpretation, proper meaning and sense to provisions that purposefully remained ambiguous and unclear, issue decisions that do not prove satisfactory to all.

4.2 Exhaustiveness of the list of prohibitions in Article XVI:2

One of the most crucial issues with respect to Article XVI of the GATS is whether it prohibits only those types of limitations described in Article XVI:2. A question that has often been raised is whether Article XVI:1 has any residual application beyond the specific types of measures prohibited under the second paragraph of that Article. In other words, does the first paragraph only 'inform' paragraph 2 and restate the (obvious) fact that market access commitments apply on a MFN basis, or, based on the principle of *effet utile*, does it contain an overarching obligation that may go beyond the scope of the second paragraph?

In *US – Gambling*, the Panel's clear answer was that the scope of Article XVI is defined exhaustively in its second paragraph.[70] This is in accordance with the 1993 Scheduling Guidelines and, to the author's knowledge, the manner in which most, if not all, Members have scheduled their commitments.[71] This provided a sigh of relief, as any other interpretation would have disastrous consequences for the WTO membership as a whole.

The Panel's finding was challenged by Antigua before the Appellate Body. Unfortunately, however, the Appellate Body exercised judicial economy – having already found a violation of Article XVI:2(a) and (c) – and decided to reserve its judgment on this issue for another day.[72] As a result, and while the Panel's finding is correct and helpful as a precedent, this issue, which is crucial for all Members, remains somewhat undecided and *en suspens*.

This is all the more true given some ambiguity on this question in the previous *Mexico – Telecoms* decision.[73] The Panel in that case was faced with the interpretation of a mode 3 (commercial presence) commitment

[70] *US – Gambling*, Panel Report, para. 6.318.
[71] 1993 Scheduling Guidelines, para. 4. See also 2001 Scheduling Guidelines, para. 8.
[72] *US – Gambling*, Appellate Body Report, para. 256.
[73] The dispute, which opposed the United States to Mexico, arose as a result of the US telecommunications industry, in particular AT&T, considering that its access to the Mexican telecommunications market for, e.g., international calls originating in the United

by Mexico with respect to the supply of telecommunications services by so-called 'commercial agencies'. The issue turned on the interpretation of a market access reservation taken by Mexico, which, in essence, states that a permit is required to supply those services and that such permit cannot be obtained until Mexico issues the relevant regulations to that effect.[74] Relying heavily on the terms of Article XX:1, the Panel concluded that Mexico's reservation is a temporal limitation that is not a market access limitation within the meaning of Article XVI:2.[75] As a consequence, the Panel opined, Mexico has in effect granted market access and cannot prohibit the supply of services by commercial agencies based on the absence of a regulatory framework providing for the issuance of permits.[76]

While this is likely an inadvertent result of the particular facts of that case, and the Panel recalled, at the beginning of the report, that its legal findings were limited to the particular context of that bilateral dispute involving the telecommunications sector,[77] it remains that there is a suggestion in that decision that a market access restriction that is not

States and terminating in Mexico, was unduly restricted, contrary to Mexico's obligations under the GATS. The United States made three claims before the Panel, as follows: (i) failure by Mexico to ensure that its major telecommunications supplier provides interconnection on terms, conditions and cost-oriented rates that are reasonable, in accordance with Section 2 of the Reference Paper; (ii) failure by Mexico to maintain appropriate measures to prevent Telmex, a major supplier and former government monopoly, from engaging in anticompetitive practices, in accordance with Section 1 of the Reference Paper; (iii) failure by Mexico to ensure access to and use of its public telecommunications transport networks and services, including private leased circuits, on reasonable and non-discriminatory terms and conditions, in accordance with Section 5 of the Annex on Telecommunications. For a discussion on the GATS regulatory framework for telecommunications services, see: M. Bronckers and P. Larouche, 'The WTO Regime for Telecommunications Services', in P. F. J. Macrory, A. E. Appleton and M. G. Plummer (eds.), *The World Trade Organization: Legal, Economic and Political Analysis* (New York: Springer, 2005), pp. 989–1040; E. H. Leroux, 'L'Accord général sur les services (AGCS): règles propres à des secteurs particuliers', *Cahiers de Droit* 43 (2002), p. 379, at 407–419.

74 *Mexico – Telecoms*, para. 7.353.

75 The provision at issue was Article XVI:2(a). Mexico's argument was that its reservation constitutes a limitation on the number of service suppliers under that provision.

76 *Mexico – Telecoms*, paras. 7.353–7.371.

77 *Ibid.*, para. 7.3:

> Our legal findings are thus limited to the disputed meaning and scope of certain GATS obligations and commitments of Mexico in the very particular context of this bilateral dispute, and do not go beyond what we consider indispensable for deciding on the legal claims submitted to this Panel. Our focus on telecommunications services may mean that certain elements of our findings in this particular service sector may not be relevant for other service sectors with different legal, economic and technical contexts.

covered by one of the subparagraphs in Article XVI:2 is prohibited. This has the effect of turning Article XVI on its head, as a market access restriction that does not fall within the scope of Article XVI:2 is permitted, as correctly decided by the Panel in *US – Gambling*. An interpretation more in line with the exhaustive nature of Article XVI:2 might have been to conclude that Mexico's reservation constitutes a (protected) quantitative limitation (zero quota) on the number of service suppliers until the issuance of regulations by Mexico.[78] However, since Mexico's scheduled entries had created legitimate expectations that such regulations would be issued within a reasonable period of time after the entry into force of the GATS, nullification and impairment of benefits under Article XXIII:3 of the GATS (so-called 'non-violation' claims)[79] had occurred.[80]

Considering the importance of this issue, it would have been useful for the Appellate Body to confirm and uphold the finding of the Panel in *US – Gambling* that the only market access limitations that are prohibited under Article XVI are those specified in the second paragraph of that provision. Pending such confirmation by the Appellate Body, one can expect this issue to resurface and be debated again in a future GATS case. It is to be hoped that the finding of the Panel in *US – Gambling* will then be followed and firmly adopted.

[78] This would also have been more in line with the previous finding of the Panel, at paras. 7.80–7.86, that a requirement that international traffic 'be routed through the facilities' of a Mexican concessionaire – scheduled by Mexico as a market access restriction – was in effect a 'zero quota' within the meaning of Article XVI:2(a), (b) and (c) of the GATS. In other words, the Panel considered that although the routing requirement did not take the form of a quota, it had the same effect, thereby meaning that it was a market access restriction (quota) under Article XVI:2 of the GATS. In the light of that finding, one would have expected the Panel to also conclude that the mode 3 reservation for commercial agencies had the effect of imposing a zero quota until such time as the regulatory framework for the issuance of permits was put in place. These two findings of the Panel are difficult to reconcile.

[79] Article XXIII:3 reads, in relevant part:

> If any Member considers that any benefit it could reasonably have expected to accrue to it under a specific commitment of another Member under Part III of this Agreement is being nullified or impaired as a result of the application of any measure which does not conflict with the provisions of this Agreement, it may have recourse to the DSU.

[80] The complainant in that case did not make a 'non-violation' claim under Article XXIII:3. Hence, the Panel could not have made a finding in favour of the complainant under that provision, as that claim was not part of the Panel's terms of reference. This, however, did not prevent the Panel from concluding that Mexico's measures only allowed for the possibility of a claim under Article XXIII:3.

4.3 Consistency of prohibitions on the supply of listed services with Article XVI

As indicated previously, Article XVI of the GATS is meant to capture measures that restrict trade and competition – and therefore effective access to a market – through the application of quantitative-type limitations. While several such measures could, in many instances, be considered to constitute a de facto breach of the national treatment obligation (e.g. limiting the number of banking licences to ten, while most or all of them have already been accorded to national banks), there may be cases where such measures would be non-discriminatory (same example, but five licences are accorded to foreign banks) but still serve, in a market-oriented policy environment favoured by the Agreement, the 'illegitimate' purpose of imposing maximum quantitative limitations designed to restrict trade and competition.

In order for Article XVI – more specifically the prohibitions in paragraph 2 – to have an object, access to the market of a Member must generally be allowed. Otherwise, such prohibitions are mere abstractions that do not have any real and concrete application. It follows that when a Member inscribes a 'None' entry in the market access column of its Schedule in connection with a listed sector and a specific mode of supply, it is generally assumed that access to the market is not completely prohibited for that sector and mode of supply. Otherwise, the Member would or should have used one of the various options at its disposal to express the absence of market access, such as listing a monopolistic situation, inscribing an 'Unbound' or 'Unbound*'.[81] entry, or not including a particular sector at all.

The *US – Gambling* dispute gave rise to the probably rare situation where a Member was found to have undertaken a full market access commitment for the supply of gambling services under mode 1 (cross-border trade), yet measures maintained by that Member in effect denied any access to its market for that sub-sector and mode of supply. The Panel, and then the Appellate Body, concluded that certain United States measures prohibiting the remote supply of gambling services are equivalent to a zero quota and thus are captured by the prohibitions in Article XVI:2(a) and (c).

While it is true that these provisions generally refer to the form of a measure, this should not prevent one from concluding, in certain cases,

[81] This means that it is not considered technically feasible to supply a service under the mode at issue. Such an entry can be used, for instance, if a Member considers that the supply of a service over the Internet is not technically feasible. See 1993 Scheduling Guidelines, para. 28, and 2001 Scheduling Guidelines, para. 47.

that a measure not using the specific word 'quota' has the exact same effect and purpose and thus is captured by the prohibitions in Article XVI:2.[82] It is likely that this is what the 1993 Scheduling Guidelines (and now the 2001 Scheduling Guidelines) mean when they use the example of a nationality requirement equivalent to a zero quota.[83] On its face, a citizenship requirement has, in a trade context, no other purpose than to be an arbitrary trade measure limiting the number of foreign service suppliers to zero. In other words, such a measure has the same effect and rationale (or absence thereof) as a quota.[84] It is also in that light that one must understand the fact – noted by the Appellate Body in *US – Gambling* – that 'monopolies' and 'exclusive service suppliers' under Article XVI:2(a) can be interpreted to cover monopolies and exclusive service suppliers authorised or established formally *or in effect*.[85] Monopolies and exclusive service suppliers will have the same effect and purpose whether they are authorised or established on a de jure or de facto basis.

Let us take the other example of a full mode 3 market access commitment for life insurance services. No one would suggest that a law simply stating

[82] While Article XI of the GATT and Article XVI of the GATS are different, they share the objective of preventing the application of restrictions of a quantitative nature. It may be worth noting that panels have in the past determined that Article XI of the GATT can apply to restrictions of a de facto nature. This suggests an approach whereby measures that exhibit both the rationale and the elements of export or import controls can fall within the scope of Article XI. See: *India – Measures Affecting the Automotive Sector*, Panel Report, WT/DS146/R, WT/DS175/R, 21 December 2001, paras. 7.254–7.276; *Argentina – Hides and Leather*, Panel Report, WT/DS155/R, 16 February 2001, para. 11.17. As also indicated above, the Panel in *Mexico – Telecoms*, paras. 7.80–7.86, based a finding that a 'routing' requirement constituted a 'zero quota' within the meaning of Article XVI on the effect of that requirement. Later on, however, at paras. 7.353–7.376, the Panel seemed to disregard the similar 'zero quota' effect of another reservation that prevented the establishment of commercial agencies until such time as a regulatory scheme providing for the issuance of permits would be in place. That requirement was determined not to be a market access restriction (zero quota) within the meaning of Article XVI:2, leading to the conclusion by the Panel that Mexico had granted market access under Article XVI. See above, section 4.2 of this chapter.

[83] 1993 Scheduling Guidelines, para. 6; 2001 Scheduling Guidelines, para. 12.

[84] Most, if not all, Members have taken market access reservations for citizenship requirements.

[85] *US – Gambling*, Appellate Body Report, paras. 228–230. Such an interpretation is based on the definition of 'monopoly supplier of a service', which covers monopolies that are authorised or established formally or in effect by a Member. GATS Article XXVIII(h). Likewise, Article VIII:5 specifies that the obligations of Article VIII apply with respect to 'exclusive service suppliers' authorised or established formally or in effect. While Article VIII:5 and the definition of 'monopoly service supplier' relate directly to the obligations of Article VIII, they can also inform the meaning to be ascribed to the same terms used in other provisions of the GATS.

that such activities are prohibited or illegal should not be captured by Article XVI, simply because it does not use the specific term 'zero quota'. It is in fact rather unlikely that a law prohibiting an activity will ever use that term. In that example, anyone would find it absurd if, notwithstanding a full market access commitment, the Member having taken that commitment would be permitted to completely prohibit access to its market in respect of these services and mode of supply. Market access under Article XVI would not mean much if, notwithstanding a full market access commitment in respect of a specific sector and mode of supply, a Member could, in any circumstances and at any time, adopt the most trade restrictive measure that exists. This would eliminate any notion of security and predictability of market access commitments under the GATS.

What is the difference, then, between a citizenship requirement or a law prohibiting the supply of life insurance services under mode 3, on the one hand, and, for instance, a prohibition on the advertisement of pornographic material or on embryonic stem cell research, on the other? The answer is of course that in the latter cases, the prohibitions have a clear and apparent legitimate (and non-discriminatory) public policy purpose or rationale. One may thus need to look at, and consider carefully, the primary purpose or rationale of a measure in order to resolve the issue of whether, notwithstanding its possible effect as a zero quota on the supply of a service, it constitutes a prohibition (zero quota) within the meaning of Article XVI:2. When interpreting the terms of that provision in context, in the light of its object and purpose and that of the GATS more generally, one can reasonably conclude that a distinction should be made between, on the one hand, prohibitions that have a clear and apparent legitimate public policy purpose, and prohibitions that seemingly have no other purpose than to impose quantitative limitations.

The fact that this may entail taking into account considerations or elements that may also form part of an analysis under the general exceptions of Article XIV is not an impediment to such an interpretive approach under Article XVI. One can draw an analogy with *EC – Asbestos*, where the Appellate Body took into account health risks when determining the 'likeness' of products under Article III:4 of the GATT.[86] The Appellate Body emphasised that doing so is not contrary to the principle of *effet utile*, that is, it does not nullify the effect of

[86] *EC – Asbestos*, European Communities – Measures Affecting Asbestos and Asbestos-Containing Products, Appellate Body Report, WT/DS135/AB/R, 12 March 2001, paras. 113–116.

Article XX(b) of the GATT.[87] Likewise, taking into account elements that will allow one to more accurately identify those quantitative measures that are meant to be captured by Article XVI does not take anything away from Article XIV. Rather, this is a matter of defining correctly the scope of Article XVI. That scope should be limited to those measures described in paragraph 2, including measures that have the same quantitative effect and purpose/rationale so as not to allow the circumvention of one's obligations. This issue is crucial so as not to impose a test of necessity – the initial burden of proof being on the Member taking the measure – where none was meant to apply. Such an approach would be conducive to ensuring the desired general distinction between non-discriminatory measures that should be prohibited outright and others that should rather be controlled through the application of criteria such as those found in Articles VI:4 and VI:5.

The above would tend to favour a conclusion where the three federal measures at issue in *US – Gambling*,[88] which prohibit the remote supply of gambling services by both foreign and domestic suppliers, are not inconsistent with Article XVI of the GATS (that is, do not constitute a 'zero quota'). It is likely, however, that the apparent existence of an exemption from the prohibition only for the benefit of domestic remote suppliers of horseracing betting services[89] affected the respondent's

[87] *EC – Asbestos*, para. 115. The Appellate Body stated:

> We do not agree with the Panel that considering evidence relating to the health risks associated with a product, under Article III:4, nullifies the effect of Article XX(b) of the GATT 1994. Article XX(b) allows a Member to 'adopt and enforce' a measure, *inter alia*, necessary to protect human life or health, even though that measure is inconsistent with another provision of the GATT 1994. Article III:4 and Article XX(b) are distinct and independent provisions of the GATT 1994 each to be interpreted on its own. The scope and meaning of Article III:4 should not be broadened or restricted beyond what is required by the normal customary international law rules of treaty interpretation, simply because Article XX(b) exists and may be available to justify measures inconsistent with Article III:4. The fact that an interpretation of Article III:4, under those rules, implies a less frequent recourse to Article XX(b) does not deprive the exception in Article XX(b) of *effet utile*. Article XX(b) would only be deprived of *effet utile* if that provision could *not* serve to allow a Member to 'adopt and enforce' measures 'necessary to protect human ... life or health'. (emphasis in text).

[88] The Illegal Gambling Business Act, the Wire Act and the Travel Act. These are the three measures determined by the Appellate Body to be at issue in the dispute between Antigua and the United States.

[89] Pursuant to the Interstate Horseracing Act. While that Act was not a 'measure at issue' before the Appellate Body, it was specifically considered in the context of the *chapeau* of Article XIV. See section 5.3 of this chapter.

argument and the final outcome under Article XVI.[90] Where the same public policy issues are found to arise notwithstanding the origin of services and service suppliers, the application of a prohibition only to foreign service suppliers and their services will naturally tend to undermine the argument that although the measure at issue has the effect of a zero quota, it does not serve (like a quota) a quantitative/trade restrictive purpose. In the end, that is the only basis on which the United States was found not to be fully compliant with its GATS obligations, as is discussed more fully in section 6 below.

In any event, one must acknowledge the particular interpretive difficulty that was faced in that case: if the prohibition found to exist was determined not to breach the full market access commitment taken by the United States, it could suggest that a 'None' entry inscribed in respect of a specific sector and mode of supply is akin to an 'Unbound' entry, thereby depriving that entry and the prohibitions of Article XVI:2 of any meaning as they would have no object.[91] A priori, this appears inconsistent with the principle of *effet utile* pursuant to which a 'treaty interpreter must read all applicable provisions of a treaty in a way that gives meaning to *all* of them, harmoniously'.[92] As explained above, a full market access commitment normally implies that a market is not closed. Otherwise, a Member is expected to use one of the various options at its disposal to express the absence of market access, such as listing a monopolistic situation, inscribing an 'Unbound' or 'Unbound*' entry, or not including a particular sector at all. The procedures of Article XXI can also be used to remove a commitment that is no longer desirable.[93]

[90] See S. Wunsch-Vincent, *Cross-Border Trade in Services and the GATS: Lessons from the WTO US-Internet Gambling Case*, December 2005, p. 31, where a similar remark is made.

[91] The types of limitations specified in Article XVI:2 can only apply where access to a market is permitted, at least to some extent. In the absence of any market access, a prohibition on the application of such limitations becomes meaningless and without any real effect.

[92] *US – Cotton*, United States – Subsidies on Upland Cotton, Appellate Body Report, WT/DS267/AB/R, 3 March 2005, para. 549 (emphasis in text). WTO panels and the Appellate Body have recalled countless times the importance of the principle of *effet utile* when interpreting the provisions of a treaty.

[93] Article XXI of the GATS sets out procedures for the modification of a Member's GATS Schedule. In the case of a reduction of the level of commitments, compensation may have to be provided to other Members. For this reason, this process is not necessarily easy to use. It may involve extensive negotiations with other Members, as well as recourse to arbitration in the case of disagreement over compensation.

The Panel and the Appellate Body in *US – Gambling* favoured an interpretation whereby a 'None' entry for a specific sector and mode of supply necessarily entails that at least some degree of market access exists for that sector and mode of supply.[94] Recognising the sensitivity of this issue, however, and mindful of preserving the regulatory autonomy of Members where justified, the Appellate Body clearly showed deference towards regulators and flexibility in the application of the conditions under Article XIV, in particular the 'necessity' requirement, discussed below.[95]

The *US – Gambling* case will likely prove to be a rare and isolated case, and the findings of the WTO adjudicatory bodies under Article XVI should be understood and interpreted in the light of the particular facts and context of that dispute. Importantly, the general distinction between Article VI:4–5 measures and quantitative measures covered by Article XVI was recognised. It was not suggested that any regulatory measure having the effect of restricting access to a market is captured by the prohibitions of Article XVI. The Appellate Body limited its findings to the particular factual situation that was presented to it, that is, the taking of a full market access commitment in respect of a specific sector and mode of supply combined with a complete prohibition effectively matching that sector and mode of supply.

In future cases, panels and the Appellate Body should clarify that Article XVI only captures those measures described in paragraph 2, which may include measures that are found to have the same quantitative effect and purpose/rationale so as not to allow the circumvention of one's obligations.[96] This is the interpretation that best reconciles the text of the

[94] *US – Gambling*, Panel Report, paras. 6.319 *et seq*.

[95] See section 5 of this chapter where this is addressed more fully. It should be noted that an overt contradiction between a Member's full market access commitment and a complete denial of any access for a listed sector and committed mode could provide grounds for a 'non-violation' claim under Article XXIII:3 of the GATS. One could indeed argue that a 'None' entry creates reasonable expectations that at least some degree of access to the market of the host Member will be provided. Such access (benefit) that could reasonably be expected to accrue from the 'None' entry is nullified or impaired by the maintenance or adoption of a complete ban by the host Member. In *EC – Asbestos*, Appellate Body Report, para. 188, the Appellate Body has not ruled out the possibility of making a 'non-violation' claim with respect to measures that might fall within the scope of general exceptions – in that case, measures taken for health reasons.

[96] This would strike the right balance, called for by Trachtman, between measures with a quantitative nature (subject to Article XVI) and those with a qualitative nature (not subject to Article XVI even if they have a zero-quota effect). See J. P. Trachtman, 'United States – Measures Affecting the Cross-Border Supply of Gambling and Betting Services', *American Journal of International Law* 99 (2005), p. 861, at 866.

GATS, the 1993 Scheduling Guidelines followed by Uruguay Round participants (and the 2001 Scheduling Guidelines used in the Doha Round), the integrity and predictability of market access commitments and the preservation of Members' regulatory autonomy.

5. General exceptions

5.1 Introductory remarks

When a measure of a Member is found to be in breach of an obligation under the GATS, it can still be 'saved' through the application of the general exceptions found in Article XIV, which has the same structure and purpose as Article XX of the GATT.[97]

US – Gambling is the first case where Article XIV of the GATS was applied. Because of the similarities between Article XX of the GATT and Article XIV of the GATS, both the Panel and the Appellate Body relied on GATT precedents to interpret and apply Article XIV.[98] Accordingly, one must first determine whether an offending measure falls within the ambit of one of the paragraphs of Article XIV. If that leads to a conclusion in the affirmative, one must then determine whether the measure also meets the requirements of the *chapeau*, that is, whether it is applied in a manner which constitutes a means of arbitrary or unjustifiable discrimination between countries where like conditions prevail, or a

[97] Article XIV provides, in relevant part:

> Subject to the requirement that such measures are not applied in a manner which would constitute a means of arbitrary or unjustifiable discrimination between countries where like conditions prevail, or a disguised restriction on trade in services, nothing in this Agreement shall be construed to prevent the adoption or enforcement by any Member of measures:
> (a) necessary to protect public morals or to maintain public order;
> (b) necessary to protect human, animal or plant life or health;
> (c) necessary to secure compliance with laws or regulations which are not inconsistent with the provisions of this Agreement including those relating to:
> (i) the prevention of deceptive and fraudulent practices or to deal with the effects of a default on services contracts;
> (ii) the protection of the privacy of individuals in relation to the processing and dissemination of personal data and the protection of confidentiality of individual records and accounts;
> (iii) safety; … (footnote omitted)

[98] Cf. *US – Gambling*, Appellate Body Report, para. 291.

disguised restriction on trade in services.[99] What is at stake under the *chapeau* is not so much the impugned measure or its specific content, but rather the manner in which it is applied. The purpose of the *chapeau* is essentially to prevent the abuse of the specific exceptions set out in Article XIV.[100]

The United States invoked Article XIV(a) and (c) in *US - Gambling*. That defence was rejected by the Panel on the basis that the 'necessity' test and the requirements of the *chapeau* were not met. On appeal, the Appellate Body reversed the findings of the Panel on 'necessity' and determined that the three federal measures at issue – the Illegal Gambling Business Act, the Wire Act and the Travel Act – were provisionally justified as measures 'necessary to protect public morals or to maintain public order' under Article XIV(a).[101] It maintained, however, the conclusion that the requirements of the *chapeau* were not satisfied because the United States had not demonstrated that, in the case of betting services for horseracing, the prohibition on the remote supply of gambling services is applied to both foreign and domestic service suppliers. In other words, the United States did not convince the Panel and the Appellate Body that the Interstate Horseracing Act does not provide domestic remote suppliers of horseracing betting services with an exemption from the prohibition embodied in the three federal measures at issue.

5.2 Deference towards domestic regulators and flexibility in the application of the necessity test

The *US – Gambling* case represents the first time where the general exception concerning public morals – common to both the GATT and

[99] *US – Gambling*, Appellate Body Report, para. 292. With regard to the interpretation of similar terms in the context of Article XX of the GATT, see: *United States – Import Prohibition of Certain Shrimp and Shrimp Products*, Appellate Body Report (Recourse to Article 21.5 of the DSU by Malaysia), WT/DS58/AB/RW, 22 October 2001, section VI; *United States – Import Prohibition of Certain Shrimp and Shrimp Products*, Appellate Body Report, WT/DS58/AB/R, 12 October 1998, paras. 146 seq.; *US – Gasoline*, United States – Standards for Reformulated and Conventional Gasoline, Appellate Body Report, WT/DS2/AB/R, 29 April 1996, pp. 22 seq.

[100] *US – Gambling*, Appellate Body Report, para. 339. *US – Gasoline*, Appellate Body Report, p. 22.

[101] Having found that the measures were provisionally justified under Article XIV(a), the Appellate Body exercised judicial economy and did not address the other exception under Article XIV(c). For the interpretation of that exception, see *Korea – Beef*, Korea – Measures Affecting Imports of Fresh, Chilled, and Frozen Beef, Appellate Body Report, WT/DS161/AB/R, WT/DS169/AB/R, 11 December 2000, paras. 152 *et seq.*

the GATS – has been addressed by dispute settlement organs.[102] Both the Panel and the Appellate Body readily accepted that the objectives of preventing money laundering, organised crime, fraud, underage gambling and pathological gambling fall within the scope of the concepts of 'public morals' and 'public order' within the meaning of Article XIV(a) of the GATS.[103]

The main issue concerned whether the Illegal Gambling Business Act, the Wire Act and the Travel Act are 'necessary' to achieve those objectives.[104] Following in the footsteps of *Korea – Beef* and *EC – Asbestos*, the Appellate Body stated that whether a measure is 'necessary' is to be determined through a process of weighing and balancing a series of factors; which process is comprehended in the determination of whether a WTO-consistent (or less WTO-inconsistent) alternative measure is reasonably available. The Appellate Body described this legal exercise as follows:

> 306. The process begins with an assessment of the 'relative importance' of the interests or values furthered by the challenged measure. Having ascertained the importance of the particular interests at stake, a panel should then turn to the other factors that are to be 'weighed and balanced'. The Appellate Body has pointed to two factors that, in most cases, will be relevant to a panel's determination of the 'necessity' of a measure, although not necessarily exhaustive of factors that might be considered. One factor is the contribution of the measure to the realization of the ends pursued by it; the other factor is the restrictive impact of the measure on international commerce.
>
> 307. A comparison between the challenged measure and possible alternatives should then be undertaken, and the results of such comparison should be considered in the light of the importance of the interests at issue. It is on the basis of this 'weighing and balancing' and comparison of measures, taking into account the interests or values at stake, that a panel determines whether a measure is 'necessary' or, alternatively, whether another, WTO-consistent measure is 'reasonably available'.

[102] The exception for 'public order' is specific to the GATS.

[103] Cf. *US – Gambling*, Appellate Body Report, para. 296.

[104] It was recalled that a Member has the right to determine its desired level of protection with respect to an objective covered under the general exceptions. *US – Gambling*, Appellate Body Report, para. 308. This was first made clear in *EC – Asbestos*, Appellate Body Report, para. 168.

308. The requirement, under Article XIV(a), that a measure be 'necessary' – that is, that there be no 'reasonably available', WTO-consistent alternative – reflects the shared understanding of Members that substantive GATS obligations should not be deviated from lightly. An alternative measure may be found not to be 'reasonably available', however, where it is merely theoretical in nature, for instance, where the responding Member is not capable of taking it, or where the measure imposes an undue burden on that Member, such as prohibitive costs or substantial technical difficulties. Moreover, a 'reasonably available' alternative measure must be a measure that would preserve for the responding Member its right to achieve its desired level of protection with respect to the objective pursued under paragraph (a) of Article XIV.

309. It is well-established that a responding party invoking an affirmative defence bears the burden of demonstrating that its measure, found to be WTO-inconsistent, satisfies the requirements of the invoked defence. In the context of Article XIV(a), this means that the responding party must show that its measure is 'necessary' to achieve objectives relating to public morals or public order. In our view, however, it is not the responding party's burden to show, in the first instance, that there are *no* reasonably available alternatives to achieve its objectives. In particular, a responding party need not identify the universe of less trade-restrictive alternative measures and then show that none of those measures achieves the desired objective. The WTO agreements do not contemplate such an impracticable and, indeed, often impossible burden.

310. Rather, it is for a responding party to make a *prima facie* case that its measure is 'necessary' by putting forward evidence and arguments that enable a panel to assess the challenged measure in the light of the relevant factors to be 'weighed and balanced' in a given case. The responding party may, in so doing, point out why alternative measures would not achieve the same objectives as the challenged measure, but it is under no obligation to do so in order to establish, in the first instance, that its measure is 'necessary'. If the panel concludes that the respondent has made a *prima facie* case that the challenged measure is 'necessary'–that is, 'significantly closer to the pole of 'indispensable' than to the opposite pole of simply 'making a contribution to'– then a panel should find that challenged measure 'necessary' within the terms of Article XIV(a) of the GATS.

311. If, however, the complaining party raises a WTO-consistent alternative measure that, in its view, the responding party should have taken, the responding party will be required to demonstrate why its

> challenged measure nevertheless remains 'necessary' in the light of that alternative or, in other words, why the proposed alternative is not, in fact, 'reasonably available'. If a responding party demonstrates that the alternative is not 'reasonably available', in the light of the interests or values being pursued and the party's desired level of protection, it follows that the challenged measure must be 'necessary' within the terms of Article XIV(a) of the GATS.[105] (italics in text; underline added)

Such a 'test' or process to determine whether a measure is 'necessary' reflects deference towards domestic regulators and, further to *Korea – Beef* and *EC – Asbestos*, additional flexibility in the application of the 'necessity' standard.[106] While the overarching standard is still described as whether a WTO-consistent (or less WTO-inconsistent) alternative is reasonably available to the Member invoking the general exception, that Member is not required to address or discuss any alternatives in order to make out a prima facie case of 'necessity'. This can be done by solely addressing the challenged measure in the light of the following factors: the importance of the interests or values that the measure is intended to protect; the extent to which the measure contributes to the realisation of the ends pursued by it; and the trade impact of the measure.

This suggests that the initial burden of the respondent can, in most cases, likely be met by demonstrating the bona fide and reasonable nature of a measure in the light of a particular public policy objective. The burden then shifts to the complainant to present a credible case that a reasonably available, and WTO-consistent (or less WTO-inconsistent), alternative exists. This evidences significant deference towards a Member's domestic regulators. It signals that panels will not second-guess domestic regulators unless a complainant has first clearly made the case that a WTO-consistent (or less WTO-inconsistent) alternative to the challenged measure is reasonably available to the respondent.

It is likely that such deference towards regulators and flexibility evidenced in the application of the necessity requirement under Article XIV of the GATS was seen by the Appellate Body as a (required) balancing factor against the stricter approach taken with respect to the interpretation of

[105] *US – Gambling*, Appellate Body Report, paras. 306–311.

[106] See M. J. Trebilcock and R. Howse, *The Regulation of International Trade*, 3rd edn (New York: Routledge, 2005), pp. 371–372, where the authors also note that the Appellate Body's decision displays sensitivity to domestic regulatory concerns. See also S. Wunsch-Vincent (2005), p. 35.

Article XVI. Such a perceived need to be much more flexible under Article XIV may constitute an indication that some leeway is needed under Article XVI in the first place. In any event, this is arguably a welcome approach in the highly regulated services context, as it is conducive to alleviating the fears of service regulators about their regulatory autonomy being unduly restrained. While this more flexible 'necessity' standard may initially have been the result of the specific services (GATS) context, it has now been clearly espoused under the GATT as well.[107]

The application of the above necessity standard in *US – Gambling* led the Appellate Body to reverse the finding of the Panel that the Illegal Gambling Business Act, the Wire Act and the Travel Act are not 'necessary' to protect public morals or to maintain public order. The conclusion of the Panel in essence hinged on the fact that the United States had refused to consult with Antigua, therefore evidencing that the United States had not 'explored and exhausted' reasonably available alternatives. The Appellate Body determined that such consultations do not need to take place for the necessity standard to be met. In doing so, however, the Appellate Body may have misunderstood the Panel. The Appellate Body faulted the Panel for having found that consultations with Antigua constituted a reasonably available alternative.[108] It appears, however, that the Panel simply used the United States' refusal to consult with Antigua as evidence that the United States had not considered or explored possible alternatives to its prohibition, not as a substantive alternative to such prohibition.

5.3 *Consistency requirement*

Although the Panel in *US – Gambling* did not need to consider the *chapeau* of Article XIV, it did so in an effort to assist the parties to resolve the underlying dispute. It considered the alleged non-enforcement of the Illegal Gambling Business Act, the Wire Act and the Travel Act against domestic remote suppliers such as Youbet.com, TVG, Capital OTB and Xpressbet.com. It also considered the possible exemption of domestic remote suppliers of horseracing betting services from the prohibition embodied in those measures pursuant to the Interstate Horseracing Act.

[107] *Dominican Republic – Cigarettes*, Dominican Republic – Measures Affecting the Importation and Internal Sale of Cigarettes, Appellate Body Report, WT/DS302/AB/R, 25 April 2005, para. 70.

[108] *US – Gambling*, Appellate Body Report, paras. 317, 321 and 326.

It found that the United States had not demonstrated that the prohibition is applied in a consistent manner between domestic and foreign suppliers. As a result, it concluded that the prohibition is applied in a manner that constitutes arbitrary or unjustifiable discrimination and/or a disguised restriction on trade in services within the meaning of the *chapeau* of Article XIV.[109]

On appeal, the Appellate Body upheld the Panel's application of a 'consistency' standard under the *chapeau* of Article XIV.[110] All other things being equal, a Member must apply restrictions on the supply of services in a consistent manner as between domestic and foreign service suppliers in order to satisfy the requirements of the *chapeau*. This reflects mere common sense. Applying the same legal standard as the Panel, the Appellate Body, however, only maintained the finding of 'inconsistent' application of the prohibition on the basis that the Interstate Horseracing Act solely exempts domestic remote suppliers from that prohibition. The finding of inconsistent enforcement of the prohibition as between foreign and domestic suppliers was reversed based on the insufficiency of evidence relating, in particular, to patterns of enforcement and the reasons for particular instances of non-enforcement .[111]

6. Conclusion

While the GATS case law is still very limited, it has thus far settled a few key issues. To begin with, the GATS has a very broad scope of application. It applies to any measure that has a demonstrable effect on the supply of services through one of the four modes of supply covered by the Agreement. This includes, in particular, a measure that involves a service relating to a particular good or a service supplied in conjunction with a particular good. In such a case, the same measure can be reviewed under both the GATT and the GATS. The specific aspects of the measure examined under each agreement are different, however. Under the GATS, the focus is on how the measure affects the supply of the service or the service suppliers involved. A determination that the GATS applies – that it 'affects' trade in services – cannot be based on mere assumptions; it must be made based on an examination of relevant facts, including who supplies the service at issue and how that service is supplied. This should

[109] *US – Gambling*, Panel Report, paras. 6.583 *et seq.*
[110] *US – Gambling*, Appellate Body Report, paras. 348–351.
[111] *US – Gambling*, Appellate Body Report, paras. 352–357.

not require the actual existence of trade flows, as they may be prevented by the very measure that is challenged.

It has also been clarified that a Member's specific commitments are to be interpreted in accordance with the rules of treaty interpretation of the Vienna Convention. Like tariff commitments under the GATT, specific commitments under the GATS represent a common agreement among all WTO Members. Accordingly, the task of the interpreter when ascertaining the meaning of such commitments is to identify the common intention of Members. In carrying out that task, the interpreter will likely give significant weight to the W/120 and the relevant scheduling guidelines, even though they 'only' constitute supplementary means of interpretation.[112] This is because Members' specific commitments under the GATS are often unclear on their face, and recourse to supplementary means of interpretation will more often than not prove necessary and a useful interpretive tool. This is all the more true in the light of the *EC – Chicken Cuts* decision, which suggests a move towards a holistic approach to interpretation and broad recourse to supplementary means of interpretation when ascertaining the meaning of commitments.[113] Unless a Member has clearly indicated a departure from the W/120's nomenclature, the latter will constitute the general benchmark against which that Member's commitments are interpreted.

As regards the general exceptions of Article XIV, deference towards domestic regulators and flexibility in the application of the 'necessity' requirement has been shown. Once the bona fide and legitimate nature of a measure in the light of a particular public policy objective has been established, WTO adjudicatory bodies will not second-guess domestic regulators unless a complainant has first clearly made the case that a WTO-consistent (or less WTO-inconsistent) alternative to the challenged measure is reasonably available to the respondent. Notwithstanding disagreements over the particular interpretation of Article XVI, this should serve to alleviate the fears of service regulators about their regulatory autonomy being unduly restrained by trade rules. A trade restriction 'necessary' to achieve the objectives set out in Article XIV must be applied in a consistent manner as between foreign and domestic suppliers and

[112] As discussed in section 3.2 of this chapter, one could take issue with the fact that the W/120 does not qualify as 'context' under Article 31(2) of the Vienna Convention.

[113] While *EC – Chicken Cuts* dealt with tariff commitments under the GATT, the reasoning is equally applicable in the context of specific commitments under the GATS.

their services in order to not constitute arbitrary or unjustifiable discrimination, or else a disguised restriction on trade in services.[114]

A number of other issues have been addressed, but need to be further debated and clarified. One such issue concerns the interpretation of Article XVI on market access. It remains for the Appellate Body to firmly decide that the only market access limitations that are prohibited under Article XVI are those quantitative-type limitations set out in the second paragraph of that provision. WTO dispute settlement organs should also further elaborate upon *US – Gambling* to clarify that only those measures that are found to have the same quantitative effect and purpose/rationale as those in paragraph 2 are captured under Article XVI. The effect of a measure can be considered, but only to avoid circumvention of one's market access obligations. This is the interpretation that best reconciles the text of the GATS, the 1993 Scheduling Guidelines followed by Uruguay Round participants (and the 2001 Scheduling Guidelines), the integrity and predictability of market access commitments, and the preservation of Members' regulatory autonomy.

Pursuant to such an approach, a citizenship requirement or a complete prohibition on the supply of life insurance services can be considered akin to a zero quota and therefore captured under Article XVI. Such would not be the case, however, with a prohibition on the advertisement of pornographic material or on embryonic stem cell research. The fact that this may involve taking into account elements that may also come into play in the context of the general exceptions of Article XIV is not an impediment to adopting such an interpretive approach, as evidenced by *EC – Asbestos* in the GATT context. The clarification of the proper scope of Article XVI is important so as not to unduly subject regulatory measures that were not intended to be captured by its prohibitions to a 'necessity' test under Article XIV. More generally, one could say that such an interpretive approach would also be more conducive to supporting the legitimacy of GATS rules, as there would generally be no suggestion that a measure that is perfectly legitimate on its face – for instance a prohibition on the advertisement and distribution of child pornography material over the Internet – breaches a positive obligation of the GATS.[115]

[114] Cf. *chapeau* of Article XIV of the GATS.

[115] Even though one might argue that such a measure could ultimately be 'saved' under the general exceptions of Article XIV, it would likely be damageable to the legitimacy of GATS positive rule-making if it were considered to be, in and of itself, in breach of an obligation like Article XVI.

The above would tend to favour a conclusion where the three federal measures at issue in *US – Gambling*, which prohibit the remote supply of gambling services by both foreign and domestic suppliers, are not inconsistent with Article XVI of the GATS (do not constitute a 'zero quota'). However, the specific facts of that case, in particular the apparent existence of an exemption from the prohibition only for the benefit of domestic remote suppliers of horseracing betting services, likely affected the respondent's argument and the final outcome under Article XVI. Where the same public policy issues are found to arise notwithstanding the origin of services and service suppliers, the application of a prohibition only to foreign service suppliers and their services will naturally raise suspicion and tend to undermine the argument that although the measure has the effect of a zero quota, it does not serve, like a quota, a quantitative/trade restrictive purpose. For this reason, the *US – Gambling* findings on Article XVI should be seen in their context and not be unduly extrapolated. The general distinction between Article VI:4–5 measures and quantitative measures covered by Article XVI was recognised, and it was not suggested that any regulatory measure having the effect of restricting access to a market is captured by the prohibitions of Article XVI.

Among the issues that have yet to be addressed and are sure to also raise difficult and sensitive questions, one can point to the exemption for 'services supplied in the exercise of governmental authority' in Article I:3 (b) and (c) of the GATS. This concept refers to services that are supplied neither on a commercial basis, nor in competition with one or more service suppliers. In an era where semi-privatisations and public-private partnerships are commonplace, it may be difficult to draw the line as to where the protection of the exemption starts and ends. This question should mostly impact areas pertaining to social services.

Bibliography

Adlung, R., *Public Services and the GATS*, World Trade Organization, Economic Research and Statistics Division, Working Paper ERSD-2005–03, July 2005.

Ahnlid, A., 'Comparing GATT and GATS: Regime Creation under and after Hegemony', *Review of International Political Economy* 3 (1996), p. 76.

Bronckers, M. and P. Larouche, 'The WTO Regime for Telecommunications Services', in P. F. J. Macrory, A. E. Appleton and M. G. Plummer (eds.), *The World Trade Organization: Legal, Economic and Political Analysis* (New York: Springer, 2005).

Krajewski, M., 'Playing by the Rules of the Game?', *Legal Issues of Economic Integration* 4 (2005), p. 417.

Leroux, E. H., 'What Is a "Service Supplied in the Exercise of Governmental Authority" under Article I:3(b) and (c) of the GATS?', *Journal of World Trade* 3 (2006), p. 345.

——'Trade in Financial Services under the World Trade Organization', *Journal of World Trade* 3 (2002), p. 413.

——'L'Accord général sur les services (AGCS): règles propres à des secteurs particuliers', *Cahiers de Droit* 43 (2002), p. 379.

Ortino, F., 'Treaty Interpretation and the WTO Appellate Body Report in *US–Gambling*: A Critique', *Journal of International Economic Law* 1 (2006), p. 117.

Pauwelyn, J., '*Rien Ne Va Plus*? Distinguishing Domestic Regulation from Market Access in GATT and GATS', *World Trade Review* 2 (2005), p. 131.

Sinclair, I., *The Vienna Convention on the Law of Treaties*, Second Edition, (Manchester University Press, 1984).

Trachtman, J. P., 'United States – Measures Affecting the Cross-Border Supply of Gambling and Betting Services', *American Journal of International Law* 99 (2005), p. 861.

Trebilcock, M. J., and R. Howse, *The Regulation of International Trade*, 3rd edn, (New York: Routledge, 2005).

Wunsch-Vincent, S., 'The Internet, Cross-Border Trade in Services and the GATS: Lessons from US–Gambling', *World Trade Review* 5 (2006), p. 319.

12

Specificities of WTO dispute settlement in services cases

WILLIAM J. DAVEY

This chapter considers the overall record of GATS claims in WTO dispute settlement. Part I examines the GATS-specific rules of the WTO dispute settlement and the role they have (or have not) played to date in the GATS cases heard in the WTO dispute settlement system. Part II catalogues the consultation requests where GATS issues have been raised and the results of those requests and the Panel/Appellate Body decisions on GATS issues and the implementation results. Part III then considers (a) preliminary issues that have arisen or might arise in GATS cases (e.g. the effective date of GATS; how conflicts with other WTO agreements are treated); (b) the consequences of overlapping obligations in GATS and other WTO agreements (e.g. those that arose in *Canada – Periodicals* and *EC – Bananas*) and (c) the rules of interpretation that have been applied in GATS cases with specific reference to the interpretation of commitments (*Mexico – Telecoms* and *US – Gambling*).

I. GATS provisions on dispute settlement

GATS contains several distinct provisions on dispute settlement. The basic provisions on dispute settlement are GATS Articles XXII and XXIII. Article XXII:1 sets out a general consultation provision modelled on GATT Article XXII:1, with the proviso (not in GATT) that the consultations are to be held pursuant to the WTO Dispute Settlement Understanding (DSU). Specifically, Article XXII:1 provides:

> Each Member shall accord sympathetic consideration to, and shall afford adequate opportunity for, consultation regarding such representations as may be made by any other Member with respect to any matter affecting the operation of [GATS].

GATS Article XXII:2, which is modelled on GATT Article XXII:2, provides that the Services Council or the Dispute Settlement Body may consult with a WTO Member at the request of another Member if the consultations under Article XXII:1 have not led to a satisfactory solution. The GATT provision was seldom used[1] and this GATS provision has not been used to date.

GATS Article XXII:3 provides that a Member may not invoke Article XVII (national treatment) under GATS Articles XXII or XXIII with respect to another Member when a measure falls within the scope of an international agreement between them relating to the avoidance of double taxation. If there is a disagreement as to whether a measure falls within the scope of such an agreement, either Member may refer the matter to the Services Council, except in the case of agreements that existed as of 1 January 1995, in which case both Members must agree to make the reference. The Services Council is to refer such matters with a relation to double taxation to arbitration. Article XXII:3 provides that the decision of the arbitrator will be final and binding, but otherwise provides no guidance on how the arbitration is to be set up and conducted.

GATS Article XXIII contains the general dispute settlement provisions of GATS. It is modelled on GATT Article XXIII, but is much shorter. It provides in its first paragraph that if one Member considers that another Member is failing to carry out its obligations or specific commitments, it may have recourse to the WTO Dispute Settlement Understanding. Thus, for violation complaints, GATS and GATT are essentially the same, except that for GATS, it is not necessary to establish the nullification or impairment of benefits or the impeding of objectives in order to establish a case.[2]

GATS does not allow for so-called 'situation' complaints,[3] but GATS Article XXIII:3 provides for non-violation complaints. The provisions

[1] GATT, Analytical Index 618–620 (6th rev. edn, 1995).

[2] In the case of alleged violations of GATT and other agreements, nullification or impairment of benefits or impeding the objectives of the agreement is required, but the requirement is of little consequence, since nullification or impairment is virtually always found without any special showing. Cf. DSU, Art. 3.8 (the suggestion that the presumption of nullification or impairment is rebuttable has to date been a dead letter).

[3] GATT Article XXIII permits cases to be brought in the event that 'the existence of any other situation', i.e. besides a violation or non-violation situation, if there has been nullification or impairment or the impeding of GATT objectives. There has never been a successful 'situation' complaint in GATT although the issue has occasionally been raised. GATT, Analytical Index 668–671 (6th rev. edn, 1995). The DSU explicitly

of paragraph 3 are somewhat different from GATT Article XXIII. To begin with, a GATS non-violation complaint has to be based on the nullification or impairment of benefits that a Member 'could reasonably have expected to accrue to it'. While such a requirement has effectively been read into GATT non-violation claims,[4] the requirement is not explicitly set out in GATT Article XXIII. GATS Article XXIII also specifies that nullification or impairment must result from the application of a measure 'which does not conflict with the provisions of [GATS]'. This wording is different from the analogous GATT Article XXIII provision, although not in an important way. In the event of a successful complaint, the complainant is 'entitled to a mutually satisfactory adjustment' on the basis of GATS Article XXI:2 negotiations. If that is not achieved, DSU Article 22 on the suspension of concessions shall apply. The specific DSU rules on non-violation complaints found in DSU Article 26.1 are not made applicable to GATS; they apply only to non-violation complaints based on GATT Article XXIII:1(b). Thus, there is (i) no requirement for a detailed justification supporting the complaint, (ii) no provision for modifying the scope of arbitration under DSU Article 21.3, and (iii) no provision that compensation may be a permanent solution notwithstanding DSU Article 22.1. The first and third differences do not seem significant, but the second suggests that there may be no way to determine the level of nullification or impairment for suspension of concession purposes in GATS non-violation cases, although such a conclusion would seem to make the reference in GATS Article XXIII to DSU Article 22 meaningless – a conclusion that would not be acceptable under standard rules of treaty interpretation. Thus, some creative interpretation may be necessary if the issue arises.

There are a few other special dispute settlement provisions in GATS. In the 'Decision on Certain Dispute Settlement Procedures for [GATS]', one of the decisions adopted by ministers at Marrakesh, it was provided that there should be a roster of panellists (para. 1), but in practice there is only one roster – the Indicative List – which lists potential panellists and does indicate whether they have GATT, GATS and/or TRIPS

provides that the old GATT dispute settlement rules (and, in particular, the need for consensus to adopt a Panel report) apply to 'situation' cases: DSU, Art. 26.2.

[4] The criteria for non-violation complaints are examined in detail in *Japan – Measures Affecting Photographic Film and Paper*, WT/DS44/R, at 380–396 (31 March 1998), not appealed, adopted 22 April 1998.

experience.[5] The decision repeats in part the DSU qualification requirements for panellists (para. 3), but goes on to specify that for disputes regarding sectoral matters, Panels shall have the necessary expertise relevant to the specific service sector in dispute (para. 4). There is also a GATS Annex on Financial Services that provides that Panels for disputes on prudential issues and other financial matters shall have the necessary expertise relevant to the specific financial service in dispute.

To date, none of the special dispute settlement rules for GATS disputes has played a significant role in any dispute.

II. Claims under GATS in WTO dispute settlement

There have been only twelve disputes raising GATS issues in the first twelve years of WTO dispute settlement.[6] Of those, seven consultation requests were either settled or dropped, while four requests led to adopted Panel and/or Appellate Body reports. The twelfth case – *Canada – Periodicals* – involved the invocation of GATS as a defence. As such, it is fair to say that GATS to date has not figured very prominently in WTO dispute settlement. Why this is so is not clear. It has been suggested that the likely explanation is that no significant new market opening commitments were made in the Uruguay Round negotiations. Rather, the accomplishment of the Uruguay Round was the creation of the GATS structure and the binding of existing market access opportunities. This is not to say that there were no significant new commitments

[5] See the current Indicative List (WT/DSB/33 & Add. 1–6 (6 March 2003–26 July 2006), which contains as an Annex the rules for administering the list, which were adopted in 1995 by the DSB. Item 7 reads as follows: 'The Decision on Certain Dispute Settlement Procedures for the GATS (S/L/2 of 4 April 1995), adopted by the Council for Trade in Services on 1 March 1995, provides for a special roster of panelists with sectoral expertise. It states that "panels for disputes regarding sectoral matters shall have the necessary expertise relevant to the specific services sectors which the dispute concerns". It directs the Secretariat to maintain the roster and "develop procedures for its administration in consultation with the Chairman of the Council". A working document (S/C/W/1 of 15 February 1995) noted by the Council for Trade in Services states that "the roster to be established under the GATS pursuant to this Decision would form part of the indicative list referred to in the DSU". The specialized roster of panelists under the GATS should therefore be integrated into the indicative list, taking care that the latter provides for a mention of any service sectoral expertise of persons on the list'.

[6] I have counted related consultation requests as involving one dispute. In the case of GATS, this means that I have considered as involving one dispute (i) the various *EC – Bananas* requests (DS16, DS27, DS105 and DS158) and (ii) the two requests challenging Canada's automobile import regime (DS139 and DS142).

made by some developing countries in some specific services – such as tourism. Some of the sectoral negotiations were in fact quite difficult – especially telecommunications and financial services. But overall, it seems that the paucity of dispute settlement cases is explainable, at least in part, by the limited achievements of the negotiators.

Indeed, it is instructive to consider the record of the United States, which was a major *demandeur* in the GATS negotiations, in bringing GATS cases. As described below, the US has not initiated many cases and it is interesting to review its annual catalogue of trade barriers to see how many complaints there are of failures to live up to GATS commitments. In reviewing the 2006 version,[7] it is my impression that the US has relatively few complaints about failures to implement GATS commitments. There are, of course, many complaints about the lack of access to services markets, but the focus is often on sectors where there was never much liberalisation (e.g., audiovisual and professional services) and the complaint is that countries should open their markets, not that they are violating existing commitments. Generally speaking, in the report's discussion of services in the major developed and developing countries, there are few assertions of WTO violations, but rather comments on the existing lack of full commitments and the need for improvement for the Doha Round. The main exception to the foregoing statement is China.[8]

In short, the paucity of GATS cases would seem to be explained by the limited achievements in the Uruguay Round market access commitments.

A. *Consultation requests*

There have been seven GATS cases that did not result in a Panel report. In this section, I briefly describe the GATS issues raised in those consultation requests.

1. The *Helms-Burton* case (DS38)

The first such case was the so-called *Helms-Burton* case (the proper name was *United States – The Cuban Liberty and Democratic Solidarity Act*), an EU challenge to a US law that, inter alia, reaffirmed the US boycott of

[7] USTR, 2006 National Trade Estimate on Foreign Trade Barriers (2006) available at: www.ustr.gov/Document_Library/Reports_Publications/2006/2006_NTE_Report/Section_Index.html, last accessed 26 July 2007.

[8] USTR, 2006 National Trade Estimate on Foreign Trade Barriers (2006) available at: www.ustr.gov/Document_Library/Reports_Publications/2006/2006_NTE_Report/Section_Index.html, last accessed 26 July 2007, pp. 128–149.

Cuba. In addition, the US law created a cause of action for US nationals against traffickers in expropriated Cuban property and provided for the denial of entry into the United States of certain persons connected with such trafficking (and their families). The President was given the power to postpone the creation of the cause of action and did so, but a number of individual 'traffickers' were denied entry into the United States. The EU claimed in its consultation request that the Act contained 'measures which may lead to the refusal of visas and the exclusion of non-US nationals from US territory in a way which may contravene US commitments under GATS … [and] may not be in conformity with at least the following provisions: … Articles I, III, VI, XVI and XVII of GATS and in particular in relation to the Annex on Movement of Natural Persons Supplying Services under the Agreement'.[9] The Panel request elaborated on the GATS issues as follows:[10]

> (d) the prohibition pursuant to Section 103 Libertad Act of the provision of 'any loan, credit or other financing' (which includes such matters as provision of performance guarantees, insurance and some payments) by US persons to any person for the purpose of transactions involving any confiscated property the claim to which is owned by a United States national;
>
> (e) under Title III of the Libertad Act, the creation of a right of action in favour of US citizens to sue EC persons and companies in US courts in order to obtain compensation for Cuban properties to which these US nationals have a claim, in cases where the EC persons or companies concerned have 'trafficked' in such property that was confiscated by the Cuban Government from persons who were or are now US nationals;
>
> (f) under Title IV of the Libertad Act, the denial of visas and exclusion from the US (or threat thereof) of persons involved in confiscating or 'trafficking' in confiscated property a claim to which is owned by a US national and persons who are corporate officers, principals or shareholders with a controlling interest of an entity which has been involved in 'trafficking' etc. in such property. Spouses, minor children and agents of such persons are also denied visas and excluded from the US under this provision.
>
> …
>
> The EC will in particular request that the panel consider and find that:
>
> …

[9] WT/DS38/1 (13 May 1996).

[10] WT/DS38/2 & Corr. 1 (4 October 1996 & 14 October 1996).

(iv) the measures described in point (d) above are inconsistent with Article XI of GATS [which prohibits restriction on international transfers and payments for current transactions related to specific commitments];

(v) the measures described in points (e) and (f) above are inconsistent with Articles II [MFN], III [transparency], VI [domestic regulation], XVI [market access]and XVII [national treatment] of GATS and the measures described in point (f) are also inconsistent with paragraphs 3 and 4 of the GATS Annex on the Movement of Natural Persons;

...

(viii) even if wholly or partly not in conflict with any of the provisions of GATS, the measures described in points (d), (e) and (f) above nullify and impair benefits which the EC could reasonably expect to have accrued to it under the specific commitments of the US and Cuba under GATS. These benefits are trade in services between the EC and the US and between the EC and Cuba unhindered by the interruption of financial services, the threat of seizure of assets for the purposes of satisfying compensation claims in respect of 'trafficking' and by the harassment of its citizens through the denial of visas and exclusion from the US (or the threat thereof).

A Panel was established on 20 November 1996 and was composed by the Director-General on 20 February 1997.[11] On the day its first written submission was due, the EU requested the Panel to suspend its work indefinitely, which the panel did as of 21 April 1997,[12] and, pursuant to Article 12.12 of the DSU, the authority of the Panel lapsed twelve months later.[13] Although the parties never notified the DSB of a mutually agreed solution, press reports indicate that one was reached in April 1997.[14] The settlement was further elaborated in May 1998.[15] In essence, the US agreed that the President would continue to postpone the effective date of the cause of action created by the act (such postponements have continued to date) and that the visa restrictions would not be given effect. The agreement called for legislation to allow implementation of a waiver of the visa restrictions, which Congress never approved, but

[11] WT/DS38/3 (20 February 1997). The Panel chair was Arthur Dunkel, who had been the Director-General of GATT from 1980 to 1993; the other panellists were Tommy Koh of Singapore and Edward Woodfield of New Zealand.

[12] WT/DS38/5 (25 April 1997). [13] WT/DS38/6 (24 April 1998).

[14] 'U.S., EU Approve Plan to Resolve Dispute over Helms-Burton, Officials Say', 14 *BNA International Trade Reporter* 686 (16 April 1997).

[15] 'U.S., EU Reach Accord to End Dispute over Helms-Burton, but Helms Objects', 15 *BNA International Trade Reporter* 855 (20 May 1998).

there have been no further complaints about visa problems from the EU or other affected parties, such as Canada; indeed, instead there have been complaints about non-enforcement by Congress.[16] Although the case could come back to life if the status quo changes, that currently seems unlikely.

Had the *Helms-Burton* case gone forward, it would have raised a number of very interesting issues under GATS, as well as GATT. In particular, there was the issue of national security – the United States claimed that the whole case was an inappropriate one for consideration by a WTO Panel and threatened not to participate in the proceedings.[17] The EU, presumably as a way around any national security defence, raised a non-violation claim, and the interaction of an exception and a non-violation claim would have been interesting.

2. *Japan – Distribution Services* (DS45)

This case was initiated by the United States on 13 June 1996.[18] The consultation request claimed that Japan's Large Retail Stores Act violated Articles III (transparency) and XVI (market access commitments) of GATS. The US also raised a non-violation claim under GATS Article XXIII:3. Following consultations held in July 1996, the US requested further consultations on a variety of Japanese laws affecting industry. According to the further request, which was made on 20 September 1996, these measures violated GATS Articles III, VI (domestic regulation), XVI, and XVII (national treatment).[19] This case was not pursued by the US and is currently listed by USTR as in monitoring or inactive.[20] The main target of the request – the Large Retail Stores Act – was one of the subjects of the *Japan – Film* case, which was argued mainly as a GATT non-violation case, although it also involved claims under GATT Articles III (national treatment) and X (transparency). Having lost that case,[21] the US may have concluded that there was little likelihood of succeeding with the GATS case. In any event, Japan's Large Retail Stores

[16] 'Menendez Blasts Clinton Administration On Enforcement of Helms-Burton Title IV', *16 BNA International Trade Reporter* (No., 13, 31 March 1999).

[17] 'U.S. Says WTO Panel Not Competent To Judge Cuba Dispute, Hopes To Settle', 15 *BNA International Trade Reporter* 351 (26 February 1997).

[18] WT/DS45/1 (20 June 1996). [19] WT/DS45/1/Add.1 (26 September 1996).

[20] Snapshot of WTO Cases Involving the United States, www.ustr.gov/Trade_Agreements/Monitoring_Enforcement/Dispute_Settlement/WTO/Section_Index.html (visited 30 August 2006).

[21] WT/DS44/R (31 March 1998)

Act was replaced in 1998, and recent USTR reports on foreign trade barriers do not highlight distribution services as a pending concern.[22]

3. *Belgium – Telephone Directory Services* (DS80)

This case was initiated by the United States on 2 May 1997.[23] The consultation request alleged that certain Belgian conditions for obtaining a licence to publish commercial directories in Belgium and measures governing a Belgian company (BELGACOM N.V.) with respect to telephone directory services violated GATS Articles II (most-favoured-nation treatment), VI (domestic regulation), VIII (monopolies) and XVII (national treatment). No settlement was reported and the case appears to have been essentially dropped for lack of continuing commercial interest, although USTR currently lists the case in its 'monitoring progress or inactive' category.[24] Shaffer reports that the commercial interest involved – ITT – felt that the initiation of the case helped in its commercial discussions with Belgian authorities.[25]

4. *Canada – Film Distribution* (DS117)

This case was initiated by the EC on 20 January 1998. The EC claimed that Canada's 1987 Policy Decision on film distribution and its application to European companies contravened GATS Articles II (most-favoured-nation treatment) and III:1 (transparency). No settlement was announced, but it is understood that the commercial interest behind the EC complaint had been bought by a Canadian company, thereby eliminating the problem.[26]

5. *Nicaragua – Imports from Colombia and Honduras* (DS188 and DS201)

Colombia requested consultations with Nicaragua on 17 January 2000 in respect of Nicaraguan measures that taxed certain goods and services from Colombia and Honduras. It alleged that the measures violated GATT Articles I and II.[27] Following the failure of the consultations to resolve the matter, Colombia requested the establishment of a Panel,

[22] See, e.g., reports for 2004 and 2005. [23] WT/DS80/1 (13 May 1997).

[24] Snapshot of WTO Cases Involving the United States, www.ustr.gov/Trade_Agreements/Monitoring_Enforcement/Dispute_Settlement/WTO/Section_Index.html (visited 30 August 2006). The issue has not been listed in 1998 or subsequent USTR Annual Reports as active.

[25] Gregory C. Shaffer, *Defending Interests: Public-Private Partnerships in WTO Litigation* (Washington, DC: Brookings Institution, (2003).

[26] Shaffer, (2003), at p. 196. [27] WT/DS188/1 (20 January 2000).

alleging, in addition to the GATT violations, violations of GATS Articles II (most-favoured-nation treatment) and XVI (market access).[28] The Panel was established on 18 May 2000. Later, on 6 June 2000, Honduras requested consultations in respect of the same measures, alleging violations of GATT Articles I and II and GATS Articles II and XVI.[29] The Panel has never been composed.[30] The case apparently grew out of a territorial dispute between Nicaragua and Colombia (and between Nicaragua and Honduras). The territorial disputes are now pending before the International Court of Justice, where they are proceeding slowly.[31]

6. *Turkey – Fresh Fruit* (DS237)

Ecuador requested consultations with Turkey in respect of a particular document that Turkey required to be issued in order to permit fresh fruit, and, particularly, bananas, to be submitted to SPS control, a prerequisite for importation. In its consultation request of 31 August 2001, Ecuador claimed that this requirement violated various provisions of GATT, the Import Licensing Agreement, the SPS Agreement and GATS.[32] In particular, it cited GATS Articles VI (domestic regulation) and XVII (national treatment). In its Panel request, Ecuador elaborated on the complaint, which was essentially that the issuance of this document was being used to limit imports. In the Panel request, however, there was no allegation of a GATS violation.[33] The matter was settled and the DSB was notified.[34] Essentially Turkey agreed to issue the document in the quantities requested by importers.

7. *China – Integrated Circuits* (DS309)

The United States requested consultations with China in respect of exemptions from its value-added tax on integrated circuits on 18 March 2004.[35] The US alleged that China granted a partial refund of such taxes for circuits produced in China and circuits designed in China but produced

[28] WT/DS188/2 & Corr.1 (28 March 2000 & 5 May 2000).

[29] WT/DS201/1 (13 June 2000).

[30] WTO website at www.wto.org/english/tratop_e/dispu_e/cases_e/ds188_e.htm (visited 30 August 2006).

[31] Nicaragua filed a case against Honduras at the ICJ in December 1999; a public hearing on the merits is scheduled to open on March 2007. Nicaragua filed a case against Colombia in December 2001; a hearing on the merits has not been scheduled. See case information at the ICJ website at www.icj-cij.org/icjwww/idocket.htm (visited 30 August 2006).

[32] WT/DS237/1 (10 September 2001).

[33] WT/DS237/3 (14 June 2002).

[34] WT/DS237/4 (29 November 2002).

[35] WT/DS309/1 (23 March 2004).

elsewhere for technical reasons. The latter aspect of the refund was alleged to violate GATS Article XVII (national treatment). The parties announced a settlement of the matter, pursuant to which China agreed to end the refunds, in July 2004.[36]

8. Summary

With the exception of the *Helms-Burton* case, the GATS consultations to date that did not lead to Panel reports were fairly mundane cases and in most instances the non-GATS issues appeared to be more important than the GATS issues.

B. Panel and Appellate Body cases

There have been five disputes where GATS issues were raised that led to adopted reports: *Canada – Periodicals* (DS31), *EC – Bananas* (DS27), *Canada – Autos* (DS139), *Mexico – Telecoms* (DS204) and *US – Gambling* (DS285). Only the latter two were true GATS cases. GATS was raised as a defence in *Periodicals*, and *Bananas* and *Autos* were essentially GATT cases, with the GATS issues arising because restrictions on imports of goods had an impact on distribution services for those goods. In this section, I summarise briefly the gist of these cases. Procedural and certain other issues regarding the cases are discussed in more detail in parts II and III.

1. *Canada – Periodicals* (DS31)

On 11 March 1996 the United States requested consultations with Canada concerning measures restricting the importation into Canada of certain periodicals.[37] The US claimed that the measures violated GATT Article XI and that the tax treatment of so-called 'split-run' periodicals[38] and the application of favourable postage rates to certain Canadian periodicals were inconsistent with GATT Article III. The panel found that the restrictions violated GATT Article XI and were not justified by GATT

[36] WT/DS309/7 (16 July 2004). Satisfactory implementation of the settlement was noted in WT/DS309/8 (6 October 2005). One interesting note: Chinese Taipei requested to join the consultations, along with the EC, Japan and Mexico. China accepted the requests to join of only the latter three. WT/DS309/6 (28 April 2004).

[37] WT/DS31/1 (14 March 1996).

[38] Split-run periodicals imported into Canada were periodicals that were largely the same as those sold in the United States, but contained advertising and some editorial content designed for the Canadian market.

Article XX; that the tax treatment violated Article III:2, first sentence; and that the favourable postage rates violated Article III:4, although one such rate was found to fall within the exception for domestic subsidies found in Article III:8(b).[39] Canada did not appeal the finding of an Article XI violation, except to argue that the measure at issue was a 'services' measure not subject to GATT. The Appellate Body rejected that argument, as discussed in part III below. It also reversed the panel's conclusion that the tax treatment violated Article III:2, first sentence, concluding that the panel had not properly found that the products at issue were 'like' products. The Appellate Body concluded instead that the products were competing products and that the discrimination violated Article III:2, second sentence.[40] The Appellate Body also reversed the Panel's conclusion that one of the favourable postage rates was permitted under GATT Article III:8(b).[41] The reports were adopted on 30 July 1997 and Canada eventually reached a mutually agreed arrangement with the United States.[42]

2. *EC – Bananas* (DS27)

EC – Bananas was a complex case brought by five countries (Ecuador, Guatemala, Honduras, Mexico and the United States) to challenge the EC's import regime for bananas.[43] The case involved many issues, but the key complaints concerned (i) the EC's preferences favouring the so-called ACP (African, Caribbean and Pacific) countries and the BFA (Banana Framework Agreement) countries; and (ii) its rules favouring entities either dealing in ACP bananas in the EC or distributing other bananas in the EC by reserving certain percentages of import licences of non-ACP bananas for them. The impact of the preferences was to discriminate against dollar-area bananas, although the discrimination was reduced as a result of the BFA for BFA-origin bananas. The impact of the licencing scheme was to shift market share and/or to raise import costs for dollar-area banana producers and exporters, which included US

[39] WT/DS31/R (14 March 1997).

[40] WT/DS31/AB/R, at 20–32 (30 June 1997). This was the first instance where the Appellate Body 'completed the analysis' of a case after reversing a Panel finding. It found that uncontroverted evidence on the record and the Panel findings were sufficient to establish the existence of competing products, which were taxed dissimilarly so as to afford protection to domestic industry.

[41] *Ibid.* at 32–35.

[42] The agreement is described in USTR, 2000 Trade Policy Agenda and 1999 Annual Report 259 (2000).

[43] WT/DS27/1 (12 February 1996).

companies. The panel found violations of GATT Articles I:1, III:4, X:3 and XIII:1, the Import Licensing Agreement and GATS Articles II (MFN) and XVII (national treatment).[44] On appeal, the Appellate Body dealt with a number of preliminary GATS issues that are examined in more detail below.[45] The substantive GATS issues in the case were directly related to the GATT issues – essentially involving distribution services for bananas. The EC reformed its banana import regime, but the new regime was challenged and found to violate GATT and GATS rules for similar reasons.[46] The EC received a waiver to exempt its regime from GATT rules until 1 January 2006,[47] at which point there would be a tariff-only regime, albeit with certain preferences for ACP countries. The level of the tariffs was twice rejected in arbitrations under the waiver.[48] The EC's current tariffs, which are lower than what had been proposed prior to the arbitrations, are still not accepted by a number of Latin American countries, and Honduras, Nicaragua and Panama have requested consultations on the matter.[49]

3. *Canada – Autos* (DS139)

Japan and the EU initiated a panel proceeding challenging aspects of the Canada–US Auto Pact, which provided duty-free treatment on the import into Canada of automobiles by certain US companies. The duty-free treatment was dependent on the specified companies meeting certain export and Canadian value-added requirements. As in the *EC – Bananas* case, the GATS issues were directly related to the GATT issues and involved automobile distribution services. The Panel found a violation of GATS Article II (MFN), which was reversed by the Appellate Body on the grounds that the panel had not properly evaluated the GATS issues and had not explained how it had considered the relevant evidence.[50]

44 WT/DS27/R/ECU; GUA & HON; MEX; USA (22 May 1997).

45 WT/DS27/AB/R, at 93–104 (9 September 1997).

46 WT/DS27/RW/ECU (12 April 1999) (no appeal).

47 The mutually agreed solution was notified in WT/DS27/58 (2 July 2001); the waiver was adopted at the Doha Ministerial – WT/MIN(01)/15 (14 November 2001).

48 European Communities – The ACP–EC Partnership Agreement – Recourse to Arbitration Pursuant to the Decision of 14 November 2001, Award of the Arbitrator, WT/L/616 (1 August 2005); European Communities – The ACP–EC Partnership Agreement – Second Recourse to Arbitration Pursuant to the Decision of 14 November 2001, Award of the Arbitrator, WT/L/625 (27 October 2005).

49 WT/DS27/62 (5 December 2005) (Honduras); WT/DS27/63 (6 December 2005) (Panama); WT/DS27/64 (7 December 2005) (Nicaragua).

50 WT/DS139/AB/R, at 48–60 (31 May 2000).

Canada removed the challenged measures within the allotted reasonable period of time.[51]

4. *Mexico – Telecoms* (DS204)

The US challenge to Mexico's telecommunications regime was the first real GATS case, as it was focused exclusively on the interpretation of GATS rules. In its consultation request of 17 August 2000, the US alleged that '[s]ince the entry into force of the GATS, the Government of Mexico has adopted or maintained anti-competitive and discriminatory regulatory measures, tolerated certain privately-established market access barriers, and failed to take needed regulatory action in Mexico's basic and value-added telecommunications sectors'.[52] According to the US such actions had led to violations of GATS Articles VI, XVI and XVII, as well as of Mexico's additional commitments under Article XVIII as set forth in the Reference Paper inscribed in Mexico's Schedule of Specific Commitments and of the GATS Annex on Telecommunications. The Panel, whose decision was not appealed, ruled that Mexico violated various aspects of the Reference Paper and the Annex.[53] Mexico implemented the changes required by the Panel report to US satisfaction.[54]

5. *US – Gambling* (DS285)

Antigua's challenge to the US ban on internet gambling was the second pure GATS case. The two issues in the case were whether the US had made a commitment to allow cross-border supply of internet gambling services (the Panel and the Appellate Body concluded that it had done so, whether intentionally or not) and whether the US ban could be justified by the public morals exception in GATS Article XIV(a). For different reasons, the Panel and the Appellate Body found that it could not be so justified.[55] At the appellate level, this conclusion was based on the fact that the US apparently allowed certain internet gambling on horse racing. The US position is that the Appellate Body misapprehended US law, which does not allow such gambling. As such, the US claims that it is in compliance with its WTO obligations because, if US law is properly interpreted, then the GATS Article XIV(a) exception applies.[56] Antigua

[51] WT/DSB/M/101, at 25 (8 May 2001). [52] WT/DS204/1 (29 August 2000).
[53] WT/DS204/R (2 April 2004). [54] WT/DSB/M/196, at 8 (30 September 2005).
[55] WT/DS285/R (10 November 2004); WT/DS285/AB/R (7 April 2005), adopted 20 April 2005.
[56] WT/DSB/M/210, at 8–10 (30 May 2006).

disagrees and a compliance Panel established in July 2006 was composed in August 2006.[57]

6. Summary

With the exception of the *US – Gambling* case, the services issues raised in the foregoing cases have been resolved. The removal of the GATT violations in *Canada – Autos* also removed the GATS issues that had been left unresolved in the Appellate Body report. The *EC – Bananas* case continues, but the current issues concern tariff levels and tariff discrimination, not services issues. The *Canada – Periodicals* and *Mexico – Telecoms* cases have been resolved to the satisfaction of the United States, which was the complainant in both cases.

III. Major GATS interpretative issues

In this part, I examine the general GATS issues that have arisen in five cases discussed in Part II:B above. I have not addressed the substantive issues in the cases, as those issues will be discussed in other chapters.[58] I have divided the discussion into three sections: (a) general issues, such as the effective date of the GATS obligations (*EC – Bananas)*; (b) the relationship of GATS and other WTO agreements (*Canada – Periodicals* and *Canada – Autos*); and (c) the interpretation of schedules (*EC – Bananas, Mexico – Telecoms* and *US – Gambling*).

A. General preliminary issues

1. Effective date

The temporal effectiveness of GATS was raised in the *EC – Bananas* case because the EC Regulations at issue had been adopted prior to the effective date of the WTO Agreement (1 January 1995) and some of the evidence relied upon by the complainants was from the pre-WTO period. As to the effectiveness of the WTO obligations, both the panel and the Appellate Body found that the Vienna Convention on the Law of Treaties (VCLT) quite clearly stated that a treaty applied to rules that had

[57] WT/DS285/19 (16 August 2006) (two of the original panellists were not available and had to be replaced).

[58] See Cossy, Mireille, 'Determining "Likeness" under the GATS: Squaring the Circle?', in: Marion Panizzon/Nicole Pohl/Pierre Sauvé (eds.), *GATS and the Regulation of International Trade in Services* (ch. 14 in this volume).

been adopted in the past and that continued to be in force after the treaty had come into effect. Indeed, the result was not particularly controversial since the VCLT states: Article 28 specifies that absent a contrary intent '[a treaty's] provisions do not bind a party in relation to ... any situation which ceased to exist before the date of entry into force of the treaty'.[59] The contrary implication as to situations which have not ceased to exist seems clear. As to the evidentiary question, the Appellate Body noted that, as a factual matter, the contested discrimination continued after the entry into force of the WTO Agreement and that as a factual matter, the Panel's conclusions were not subject to appeal.[60] These issues are essentially transitional in nature and are unlikely to arise in the future in GATS.

2. The issue of conflicts

The issue of conflicts between WTO agreements has not much arisen in WTO disputes, except in transitional settings.[61] One area where such conflicts seem inevitable involves the interaction of the three general agreements – GATT, GATS and TRIPS – because the coverage of each of these agreements is expressed in very broad terms. The coverage of GATT has long been interpreted expansively, particularly with respect to its MFN and national treatment obligations. The scope of GATS has been defined broadly as applying to measures affecting trade in services, while the MFN and national treatment provisions of TRIPS apply generally to the protection of intellectual property. It seems clear that some measures will likely be covered by two or even all three agreements. I wrote on this issue at a previous World Trade Forum and will not further address the issue here.[62]

B. Overlapping obligations in GATS and other WTO agreements

In considering the question of overlapping obligations, there is first a problem of terminology.[63] Such obligations are generally thought of as

59 WT/DS27/AB/R, para. 235. 60 WT/DS27/AB/R, paras. 236–237.

61 The *Bananas* Panel speculated on a potential ATC/GATT conflict and the *Indonesia Autos* panel dealt with a claimed conflict arising out of transitional provisions in the TRIMS and Subsidies Agreement.

62 William J. Davey and Werner Zdouc, 'The Triangle of TRIPS, GATT and GATS', in Thomas Cottier and Petros C. Mavroidis (eds.), *Intellectual Property: Trade, Competition and Sustainable Development* (Ann Arbor, The University of Michigan Press, 2003), pp. 53–84.

63 This section is taken from William J. Davey, 'The Quest for Consistency: Principles Governing the Interpretation of the WTO Agreements', in Stefan Griller (ed.), *The WTO and the Doha Round. At the Brink of Failure?* (Springer 2006).

not conflicting, but rather consisting of two obligations, both of which could be complied with, but where it can be argued that one of the obligations is more basic and somehow replaces the other obligation. This sort of situation arose early in WTO dispute settlement, and, generally speaking, the Appellate Body has concluded that overlapping obligations should be viewed as cumulative. Several examples will serve to illustrate the kind of issues that arise.

The first GATS case raising this issue was the *Canada – Periodicals* case.[64] There, Canada argued that since it had made no specific commitment in GATS on advertising services, it could not be held responsible under GATT for a measure regulating advertising that indirectly affected trade in goods. In that connection, it argued that overlaps between GATT and GATS should be avoided. The Panel noted that

> [O]bligations under GATT 1994 and GATS can co-exist and … one does not override the other. … Overlaps between the subject matter of disciplines in GATT 1994 and in GATS are inevitable … In fact, certain types of services such as transportation and distribution are recognized as a subject-matter of GATT Article III:4.[65]

Accordingly, the Panel found that GATT Article III:4 applied to the Canadian measure. On appeal, the Appellate Body agreed with the panel that the Canadian measure indirectly affected imported products and was accordingly covered by GATT Article III:4.[66] In doing so, it noted 'The entry into force of the GATS … does not diminish the scope of application of the GATT 1994.'[67]

Soon thereafter, the relationship of GATT and GATS arose in the context of the *Bananas* case.[68] The EC argued in essence that a measure taken to regulate trade in goods could not be inconsistent with that Member's GATS obligations. The argument was rejected given the broad scope of the GATS obligations, which apply generally to measures 'affecting' trade in services. This broad definition does not suggest that only regulatory measures aimed at a particular service sector are covered. In the

[64] Panel and Appellate Body Reports on *Canada – Certain Measures Concerning Periodicals*, WT/DS31/R & WT/DS31/AB/R, adopted by the WTO Dispute Settlement Body on 30 July 1997.

[65] WT/DS31/R, paras. 5.17–5.18. [66] WT/DS31/AB/R, at 17–20.

[67] WT/DS31/AB/R, at 19.

[68] Appellate Body Report on *European Communities – Regime for the Importation, Distribution and Sale of Bananas*, WT/DS27/AB/R, paras. 217–222, adopted by the WTO Dispute Settlement Body on 25 September 1997.

view of the Appellate Body,[69] there could be three different types of measures – those affecting only trade in goods, those affecting only trade in services and those affecting both, such as measures involving a good that relates to a particular service or a service supplied in conjunction with a particular good falling under the scope of GATS. In its view, in the third case, the measures at issue could be examined under both GATT and GATS. The Appellate Body noted, however, that the specific focus of the examination of the measure under each agreement would likely be different. Under GATT, the focus would be on how the measure affects the goods involved, while under GATS the focus would be on how the same measure affects the supply of the service or the service supplier involved.

The need to focus on the different nature of the GATT and GATS obligations affecting a single measure was highlighted in the *Canada – Autos* case.[70] The case involved Canadian measures that gave duty-free treatment to imports of automobiles by specified companies, which were required to meet certain Canadian value-added and export requirements. The Canadian measures were found to violate GATT Article I and the WTO Subsidies Agreement. In addition, the Panel found violations of GATS because the measures at issue affected trade in services and denied MFN treatment to distribution services and service suppliers of other WTO Members. On appeal, the Appellate Body reversed the GATS findings. First, it found that the Panel should have in the first instance determined whether the challenged measures 'affected' trade in services before considering whether they violated GATS. In its view, the Panel had failed to examine the relevant facts and, on the basis thereof, to determine that the measures in fact affected trade in services. In reaching its conclusion, the Appellate Body noted that the complainants 'may well be correct in their assertions that [the measure] "affects" those wholesale trade service suppliers in their *capacity as service suppliers*. However, the Panel did not examine this issue.'[71] Second, the Appellate Body also rejected the Panel's findings under GATS Article II, essentially finding that the Panel had failed to analyse the relevant facts. In large part, this seemed to be due to the fact that the Panel had failed to differentiate the sort of analysis appropriate for goods in a GATT case from one appropriate for analysing the effect of a measure on services and service suppliers.[72]

[69] WT/DS27/AB/R, at para. 221.

[70] WT/DS139/R & WT/DS139/AB/R, *Certain Measures Affecting the Automotive Industry*, adopted by the WTO Dispute Settlement Body on 19 June 2000.

[71] WT/DS139/AB/R, para. 166. [72] WT/DS139/AB/R, paras. 168–184.

For me, these results that impose overlapping or cumulative obligations seem appropriate. They essentially go back to the idea that a treaty interpreter should avoid reading provisions out of a treaty. Where there is no question of true conflict, nor any question of an obligation, such as an explicit prohibition in tension with a right such as an explicit permission, it seems appropriate to apply each obligation. Of course, as the Appellate Body found in *Bananas*,[73] it may be appropriate and sufficient to find only a violation of a single agreement only as a matter of judicial economy, but that should not imply that the other obligation was inapplicable.

C. *Interpretation of schedules*

The interpretation of GATS schedules has presented particular problems in two GATS cases – *Mexico – Telecoms* and *US – Gambling*.[74] From my perspective, the conclusions that Mexico and the United States had made commitments were not at all surprising. While it may be true that the US did not intend to make a commitment on gambling (or, more likely, did not specifically consider the issue), the interpretative materials available made that conclusion inevitable. As to the methodology of interpretation, i.e. the way in which the rules on treaty interpretation of the Vienna Convention on the Law of Treaties were applied, one might criticise some aspects of the approach, but since these cases predate the more thorough analysis of the Appellate Body as to the methodology applying the Vienna Convention's rules to schedules in the *Chicken Cuts* case, there is little to be gained from a close examination of the methodology in these two cases.[75]

Conclusion

Dispute settlement experience under the General Agreement on Trade in Services has been quite limited. Only a few consultation requests have been brought and in many of them, the services issues have been relatively minor. In fact, there have been only two real GATS cases to

[73] Appellate Body Report on *European Communities – Regime for the Importation, Distribution and Sale of Bananas*, WT/DS27/AB/R, para. 204, adopted by the WTO Dispute Settlement Body on 25 September 1997.

[74] *Mexico – Measures Affecting Telecommunication Services*, WT/DS204/R, adopted 1 June 2004; *United States – Measures Affecting the Cross-Border Supply of Gambling and Betting Services*, WT/DS285/AB/R, adopted 20 April 2005.

[75] *European Communities – Customs Classification of Frozen Boneless Chicken Cuts*, WT/DS269/AB/R, adopted 27 September 2005.

date – *Mexico – Telecoms* and *US – Gambling*. While those cases raised some interesting substantive issues – competition issues arising out of the Reference Paper in *Telecoms* and the interpretation of the 'public morals' exception in *Gambling* – there has been much in the way of interesting procedural or preliminary issues raised in GATS cases.

Bibliography

BNA International Trade Reporter, 'U.S. Says WTO Panel Not Competent to Judge Cuba Dispute, Hopes To Settle', Vol. 15, 26 February 1997, p. 351.

——'U.S., EU Approve Plan to Resolve Dispute over Helms-Burton, Officials Say', Vol. 14, 16 April 1997, p. 686.

——'U.S., EU Reach Accord to End Dispute over Helms-Burton, but Helms Objects', Vol. 15, 20 May 1998, p. 855.

——'Menendez Blasts Clinton Administration on Enforcement of Helms-Burton Title IV', Vol. 16, 31 March 1999, p. 13.

Cossy, Mireille, 'Determining "Likeness" under the GATS: Squaring the Circle?', in Marion Panizzon, Nicole Pohl and Pierre Sauvé (eds.), *GATS and the Regulation of International Trade in Services* (ch. 14 in this volume).

Davey, William J. 'The Quest for Consistency: Principles Governing the Interpretation of the WTO Agreements', in Stefan Griller (ed.), *The WTO and the Doha Round. At the Brink of Failure?* (Springer 2006).

Davey, William J., and Werner Zdouc, 'The Triangle of TRIPS, GATT and GATS', in Thomas Cottier and Petros C. Mavroidis (eds.), *Intellectual Property: Trade, Competition and Sustainable Development* (The University of Michigan Press, 2003).

GATT, Analytical Index: Guide to GATT Law and Practice, 6th updated edn (Geneva: GATT 1995).

Shaffer, Gregory C., *Defending Interests: Public-Private Partnerships in WTO Litigation* (Washington, DC: Brookings Institution, 2003).

USTR, 2000 Trade Policy Agenda and 1999 Annual Report (2000).

USTR, 2004 Trade Policy Agenda and 2003 Annual Report (2004).

USTR, 2006 National Trade Estimate on Foreign Trade Barriers (2006) available at: www.ustr.gov/Document_Library/Reports_Publications/2006/2006_NTE_Report/Section_Index.html, last accessed 26 July 2007.

WTO, CTS, 'First Meeting of the Council for Trade in Services', Note by the Secretariat, S/C/W/1, 15 February 1995.

——'Decision on Certain Dispute Settlement Procedures for the General Agreement on Trade in Services', S/L/2, 4 April 1995.

WTO, DSB, 'Indicative List of Governmental and Non-Governmental Panelists', DSB/33 & Add. 1–6, 6 March 2003–26 July 2006.

13

Can foreign investors in services benefit from WTO dispute settlement? Legal standing and remedies in WTO and international arbitration

MARTÍN MOLINUEVO*

1. Introduction

Disputes involving trade and investment in services are a rarity in the WTO. Up to now, the WTO dispute settlement mechanism (DSM) has addressed over 130 cases, of which only a handful concerned services. Furthermore, only two disputes were true General Agreement on Trade in Services (GATS) cases, as the other three were primarily 'goods' cases, with only a secondary services dimension concerning the disciplines on the importation of goods – bananas and cars.[1]

In addition, investment in services has received minimal consideration in these disputes. Of the two GATS cases, only *Mexico – Telecom* paid some attention to trade in services through 'commercial presence' (or 'mode 3', GATS jargon for 'foreign investment'), but the dispute concerned mostly cross-border trade. The three goods cases involving the GATS also said little about the disciplines concerning investment in services, although some clarifications can be found in the bananas case.

It is possible to identify three reasons that may explain, at least partially, the marginal attention that WTO dispute settlement has paid to investment in services.

* The author is grateful to Panos Delimatsis, Carsten Fink, Marion Panizzon, Pierre Sauvé and Werner Zdouc for helpful comments and suggestions. A lengthier version of this chapter can be found at http://www.nccr-trade.org/nccr-publications/8.html.

[1] For a detailed review on WTO dispute concerning the GATS, see Werner Zdouc, 'WTO Dispute Settlement Procedures Relating to the GATS', *Journal of International Economic Law* (1999), pp. 295–346. and William Davey, 'Specificities of WTO Dispute Settlement in Services Cases', Chapter 12 in this volume.

First, multilateral commitments in services, like tariff bindings in goods, feature an important level of 'water' between bound policies and applied measures. That is, domestic policies towards foreign services suppliers are commonly more liberal than those to which Members have committed under GATS rules. Indeed, the GATS has been accused of providing for very little real liberalisation.[2] Therefore, to the extent that the GATS does not really impose strong liberalisation obligations on the WTO Members, violations of GATS disciplines are less likely. Nonetheless, the above-mentioned cases that have tackled GATS disciplines show that breaches of GATS general disciplines and specific commitments do take place.[3]

A further explanation of the small number of services disputes brought before the WTO dispute settlement bodies lies in the common perception that the GATS does not provide for national treatment obligations with regard to pre-establishment rights.[4] This is matched by the belief that countries tend to impose pre-establishment restrictions on foreign investment, rather than post-establishment discriminatory measures. In other words, once the foreign investors are allowed into the host country, they would not usually face discriminatory policies, which could violate the national treatment obligation. This assumption, however, may not be justified. UNCTAD has found that in a number of investment agreements covering services, most of the restrictions affected the post-establishment operation of the services companies, rather than the ability of foreign services suppliers to establish themselves in the host country. Indeed, in an analysis of reservations lists in investment agreements, UNCTAD recorded almost four times more measures inconsistent with national treatment than barriers to the establishment of foreign services suppliers.[5]

2 *Ibid.*

3 The exception being *Canada – Automotive Industry*, where the Appellate Body reversed the Panel's findings on Canada's violation of Article II of the GATS. See Appellate Body Report on *Canada – Autos*, paras. 83–184.

4 Despite the perception that the GATS provides limited rules on the pre-establishment rights of foreign investors, mostly under market access disciplines (Art. XVI), measures affecting the ability of foreign services suppliers to establish a commercial presence in the host country also fall under the scope of the GATS, by means of the definition of 'commercial presence' adopted in GATS Art. XXVIII(d).

5 UNCTAD, 2006, 'Preserving Flexibility in IIAs: The Use of Reservations', UNCTAD Series on International Investment Policies for Development, United Nations, New York and Geneva.

One further reason, independent of the WTO disciplines and commitments, may also help to explain the relative lack of investment in services disputes in the WTO: the WTO is not the main forum involved with investment disputes.[6] Unlike 'trade' disputes, controversies concerning investment have not been so much disputes between countries, as disputes between multinational corporations and States.[7] Foreign investors have traditionally had access to international arbitration fora to address claims against their host country governments.

This is an important reason for the lack of disputes regarding investment in services in the WTO. Indeed, investor–State arbitration is considered to offer a number of advantages for investors, which make it a more attractive option.

This study attempts to explore two aspects of international disputes over investment in services. The first part focuses on the international agreements granting standing for private parties in international dispute settlement procedures. With regard to the WTO dispute settlement mechanism, the study attempts to explore how the disciplines of the Understanding on Dispute Settlement Procedures (DSU) together with the disciplines adopted in the GATS relate to foreign investors in services. It also addresses whether and how private parties are involved in WTO dispute settlement procedures. The second part of the study addresses the remedies offered by investor-State arbitration on the one hand and WTO dispute settlement mechanism on the other to resolve an investment-in-services dispute. Ultimately, the study attempts to answer the question of whether WTO dispute settlement procedures could become a valid alternative to investor-State dispute settlement. The final section discusses the main conclusions of the study.

[6] UNCTAD notes that 'the economic sectors that have seen treaty-based disputes include construction, water and sewage services, brewing, telecommunications concessions, banking and financial services, hotel management, television and radio broadcasting, hazardous waste management, textile production, gas and oil production, and various forms of mining' See UNCTAD, 2005c, 'Investor – State Disputes and Policy Implications', Note by UNCTAD Secretariat, document number TD/B/COM.2/62, available at www.unctad.org/en/docs/c2d62en.pdf (8/2006). While this list is merely indicative, it is remarkable that nine out of twelve of the activities listed belong to the services sector.

[7] Throughout this study we refer to 'countries' or 'States' in a broad sense, so as to encompass any geographical entity with international personality and capable of implementing an independent foreign economic policy.

2. Legal standing in WTO and investment disputes

2.1. Investor–State arbitration

International arbitration in investment disputes is characterised by the rights of individual investors (rather than States)[8] to raise claims directly against States. In a typical case of investor–State arbitration, the sovereign immunity of the State concerned is waived, to allow a State to be tried by a privately constituted international arbitration tribunal. By this token, international investment agreements allow private parties to bring claims against States in a similar way to international commercial arbitrations between private parties.[9]

The ability to bring claims in fora other than the domestic courts of the host country acts as a guarantee for foreign investors that any disputes will be addressed by a highly specialised, cost-efficient and, most importantly, unbiased court. This exceptional ability – investor–State arbitration is indeed the only non-human-rights-related international forum that foresees such possibility[10] – is meant to reduce the risks related to the investment, thus allowing for greater flows of foreign capital into developing countries.[11]

The right of foreigners to access international arbitration fora usually stems from bilateral investment treaties (BITs). The majority of the BITs signed to date feature such disciplines. Furthermore, recent free trade agreements (FTAs) generally feature investment disciplines, where they also provide for investor–State arbitration.[12]

This vast array of international investment agreements (IIAs) is not entirely consistent in the precise wording of the relevant provisions and the specific elements that investor–State dispute settlement mechanisms

[8] Investment agreements also typically provide for State–State arbitration for disputes concerning the interpretation or application of the treaties. These State–State mechanisms are 'however' less well developed than those of the WTO DSM and are rarely used.

[9] Marc Friedman, and Gaetan Verhoosel, 'Arbitrating over BIT claims', *The National Law Journal* (15 September 2003).

[10] With the important exception of the European Court of Justice.

[11] Arguably, investor–State arbitration has led to unexpected developments in recent years, that may cast some doubt as to whether such procedures are currently achieving any of these intended goals. Regarding some limitations and problems currently arising in international arbitration, see Mark Kantor, 'The Limits of Arbitration', *Transnational Dispute Management* 1(2) (2004).

[12] The most notable exception being the US–Australia FTA signed in 2004.

feature in each case.[13] In regard to investor-State arbitration, most IIAs allow for ad hoc arbitration under the Arbitration Rules of the United Nations Commission on International Trade Law (UNCITRAL). At the same time, most of them also provide for arbitration procedures at the International Centre for Settlement of Investment Disputes (ICSID). Some investment agreements allow investor–State disputes to be conducted in other fora, such as the International Chamber of Commerce (ICC), or the Arbitration Institute of the Stockholm Chamber of Commerce. Of these institutions, ICSID has grown to be the most prominent international setting for investor–State disputes, currently accounting for over 60 per cent of all known treaty-based claims.[14]

Despite the particular characteristics that each IIA may adopt, the core features of investor–State arbitration are the same across all agreements. Essentially, IIAs grant foreign investors covered by the agreement the right to invoke the treaty's provisions directly against the host country's government in an international court. In other words, international investments grant legal standing to the covered investors and investments to challenge the host State's compliance with the international obligations.

2.2. Legal standing in investor–State arbitration

The definition of investment determines the substantial scope of the agreement. The ability to bring an investor-State dispute to arbitration is no more than one of the trade benefits enshrined in the agreement. Hence the assessment of whether a private party has legal standing before international arbitral tribunals is equivalent to the determination of whether the foreign investor is covered by the investment agreement concerned.

The legal standing of the investor requires, first, a finding on whether the person concerned has made an 'investment' under the terms of the agreement, and is, therefore, an 'investor'; secondly, it is necessary to check whether that foreign investor is among those allowed to benefit from the preferential concessions granted in the agreement.

[13] For a review of some alternative clauses relating to investor–State disputes in investment agreements and related arbitral jurisprudence, see Christoph Schreuer, 'Travelling the BIT Route. Of Waiting Periods, Umbrella Clauses and Forks in the Road', *Journal of World Investment & Trade* 5(2) (2004).

[14] UNCTAD, 2005a, 'Latest Developments in Investor-State Dispute Settlement', IIA MONITOR No. 4 (2005), document number UNCTAD/WEB/ITE/IIT/2005/2.

2.2.1. Definition of investment

Typically, IIAs adopt a broad definition of investment that refers to 'every kind of asset', suggesting that any economic value is covered by the agreement. This sort of broad asset-based definition is usually followed by an illustrative list of assets, which includes movable and immovable property and other property rights; interests in the property of companies, such as shares, stock and debentures; claims to money and claims to a performance under a contract having financial value; and intellectual property rights.[15]

In these terms, an 'investor' is a juridical or physical person who holds any of the rights listed above, or 'any kind of asset' that otherwise falls under that definition and is not elsewhere carved out from the scope of the agreement.

Regarding investments made through the acquisition of equity share in domestic companies – a common form of foreign participation in the services market – it is noteworthy that asset-based definitions of investment do not require the investor to be in a position of ownership or control over that investment in order to be protected by the agreement. Indeed, investment agreements refer broadly to 'shares, stocks or any other kind of equity participation in a company'[16] or use similar wording, without referring to the level of participation or other qualifications regarding the relationship between the foreign investor and the domestically incorporated company.

In these cases, investors have standing not because they control the enterprise but because their shares constitute the investment in their own right. It is logical, therefore, that, to date, no case is known in which a lower limit has been set on the level of shareholding in order to allow procedures in an investor–State dispute settlement to begin, unless such a requirement is set out in the text of the treaty itself.[17] In that sense, the ICSID arbitral tribunal in *CMS Gas v. Argentina* found nothing in international law, the ICSID Convention or the agreement at issue (US–Argentina BIT) that required foreign investors to hold a majority

[15] For a detailed discussion on the scope of investment agreements, see UNCTAD, 1999, 'Scope and Definition', UNCTAD Series on issues in international investment agreements, United Nations, New York and Geneva.

[16] Korea – EFTA BIT, Article 1, para. 2(c).

[17] UNCTAD, 2005b, 'Investor-State disputes arising from investment treaties: a review', UNCTAD Series on International Investment Policies for Development, United Nations, New York and Geneva.

equity share or to own or control the domestic enterprise in order to have *jus standi* before the tribunal.[18]

2.2.2. Rules of origin

The legal standing in investor–State disputes stems principally from bilateral and regional preferential trade and investment agreements. The ability of the investor to bring an international claim depends on whether the investor is among those that benefit from the preferential treatment. In the field of services and investment disciplines, the rules on nationality useful in determining whether the investor concerned has legal standing based on its country of origin are given by the more general rules of origin enshrined in the agreement. Indeed, in conceptual terms, the right to access to international arbitration in a dispute with the host country is no different from other trade preferences granted by the investment agreement. Rules of origin in investment are used to ensure that the foreign investor holds a relevant link with one of the signatory countries party to the agreement, which accords them – and not others – the preferences enshrined in the instrument.[19]

Since investment and services disciplines deal directly with subjects, that is, with the foreign investor itself, the rules of origin foresee nationality requirements for natural persons as well as juridical persons. With respect to natural persons, most IIAs give protection to persons who are 'nationals' of one of the contracting countries concerned. The general practice provides that a natural person is a 'national' of a State according to the domestic laws of that country. This is the case, for instance, in the Japan–Mexico FTA, which provides that 'the term "national" means a natural person possessing the nationality of a Party under its domestic laws'.[20] In addition, some IIAs extend the benefits to natural persons who are permanent residents of one of the contracting parties.[21]

[18] *CMS Gas Transmission Company v. The Argentine Republic*, ICSID Case No. ARB/01/8, Decision on Jurisdiction of 17 July 2003, paras. 48, 51 and 65.

[19] For a discussion on rules of origin in services and investment and its main economic implications, see Americo Beviglia-Zampetti and Pierre Sauvè, 2004, 'Rules of Origin in Services – A Review of Current Practice', and Carsten Fink and Deunden Nikomborirak, 'Rules of Origin in Services: A Case Study of Five ASEAN Countries', chapter 4 in this volume.

[20] Japan–Mexico FTA, Art. 2.1(l).

[21] Singapore–EFTA FTA, Article 37(d), defines 'investor of a Party', inter alia, as 'a natural person having the nationality of that Party or having the right of permanent residence of that Party in accordance with its applicable laws'.

However, international investor–State disputes usually involve a claimant who is a juridical person, rather than a natural person. The rules of origin for juridical persons in investment agreements are commonly construed by two provisions that set out one positive and one negative element. These two elements work together to identify the nationality of the investor:

- first, a provision identifies the juridical persons covered by the agreement by linking those persons to one of the contracting parties. For this purpose, the place of incorporation, organisation or constitution of the legal person is the most frequently used. Such a test lends itself to granting nationality to a company that has only a formal link with the country of incorporation and does not engage in any economic activity there. Indeed, the place of constitution could be chosen exclusively to enable the enjoyment of treaty advantages reserved for nationals of signatories.[22] In this sense, the ability to resort to international arbitration is a major benefit for a foreign investor, which may lead in some cases to 'nationality shopping';[23]
- secondly, a 'denial of benefits' provision allows exclusion from an agreement of those foreign investors who do not maintain a genuine link with the country in which they are located – albeit they may meet the place of constitution test. To this end, investment (and services) agreements tend to focus on the ownership or control over the investment together with a substantial business operation test. The party may thus deny the benefits of the agreement – including access to international arbitration – to those investors who, although they are incorporated in one of the contracting parties, are owned or controlled by an investor from a non-party and have no substantial business activities in the territory of the contracting party.

In sum, while international investment agreements are instruments signed between States, and it is to them that the obligations apply, the ability to demand enforcement of such obligations is given to the private

[22] For instance, the Trans-Pacific Strategic Economic Partnership agreement between Brunei, Chile and New Zealand, Art. 2.1 provides that an 'enterprise of a Party means an enterprise constituted or organised under the law of a Party'.

[23] Von Mehren *et al.*, 2004, point out the case of Bechtel Corp.'s claim against Bolivia, where Bechtel changed its location of registration from the Cayman Islands to the Netherlands in order to be able to bring the arbitration under the Netherlands–Bolivia BIT. See also the arbitral decision on the matter: *Aguas del Tunari S.A. v. Republic of Bolivia*, ICSID Case No. ARB/02/3, Decision on Jurisdiction, 21 October 2005.

parties covered by the agreement. The legal standing of the investor bringing such claims arises from the agreement itself, requiring the claimant to prove coverage by the disciplines in the agreement, both in terms of the activities performed as well as in the relevant link with the contracting parties of the agreement concerned.

2.3. WTO Members' standing in dispute settlement

At first glance, the WTO dispute settlement mechanism (DSM) seems to have little in common with international investor–State arbitration. The possible links between these two fora have received very little attention from scholars, and practitioners tend to specialise in either WTO law or international investment law. Additionally, the failure of the negotiations on a multilateral investment agreement under the umbrella of the WTO sealed the common perception that investment law and WTO law – or 'trade law'– are two separate branches of international economic law with no major links.

This is all the more so for dispute settlement procedures where, although the main obligations remain substantially the same between investment and 'trade' agreements (i.e. most-favoured nation, national treatment), the important differences between the two systems have discouraged closer attention to the interaction between them.[24]

The legal basis for a WTO dispute is established by the WTO agreements. Art. 1.1 of the Understanding on Rules and Procedures Governing the Settlement of Disputes (DSU) provides that the rules and procedures of DSU shall apply to disputes brought pursuant to the 'covered agreements'. Appendix 1 provides a list of such agreements, which encompasses the Agreement Establishing the World Trade Organization (the 'WTO Agreement' or 'Marrakesh Agreement') together with all multilateral trade agreements and the four plurilateral trade agreements.[25] The

[24] For instance, although the decisions of the WTO Panels and the Appellate Body frequently cite decisions of other international tribunals, in particular the ICJ, no decisions have referred to arbitral awards although the concepts under review are commonly very similar. Arbitral awards seldom refer to WTO jurisprudence.

[25] Namely, the Agreement on Trade in Civil Aircraft, the Agreement on Government Procurement (GPA), International Dairy Agreement (no longer in force) and the International Bovine Meat Agreement (no longer in force). However, the DSU is currently only applicable to the GPA, whose parties so decided pursuant to the requirements of Appendix 1 of the DSU. See Notification Under Appendix 1 of the DSU, Communication from the Chairman of the Committee on Government Procurement, 12 July 1996, WTO Document No. WT/DSB/7.

covered agreements concerned in each dispute are also the ones that delimit the jurisdiction of the Panels and the Appellate Body. Claims that do not refer to a covered agreement fall outside the Panels' terms of reference.[26]

Only countries that are signatories to the WTO Agreement, i.e. 'WTO Members', are subject to the obligations enshrined in the WTO agreements and may benefit from the rights recognised therein. In the terms of the Panel in *Japan – Film*, 'the WTO Agreement is an international agreement, in respect of which only national governments and separate customs territories are directly subject to obligations'.[27]

Consequently, the rights and obligations relating to dispute settlement procedures as covered by the DSU are also reserved for WTO Members. Throughout the agreement, the DSU refers exclusively to the 'Members', allowing them to take part in the dispute settlement proceedings either as claimant, respondent or third-party. Neither private entities (natural or juridical persons), nor countries that are not WTO Members are granted any rights in the dispute settlement mechanism. As stated by the Appellate Body in *US – Shrimp*, '[o]nly Members may become parties to a dispute of which a panel may be seized, and only Members "having a substantial interest in the matter before a panel" may become third parties in the proceedings before that panel'.[28]

The WTO dispute settlement procedures are thus established for the resolution of purely State-to-State conflicts. The obligations enshrined in the WTO agreements apply exclusively to WTO Members as do the rights and the ability to seek their enforcement. The legal standing in WTO disputes thus remains an exclusive right of the States.

2.3.1. Legal standing in services disputes

In disputes concerning trade and investment in services governed by the GATS, the Members' legal standing in relation to bringing a dispute arises from Articles XXII and XXIIII. In particular, GATS Art. XXIII:1 provides that:

> [i]f any Member should consider that any other Member fails to carry out its obligations or specific commitments under this Agreement, it may with a view to reaching a mutually satisfactory resolution of the matter have recourse to the DSU.

[26] Panel Report on *Canada – Aircraft*, WT/DS222/R and Corr.1, para. 7.49.
[27] Panel Report on *Japan – Film*, para. 10.52.
[28] Appellate Body Report on *US – Shrimp*, para. 101.

Like the GATT, the GATS admits 'violation complaints' as one of the bases for a dispute. For this sort of claim, the GATS abandoned the reference to 'nullification or impairment' of trade benefits that appeared in GATT Art. XXIII:1. Members are granted the right to bring a dispute regardless of the potential economic effects that the challenged measures may or may not have on the other Members.[29] In this sense, the legal right to bring a violation complaint on services matters has de jure a broader scope than disputes related to goods, as the claimant is not required to demonstrate any material adverse effect of the challenged measures. For services disputes, the mere consideration that a Member 'fails to carry out its obligations or specific commitments' under the GATS is sufficient to establish the standing to bring the dispute.

In other words, the only effective requirement to benefit from legal standing in GATS violation complaints is to be a WTO Member. This has important implications, especially for investment in services: any WTO Member may initiate a dispute on GATS disciplines even in cases where the foreign investor does not meet the 'rules of origin' – or nationality requirements – of the agreement. Hence, any WTO Member may launch a case for the benefit of any foreign investor in services, even if that investor is not originally from its territory.

Further, GATS admits 'non-violation complaints' as another legal basis for a dispute. Non-violation remedies seek to protect the balance of concessions under the WTO agreements by providing a means to redress government actions not otherwise regulated by WTO rules that nonetheless nullify or impair a Member's legitimate expectations of benefits from trade negotiations.[30]

Non-violation remedies, being an exceptional alternative,[31] feature stricter requirements than those imposed for violation complaints. The claimant is required to demonstrate that the challenged measure nullifies or impairs specific commitments on services, and that these measures were not in force or could not have reasonably been expected at the time of the negotiations. Specific commitments, which could be nullified or impaired, may relate to market access, national treatment or additional commitments under GATS Arts. XVI, XVII and XVIII. Due to these

[29] Previous GATT jurisprudence had evolved into creating an almost irrefutable presumption of the existence of nullification or impairment of trade benefits when a violation of GATT disciplines had been found. With the creation of the new WTO dispute settlement mechanism, Art. 3.8 of the DSU codified that presumption into the new disciplines.

[30] Panel Report on *Japan– Film*, para. 10.50. See also, Werner Zdouc, note 1 above.

[31] Panel Report on *Japan– Film*, para. 10.36.

stricter requirements, a country raising a non-violation complaint must demonstrate that the investor experiencing the negative effects originated in its territory.

In any case, GATS provisions on dispute settlement grant only WTO Members the legal standing to bring a claim under its disciplines, even though GATS rules may directly concern private individuals.

2.3.2. Private parties in WTO dispute settlement

Unlike investor-State arbitration, WTO dispute settlement is an intergovernmental forum. As mentioned above, private parties have no legal standing in WTO disputes, but this does not mean that they do not get involved in WTO disputes.

It is clear that 'behind the formal "public international law" structure of the multilateral trading system lies a multiplicity of private interests. Indeed, private entities, be they citizens, consumers, workers or companies, are normally the intended ultimate beneficiaries of WTO rules'.[32] The impact of WTO rules on private business operators has also been recognised by the Panel in the *US – Section 301* decision, noting that:

> [t]he lack of security and predictability [of the multilateral trading system] affects mostly ... individual operators. Trade is conducted most often and increasingly by private operators. It is through improved conditions for these operators that Members benefit from WTO disciplines. The denial of benefits to a Member which flows from a breach is often indirect and results from the impact of the breach on the market-place and the activities of individuals within it.[33]

The concerns of private parties in WTO law are also perceived in dispute settlement procedures. Their involvement takes place behind the veil of 'inter-governmentality' since only the interests of WTO Members' governments are formally represented in WTO disputes. But the shadows of private parties can be distinguished in every case where WTO law impacts on economic opportunities.

To begin with, the involvement of private parties in WTO litigation commonly takes place through the submission of *amicus curiae* briefs to the WTO Panels and Appellate Body. The participation through *amicus*

[32] Kerry Allbeury, 'Behind the Curtain of Intergovernmental Trade Disputes', paper presented at the conference on 'Changing Patterns of Authority in the Global Political Economy', organised by the Univeristy of Tübingen, in Tübingen, Germany, 14–16 October 2004.

[33] Panel Report on *US – Section 301*, paras. 7.76–77.

curiae briefs does not rest on the international personality of individuals as subjects of international law. Instead, it provides an instrument for allowing private parties to take part in the WTO dispute settlement process as non-subjects of international law. 'Unlike "legal standing", the operation of *amicus curiae* submissions does not concern the execution of a right of the individuals to be heard in defence of their particular interests, but rather it is understood as providing assistance to the tribunals in a way that allows for the expression of public or private interests not otherwise formally represented in the jurisdictional process'.[34]

However, the involvement of private parties in WTO dispute settlement goes well beyond the narrow scope of *amicus curiae* submissions. Their involvement concerns more significant roles too. Business operators stand side by side with the governments of WTO Members in the preparation, initiation and pursuit of a WTO dispute.

First, 'it is very unlikely that a government would engage in international litigation with another country without a strong incentive grounded in a trade interest, if only because of the potential political and resource costs involved. Indeed, many disputes are known, inside and outside trade circles, by the name of the main industrial interests behind them (e.g Kodak-Fuji, Havana Club)'.[35]

Further, according to Shaffer, government officials and diplomats are seldom familiar with the economic and legal details that a WTO dispute entails. Such details are the province of private business executives and individual legal advisors. 'To litigate effectively in the WTO system, government officials need the specific information that businesses and their legal representatives can provide. Officials therefore strive to establish better working relations with industry on trade matters.'[36] Government officials and private entities therefore form 'public–private partnerships' to tackle WTO disputes in a mutually advantageous way.

[34] Schwartmann, Rolf, *Private in Wirtschaftsvölkerrecht* (Tübingen: Mohr Siebeck, 2005), p. 428. *Amicus curiae* submissions, however, remain a controversial topic. A number of WTO Members, especially developing countries, have been uncomfortable with their acceptance in the dispute settlement process, which they feel is not in line with the nature of WTO dispute settlement as an intergovernmental procedure, and raises significant questions as to exactly what interests are being represented through these submissions and in what capacity, especially when such notes are presented by private entities invoking a general interest – rather than their own.

[35] Allbeury, note 32 above, p. 2.

[36] Gregory Shaffer, *Defending Interests. Public-Private Partnerships in WTO Litigation* (Washington, DC: Brookings Institution Press, 2003), p. 143.

As a result, while the subjects of law under the WTO agreements are and remain the States, governments are espoused by private parties in order to challenge the trade-restrictive measures of other countries. This domestic support for governmental action comes from the industries or individual companies affected by the restrictions at issue.

2.3.3. Foreign investors in GATS disputes

While the above findings apply to all WTO disputes, regardless of the industries involved, they are all the more relevant to disputes relating to investment in services.

GATT disciplines typically apply to the importation of 'goods' in general, with no special consideration or disciplines directly relating to the operators involved in such activities. GATS disciplines, by contrast, address directly the rights of private operators involved in trade and investment in services. GATS disciplines refer to the treatment of 'services' per se, but also to 'service suppliers'. Furthermore, foreign investors in services are directly invoked when such disciplines apply to a 'commercial presence'.

The domestic 'treatment' of foreign investors involves not only the main national law which applies across the board to all foreign investments, but also includes all domestic measures that in one way or another affect the supply of services. In this sense, disciplines as different as those concerning taxation, the ownership of property and real estate, employment, transfer of funds, registration of juridical persons, corporate governance, environment and professional qualifications, among others, may be encompassed within the concept of treatment of foreign service suppliers.

A successful claim under WTO law would require, inter alia, the precise identification from among this vast array of regulatory disciplines of the particular measures that affect the foreign investor in a manner inconsistent with GATS disciplines. From this perspective, it seems highly unlikely that a foreign government would be in a position to undertake such a detailed scan of its trading partners' regulatory framework on its own. Indeed, it would seem that only the foreign investor itself could perform this task satisfactorily.

Furthermore, in order for GATS disciplines to apply, the measures must concern a foreign investor. Services suppliers are 'foreign' under GATS rules when they meet the conditions of being a 'juridical person of another Member'. According to GATS Article XVIII:m a commercial presence is 'of another Member' (i.e. 'foreign') when: a) it is owned or controlled by natural persons of another WTO Member (e.g. natural persons of its home state); or b) it is owned or controlled by a juridical person constituted in another WTO Member, as long as this person is engaged in substantive business activities in the territory of any country Member of the WTO.

The 'nationality' analysis of the commercial presence thus entails the examination of the regime of ownership of the juridical person concerned. This may prove a daunting task for any subject other than the company itself. Indeed, depending on the national regulatory framework and the type of juridical person, the required information may not be publicly available. Furthermore, the linkage between the owner or controller with the final service supplier is often indirect; there may be a number of successive links with branches and other controlled companies, in many cases registered in different countries, so that an accurate description of the relationship between all the juridical persons may be impossible without the assistance of the company concerned.

Finally, a breach of national treatment obligations under GATS requires that foreign investors established in the host state are subject to an unfavourable regulatory framework, which biases the conditions of competition in favour of the domestic services suppliers. In that sense, GATS violations affect directly one – or several – foreign investors in services, as they have to face trade restrictions that do not apply to other suppliers.

As a whole, this set of disciplines leads to the link between GATS disciplines and private parties being stronger than the linkages of private parties and the other WTO agreements, especially those related to goods. Indeed, rather than being the ultimate beneficiaries of multilateral disciplines, foreign investors in services seem to be the direct beneficiaries of the GATS disciplines when they apply to commercial presences.

In sum, several factors accord a particular importance to private parties in WTO dispute settlement. First, it appears that private parties are best positioned to be familiar with the regulatory framework of the country whose measures are to be challenged and to know how these measures operate. Furthermore, GATS disputes require the demonstration of facts relating directly to the private operators – such as their own internal organisation – that are seldom accessible to bodies other than the private party itself. And, finally, foreign investors in services are the direct beneficiaries of GATS disciplines relating to commercial presence. Foreign investors are therefore the party most interested in the correct compliance of the host country government with its WTO obligations concerning foreign investment.

These various factors suggest that the participation of foreign investors in services in WTO dispute settlement is not simply a fortuitous result of shared interests between the government and the investors, but rather, is a necessary element in ensuring the successful outcome of a WTO dispute concerning a commercial presence as covered by the GATS.

However, as this element of privates parties' involvement is not reflected in the formal rules on legal standing recognised in the GATS and the DSU, private parties are to remain behind the veil of the government sponsoring their claim and it is only through their formal representation that foreign investors can avail themselves of WTO dispute settlement.

3. Remedies in investor–State and WTO disputes

It has been seen thus far that foreign investors in services – in addition to the possibility of resorting to investor-State arbitration – may, together with the government of a WTO Member, challenge those measures under the WTO dispute settlement mechanism.

Arbitration, at least in terms of its specificity, is traditionally regarded as the natural, if not the most advantageous, forum for foreign investors. The question is then whether there are any incentives for a foreign investor to resort instead to WTO dispute settlement, despite their lack of legal standing and the need to turn to government authorities to bring the claim.

A number of elements are significant in a comparison between two systems as different as investor–State arbitration and WTO State–State dispute settlement. Possible considerations in the selection of the appropriate forum may range from time- and cost-efficiency of the proceedings, to the particular international disciplines that may give legal basis to the claim.[37] The political implications of a claim in one or another forum may be also relevant. For a WTO dispute, as mentioned above, the investor claimant needs to be able to count on the active support of its government to launch the dispute, which may not always be possible.

One particularly important element in this decision is the legal remedies provided by the chosen forum. The legal remedies constitute the legal outcome of the dispute and reflect the rights and obligations of the parties that stem from the final decision of the selected tribunal. In other

[37] For a comparison of substantive provisions in investment in the GATS and IIAs, see UNCTAD 2004 and Molinuevo 2006. For the purpose of this study we assume that a claim based on national treatment is covered by the GATS and IIAs in the same manner.

words, remedies represent the response to the question 'what does the claimant win, if it wins?'. Ultimately, the rights and obligations stemming from the a final decision in the case determine whether the dispute, even if won, can be considered successful.

Investor–State arbitration and WTO dispute settlement offer two different approaches towards remedies for international disputes. While arbitration focuses on the reparation of the consequences of the lack of non-compliance with the State's international obligations, WTO dispute settlement concentrates on ensuring compliance with the WTO Member's multilateral obligations.

3.1. Compensation for damages in international arbitration

3.1.1. Nature of the remedy

The remedies in investor–State procedures follow the general principle recognised by international customary law on State's responsibility which obliges States to repair the economic damages suffered by the other party due to the violation of international law. The principle was set out by the Permanent Court of International Justice in the *Chorzów Factory* case and is widely recognised as authoritative and commonly applied in investor–State arbitration.[38]

> The essential principle contained in the actual notion of an illegal act is that reparation must, as far as possible, wipe out all the consequences of the illegal act and re-establish the situation which would, in all probability, have existed if that act had not been committed. Restitution in kind or, if this is not possible, payment of a sum corresponding to the value which a restitution in kind would bear; the award, if need be, of damages for loss sustained which would not be covered by restitution in kind or payment in place of it – such are the principles which should serve to determine the amount of compensation for an act contrary to international law.[39]

Following this approach, the claimant may demand either a monetary payment or, where possible, the restitution of the lost property.[40] This

[38] See, for instance, *CME Czech Republic B.V. (The Netherlands) v. Czech Republic*, Final Award, March 14 2003, and *CMS Gas Transmission Company v. The Argentine Republic*, Award, ICSID case No. ARB/01/8, 12 May 2005.

[39] Decision of the Permanent Court for International Justice in the Case Concerning the Factory at Chorzów (claim for indemnity) (merits), p. 47. 13 September 1928.

[40] This solution is expressly foreseen in some investment agreements, such as Art. 1135 of the NAFTA.

latter option, however, is only applicable to a limited number of cases, namely, those where the foreign investor's property has been unlawfully expropriated and the restitution is possible. Where the violation does not entail the seizure of property, such as in breaches of the treatment obligations, the foreign investor is prevented from seeking any relief other than a monetary payment.

The ICSID Convention does not feature an explicit provision on the matter. However, it recognises the monetary nature of the remedies by stating that the contracting parties shall recognise the awards rendered under its rules and 'enforce the pecuniary obligations imposed by that award' (ICSID Convention, Art. 54(1)).

The UNCITRAL Arbitration Rules, frequently used by ad hoc (non-institutional) arbitral tribunals, provide that the claimant may include in its petition 'the relief or arbitration sought' (UNCITRAL Rules, Art. 18.2 (d)). In investor–State cases, the practice under the UNCITRAL rules is to provide for the reparation of the damages suffered by the claimant through monetary compensation.

In cases regarding expropriation, full compensation would include the future profits lost by reason of the expropriation in addition to the actual damages incurred. However, some arbitral panels have rejected the inclusion of lost profits in the calculation of the award in cases where the investment was not yet operative, as it was noted that, given the lack of historical records on the business operations of the investment, the calculation of lost profits would have been 'wholly speculative'.[41] For cases involving other types of violations, including of treatment obligations, the calculation of lost profits is even more difficult.

The remedies foreseen in arbitration on investor–State disputes thus focus on eliminating the consequences of the violation of international obligations, by compensating for the financial damages suffered by the investor, so as to return the claimant to the economic situation it would have been in if the breach had not taken place.

Arbitral courts are prevented from addressing the cause of the damages, that is, the State's internationally unlawful conduct. Arbitral courts do not have the power to order a State to adjust its behaviour to fulfil its international obligations. Therefore, the investor sees no relief of its current situation, as the host State is not obliged to lift the inconsistent

[41] See *Metalclad Corporation v. The United Mexican States*, Award, ICSID case No. ARB (AF)/97/1, 30 August 2000, paras. 121–122.

measures. It has been said, in this regard, that 'the main focus of investor-State arbitration is not a matter of principle but a matter of money'.[42]

The remedy of compensation for damages, as provided for in investor–State arbitration, may thus be particularly suitable for situations in which the investor is prevented from continuing its business in the host country. This situation typically arises in expropriation claims. However, where the harm stems from violations of treatment obligations – such as national treatment – the foreign investor may be compensated for the economic damages that the discriminatory regulation has provoked, while the mistreatment suffered under the host country's regulatory framework may persist. The State sees no obligation to withdraw the measures and to ensure the investor operates under conditions of competition equal to those of the domestic operators.

Furthermore, investor–State disputes create great political tensions between the foreign investor and the domestic authorities. This often leads to cases in which the investor is faced with the option of either accepting the challenged measures or pursuing the international claim which may lead to exacerbation of the conflict with the domestic government to a point where the operation of the business in the host country may no longer be feasible.

Therefore, where the interest of the foreign investor is to continue its business in accordance with the host State's international obligations, investor–State arbitration does not provide a fully satisfactory remedy.

3.1.2. Enforcement

The remedies provided by investor–State arbitration are not backed up by international jurisdiction in regard to the enforcement of the arbitral mandate. Awards rendered in international arbitration are to be enforced through the domestic jurisdictional system of the country against which the enforcement is sought.

Consequently, foreign investors will ultimately have to face the domestic courts whose jurisdiction they initially attempted to avoid through international arbitration. While international instruments accept only a limited number of substantial reasons for national courts to refuse the recognition and enforcement of arbitral awards (such as the Convention on the Recognition and Enforcement of Foreign Arbitral Awards of

[42] Sumio Kozawa, 'Depoliticization of International Dispute Settlement. A Comparison of the Dispute Settlement Provisions of the WTO and the Energy Charter Treaty', *Journal of World Investment* 3(5) (2002), 821.

1958 – New York Convention) or virtually no grounds (ICSID Convention), domestic law finds its way into international litigation. In particular, national laws still govern entirely the execution procedures of the award, setting out the manner in which the payment by the State to the claimant should take place, which may pose an obstacle for the successful satisfaction of the claimant's interests.[43]

3.2. Withdrawal of WTO-inconsistent measures

WTO dispute settlement procedures provide a different approach towards remedies. The focus is on ensuring compliance by the WTO Members with their multilateral obligations, rather than providing for the reparation of the damages caused by the Member's violations.

3.2.1. Nature of the remedy

Article 3.7 of the DSU expresses that 'the aim of the dispute settlement mechanism is to secure a positive solution to the dispute', and that, to that end, where a mutually agreed solution between the parties cannot be reached, 'the first objective of the dispute settlement mechanism is usually to secure the withdrawal of the measures concerned if these are found to be inconsistent with the provisions of any of the covered agreements'. Accordingly, Article 19 of the DSU provides that 'where a panel or the Appellate Body concludes that a measure is inconsistent with a covered agreement, it shall recommend that the Member concerned bring the measure into conformity with that agreement'.

Under these terms, the DSU establishes that the relief provided under WTO dispute settlement procedures consists in the removal of the inconsistent measure, so as to assure the complainant that the benefits accrued under the WTO agreements are maintained.

By contrast to the compensation for damages foreseen by investor–State procedures, this remedy is clearly prospective. In this regard, the Panel on *US – Section 129(c)(1) URAA* stated that:

> panels and the Appellate Body have … recogniz[ed] that a Member's obligation under the DSU is to provide prospective relief in the form of withdrawing a measure inconsistent with a WTO agreement, or bringing

[43] In this regard, Kantor remarks that 'litigation has proven an uncertain means of enforcing agreements to arbitrate project disputes' (Mark Kantor, 2004, p. 9).

> that measure into conformity with the agreement by the end of the reasonable period of time.[44]

This remedy, in the context of disputes concerning a commercial presence, implies that the country concerned is required to remove the measures negatively affecting the foreign investor in services. Where the breach of GATS disciplines concerns national treatment, the foreign investor benefits from the withdrawal of the discriminatory regulation and enjoys conditions of competition equal to those of the domestic service suppliers.

This remedy meets the needs of those foreign investors that intend to continue their commercial activities in the host country in fair competition with the domestic services suppliers. This may be the case, for instance, in service sectors with significant entry costs, such as telecoms, some distribution services, transport or construction services. Investors in these sectors, where sunk costs are high, may see greater relief in the removal of the discriminatory measures that may allow them greater earnings in the medium to long term than in the possible economic gains of an investor–State dispute.

3.2.2. Enforcement

Article 22 of the DSU provides for the enforcement mechanism available to the claimant when the respondent fails to comply with the obligation of bringing its measures into conformity with the WTO agreements. It sets out two alternative channels: compensation and suspension of concessions (i.e. retaliation). However, none of these means is preferred to full compliance with the WTO agreements.

Article 22.1 establishes that compensation is 'voluntary and, if granted, shall be consistent with the covered agreements'. No WTO case has so far implemented this alternative, and parties have commonly resorted to retaliation. If no compensation or otherwise mutually agreed solution is reached, the claimant may suspend trade concessions as a means of enforcing the WTO ruling. By way of retaliation, the complainant Member is entitled to withdraw trade concessions in regard of the non-complying party. According to Article 22.8, 'the suspension of concessions or other obligations shall be temporary and shall only be applied until such time as the measure found to be inconsistent with a covered agreement has been removed, or the Member that must implement recommendations

[44] Panel Report on *US – Section 129(c)(1) URAA*, paras. 3.90 and 3.93.

or rulings provides a solution to the nullification or impairment of benefits, or a mutually satisfactory solution is reached'.

Article 22.3 of the DSU sets out the requirements for the suspension of a concession, stating that 'the general principle is that the complaining party should first seek to suspend concessions or other obligations with respect to the same sector(s) as that in which' the violation occurred; 'if that party considers that it is not practicable or effective to suspend concessions or other obligations with respect to the same sector(s), it may seek to suspend concessions or other obligations in other sectors under the same agreement;' finally, 'if that party considers that it is not practicable or effective to suspend concessions or other obligations with respect to other sectors under the same agreement, and that the circumstances are serious enough, it may seek to suspend concessions or other obligations under another covered agreement'. Furthermore, Article 22.4 provides that 'the level of the suspension of concessions or other obligations authorized by the DSB shall be equivalent to the level of the nullification or impairment'.

3.2.3. Implications for private parties

For the service suppliers involved in the dispute, the ability of the claimant WTO Member to resort to suspension of concessions has the benefit of keeping the dispute at the international level and not needing to turn to other fora to seek enforcement of the international rulings. However, the procedures defined by Article 22.3 and 22.4 may also have negative implications in a dispute involving services suppliers.

The requirements imposed by Article 22.3 and, in particular, the general principle that suspension of concessions is to be imposed primarily 'with respect to the same sector(s)' as those where the inconsistent measures have been found, may have unexpected consequences for foreign investors in services where the dispute concerns modes of supply other than commercial presence. Theoretically, the rules of procedure established by the DSU might ultimately lead to the imposition of trade sanctions on the same foreign investor that helped to bring the claim. This may happen where a foreign investor has established itself in the host state not only to provide services within the territory of that state, but also – or primarily – to provide cross-border services to its home state.[45] If the rules set out by Article 22.3 were to be applied strictly, the claimant would have to impose the sanctions in the service sector in

[45] This is the case, for instance, in the *US – Gambling* dispute.

which the violation occurred. Paradoxically, this sector would in fact be composed of the foreign companies that, by being established in the territory of the claimant, are 'commercial presences' of the respondent. Should a dispute in these terms take place, the analysis made by the arbitrator should take due account of the activities and interests of the private parties on whom the trade restrictions should be applied.[46]

Furthermore, pursuant to Article 22.4, the claimant may be authorised to suspend concessions up to a level 'equivalent to the level of nullification or impairment'. As mentioned above, the nullification or impairment of trade benefits is not a requirement for the legal standing. Any WTO Member may bring a dispute under GATS disciplines, regardless of the trade effects that it may or may not suffer. Accordingly, a WTO Member could bring a dispute in support of its own commercial presences, as well as the commercial presence of other Members.[47] In such a case, however, the claimant may be unable to enforce a favourable ruling. Under GATS rules of origin, the investors concerned would not be 'services suppliers' of the Member bringing the dispute; it follows that the level of nullification or impairment suffered by the claimant will in fact be zero. This implies that whereas the nationality of the commercial presence is not relevant as a prerequisite for bringing the dispute, the link of nationality between the claimant Member and the concerned commercial presence is essential for the enforcement of a favourable decision.

In brief, remedies under WTO dispute settlement procedures provide a valuable option for foreign investors. In particular, the obligation to withdraw the inconsistent measures offers special benefits to investors that wish to continue to operate their commercial presence in the host country. Furthermore, the enforcement mechanism foreseen by the DSU provides an extra benefit for private parties, as they do not need to resort to other fora to ensure compliance with the WTO recommendations and rulings. However, the procedures for the suspension of concessions established by the DSU do not take proper account of the particular features of disputes involving GATS disciplines, which may ultimately

[46] This could be done, for instance, under the analysis of 'effectiveness' of the sector selected for the suspension of concessions. Under this concept, the imposition of trade sanctions on foreign commercial presences whose main interest lies in the supply of services to its home country through cross-border trade – facing the trade restrictions maintained by the respondent – would not make an impact on the respondent Member sufficient to induce compliance.

[47] See section 2.3.1 above.

have negative implications for investors in services involved in WTO disputes.

4. Conclusion

Foreign investors in services hold a particular position in international economic law: they are covered by international investment agreements as well as by multilateral disciplines on trade in services. These agreements, albeit of very different nature, feature common principles that favour international investment in services. In particular, both sets of agreements enshrine obligations on non-discrimination between foreign and domestic investors in services. In this situation, foreign investors profit equally from the obligations that both sets of instruments impose on the contracting States. These instruments provide strong dispute settlement mechanisms in case of breach of their obligations. Foreign investors in services, therefore, may choose between two alternative dispute settlement mechanisms to challenge those of their host countries' measures that infringe international obligations.

International investment agreements grant foreign investors access to international arbitration tribunals. WTO disciplines, by contrast, provide for a purely intergovernmental dispute settlement mechanism, to which access is reserved to its Member States. This does not mean that private parties are completely excluded from WTO disputes. Private parties are actively involved in WTO dispute settlement procedures, not only through the limited means of *amicus curiae* briefs, but through business operators collaborating closely with the governments of WTO Members in their litigation procedures.

In WTO disputes regarding investment in services, the need for public–private partnerships is even greater than in other trade issues. GATS disciplines directly concern foreign investors in a way that makes the active involvement of foreign investors in services a de facto requirement for successful litigation in a WTO dispute regarding commercial presence. However, the ability to bring a claim under WTO disciplines entails a further effort from foreign investors, as they are subordinated to the governmental policies and they need to work together to ensure the successful outcome of a case.

The remedies provided by the different fora are relevant to the selection of the forum to bring the claim, as, ultimately, it is these factors that will determine the satisfaction of the claimants' demands. WTO and investor–State arbitration provide two radically different solutions.

While investor–State arbitration focuses on the reparation of the economic damages suffered as a result of the unlawful measures imposed by the host State, WTO procedures seek to ensure the removal of the inconsistent measures. Each of these alternatives has advantages and disadvantages for foreign investors in services. On the one hand, compensation for damages may be particularly interesting for investors whose investment has been seized by the host country authorities and for whom continuation of business activities has become impossible. On the other hand, the guarantee of withdrawal of the WTO-inconsistent measures may be an appealing solution for foreign investors in services that are interested in the normal continuation of their investment in the host country. For foreign investors in services, WTO dispute settlement procedures may prove a more effective means to ensure an appropriate competitive environment in the host State.

In conclusion, the WTO dispute settlement procedures may offer, according to the investor's needs, significant benefits for foreign investors in services willing to bear the burden of the intergovernmental nature of WTO litigation with a view to a long-term profitable business activity in the host State.

Bibliography

Allbeury, Kerry, 'Behind the Curtain of Intergovernmental Trade Disputes', paper presented at the Conference 'Changing Patterns of Authority in the Global Political Economy', organised by the Univeristy of Tübingen, in Tübingen, Germany, 14–16 October 2004.

Beviglia-Zampetti, Americo and Pierre Sauvé, 'Rules of Origin in Services – A Review of Current Practice', mimeo, 2004.

Clark, Peter and Gordon LaFortune, 'Why Can't NAFTA Chapter 11 be More Like the WTO?', *Transnational Dispute Management* 1(2) (2003).

Davey, William, 'Specificities of WTO Dispute Settlement in Services Cases', Chapter 12 in this volume.

Fink, Carsten and Deunden Nikomborirak, 'Rules of Origin in Services: A Case Study of Five ASEAN Countries', Chapter 5 in this volume.

Friedman, Marc and Gaetan Verhoosel, 'Arbitrating over BIT claims', *The National Law Journal* (15 September 2003).

Gaillard, Emmanuel, 'Enforcement of Arbitral Awards – The Next "Noga" Episode', *New York Law Journal* (3 April 2003).

Hallward-Driemeier, Mary (2003), 'Do Bilateral Investment Treaties Attract FDI? Only a bit … and they could bite', World Bank Policy Research Working Paper, document number WPS3121, available at econ.worldbank.org (8/2006).

International Law Association Committee on International Commercial Law, 2002, 'Final Report on Public Policy as a Bar to Enforcement of International Arbitration Awards', reproduced in *Transnational Dispute Management* 1(1) (February 2004).

Kessie, Edwini, 'Enhancing Security and Predictability for Private Business Operators under the Dispute Settlement System of the WTO', *Journal of World Trade* 34(6) (2000).

Kantor, Mark, 'The Limits of Arbitration', *Transnational Dispute Management* 1 (2) (2004).

Kozawa, Sumio, 'Depoliticization of International Dispute Settlement. A Comparison of the Dispute Settlement Provisions of the WTO and the Energy Charter Treaty', *Journal of World Investment* 3(5) (2002).

Jansen, Bernhard, 'The GATT/WTO Dispute Settlement Mechanism: an Introduction', in Malcolm Evans, (ed.), *Remedies in International Law. The Institutional Dilemma*, (Oxford: Hart Publishing, 1998).

Marceau, Gabrielle, 'The Dispute Settlement Rules of the North American Free Trade Agreement: a Thematic Comparison with the Dispute Settlement Rules of the World Trade Organization', in Ernst-Ulrich Petersmann, (ed.), *International Trade Law and the GATT/WTO Dispute Settlement System* (The Hague: Kluwer Law International, 1997).

Mavroidis, Petros and Werner Zdouc, 'Legal Means to Protect Private Parties' Interests in the WTO. The Case of the EC New Trade Barrier Regulation', *Journal of International Economic Law* 1(3) (1998), p. 407.

Molinuevo, Martín, 2006, 'WTO Disciplines on Foreign Investment: Wasn't the GATS about trade in services?', Master thesis presented at the Università degli Studi di Bologna, available at www.nccr-trade.ch/ip/ip8/publications.html.

Morrison, Peter, 'WTO Dispute Settlement in Services: Procedural and Substantive Aspects', in Ernst-Ulrich Petersmann, (ed.), *International Trade Law and the GATT/WTO Dispute Settlement System* (The Hague: Kluwer Law International, 1997).

Neumayer, Eric and Laura Spess, 'Do Bilateral Investment Treaties Increase Foreign Direct Investment to Developing Countries?', *World Development* 33(10) (2005), p. 1567.

Palmeter, David and Petros Mavroidis, *Dispute Settlement in the World Trade Organization* (Cambridge University Press, 2004).

Petersmann, Ernst-Ulrich, *The GATT/WTO Dispute Settlement System. International Law, International Organizations and Dispute Settlement* (The Hague: Kluwer Law International, 1997).

Rose-Ackerman, Susan and Jennifer Tobin, 'Foreign Direct Investment and the Business Environment in Developing Countries: The Impact of Bilateral Investment Treaties' (2 May 2005), Yale Law & Economics Research Paper No. 293. Available at http://ssrn.com/abstract=557121.

Rubins, Noah, 'Must the Vistorious Investor-Claimant Relinquish Title to Expropriated Property?', *Journal of World Investment* 4(3) (2003).

Rutsel Silvestre, Martha, 'Capacity to Sue and be Sued under WTO Law', *World Trade Review* 3(1) (2004).

Schreuer, Christoph, 'Travelling the BIT Route. Of Waiting Periods, Umbrella Clauses and Forks in the Road', *Journal of World Investment & Trade* 5(2) (2004).

——'Calvo's Grandchildren: The Return of Local Remedies in Investment Arbitration', *The Law and Practice of International Courts and Tribunals* 4 (1) (2005).

Schwartmann, Rolf, *Private in Wirtschaftsvölkerrecht* (Tübingen: Mohr Siebeck, 2005).

Shaffer, Gregory, *Defending Interests. Public-Private Partnerships in WTO Litigation*, (Washington, DC: Brookings Institution Press, 2003).

Smutny, Abby, 'Arbitration Before the International Centre for Settlement of Investment Disputes', *Transnational Dispute Management* 1(1) (2004).

UNCTAD, 1999, 'Scope and Definition', UNCTAD Series on issues in international investment agreements, United Nations, New York and Geneva.

UNCTAD, 2003a, 'World Investment Report 2003 – FDI Policies for Development: National and International Perspectives', United Nations, New York and Geneva.

UNCTAD, 2003b, 'Dispute Settlement. Investor-State', UNCTAD Series on issues in international investment agreements, United Nations, New York and Geneva.

UNCTAD, 2003c, 'Course on Dispute Settlement – International Centre for the Settlement of Investment Disputes. 2.1 Overview', United Nations, New York and Geneva.

UNCTAD, 2003d, 'Course on Dispute Settlement – International Centre for the Settlement of Investment Disputes. 2.8 Post-Award Remedies and Procedures', United Nations, New York and Geneva.

UNCTAD, 2003e, 'Course on Dispute Settlement – International Centre for the Settlement of Investment Disputes. 2.9 Binding Force and Enforcement', United Nations, New York and Geneva.

UNCTAD, 2003f, 'Course on Dispute Settlement – World Trade Organization. 3.13 GATS', United Nations, New York and Geneva.

UNCTAD, 2003g, 'Dispute Settlement: State-State', UNCTAD Series on issues in international investment agreements, United Nations, New York and Geneva.

UNCTAD, 2004, 'World Investment Report 2004 – The Shift Towards Services', United Nations, New York and Geneva.

UNCTAD, 2005a, 'Latest Developments in Investor-State Dispute Settlement', IIA MONITOR No. 4 (2005), document number UNCTAD/WEB/ITE/IIT/2005/2.

UNCTAD, 2005b, 'Investor-State Disputes Arising from Investment Treaties: A Review', UNCTAD Series on International Investment Policies for Development, United Nations, New York and Geneva.

UNCTAD, 2005c, 'Investor–State Disputes and Policy Implications', Note by UNCTAD Secretariat, document number TD/B/COM.2/62, available at www.unctad.org/en/docs/c2d62_en.pdf (8/2006).

UNCTAD, 2006, 'Preserving Flexibility in IIAs: The Use of Reservations', UNCTAD Series on International Investment Policies for Development, United Nations, New York and Geneva.

Verhoosel, Gaetan, 'The Use of Investor-State Arbitration under Bilateral Investment Treaties to Seek Relief for Breaches of WTO Law', *Journal of International Economic Law* 6(2) (2003).

Von Mehren, George, Claudia Salomon and Aspasia Paroutsas, 'Navigating Through Investor–State Arbitrations – An Overview of Bilateral Investment Treaty Claims', *Dispute Resolution Journal* 59(1) (Feb.–April 2004).

Weiss, Friedl, 'Dispute Settlement Under the General Agreement on Trade in Services', in James Cameron and Karen Campbell, (eds.), *Dispute Resolution in the World Trade Organization* (London: Cameron May, 1998).

Zdouc, Werner, 'WTO Dispute Settlement Procedures Relating to the GATS', *Journal of International Economic Law* (1999), pp. 295–346.

PART 5

Market access, national treatment and domestic regulation

14

Some thoughts on the concept of 'likeness' in the GATS

MIREILLE COSSY*

A. Introduction

The concept of 'like services and service suppliers' under the General Agreement on Trade in Services (GATS) is still very much uncharted territory. One explanation may be the limited jurisprudence – only five disputes – existing so far under the GATS. In two disputes, the Panels and the Appellate Body made findings with respect to national treatment, but likeness was addressed in a very cursory manner. Moreover, in WTO services bodies, Members have shown little interest in discussing these issues *in abstracto* and have expressed a preference for leaving it to the Panels and the Appellate Body to determine likeness on a case-by-case basis, as has been done under the GATT.

There is perhaps one point on which there is general agreement: that the application of the national treatment obligation and the determination of likeness give rise to a wider range of questions – and uncertainties – under the GATS than under the GATT. The intangibility of services, the difficulty of drawing a line between the product and the producer, the existence of four modes of supply, the combined reference to services and service suppliers, the lack of a detailed nomenclature and the customised nature of many transactions are some of the factors that complicate the task of establishing likeness in services trade. In brief, 'the concept of likeness … is more elusive in services than in goods'.[1]

* The author would like to thank Rolf Adlung, Kerry Allbeury, Antonia Carzaniga, Carlo Gamberale, Gabrielle Marceau and Martin Roy for useful comments and suggestions. The views expressed are the author's only and cannot be attributed to WTO Members or the WTO Secretariat.

[1] Subsidies and Trade in Services, Note by the Secretariat, S/WPGR/9, 6 March 1996 at 3.

However, defining some basic parameters concerning the scope of the national treatment obligation, including the concept of likeness, would be useful given that, under the GATS, the application of national treatment is negotiable. Members should be able to know more precisely the extent of the obligations they contract when undertaking a national treatment commitment, and be better able to assess the potential for de facto discrimination entailed by such a commitment. As under the GATT, the definition of likeness and the scope of the national treatment obligation will have a direct impact on regulatory sovereignty. This is even more so in services, which are generally more regulated than goods.

This chapter will focus on the concept of likeness in the context of the national treatment obligation (GATS Article XVII). It is concerned mainly with situations of de facto national treatment violations[2] as these raise the thorniest questions. After a brief review of the relevant GATS provisions and the existing jurisprudence, we shall examine whether the criteria developed by GATT case law (physical characteristics, classification, end-use and consumer tastes) can be transposed to services trade and to what extent they may contribute to establishing likeness under the GATS. We shall then discuss whether 'something different' should be envisaged under the GATS.

B. Where do we start?

As under the GATT, the GATS national treatment obligation has to be understood in terms of competitive opportunities: Article XVII aims at ensuring that foreign services and service suppliers benefit from conditions of competition no less favourable than those benefiting like national services and service suppliers. GATS Article XVII reads as follows:

> 1. In the sectors inscribed in its Schedule, and subject to any conditions and qualifications set out therein, each Member shall accord to services and service suppliers of any other Member, in respect of all measures

[2] These are situations in which, although the measure does not formally distinguish services and service suppliers on the basis of national origin (we are talking about 'origin-neutral measures'), it de facto grants less favourable treatment to foreign services and service suppliers because they are less likely to be able to comply with the measure than services and suppliers of national origin. Example: a measure establishes a prior residency requirement for suppliers to be able to supply a service. De jure discrimination refers to measures which explicitly distinguish between services or suppliers on the basis of their origin.

affecting the supply of services, treatment no less favourable than that it accords to its own like services and service suppliers.[10]

2. A Member may meet the requirement of paragraph 1 by according to services and service suppliers of any other Member, either formally identical treatment or formally different treatment to that it accords to its own like services and service suppliers.
3. Formally identical or formally different treatment shall be considered to be less favourable if it modifies the conditions of competition in favour of services or service suppliers of the Member compared to like services or service suppliers of any other Member.

[10] Specific commitments assumed under this Article shall not be construed to require any Member to compensate for any inherent competitive disadvantages which result from the foreign character of the relevant services or service suppliers.

References, in paragraphs 2 and 3 of Article XVII, to formally identical or different treatment, and to the modification of the conditions of competition are directly borrowed from GATT jurisprudence on Article III. The concept 'modify the conditions of competition' was first established in the *Italian Agricultural Machinery* case. It was subsequently endorsed by the *US – Section 337* Panel, which found that '[t]he words "treatment no less favourable" in paragraph 4 [of GATT Article III] call for effective equality of opportunities for imported products' and that the purpose of that provision was to protect 'expectations on the competitive relationship between imported and domestic products'.[3]

There are also several differences between the national treatment obligations in GATT Article III and GATS Article XVII. First, whereas the GATT covers only products, the GATS national treatment obligation includes both products (services), and producers, i.e. service suppliers. Second, GATS Article XVII does not distinguish between tax and other regulatory measures. Third, GATS Article XVII does not contain a reference to 'directly competitive products', but only to 'like' services and service suppliers.

Neither the GATS nor the Guidelines for the Scheduling of Specific Commitments under the GATS[4] provide guidance as to which criteria

[3] Panel report in *US – Section 337*, paras. 5.11 and 5.13.

[4] Adopted by the Council for Trade in Services on 23 March 2001, S/L/92 (hereinafter the 'Scheduling Guidelines') and updating the 1993 Explanatory Note (MTN.GNS/W/164 + Add.1) circulated during the Uruguay Round. As stated in paragraph 1, the Scheduling Guidelines aim at explaining 'how specific commitments should be set out in schedules in order to achieve precision and clarity'; however, they 'should not be considered as a legal

should be taken into account to determine likeness. One should note, though, that the Scheduling Guidelines address the scope of national treatment in a way which might be indirectly relevant for likeness. Paragraph 15, in the section dealing with national treatment, stipulates that

> [t]here is no obligation in the GATS which requires a Member to take measures outside its territorial jurisdiction. It therefore follows that the national treatment obligation in Article XVII does not require a Member to extend such treatment to a service supplier located in the territory of another Member.

The last sentence of paragraph 16 adds that 'a binding under Article XVII with respect to the granting of a subsidy does not require a Member to offer such subsidy to a services supplier located in the territory of another Member'. The potential legal implications of this statement are unclear. For instance, does this imply that, as far as modes 1 and 2 are concerned, the national treatment obligation applies only to the service, and that likeness of the supplier becomes irrelevant?[5]

Discussions in WTO services bodies, such as the Services Council and the Working Party on GATS Rules, showed that most Members had little enthusiasm for discussing these issues *in abstracto*, but tend to share the view that it must be left to Panels and the Appellate Body to determine likeness on a case-by-case basis. One can also detect certain doubts about a mechanical transposition of the GATT approach to services trade.[6]

The limited case law on the GATS has not provided much clarification on the interpretation of likeness. As under the GATT, the burden of proof remains on the party asserting that services are like.[7] Beyond that, very little information can be gathered, either from Panel or Appellate Body reports, as to which criteria should come into play. In *EC – Bananas III*, the Panel accepted that foreign and domestic services and services suppliers

interpretation of the GATS'. In the dispute on *US – Gambling*, the Appellate Body considered that the 1993 Guidelines constituted supplementary means of interpretation, within the meaning of Article 32 of the Vienna Convention, for the interpretation of Uruguay Round schedules of specific commitments.

[5] The correlation between 'like services and service suppliers' and the possible implications of this combined reference in national treatment claims will be discussed in another publication.

[6] See, for instance, reports of the Council for Trade in Services (S/C/M/56; -59; 60) and reports of the Working Party on GATS Rules (S/WPGR/M/26; -27). See also the arguments of the parties and third parties in the panel report in *US – Gambling*.

[7] Panel report in *Canada – Autos*, para. 10.289.

were like without justifying its decision in detail. Reference was made to the 'nature' and 'characteristics' of the services at stake, but the Panel did not explain what these were. Also, the restraint exercised by the Panel when looking at the likeness of service suppliers ('to the extent that entities provide these like services, they are like service suppliers') has been criticised by various commentators.[8] This finding was repeated in the *Canada – Autos* dispute, with the useful clarification that it was applied 'for the purpose of the case', thus leaving the door open for a different approach in future cases. Moreover, in the *Canada – Autos* dispute, the Panel introduced the questionable concept of 'likeness across modes'.[9] In the latest services dispute, *US – Gambling*, the Panel exercised judicial economy with respect to the complaint of national treatment violation made by Antigua and Barbuda (hereafter 'Antigua') under Article XVII. The arguments of the parties and third parties, reflected in the descriptive part of the Panel report, offer nevertheless a good idea of the issues arising in a mode 1 national treatment claim.[10]

Another important step in the GATS national treatment case law is the rejection of the so-called 'aims and effects' test by the Appellate Body in the *EC – Bananas III* dispute (see below for a discussion on aims and effects). However, although the Appellate Body categorically condemned aims and effects, it did not indicate which criteria should be used instead to guide an assessment of national treatment claims under the GATS. We can only presume that the Appellate Body intends to use an approach based on the four-pronged GATT test (see next section).

Does the paucity of the discussion on likeness mean that, as argued by Antigua in the *US – Gambling* dispute, this concept 'will often be less important in disputes concerning trade in services than in disputes on trade in goods'?[11] There is no reason why this should be the case. In fact, we would be tempted to argue that the difficulty of apprehending likeness in services trade may be a more convincing explanation of why Panels and the Appellate Body have so far avoided engaging in the exercise.

[8] Panel report in *EC – Bananas III*, para. 7.322. This finding was made in the context of a MFN claim and was not reviewed by the Appellate Body. It is true that the issue of likeness of service suppliers was not really addressed by the parties.

[9] Panel report in *Canada – Autos*, para. 10.307. The issue of 'likeness across modes' will be discussed in another publication.

[10] Panel report in *US – Gambling*, Sections III and IV.

[11] Panel report in *US – Gambling*, para. 3.149.

C. Applying the GATT approach to assess likeness under the GATS

1. *The four criteria used under the GATT*

The basic criteria for determining likeness under the GATT were laid down in the Report of the Working Party on Border Tax Adjustments. They included 'the product's end-uses in a given market, consumers' tastes and habits, which change from country to country; the product's properties, nature and quality'.[12] Putting aside the brief – and frustrated – attempt to introduce the so-called aims and effects test, these criteria have been used consistently by GATT and WTO Panels and the Appellate Body. In the *EC – Asbestos* case, the Appellate Body summarised as follows the now well-established approach for determining likeness under the GATT:

> This approach has, in the main, consisted of employing four general criteria in analyzing 'likeness': (i) the properties, nature and quality of the products; (ii) the end-uses of the products; (iii) consumers' tastes and habits – more comprehensively termed consumers' perceptions and behaviour – in respect of the products; and (iv) the tariff classification of the products. [footnote omitted] We note that these four criteria comprise four categories of 'characteristics' that the products involved might share: (i) the physical properties of the products; (ii) the extent to which the products are capable of serving the same or similar end-uses; (iii) the extent to which consumers perceive and treat the products as alternative means of performing particular functions in order to satisfy a particular want or demand; and (iv) the international classification of the products for tariff purposes.[13]

Concerning the delicate task of assessing likeness, the Appellate Body admitted that, in applying these criteria to the facts of a particular case, 'Panels can only apply their best judgement' and that '[t]his will always

[12] Border Tax Adjustments, Report of the Working Party adopted 2 December 1970, BISD/18 (97–109).

[13] Appellate Body report in *EC – Asbestos*, WT/DS135/AB/R, para. 101. The Appellate Body noted that the fourth criterion, tariff classification, was not mentioned by the 1970 Working Party on Border Tax Adjustments, but was included by subsequent panels. It should also be remembered that the Working Party added that 'the term "… like or similar products …" causes some uncertainty and … it would be desirable to improve on it; however, no improved term was arrived at'. Thus, the Working Party itself was not convinced that the criteria it had identified were the last word for the purpose of determining likeness.

involve an unavoidable element of individual, discretionary judgement'.[14] The Appellate Body also developed the metaphor of the 'accordion' to explain that likeness does not necessarily have the same scope in the different provisions in which it appears.

> The concept of 'likeness' is a relative one that evokes the image of an accordion. The accordion of 'likeness' stretches and squeezes in different places as different provisions of the WTO Agreements are applied. The width of the accordion in any of these places must be determined by the particular provision in which the term 'like' is encountered as well as by the context and the circumstances that prevail in any given case to which that provision may apply.[15]

The key question is then whether the approach developed under the GATT to assess likeness of goods can, if transplanted to the GATS, allow an appropriate assessment of the likeness of transactions of intangible services. So far, neither the Panels nor the Appellate Body have consistently used these criteria with respect to claims regarding national treatment – or MFN – under the GATS, although reference has been made at times to one or the other (for instance, classification).

2. *Classification instruments*

(a) Likeness of services

Two main instruments have been used by Members to describe the sectors/sub-sectors covered in their specific commitments: the Services Sectoral Classification List, established by the Secretariat in 1991 ('SSCL'), and the 1991 UN Provisional Central Product Classification ('CPC prov.'). The SSCL, which is based on, and cross-refers to, the CPC, categorises services into twelve sectors and about 160 sub-sectors.[16] These two instruments are complemented by ad hoc sectoral classifications, such as the list contained in the Annex on Financial Services or the

[14] Appellate Body report in *Japan – Alcoholic Beverages II*, at 20.

[15] Appellate Body report in *Japan – Alcoholic Beverages II*, at 21.

[16] It should be noted that both the SSCL and the CPC prov. are fifteen years old and are outdated in a number of sectors. Work has been under way for the past eight years in the Committee on Specific Commitments to try to update the SSCL, but no concrete results have been achieved so far. Beyond the technical difficulties, there are also legal uncertainties relating to the consequences that new definitions – or breakdowns – could have on existing commitments (see reports of the Committee on Specific Commitments, S/CSC/M/–).

telecom model schedule. Members have a broad margin of discretion to define the services they are ready to commit on; they are encouraged, but not obliged to use these instruments.[17] This flexibility might have the potential for reducing the comparability of schedules and diminishing the usefulness of the CPC and SSCL as a basis for comparing the likeness of services transactions. In practice, however, the vast majority of existing GATS schedules are based on the SSCL, which means that they follow its structure, headings and codes. Moreover, most Members have chosen to refer to CPC numbers to define the scope of their commitments.

Despite their widespread use, the SSCL and the CPC may be less reliable than the Harmonised System ('HS'), used with respect to tariff schedules, for identifying and defining service activities. Compared to the HS and its 8,000 entries, the SSCL is characterised by a high level of aggregation (11 sectors and some 160 sub-sectors). Although the CPC is more detailed than the SSCL, its definitions remain broad, even at a five-digit level. To take one example, should services provided by cardiologists and dermatologists be considered 'like' because they fall under the same CPC category of 'specialised medical services' (CPC 93122)? In some sectors, nevertheless, the CPC breakdown may be considered to refer to clearly-defined activities: 'taxi services' (CPC 71221) is one possible example. Also, in financial services, the nature of the activities listed in the Annex seems clear.

Overall, services classification instruments appear to be less reliable than the HS for determining likeness of services, but cannot be considered totally irrelevant. On the one hand, the fact that two services fall under the same CPC category will generally be insufficient to establish likeness; at best, it will create a presumption thereof. On the other hand, there will be a strong presumption that two services falling under different categories are unlike.[18]

(b) Likeness of suppliers

The CPC defines service activities and does not consider the quality or characteristics of the supplier.[19] Hence, it can at best be indirectly relevant to compare service suppliers. In the *Canada – Autos* case, the

[17] See Scheduling Guidelines, Part II, Section A.

[18] In the same sense, see A. Mattoo, 'National Treatment in the GATS – Corner-Stone or Pandora's Box', *Journal of World Trade* 31(1) (1997), 107–135, at p. 128.

[19] The only exception is 'Postal and courier services' (CPC 751) which defines postal services as those rendered by 'national postal administration', while 'courier services' are rendered 'other than by the national postal administration'.

Panel assessed summarily the likeness of Canadian vis-à-vis Japanese companies against the relevant definition contained in the CPC. It found that, contrary to the claim made by Japan, the Canadian companies cited by Japan did not 'seem to be supplying "wholesale trade services of motor vehicles" as defined in CPC 6111'. Hence, in the absence of domestic 'like' suppliers, discrimination could not occur.[20] More generally, using the definition of services activities to deduce the likeness of suppliers would lead to the conclusion reached by the *EC – Bananas III* Panel, which was much debated by commentators, that entities providing like services are like service suppliers.

3. *Characteristics of services and service suppliers*

(a) Likeness of services

A criterion focusing on the 'physical' characteristics of products, as used in the GATT context, is a contradiction in terms for intangible and non-storable services transactions. However, leaving aside 'physical' characteristics, one could explore whether there is a role for 'intrinsic' characteristics that could distinguish one service from another. In *EC – Bananas III*, the Panel referred in general terms to the 'nature' and 'characteristics' of the transactions at issue, but did not elaborate further on these two criteria.

> [t]he nature and the characteristics of wholesale transactions as such, as well as of each of the different subordinated services mentioned in the headnote to section 6 of the CPC, are 'like' when supplied in connection with wholesale services, irrespective of whether these services are supplied with respect to bananas of EC and traditional ACP origin, on the one hand, or with respect to bananas of third-country or non-traditional ACP origin, on the other. Indeed, it seems that each of the different service activities taken individually is virtually the same and can only be distinguished by referring to the origin of the bananas in respect of which the service activity is being performed.[21]

In the *US – Gambling* dispute, the parties developed detailed arguments regarding the characteristics of the types of games found in the gambling industry, coming very close to a physical test.[22] For instance, the nature of the different types of games was discussed in detail and a comparison

[20] Panel report in *Canada – Autos*, paras. 10.283–10.289. These finding were not reviewed by the Appellate Body.
[21] Panel report in *EC – Bananas III*, para. 7.322.
[22] Panel report in *US – Gambling*, section III.B.5(a).

was made between betting on software algorithms, as is the case for Internet gambling, and using physical gambling paraphernalia as in a casino. Quoting the *EC – Asbestos* Appellate Body report,[23] the United States also looked at the differential risks of games to support its view that online gambling is not like other forms of gambling, in particular casino gambling.

The characteristics of intangible services transactions are undoubtedly more elusive than those of tangible goods, and even more so in sectors where services transactions are customised. This being said, could a criterion relating to the 'intrinsic' characteristics of services play a useful role? Such characteristics could relate, for instance, not only to the result of the service being supplied, but also to how the service is actually being supplied (operational characteristics), among others. The ordinary meaning of the activities concerned might contribute to the identification of such intrinsic characteristics (for example, in the case of hairdressing services, the intrinsic characteristics of the service would involve cutting, dressing and styling the hair). Perhaps the main difficulty is to determine how detailed an examination of intrinsic characteristics should be; the discussion which took place between the parties in the *US – Gambling* dispute offers a good illustration of this problem.[24] Moreover, the criterion relating to intrinsic characteristics may complement, but also overlap to some extent with other criteria used in the determination of likeness, in particular CPC definitions and end-uses.

(b) Likeness of service suppliers

Which characteristics of the supplier could be usefully taken into account in a determination of likeness? Some commentators have suggested that criteria such as skills, size of the company, number of employees, type of assets, technological equipment, traditional fields of business, experience and know-how could be relevant.[25]

[23] '[E]vidence relating to the health risks associated with a product may be pertinent in an examination of "likeness" under Article III:4 of the GATT 1994'. Appellate Body report in *EC – Asbestos*, para. 113.

[24] In *US – Gambling*, the parties argued at length over the characteristics of gambling paraphernalia: type of technology, sound and visual effects, surroundings, etc. See Panel report, paras. 3.152 *ff.*

[25] See, for instance, W. Zdouc, 'WTO Dispute Settlement Practice Relating to the GATS', *Journal of International Economic Law* 2 (1999), pp. 295–346, at 333 and M. Krajewski, *National Regulation and Trade Liberalization in Services – The Legal Impact of the General Agreement on Trade in Services (GATS) on National Regulatory Autonomy* (The Hague: Kluwer Law International, 2005) at p. 105.

So far, Panels have not relied on such criteria to assess the likeness of services suppliers, although parties have invoked them to support claims of likeness or 'unlikeness'. For instance, in *EC – Bananas III*, the United States argued that EC/ACP distribution suppliers were 'like' Latin American suppliers because '[t]heir respective activities, equipment, types of personnel employed and marketing stages were either identical or virtually so and the extent to which they had competed directly with each other in the EC market had been limited only by the restrictive regulatory regimes established by certain member States … and by traditional marketing relationships built up over time'.[26] In *Canada – Autos*, Canada argued that the 'size, sales volumes and the products [the Canadian company] manufactures are vastly different from those of any of the establishments identified by Japan as suppliers of wholesale trade services of motor vehicles'.[27] In *US – Gambling*, the United States proposed a distinction based on the ownership and structure of suppliers, by arguing that state monopolies of gambling services are not like non-state private suppliers.[28]

At first glance, supplier-related criteria are attractive because they could provide Panels and the Appellate Body with seemingly straightforward and objective criteria, which might help to distinguish among a range of possible like suppliers. However, these criteria raise a number of questions as, in the real world, it is impossible to find two wholly similar suppliers. For instance, it is not clear why the size of a company, the number of employees or the technological equipment should matter, when the services they supply compete on a given market. And where should the line be drawn between a 'small' and a 'big' firm?[29] Why should the ownership justify different treatment if both state- and privately owned companies behave in a commercial way and supply competitive services?[30]

[26] Panel report in *EC – Bananas III*, para. 4.677.

[27] Panel report in *Canada – Autos*, paras. 10.284–10.285.

[28] Panel report in *US – Gambling*, para. 3.154.

[29] In fact, debates in the Special Session of the Council for Trade in Services show that Members are careful to avoid discrimination among enterprises based on their size. See, for instance, Communication from Canada, Initial Proposal on Small- and Medium-Sized Enterprises, S/CSS/W/49, as well as the reports contained in S/CSS/M/8 to S/CSS/M/13. The debate also shows the difficulty of defining what a small- and medium-sized enterprise (SME) is, since definitions seem to vary widely among Members.

[30] Nothing in the GATS appears to allow for a differentiation between state-owned and privately owned companies. On the contrary, various provisions suggest that the GATS is neutral with respect to ownership. Article XXVIII(h), defines a monopoly supplier as 'any person, public or private …'; Article XXVIII(l) defines a juridical person as 'any

Taking into account such supplier-related criteria may make sense in an aims and effects type of test, where they would be assessed against the policy objective of a measure. However, in the four-pronged test currently used under the GATT, these criteria would result in an artificial selection of suppliers which may provide like – and perfectly competitive – services. As argued by Zdouc, 'the existence of *like* suppliers would become a theoretical construct which could hardly be found in the real world'.[31] This might lead to an arbitrary reduction in the scope of the national treatment obligation.

4. *The criteria of 'consumer tastes and habits' and 'end-uses'*

(a) Likeness of services

Of the various criteria used in the context of the GATT, services' 'end-uses', and, to a lesser extent, 'consumer tastes and habits' may be the most useful for comparing two services in the context of the GATS. Both criteria contribute to a determination as to whether two products are substitutable in a given market and, hence, are good indicators of a competitive relationship, the protection of which is the very purpose of GATS Article XVII.

The analysis made by the Appellate Body in the *EC – Asbestos* dispute can arguably be transposed to the services context. The concept of 'end-uses' would entail a determination of the 'extent to which products are capable of performing the same, or similar, functions (end-uses)'. The criterion of 'consumer tastes' would refer to 'the extent to which consumers are – or would be – willing to choose one product instead of another to perform those end-uses',[32] or, in other words, whether consumers regard two services as substitutable in a given market. The application of these criteria would have to rely on a significant quantity of factual evidence (will it always be available?) and will typically require a case-by-case determination.

(b) Likeness of service suppliers

Again, the criteria of end-uses and consumer tastes would be primarily relevant for comparing services and indirectly for service suppliers. A

legal entity ... whether privately owned or governmentally owned'. Allowing for an a priori distinction based on ownership would greatly reduce the value of specific commitments in sectors where public monopolies or enterprises coexist with private suppliers (telecoms, postal services, energy, etc).

[31] Zdouc (1999), at p. 333. [32] Appellate Body report in *EC – Asbestos*, para. 117.

determination of whether suppliers compete for a given market will inevitably entail an assessment of whether their services can have similar end-uses and are treated as substitutable by consumers. Nevertheless, in some sectors, it may be difficult to establish a clear distinction between the service and the supplier, especially when it comes to assessing the taste and perceptions of the consumers. This is so because, if tastes and perceptions bear directly on the service, the characteristics and qualities of the suppliers are likely to have an important influence on these tastes and perceptions. For example, the particular qualifications of certain suppliers may make them like or unlike from a consumer's point of view.

Although they tend to be recognised as the most pertinent criteria for determining a competitive likeness under the GATS,[33] end-uses and consumers' tastes have not been used so far by Panels in their assessment of likeness in services disputes. Neither *Canada – Autos*, nor *EC – Bananas III* contains a discussion of end-uses or consumers' perceptions. In *US – Gambling*, the parties had presented detailed arguments on these two criteria, but the Panel exercised judicial economy with respect to the claim of national treatment violation.

5. *Is there a need for 'something different' under the GATS?*

The approach developed in the context of the GATT to establish likeness of goods can be used to a certain extent under the GATS to establish likeness of services. It is possible that Panels and the Appellate Body will be able to improve these criteria over time, to take better account of the specificities of services trade. Nevertheless, the concept of the like supplier is likely to remain largely empty since, by their very nature, all four criteria tend to focus on the service. The use of the GATT test also means that any other justification for regulatory distinction would have to be addressed under GATS Article XIV.

However, both Members and commentators are uneasy about simply transplanting the GATT approach into the GATS. The intangibility of services activities, the existence of the four modes of supply, the difficulty in separating the service from the supplier, and the fact that regulation for services is generally more complex than for goods would seem to call

[33] In the same sense, see Mattoo, at p. 128, and W. Zdouc, 'WTO Dispute Settlement Practice Relating to the General Agreement on Trade in Services', in F. Ortino and E.-U. Petersmann (eds.), *The WTO Dispute Settlement System 1995–2003* (The Hague: Kluwer Law International, 2004), pp. 381–420 at 395.

for a more subtle approach. Legal definitions and jurisprudence show that the GATS bites deep[34] and GATS Article XIV offers even less scope than GATT Article XX for justifying exceptions.[35] Against this background, a likeness test based exclusively on the four criteria used in GATT jurisprudence may have liberalising effects beyond those anticipated by the drafters of the GATS (and by Members when they undertake national treatment commitments).[36]

A look at the approach chosen in other trade and investment instruments may also be informative. NAFTA, for instance, has a different standard of likeness for national treatment in goods and in services. Also, the concept of 'like circumstances', found in the national treatment provisions related to investment (chapter 11) and cross-border trade in services (chapter 12), appears to be broader than a simple competitive test as it may allow a panel to take into account regulatory distinctions and weigh them in the light of a 'legitimate objective'. NAFTA parties and case law seem to prefer to define likeness in services on the basis of broader concepts than those used in the WTO jurisprudence in goods.[37] The OECD Declaration on International Investment and Multinational Enterprises seems to be based on a similar idea.[38]

[34] Keeping in mind the definition of 'the supply of a service', any regulation touching upon 'the production, distribution, marketing, sale and delivery of a service' (GATS Article XXVIII(b)) could arguably be relevant. A measure affecting trade in services is 'any measure by a Member, whether in the form of a law, regulation, rule, procedure, decision, administrative action, or any other form' (Art. XXVIII(a)). Moreover, in *EC – Bananas III*, the Panel found that '[n]o measures are excluded a priori from the scope of the GATS as defined by its provisions. The scope of the GATS encompasses any measure of a Member to the extent it affects the supply of a service regardless of whether such measure directly governs the supply of a service or whether it regulates other matters but nevertheless affects trade in services'. Panel report, para. 7.285.

[35] For instance, Article XIV does not contain an exception relating to the protection of natural resources equivalent to GATT Article XX(g).

[36] In the same sense, see Zdouc (1999), at p. 342: 'overtly strict interpretations of the GATS non-discrimination clauses – irrespective of possibly *legitimate policies* pursued by national legislators – could in effect undermine sovereign regulatory powers of WTO Member governments to a larger degree than similarly strict interpretations of corresponding GATT provisions'. Other commentators share the same view.

[37] See, in particular, Dolzer R., 'National Treatment: New Developments', ICSID/OECD/UNCTAD Symposium on Making the Most of International Investment Agreements: A Common Agenda, Paris (2005).

[38] The Declaration defines national treatment as treatment 'no less favourable than that accorded in *like situations* to domestic enterprises'; according to the Investment Committee, the expression 'like situations' implies that the comparison must be made 'between firms operating in the same sector' and that 'the key to determining whether a

The question is therefore: is there a need for something different when assessing national treatment violations under the GATS, and in particular for determining likeness? This 'something different' would broaden the terms of reference which would be used to determine when there is a violation of national treatment and could thus allow regulatory distinctions not necessarily based on the four criteria used in the GATT case law to be taken into account. A key issue which, in our view, should be further discussed is whether elements related to the 'regulatory context' of the service and/or of the supplier should play a role in relation to GATS national treatment. We are aware that an approach involving regulatory distinctions not based on the four GATT criteria is currently not viewed favourably by the Appellate Body, in particular if it is called 'aims and effects'.[39] However, we believe that this issue ought to be revisited, especially considering that, in recent jurisprudence, the Appellate Body itself hinted that regulatory considerations, including governments' regulatory objectives, are relevant in a determination of national treatment violation.

D. Possible parameters for determining 'likeness' under the GATS

1. *The 'aims and effects' test in GATT/WTO*

The aims and effects approach was used in two GATT panel reports as an alternative to the traditional approach first enunciated by the Working Party on Border Tax Adjustments. It first appeared in the *US – Malt Beverages* case and was further elaborated by the Panel in *US – Taxes on Automobiles*, whose report was never adopted.[40]

This approach was based on GATT Article III:1, which provides that internal measures 'should not be applied … so as to afford protection to

discriminatory measure applied to foreign-controlled enterprises constitutes an exception to National Treatment is to ascertain whether the discrimination is motivated, at least in part, by the fact that the enterprises concerned are under foreign control'. Declaration on International Investment and Multinational Enterprises and Clarifications of the National Treatment Instrument, 27 June 2000, National Treatment for Foreign-Controlled Enterprises, OECD 2005, Annexes A and C.

39 We share Zdouc's doubts as to 'whether it was an act of judicial wisdom for the Appellate Body to engage in such merciless condemnation of "aims and effects" once and forever in the context of the GATS non-discrimination clauses'. Zdouc (1999), at p. 342.

40 According to the Appellate Body, 'unadopted Panel reports have no legal status in the GATT or WTO system … a Panel could nevertheless find useful guidance in the reasoning of an unadopted Panel report that it considered to be relevant'. See Appellate Body report in *Japan – Alcoholic Beverages II*, at 15–16.

domestic production'. At issue was Article III:2 of the GATT, dealing with discriminatory taxes, and whose second sentence makes an explicit reference to paragraph 1 of Article III. The 'aims and effects' test is intended for use in cases where the measure does not distinguish between products on the basis of their origin (i.e. cases of possible de facto discrimination). The underlying idea is that the four-criteria likeness test is too narrow because it does not allow non-protectionist government policies requiring regulatory distinctions which would be based on other criteria to be taken into account.[41] Pursuant to aims and effects, a panel considers whether a regulatory distinction between products has a bona fide aim and whether it creates a protectionist effect in favour of domestic products.[42] A regulator is allowed to treat two products differently if the regulation which distinguishes between them has neither the aim nor the effect of affording protection to domestic products. In other words, there is a determination of likeness if and when the regulation at issue has the aim and the effect of affording protection. Thus, the purpose and the market effect of a measure become an integral part of the likeness test. As explained by the Panel in *Malt Beverages*, such an approach is meant to give more deference to the regulator. Taking into account that the 'limited purpose of Article III' had to be considered in the interpretation of likeness, that Panel stated:

> [t]he purpose of Article III is thus not to prevent contracting parties from using their fiscal and regulatory powers for purposes other than to afford protection to domestic production. Specifically, the purpose of Article III is not to prevent contracting parties from differentiating between different product categories for policy purposes unrelated to the protection of domestic production.[43]

According to Hudec, the aims and effects approach had two advantages over the traditional analysis of likeness. First, it 'made the question of

[41] Panel report in *US – Taxes on Automobiles*, para. 5.8.

[42] 'A measure could be said to have the *aim* of affording protection if an analysis of the circumstances in which it was adopted, in particular an analysis of the instruments available to the contracting party to achieve the declared domestic policy goal, demonstrated that a change in competitive opportunities in favour of domestic products was a desired outcome and not merely an incidental consequence of the pursuit of a legitimate policy goal'. As to 'effect', the Panel stated that 'a measure could be said to have the *effect* of affording protection to domestic production if it accorded greater competitive opportunities to domestic products than to imported products'. *Ibid.*, para. 5.10, emphasis in the original.

[43] Panel report in *US – Malt Beverages*, para. 5.25.

violation depend primarily on the two most important issues that separate bona fide regulation from trade protection – the trade effects of the measure and the bona fides of the alleged regulatory purpose behind it'. Second, it avoided 'both the premature dismissal of valid complaints on grounds of "un-likeness" alone and excessively rigorous treatment given to claims of regulatory justification under Article XX'.[44]

The aims and effects test was rejected by both the panel and the Appellate Body in one of the first WTO cases, the so-called *Japan – Alcoholic Beverages II*, which involved a claim of violation of GATT Article III:2.[45] The first argument invoked against aims and effects was based on textual grounds: the first sentence of GATT Article III:2, which contains the concept of 'like' product, does not refer to the general policy statement of 'so as to afford protection to domestic production' contained in the first paragraph of the same provision.[46] The second concern, expressed by the panel, was the possible overlap with GATT Article XX.[47] The main problem associated with aims and effects, although not expressed directly by the Appellate Body in this dispute, seems to be the fear of having to second-guess the motivation of a regulator and the possible high level of subjectivity that this may entail.[48] In *Japan – Alcoholic Beverages II*, the Panel and the Appellate Body applied a strict

[44] R. Hudec, 'GATT/WTO Constraints on National Regulation: Requiem for an "Aim and Effects" Test', *The International Lawyer* 32(3) (1998), pp. 619–649, at 628.

[45] Appellate Body report in *Japan – Alcoholic Beverages II*, at p. 25 and Panel report, paras. 6.15–6.19.

[46] 'Article III:2, first sentence does not refer specifically to Article III:1. There is no specific invocation in this first sentence of the general principle in Article III:1 that admonishes Members of the WTO not to apply measures "so as to afford protection". This omission must have some meaning. We believe that the meaning is simply that the presence of a protective application need not be established separately from the specific requirements that are included in the first sentence in order to show that a tax measure is inconsistent with the general principle set out in the first sentence'. Appellate Body report in *Japan – Alcoholic Beverages II*, at p. 19.

[47] 'The Panel further noted that the list of exceptions contained in Article XX of GATT 1994 could become redundant or useless because the aim-and-effect test does not contain a definitive list of grounds justifying departure from the obligations that are otherwise incorporated in Article III'. According to the Panel, the 'aims and effects' test would circumvent the burden of proof established in Article XX, and might even shift this burden of proof on the complainant. Panel report in *Japan – Alcoholic Beverages II*, para. 6.17.

[48] The Panel did discuss these issues, though: 'The Panel also noted that very often there is a multiplicity of aims that are sought through enactment of legislation and it would be a difficult exercise to determine which aim or aims should be determinative for applying the aim-and-effect test. Moreover, access to the complete legislative history … could be difficult or even impossible for a complaining party to obtain. Even if the complete

reading of likeness, based on the test elaborated in the 1970s by the Working Party on Border Tax Adjustment. This approach, which is seen as resting on 'objective' criteria, has prevailed until now.

Shortly thereafter, the aims and effects approach was rejected in the context of the GATS. In the *EC – Bananas III* case, in response to EC arguments, the Appellate Body stated categorically that:

> We see no specific authority either in Article II or in Article XVII of the GATS for the proposition that the 'aims and effects' of a measure are in any way relevant in determining whether that measure is inconsistent with those provisions. In the GATT context, the 'aims and effects' theory had its origins in the principle of Article III:1 that internal taxes or charges or other regulations 'should not be applied to imported or domestic products so as to afford protection to domestic production'. There is no comparable provision in the GATS. Furthermore, in our Report in *Japan – Alcoholic Beverages*, the Appellate Body rejected the 'aims and effects' theory with respect to Article III:2 of the GATT 1994. The European Communities cites an unadopted panel report dealing with Article III of the GATT 1947, *United States – Taxes on Automobiles*, as authority for its proposition, despite our recent ruling.[49]

Is *EC – Bananas III* the requiem for any approach taking into account the regulatory context in the GATS? In fact, there are signs in more recent GATT jurisprudence that 'aims and effects' is making a discreet return, but linked to the determination of 'less favourable treatment' rather than of likeness.[50]

In *Japan – Alcoholic Beverages II*, the Appellate Body interpreted the statement of 'so as to afford protection' in Article III:1 as calling for an investigation of the 'protective application' of a measure, which 'can most often be discerned from the design, the architecture and the revealing structure of a measure'.[51] Some commentators, such as Hudec, consider that this statement is no different from aims and effects

legislative history is available, it would be difficult to assess which kinds of legislative history (statements in legislation, in official legislative reports, by individual legislators, or in hearings by interested parties) should be primarily determinative of the aims of the legislation'. Panel report in *Japan – Alcoholic Beverages II*, para. 6.16, footnotes omitted.

49 Appellate Body report in *EC – Bananas III*, para. 241, footnotes omitted.

50 See A. Porges and J. Trachtman, 'Robert Hudec and Domestic Regulation: The Resurrection of Aim and Effects', *Journal of World Trade* 37(4) (2003), pp. 783–799.

51 The full quote reads: 'Although it is true that the aim of a measure may not be easily ascertained, nevertheless its protective application can most often be discerned from the design, the architecture and the revealing structure of a measure'. Appellate Body report in *Japan – Alcoholic Beverages II*, at p. 18.

or 'at least some understanding of the "aim and effects" approach'.[52] According to Verhoosel, '[t]he concept of "protective application" is nothing but a painfully far-fetched attempt to define objective parameters which may be revealing of subjective intent'.[53] And indeed, one can draw a parallel with the statement made by the Panel in *US – Taxes on Automobiles* that 'an assessment of the aim of the legislation could not be based solely on ... statements or on other preparatory work. The aim of the legislation had also to be determined through the interpretation of the wording of the legislation as a whole.'[54]

Furthermore, in *EC – Asbestos*, the Appellate Body adopted a less literal approach in the context of GATT Article III and considered effects despite the absence of a reference to 'so as to afford protection' in Article III:4:

> the term 'less favourable treatment' expresses the general principle, in Article III:1, that internal regulations 'should not be applied ... so as to afford protection to domestic production'. ... However, a Member may draw distinction between products which have been found to be 'like', without, for this reason alone, according to the group of 'like' *imported* products 'less favourable treatment' than that accorded to the group of 'like' *domestic* products.[55]

This statement has been interpreted by some commentators as supporting the aims and effects approach.[56] More recently, the Appellate Body may have gone one step further in *Dominican Republic – Cigarettes*,

[52] Hudec, at p. 631.

[53] G. Verhoosel, *National Treatment and WTO Dispute Settlement – Adjudicating the Boundaries of Regulatory Autonomy* (Oxford and Portland, Oregon: Hart Publishing, 2002), at pp. 55–56.

[54] Panel report in *US – Taxes on Automobiles*, para. 5.12 (emphasis added).

[55] Appellate Body report in *EC – Asbestos*, para. 100. This is a 180 degree turn compared to the *EC – Bananas III* jurisprudence, where the Appellate Body said that a determination of whether there has been a violation of Article III:4 'does not require a separate consideration of whether a measure "afford[s] protection to domestic production" because Article III:4 does not refer specifically to Article III:1'. Appellate Body report in *EC – Bananas III*, para. 216.

[56] R. Howse and E. Türk, 'The WTO Impact on Internal Regulation – A Case Study of the Canada – EC Asbestos Dispute', in Gráinne de Búrca and Joanne Scott (eds.), *The EU and the WTO: Legal and Constitutional Aspects* (London: Hart Publishing, 2001), at p. 299. However, other commentators do not necessarily share this view (see L. Ehring, 'De Facto Discrimination in World Trade Law – National and Most-Favoured-Nation Treatment – or Equal Treatment?', *Journal of World Trade* 36(5) (2002), pp. 921–977). In fact, this finding could be a restatement of the principle that a foreign product can be treated differently, as long as this does not result in less favourable treatment. See Appellate Body report in *Korea – Beef*, para. 132.

where it found that 'the existence of a *detrimental effect* on a given imported product resulting from a measure does not necessarily imply that this measure accords less favourable treatment to imports if the detrimental effect is explained by factors or circumstances *unrelated to the foreign origin of the product*, such as the market share of the importer in this case'.[57] This finding, in particular the concept of 'detrimental effect' merits clarification – does it amount to discriminatory treatment? How 'detrimental' must the effect be for a finding of less favourable treatment to be made? However, allowing 'factors or circumstances unrelated to the foreign origin of the product' to be taken into account could arguably open the door to an aims and effects test.

2. What scope is there for regulatory distinctions in GATS Article XVII?

Distinguishing services and service suppliers based on the 'regulatory context' may bring us back to an aims and effects type approach. Two main questions would then merit further consideration. The first is whether aims and effects can be read in GATS Article XVII. The second is whether this test can be improved in order to ensure that only bona fide regulatory distinctions would be accepted, and that the effect on foreign services and suppliers is not disproportionate. In other words, the rationale underlying aims and effects should be kept, while correcting the weaknesses that affected its application.

Turning to the first question, we note that the concept of 'like services and service suppliers' is fluid: the ordinary meaning of 'like' is not directly applicable and requires a broader theoretical construct to establish the parameters by which likeness can be established.[58] In this context, it could be argued that looking at the aim and the effect of a measure to distinguish services and service suppliers is a priori no more arbitrary or artificial than relying on classification or consumer tastes, for instance. As already noted, the text of Article XVII does not contain a reference to the concept of 'so as to afford protection', which was used as a basis for formulating the original aims and effects test. But a possible textual link for reading aims and effects into the GATS could be found in footnote 10

[57] Appellate Body report in *Dominican Republic – Import and Sale of Cigarettes*, para. 96.

[58] The definition in the Oxford English Dictionary reads: 'Having the same characteristics or qualities as some other person or thing; of approximately identical shape, size, colour, character, etc., with something else; similar; resembling; analogous'.

to paragraph 1 of Article XVII, which stipulates that Members are not obliged to 'compensate for any inherent competitive disadvantages which result from the foreign character of the relevant services or service suppliers'.[59] Arguably, a disadvantage which is 'inherent'[60] is not due to an intent to discriminate and cannot be assimilated with a de facto discrimination; hence, to paraphrase GATT Article III:1, it is not 'so as to afford protection' to domestic services and producers. This interpretation could give meaning to footnote 10, whose role has remained unclear so far.[61] Hudec is of the view that paragraph 3 of Article XVII explicitly invites an aims and effects enquiry because a 'one-dimensional analysis of competitive impact', which some could be tempted to read in the text, might lead to invalidation of a measure on the basis of 'fortuitous market circumstances'.

Moreover, the preamble of the GATS, which provides the context for interpreting its provisions, could be invoked as a basis for considering regulatory distinctions in their own right, as it explicitly recognises 'the right for Members to regulate, and to introduce new regulations, on the supply of services within their territories in order to meet national policy objectives'. And, as discussed above, applying the criteria used in GATT jurisprudence makes little sense for determining likeness of suppliers, thus leaving this concept largely without substance; this is paradoxical considering that services regulations are most often directed at the supplier.

Against this background, regulatory distinctions could be taken into consideration to the extent that they are based on objective differences in the services and service suppliers concerned – other than classification and end-uses – and pursue non-protectionist policy objectives. Under this approach, aims and effects would replace rather than complement the GATT likeness test.

Alternatively, aims and effects could be linked to the concept of 'less favourable' in Article XVII, which would presuppose a 'traditional'

[59] In the same sense, see Zdouc (2004) and Verhoosel. Note that the use of the word 'compensate' raises several interpretative questions.

[60] The Oxford English Dictionary (on-line version) defines 'inherent' as follows: 'Existing in something as a permanent attribute or quality; forming an element, esp. a characteristic or essential element of something; belonging to the intrinsic nature of that which is spoken of; indwelling, intrinsic, essential'.

[61] The Panel in *Canada – Autos* stated that footnote 10 'does not provide cover for actions which might modify the conditions of competition against services and service suppliers which are already disadvantaged due to their foreign character'. The Panel does not clarify the meaning of 'inherent'. See Panel report, para. 10.300.

determination of likeness, probably based on a GATT-type test; however, this approach would probably diminish the importance of likeness in national treatment claims. Linking aims and effects with the determination of less favourable treatment would have the advantage of fitting with the trend in the Appellate Body's jurisprudence described above. Ultimately, whether aims and effects are considered under likeness or under 'less favourable' should not make a practical difference in terms of the final result.

The second issue: how to strengthen aims and effects raises two questions. First, there is a need to ensure that a truly objective assessment of governments' regulatory intent can be made. The Appellate Body apparently considered that such an assessment was possible when it referred to the 'protective application' of a measure which 'can most often be discerned from the design, the architecture and the revealing structure of a measure'.[62] It might also be useful to recall *Canada – Periodicals*, where the Appellate Body concluded, on the basis of, inter alia, 'the several statements of the Government of Canada's explicit policy objectives in introducing the measure and the demonstrated actual protective effect of the measure' that the 'design and structure' of the tax in question was to afford protection;[63] and in *Chile – Taxes on Alcoholic Beverages*, the Appellate Body considered that it was pertinent to take into consideration 'the statutory purposes or objectives – that is, the purpose or objectives of a Member's legislature and government as a whole – to the extent that they are given *objective* expression in the statute itself'.[64]

Second, the main problem with the aims and effects approach as applied by the panel in *US – Taxes on Automobiles*, is not that governments should be allowed to define likeness on the basis of certain regulatory objectives of their choice. It is rather that, in this dispute, the Panel opened the door to all kinds of market barriers by refusing to examine the efficiency of the measure, and by introducing an 'inherency' test which allowed claims that imported products bore a heavier burden of tax to be easily dismissed.[65] These weaknesses in the application of the aims and effects test no doubt contributed to its being discredited. Hence, should an aims and effects type approach be used under the GATS, it

[62] Appellate Body report in *Japan – Alcoholic Beverages*, at p. 18.
[63] Appellate Body report in *Canada – Periodicals*, at p. 32
[64] Appellate Body report in *Chile – Taxes on Alcoholic Beverages*, para. 62 (emphasis in the original).
[65] For a detailed critique of the panel's approach in *US – Taxes on Automobiles*, see Mattoo, at p. 131 and Verhoosel, at p. 53.

would have to be strengthened so as to ensure that a reasonable nexus exists between the measure and the policy objective in question. In other words, a solution must be found to prevent situations where a truly bona fide regulation would have a disproportionate effect on foreigners.

This leads us to argue, as other commentators have done, that an 'improved aims and effects' approach would almost inevitably entail the introduction of some kind of proportionality or necessity test in Article XVII. Mattoo seems to suggest that such a test could be inferred in relation to the supplier, but would prefer that its explicit inclusion be considered by Members in negotiations.[66] Verhoosel is in favour of an 'integrated necessity test' to be read into WTO national treatment provisions and considers that existing jurisprudence has already condoned de facto an 'in-depth' necessity test under GATT Article III:2.[67] The question is whether and how such a test could be read into GATS Article XVII.

A possible hook for ensuring that a measure has 'least trade-restrictive effects' could be found in the concept of 'inherence' contained in the footnote 10 to Article XVII. Paraphrasing the definition quoted above, an inherent competitive disadvantage 'exists as a permanent attribute or quality' in the foreign service or supplier and will thus persist irrespective of the type of regulatory measure in force. All other conditions being equal, foreign services and suppliers suffer from the very – and only – fact that they are foreign. However, determination of whether, in practice, a disadvantage does or does not result from the 'inherent' foreign character of the service or the supplier is fraught with difficulties. A reliable test has yet to be developed to give meaning to this concept of 'inherence'. Two commentators have made suggestions in this regard.

Verhoosel argues that reading a necessity test into footnote 10 'follows inevitably from the concept of "inherence", which requires a counterfactual

[66] Mattoo, at p. 133.

[67] In *Chile – Taxes on Alcoholic Beverages*, the panel examined 'the *relationship* between the stated objective and the measure in question. If a rational relationship between the stated objective and the measure is lacking, this may provide evidence of protective application' (Panel report, para. 7.148, emphasis in the original). The Appellate Body approved this approach: 'It appears to us that the Panel did no more than try to relate the observable structural features of the measure with its declared purposes, a task that is unavoidable in appraising the application of the measure as protective or not of domestic production' (para. 72). Verhoosel (pp. 29–30) argues that, in *Chile – Taxes on Alcoholic Beverages*, both the Panel and the Appellate Body held that 'the discriminatory character of a domestic regulation is revealed under GATT Article III:2, second sentence, by the lack of a "necessary" relationship between the measure and the purported policy goal'.

analysis of whether the regulation at hand constitutes a necessary condition for the same adverse effect to occur, the foreign character remaining the same'.[68] The 'counterfactual' analysis would require a Panel to examine various measures for attaining the same regulatory objective; if the adverse effects on foreign services and suppliers persist when applying these various measures, it would mean that they are 'inherent' to the foreign character, and, hence, the measure at stake would not be considered as affording less favourable treatment. This raises several questions, however. In practice, is it feasible for a Panel to assess whether different measures pursue the same objective and whether they would lead to similar adverse effects on foreigners? Should it be up to a Panel or to the parties concerned to identify the range of possible measures and their capability to pursue the same regulatory objective? Is it possible to determine *in abstracto* whether different measures present the same 'inherent' competitive disadvantage to foreign services and suppliers?

Zdouc reads a 'de facto discrimination test' into footnote 10 and proposes a three-step test to distinguish the adverse effects caused by the origin-neutral regulation at issue from those due to the foreign character of the service or the service supplier. The first step is to measure the inherent competitive disadvantages 'on the basis of a comparison between foreign and like domestic services and service suppliers'. The second is to assess the restrictive impact of the measure at stake on domestic services and service suppliers, and the third to ascertain the restrictive impact of the same measure on the foreign services and service suppliers. Then, one would compare the third variable 'with the sum of the first and second variables' and 'if these sums are equal, no de facto discriminatory domestic regulation has been taken'. Zdouc acknowledges that this approach presupposes that each of these three elements is susceptible to 'some form of quantification', but he is silent on the parameters which could be used for that purpose.[69] And that is certainly the key to implementing this test. The main challenge may well be the quantification of the first variable, which entails the identification of parameters to 'measure' an inherent competitive disadvantage. While this author does not refer explicitly to a necessity test, he notes that his proposed approach resembles the one which would normally be used under GATT Article XX or GATS Article XIV.

[68] Verhoosel, at pp. 90–91. [69] Zdouc (2004), at p. 412.

These two approaches are conceptually innovative and provide an interesting framework for further analysis. They would need to be further elaborated upon with a view to their possible implementation.

Another possible basis for reading a necessity test into Article XVII could be found in GATS Article VI dealing with domestic regulation. Article VI:5 stipulates that, in sectors where Members have undertaken specific commitments, they shall not apply 'licensing and qualification requirements and technical standards' which are, inter alia, 'more burdensome than necessary to ensure the quality of the service'. Reading Article XVII in the light of Article VI:5 could allow application of this test to origin-neutral measures in order to identify de facto national treatment discrimination. However, there may be several difficulties with this approach. First, paragraph 5 of Article VI contains the additional condition that the measure in question 'could not reasonably have been expected of the Member at the time the specific commitments … were made'. It is generally acknowledged that this condition, taken from GATT jurisprudence on non-violation cases, makes Article VI:5 an extremely weak discipline. This weakness might nevertheless disappear in the future as paragraph 4 of Article VI contains a mandate to develop disciplines on domestic regulation, containing, inter alia, the 'no more burdensome than necessary' criterion. In 1998, Members completed part of this mandate when they adopted the Disciplines on Domestic Regulation in the Accountancy Sector, which contain an elaborated necessity test inspired by Article 2.2 of the Agreement on Technical Barriers to Trade.[70] Negotiations aiming at agreeing on generally applicable disciplines are still underway.

The main obstacle, however, is that the disciplines contained in paragraphs 4 and 5 of Article VI have so far been understood by Members as applying only to non-discriminatory measures. The fact that Article VI:4

[70] Adopted by the Council for Trade in Services on 14 December 1998, S/L/64 ('Accountancy Disciplines'). They have not yet entered into force. Paragraph 2 of the Disciplines elaborated the necessity test as follows: 'Members shall ensure that measures not subject to scheduling under Articles XVI or XVII of the GATS, relating to licensing requirements and procedures, technical standards and qualification requirements and procedures are not prepared, adopted or applied with a view to or with the effect of creating unnecessary barriers to trade in accountancy services. For this purpose, Members shall ensure that such measures are not more trade-restrictive than necessary to fulfil a legitimate objective. Legitimate objectives are, *inter alia*, the protection of consumers (which includes all users of accounting services and the public generally), the quality of the service, professional competence, and the integrity of the profession'.

and 5, on the one hand, and Article XVII on the other, are mutually exclusive is not found in the GATS itself, but is expressed, for instance, in the Accountancy Disciplines, which state that they 'do not address measures subject to scheduling under Articles XVI and XVII of the GATS'.[71] Arguably, there is nothing to prevent Members from modifying this understanding and deciding that the criteria contained in Article VI:4, in particular its necessity test, can be used as context for assessing the conformity of measures under Article XVII. However, in the absence of an explicit decision by Members on this issue, resorting to the Article VI necessity test in an analysis made under Article XVII may be a long way for a Panel to go.

It is noteworthy in this regard that the current understanding that Articles VI:4 and 5 apply to non-discriminatory measures means that WTO judiciary organs could be in a position to condemn a particular measure on the ground that it is more burdensome than necessary, even though the possible negative effects are the same for both national and foreign services and suppliers, and even though the measure may be motivated by legitimate policy objectives, such as consumer or environmental protection. Now, in the absence of agreed benchmarks and standards, what would be the basis for ruling that technical standard A is more trade-restrictive than necessary, while technical standard B is acceptable? Should a non-discriminatory environmental regulation, for example, be looked at mainly through the lens of trade considerations? In practice, such a necessity test might mean, in the medium- to long-term, harmonisation of regulation through judiciary organs. Allowing the WTO judiciary system to dictate 'sound' regulation is likely to be politically unacceptable for many Members. It would also depart from the historical role of GATT/WTO, which is to ensure access of foreigners to markets and fair conditions of competition between foreigners and nationals in the market, and not to harmonise regulation. This is expressed in the third paragraph of the WTO Agreement, which states that Members desire to contribute to the 'objectives [expressed in the first paragraph] by entering into reciprocal and mutually advantageous arrangements directed to the substantial reduction of tariffs and other barriers to trade and to the elimination of discriminatory treatment in

[71] *Ibid.*, para. 1. The same idea is found in the *Scheduling Guidelines* (S/L/92), para. 14 and Attachment 4, as well as *US – Gambling*, report by the Panel, paras. 6.301–6.313.

international trade relations'. Hence, we would agree with Marchetti and Mavroidis that a necessity test 'has its limits'.[72]

Assessing national treatment claims under Article XVII in the light of a necessity test would be likely to reduce, in practice, the role of the exceptions contained in Article XIV, which might then be resorted to mainly in cases of de jure discrimination. But the Appellate Body may have already provided the answer to this type of concern when it stated that '[t]he scope and meaning of Article III:4 should not be broadened or restricted beyond what is required by the normal customary international law rules of treaty interpretation, simply because Article XX(b) exists and may be available to justify measures inconsistent with Article III:4. The fact that an interpretation of Article III:4, under those rules, implies a less frequent recourse to Article XX(b) does not deprive the exception in Article XX(b) of *effet utile*'.[73] This jurisprudence could apply *mutatis mutandis* to the relationship between GATS Articles XIV and XVII. A diminished role for Article XIV should be weighed against the possibility that Members could make regulatory distinctions beyond the limited list of exceptions contained in that provision (and the fact there would be no need to formally amend Article XIV, which is anyway an unrealistic prospect).

Finally, applying an improved aims and effects test under the GATS would be without prejudice to the approach taken under the GATT. As made clear by the Appellate Body with its 'accordion metaphor', likeness does not need to have the same scope across the different provisions of a given agreement, let alone across different WTO agreements.

E. Conclusion

The main purpose of this chapter is to contribute to a much-needed brainstorming on a question which has so far attracted surprisingly little

[72] 'On the one hand, [a necessity test] may raise interpretative problems in the future, and it is not readily apparent how such a test would be applied in the absence of internationally agreed standards or regulations that could be used as a benchmark against which to judge specific measures. On the other hand, the necessity test does not provide positive guidance for the design of a regulatory regime, since it lacks appropriate details for such an endeavour. Although this may eventually be a drawback in terms of the potential of the GATS to promote efficient regulation, it is also the reasonable outcome for an organisation such as the WTO that promotes liberalisation while respecting regulatory diversity'. J. A. Marchetti and P. C. Mavroidis, 'What Are the Main Challenges for the GATS Framework? Don't Talk About Revolution', *European Business Organization Law Review* 5 (2004), pp. 511–562 at 552.

[73] Appellate Body report in *EC – Asbestos*, para. 115.

PRIFYSGOL BANGOR UNIVERSITY LLYFRGELL LIBRARY

attention, considering its potential importance for the application of the GATS. The interpretation of the national treatment obligation in the context of services trade raises unprecedented questions in the WTO legal system. The limited GATS case-law has provided little clarification on the concept of 'like services and service suppliers' and discussions in WTO services bodies tend to indicate that most Members have little interest in discussing these issues.

The four-pronged test developed under the GATT to establish likeness of goods (classification, physical characteristics, end-uses and consumer tastes) can be used to a certain extent under the GATS, but has limits. End-uses and consumer tastes are the most useful criteria because they help to determine whether two services are substitutable in a given market and, hence, are a good indicator of a competitive relationship. The aggregated nature of services classification instruments severely restricts their relevance as possible tools for determining likeness. 'Physical characteristics' is a contradiction in terms for intangible services transactions and it is not clear whether a criterion related to the 'intrinsic' characteristics of services could prove useful in practice; furthermore, attempting to distinguish among suppliers with criteria based on 'characteristics' such as size or skills may result in artificial distinctions. Also, all four criteria bring the analysis back to the service, thus failing to address the concept of like supplier. Overall, these criteria appear to offer too narrow a base for determining likeness of services and service suppliers, and may have liberalising effects exceeding those necessary to protect conditions of competition for foreign services and service suppliers.

Hence, we would argue that a mechanical transposition of the four-pronged GATT test to assess national treatment claims under the GATS may not do justice to the more complicated nature of services trade (including different modes of supply, intangibility of transactions, application of national treatment to services and service suppliers and more complex regulations). There seems to be a need to consider something different, which would broaden the terms of reference used to determine whether there is a violation of national treatment in international services trade. Focusing on new criteria would allow different parameters to enter the equation in order to allow non-protectionist regulatory objectives (other than those deriving from the GATT likeness test or GATS Article XIV) to be taken into consideration. What is known as the aims and effects approach could offer a starting point for dealing with national treatment claims in services trade. However, while the thrust of the aims and effects approach has merits, its application should be strengthened so as to ensure that only good faith measures, having a reasonable nexus with the regulatory objective sought, would be found compatible with Article XVII. This, in turn, would mean reading some kind of necessity test into GATS Article XVII.

We are aware that the aims and effects test has been declared *non grata* by the Appellate Body. But there are signs in recent Appellate Body jurisprudence that some elements of this approach can find their way into WTO case law. This should offer an opportunity for reopening the debate.

Bibliography

Publications

Abu-Akeel, A. K., 'The MFN as it Applies to Service Trade – New Problems for an Old Concept', *Journal of World Trade* 33(4) (1999), pp. 103–129.

Davey, W. J. and J. Pauwelynn, 'MFN Unconditionality: A Legal Analysis of the Concept in View of its Evolution in the GATT/WTO Jurisprudence with Particular Reference to the Issue of "Like Product"', in Th. Cottier and P. Mavroidis (eds.), *Regulatory Barriers and the Principle of Non-Discrimination in World Trade Law* (Ann Arbor: The University of Michigan Press, 2000).

Dolzer, R., 'National Treatment: New Developments', ICSID/OECD/UNCTAD Symposium on Making the Most of International Investment Agreements: A Common Agenda, Paris (2005).

Ehring, L., 'De Facto Discrimination in World Trade Law – National and Most-Favoured-Nation Treatment – or Equal Treatment?', *Journal of World Trade* 36(5) (2002), pp. 921–977.

Howse R. and E. Türk, 'The WTO Impact on Internal Regulation – A Case Study of the Canada – EC Asbestos Dispute', in Gráinne de Búrca and Joanne Scott (eds.), *The EU and the WTO: Legal and Constitutional Aspects* (London: Hart Publishing, 2001).

Hudec, R. E, 'GATT/WTO Constraints on National Regulation: Requiem for an "Aim and Effects" Test', *The International Lawyer* 32(3) (1998), pp. 619–649.

Kajewski, M., *National Regulation and Trade Liberalization in Services – The Legal Impact of the General Agreement on Trade in Services (GATS) on National Regulatory Autonomy* (The Hague: Kluwer Law International, 2005).

Marchetti, J. A. and P. C. Mavroidis, 'What Are the Main Challenges for the GATS Framework? Don't Talk about Revolution', *European Business Organization Law Review* 5 (2004), pp. 511–562.

Marconini, M. 'The Uruguay Round Negotiations on Services: An Overview', in P. Messerlin and K. Sauvant (eds.), *The Uruguay Round – Services in the World Economy* (The World Bank, Washington D.C., 1990), pp. 19–26.

Mattoo A., 'National Treatment in the GATS – Corner-Stone or Pandora's Box', *Journal of World Trade* 31(1) (1997), pp. 107–135.

Nicolaïdis K. and J. P. Trachtman'From Policed Regulation to Managed Recognition in GATS', in P. Sauvé and R. M. Stern (eds.), *GATS 2000 – New Directions in Services Trade Liberalization* (Washington D.C: Brookings, 2000), pp. 241–282.

Porges A. and J. P. Trachtman, 'Robert Hudec and Domestic Regulation: The Resurrection of Aim and Effects', *Journal of World Trade* 37(4) (2003), pp. 783–799.

Verhoosel G., *National Treatment and WTO Dispute Settlement – Adjudicating the Boundaries of Regulatory Autonomy* (Oxford and Portland, Oregon: Hart Publishing, 2002).

Weiss F., 'The General Agreement on Trade in Services 1994', *Common Market Law Review* 32 (1995), pp. 1177–1225.

Zdouc W., 'WTO Dispute Settlement Practice Relating to the GATS', *Journal of International Economic Law* 2 (1999), pp. 295–346.

——'WTO Dispute Settlement Practice Relating to the General Agreement on Trade in Services', in F. Ortino and E.-U. Petersmann (eds.), *The WTO Dispute Settlement System 1995–2003* (The Hague: Kluwer Law International, 2004), pp. 381–420.

GATT/WTO documents

Border Tax Adjustments, Report of the Working Party adopted on 2 December 1970, BISD18/97–109.

Scheduling of Initial Commitments in Trade in Services: Explanatory Note, MTN. GNS/W/164, 3 September 1993 (1993 Scheduling Guidelines).

Subsidies and Trade in Services, Note by the Secretariat, S/WPGR/9, 6 March 1996.

Guidelines for the Scheduling of Specific Commitments under the General Agreement on Trade in Services (GATS), adopted by the Council for Trade in Services on 23 March 2001, S/L/92 (Scheduling Guidelines).

GATT/WTO Disputes

GATT disputes

Italian Discrimination of Imported Agricultural Machinery, report adopted 23 October 1958, BISD 7S/60.

United States – Section 337 of the Tariff Act of 1930, report adopted 7 November 1989, BISD 36S/345 (US – Section 337).

United States – Measures Affecting Alcoholic and Malt Beverages, report adopted 19 June 1992, 39S/206 (US – Malt Beverages).

United States – Taxes on Automobiles, report dated 11 October 1994, unadopted (US – Taxes on Automobiles).

WTO disputes

Canada –Periodicals, Canada – Certain Measures Concerning Periodicals, Panel Report, WT/DS31/R, adopted 30 July 1997, as modified by Appellate Body Report, WT/DS31/AB/R.

Canada – Autos, Canada – Certain Measures Affecting the Automotive Industry, Panel Report, WT/DS139/R, WT/DS142/R, adopted 19 June 2000, as modified by Appellate Body Report, WT/DS139/AB/R, WT/DS142/AB/R.

Chile – Alcoholic Beverages, Chile – Taxes on Alcoholic Beverages, Panel Report, WT/DS87/R, WT/DS110/R, adopted 12 January 2000, as modified by Appellate Body Report, WT/DS87/AB/R, WT/DS110/AB/R.

Dominican Republic – Import and Sale of Cigarettes, Dominican Republic – Measures Affecting the Importation and Internal Sale of Cigarettes, Panel Report, WT/DS302/R, adopted 25 April 2005, as modified by Appellate Body Report, WT/DS302/AB/R.

EC – Bananas III (US), European Communities – Regime for the Importation, Sale and Distribution of Bananas, Panel Report, WT/DS27/R/USA, adopted 25 September 1997, as modified by Appellate Body Report, WT/DS27/AB/R.

EC – Asbestos, European Communities – Measures Affecting Asbestos and Asbestos-Containing Products, Panel Report, WT/DS135/R and Add.1, adopted 5 April 2001, as modified by Appellate Body Report, WT/DS135/AB/R.

Japan – Alcoholic Beverages II , Japan – Taxes on Alcoholic Beverages, Panel Report, WT/DS8/R, WT/DS10/R, WT/DS11/R, adopted 1 November 1996, as modified by Appellate Body Report, WT/DS8/AB/R, WT/DS10/AB/R, WT/DS11/AB/R, DSR.

Korea – Various Measures on Beef, Korea – Measures Affecting Imports of Fresh, Chilled and Frozen Beef, Panel Report, WT/DS161/R, WT/DS169/R, adopted 10 January 2001, as modified by Appellate Body Report, WT/DS161/AB/R, WT/DS169/AB/R.

US – Gambling, United States – Measures Affecting the Cross-Border Supply of Gambling and Betting Services, Panel Report, WT/DS285/R, adopted 20 April 2005, as modified by Appellate Body Report, WT/DS285/AB/R.

15

Comment: The unbearable lightness of likeness

JOOST PAUWELYN

Overview

In the previous chapter Mireille Cossy essentially does three things. First, she describes the state-of-play of 'like products' under GATT national treatment: on the one hand, the four criteria of physical characteristics, end-use, consumer tastes and tariff classification; on the other hand, the formal rejection by the Appellate Body of the aims-and-effects test (both in GATT and GATS). Second, Cossy argues that likeness under GATS needs 'something different'. In her words (at pp. 339–340):

> The intangibility of services activities, the existence of the four modes of supply, the difficulty in separating the service from the supplier, and the fact that regulation for services is generally more complex than for goods would seem to call for a more subtle approach.

Third, and finally, according to Cossy, this 'something different' is an improved aims-and-effects test according to which 'elements related to the "regulatory context" of the service and/or of the supplier should play a role in relation to GATS national treatment' (at p. 341). Cossy calls her proposal an improved aims-and-effects test in that, contrary to previous GATT cases that upheld aims and effects, Cossy's test would 'ensure that only bona fide regulatory distinctions would be accepted, and that the effect on foreign services and suppliers is not disproportionate' (at p. 346). This would be achieved, argues Cossy, by strengthening the aims-and-effects test 'so as to ensure that a reasonable nexus exists between the measure and the policy objective in question' (at p. 349). This, in turn, 'would almost inevitably entail the introduction of some kind of proportionality or necessity test in Article XVII' (at p. 349), that is, a 'necessity test' within the very notion of discrimination (i.e. even before one reaches the general exceptions under Article XIV of GATS).

For a WTO staff working paper (published also on the WTO website at www.wto.org/english/res_e/reser_e/ersd200608_e.pdf) this is an important and daring analysis. In response, this comment raises two points.

Firstly, although it follows most GATT and WTO jurisprudence, as well as most commentators,[1] Cossy's focus on 'likeness' as the core element of a national treatment test, is misguided. It begs more questions than it resolves. Instead, the focus of a national treatment analysis ought to be on how to define 'less favourable treatment of foreign services or service suppliers', in particular: what qualifies as de facto discrimination? In the words of GATS Article XVII:3: What 'modifies the conditions of competition in favour of [domestic] services or service suppliers'? Similarly (but not further addressed in this comment[2]), more important than 'likeness' is the GATS expansion from like 'products' (under GATT) so as to include both like 'products' (i.e. services) and like 'service suppliers' (or what, under GATT, would be 'producers'). The coverage of both services and service suppliers under GATS national treatment not only expands the prohibitive effect of national treatment (in that discrimination of foreign suppliers also becomes actionable). Perhaps more importantly, it equally expands the permissive effect of national treatment: under GATS, differences not related to the product (i.e. service), but related rather to the production or process (i.e. service supplier), can clearly justify at least certain forms of differential treatment (otherwise Article XVII would not include a reference to like service 'suppliers').

This first point – 'likeness' is not, or should not be, central to a national treatment analysis – does not amount to saying that Cossy should have written a paper on a different topic. Rather, my point is that Cossy's proposal for what she calls an 'improved aims-and-effects' test within the definition of likeness is a dead end (or, in any event, does not resolve the core question of GATS national treatment), and that many of the questions she struggles with under 'likeness' are better addressed head-on under 'less favorable treatment of foreign services or service suppliers'.[3]

[1] For a recent example, see Julia Ya Qin, 'Defining Nondiscrimination under the Law of the WTO', *Boston University International Law Journal* 23 (2005), pp. 215–297.

[2] An earlier draft of Cossy's chapter had an entire section on likeness of services and/or service suppliers, not reflected in the final version. In footnote 5, however, Cossy promises that this will be the subject of another publication.

[3] For a similar argument in respect of GATT, see William Davey and Joost Pauwelyn, 'MFN Unconditionality: A Legal Analysis of the Concept in View of its Evolution in the GATT/WTO Jurisprudence with Particular Reference to the Issue of "Like Product"', in Petros Mavroidis and Thomas Cottier (eds.), *Regulatory Barriers and the Principle of Non-Discrimination in World Trade Law* 13–50 (University of Michigan Press, 2000), at

The second point raised in this comment is that the wedge that Cossy attempts to drive between GATT (no aims-and-effects test) and GATS (an improved aims-and-effects test) is untenable. Notwithstanding important differences between trade in services as opposed to trade in goods, to argue that GATS national treatment should focus on regulatory purpose and protectionism (improved aims-and-effects), but at the same time pretend that such 'would be without prejudice to the approach taken under the GATT' (at p. 353), is unconvincing and unrealistic. Many differences amongst goods industries or amongst services sectors are as deep as the differences pointed out by Cossy between the broad categories of goods, on the one hand, and services, on the other. Moreover, the rationale for looking at regulatory purpose and requiring proof of protectionism amounts, in the final analysis, to recognition that national treatment (both in GATS and GATT) is, and remains, about discrimination based on origin. Its rationale is not grounded in real or perceived differences between goods and services. In other words, if aims and effects is to return, in whatever guise, it should return in both GATS and GATT.

From likeness 'in the air' to concrete proof of de facto discrimination

The obsession with 'likeness' in the GATT/WTO is unheard of in any other legal arena that needs to decide cases of alleged discrimination, be it in EU law, US constitutional law or before the European Court of Human Rights. In each of these other fora, the big question is rather: how to define de facto discrimination? If a law or regulation explicitly differentiates based on sex, race or nationality, de jure discrimination is easily found (even though such discrimination might still be justified under exceptions). The sticking point, of course, is to decide whether laws or regulations that are sex-, race- or origin-neutral on their face amount to de facto discrimination of, for example, women, blacks or foreigners.

Instead of tackling this question head-on – i.e. although the law or regulation is origin-neutral on the books, is it nonetheless more burdensome on imports? – especially WTO Panels and the Appellate Body have spent most of their energy on deciding whether the domestic products and imports compared are 'comparable' or 'like' in the first place. Once

pp. 39–41 (referring to a requirement of discriminatory effect or origin-based discrimination under both Article III and Article I of GATT).

they find 'likeness', discrimination almost follows naturally, as an afterthought. Yet, this bottom-up approach of deciding, in the abstract, whether two products referred to by the complainant are 'like' – be it shochu and vodka, asbestos and other fibres, GMOs and conventional crops – is tackling the question from the wrong end. Instead of examining whether products are 'like' with reference to some purportedly neutral criteria of physical characteristics, end use, consumer tastes and tariff classifications – all of which are portrayed as permissible features on which to base regulatory distinctions – Panels ought to focus on the specific law or regulation that is at issue, and ask the following question: does the law or regulation differentiate, de jure or de facto, based on the one and only impermissible criterion, namely: national origin. Instead of approaching the question from what is permissible (the universe of features that validly make products unlike), Panels ought to approach the question from what is not permissible (the specifics of whether the regulation distinguishes based on origin).

Put differently, if a tribunal asked to decide on sex-based discrimination were to follow the WTO's (likeness) approach to nationality-based discrimination, this tribunal would, oddly enough, proceed as follows: it would focus its analysis on what makes people, in general, 'like' or 'comparable' in the abstract, and what are permissible features to differentiate between human beings (say, a person's formal education, skills or experience), rather than examine the specific law or regulation head on, and ask the obvious question: does the law or regulation differentiate based on the one and only impermissible criterion, namely: gender? In both the WTO and sex discrimination cases, the legal discipline only prohibits one single type of differentiation, namely: differentiation based on national origin or differentiation based on sex, respectively. All other real or perceived differences are ultimately irrelevant and any differentiation based on distinctions not related to sex or origin are permissible. Rather than spend time on deciding what are permissible distinctions in the abstract (making products or persons 'unlike'), adjudicators must check whether the concrete law or regulation before it distinguishes, in form or effect, based on the one impermissible feature (national origin or gender). Rather than focus on the similarity or likeness between two types of products (e.g. GMOs and conventional crops) or between two persons (e.g. men and women, blacks and whites) in the abstract, adjudicators ought to focus on whether the concrete regulation differentiates, de jure or de facto, based on the one differential that is prohibited, namely origin, sex or race.

Likeness as a mere threshold question which ultimately may be irrelevant

Granted, before one can even compare foreign products as opposed to domestic products, these products must be 'comparable'. But this is only a threshold question to the real test: assuming that the two products (or, in sex discrimination cases, the woman and man compared) are broadly speaking comparable, does the regulation distinguish, de jure or de facto, between the two, based on origin (or sex)? In other words, 'likeness' is only the trigger or threshold, not the substantive test. Broadly defining likeness activates the test more often. Yet, it should not normally lead to more findings of violation: If the regulation distinguishes between products based on genuine features that are not origin-based (e.g. physical characteristics, end use, consumer tastes or other non-protectionist reasons), then the regulation, even where the adjudicator presumed 'likeness', would not be found to distinguish based on origin anyhow. Thus, the regulation would be permissible not so much because it distinguishes between 'unlike' products, but because the complainant could not prove that it distinguishes based on origin. For example, even if one were to define like products so extravagantly broadly as to find that luxury cars and bread become comparable, a higher tax on luxury cars than bread would still not breach national treatment, as it would be very hard for the complainant to demonstrate that such tax distinction is based on national origin rather than legitimate tax objectives such as taxing luxury products higher than daily necessities (a form of progressive taxation). From this perspective, the test of likeness becomes irrelevant: Any argument that could have been made under 'likeness' (e.g. GMOs are not 'like' conventional crops because of health risks, consumer preferences, etc.) will anyhow be fished up under the real test of whether the regulation differentiates based on origin (e.g. the GMO regulation is based on health or consumer concerns, not on national origin or protectionism).

An 'improved aims-and-effects test' to check de facto discrimination (not likeness)

At this juncture, Cossy's improved aims-and-effects test becomes crucial. Again, not to decide on 'likeness' between services or service suppliers, but to decide on whether the services regulation amounts to de facto discrimination. In the words of GATS Article XVII:3: does the regulation 'modify the conditions of competition in favour of [domestic] services or service suppliers'? Since the regulation does not do so on the books, i.e. de jure, the question of the regulation's effect (does it impose a heavier burden on imports?) and/or objective purpose (is the regulation's structure and/or operation protectionist or rather based on non-protectionist goals?) must, as Cossy argues, play a decisive role. In contrast to Cossy's approach, however, it is difficult to conceive how such a search for de facto discrimination could or should be different between GATS and GATT. As noted earlier, the rationale for looking at regulatory purpose and requiring proof of protectionism amounts, at the end of the day, to recognition that national treatment (both in GATS and GATT) is, and remains, about discrimination based on origin. Its rationale is not grounded in real or perceived differences between goods and services. In other words, if aims-and-effects is to return, in whatever guise, it should return in both GATS and GATT.

As Cossy recognises, there are important signs in recent case law that some form of aims-and-effects test is back even within the GATT. Yet, the importance of a regulation's effects and objective purpose was not, in any of these cases, considered under 'likeness', but under other headings of the national treatment test. For tax distinctions between directly competitive or substitutable products (GATT Article III:2, second sentence), effect and purpose matter under the requirement that the regulation must be shown to be applied 'so as to afford protection to domestic production'. As the Appellate Body noted in *Chile – Taxes on Alcoholic Beverages*:

> we consider that a measure's purposes, objectively manifested in the design, architecture and structure of the measure, *are* intensely pertinent to the task of evaluating whether or not that measure is applied so as to afford protection to domestic production.[4]

In that same dispute, the Appellate Body was also willing to check whether objectives other than protectionism (e.g. health or progressive taxation) could rebut the claim that Chile's tax was applied 'so as to afford protection to domestic production'. In the case at hand, however, the Appellate Body found that the mere reference to such other objectives was not sufficient:

[4] Appellate Body Report on *Chile – Taxes on Alcoholic Beverages*, WT/DS87/AB/R, adopted on 12 January 2000, para. 71, emphasis in the original.

> The conclusion of protective application reached by the Panel becomes very difficult to resist, in the absence of countervailing explanations by Chile. The mere statement of the four objectives pursued by Chile does not constitute effective rebuttal on the part of Chile.[5]

Equally, even in respect of domestic regulations other than taxes (GATT Article III:4) where the requirement of 'so as to afford protection to domestic production' was not found to apply[6], the Appellate Body has stressed the importance of (1) the regulation's effect on imports as opposed to domestic production, as well as (2) the role of alternative, non-protectionist objectives. Both this 'effects' and this 'aims' or purpose analysis was conducted not under the question of likeness, but under the question of whether the regulation provides less favourable treatment to imports as opposed to domestic products.

In *EC – Asbestos*, the Appellate Body stressed that the requirement of less favourable treatment of imports is not a simple guillotine approach of finding one single imported product that is banned (say, imported asbestos) as compared to one single domestic product that is permitted (say, an alternative fibre). In addition, proof of less favourable treatment of the entire group of imports (imported asbestos and alternative fibres) as opposed to the entire group of domestic production (domestic asbestos and alternative fibres) must be demonstrated. In other words, and highlighting once more the relative unimportance of 'likeness', even where 'likeness' (between asbestos and alternative fibres) is found, we are unavoidably back to square one. Indeed, after spending pages on 'likeness' and ultimately finding 'likeness' pursuant to an intricate test, we are led back to the original and core question with which we started the national treatment analysis, namely: does the regulation favour the group of domestic products over the group of imports? Put differently, although there is no de jure discrimination (all asbestos is treated alike notwithstanding its origin; and all alternative fibres are treated alike, notwithstanding their origin), is there de facto discrimination of imports? Other than setting the trigger for application of this question, the 'likeness' analysis has not brought us one step forward. In the words of the Appellate Body:

5 *Ibid.*

6 Appellate Body Report on *EC – Bananas*, WT/DS27/AB/R, adopted on 25 September 1997, para. 216 ('a determination of whether there has been a violation of Article III:4 does *not* require a separate consideration of whether a measure "afford[s] protection to domestic production"').

> even if two products are 'like', that does not mean that a measure is inconsistent with Article III:4. A complaining Member must still establish that the measure accords to the group of 'like' *imported* products 'less favourable treatment' than it accords to the group of 'like' *domestic* products ... a Member may draw distinctions between products which have been found to be 'like', without, for this reason alone, according to the group of 'like' *imported* products 'less favourable treatment' than that accorded to the group of 'like' *domestic* products.[7]

In *Dominican Republic – Cigarettes*, the Appellate Body went a step further. In that case, there clearly was a disparate impact or effect on the group of imported cigarettes as opposed to the group of domestic cigarettes: on a per cigarette basis, the bond of five million pesos to be paid by both importers and domestic producers of cigarettes imposed a higher burden on an imported cigarette as compared to a domestic cigarette (for one thing, because importers sell fewer cigarettes in the Dominican Republic then domestic cigarette producers). In the view of the Appellate Body, however, this disparate effect on imports was not enough to find a violation of national treatment:

> the existence of a detrimental effect on a given imported product resulting from a measure does not necessarily imply that this measure accords less favourable treatment to imports *if the detrimental effect is explained by factors or circumstances unrelated to the foreign origin of the product*, such as the market share of the importer in this case. In this specific case, the mere demonstration that the per-unit cost of the bond requirement for imported cigarettes was higher than for some domestic cigarettes during a particular period is not, in our view, *sufficient* to establish 'less favourable treatment' under Article III:4 of the GATT 1994.[8]

In other words, even if a regulation has a detrimental effect on imports as opposed to like domestic products, that effect alone may not be sufficient proof of less favourable treatment of imports, i.e. protectionism of domestic production: a non-protectionist explanation – here market share, but possibly in other cases a non-protectionist alternative purpose – may demonstrate that the regulation is not de facto discriminatory based on origin.

[7] Appellate Body on *EC – Asbestos*, WT/FD135/AB/R, adopted on 5 April 2001, para. 100, emphasis in the original.

[8] Appellate Body report on *Dominican Republic – Cigarettes*, WT/DS302/AB/R, adopted on 19 May 2005, para. 96, emphasis added.

This implied requirement of something more than differential treatment between like products, and even something more than a disparate impact on the group of imports as opposed to domestic production, was reiterated most recently in the Panel report on *EC – Biotech*. In that case, the Panel assumed that biotech products and non-biotech products were like (thereby cleverly skipping the likeness question altogether), but pointed out that the EC treats all biotech products alike irrespective of origin, and also treats all non-biotech products alike irrespective of origin. The Panel then found as follows:

> Argentina is not alleging that the treatment of products has differed depending on their origin. In these circumstances, it is not self-evident that the alleged less favourable treatment of imported biotech products is *explained by the foreign origin of these products* rather than, for instance, a perceived difference between biotech products and non-biotech products in terms of their safety, etc. In our view, Argentina has not adduced argument and evidence sufficient to raise a presumption that the alleged less favourable treatment is explained by the foreign origin of the relevant biotech products.[9]

In sum, if the above-cited cases illustrate a trend, it is that in the future, most of the attention is likely to go not to likeness but to whether the regulation differentiates, either de jure or de facto, based on origin. The burden of proving de facto discrimination, or less favourable treatment of imports, rests on the complaining party. From the case law above, it seems that proof of de facto discrimination will be decided on a case-by-case basis, looking at a number of elements: the structure, design and architecture of the regulation; the way the regulation is applied; the effect of the regulation on the group of imports as opposed to the group of like domestic products; evidence of a protectionist purpose (objectively proven; not subjective intent); evidence of alternative non-protectionist purposes that explain the regulation and why it distinguishes between like products, etc. In most cases, the fulfilment of only one of these criteria will not be enough. For example, a merely incidental effect of a higher burden on imports as opposed to domestic production may not be enough to prove a violation; nor may evidence of protectionist purpose, without any disparate effect on imports. Within this mix of elements, proof of a non-protectionist purpose that justifies the regulation can play

[9] Panel Report on *EC – Biotech Products*, WT/DS291/R, adopted on 21 November 2006, para. 7.2514.

a role. In most cases, the presence of a non-protectionist purpose (say, health, the environment or consumer protection), or the absence of a discriminatory effect, will come up as evidence submitted by the defendant so as to rebut the complainant's claim of protectionism. In the end, it will be for the adjudicator to weigh everything together and to decide whether the complainant has met its burden of proving that the regulation treats imports less favourably as opposed to domestic production.

A 'necessity test' within national treatment?

The weighing exercise for finding less favourable treatment of imports or foreign services or service suppliers, depicted earlier, is unlikely to focus exclusively on whether a non-protectionist purpose explains the measure. In other words, contrary to Cossy's prediction, national treatment in either GATT Article III or GATS Article XVII is unlikely to transform into a type of 'necessity test', where the Panel would decide, as a separate matter, whether the regulation is 'necessary', for example, to protect health within the very definition of national treatment. Moreover, if, under GATT Article III or GATS Article XVII, there is to be a link between the regulation and the non-protectionist objective it aims for, this link or nexus should, in the view of the Appellate Body, be something less than 'necessity'. Indeed, in *Chile – Taxes on Alcoholic Beverages*, in response to Chile's argument that, under GATT Article III, it was not for Chile to demonstrate that the tax was 'necessary' to achieve the non-protectionist objectives of health protection and progressive taxation, the Appellate Body found as follows:

> we agree with Chile that it would be inappropriate, under Article III:2, second sentence, of the GATT 1994, to examine whether the tax measure is *necessary* for achieving its stated objectives or purposes ... It appears to us that the Panel did no more than try to relate the observable structural features of the measure with its declared purposes, a task that is unavoidable in appraising the application of the measure as protective or not of domestic production.[10]

Cossy is right, however, to 'improve' the old GATT aims-and-effects test by requiring at least some kind of nexus between the measure and the alleged non-protectionist objective that it pursues. Such reference to non-protectionist objectives, including a related nexus test, does not

[10] *Supra* note 4, para. 72 (emphasis in the original).

make the exceptions in GATT Article XX or GATS Article XIV *inutile*. To be sure, those exceptions remain fully operational for de jure discrimination (no non-protectionist objective can excuse de jure discrimination within GATT Article III or GATS Article XVII itself). But, as the Appellate Body in *Chile – Taxes on Alcoholic Beverages* implied, to require the strict test of 'necessity' in national treatment itself could lead to odd results: knowing that under the exceptions to national treatment some justifications (such as conservation of exhaustible natural resources) are acceptable under a weaker 'related to' test, to require 'necessity' within national treatment itself would somehow mean that the rule ('necessity') is stricter than the exception ('related to'). In that scenario, it would also be easier to justify de jure discrimination ('related to' test under GATT Article XX(g)), than to avoid or justify a claim of de facto discrimination ('necessity' test under GATT Article III) – another absurd result. So, should the nexus within national treatment itself be the somewhat weaker test of 'related to' or 'rational relationship' between the measure and the objective allegedly pursued? Here as well, surprising consequences may follow: knowing that some exceptions to national treatment require 'necessity' (such as GATT Article XX(b) on human health), once a Panel does find de facto discrimination under GATT Article III (i.e. the measure is not 'related to' health), then, a fortiori, the exception in GATT Article XX(b) cannot possibly be met. Although other uses remain for Article XX, in this scenario, there would simply be no exception available (once a measure was found, under Article III, not to be 'related to' health, then, for sure, it cannot possibly be 'necessary' to protect health under Article XX(b)). Yet, if one adopts a 'related to' test in national treatment for finding de facto discrimination, then at least it makes sense to be less strict on a claim of de facto discrimination (one only needs to show that the measure 'relates to' health) and more strict before justifying de jure discrimination (under Article XX, one needs to show that the measure is 'necessary' to protect health). In the end, and recalling how the reference to non-protectionist objectives within national treatment is, or should be, part of a broader weighing exercise to check whether imports or foreign services/service suppliers are treated less favourably, the nexus requirement is best held flexible. The Appellate Body has varied the strictness of the 'necessity test' under GATT Article XX and GATS Article XIV depending on 'the relative importance of the interests or values furthered by the challenged measure'; similarly, the nexus required within national treatment itself could vary depending on the 'relative importance' of the non-protectionist objective put on the table by the defendant. In that event, the required nexus could be 'necessity', 'related to' or 'rational relationship' or any other test, depending on the non-protectionist objective in question.

Moreover, if, as Cossy argues, there is already now a 'necessity test' built into the national treatment discipline of GATS Article XVII, what are the negotiators under GATS Article VI currently negotiating about? As the next chapter by Panagiotis Delimatsis demonstrates, the holy grail of Article VI negotiations seems to be a 'necessity test' for all domestic services regulations. Yet, if such test is, as Cossy claims, already present within GATS Article XVII (national treatment) what more is there to negotiate (other than to expand the services sectors in which WTO Members commit to national treatment)?

Concluding remark

When it comes to national treatment, as well as MFN, most Panels and commentators focus on the peripheral question of 'likeness'. The more important question of what factors matter, and how much, in the weighing exercise of whether a regulation affords less favourable treatment to imports or foreign services or service suppliers, has received surprisingly little attention.[11] For trade in goods, the importance of the national treatment discipline and how to define de facto discrimination was seriously reduced with the introduction of the SPS and TBT Agreements. Those agreements impose different types of 'necessity tests' even for measures that are not discriminatory. In other words, these 'necessity tests' can be applied directly, without any need for a prior finding of discrimination. The same is not true for trade in services. As the chapter by Delimatsis illustrates, negotiations on a 'necessity test' for domestic services regulations are still ongoing. Thus, until these negotiations conclude, within GATS, discrimination is the central discipline and with it, the core question of defining de facto discrimination (not so much likeness) remains crucial.

[11] For two notable exceptions, see Lothar Ehring, 'De Facto Discrimination in WTO Law: National Treatment and Most-Favoured-Nation Treatment – or Equal Treatment'?, *Journal of World Trade* 36 (2002), pp. 921–977 and Federico Ortino, 'From "Non-Discrimination" to "Reasonableness": A Paradigm Shift in International Economic Law'? Jean Monnet Working Paper 01/05, available at www.jeanmonnetprogram.org/papers/05/050101.pdf.

16

Towards a horizontal necessity test for services: Completing the GATS Article VI:4 mandate

PANAGIOTIS DELIMATSIS*

Introductory remarks

The successful culmination of the General Agreement on Trade in Services (GATS), while unsatisfactory in terms of the 'teeth' of general obligations or the level of liberalisation commitments,[1] provides the legal framework for liberalising the services trade. The breadth of the GATS coverage; the novelty of the issues at stake; the sectoral diversity; the specificities associated with services of which the state used to be the monopoly supplier or was involved in supplying; the regulatory intensity of several services sectors and the inherent complexity of the GATS due to the multiple modes of supply, are only few of the justifications for the deficiencies of the GATS. Thus, the GATS can still be seen as a work in progress, more than a decade after its inception.

Although WTO Members concluded the drafting of Articles XVI and XVII, they failed to agree on a provision that would tackle origin-neutral domestic regulations with an unduly trade-distortive effect.[2] Consequently, at the end of the Uruguay Round, Members adopted the current (weak and provisional) wording of Article VI:4 GATS. Leaving this provision unfinished, together with the choice of making the national treatment obligation a negotiable commitment, has considerably weakened the potential 'bite' of the GATS.

For want of anything better, Members explicitly conveyed in Article VI:4 their willingness to develop, through a work programme, concrete

* I am indebted to Petros Mavroidis for his mentoring during the preparation of this chapter.

[1] Rudolf Adlung and Martin Roy, 'Turning Hills into Mountains? Current Commitments under the GATS and Prospects for Change', *Journal of World Trade* 39(6) (2005), p. 1168.

[2] Panagiotis Delimatsis, 'Due Process and "Good" Regulation Embedded in the GATS – Disciplining Regulatory Behaviour in Services through Article VI of the GATS', *Journal of International Economic Law* 10(1) (2007), p. 17.

disciplines on domestic regulation. The Council for Trade in Services (CTS) established two bodies for this purpose: the Working Party on Professional Services (WPPS),[3] and its successor, the Working Party on Domestic Regulation (WPDR).[4] Thus, Article VI:4 does not incorporate a direct, horizontally (i.e. across sectors) applicable necessity test; rather, it sets up a work programme which, inter alia, contains an obligation for Members to negotiate with a view to adopting a horizontal necessity test.

This paper addresses the challenge that Members face in creating a horizontal necessity test amid extensive sectoral diversity until the end of the ongoing negotiating round. The function of this test would be to validate the GATS consistency of a measure relating to qualifications, licensing and technical standards if it is not more trade-restrictive than necessary to fulfil a Member's policy objectives. The paper argues that Members will not fulfil the mandate of Article VI:4 unless they create a necessity test. This is a conclusion that can be plausibly drawn from Article VI:4 and the related negotiating documents. In addition, the future disciplines will have limited value without some kind of necessity test, since necessity is a key proxy for drawing the line between legitimate regulatory interference and protectionism.[5]

Section 1 of this chapter addresses the objective function of Article VI:4. Section 2 identifies elements and concepts that could be relevant in creating a horizontal necessity test for services. Finally, Section 3 pinpoints common elements among the proposals submitted to date, as well as tendencies and concerns.

1. The objective function of Article VI:4

Article VI touches on the interface of services trade liberalisation and domestic policy autonomy.[6] Paragraph 4 is aimed at measures that do not discriminate (either de jure or de facto) against foreign services or service suppliers. Furthermore, such measures are predominantly qualitative, as they normally strive to ensure the quality of the service supplied. These measures usually entail minimum requirements. For instance, domestic measures that foresee the minimum requirements

[3] WTO, 'Decision on Professional Services', S/L/3, 4 April 1995, para. 1.

[4] WTO, 'Decision on Domestic Regulation', S/L/70, 28 April 1999, para. 1.

[5] Cf. WTO, WPDR, 'Report of the Meeting Held on 19 and 20 June 2006', S/WPDR/M/35, 14 August 2006, paras. 78.

[6] *In extenso*, Delimatsis, above note 2.

that a service supplier must fulfil to be eligible, under domestic law, to obtain a licence come under this provision. The aforementioned attributes of this provision are drawn from the 1993 Scheduling Guidelines[7] and reiterated in the 2001 Scheduling Guidelines.[8] Importantly, the thorny interplay between Article VI, XVI, XVII and XVIII GATS can be clarified only with reference to these Guidelines.[9] Hence, these Guidelines have been an indispensable instrument for the interpretation of the GATS.[10]

The substantive obligation of Article VI:4 provides the negotiating framework and the basic principles that Members should transform into disciplines.[11] This built-in mandate seeks to guarantee that measures relating to licensing, qualifications and technical standards are, inter alia:

a) based on objective and transparent criteria, such as competence and the ability to supply the service;
b) not more burdensome than necessary to ensure the quality of the service; and
c) with respect to licensing procedures, not in themselves a restriction on the supply of the service in question.

These criteria constitute an indicative list of minimum characteristics that the prospective regulatory disciplines should exhibit. Of course, Members are free to introduce additional features, e.g. the reasonableness of licence fees or the independence of the supervisory authority.

Paragraph 4 envisages a positive-integration-type obligation, as Members enter into multilateral negotiations with a view to creating minimum requirements for qualifications, licensing and standards that their regulatory frameworks must abide by. In the long run, such requirements will bring about regulatory reform domestically and induce regulatory cooperation. Minimum harmonisation and mutual recognition

[7] GATT, 'Scheduling of Initial Commitments in Trade in Services: Explanatory Note', MTN.GNS/W/164, 3 September 1993, para. 5.

[8] WTO, 'Guidelines for the Scheduling of Specific Commitments Under the General Agreement on Trade in Services (GATS)', S/L/92, 28 March 2001, para. 11.

[9] Panagiotis Delimatsis, 'Don't Gamble with GATS – The Interaction between Articles VI, XVI, XVII and XVIII GATS in the Light of the *US–Gambling* Case', *Journal of World Trade* 40(6) (2006), p. 1059.

[10] Cf. Panel Report, *US – Gambling*, para. 6.345, and Appellate Body Report, *US – Gambling*, paras. 237, 249.

[11] WTO, WPPS, 'Background Information on the Agreement on Technical Barriers to Trade and the Agreement on Import Licensing Procedures', S/WPPS/W/6, 29 February 1996, para. 2.

of domestic regulations will probably follow. Until this work programme is complete, Article VI:5 provides for the application of the main principles laid down in paragraph 4.[12]

Article VI:4 solely comprises domestic regulatory measures relating to qualification requirements and procedures (QRP), licencing requirements and procedures (LRP), and technical standards (TS).[13] All the same, these categories of measures include a vast array of domestic regulations.[14] Qualification requirements include substantive requirements that a service supplier has to fulfil, such as experience or language requirements, to obtain certification or a licence. Qualification procedures are administrative or procedural rules relating to the qualification requirements, such as the number and nature of documents to be filed or the fees to be paid. Licensing requirements include all substantive requirements that do not fall under the category of qualification requirements, compliance with which would allow a service supplier to obtain formal permission to supply a service. Any registration or establishment requirements are examples of this category. Licensing procedures are administrative procedures dealing with the submission and processing of an application for a licence, such as time frames for processing the licences or the number and nature of documents required. Finally, technical standards include requirements which can be related to the characteristics or the definition of the service itself, as well as to the manner in which the service is performed. For example, a code of conduct for lawyers would fall under this category. Arguably, voluntary standards (that is, standards with which compliance is optional) also come under this category.[15]

Furthermore, Article VI embraces measures *relating to* QRP, LRP and TS, implying a wide scope.[16] The implications of the prospective

[12] Delimatsis, above note 2.

[13] The initial provision included in the 'Dunkel Draft' was broader: GATT, 'Draft Final Act Embodying the Results of the Uruguay Round of Multilateral Trade Negotiations', MTN. TNC/W/FA, 20 December 1991; also WTO, CTS, 'Article VI:4 of the GATS: Disciplines on Domestic Regulation Applicable to All Services', S/C/W/96, 1 March 1999, paras. 2–3; also Terence Stewart (ed.), *The GATT Uruguay Round: A Negotiating History (1986–1992)*, Vol. 2: Commentary (Deventer: Kluwer Law and Taxation Publishers, 1993), p. 2429.

[14] WTO, WPPS, 'The Relevance of the Disciplines of the Agreements on Technical Barriers to Trade (TBT) and on Import Licensing Procedures to Article VI.4 of the General Agreement on Trade in Services', S/WPPS/W/9, 11 September 1996, para. 4.

[15] *Ibid.*, para. 6.

[16] Manifold regulatory measures fall outside the scope of Art. VI:4, such as the independence of the regulatory authority or universal service provisions, business advertising and marketing, access to networks and essential facilities.

disciplines for service suppliers through mode 4 can also be substantial. The current ubiquity of non-discriminatory, but still onerous and vague requirements and procedures negatively affecting individuals attempting to supply their services acts as a deterrent. Because unilateral action in these areas is inherently limited, Members, and especially those that are interested in effective mode 4 liberalisation, should make these negotiations a success.[17]

2. Essential elements for a horizontal necessity test – the paradigm of the accountancy disciplines and lessons drawn from regional experience

A. The necessity test in paragraph 2 of the accountancy disciplines

The WPPS first assumed the difficult task of operationalising the Article VI:4 mandate regarding the accountancy services[18] and concluded its work with the adoption by the CTS of the Disciplines on Domestic Regulation in the Accountancy Sector ('draft accountancy disciplines').[19] These disciplines apply only to Members that undertook specific commitments in the accountancy sector and should become part of the GATS no later than the end of the current services negotiations round.[20] The salient feature of these disciplines is the inclusion of a sector-specific necessity test in paragraph 2:

> Members shall ensure that measures not subject to scheduling under Articles XVI or XVII of the GATS, relating to licensing requirements and procedures, technical standards and qualification requirements and procedures are not prepared, adopted or applied *with a view to* or *with the effect of* creating *unnecessary* barriers to trade in accountancy services. For this purpose, Members shall ensure that such measures are *not more trade-restrictive than necessary to fulfil a legitimate objective.* Legitimate

[17] See Bernard Hoekman and Patrick Messerlin, 'Liberalizing Trade in Services: Reciprocal Negotiations and Regulatory Reform', in: Pierre Sauvé and Robert M. Stern (eds.), *GATS 2000: New Directions in Services Trade Liberalization* (Washington, DC: Brookings Institution/Harvard University, 2000), p. 493.

[18] Also Claude Trolliet and John Hegarty, 'Regulatory Reform and Trade Liberalization in Accountancy Services', in: Aaditya Mattoo and Pierre Sauvé (eds.), *Domestic Regulation and Service Trade Liberalization* (Oxford University Press/World Bank, 2003), p. 147.

[19] WTO, 'Disciplines on Domestic Regulation in the Accountancy Sector', S/L/64, 17 December 1998.

[20] WTO, 'Decision on Disciplines Relating to the Accountancy Sector', S/L/63, 15 December 1998, paras. 1, 3.

> objectives are, *inter alia*, the protection of consumers (which includes all users of accounting services and the public generally), the quality of the service, professional competence, and the integrity of the profession. (emphasis added)

First, paragraph 2 clarifies that measures falling under Articles XVI or XVII are not covered by this necessity test. Arguably, the administrative aspects of the Articles XVI or XVII measures relating to the accountancy sector would still fall under the accountancy disciplines and be covered by the necessity test. Paragraph 2 requires that trade-restrictiveness should be neither the objective nor the result of the application of the regulatory measure at stake, thereby establishing a purpose and effect test. In this respect, paragraph 2 borrows the wording of Article 2.2 TBT, which also covers intent and effect of creating unnecessary trade-restrictiveness. In addition, the accountancy disciplines impose a necessity test for relevant technical standards.[21]

This provision further contains an illustrative list of four legitimate objectives that a Member can pursue, i.e. consumer protection, quality of the service, professional competence, and integrity of the profession. By contrast, Article VI:4(b) considers the quality of the service as the only objective that can justify the burdensomeness of a measure relating to licensing, qualifications or technical standards. By expanding the list of objectives that are deemed explicitly legitimate, paragraph 2 contains a stronger necessity test than Article VI:4/5 GATS. This is so because, in the case of the accountancy disciplines, Members agreed unequivocally on four (instead of one, as under Article VI:4) legitimate objectives which the adjudicating bodies are bound to take into account when they examine the link between the measure selected and the objective sought.

This explicit reference to specific objectives in paragraph 2 is decisive, especially when compared with Articles 2.5 and 2.2 TBT. Article 2.2 contains a necessity test and an indicative list of legitimate objectives. In Article 2.5, however, the rebuttable presumption of necessity appears to cover only those technical regulations that are prepared, adopted or applied for one of the legitimate objectives explicitly mentioned in Article 2.2. Other possible legitimate objectives that could come under Article 2.2 do not benefit from the Article 2.5 presumption because they are not explicitly mentioned in Article 2.2. Consequently, this provision appears to establish a hierarchy of legitimate objectives, i.e. objectives

[21] WTO, above note 19, paras. 25–26; also WTO, WPDR, 'Report on the Meeting Held on 22 November 2004', S/WPDR/M/28, 25 January 2005, para. 25.

that enjoy the presumption and objectives that do not. Hence, the recognition of an objective as legitimate through its inclusion in an *indicative* list can have important ramifications.

Certainly, 'quality' can be construed broadly to comprehend not only the delivery to the consumer, but also reliability, efficiency, comprehensiveness, or objectives associated with externalities and public policy.[22] However, the Appellate Body (AB) has advanced a rather narrow interpretation of necessity in provisions entailing an exception, such as Article XX GATT.[23] Again, one cannot prejudge the interpretation of the phrase 'necessary to ensure the quality of the service' in a case involving an obligation provision, such as Article VI:4. As things stand, measures pertaining to licensing, qualifications or technical standards that do not relate strictly to the quality of the service would arguably be outlawed under Article VI:4. Measures that serve important social objectives could fall within this category, e.g. the obligation to supply a service in a bottleneck services sector in the underserved regions of a given Member at lower prices than in urban areas, or a regulation that aims at minimising the detrimental impact of a given service on the environment.

To date, the WTO adjudicating bodies have taken a deferential approach to Members' regulatory autonomy. However, it would be unreasonable for the AB to adopt an interpretation that would equate the phrase 'ensure the *quality* of the service' to the phrase 'ensure the *fulfilment of a legitimate objective*'. In addition, no persuasive argument can be made that, whereas 'quality of the service' should be interpreted broadly under Article VI:4 – to cover a gamut of objectives, inter alia, professional competence – under paragraph 2 of the accountancy disciplines the same objective, i.e. the quality of the service, must be interpreted narrowly, so that it does not overlap with professional competence which is listed as a separate legitimate objective. Recourse to Article XIV GATS would always be possible, but under the narrow interpretation scenario it would be for the respondent to establish the affirmative defence under one of the exceptions defined in an exhaustive manner. For these reasons, clarifying and probably expanding the list of legitimate objectives under Article VI:4 should be a priority for the current WPDR negotiations.[24]

22 WTO, WPDR, 'Communication from Australia', S/WPDR/W/1, 19 July 1999, para. 7.

23 Appellate Body Report, *Korea – Beef*, para. 161.

24 Geza Feketekuty, 'Regulatory Reform and Trade Liberalization in Services', in Sauvé and Stern, above note 17, p. 237.

Undeniably, the creation of a necessity test as laid down in paragraph 2 of the accountancy disciplines was a success. Nevertheless, until the disciplines become binding, it will not be possible to evaluate precisely the impact that the necessity test will have on the accountancy sector. Meanwhile, these disciplines, and the necessity test, are useful in guiding the work of the WPDR regarding the development of horizontal disciplines.

B. *The necessity requirement as reflected in RIAs*

Regional integration agreements (RIAs) have proliferated in recent years. Such agreements strive for deeper integration of the participants' services markets. The interaction between regional initiatives and the multilateral efforts under the GATS appears to be mutually advantageous. Many RIAs echo in their texts, and build on, several GATS provisions. Article VI in general (and paragraph 4 in particular) is one GATS provision found with somewhat altered wording in manifold RIAs. In this respect, numerous RIAs display a certain degree of standardisation. RIAs can be seen as indispensable 'laboratories' from which useful lessons are learnt, empowering the negotiating capacity of the participating countries in the multilateral arena as well as enriching and expediting multilateral services negotiations.[25]

At the regional level, the most comprehensive necessity tests regarding trade in services are to be found in MERCOSUR (the Southern Common Market) and the Trans-Pacific Strategic Economic Partnership (between Brunei, Chile, New Zealand and Singapore). Article X:4 of the MERCOSUR Protocol of Montevideo (signed in December 1997, entered into effect on 7 December 2005) establishes a clear-cut GATS-type horizontal necessity test with respect to measures relating to qualifications, licensing and technical standards. Likewise, paragraph 2 of Article 12.10 of the Trans-Pacific Strategic Economic Partnership, which entered into force on 28 May 2006, embodies a strong horizontal necessity test which reflects the criteria established under Article VI:4 GATS. The application of this necessity test can generate further services trade liberalisation and regulatory reform in the participants' markets.

Recently, the United States signed bilateral trade agreements with Chile, Singapore and Australia. These arrangements entail a binding

[25] Pierre Sauvé, 'Adding Value at the Periphery: Aiming for GATS+ Advances in Regional Agreements on Services', NCCR Working Paper, available at www.nccr-trade.org.

horizontal necessity test for measures relating to licensing, qualifications and technical standards. There are, nevertheless, two important caveats: first, the language that the respective provisions use is hortatory, simply requesting that participants 'endeavour to ensure' the objectivity, transparency and necessity of the VI:4-like measures; and, second, participants are bound to endorse the results of the WPDR negotiations on Article VI:4 when they enter into effect.[26]

The Japan–Singapore Free Trade Agreement also adopts a GATS-like approach. While Article 64:5 entails a necessity test concerning licensing, qualifications and technical standards, the similarities of this provision with Article VI:5 GATS render the bringing of a case based on this provision almost impossible. More specifically, Article 64:5 is applicable only in sectors where specific commitments were made. In addition, a successful complaint based on this provision would require the complainant to prove that the application of such measures resulted in a nullification or impairment of commitments that could not reasonably have been expected.[27] There is also a variant of this type of RIA, where participants agree to 'jointly review' the results of the WPDR negotiations. In the meantime, these participants are required to abide by an obligation which is identical to Article VI:5 GATS, i.e. that pending the WPDR negotiations they apply the criteria of Article VI:4(a), (b) and (c) in sectors where specific commitments were undertaken. This is notably the case with Singapore's RIAs with the European Free Trade Association (EFTA), Australia and New Zealand.

In addition to the GATS-type RIAs, there are also NAFTA-type RIAs, notably in the Western Hemisphere.[28] Such arrangements contain more narrowly drawn disciplines regarding the licensing and certification of professionals from participating Members.[29] In addition, they use a 'best-efforts' language. Generally, North American Free Trade Agreement (NAFTA)-type agreements incorporate a provision similar to Article 1210 NAFTA which requires that licensing or certification measures be based on objective and transparent criteria, and that these must be neither more burdensome than necessary to ensure the quality of the service, nor constitute a disguised restriction on the cross-border

[26] Arts. 11.8 of the US–Chile FTA, 8.8 of the US–Singapore FTA, and 10.7 of the US–Australia FTA.

[27] Cf. Art. 28 of the EFTA–Singapore FTA.

[28] Cf. Art. H-10 of the Canada–Chile FTA or Art. 10–12 of the Chile–Mexico FTA.

[29] The provisions regulating trade in services in NAFTA are dispersed.

supply of the service at issue. However, contrary to the GATS, NAFTA-type agreements call for comprehensive mutual recognition of foreign education credentials and professional qualifications in several professions. Work in these areas, however, has made little progress.

Although some RIAs embody a horizontal necessity test using 'best-efforts' language, many others simply declare their determination to respect Article VI:5 GATS and to incorporate the disciplines on domestic regulation that will emerge from the WPDR negotiations. In yet other RIAs, the coverage is fairly narrow and includes only licensing and certification of professionals. Such RIAs add nothing to the concept of necessity and its interpretation, but they borrow the wording of Article VI:4/5 GATS and simply adjust it depending on their needs, preferences, and the degree of homogeneity between the participants. In fact, such RTA provisions appear to be, for the most part, less far-reaching than the GATS, as participants are reluctant to expand on Article VI:4 or to include more categories of measures than this provision currently covers.[30] The sluggish progress at the regional level runs counter to the idea of encouraging the creation of optimum harmonisation areas as an optimal first step towards further multilateral liberalisation.[31] At least with respect to non-discriminatory non-quantitative domestic regulations, the lessons that can be learnt from the examination of RIAs are few and add nothing to the prospective multilateral VI:4 disciplines. Several RIAs have nevertheless made important progress regarding transparency. Indeed, in this case one could already speak of noteworthy GATS+ outcomes regionally.

Among RIAs, the EU experience constitutes an exception. The EU, however, has benefited from the political determination to move towards deeper and wider integration. This process has been facilitated by an integration-promoting supranational judiciary, which has made its presence felt through far-reaching interpretations that, although not always based on the Treaties, have gained the assent of the EU Member States. One of the concepts that the European Court of Justice (ECJ) has fashioned is the principle of proportionality which has its roots in German law. Whereas Article 5:3 ECT embodies one part of the three-pronged

[30] Also Sherry Stephenson, '"Deeper" Integration in Services Trade in the Western Hemisphere: Domestic Regulation and Mutual Recognition', in OECD, *Trade and Regulatory Reform – Insights from Country Experience* (Paris, OECD, 2001), p. 90.

[31] Aaditya Mattoo and Carsten Fink, 'Regional Agreements and Trade in Services – Policy Issues', June 2002.

proportionality test, i.e. the necessity requirement, and there is also a Protocol clarifying the meaning of the principle,[32] the ECJ does not search for a legal basis to justify its decision to use proportionality, but simply notes that it is a general principle of EC law.[33]

According to established case law, a measure is proportionate if it is: (a) suitable or appropriate to achieve the objective pursued; (b) necessary, i.e. the least onerous among several appropriate measures (proportionality *lato sensu*); and (c) *stricto sensu* proportionate, that is, the disadvantages (these are usually the damages to individual interests) should not be disproportionate to the objectives pursued (these usually serve the public or the Community interest).[34] *Stricto sensu* proportionality entails a cost–benefit analysis, the only difference being that the Court will not necessarily invalidate an act solely because the costs exceed the benefits. In general, the application of proportionality has been fairly flexible and applied differently to protect different interests; thus the degree of judicial review has varied considerably.[35] By the same token, in many cases the ECJ, instead of expressly scrutinising whether the measure at stake was *stricto sensu* proportionate, has favoured conducting a 'marginal review' of the costs and benefits of the contested measure under the guise of necessity.[36] Again, this does not suggest that the judicial review focuses on the existence of alternatives, since the quintessence of proportionality seems to be a balancing test weighing the objective of a given measure against its adverse effects.[37]

[32] Protocol No. 30, attached to the Amsterdam Treaty, on the application of the principles of subsidiarity and proportionality (1997).

[33] Case C-180/96, *United Kingdom v. Commission (BSE)* [1998] ECR I-2265, para. 96.

[34] Joined cases T-125/96 and 152/96, *Boehringer Ingelheim Vetmedica GmbH and C.H. Boehringer Sohn v. Council of the European Union* (T-125/96) and *Commission* (T-152/96) [1999] ECR II-3427, paras. 73ff. See also Joel Trachtman, 'Trade and … Problems, Cost-Benefit Analysis and Subsidiarity', *European Journal of International Law* 9(1) (1998), p. 35.

[35] Francis Jacobs, 'Recent Developments in the Principle of Proportionality in European Community Law', in Evelyn Ellis (ed.), *The Principle of Proportionality in the Laws of Europe* (Oxford: Hart Publishing, 1999), p. 20. See also Case C-124/97, *Markku Juhani Läärä Cotswold Microsystems Ltd and Oy Transatlantic Software Ltd v. Kihlakunnansyyttäjä (Jyväskylä) and Suomen valtio (Finnish State)* [1999] ECR I-6067, para. 36; also Case C-384/93, *Alpine Investments BV v. Minister van Financiën* [1995] ECR I-1141, para. 51.

[36] J. Snell, 'True Proportionality and Free Movement of Goods and Services', *European Business Law Review* 11 (2000), pp. 52ff.

[37] Case C-169/91, *Council of the City of Stoke-on-Trent and Norwich City Council v. B & Q plc.* [1992] ECR I-6635, para. 15.

C. *Elements and wording for a prospective horizontal necessity test*

For the creation of an effective, enforceable and operationally useful horizontal necessity test, WPDR negotiators could build on elements and wordings adopted in other WTO Agreements. As to the RIAs, the only arrangement that appears to be of interest for the work of the WPDR is that of the European Union. All the other arrangements are either contemporary with, or proliferated in the aftermath of, the GATS and, consequently reflect the structure, scope and concepts of Article VI:4 GATS. Therefore, guidance cannot be sought from such agreements. In contrast, paragraph 2 of the accountancy disciplines plays a significant role, as acknowledged by Members in their WPDR discussions. Overall, the following elements emerged as common denominators relating to the concept of necessity in the WTO. These denominators extend beyond the strict confines of any particular WTO agreement and seem to be independent of whether necessity forms part of a WTO provision foreseeing an obligation or, rather, an exception.[38]

Burden of proof

The allocation of the burden of proof is clear-cut as regards provisions establishing a positive obligation (such as paragraph 2 of the accountancy disciplines or the prospective necessity test under Article VI:4). The complainant bears the initial *onus probandi* and, once the violation of the necessity requirement is established, it is for the respondent to rebut the charge.[39]

Justiciability of instruments/level of protection/legitimate objectives

Consistent WTO case law suggests that the objectives a Member seeks to pursue will not be subject to judicial review. The legitimacy of the desired ends or the level of protection that the respondent deems appropriate are unilaterally defined and may entail a zero-risk level of attainment. Rather, what is examined is the choice of means that a Member favours.[40] As to the legitimate objectives, it is still questionable within the WPDR discussions whether a (possibly indicative) list of legitimate objectives

[38] Also WPDR, 'Application of the Necessity Test: Issues for Consideration', Job No. 5929, 8 October 1999.

[39] Appellate Body Report, *EC – Hormones*, para. 98.

[40] Cf. Appellate Body Reports, *US – Gasoline*, pp. 30–31; *Korea – Beef*, para. 176; *EC – Asbestos*, para. 168; and *US – Shrimp*, para. 121.

should be endorsed.[41] Such a list would not overlap with Article XIV GATS, but would include additional legitimate objectives. Articles 2.2 TBT, 5.6 SPS and paragraph 2 of the accountancy disciplines include an illustrative list of legitimate objectives. As Article VI:4(b) GATS identifies quality of the service as the only legitimate objective, Members have to address this issue which could be germane to all services sectors. There are three options available: (a) having no list, but simply referring to the Members' prerogative to fulfil legitimate objectives; (b) creating an open-ended list of objectives; (c) creating an indicative list of objectives horizontally and then seeking to add sector-specific objectives when developing sectoral disciplines. In any case, although a list of objectives is not indispensable,[42] a clarification of what Members understand by 'quality of the service' definitely is.

Less trade-restrictiveness/reasonable availability, and comparison of alternatives/'third aspect of necessity'

The AB has interpreted the term 'necessary' as implying 'a range of degrees of necessity'. In its view, this term would hardly encompass a measure that simply 'contributes' to the achievement of a legitimate objective.[43] According to established WTO case law,[44] a measure is deemed necessary if it is designed to protect the interest at issue or to fulfil the objective pursued. The 'nexus' – or degree of connection – between the measure and the legitimate objective sought should be sufficiently tight. Of course, necessity cannot be determined *in abstracto*; rather, a measure is 'necessary' when there is no reasonably available alternative which is less trade-restrictive and which could attain the same level of protection or fulfil the same legitimate objective as the contested measure.[45] Hence, the adjudicating bodies will first look for concrete alternative measures. In so doing, the Panels will determine whether less trade-restrictive measures are already being applied by the respondent to attain the same objectives as the challenged WTO-inconsistent measure.[46] After having identified a specific alternative measure that is

[41] Also WTO, WPDR, 'Report on the Meeting Held on 2 October 2001', S/WPDR/M/13, 21 November 2001, para. 21.

[42] Also WTO, WPDR, 'Report on the Meeting Held on 20 March 2001', S/WPDR/M/10, 10 May 2001, para. 25. See also the discussion under Section 2.A.

[43] Appellate Body Report, *Korea–Beef*, para. 161. *But* see Panel Report, *Mexico – Telecoms*, paras. 7.337–7.343.

[44] *Ibid.*, para. 157. [45] Cf. GATT Panel Report, *US* – Section 337, para. 5.26.

[46] Appellate Body Report, *Korea – Beef*, paras. 170–172. Also Gabrielle Marceau and Joel Trachtman, 'The Technical Barriers to Trade Agreement, the Sanitary and Phytosanitary Measures Agreement, and The General Agreement on Tariffs and Trade: A Map of the

reasonably available to the respondent,[47] the Panels will proceed to compare this measure with the contested one. The comparison of available alternatives is crucial and inherent in any objective evaluation of necessity. When comparing the measures it is taken for granted that both protect the interest at stake or achieve the legitimate objective equally effectively. The comparison will be made on the basis of the 'weighing and balancing' of a list of factors,[48] i.e. (a) the relative importance of the interests at stake; (b) the contribution of each of the measures to the realisation of the ends pursued and whether the design of the measures is suitable to fulfil the objective (i.e. means–ends test); and (c) the degree of trade-restrictiveness. These criteria, while illustrative, dominate in an examination of necessity by the WTO judiciary.[49] Under this necessity analysis, it is apparent that a considerable margin of appreciation exists and that second-best measures may still be deemed necessary, depending on the circumstances and the interests at stake. In any case, the analysis undertaken by the WTO judiciary will be qualitative in nature. It also goes without saying that, depending on the importance of the interests or values a measure serves, the WTO judiciary will apply differing levels of scrutiny in that the standard of review becomes more deferential and thus less intrusive when the objective is of vital importance.[50]

In the WPDR jargon, the idea that a measure that restricts trade can still be deemed necessary if there is no alternative, less disruptive and reasonably available measure that a Member could take to achieve the same policy objective echoes the 'third aspect' of the necessity test. While it has been suggested that the 'third aspect' is an important part of any

World Trade Organization Law of Domestic Regulation of Goods', *Journal of World Trade* 36(5) (2002), p. 847. If *other* Members employ less restrictive measures to tackle similar situations, this does not render a measure in a given Member unnecessary. Cf. ECJ Case C-384/93, *Alpine Investments*, above note 35, para. 51.

47 An alternative measure is to be regarded as *not* being reasonably available when its implementation is associated with significant administrative burden and excessive costs. See Appellate Body Reports, *Dominican Republic – Cigarettes*, para. 70; *US – Gambling*, para. 308; also Panel Report, *EC – Asbestos*, paras. 8.207–8.216, and Appellate Body Report, *EC – Asbestos*, para. 174.

48 Appellate Body Report, *Korea – Beef*, paras. 162–164.

49 Cf. Appellate Body Reports, *US – Gambling*, para. 306; *Dominican Republic – Cigarettes*, paras. 71–72.

50 Appellate Body Report, *EC – Asbestos*, para. 172; and Alan Sykes, 'The Least Restrictive Means', *University of Chicago Law Review* 70(1) (2003), p. 416; also Appellate Body Report, *US – Gambling*, para. 307.

necessity test, as it contains the comparison of alternatives, during the WPDR negotiations, several Members expressed the view that it is too burdensome a concept to be applied horizontally.[51] This burden could be removed by considering the introduction of concepts available under TBT or SPS. In the TBT necessity test analysed earlier, the adjudicating bodies take into account 'the risks non-fulfilment [of the legitimate objective at issue] would create'.[52] This implies a delicate balancing of costs against benefits where costs (or risks) should be carefully evaluated. In Article 5.6 SPS there are also elements that Members could consider in the process of creating a necessity test for the purposes of Article VI:4, first and foremost the *de minimis* requirement that the alternative measure should meet, namely that it should be significantly less restrictive than the measure actually chosen. Another important element in the SPS provision is the technical and economic feasibility concept, although this concept appears to encapsulate the WTO jurisprudence on the conditions that render a measure not reasonably available.

Proportionality/balancing/means–ends test

After an examination of the WTO jurisprudence on necessity and the ECJ application of proportionality,[53] similarities and differences are easily discernible. Notably since *Korea – Beef*, the WTO adjudicating bodies have come closer to the tests that the ECJ applies to pronounce on the legality of national regulatory measures. The necessity test as it is applied in the WTO also entails two of the three conditions that render a measure proportionate in the EC context: first, the suitability requirement, which examines whether the measure is suitable to attain the Member's desired objective or the level of protection (causal relationship);[54] and, second, the necessity requirement, which examines whether the measure is *necessary* for the achievement of a given objective. In *US – Gambling*, the Appellate Body emphasised that necessity is an objective standard and, therefore, a

[51] WTO, WPDR, 'Report on the Meeting Held on 19 October 1999', S/WPDR/M/3, 18 January 2000, para. 5, and 'Report on the Meeting Held on 2 October 2000', S/WPDR/M/8, 17 November 2000, p. 5; also WPDR, above note 38.

[52] Article 2.2 TBT.

[53] For a thorough analysis of the case law regarding necessity in the WTO and proportionality in the EC legal order, see Panagiotis Delimatsis, *International Trade in Services and Domestic Regulations: Necessity, Transparency, and Regulatory Diversity* (Oxford University Press, 2007), chapter iv.

[54] Cf. Appellate Body Report, *Mexico – Soft Drinks*, para. 74.

Panel is obliged, when interpreting a measure, to 'independently and objectively assess the "necessity" of the measure before it'.[55]

As the ECJ very often does not have recourse to the third requirement of the proportionality test (*stricto sensu* proportionate) to consider a measure as proportionate, the differences between the tests that the EC and the WTO judiciaries apply are not so intractable. Again, this by no means implies that the proportionality test as applied by the ECJ can be transposed to the WTO legal order. The means–ends test is also inherent to both tests, and so is balancing. Cost–benefit analysis, on the other hand, could arguably be read in the *stricto sensu* proportionality,[56] but such a primarily quantitative analysis is unlikely for an international court to undertake, first, because of the absence of legitimacy, but more fundamentally, because of the absence of factual information. In this regard, it is noteworthy that in many cases the ECJ, while having the appropriate degree of legitimacy, exercises judicial self-restraint and leaves the final decision on whether the measure satisfies the proportionality standard to the national court. Before doing this, however, the ECJ will provide the national court with some guidelines.[57]

Burdensomeness vs. trade-restrictiveness

This issue arose early in the WPDR discussions and Members appear to agree that these concepts have the same meaning.[58] This approach is perhaps convenient from a negotiator's viewpoint, but it does not seem to derive from the Article VI:4 text itself. This provision seems to suggest a two-fold task for the WPDR, one under the *chapeau* and another under the body of the provision: first, Members shall ensure that measures relating to QRP, LRP and TS do not constitute unnecessary trade barriers. This is the ultimate objective of the Article VI:4 work programme. Second, the disciplines that Members are called on to develop must ensure that such measures are not more burdensome than necessary to

[55] Appellate Body Report, *US – Gambling*, para. 304.

[56] Also Joel Trachtman, 'Negotiations on Domestic Regulation and Trade in Services (Article VI GATS): A Legal Analysis of Selected Current Issues', in Ernst-Ulrich Petersmann (ed.), *Reforming the World Trading System – Legitimacy, Efficiency, and Democratic Governance* (Oxford University Press, 2005), p. 216.

[57] Cf. Case C-368/95, *Vereinigte Familiapress Zeitungsverlags- und Vertriebs GmbH v. Heinrich Bauer Verlag* [1997] ECR I-3689.

[58] WTO, WPDR, 'Domestic Regulation: Necessity and Transparency', Communication from the EC and their Member States, S/WPDR/W/14, 1 May 2001, para. 17; also David Leebron, 'Regulatory Discrimination in Domestic United States Law: A Model for the GATS?', in Mattoo and Sauvé, above note 18, p. 52.

ensure the quality of the service (and, arguably, of the service supplier). The accountancy disciplines replaced the latter phrase with the phrase 'not more trade-restrictive than necessary to fulfil a legitimate objective', thereby adopting a TBT-type language. In paragraph 15 of the disciplines, however, Members are required to ensure that application procedures and the related documentation are not more burdensome than necessary to ensure that applicants fulfil the qualification and licensing requirements at issue and that the establishment of the authenticity of documents be sought through the least burdensome procedure. Therefore, following an interpretation that is faithful to the texts of Article VI:4 and the accountancy disciplines, trade-restrictiveness and burdensomeness can be construed to mean two different things.[59]

There are two possibilities for overcoming this interpretative conundrum. The first would advocate that, while trade-restrictiveness is not mentioned in Article VI:4, the objective of a prospective necessity test is to discipline measures relating to LRPs, QRPs and TS so that they do not create unnecessary trade barriers.[60] Therefore, only the existence of an unnecessary trade-restrictive measure could give rise to a successful complaint before the WTO adjudicating bodies. Merely arguing that a measure is inefficient or overly burdensome, while *not* trade-restrictive, would not suffice to challenge it under Article VI:4 and the nascent disciplines thereunder. The second possibility is to stick to the text and suggest that a prospective necessity test should consist of two subsets, an external and an internal layer of judicial review. First, the adjudicating bodies would examine whether the measure at issue (relating to licensing, qualifications, or technical standards) unnecessarily hampers trade in services. If so, then, under the internal layer, the judicial scrutiny would focus on the burdensomeness of the measure vis-à-vis the legitimate objective pursued, e.g. ensuring the quality of the service. If, however, a given measure is found not to be more trade-restrictive than necessary, would the adjudicating bodies have the right to outlaw such a measure on the basis that it is unduly burdensome? If so, this would mean that in the absence of a trade restriction, the WTO adjudicating bodies would still have a say in unduly burdensome regulations. A similar interpretation would undermine Members' regulatory

[59] Also WTO, WPDR, above note 12, p. 10.

[60] Also Markus Krajewski, *National Regulation and Trade Liberalization in Services – The Legal Impact of the General Agreement on Trade in Services (GATS) on National Regulatory Autonomy* (London: Kluwer Law International, 2003), p. 142.

sovereignty, something that Members would never consent to. In reality, in the WPDR discussions, Members use the two terms interchangeably.[61]

Drawing on relevant jurisprudence and several lessons learnt from RIAs, this section has identified key elements and concepts that could be relevant for the creation of an effective necessity test aimed at disciplining the trade-inhibitory effects of non-discriminatory domestic regulations in services. No doubt, legal drafting and judicial rulings already existent in other WTO agreements, such as the TBT, the SPS and the GATT, as well as the draft accountancy disciplines under the GATS, and the EU experience, can all inform the development of a horizontally applicable necessity test pursuant to Article VI:4 GATS. Importantly, the choice of wordings similar to those used in other WTO Agreements, especially in the TBT or the SPS, will also conduce to similar interpretations of the necessity requirement, bringing a considerable degree of legal certainty and textual uniformity. Members could add to these concepts the clarifications that they deem apposite for services trade and thus reduce the probability of judicial activism.[62]

3. Common ground among the WPDR proposals and services-inherent vs. political concerns

Seven communications have been submitted to the WPDR to date proposing a horizontal necessity test covering the five types of measures identified under the Article VI:4 *chapeau*.[63] Several elements are evident from these proposals. First, Members appear to agree that future disciplines will apply only to sectors with specific commitments. Again, this is in sharp contrast to the text of Article VI:4, which, contrary to paragraphs 1, 3, 5 and 6 of Article VI, does not include a similar qualification. Members disregarded this in the case of accountancy, and it seems that

[61] WTO/WPDR, 'Report of the Meeting Held on 7 and 18 February 2005', S/WPDR/M/29, 11 July 2005, para. 112.

[62] Cf. footnote 3 to Art. 5.6.

[63] Communication from Australia (S/WPDR/W/1, 19 July 1999; and S/WPDR/W/8, 15 September 2000); Communication from Korea (S/WPDR/W/9, 28 September 2000); Communication from the EC (S/WPDR/W/14, 1 May 2001); Communication from Japan (JOB(03)/45, 3 March 2003, and Rev.1 of 2 May 2003); Communication from Switzerland (JOB(05)/68, 2 May 2005); Communication from Brazil *et al.* (JOB(06)/34, 24 February 2006); Communication from Australia *et al.* (JOB(06)/193, 19 June 2006). There have also been proposals for introducing a necessity test with respect to a *specific* category of VI:4 measures, e.g. on licensing procedures (EC), on qualification requirements and procedures (Chile *et al.*) or even on technical standards (Switzerland).

they will iterate this error. Second, Members prefer an indicative list of national policy objectives, the legitimacy of which should not be questioned. This list may include ensuring the quality of the service as an example of objectives of this kind. Another interesting element is that there will definitely be derogations/transitional periods/sunset provisions, or, alternatively, best-endeavours language for the LDCs and perhaps for the developing countries as well, depending on the level of development of their services sectors. Final modalities will be a matter for negotiations.

A (services-inherent) concern expressed at the beginning of the services negotiations was whether the creation of a horizontally applicable necessity test is feasible given the extensive sectoral diversity. However, because the reasons for regulating, e.g. market failures, externalities, abuse of market power or information asymmetries, are similar regardless of the services sector concerned, a horizontal approach makes sense. Besides, Members have never excluded the possibility of developing sector-specific disciplines. In fact, the two approaches are considered as reinforcing and complementary. In a horizontal approach, however, there is always the risk that the negotiations will not reach closure because of the amount of substantial issues that have to be addressed. Nevertheless, the proposals analysed above demonstrate that a horizontal approach can bring fairly satisfactory results. In addition, in negotiations of such magnitude, the mutual interests are more easily identifiable. For instance, objective, transparent and least trade-restrictive licensing and qualification requirements and procedures have obvious implications for modes 3 and 4. Under the current WPDR negotiations, Members demonstrated in essence their willingness to conclude their discussions with the creation of horizontal disciplines, no matter how unsatisfactory these disciplines may be to start with due to possible derogations, transitional periods or because of the weak bite of the disciplines. Hence, the momentum for creating horizontal disciplines under Article VI:4 is considerable and, for many, a necessity test should form part of such disciplines.

The quality of the outcome of the WPDR negotiations cannot be prejudged. The quality will also depend on the degree of involvement of national regulators in the negotiations. National regulators' involvement to date has been marginal. As time for the creation of a final text approaches, national regulators at home start becoming more active regarding the drafting of proposals submitted to the WPDR. Their growing involvement will greatly enhance the quality and enforceability of the final text.

Another services-inherent concern is the absence of international standards and how this lack may have a negative influence on the effectiveness of a horizontal necessity test. International standards could constitute a yardstick against which the necessity of a given measure could be tested. Arguably, the availability of international standards would allow the introduction of a TBT/SPS-like rebuttable presumption of necessity for those measures that conform to these standards.[64] Theoretically, such a presumption would facilitate the task of the adjudicating bodies by making their judgments more informed and objective. In practice, however, the manner in which several of the standard-setting bodies operate makes this assumption problematic. Experience shows that there have been standards that benefit from the TBT/SPS-like presumption and which have not been adopted by consensus. Sometimes, they do not even reflect the views of the majority in the standard-setting body.[65] Another issue is that it may be erroneous to allow voluntary standards to benefit from this presumption because it distorts preferences and, in the long run, transforms such standards into de facto mandatory ones, as countries are willing to adopt them to avoid litigation. This could even lead to a race to the bottom in the case of countries that had initially opted for a higher level of protection. For these reasons, the absence of international standards can be less problematic than initially thought.

The room for manoeuvre that should be available to the adjudicating bodies when interpreting the necessity test is a significant political concern. Based on the earlier analysis of the proposals, one can infer that guidance to the WTO judiciary as to how it should construe concepts, such as necessity, burdensomeness, trade-restrictiveness, professional competence or quality of the service, is nominal. This could mean that Members feel comfortable with the interpretations that the adjudicating bodies advanced when dealing with similar concepts in other WTO Agreements. Alternatively, this might imply that Members could not be more specific without jeopardising the effectiveness of a necessity test destined to apply horizontally. Or, perhaps, that Members could not agree on more specific provisions, for instance on a provision similar to

64 Even though international standards in services are currently scarce, there are RIAs that introduce a similar presumption. Cf. Arts. 28.6 EFTA–Singapore FTA, 28.6 EFTA–Chile FTA, and 21.4 New Zealand–Singapore CEP.

65 Doaa Abdel Motaal, 'The "Multilateral Scientific Consensus" and the World Trade Organization', *Journal of World Trade* 38(5) (2005), pp. 871–872.

footnote 3 to Article 5.6 SPS, and hence this was the only solution to avoid the deadlock and, a fortiori, the incremental transaction costs.

Nonetheless, the most important challenge that the proponents of a necessity test appear to face is that of allaying the fears of those Members that oppose the adoption of a horizontal necessity test on the grounds that it curtails the regulatory flexibility they enjoy.[66] This fear recurs time and again despite the numerous assurances in Members' proposals and during the WPDR discussions that Members' right to regulate, including the right to introduce or to maintain regulations that aim to ensure the fulfilment of national policy objectives, and to adopt certain regulatory approaches or regulatory provisions, is non-negotiable. After all, similar necessity tests are also present in other WTO Agreements and the experience from the case law demonstrates that this right has been adequately preserved. A necessity test is crucial for effective and operationally useful disciplines under Article VI:4. This view is strongly corroborated by the proposal submitted by Australia *et al.* Necessity tests are envisaged for all categories of measures, simply because a criterion or benchmark is needed against which the future disciplines should be judged. In other words, necessity will be part of the final outcome of the WPDR negotiations to give meaning to the adopted rules. Therefore, it is in Members' interests to spell out the content of a prospective horizontal necessity test, rather than to entrust the interpretation of any ambiguous wording to the WTO judiciary.

Because Article VI:4 can be likened to a potentially powerful provision promoting positive integration, the completion of the Article VI:4 mandate may contribute to greater regulatory cooperation and convergence, and/or pressures towards harmonisation and recognition of domestic regulations dealing with licensing, qualifications or technical standards.[67] Although this is not going to occur any time soon, it leads to caution and wariness on the side of regulators in capitals and negotiators in Geneva. For instance, in May 2006, Brazil *et al.* revised their proposal to withdraw the horizontal necessity test that they had initially proposed.[68] To justify this decision they contended – wrongly in my view – that Article VI:4 does not require the incorporation of a

[66] Aaditya Mattoo, 'Services in a Development Round: Three Goals and Three Proposals', *Journal of World Trade* 39(6) (2005), p. 1229.

[67] In fact, the necessity test is a form of 'forced recognition'. See Productivity Commission/ Australian National University, *Achieving Better Regulation of Services, Conference Proceedings* (Canberra, AusInfo: 2000), p. 56.

[68] See above, note 63.

horizontally applicable necessity test in future disciplines. The African, Caribbean and Pacific Group of States (ACP) likewise expressed their opposition to the incorporation of a necessity test in the future disciplines because it would hamper their flexibility to regulate.[69]

To allay the worries expressed mostly by developing countries or LDCs, Members could allow for derogations that would apply to the developing country Members for a certain period. An additional safeguard in this respect is the decision to apply the future disciplines only to sectors where specific commitments are made. Hence, when a Member decides to liberalise a sector, it should be aware that this sector is also covered by a necessity test for those measures that relate to licencing, qualifications or technical standards. While Article VI:4 does not embody such a qualification, the conditional application of a horizontal necessity test may be a crucial element in its political acceptance. Therefore, political reality suggests that a horizontal necessity test will apply only to committed sectors.

Of course, developed countries may also oppose a necessity test. Discussions in the WPDR have, for instance, revealed the considerable reluctance of the United States government, and of its powerful domestic regulatory agencies, to contemplate the adoption of a necessity test under the GATS that might subject sovereign non-discriminatory regulatory conduct to a trade or market-access test.[70] This is somewhat paradoxical for a country that has such a long tradition of applying cost–benefit analysis in domestic regulation; whose goods producers are already subject to a necessity test under the TBT and SPS agreements; and whose services industry is the world's most internationalised, and hence the most likely to suffer from unduly burdensome regulatory conduct overseas. To date, the United States government has argued in favour of a strengthening of the GATS transparency disciplines rather than a horizontal necessity test and has advanced proposals on such disciplines.[71] Nevertheless, it is not clear whether the United States would mind agreeing on a horizontal necessity test in the final outcome of the WPDR negotiations on condition that its proposal for horizontal transparency disciplines finds acceptance among Members. From a public-interest

[69] JOB(06)/136, 2 May 2006.

[70] WPDR, 'Outline of US Position on a Draft Consolidated Text in the WPDR', Communication from the United States, JOB(06)/223, 11 July 2006, para. 3.

[71] The most recent version of the US proposal is contained in WPDR, 'Horizontal Transparency Disciplines in Domestic Regulation', JOB(06)/182, 9 June 2006.

point of view, a trade-off between necessity and transparency would appear a desirable means of enhancing the GATS. Such a combination would arguably help improve the quality of domestic rule-making in both substantive and procedural terms. Transparency, together with necessity, can indeed be expected to reduce the trade-restrictiveness and burdensomeness of regulatory measures by increasing accountability, predictability and legal certainty, while also reducing protectionist bias, regulatory capture and similar 'sirens'.

Finally, Members have to decide carefully on the legal status of the prospective disciplines. The option that appears the most suitable is to incorporate the text of the disciplines in an Annex on Domestic Regulation, as first proposed by Japan. By virtue of Article XXIX GATS, the disciplines would then become an integral part of the GATS. Another option would be to create a reference paper. In this case, no consensus would be required. Members could also agree to list the disciplines in the form of additional commitments in their schedules. Nevertheless, this option would involve negotiations of a request–offer nature.[72]

Conclusions

This chapter discussed issues of legal interpretation, political realism and intense bargaining regarding the fulfilment of the Article VI:4 mandate. The creation of a necessity test covering all services sectors and all five categories of measures identified in the *chapeau* of this provision is the nucleus of this mandate. Necessity remains a highly controversial concept, as it touches upon domestic regulations and questions their rationale vis-à-vis trade liberalisation.

Theoretical and practical issues associated with the possible creation of a horizontal necessity test were presented. The essential elements of any necessity test set out in numerous WTO Agreements, such as the less/least trade-restrictiveness, balancing, means–ends test, comparison between alternatives and reasonable availability, do not seem to be Agreement-specific. Therefore, several interpretations made by the adjudicating bodies relating to necessity tests embodied in other WTO Agreements or RIAs (notably the EU proportionality test) can be helpful in clarifying similar notions under Article VI:4.

[72] For instance, the regulatory disciplines of the Reference Paper on Telecommunications were negotiated as additional commitments and Members inscribed them under the Additional Commitments column in their Schedules of Commitments.

Members should seek to create a horizontal necessity test that will build on these concepts and be flexible enough to encompass several qualifications, thereby addressing Members' worries regarding the preservation of their regulatory autonomy and allowing a margin of appreciation and room for manoeuvre to national regulatory authorities. For instance, Members should consider the *de minimis* requirement laid down in Article 5.6 SPS with respect to the possible alternative measures that could outlaw the measure actually chosen. Equally interesting for the WPDR negotiations could be the TBT language. The risks of non-fulfilment of the objective should be taken into account when examining the necessity of a given measure. However, a necessity test that covers measures having an unnecessarily trade-restrictive *effect* has little chance of being accepted horizontally, as it can be very intrusive. Such coverage can be accepted only at a sectoral level, as the accountancy disciplines demonstrated. Provisions that foresee transitional periods and flexibility of compliance for developing countries and LDCs depending on the level of development of their service sector are equally crucial for the overall acceptance of the future VI:4 disciplines.

Recently, the WPDR Chairman presented a consolidated draft text of VI:4 disciplines which embodies several necessity tests.[73] However, he takes note of many Members' opposition against the adoption of such tests. Again, the creation of a horizontal necessity test as part of the prospective horizontal disciplines of Article VI:4 is both feasible and essential. If no necessity test is created at the end of the negotiations, Members will not have fulfilled the mandate prescribed in Article VI:4. The absence of a kind of necessity test would effectively render the new disciplines without any real value, as no benchmark would be available to the WTO judiciary against which to judge the challenged measures. Since operational regulatory disciplines under Article VI:4 are in all Members' interests, the inclusion of a necessity test appears to be a 'necessary evil'.

Bibliography

Adlung, Rudolf and Martin Roy, 'Turning Hills into Mountains? Current Commitments under the GATS and Prospects for Change', *Journal of World Trade* 39(6) (2005), pp. 1161–1194.

[73] WPDR, 'Disciplines on Domestic Regulation Pursuant to GATS Article VI:4 – Consolidated Working Paper', Note by the Chairman, JOB(06)/225, July 2006.

Delimatsis, Panagiotis, 'Don't Gamble with GATS – The Interaction between Articles VI, XVI, XVII and XVIII GATS in the Light of the *US–Gambling* Case', *Journal of World Trade* 40(6) (2006), pp. 1059–1080.

——'Due Process and Good Regulation Embedded in the GATS – Disciplining Regulatory Behaviour in Services through Article VI of the GATS', *Journal of International Economic Law* 10/1 (2007), pp. 13–50.

——*International Trade in Services and Domestic Regulations: Necessity, Transparency, and Regulatory Diversity* (Oxford University Press, 2007).

Feketekuty, Geza, 'Regulatory Reform and Trade Liberalization in Services', in: Pierre Sauvé and Robert M. Stern (eds.), *GATS 2000: New Directions in Services Trade Liberalization* (Washington, DC: Brookings Institution/ Harvard University, 2000).

GATT, 'Draft Final Act Embodying the Results of the Uruguay Round of Multilateral Trade Negotiations', MTN.TNC/W/FA, 20 December 1991.

——'Scheduling of Initial Commitments in Trade in Services: Explanatory Note', MTN.GNS/W/164, 3 September 1993.

Hoekman, Bernard and Patrick Messerlin, 'Liberalizing Trade in Services: Reciprocal Negotiations and Regulatory Reform', in Pierre Sauvé and Robert M. Stern (eds.), *GATS 2000: New Directions in Services Trade Liberalization* (Washington, DC: Brookings Institution/Harvard University, 2000).

Jacobs, Francis, 'Recent Developments in the Principle of Proportionality in European Community Law', in Evelyn Ellis (ed.), *The Principle of Proportionality in the Laws of Europe* (Oxford: Hart Publishing, 1999).

Krajewski, Markus, *National Regulation and Trade Liberalization in Services – The Legal Impact of the General Agreement on Trade in Services (GATS) on National Regulatory Autonomy* (Kluwer Law International, 2003).

Leebron, David, 'Regulatory Discrimination in Domestic United States Law: A Model for the GATS?', in Aaditya Mattoo and Pierre Sauvé (eds.), *Domestic Regulation and Service Trade Liberalization* (OUP/World Bank, 2003).

Marceau, Gabrielle and Joel Trachtman, 'The Technical Barriers to Trade Agreement, the Sanitary and Phytosanitary Measures Agreement, and The General Agreement on Tariffs and Trade: A Map of the World Trade Organization Law of Domestic Regulation of Goods', *Journal of World Trade* 36(5) (2002), pp. 811–881.

Mattoo, Aaditya, 'Services in a Development Round: Three Goals and Three Proposals', *Journal of World Trade* 39(6) (2005), pp. 1223–1238.

Mattoo, Aaditya and Carsten Fink, 'Regional Agreements and Trade in Services – Policy Issues', Policy Research Working Paper No.2852, World Bank, June 2002.

Motaal, Abdel Doaa, 'The "Multilateral Scientific Consensus" and the World Trade Organization', *Journal of World Trade* 38(5) (2005), pp. 855–876.

Productivity Commission and Australian National University, *Achieving Better Regulation of Services, Conference Proceedings* (Canberra, AusInfo: 2000).

Sauvé, Pierre, 'Adding Value at the Periphery: Aiming for GATS+ Advances in Regional Agreements on Services', NCCR Working Paper, available at www.nccr-trade.org.

Snell, Jukka, 'True Proportionality and Free Movement of Goods and Services', *European Business Law Review* 11 (2000), pp. 50–57.

Stephenson Sherry, '"Deeper" Integration in Services Trade in the Western Hemisphere: Domestic Regulation and Mutual Recognition', in OECD, *Trade and Regulatory Reform – Insights from Country Experience* (Paris: OECD, 2001).

Stewart, Terence (ed.), *The GATT Uruguay Round: A Negotiating History (1986–1992)*, Vol. 2: Commentary (Deventer: Kluwer Law and Taxation Publishers, 1993).

Sykes, Alan, 'The Least Restrictive Means', *University of Chicago Law Review* 70(1) (2003), pp. 403–416.

Trachtman, Joel, 'Trade and ... Problems, Cost-Benefit Analysis and Subsidiarity', *European Journal of International Law* 9(1) (1998), pp. 32–85.

——'Negotiations on Domestic Regulation and Trade in Services (Article VI GATS): A Legal Analysis of Selected Current Issues', in Ernst-Ulrich Petersmann (ed.), *Reforming the World Trading System – Legitimacy, Efficiency, and Democratic Governance* (OUP, 2005).

Trolliet, Claude and John Hegarty, 'Regulatory Reform and Trade Liberalization in Accountancy Services', in Aaditya Mattoo and Pierre Sauvé (eds.), *Domestic Regulation and Services Trade Liberalization* (OUP/World Bank, 2003).

WPDR, 'Application of the Necessity Test: Issues for Consideration', Job No. 5929, Informal Note by the WTO Secretariat, 8 October 1999.

——'Draft Annex on Domestic Regulation', Communication from Japan, JOB (03)/45, 3 March 2003, and Rev.1 of 2 May 2003.

——'Initial Elements for Modalities for Negotiations on Disciplines on Domestic Regulation', Communication from Switzerland, JOB(05)/68, 2 May 2005.

——'Elements for Draft Disciplines on Domestic Regulation', Communication from Brazil, Colombia, Dominican Republic, Indonesia, Peru and the Philippines, JOB(06)/34, 24 February 2006.

——'Pro-Development Principles for GATS Article VI:4 Negotiations', Communication from the ACP Group, JOB(06)/136, 2 May 2006.

——'Horizontal Transparency Disciplines in Domestic Regulation', Communication from the United States, JOB(06)/182, 9 June 2006.

——'Article VI:4 Disciplines – Proposal for a Draft Text', Communication from Australia, Chile, Colombia, Hong Kong, China, Korea, New Zealand, and the Separate Customs Territory of Taiwan, Penghu, Kinmen and Matsu, JOB (06)/193, 19 June 2006.

——'Outline of US Position on a Draft Consolidated Text in the WPDR', Communication from the United States, JOB(06)/223, 11 July 2006.

——'Disciplines on Domestic Regulation Pursuant to GATS Article VI:4 – Consolidated Working Paper', Note by the Chairman, JOB(06)/225, July 2006.

WTO, 'Decision on Professional Services', S/L/3, 4 April 1995.

——'Decision on Disciplines Relating to the Accountancy Sector', adopted by the CTS on 14 December 1998, S/L/63, 15 December 1998.

——'Disciplines on Domestic Regulation in the Accountancy Sector', adopted by the CTS on 14 December 1998, S/L/64, 17 December 1998.

——'Decision on Domestic Regulation', S/L/70, 28 April 1999.

——'Guidelines for the Scheduling of Specific Commitments Under the General Agreement on Trade in Services (GATS)', adopted by the CTS on 23 March 2001, S/L/92, 28 March 2001.

WTO, CTS, 'Article VI:4 of the GATS: Disciplines on Domestic Regulation Applicable to All Services', S/C/W/96, 1 March 1999.

WTO, WPDR, 'Communication from Australia', S/WPDR/W/1, 19 July 1999.

——'Report on the Meeting Held on 19 October 1999', S/WPDR/M/3, 18 January 2000.

——'The Necessity Test', Communication from the Republic of Korea, S/WPDR/W/9, 28 September 2000.

——'Report on the Meeting Held on 2 October 2000', S/WPDR/M/8, 17 November 2000.

——'Domestic Regulation: Necessity and Transparency', Communication from the EC and their Member States, S/WPDR/W/14, 1 May 2001.

——'Report on the Meeting Held on 20 March 2001', S/WPDR/M/10, 10 May 2001.

——'Report on the Meeting Held on 2 October 2001', S/WPDR/M/13, 21 November 2001.

——'"Necessity Tests" in the WTO', S/WPDR/W/27, 2 December 2003.

——'Report on the Meeting Held on 22 November 2004', S/WPDR/M/28, 25 January 2005.

——'Report of the Meeting Held on 7 and 18 February 2005', S/WPDR/M/29, 11 July 2005.

——'Report of the Meeting Held on 19 and 20 June 2006', S/WPDR/M/35, 14 August 2006.

WTO, WPPS, 'Background Information on the Agreement on Technical Barriers to Trade and the Agreement on Import Licensing Procedures', S/WPPS/W/6, 29 February 1996.

——'The Relevance of the Disciplines of the Agreements on Technical Barriers to Trade (TBT) and on Import Licensing Procedures to Article VI.4 of the General Agreement on Trade in Services', S/WPPS/W/9, 11 September 1996.

17

Comment: *Quis custodiet necessitatem?* Adjudicating necessity in multilevel systems and the importance of judicial dialogue

MARKUS KRAJEWSKI

Necessity as a (contentious) element of world trade law

The requirement that a measure should not be more trade-restrictive or burdensome than necessary to achieve a specific goal is a central, but contentious element of the multilateral trading system.[1] Two functionally different contexts of a necessity test need to be distinguished: necessity can be part of the requirements of an exception clause, such as Article XX GATT. In this case, necessity only becomes relevant for the justification of a measure, which would otherwise be GATT-inconsistent. This context is the traditional *sedes materiae* of necessity and has been part of the world trading system since 1948. More recently, and especially with the entry into force of the WTO Agreement, necessity tests have also been integrated in positive obligations, in particular in the TBT and SPS Agreements. Necessity tests are not restricted to the multilateral trading system. In various degrees, they can also be found in exception clauses and positive obligations of regional integration and bilateral trade agreements.[2]

The GATS contains references to both types of necessity tests: the general exception clause of Article XIV GATS includes necessity tests

[1] For a useful summary see Jan Neumann and Elisabeth Türk, 'Necessity Revisited: Proportionality in World Trade Law After *Korea – Beef, EC – Asbestos* and *EC – Sardines*', *Journal of World Trade* 37(1) (2003), pp. 199–233.

[2] Panos Delimatsis discusses some examples in his contribution to this volume. For an analysis of other examples, see Markus Krajewski, 'Services Liberalization in Regional Trade Agreements: Lessons for GATS 'Unfinished Business'?', in Lorand Bartels and Federico Ortino (eds.), *Regional Trade Agreements and the WTO Legal System* (Oxford University Press, 2006), p. 175, at pp. 186–191.

which are similar to the ones in Article XX GATT. The necessity test in the negotiating mandate of Article VI:4 GATS envisages a positive requirement. As Panos Delimatsis rightly recalls, this necessity test is a controversial subject of the negotiations on disciplines on domestic regulation in the WTO. Many WTO Members have doubts regarding the usefulness and desirability of a necessity test in future disciplines. Others regard disciplines without a necessity test as worthless. The views in the literature are also divided: while some commentators, including Panos Delimatsis, argue strongly in favour of the inclusion of a necessity test,[3] others question the feasibility of the approach and point to the limitation of domestic regulatory and policy space as a result of such a test. These political and academic debates focus on the substantive aspects of a necessity test, i.e. its coverage and its contents.

The comment in this chapter will not address substantive questions, which have been aptly analysed in the contribution by Panos Delimatsis (Chapter 16). Instead, the comment will focus on the capability of the WTO dispute settlement system to adequately adjudicate a necessity test in light of domestic regulatory interests. In this comment, I will argue that the core of the controversy around necessity in the multilateral trading system is of procedural and not of substantial nature. The short version of the argument goes as follows: WTO Members do not oppose the substantive requirement that measures should be not more restrictive than necessary, but do not want the WTO dispute settlement organs to decide on this issue. Admittedly, this argument is not novel.[4] However, so far it has only been put forward on the basis of a general distrust of national policy-makers and regulators vis-à-vis 'faceless WTO judges' in Geneva. The present comment will argue that this perception, though intuitive, is not the full picture. Another fundamental problem lies in a specific deficit of the WTO dispute settlement procedures regarding the role and function of national courts. This will become particularly apparent when comparing the DSU in this respect to the judicial system of the EC.

[3] See also Margareta Djordjevic, 'Domestic Regulation and Free Trade in Services – A Balancing Act', *Legal Issues of Economic Integration* 29 (2002), p. 305 at p. 321.

[4] For a summary of the arguments see Jan Wouters/Dominic Coppens, Domestic Regulation within the Framework of GATS, Working Paper 93, Institute for International Law, K.U.Leuven, www.internationallaw.be, 2006, at pp. 45–46.

Necessity as a (non-contentious) element of public international, European and domestic law

The requirement that an action should not be pursued if less restrictive alternatives are available is a concept which can be found in many legal systems at different levels, often as part of the principle of proportionality. The proportionality principle has been accepted as a general principle of public international law by the International Court of Justice in the *Gabcíkovo–Nagymaros* judgment.[5] Proportionality and necessity can also be found in Articles 51 and 52 of the ILC's Draft Articles on State Responsibility regarding countermeasures. Necessity is also a key requirement of restrictions of international human rights both under the system of the European Convention on Human Rights (see e.g. Article 10 (3) ECHR) and the International Covenant on Civil and Political Rights (see e.g. Article 19 (3) CCPR).

In European Law, necessity – again as part of the principle of proportionality – is also accepted far and wide as a principle of Community law.[6] According to the ECJ, proportionality entails that 'measures are appropriate and necessary in order to achieve the objectives legitimately pursued by the legislation in question; when there is a choice between several appropriate measures, recourse must be had to the least onerous, and the disadvantages caused must not be disproportionate to the aims pursued'.[7]

Notions of necessity and proportionality are also fundamental elements of many domestic administrative or constitutional legal orders. This is not only the case for constitutional systems with a traditional and differentiated approach to proportionality such as the German system,[8] but also for systems which have embraced this concept only recently, such as British constitutional law.[9]

[5] ICJ, Case concerning the Gabcíkovo-Nagymaros Project (Hungary/Slovakia), ICJ Reports 1997, 7, para. 85.

[6] Paul Craig and Gráinne de Búrca, *EU Law*, 3rd edn (Oxford University Press, 2003), at pp. 371–374 with further references.

[7] ECJ, Case C-331/88, *Fedesa*, [1990] ECR I-4023, para. 12 and ECJ, Case C-380/03, *Germany/Parliament and Council*, Judgment of 12 December 2006, not yet reported, para. 144.

[8] B. Pieroth and B. Schlink, *Grundrechte, Staatsrecht II*, 22nd edn (Heidelberg: Müller, 2006), at pp. 64–66.

[9] Paul Craig, *Administrative Law*, 4th edn. (London: Sweet and Maxwell, 1999), at pp. 586–603 and Adam Tomkins, *Public Law* (Oxford University Press, 2003), at pp. 197–199.

Necessity and the WTO dispute settlement system

If necessity seems to be a universally accepted principle, why is it so controversial in the context of Article VI:4 GATS? Arguably, the allocation of judicial authority to decide whether the necessity test is fulfilled or violated is of greater importance than the exact scope and requirements of such a test. In other words, countries distrust the courts, not the law. The assessment of the availability of an alternative, less trade-restrictive measure and its ability to fulfil the desired policy goal requires, as stated by the Appellate Body in *Korea – Beef*, 'in every case a weighing and balancing of factors'.[10] This involves an evaluation of various and often conflicting legal, political, economic and social circumstances in diverging national regulatory systems in order to determine whether a less trade-restrictive measure is available and to which extent the alternative measure would fulfil the desired policy objective. Such an exercise not only requires a thorough understanding of the domestic values, principles and circumstances, but also an assessment and appreciation of their relative importance. This is a balancing exercise, which is at the heart of every regulatory decision-making process. It is doubtful whether the composition of the dispute settlement organs and the structure of the WTO dispute settlement system is adequately equipped for an evaluation of national regulatory contexts.[11]

A comparison: Proportionality, the ECJ and national courts

The arguments questioning the capacity of the WTO dispute settlement system to adequately apply a necessity test can also be brought forward regarding the capacity of the European Court of Justice (ECJ) to assess the proportionality of measures of the EC Member States. However, the Member States, including their regulators and courts, generally seem to accept the judgments of the ECJ on proportionality and necessity. Why is the ECJ different? It could, of course, be argued that the judges of the ECJ are 'closer to home' and that the European legal order in general is more coherent and more closely related to the domestic legal systems of the EC Member States.

[10] *Korea – Measures Affecting Imports of Fresh, Chilled and Frozen Beef*, WT/DS161/AB/R and WT/DS169/AB/R, Report of the Appellate Body adopted on 10 January 2001, para. 164.

[11] For a comprehensive version of this argument see Markus Krajewski, *National Regulation and Trade Liberalization in Services* (The Hague: Kluwer Law International, 2003), at pp. 154–157. See also Neumann and Türk, above note 1, at pp. 231–233.

There is, however, also a procedural side to the picture which distinguishes the ECJ from WTO dispute settlement. The majority of the cases which reach Luxembourg are cases for a preliminary ruling on the basis of Article 234 ECT. These cases are referred to the ECJ from national courts. This mechanism ensures that the question placed before the ECJ is already contextualised by a specific case and proceedings in a national court. The legal questions are asked against the background of the case, the arguments of the parties are included in the reference and often the referring court indicates to the ECJ which aspects are of particular importance in the case. The ECJ has therefore a better understanding of the concrete circumstances of a measure and its application which the Court uses in its evaluation of the measure.

Furthermore, and this should not be underestimated, the ECJ does not formally decide on the compatibility of a domestic measure with EC law. Rather, the Court only interprets EC law and leaves the concrete decision to the referring court. In most cases, however, the answer of the ECJ is clear and leaves little substantive discretion to the national court. However, the (formal) right to reach a different solution, for example on the basis of a reinterpretation of domestic law, is an important tool to balance domestic and European interests in controversial cases.

The ECJ even has the power to refer the application of the proportionality test back to the national court: In *Gourmet International*, the ECJ was asked by a Swedish court whether a Swedish law prohibiting advertisements for alcoholic beverages in periodicals violated the free movement of goods and services. The Court concluded that the law was an obstacle to trade between the Member States and that such an obstacle could be justified on grounds of public health if it was proportionate. However, after pointing out that there was no evidence for a discriminating intention on behalf of the Swedish authority, the ECJ held that the decision whether the measure was proportionate should be left to the national court. The ECJ's reasoning is worth recalling: '[T]he decision as to whether the prohibition on advertising … is proportionate, and in particular as to whether the objective sought might be achieved by less extensive prohibitions or restrictions or by prohibitions or restrictions having less effect on intra-Community trade, calls for an analysis of the circumstances of law and of fact which characterise the situation in the Member State concerned, which the national court is in a better position than the Court of Justice to carry out.'[12] The

[12] ECJ, Case C-405/98, *Gourmet International*, [2001] ECR I-1795, para. 33.

Court reached the same conclusion in the recent *Ahokainen and Leppik* case, which concerned the Finnish licensing system for alcoholic beverages.[13]

In the passage of the judgment quoted above, the ECJ shows its appreciation for the concerns which are connected with the application of a proportionality test to measures of sensitive domestic policies. Even though the Court only rarely leaves it to the national court to 'finalise' the application of the proportionality principle, the existence of this possibility shows that the 'judicial dialogue' between the ECJ and the national courts allows for institutional self-restraint in cases which cut deeply into national regulatory autonomy.

The missing communicative link between national courts and the WTO dispute settlement system

It is well known, that the WTO dispute settlement system does not provide for any formal communication between the dispute settlement organs and national courts.[14] Often, the WTO dispute settlement organs are faced with cases which have not yet been tried at the domestic level. Hence, there is usually no specific case which provides the context for the evaluation of the necessity of a regulatory measure. Furthermore, WTO dispute settlement has to reach a final and definite conclusion on the legality of a national measure. The DSB cannot leave the formal, let alone the substantive decision on the legality of a measure to a national court. A *Gourmet*-type jurisprudence in the WTO is not possible.

The missing communicative link between national courts and the WTO dispute settlement system could be a key element of the reluctance of WTO Members to trust the WTO dispute settlement with regard to decisions on necessity. Yet, judicial dialogue could create mutual understanding, which in turn could lead to mutual trust as seen in the experience of the ECJ and the national courts. Introducing such communicative elements into the dispute settlement system would, however, dramatically

[13] ECJ, Case C-434/04, *Ahokainen and Leppik*, Judgment of 28 September 2006, not yet reported, para. 39.

[14] For a comprehensive and early exposition of the different facets of this problem see Meinhard Hilf, 'The Role of National Courts in International Trade Relations', *Michigan Journal of International Law* 18(2) (1997), pp. 321–356.

change the nature of the system. In particular, it would also require that WTO law is directly applicable in the domestic legal systems. This is a step which most WTO Members consider as too far for various reasons. For the time being, it is therefore not surprising that necessity continues to be a controversial subject in the WTO.

PART 6

Unfinished business: Safeguard and subsidy disciplines for services

18

Recognition, standardisation and harmonisation: Which rules for GATS in times of crisis?

MARKUS KRAJEWSKI*

I. Introduction

With the suspension of the multilateral trade negotiations in July 2006,[1] discussions about the scope of future rules in the WTO framework may seem futile. Although formally the suspension concerns only the Doha Development Agenda (DDA) and WTO Members can always revive the negotiations, it is unlikely that new rules will be agreed upon in the near future. Instead of reducing scholarly interest in the scope and content of future rules, the current situation should stimulate reflection and discussion. In fact, without the straitjacket of ongoing negotiations and the necessity of commenting on existing negotiation proposals, academics should seize the opportunity to reconsider some aspects of the conventional wisdom of the WTO system and engage in a critical and radically different discourse about the future of the trading system.

This chapter aims to contribute to such an exercise with regard to a limited area of WTO law. It concerns the content and scope of future General Agreement on Trade in Services (GATS) rules, in particular whether and to what extent GATS should incorporate provisions on recognition, standardisation or harmonisation. Recognition, standardisation and harmonisation are advanced instruments of trade liberalisation which can already be found in some WTO agreements, notably

* I would like to thank Johannes Bernabé, Thomas Cottier, Marion Panizzon, Nicole Pohl and Pierre Sauvé for useful and stimulating comments on an earlier draft of this chapter.

[1] The Doha negotiations effectively came to a halt in 2006 after the General Council 'took note' of WTO Director-General Lamy's recommendation to suspend the negotiations at the 27–28 July meeting of the General Council. However, no formal vote was taken. See 'Doha Round Suspension Receives Support of General Council', *Bridges Weekly Trade News Digest* – Vol. 10, Number 28, 2 August 2006.

the Agreement on Sanitary and Phytosanitary Measures (SPS) and the Agreement on Technical Barriers to Trade (TBT).[2] The aim of these instruments is to reduce the trade-distorting effect of diverging domestic regulations in the territories of different WTO Members. In the GATS context, these instruments have been partly recognised in Articles VI and VII GATS. They also play an important role in the negotiations on disciplines for domestic regulation. This chapter will critically assess the function and potential effects of various options for incorporating these instruments into the GATS. The paper will place this assessment in the context of the current crisis of the WTO system and will suggest approaches which ensure that future WTO rules will contribute to a solution to the crisis instead of aggravating it.

The chapter is organised as follows: section II will provide a critical assessment of the current state of WTO law and argue that the conventional wisdom about the role and function of multilateral trade rules must be reconsidered. It will claim that a new paradigm of WTO law is necessary but does not offer a thoroughly developed theoretical framework. Instead, it will make some preliminary suggestions in the hope of encouraging further debate. The main argument of this section will be that future WTO rules should be based on a redefined understanding of the functions of the WTO. The next section (III) will turn to the three key concepts in the chapter, i.e. recognition, standardisation and harmonisation. These concepts will be presented as advanced instruments of trade liberalisation and will be placed in a framework of different generations or dimensions of liberalisation instruments. In an in-depth look at each of these instruments, I turn first to recognition (section IV), because this concept is explicitly recognised in the GATS agreement itself (Article VII GATS). I consider standardisation and harmonisation jointly in section V because the two concepts are closely related. Sections IV and V provide definitions of the key concepts and show their use in other WTO agreements, notably the TBT and SPS Agreements. Each section then analyses the extent of these concepts in current GATS law, discusses potentials for future GATS rules and makes concrete suggestions regarding the scope and content of recognition, standardisation and harmonisation in the GATS framework. Discussion and proposals will be informed by the perspective sketched in section II. The concluding section will summarise the main arguments of the chapter.

[2] See below sections IV.2 and V.1.

II. Options for GATS and the crisis of the WTO

By asking which rules GATS ought to include, the paper addresses a question *de lege ferenda* and not *de lege lata*. This has implications for the scope and the methodology of the paper. It needs to go beyond standard analysis of the law and must include normative claims and arguments. This implies debates about policy choices and objectives and the assessment of different options from a broader perspective, which also opens the door to economic, political and social considerations. A debate about potential future WTO rules must begin with a critical and fundamental assessment of the current state of the WTO legal system. While it is true from a formal point of view that the collapse of the negotiations has no direct implications for the application and implementation of existing WTO rules, discussions about future WTO rules cannot ignore the overall structural and systemic crisis. In this sense, some fundamental 'mantras' must be revisited.[3]

1. The WTO crisis and current challenges to trade liberalisation

Even the most optimistic observers will agree that the political system of the WTO is currently in a crisis which is epitomised by the collapse of the Doha Development Agenda. The crisis of the political system must be distinguished from the situation of world trade in general, which continues to grow, and other elements of the world trading system, in particular the WTO dispute settlement mechanism, which is still functioning well.[4] However, in light of the often repeated, seldom seriously challenged mantra that the world trading system requires an ever increasing broadening and deepening of trade liberalisation ('bicycle theory'),[5] the suspension of the negotiations is severe enough to be considered a clear sign of a larger problem.

There are a number of reasons for the current situation: internal politics such as elections in key WTO Members and an apparent refocusing of business interests from the multilateral trading system to strategic

[3] The term is taken from John Jackson, 'The WTO "constitution" and proposed reforms: seven "mantras" revisited', *JIEL* 4 (2001), p. 67, who, however, revisits different mantras.

[4] For an overview of the first eight years see Federico Ortino and Ernst-Ulrich Petersmann (eds.), *The WTO Dispute Settlement System 1995–2003* (The Hague: Kluwer Law International, 2004).

[5] James Bacchus, 'The Bicycle Club: Affirming the American Interest in the Future of the WTO', Address to the Washington International Trade Association, 12 November 2002, www.worldtradelaw.net/articles/bacchusbicycle.pdf, p. 2 *et seq.* with further references.

bilateral and regional agreements are among the most important. It is submitted, however, that the WTO's crisis is also one of trade liberalisation in general. Governments and populations of a growing number of WTO Members do not seem to be willing to follow this paradigm any longer. They question, for a number of different reasons, the validity of the two-hundred-year-old claim that liberalisation of trade will be beneficial for everyone.[6] Whether or not this scepticism is justified on the basis of neoclassical economics is not the most relevant question. Rather, the dissatisfaction of large constituencies with the politics and the policies of the WTO is a social fact, which must be taken into account when formulating options for future GATS rules.

At the risk of oversimplifying, two perceptions seem to be at the core of the dissatisfaction and are hence the key challenges to WTO law at present. First, in many developing countries, in particular the poorer ones, ruling elites and ordinary citizens increasingly question whether the WTO benefits them. They see that the participation of their countries in the multilateral trading system has not changed their trade patterns nor has the economic basis of their countries benefited in a way which contributes to development and the eradication of poverty. In light of the dramatic economic and social crises in many African, Asian and Latin American countries, it is no longer sufficient to claim that trade liberalisation will have benefits in the long-term,[7] in particular if it may have negative effects in the short term. Recent studies have shown that least-developed countries are most likely to be the net losers if there is further trade liberalisation, irrespective of the outcome of the Doha round.[8] Leaders of developing countries, and increasingly their populations, demand that trade liberalisation and the world trading system in general contribute directly and recognisably to development objectives. New WTO rules must therefore live up to the claim of a 'development agenda'.[9] This is especially true for GATS rules, because many developing countries approached the services negotiations during the Uruguay

[6] For an overview of this thinking see Alan O. Sykes, 'Comparative Advantage and the Normative Economics of International Trade Policy', *JIEL* 1 (1998), pp. 49–82.

[7] John Maynard Keynes' famous remark 'In the long run we are all dead' receives a dramatic connotation in light of poverty and pandemics in many least-developed countries.

[8] See e.g. Sandra Polaski, *Winners and Losers – Impact of the Doha Round on Developing Countries* (Washington, DC: Carnegie Endowment, 2006), pp. viii–xi.

[9] For a critical assessment of the development perspective in the WTO see B. S. Chimni, 'The World Trade Organization, Democracy and Development: A View From the South', *JWT* 40 (2006), pp. 25–34.

Round with reservations. For them, GATS is still often perceived as an instrument designed for large finance, telecommunications and consulting companies from the developed world targeting new markets.

Second, the populations of many developing and developed countries increasingly question the consequences of the intrusion of WTO law into domestic regulatory systems. As evidenced by the public controversies on the *US – Shrimp*, *EC – Hormones* and *EC – Biotech* Products ('GMO') cases, among others, it is not acceptable to the general public that trade rules override regulatory policies and instruments. In the GATS context, the relationship between GATS and domestic regulatory autonomy is one of the most important questions. It is at the heart of public debate about and political campaigns against the GATS. The core problems of the only two 'real' GATS cases, *Mexico – Telecommunications (Telmex)*[10] and *US – Betting and Gambling*[11] also relate to the impact of GATS on national regulation.

2. *Revisiting the classic paradigm of trade liberalisation*

Both of the challenges to WTO law and practice just mentioned need to be addressed in the development of future WTO rules. This is the task of politicians, negotiators and those observing the negotiations. Both challenges, however, also question a fundamental paradigm of WTO law. Addressing this challenge and reconceptualising the functions of WTO law is a task for academic commentators. One, if not the, leading theoretical approach to the functions of multilateral trade rules is the perception that these rules assist policy-makers in overcoming protectionism by binding them to international rules, hence locking in achievements of trade liberalisation and requiring further liberalisation steps.[12] This approach is based on two assumptions: first, trade liberalisation is per se beneficial and second, policy-makers will not achieve trade liberalisation unilaterally because they are pressured by organised groups demanding protectionism. Multilateral trade rules should therefore tie

[10] *Mexico – Telecoms*, Mexico – Measures Affecting Telecommunications Services, Report of the Panel, WT/DS204/R, adopted 1 June 2004.

[11] *US – Gambling*, United States – Measures Affecting the Cross-Border Supply of Gambling and Betting Services, Report of the Appellate Body, WT/DS285/AB/R, adopted on 20 April 2005.

[12] Jan Tumlir, 'International Economic Order and Democratic Constitutionalism', *ORDO* 34 (1983), pp. 71–83 and Heinz Hauser, 'Domestic Policy Foundation and Domestic Policy Functions of International Trade Rules', *Aussenwirtschaft* 41 (1986), pp. 171–184.

the hands of the decision-makers in order to counterbalance this demand for protectionism, even if this includes restricting democratic decision-making at the domestic level. The assumptions of this approach are rooted in economic theory (neoclassical trade theory and political economy of trade policy) and have been used as a basis for legal analysis as well.[13] In the legal context, it is sometimes even argued that multilateral trade agreements serve the same functions as national constitutional law, because they restrict discretionary external economic policy-making in a similar way to constitutional limitations of domestic policy-making. Hence, WTO law serves economic constitutional functions.[14]

This approach, however, cannot offer the much-needed answers to the challenges outlined in the previous section. Rather, it would seem to aggravate the critics' claims. The developing country critics would argue that the assumption of the benefits of trade liberalisation does not hold true; the developed country critics would claim that disciplining governments and regulators amounts to circumventing democratically legitimised policies at the domestic level. Based on the problems of the conventional approach, WTO law should be based on a new understanding of its main functions. Rather than placing domestic regulation under the general suspicion of protectionism, one should accept that many obstacles to the international exchange of goods and services are caused not by burdensome regulations, but by the differing regulatory systems throughout the world. Based on this perception, the main focus of international trade law should not be a reduction of regulations per se, but the sound management of regulatory diversity. International trade law should enable and steer the international exchange of goods and services and should not serve domestic constitutional economic functions.

This approach should be complemented by scrutinising existing trade rules, first and foremost to assess their contribution to development. For each and every rule of the international trading system, one should ask to what extent it contributes to the reduction of poverty and/or the economic and social development of a country or region. Future WTO

[13] See e.g. Peter Van den Bossche, *The Law and Policy of the World Trade Organization* (Cambridge University Press, 2005), p. 36 and Peter-Tobias Stoll and Frank Schorkopf, *WTO–World Economic Order, World Trade Law* (Leiden and Boston: Martinus Nijhoff, 2006), pp. 34–35.

[14] Ernst-Ulrich Petersmann, *Constitutional Functions and Constitutional Problems of International Economic Law* (University of Fribourg Press, 1991). For a critique of this approach see Markus Krajewski, 'Democratic Legitimacy and Constitutional Perspectives of WTO Law', *JWT* 35 (1) (2001), pp. 167–186.

law, including new GATS rules, should meet the standards of these approaches if they are to contribute to a resolution of the current WTO crisis. Multilateral trade rules based only on neoclassical economic theory and approaches that use WTO law to control and limit democratically legitimised decisions at the domestic level should be treated with great caution. Arguably, such proposals will deepen the current crisis. To the contrary, proposals based on policy objectives of developing countries and aimed at reconciling domestic regulatory autonomy with the need for managing the interface between regulation and trade will contribute to a reconfiguration of the world trading system leading out of the current crisis. This will be the case, even though or perhaps precisely because such new rules may be less liberalising than trade proponents would hope for.

III. Instruments of trade liberalisation and their impact on domestic regulatory autonomy

Recognition, harmonisation and standardisation are instruments aimed at the liberalisation of trade. They can therefore be compared and contrasted with other liberalisation instruments which will highlight the potential gains and dangers of standardisation, harmonisation and mutual recognition in a broader context. I propose a taxonomy of liberalisation instruments developed on the basis of the idea of different 'generations' of approaches to the liberalisation of trade.[15]

A first generation of liberalisation instruments aims at the reduction of traditional border measures, such as tariffs, and of other market access restrictions. These instruments are at the heart of the trading system: the binding reduction of tariffs (Articles II and XXVIIIbis GATT) and the prohibition of quantitative restrictions (Article XI GATT) guarantee a predictable standard of market openness for trade in goods. Regarding services, the obligation to provide market access does not aim at 'border' measures, but at quantitative restrictions, which make it difficult or impossible to provide a service on a given market. Subject to specific commitments, GATS Article XVI provides for the abolition of key restrictions to market access. Trade rules aiming at reducing or abolishing market

[15] Gabrielle Marceau and Joel Trachtman, 'The Technical Barriers to Trade Agreement, the Sanitary and Phytosanitary Measures Agreement, and the General Agreement on Tariffs and Trade', *JWT* 36 (2002), p. 811 and Joel Trachtman, 'Lessons for the GATS from Existing WTO Rules on Domestic Regulation', in Aaditya Mattoo and Pierre Sauvé (eds.), *Domestic Regulation and Service Trade Liberalization* (Washington: World Bank, 2003), p. 57 apply similar, but more detailed typologies of instruments.

access restrictions are complemented by the general principles of non-discrimination, most-favoured nation treatment (Article I GATT and Article II GATS) and national treatment (Article III GATT and Article XVII GATS). The connection of these core principles to the objective of trade liberalisation is clearly described in the third paragraph of the GATT preamble.

In general, the first-generation approaches to trade liberalisation establish the least constraints on domestic regulatory autonomy. Non-discrimination rules generally leave instruments and objectives of domestic regulation untouched, because they only aim at special regulations for foreign goods and services. It should be noted, however, that a broad interpretation of de facto discrimination may put pressure on origin-neutral regulation and can therefore have a restrictive effect on regulatory autonomy.[16] In addition, the market access provision of the GATS (Article XVI GATS) covers certain instruments of domestic regulation, such as exclusive suppliers or economic needs tests.[17] They can therefore also place constraints on regulatory autonomy.

A second generation of liberalisation obligations formulates tests for domestic laws and regulations and establishes general standards which these laws and regulations must meet. The various necessity tests of WTO law fall into this category.[18] Typically, a necessity test requires a national measure to be no more trade-restrictive or burdensome than necessary.[19] Necessity requires that the measure in question contributes to the objective and that there is no reasonably available alternative measure which would have a similar effect.[20] Other disciplines on domestic regulation, such as requirements of transparency and due process can also be seen as second-generation instruments of trade liberalisation.

[16] Markus Krajewski, *National Regulation and Trade Liberalization in Services – The Legal Impact of the General Agreement on Trade in Services (GATS) on National Regulatory Autonomy* (London: Kluwer Law International, 2003), chapter 4.

[17] See e.g. *United States – Gambling*, above note 11, paras. 221 *et seq*. For a critical assessment of this decision from the perspective of regulatory autonomy see Joost Pauwelyn, 'Rien ne va plus? Distinguishing domestic regulation from market access in GATT and GATS', *WTRev* (2005), p. 131.

[18] On these tests see Axel Desmedt, 'Proportionality in WTO Law', *JIEL* 4 (2001), 441 and Jan Neumann and Elisabeth Türk, 'Necessity Revisited – Proportionality in World Trade Organization Law after *Korea – Beef, EC – Asbestos* and *EC – Sardines*', *JWT* 37 (2003), p. 199.

[19] See e.g. Art. 2.2 TBT and Art. VI:4 (b) GATS.

[20] *Korea – Beef*, Korea – Measures Affecting Imports of Fresh, Chilled and Frozen Beef, Report of the Appellate Body, WT/DS161/AB/R and WT/DS169/AB/R, adopted on 10 January 2001, paras. 160, 161.

The potential impact of necessity tests on national regulatory autonomy is greater than that of first-generation obligations, in particular because second-generation tests also address non-discriminatory measures, which are often key elements of a domestic regulatory regime. However, necessity tests do not prohibit specific regulatory instruments or prescribe the use of specific instruments (e.g. technical standards, qualification and licensing requirements, quantitative restrictions). Members are free to apply whichever regulatory measure they want, as long as the measure is not more trade-restrictive than necessary. The choice of a domestic regulatory instrument is therefore not restricted by a necessity test.

A basic necessity test also does not restrict the regulatory goals of the measure in question. However, some necessity tests specify that a measure must be no more trade-restrictive than necessary to pursue a particular regulatory goal (see e.g. Article VI:4 (b) GATS 'quality of the service'). Arguably this means that a measure aimed at a regulatory objective other than the one mentioned in the norm in question does not meet the requirements of such a specific necessity test. Therefore, such necessity tests amount to a restriction of national regulatory autonomy.

Recognition, standardisation and harmonisation are the most advanced instruments of liberalisation.[21] They often require a greater degree of economic and political integration than the other instruments of liberalisation. Recognition requires a minimum standard of regulatory cohesion between different systems, which exists more frequently at a regional than at the global level. Standardisation and harmonisation require institutions based on common and shared economic, social, scientific or technical understandings. Even though international harmonisation organisations exist at the global level, their standards are usually voluntary. Binding harmonisation can be found at the regional level more frequently than at the global level. Recognition and harmonisation are hence instruments of liberalisation used by countries with similar political, economic and social systems. However, the multilateral trading system also involves recognition, harmonisation and standardisation, in particular in the TBT (Articles 2.6 and 2.7) and the SPS (Articles 3 and 4). There are also references to these obligations in the GATS framework (Articles VI and VII), to which I will return in the next part of this chapter. Recognition, harmonisation and standardisation have the greatest impact on national regulatory autonomy of all approaches to

[21] For definitions and a more detailed discussion of these concepts see sections IV.1 and V.1.

liberalisation because they require that domestic rules and regulations are – at least partially – replaced with rules and regulations from another legal system. In the case of recognition, domestic regulations of the host country need to give way to the regulations of the home country. In the case of harmonisation and standardisation, domestic rules are replaced with transnational or supranational norms. This preliminary conclusion already leads to a questioning of the appropriateness of these instruments of trade liberalisation in the context of future GATS rules.

At first sight, it seems as if calls for recognition, harmonisation and standardisation in the GATS contexts are based on the classic paradigm of WTO law and therefore do not adequately address the above-mentioned challenges to the WTO system. However, the actual impact of recognition, harmonisation and standardisation on national regulatory autonomy depends on a number of aspects. A first aspect relates to the degree of bindingness: is compliance with international norms or the acceptance of home country regulations mandatory or only recommended? A second aspect concerns the competence to determine compliance: who decides whether the regulations of the home country are equivalent and on what basis? Regarding harmonisation and standardisation, a third aspect is the participation of national institutions in the rule-making process: do national regulators participate in the institutions developing transnational standards and norms, and to what extent? I will return to these issues in the next section.

IV. Recognition

1. General remarks

There is no commonly agreed definition of 'recognition'. The scope and content of this concept are determined by the legal framework in which it is used. In general, recognition can be understood as the acceptance of regulatory conditions for goods and services required in one country (exporting origin/home country) as being equivalent to the conditions necessary in another country (importing country/host country).[22] In general, three types of recognition can be distinguished: autonomous recognition, mutual recognition and the country of origin principle.

[22] Kalypso Nicolaïdis, *Mutual Recognition of Regulatory Regimes: Some Lessons and Prospects*, Jean Monnet Working Paper 7/1997, available at http://jeanmonnetprogram.org/papers/97/97-07.html.

Autonomous recognition refers to the decision of the regulatory authority of the importing country to accept compliance with certain qualifications and standards in the exporting country as equivalent to the requirements of the importing country, based on administrative discretion. Mutual recognition refers to the situation in which two countries accept the compliance with certain qualifications and standards in the other country as equivalent to its own requirements on a mutual and reciprocal basis. Often, this process is based on an international agreement between two or more countries (Mutual Recognition Agreement, MRA). In the words of Nicolaïdis and Trachtman, mutual recognition can be understood as allocating regulatory jurisdiction to the home state, whereas harmonisation establishes a (limited) transnational regulatory jurisdiction.[23] Mutual recognition is hence deference to another national regulatory regime, while harmonisation and standardisation require deference to an international regime.

The most advanced form of recognition is the country-of-origin principle.[24] It is a well-known element of the legal order of the EC internal market famously developed by the ECJ in the *Cassis de Dijon* judgment[25] and subsequent cases. Recently, it played a key role in the debates about the Services Directive.[26] Under a country of origin principle, a good or service which is lawfully produced and supplied in one country cannot be deemed illegal in another country. Countries bound by the country of origin principle do not only recognise the fulfilment of conditions in one country as equivalent. However, they recognise the 'result' of an approval process in one country as sufficient for all countries. Clearly, the establishment of a country of origin principle requires a very advanced form of economic integration and reduces regulatory autonomy to the greatest degree.

[23] Kalypso Nicolaïdis and Joel Trachtman, 'From Policed Regulation to Managed Recognition in GATS', in: Pierre Sauvé and Robert M. Stern (eds.), *GATS 2000: New Directions in Services Trade Liberalization* (Washington, DC: Brookings Institution Press, 2000), p. 242.

[24] Josephine Steiner, Lorna Woods and Christian Stigg-Flessner, *EU Law*, 9th edn (OUP, 2006), p. 334.

[25] ECJ, Case 120/78, *Rewe/Bundesmonopolverwaltung für Branntwein*, ECR 1979, 649, para. 8

[26] The two Commission proposals and the Parliament and Council opinions are available at http://ec.europa.eu/internal_market/services/services-dir/proposal_en.htm.

2. *Recognition in existing WTO and GATS law*

Examples of recognition can be found in the WTO legal order, in particular in the SPS and TBT Agreements.[27] These examples can be distinguished on the basis of their strictness. For example, Article 2.7 TBT contains a soft requirement for recognition, because it only requires Members to 'give positive consideration to accepting as equivalent technical regulations of other Members ... provided they are satisfied that these regulations adequately fulfil the objectives of their own regulations'. This requirement aims at autonomous recognition and by and large requires only that the competent authorities do not reject the possibility of recognition from the outset.

Article 4.1 SPS on the other hand is a strong requirement. It states that Members 'shall accept the sanitary or phytosanitary measures of other Members as equivalent, even if these measures differ from their own ... if the exporting Member objectively demonstrates to the importing Member that its measures achieve the importing Members' appropriate level of sanitary or phytosanitary protection'. Again, Article 4.1 SPS aims at autonomous recognition, but is stricter than Article 2.7 TBT. A Member violates its obligations under Article 4.1 SPS if it refuses to accept the SPS measures of another Member which are objectively equivalent to its own measures, even if the instruments used in the two Members are different.

Article VII GATS is entitled 'recognition'. However, its five paragraphs do not contain the legal obligation to recognise the regulatory requirements of other WTO Members as equivalent. Under Article VII:1 GATS WTO Members may recognise education or training gained or requirements met in another country, or licences and certifications obtained from another country when considering the fulfilment of their own requirements. Such recognition can 'be achieved through harmonisation or otherwise' and may be based upon an agreement or arrangement with the country concerned (mutual recognition) or may be accorded autonomously (unilateral or autonomous recognition).[28] Paragraph 1 therefore only suggests that Members may refer to mutual recognition, but unlike Article 2.7 TBT and 4.1 SPS does not impose any legal obligations on the Members to do so.

[27] On these requirements see Marceau and Trachtman, above note 15, pp. 842–844.

[28] Amerigo Beviglia Zampetti, 'Market Access through Mutual Regulation: the Promise and Limits of GATS Article VII', in: Pierre Sauvé and Robert M. Stern (eds.), *GATS 2000 – New Directions in Services Trade Liberalization* (2000), p. 283.

Article VII:1 suggests that harmonisation is a means of recognition. As will be shown below, harmonisation in the WTO legal system refers to the use of international standards. This is also shown in Article VII:5 GATS, which provides that '[w]herever appropriate, recognition should be based on multilaterally agreed criteria. In appropriate cases, Members shall work in cooperation with relevant intergovernmental and non-governmental organizations towards the establishment and adoption of common international standards and criteria for recognition and common international standards for the practice of relevant services trades and professions.' Recognition may be based on international standards. Like paragraph 1, however, paragraph 5 of Article VI GATS does not establish a binding obligation.

Paragraphs 2, 3 and 4 of Article VII GATS only establish obligations if Members use mutual recognition. Most importantly, Article VII:3 GATS requires that Members shall not accord recognition in a discriminatory manner or in a manner which would be a disguised restriction on trade. Article VII:2 GATS also contains a non-discrimination requirement, albeit a more specific one: parties to a recognition agreement shall afford adequate opportunity for other interested WTO Members to join that agreement or a comparable one. Where a Member accords recognition autonomously, it shall afford adequate opportunity for any other Member to demonstrate that requirements met in its territory should be recognised.

Finally, Article VII:4 GATS requires WTO Members to inform the Council for Trade in Services about their unilateral and mutual recognition policies and instruments. It seems that despite this clear obligation, the implementation of this provision is difficult. So far, the Council for Trade in Services has received relatively few notifications.[29] The Members have agreed to discuss this problem.[30]

A relatively weak element of recognition can also be found in Article VI:6 GATS, which holds that Members shall provide adequate procedures to verify the competence of foreign professionals in sectors with specific commitments. Though only a procedural requirement, this obligation presupposes that professionals can also gain their competence abroad and that their education and training are recognised as equivalent. Yet,

[29] See Annual Reports of the Council for Trade in Services for 1999 (S/C/10), 2000 (S/C/12) and 2004 (S/C/22).

[30] Council for Trade in Services, Report of the Meeting held on 26 November 2004, S/C/M/75, para. 46.

Article VI:6 does not specify under what circumstances a professional should be regarded as competent. However, Article VI:6 is important if Members are willing to recognise professional qualifications gained abroad as equivalent, because it requires Members to establish adequate procedures to verify these qualifications.

In summary, it can be said that existing elements of recognition in the GATS context are limited and lenient even if compared with a soft requirement of recognition such as Article 2.7 TBT. It should therefore be no surprise that an expansion of recognition has been discussed in the negotiations on domestic regulation disciplines based on Article VI:4 GATS. So far, these negotiations have led to a set of sector-specific disciplines only with regard to accountancy services, which are discussed in the next section. Negotiations on general disciplines are still in progress and were fairly advanced by the time the Doha negotiations were suspended.

3. *Accountancy Disciplines and other disciplines on domestic regulation*

The Accountancy Disciplines which were adopted by the Council for Trade in Services in 1999[31] incorporate obligations of mutual recognition. Paragraph 19 of the Accountancy Disciplines contains a general standard: the competent authorities of a Member shall take account of qualifications acquired in the territory of another Member on the basis of equivalence of education, experience and/or examination requirements. Regarding the specific issue of professional indemnity insurance, paragraph 12 of the Accountancy Disciplines states that Members shall 'take into account any existing insurance coverage, in so far as it covers activities in its territory or the relevant jurisdiction in its territory and is consistent with the legislation of the host Member'. Lastly, paragraph 21 of the Accountancy Disciplines notes the role which mutual recognition agreements can play in facilitating the process of verification of qualifications and/or in establishing equivalence of education. In this context, WTO Members adopted Guidelines for Mutual Recognition

[31] Disciplines on Domestic Regulation in the Accountancy Sector Adopted by the Council for Trade in Services on 14 December 1998, S/L/64. See on these Claude Trolliet and John Hegarty, 'Regulatory Reform and Trade Liberalisation in Accountancy Services', in Aaditya Mattoo and Pierre Sauvé (eds.), *Domestic Regulation and Service Trade Liberalization* (Washington, DC: World Bank, 2003), p. 147.

Agreements or Arrangements in the Accountancy Sector in 1997.[32] Their aim is to provide practical guidance for the negotiation of mutual recognition agreements on accountancy services. The guidelines are non-binding and are intended to be used by Members on a voluntary basis.

The concept of recognition also played an important role in the negotiations on future Disciplines for Domestic Regulations on the basis of Article VI:4 GATS. A document submitted to the Working Party on Domestic Regulation (WPDR) by Chile, India, Mexico, Pakistan and Thailand makes a number of concrete proposals in this regard, such as the recognition of equivalence of education and diplomas.[33] The importance of this issue for developing countries can also be seen in a proposal by Brazil and other developing countries.[34] A proposal by Chile and others, however, contains only a relatively weak reference to recognition.[35] Recognition is not an issue only of interest to developing countries. Switzerland proposed the general principle of country of origin regarding technical standards in mode 1 if both the home and the host country pursue the same regulatory objectives.[36]

The latest consolidated working paper produced before the suspension of the negotiations in July 2006 is a Note by the Chairman of the WPDR of 18 July 2006.[37] Though its contents do not represent a consensus in the WPDR, the paragraphs on recognition seem less controversial than other parts of it, e.g. the necessity test. It is therefore not unlikely that they will be adopted. With regard to qualification requirements, Members note 'the role which autonomous and mutual recognition can play in facilitating the process of verification of qualification and/or in establishing equivalency of education, experience or examination

[32] Council for Trade in Services, Guidelines for Mutual Recognition Agreements or Arrangements in the Accountancy Sector, S/L/38, 28 May 1997.

[33] WPDR, Communication from Chile, India, Mexico, Pakistan and Thailand, Proposed elements for disciplines on Qualification Requirements and Procedures, JOB(05)/50, 30 March 2005, para. 13 A. (iii).

[34] WPDR, Communication from Brazil, Colombia, Dominican Republic, Peru and the Philippines, Elements for Draft Disciplines on Domestic Regulation, Room Document, 26 April 2005, para. 7.

[35] WPDR, Communication from Chile; Hong Kong, China; The Separate Customs Territory of Taiwan, Penghu, Kinmen and Matsu, Article VI:4 Disciplines – Proposal for a Draft Text, Room Document, 9 June 2006, para. 30.

[36] WPDR, Communication from Switzerland, Proposal for Disciplines on Technical Standards in Services, S/WPDR/W/32, 1 February 2005, para. 19.

[37] WPDR, Disciplines on Domestic Regulation Pursuant to GATS Article VI:4 – Consolidated Working Paper – Note by the Chairman, JOB(06)/225, 18 July 2006.

requirements. Where possible, autonomous recognition shall be accorded to qualifications where they are found to be equivalent to those required for the supply of a service.'[38] This paragraph by and large repeats the contents of Article VII:1 GATS: recognition can be a useful instrument for liberalising trade in services. However, WTO Members are under no obligation to use it.

Also relating to qualification requirements, the consolidated working paper states: 'Where qualifications have been recognized as equivalent to those required for the supply of the service … each Member shall allow the service supplier to supply the service, subject to any applicable registration requirements.'[39] This provision, though it contains a legally binding obligation, is only applicable if a WTO Member makes use of recognition. It provides that once equivalence has been recognised, the service supplier shall be allowed to supply the service. This prevents Members from recognising equivalence without allowing the service supplier to benefit from it.

4. *Which rules for GATS regarding recognition?*

The crucial question in the context of recognition is: who decides about equivalence? As long as this decision rests solely with the national authority and a WTO dispute settlement organ cannot question this decision, regulatory autonomy largely remains intact. If, however, dispute settlement organs determine whether or not there is equivalence, regulatory autonomy will be reduced. It should also be noted that mutual recognition works better among countries with similar regulatory regimes. This is why it has been successfully applied by the European Court of Justice as a tool of European integration.[40] However, the concept may have limits in a system such as the WTO, where Members differ greatly in their regulatory traditions.

A 'soft' requirement for recognition along the lines of paragraph 19 of the Accountancy Disciplines or Article 2.7 TBT, which merely requires Members to give positive consideration to equivalent qualifications acquired in another country or to take those qualifications into account, respects national regulatory autonomy to a greater extent than a stricter

[38] Consolidated Working Paper, above note 37, para. H.3.

[39] Consolidated Working Paper, above note 37, para. H.6.

[40] As mentioned above, the leading case is the *Cassis de Dijon* judgment, in which the Court famously stated: 'There is therefore no valid reason why, provided that they have been lawfully produced in one of the Member States, alcoholic beverages should not be introduced into any other Member State'. ECJ, above note 25, para. 14.

obligation like the one in Article 4.1 SPS. An obligation to accept equivalent qualifications and licences would only leave national regulatory autonomy intact if the decision about equivalence would be left to the national authorities. A mere procedural obligation to consider the foreign qualification when determining the suitability of a service provider would not reduce national regulatory autonomy greatly. Only an a priori refusal to take foreign qualifications or degrees into account could be regarded as more trade-restrictive than necessary. However, it should also be noted that the appraisal of foreign qualifications can be a difficult and often onerous task for an administration as it may require a substantial amount of knowledge about the background of these qualifications.

Mutual recognition agreements (MRAs) may be a useful contribution and may avoid some of the problems raised by strong requirements for recognition.[41] MRAs allow the countries involved to assess which requirements fulfilled in the home country are equivalent to their own and can hence be recognised as such. If the negotiations of MRAs are based on equal terms, MRAs preserve national regulatory autonomy to a greater extent than strong obligations such as Article 4.1 SPS.

Finally, it should be noted that mutual recognition is easier if the specific regulatory requirements and implications of a particular sector can be taken into account. This is clearly shown by the reference to professional indemnity insurance in the Accountancy Disciplines. Solutions to a particular regulatory problem of a sector which is similarly regulated in most jurisdictions have a greater chance of being accepted as equivalent because the regulators involved can assess the scope and implications of a requirement for recognition more easily.

V. Standardisation and harmonisation

This paper distinguishes between harmonisation and standardisation even though this distinction is not based on the terminology and content of WTO law. WTO law uses only the term harmonisation and makes no reference to standardisation.[42] Nevertheless, a distinction seems useful because it allows comparisons of WTO law with the law of regional

[41] On MRAs see also Kalypso Nicolaïdis, 'Non-Discriminatory Mutual Recognition: An Oxymoron in the New WTO Lexicon?', in Thomas Cottier and Petros Mavroidis (eds.), *Regulatory Barriers and the Principle of Non-Discrimination in World Trade Law* (Ann Arbor: University of Michigan Press, 2000), pp. 267–301.

[42] See e.g. Art. 3 SPS, Art. 2. 6 TBT and Art. VII:1 GATS.

integration systems, such as NAFTA or the EC. It has therefore also been applied to WTO law in the literature.[43]

1. *General remarks*

Like the term 'recognition', the terms 'standardisation' and 'harmonisation' have not received a generally accepted definition. For the purposes of this paper, standardisation is understood as the creation of uniform laws and regulation through the implementation of rules developed by international standardisation bodies, such as the Codex Alimentarius Commission. International agreements can refer to these standards or make their use obligatory. This technique turns international standards which have often been drafted as non-binding suggestions for national legislation, into binding international norms. Examples of this form of standardisation can be found in Article 3 SPS and Article 2.4 TBT. In WTO legal language, these provisions contain rules on harmonisation (see e.g. the title of Art. 3 SPS). Similarly, some contributors to the literature view the use of international standards as one, if not the most important, means of harmonisation.[44] However, this chapter uses the term harmonisation in a way based on the approaches of EC law and general public international law.

In this regard, harmonisation is understood as the original creation of uniform laws and regulations, which apply in more than one national jurisdiction in the same way. Harmonisation can be achieved through supranational legislation, e.g. legislation based on Article 95 ECT in the EC. Some authors appear to claim that supranational law-making is in fact the only way of achieving harmonisation.[45] However, this understanding is too narrow and focuses too much on the experience of the EC. A broader understanding of harmonisation also includes international agreements creating uniform laws, in particular in the area of private international law. The agreements developed by the United Nations Commission on International Trade Law (UNCITRAL), such as the Convention on Contracts for the International Sale of Goods (CISG) are well-known examples. Arguably, TRIPS is also an international harmonisation agreement. Closely related to the creation of uniform law is the formulation of model laws, which also provide for harmonisation, but leave it

[43] Trachtman, above note 15, p. 77.
[44] Marceau and Trachtman, above note 15, 838 and Trachtman, above note 15, p. 69 and 77.
[45] Nicolaïdis and Trachtman, above note 23, p. 266.

up to the individual states to adopt the rules of the model law. Again, the work of UNCITRAL can be mentioned as an example, such as the UN model laws on commercial arbitration (1985) and conciliation (2002).

Standardisation and harmonisation therefore both lead to similar, if not identical, rules in different jurisdictions. However, they achieve this through different means. Standardisation uses existing rules and incorporates them into other legal frameworks. Harmonisation involves the creation of new rules.

2. *Article VI:5(b) GATS*

Article VI:5(b) GATS explicitly refers to international standards. Even though Article VI:5 GATS is best described as containing 'first and foremost merely a standstill obligation',[46] it can be used as a reference point for the treatment of international standards in the GATS. Article VI:5(b) requires that account shall be taken of relevant international standards applied by a Member when determining the conformity with the criteria of Article VI:4(a), (b) and (c). According to an interpretative footnote, the term 'relevant international organizations' refers to international bodies whose membership is open at least to the relevant bodies of all Members of the WTO.[47]

This obligation does not amount to a full, positive obligation to base domestic regulations on international standards. It may not even require WTO Members to actively take such standards into account when applying domestic regulations, because the passive wording of Article VI:5(b) – 'account shall be taken' – could also be understood as an interpretative guideline for WTO dispute settlement organs. While this may seem to leave national regulatory authority untouched, its practical application could have the effect of a presumption in favour of such standards. In taking international standards into account, WTO panels or the Appellate Body could decide that domestic regulations deviating from international standards are unnecessary trade restrictions.

However, Article VI:5(b) only requires that international standards applied by that Member shall be taken into account. This could be understood in such a way that a Member is presumed to have fulfilled the obligations of Article VI:5(a) if it applied international standards. However, if international standards are not applied by that Member, they should not be considered in determining compliance with Article VI:5(a).

[46] Trachtman, above note 15, p. 67. [47] Interpretative footnote 3 to Art. VI GATS.

Such an understanding differs from the presumption in favour of international standards as established by Article 2.5 TBT or 3.2 SPS, because these obligations establish a general presumption. On the one hand, compliance or non-compliance with international standards is taken into account when determining whether a WTO Member has met its obligations under the TBT and the SPS Agreements. Article VI:5(b) GATS, on the other hand, seems to suggest that international standards only play a role if the Member has actually applied them; otherwise the necessity of a domestic regulation has to be established without taking international standards into account.

3. *Standardisation in the Accountancy Disciplines and in proposals on Disciplines on Domestic Regulation*

Both the Accountancy Disciplines and proposals for future Disciplines on Domestic Regulation contain references to international standards. Paragraph 26 of the Accountancy Disciplines holds: 'In determining whether a measure is in conformity with the obligations under paragraph 2, account shall be taken of internationally recognized standards of relevant international organizations applied by that Member.' Similar to Article VI GATS, a footnote in the Accountancy Disciplines specifies that the term 'relevant international organizations' refers to international bodies whose membership is open at least to the relevant bodies of all Members of the WTO.[48]

In the negotiations on Disciplines on Domestic Regulation, Switzerland proposed provisions on the use of international standards, which are based on the model of Articles 2.4 und 2.5 TBT.[49] In contrast, Brazil and other developing countries suggested a general obligation – similar to Article VI:5 GATS – to take account of international standards in determining whether a Member is in conformity with the proposed Disciplines on Domestic Regulation.[50] Chile and a group of other countries have recently proposed a similar provision.[51] The consolidated working paper of the chairman of the

[48] Interpretative footnote 2 to paragraph 26 of the Accountancy Disciplines.

[49] WPDR, Communication from Switzerland, Proposal for Disciplines on Technical Standards in Services, S/WPDR/W/32, 1 February 2005, paras. 20 and 23.

[50] WPDR, Communication from Brazil, Colombia, Dominican Republic, Peru and the Philippines, Elements for Draft Disciplines on Domestic Regulation, Room Document, 26 April 2005, para. 3(f).

[51] WPDR, Communication from Chile; Hong Kong, China; The Separate Customs Territory of Taiwan, Penghu, Kinmen and Matsu, Article VI:4 Disciplines – Proposal for a Draft Text, Room Document, 9 June 2006, para.14.

WPDR also refers to international standards. Members 'recognize the role of international standards in facilitating trade in services, and are encouraged to consider following international standards of relevant international organizations'.[52] In addition, the working paper contains the same wording as paragraph 26 of the Accountancy Disciplines.

Obligations of the type of Article VI:5 GATS and of paragraph 26 of the Accountancy Disciplines leave national regulators a greater margin of discretion than obligations in the TBT and SPS Agreements. According to Article 2.5 TBT a technical regulation, which is in accordance with a relevant standard, shall be presumed not to create an unnecessary obstacle to trade. A similar provision can be found in Article 3.2 SPS. Even though the presumption established in these provisions is rebuttable, the obligations create a strong incentive to use international standards. International standards determining the level of necessity amount to a nearly binding obligation to comply with such standards. Requiring Members to comply with international standards introduces elements of regulatory harmonisation into WTO law and greatly reduces national regulatory autonomy.

Obligations such as Article VI:5 GATS and paragraph 26 of the Accountancy Disciplines require WTO Members to use international standards when developing or applying domestic regulations, but do not presume the outcome of this process. The main difference between these obligations and obligations such as Article 2.4 TBT becomes apparent when a Member tries to defend a domestic regulation that deviates from an international standard. If there is a presumption in favour of international standards, any deviation will be difficult to defend. If there is only a procedural obligation to take those standards into account, the substance of the regulation can be assessed independently of international standards.

4. *Harmonisation in the WTO telecommunications regime*

The WTO is not a supranational institution and most of its agreements – with the exception of TRIPS – do not contain detailed substantive requirements for national regulation. Yet, there is a nucleus of harmonisation in the telecommunications regime.[53] The post-Uruguay Round negotiations on

[52] Consolidated Working Paper, above note 37, para. C.2.

[53] See generally Marco Bronckers and Pierre Larouche, 'Telecommunications Services and the World Trade Organization', *JWT* 31 (1997), 5.

telecommunications did not focus only on specific commitments, but also produced a Reference Paper on regulatory principles in telecommunications.[54] This Reference Paper only becomes binding if a WTO Member explicitly includes the paper or parts of it in its schedule of commitments. Usually, the Reference Paper can be found in the column for additional commitments under Article XVIII GATS.

Like the Annex on Telecommunications, the Reference Paper builds on Articles VIII and IX GATS and strengthens disciplines to ensure competition. Its purpose is to ensure that the market power of a former (public) monopoly operator is not used to the detriment of new market entrants.[55] The Reference Paper also draws on elements of the transparency obligation in Article III GATS,[56] the requirement of adequate remedies in Article VI:2[57] and on the necessity test of Article VI:4 GATS.[58]

Some elements of the Reference Paper contain only general standards. For example, paragraph 1 of the Reference Paper states: 'Appropriate measures shall be maintained for the purpose of preventing suppliers who, alone or together, are a major supplier from engaging in or continuing anticompetitive practices'. Though the terms major supplier and anticompetitive practices are defined in the Reference Paper, this provision does not prescribe any specific rules or regulations which all Members who adopted the Reference Paper must incorporate into their legal system. The same applies to paragraph 3, which states the right of Members to define the kind of universal service obligation they wish to maintain.

Other elements of the Reference Paper can be seen as minimum harmonisation in the telecommunications sector. In particular, paragraph 2.2 of the Reference Paper requires that interconnection with a major supplier is ensured at any technically feasible point. Interconnection must be provided under non-discriminatory terms, conditions and rates and at a quality no less favourable than that provided to affiliates, subsidiaries and third parties. Furthermore, interconnection must be provided in a timely fashion, at cost-oriented rates that are transparent, reasonable, and sufficiently unbundled so that the supplier need not pay for network components or facilities that it does not require. The requirement to

[54] Decision of the Negotiating Group on basic telecommunications, 24 April 1996, available from www.wto.org/english/tratop_e/serv_e/telecom_e/tel23_e.htm.

[55] See paragraph 1.1 of the Reference Paper, above note 54.

[56] See paragraphs 2.3, 2.5. and 4 of the Reference Paper, above note 54.

[57] See paragraph 2.5 of the Reference Paper, above note 54.

[58] See paragraph 2.2 (b) of the Reference Paper, above note 54.

impose reasonable and unbundled rates is one of the more contentious issues of the Reference Paper. This obligation was at the heart of the *Mexico – Telecoms* case, in which the United States alleged that Mexico's major supplier Telmex did not provide for cost-oriented or reasonable interconnection and also claimed that the charges were not sufficiently unbundled.[59]

Another element of telecommunication harmonisation can be found in paragraph 5 of the Reference Paper, which obliges Members to establish an independent regulator who must be separate from, and not accountable to, any supplier of basic telecommunications services. The regulator's decisions and procedures shall be impartial with respect to all market participants. In some legal systems this obligation requires the establishment of a new type of administrative entity which may be alien to the traditional institutional structure of the administrative system. Furthermore, the requirement may have effects on the constitutional structure of some legal systems. In countries with privatised former government telecommunications operators, the establishment of an independent regulator requires a clear separation between the regulator's office and the former government operator. Yet, the government may still exercise some control over its former telecommunications operator or maintain closer links with it than with other operators, especially if the former government operator is subject to a universal service obligation. In such a situation, the WTO Member may be obliged to establish a regulatory body, which operates independently of other government branches. The existence of administrative bodies, which are independent of government or parliamentary control, gives rise to important questions about their legitimacy and accountability in constitutional systems, which require that all public authority has to be accountable to democratic or parliamentary scrutiny.

It should be noted that the harmonisation approaches of the Reference Paper follow a particular model of telecommunication regulation, i.e. a system of regulated competition in a market dominated by former monopoly suppliers. In this regard the Reference Paper draws on the experience of the telecommunications liberalisation in the US (former private monopoly) and in most European countries (former public monopolies). The Reference Paper, however, does not contain regulatory methods and instruments which could be relevant in the context of the initial setting up of a telecommunications network, which is the main

59 *Mexico – Telecoms*, above note 10.

task in many developing countries. Rather, the Reference Paper aims at solving regulatory problems if the network already exists and its use can be dominated by the former monopoly supplier. It is therefore doubtful whether the Reference Paper is a suitable framework for regulation in developing countries.

5. Which rules for GATS regarding standardisation and harmonisation?

Should future GATS rules incorporate (additional) elements of standardisation and harmonisation? Based on the impact of these obligations on national regulatory autonomy it should not be surprising that I would advise against any broadening or deepening of these concepts in the GATS context.

Regarding standardisation, it should be kept in mind that the membership of a standard-setting international organisation and the membership of the WTO can be different, even if the standard-setting organisation is open to all WTO Members. Developing countries often find it difficult to participate actively in a standard-setting organisation due to lack of capacity even if they are formally Members of that organisation. International standards are also sometimes drafted by the respective international organisation as non-binding voluntary standards. Incorporating such standards as binding standards into WTO law raises questions about the legitimacy of such a law-making process. Because of these difficulties and the reduction of regulatory autonomy it would be a sensible approach if future GATS rules employed, at most, international standards based on the approach of the Accountancy Disciplines and did not follow the stricter approaches of the TBT and SPS Agreements. International standards should be taken into account when developing technical standards for the provision of services. International standards can help Members in designing better regulation if their policy objectives coincide with the aims of the relevant international standards. However, there should be no obligation to use these standards, in particular if Members want to pursue regulatory objectives which are not (adequately) addressed in those standards.

Regarding harmonisation I would be even more cautious. The harmonisation elements of the Reference Paper on telecommunications should remain the only instances of harmonisation within the GATS system. Firstly, harmonisation of services regulation always requires a sectoral approach and would therefore require specific knowledge of and expertise in that sector, which is typically not available to trade diplomats and negotiators. In fact, the many scheduling mistakes in the schedules of specific commitments show that the trade negotiators of the Uruguay Round were often not aware of the regulatory implications of their commitments. Furthermore, given the variety of regulation of services in WTO Members, the harmonisation of services regulation would often lead to imposing the particularities of one regulatory system on all WTO Members regardless of their regulatory traditions. In light of the implications of the *Mexico – Telecoms* case for Mexico, it can even be questioned whether the Telecommunications Reference Paper is a useful addition to the WTO legal system.

VI. Conclusion

An appropriate reaction to the crisis of the WTO does not include proposals to increase the liberalisation of trade in services. Rather, it should be realised that proposals preserving or re-establishing national regulatory autonomy may be more useful in restoring the credibility of the WTO system. Future GATS rules should therefore allow for a large degree of regulatory autonomy. Rules on mutual recognition and the use of international standards should give national legislators and regulators the competence to determine whether and to what extent they wish to defer to the requirements of other domestic systems or an international system. In this context, MRAs may be an option which could be explored. However, harmonisation, i.e. the creation of uniform rules and regulations at the WTO, should not be pursued further.

Bibliography

Bacchus, James, 'The Bicycle Club: Affirming the American Interest in the Future of the WTO', Address to the Washington International Trade Association, 12 November 2002, www.worldtradelaw.net/articles/bacchusbicycle.pdf.

Beviglia Zampetti, Amerigo, 'Market Access through Mutual Regulation: The Promise and Limits of GATS Article VII', in: Pierre Sauvé and Robert M. Stern (eds.), *GATS 2000 – New Directions in Services Trade Liberalization*, 2000, p. 283.

Bronckers, Marco and Pierre Larouche, 'Telecommunications Services and the World Trade Organization', *Journal of World Trade* 31 (1997), p. 5.

Chimni, B. S., 'The World Trade Organization, Democracy and Development: A View From the South', *Journal of World Trade* 40 (2006), p. 5.

Desmedt, Axel, 'Proportionality in WTO Law', *Journal of International Economic Law* 4(2001), p. 441.

Hauser, Heinz, 'Domestic Policy Foundation and Domestic Policy Functions of International Trade Rules', *Aussenwirtschaft* 41 (1986), p. 171.

Jackson, John, 'The WTO "constitution" and proposed reforms: seven "mantras" revisited', *JIEL* 4 (2001), p. 67.

Krajewski, Markus, 'Democratic Legitimacy and Constitutional Perspectives of WTO Law', *Journal of World Trade* 35(1) (2001), p. 167.

——*National Regulation and Trade Liberalization in Services – The Legal Impact of the General Agreement on Trade in Services (GATS) on National Regulatory Autonomy* (London: Kluwer Law International, 2003).

Marceau, Gabrielle and Joel Trachtman, 'The Technical Barriers to Trade Agreement, the Sanitary and Phytosanitary Measures Agreement, and the General Agreement on Tariffs and Trade', *Journal of World Trade* 36 (2002), p. 811.

Neumann, Jan and Elisabeth Türk, 'Necessity Revisited – Proportionality in World Trade Organization Law after *Korea – Beef, EC –Asbestos* and *EC – Sardines*', *Journal of World Trade* 37 (2003), p. 199.

Nicolaïdis, Kalypso, *Mutual Recognition of Regulatory Regimes: Some Lessons and Prospects*, Jean Monnet Working Paper 7/1997, available at http://jeanmonnetprogram.org/papers/97/97–07.html.

——'Non-Discriminatory Mutual Recognition: An Oxymoron in the New WTO Lexicon?', in Thomas Cottier and Petros Mavroidis (eds.), *Regulatory Barriers and the Principle of Non-Discrimination in World Trade Law* (Ann Arbor: University of Michigan Press, 2000), pp. 267–301.

Nicolaïdis, Kalypso and Joel Trachtman, 'From Policed Regulation to Managed Recognition in GATS', in Pierre Sauvé and Robert M. Stern (eds.), *GATS 2000: New Directions in Services Trade Liberalization* (Washington: Brookings Institution Press, 2000), p. 242.

Ortino, Federico and Ernst-Ulrich Petersmann, (eds.), *The WTO Dispute Settlement System 1995–2003* (The Hague: Kluwer Law International, 2004).

Pauwelyn, Joost, 'Rien ne va plus? Distinguishing Domestic Regulation from Market Access in GATT and GATS', *World Trade Review* (2005), pp. 131–170.

Petersmann, Ernst-Ulrich, *Constitutional Functions and Constitutional Problems of International Economic Law* (University of Fribourg Press, 1991).

Polaski, Sandra, *Winners and Losers – Impact of the Doha Round on Developing Countries* (Washington, DC: Carnegie Endowment, 2006).

Steiner, Josephine, Lorna Woods, and Christian Stigg-Flessner, *EU Law*, 9th edn (Oxford University Press, 2006).

Stoll, Peter-Tobias and Frank Schorkopf, *WTO-World Economic Order, World Trade Law* (Leiden and Boston: Martinus Nijhoff, 2006).

Sykes, Alan O., 'Comparative Advantage and the Normative Economics of International Trade Policy', *Journal of International Economic Law* 1 (1998), p. 49.

Trachtman, Joel, 'Lessons for the GATS from Existing WTO Rules on Domestic Regulation', in Aaditya Mattoo and Pierre Sauvé (eds.), *Domestic Regulation and Service Trade Liberalization* (Washington: World Bank, 2003) p. 57.

Trolliet, Claude and John Hegarty, 'Regulatory Reform and Trade Liberalisation in Accountancy Services', in: Aaditya Mattoo and Pierre Sauvé (eds.), *Domestic Regulation and Service Trade Liberalization* (Washington: World Bank, 2003), p. 147.

Tumlir, Jan, 'International Economic Order and Democratic Constitutionalism', *ORDO* 34 (1983), p. 71.

Van den Bossche, Peter, *The Law and Policy of the World Trade Organization* (Cambridge University Press, 2005).

19

A safeguards regime for services

FERNANDO PIÉROLA*

Introduction

This chapter examines the main issues in the debate on the introduction of an emergency safeguard mechanism (ESM) for trade in services. After discussing the mandate under which negotiations are currently being conducted (section I), the chapter identifies some of the main challenges and opportunities that arise from the negotiations (section II), setting out the main arguments regarding the desirability of an ESM (section III) and addressing the feasibility issues that arise in developing a workable ESM (section IV). The chapter presents general views on the best way forward for the negotiating process and, should agreement to adopt a GATS ESM be reached, how such disciplines should be incorporated into the law of the World Trade Organization (WTO) (Section V).

I. The mandate of negotiations: Debating the desirability and feasibility of an emergency safeguard regime for services

While the Uruguay Round resulted in far-reaching obligations and commitments in services (as embodied in GATS), it left open a number of issues for further work and discussion after the entry into force of the Agreement Establishing the World Trade Organization (WTO Agreement).[1] One of these 'leftovers' was the negotiation and regulation

* The views expressed in this paper are exclusively those of the author and not of any of the institutions with which he is affiliated. Special thanks go to Pierre Sauvé, Cherise Valles, Martin Roy, Hunter Nottage and Johannes Bernabe for their comments on a prior draft of this article. All errors, however, remain those of the author.

[1] B. Hoekman and M. Kostecki, *The Political Economy of the World Trading System, The WTO and Beyond* (Oxford University Press, 2001), 2nd edn p. 269; G. Gauthier, E. O'Brien and S. Spencer, 'Déjà Vu, or New Beginning for Safeguards and Subsidies Rules in Services Trade?', in P. Sauvé and R. M. Stern (eds.), *GATS 2000, New Directions in Services and Trade Liberalization* (The Brookings Institution, 2000), p. 165; P. Sauvé, 'Completing the GATS Framework: Addressing Uruguay Round Leftovers' (Chapter 4), in *Trade Rules Behind*

of 'emergency safeguard measures' referred to in Article X:1 of the GATS, which states:

> *Emergency Safeguard Measures*
>
> 1. There shall be multilateral negotiations on the question of emergency safeguard measures based on the principle of non-discrimination. The results of such negotiations shall enter into effect on a date not later than three years from the date of entry into force of the WTO Agreement.

The general wording of this mandate has given rise to two different perspectives regarding the proper scope of these negotiations.[2] On the one hand, some WTO Members consider that the negotiations must focus on the question of the desirability of an ESM for services, leaving aside any discussion on how to introduce such a mechanism (provided there is consensus as to its desirability) to a second stage.[3] On the other hand, some Members consider that, while the desirability of an ESM is an issue that must be discussed, negotiations need to move beyond that aspect.[4] They argue that Article X:1 implicitly acknowledges that negotiations must lead to 'results', as referred to in the second sentence of Article XI:1, that will have to 'enter into effect'. For these Members, the term 'results' refers unequivocally to rules for the implementation of an ESM.[5] The negotiating history of Article X:1, as the WTO Secretariat describes it, appears to favour the former perspective.[6]

Borders, Essays on Services, Investment and the New Trade Agenda (Cameron May, 2003), pp. 73–76; M. Footer and C. George, 'The General Agreement on Trade in Services', in P. F. J. Macrory, A. E. Appleton and M. G. Plummer (eds.), *The World Trade Organization: Legal, Economic and Political Analysis*, volume I (Springer, 2005), p. 902.

[2] See, M. Marconini, 'Emergency Safeguard Measures in the GATS: Beyond Feasible and Desirable', UNCTAD/DITC/TNDC/2005/4, 9 March 2005, p. 4; L. P. Niscovolos, 'A Way Out of the Fruitless Debate on Services Safeguards?', *Bridges*, Year 10, Number 6, September–October 2006, p. 3.

[3] See, e.g., Hong Kong's position, Working Party on GATS Rules, Report of the Meeting of 10 February 2006, Note by the Secretariat, S/WPGR/M/54, 22 February 2006, para. 8; Chile's position, *ibid.*, para. 10; Mexico's position, *ibid.*, para. 12.

[4] See, e.g., the revised offer of Malaysia, Council for Trade in Services, TN/S/O/MYS/Rev. 1, 31 January 2006, para. 2: '[t]his revised offer is conditional upon the outcome of the negotiations stipulated by the GATS, particularly on Article X (Emergency Safeguard Measures)'.

[5] Marconini, 'Emergency Safeguard Measures', p. 4.

[6] According to the WTO Secretariat: '[t]he negotiating history … implies that prior to elaborating specific provisions, Members may wish to consider the broader question of whether or not it would be desirable to develop an emergency safeguard instrument in the field of trade in services'. Working Party on GATS Rules, Emergency Safeguard Measures under Article X of GATS, Note by the Secretariat, S/WPGR/W/1, 6 July 1995, para. 1.

The result of these diverging perspectives is that the scope of negotiations, to date, has been defined by two themes: (i) the desirability of having an ESM (or its convenience), and (ii) the feasibility of implementing an ESM.

II. The negotiations: Permanent disagreement

The negotiations pursuant to Article X:1 have been taking place since 1995. However no agreement has yet been reached.[7]

In March 1995, the Council for Trade in Services established a Working Party on GATS Rules to implement the negotiating mandates contained in the GATS on emergency safeguard measures.[8] In principle, as stated in Article X:1, the results of negotiations had to enter into effect no later than 3 years after the entry into force of the WTO, that is, no later than 31 December 1997.

Because of the Members' lack of consensus on both the desirability and feasibility of an ESM, the deadline for negotiations has been continually extended by subsequent Decisions of the Council for Trade in Services[9] – from 30 June 1998[10] to 15 December 2000,[11] 15 March 2002,[12] 15 March

[7] According to the 2006 Annual Report of the Working Party on GATS Rules '[d]ivergent views continued to be expressed on the various aspects raised in relation to emergency safeguard measures, including desirability and feasibility'. Annual Report of the Working Party on GATS Rules to the Council for Trade in Services (2006), S/WPGR/16, 23 November 2006, para. 4.

[8] Working Party on GATS Rules, Activities of the Working Party on GATS Rules, Report to the Council for Trade in Services, S/WPGR/1, 23 October 1996, para. 1.

[9] This type of decision has no legal basis in the treaty at issue. It appears, however, to be the type of decision that would fall under the general decision-making powers of Article IV:1, in conjunction with Articles IV:2 and IV:5, of the WTO Agreement. See H. Nottage and T. Sebastian 'Giving Legal Effect to the Results of the WTO Trade Negotiations: An Analysis of the Methods of Changing WTO Law', *Journal of International Economic Law* 9(4) (2006), pp. 1003–1009.

[10] Council for Trade in Services, Decision on Negotiations on Emergency Safeguard Measures, Adopted by the Council for Trade in Services on 26 November 1997, S/L/43, 2 December 1997.

[11] Council for Trade in Services, Second Decision on Negotiations on Emergency Safeguard Measures, Adopted by the Council for Trade in Services on 24 June 1999, S/L/73, 5 July 1999.

[12] Council for Trade in Services, Third Decision on Negotiations on Emergency Safeguard Measures, Adopted by the Council for Trade in Services on 1 December 2000, S/L/90, 8 December 2000.

2004[13] and currently, 'the date of entry into force of the results of the current round of services negotiations'.[14]

The main (and remaining) proponents of a GATS ESM are most of the members of the Association of Southeast Asian Nations (ASEAN). This group has submitted several documents including elements for a proposal.[15] Other Members, such as Brazil and China, 'are sympathetic to the adoption of ESMs' (rather than active supporters).[16] On the other hand, several WTO Members, among them both developed and developing countries, are either strongly opposed to or sceptical about the introduction of such a mechanism.[17]

The current stalemate would appear to stem from the following causes:

(a) Certain Members consider that the proponents have been unable to make a robust enough case in favour of an ESM and there are no clear reasons why such a mechanism is needed.[18] In particular, some of these Members wonder whose interests an ESM would protect and in what particular circumstances it would apply. Furthermore, some of these Members consider that the GATS already has considerable built-in flexibility to accommodate the interests of any Member intending protecting a particular interest.[19]
(b) Irrespective of their views on the desirability of an ESM, certain Members consider that the implementation of such a mechanism raises serious problems as to feasibility to which proponents have

[13] Council for Trade in Services, Fourth Decision on Negotiations on Emergency Safeguard Measures, Adopted by the Council for Trade in Services on 15 March 2002, S/L/102, 27 March 2002.

[14] Council for Trade in Services, Fifth Decision on Negotiations on Emergency Safeguard Measures, Adopted by the Council for Trade in Services on 15 March 2004, S/L/159, 17 March 2004.

[15] Although the WTO document containing the ASEAN proposal is not publicly available, the proposal has been posted at: www.ictsd.org/issarea/stsd/Resources/Docs/ASEAN_ESM.pdf, last visited 12 December 2006.

[16] R. Clogstoun, R. Trewin and M. Bosworth, 'Would Emergency Safeguard Measures Work for Services' in *Asian-Pacific Economic Literature* (Journal Compilation) (The Australian National University and Blackwell Publishing Asia Pty. Ltd), pp. 56–57.

[17] *Ibid.*

[18] See, e.g., Hong Kong's position, Working Party on GATS Rules, Report of the Meeting of 10 April 2006, Note by the Secretariat, S/WPGR/M/55, 4 May 2006, para. 9; Japan's position, Working Party on GATS Rules, Report of the Meeting of 20 June 2005, Note by the Secretariat, S/WPGR/M/52, 7 September 2005, para. 21; Australia's position, *ibid.*, para. 18; European Communities' position, *ibid.*, para. 22.

[19] See, e.g., Switzerland's position, *ibid.*, para. 32.

not been able to offer credible solutions.[20] Even if an ESM was desirable, in the absence of clear answers to pertinent questions,[21] the opposing Members prefer not to take a chance. Given the challenges arising from the application to safeguards in goods trade and the differing nature of trade in services, it is questionable whether the focus on a goods-type mechanism for services would be appropriate. Certain Members are clearly of the view that the answer to this question is no.[22]

(c) Certain Members appear to expect proponents of a GATS ESM to make improved services offers in exchange for the introduction of an ESM.[23] However, no such offers have materialised to date.

While the above obstacles clearly represent important challenges to the negotiations, they also provide an opportunity to establish, if agreed, a well-thought-out ESM whose operational properties may be subject to less uncertainty than in the case of the safeguard for trade in goods and, potentially, to less controversy and a reduced likelihood of trade disputes requiring recourse to litigation. Each of these issues is addressed in the following sections.

III. Is it 'desirable' to have an emergency safeguard mechanism for services?

There are divergent views among WTO Members and in policy circles for and against an ESM,[24] ranging from outright opposition to the very

[20] See, e.g., US position, Working Party on GATS Rules, Report of the Meeting of 10 April 2006, Note by the Secretariat, S/WPGR/M/55, 4 May 2006, para. 12.

[21] Ranging from the definition of the service under consideration and the like service, 'domestic industry', the surge in 'imports', the collection of data, the demonstration of injury and causal link, and the issue of enforceability, all of these are discussed below under the section on feasibility.

[22] See, e.g., US position, Working Party on GATS Rules, Report of the Meeting of 10 April 2006, Note by the Secretariat, S/WPGR/M/55, 4 May 2006, para. 12.

[23] See Thailand's statement, Working Party on GATS Rules, Report of the Meeting of 20 June 2005, Note by the Secretariat, S/WPGR/M/52, 7 September 2005, para. 9; Switzerland's position, Working Party on GATS Rules, Report of the Meeting of 24 November 2004, Note by the Secretariat, S/WPGR/M/50, 17 January 2005, para. 40.

[24] As Jara and Domínguez mention, '[f]or a few Members, in particular the ASEAN countries, the development of an ESM is a political imperative, while for others it's neither technically feasible nor politically acceptable. Thus, there is a stalemate'. A. Jara and C. Domínguez, 'Liberalization of Trade in Services and Trade Negotiations', *Journal of World Trade* 40 (1) (2006), pp. 117–118.

concept of services ESM[25] to the view that an ESM is not only a goal of the negotiations, but a requirement for further liberalisation in the services area.[26] The main arguments put forward in this debate are stated below.

A. Safeguards may provide relief to the domestic industry while it 'adjusts' to a more competitive environment or prepares to leave the market in an orderly fashion[27]

This argument is based on the premise that liberalisation is likely to adversely affect the situation of domestic industries and that an 'adjustment' may be necessary to allow the domestic industry to 'catch up' with a more competitive environment, or otherwise, to leave the market in an orderly manner. Such an 'adjustment' may, however, be costly,[28] concentrated in time and space, affect particular categories of workers, and could take some time. Under such circumstances, an emergency safeguard measure is seen as an instrument that could allow the domestic industry to receive temporary protective relief while undertaking needed adjustment efforts; in the context of services, it would provide breathing space to allow the affected domestic industry to adjust to a change in competitive conditions.[29]

It may be argued that it makes little sense to use safeguards to counter the adverse effects of increased competition for domestic industries when encouragement of that competition may have been one of the main reasons for adopting a policy of trade liberalisation in the first place. In principle, safeguards are designed to respond to particular circumstances that were not foreseen at the time of the conclusion of the agreement. The adverse effects of competition cannot be viewed per se as 'unforeseen'. Even if the unexpected results of liberalisation did somehow justify the

[25] See, e.g., Hong Kong's position, Working Party on GATS Rules, Report of the Meeting of 20 September 2004, Note by the Secretariat, S/WPGR/M/49, 27 October 2004, para. 45.

[26] See note 4 above.

[27] J. H. Jackson, *The World Trading System*, p. 176; C. Brown and M. Crowley, 'Safeguards', in P. F. J. Macrory, A. E. Appleton and M. G. Plummer (eds.), *The World Trade Organization: Legal, Economic and Political Analysis*, volume II (Springer, 2005), pp. 55–57.

[28] B. M. Hoekman, *The Uruguay Round of Multilateral Trade Negotiations: Investigating the Scope for Agreement on Safeguards, Services, and Agriculture* (The University of Michigan, 1988), p. 52.

[29] Working Party on GATS Rules, Summary of Main Views Expressed by Members on Emergency Safeguard Measures, Note by the Secretariat, JOB(06)/165, 2 June 2006, para. 6.

need for certain types of transitional relief, one could argue that the industries that are capable of adjustment should be able to obtain such relief from financial markets, and not through trade protection by their governments.[30] The question is more nuanced for industries that are less able to undertake the needed adjustments, and in such situations a safeguard that is progressively phased out may provide an optimal policy solution.[31]

B. Safeguards may facilitate further liberalisation as they would work as a safety net if liberalisation did not yield the expected benefits[32]

This argument is premised on the uncertainty of information regarding what may happen after liberalisation, triggering the need for a security mechanism or a 'safety net'. The uncertainty may relate, for instance, to the importing country's post-liberalisation growth prospects or whether international prices may change and the economic environment might be different from that prevailing at the time of the conclusion of an agreement.[33]

ESM supporters claim that if the mechanism were put in place, liberalisation in services would be faster and deeper as WTO Members could provide some security to their constituents in the event of sudden, unanticipated, changes, and would thereby be more inclined to take on new commitments.[34]

It may be argued that the underlying assumption is that importing countries are generally likely to perceive trade liberalisation without a safeguard mechanism as potentially detrimental, although for some countries trade liberalisation, even with such a mechanism, may be viewed as inherently beneficial. Indeed, some WTO Members have gone so far as to state that the introduction of a safeguards regime is unnecessary.[35]

[30] Y-S. Lee, *Safeguard Measures in World Trade, The Legal Analysis* (Kluwer Law International, 2003), pp. 8 and 61.

[31] A. O. Sykes, *The Safeguards Mess: A Critique of WTO Jurisprudence* (The University of Chicago 2003), p. 25; Brown and Crowley, 'Safeguards', pp. 56–57.

[32] Hoekman and Kostecki, *The Political Economy of the World Trading System*, p. 311; C. Brown and M. Crowley, 'Safeguards', p. 53.

[33] *Ibid.*, p. 54.

[34] See, e.g., The Philippines' position, Working Party on GATS Rules, Report of Meeting of 24 March 2004, Note by the Secretariat, S/WPGR/M/47, para. 4.

[35] See, e.g., Chile's position, S/WPGR/M/47, para. 17; Mexico's position, S/WPGR/M/47, para. 31.

Furthermore, the argument relies on the assumption that, in negotiating trade liberalisation, importing countries are risk-averse as to what may happen without a safeguard mechanism and might not assume further liberalisation commitments as a result. Such an argument disregards the fact that some importing countries may be risk-neutral or even risk-takers, and therefore less concerned than other Members by the absence of a safeguard mechanism. The Uruguay Round's services negotiations were a good example of a process that was not tied to the existence of a safeguard mechanism. Nonetheless, Members were willing to agree on new disciplines and to undertake a first harvest of market access and national treatment commitments.

It is true that some Members that have liberalised used certain forms of *ex ante* safeguards through limitations on market access and national treatment commitments, and that only because of these limitations were they able to undertake such commitments. However, such a view cannot be generalised to all WTO Members and the impact of an emergency safeguard mechanism on further liberalisation would have to be assessed on a country-specific basis.

It may be true that these *ex ante* safeguard-type measures could provide for an alternative to a generic safeguard regime, while some of them may be considered as sub-optimal. However, the fact that these limitations are *ex ante* and permanent may prevent the efficient exchange of commitments. If a Member were risk-averse, it might be inclined to assume commitments but also to include *ex ante* and permanent limitations to avoid any possible complaint from its constituents, regardless of whether that risk is likely to occur. This scenario may be different if the possibility of introducing a case-by-case safeguard measure were contemplated in the agreement. A risk-averse Member may be willing to be more flexible in its commitments because it would have a mechanism to 'adjust' on an ad hoc basis and in specific circumstances.

As some delegations have suggested, if the proponents of a GATS ESM were to indicate the additional commitments that they were likely to assume in the presence of an ESM, this might encourage the opponents to reconsider their position.[36] From an individual negotiating perspective, the cost of introducing an ESM would have to be assessed against the substantial likely benefits of further liberalisation commitments. In such a case, it may come as no surprise that, if accepted, opponents would

[36] See, e.g., US position, S/WPGR/M/52, para. 13.

request that an ESM apply only to new commitments and not to those that were made in the Uruguay Round.

To counter the argument that an ESM may encourage liberalisation, some Members argue that an ESM would introduce an element of uncertainty into the operation of the GATS, potentially diminishing the value and credibility of commitments and of the agreement itself. In particular, an argument has been raised in that an ESM could depress investment flows under mode 3 in developing countries.[37]

It is true that the introduction of an ESM may add some uncertainty to the terms and conditions of services commitments and of the GATS in general. However, such uncertainty and the possibility of withdrawing or modifying GATS commitments have always existed. Article V on Economic Integration, Article XII on Restrictions to Safeguard the Balance of Payments, Article XIV on General Exceptions, Article XIV *bis* on Security Exceptions, and Article XXI on Modification of Schedules contemplate situations in which WTO Members may undermine the expected value of commitments vis-à-vis other WTO Members by means of discriminatory treatment, imposing restrictions or modifying or withdrawing services commitments.

Furthermore, as Brazilian negotiators have noted, several of the Members opposed to the introduction of an ESM have safeguard-type provisions in their own Schedules of Commitments. Notwithstanding the lack of precision found in many GATS schedules regarding the substantive situations that could give rise to the application of such safeguard-type measures, there is little doubt that these are valid means to protect a market.[38] However, the debate of uncertainty in this context does not arise.

C. As a safety net, a safeguard regime would allow the accommodation of domestic pressures, which may otherwise favour continued or new trade protection

While this argument has not been clearly stated in the ESM negotiations, it is a consequence of the notion of a safety net. If liberalisation does not lead to the expected outcome, a services safeguard can be regarded as a safety net, a multilaterally agreed mechanism that can be used in

[37] See, e.g., Japan's position, S/WPGR/M/47, para. 31; Switzerland's position, S/WPGR/M/49, para. 51; Canada's position, S/WPGR/M/52, para. 22.

[38] Brazil's position, S/WPGR/M/53, paras. 22–24.

exceptional circumstances to address the concerns of the domestic industry in that particular context. In the absence of a safeguard mechanism, the Member affected by the unexpected results of liberalisation would have to resort to other means – such as those provided in Article XXI of the GATS – that may be more costly in political and trade terms, and have results other than those envisaged under a safeguard regime (e.g. a permanent modification or withdrawal of commitments as compared to a temporary suspension or modification, or the lack of demonstration of injury or of other conditions for the imposition of a safeguard). The use or misuse of such alternative 'safeguards' may thus yield sub-optimal outcomes relative to what might be expected to derive from recourse to a well-defined and organised safeguard procedure for services trade.[39]

If liberalisation generated unexpected dislocations such that a WTO Member might need to deviate from its services commitments, it would be better for other WTO Members if such action were taken in accordance with multilaterally-agreed rules and procedures so that the scope for discretion is reduced to a minimum. This was the intent of the negotiators of the Agreement on Safeguards in goods.[40]

In that regard, an ESM may be beneficial in the sense of disciplining discretion in the application of trade-restrictive actions within the contours of the WTO system.

IV. Practicalities: Is a GATS ESM feasible?

A. General considerations

1. Does it make sense to replicate the goods approach?

The debate on feasibility has largely focused on how to replicate relevant categories of the safeguard regime for goods in the services context. This approach generally fails to take into account the significant differences between trade in goods and trade in services. Whereas goods are tangible, storable, often homogeneous, and their production takes place separately from their delivery to buyers, most services are intangible and

[39] See China's position comparing an ESM with ENTs in Members' Schedules of Commitments, S/WPGR/M/52, para. 17.

[40] Argentina – Safeguard Measures on Imports of Footwear, Appellate Body Report, WT/DS121/AB/R, adopted 12 January 2000, para. 95.

non-storable,[41] heterogeneous,[42] and typically involve the simultaneity of production and consumption.[43]

Trade in services therefore takes place in a different manner to trade in goods. Whereas goods are traded only in one way, from the country of origin to the export market (cross-border supply – or in services jargon, mode 1), services may, in addition to cross-border delivery, be traded in three additional modes: consumption abroad, establishment of service suppliers in the importing country, and movement of natural persons.

The traditional purpose of an ESM is to provide 'import-relief' and as Sauvé has explained, there is good reason to doubt that all types of services transactions would represent 'imports' in the traditional meaning of the term.[44]

The differing innate characteristics of services and the multiplicity of modes of supply lead to an additional difference with respect to trade in goods: the means of measurement of trade and the collection of information required for trade-remedy investigations and the credible determination of injury. Since goods must typically clear customs to enter a foreign market, trade in goods can be easily monitored and measured through customs control procedures. In addition, the greater homogeneity of goods of the same nature makes it simpler to count them for purposes of customs valuation and collection of statistics. In the case of services, the situation is different. Services, however, are intangible and this makes it impossible to subject their 'importation' to the same type of border controls as apply to goods. Therefore, the collection of information at the point of 'importation' becomes irrelevant with the possible exception of mode 4 transactions (movement of service suppliers). Even if customs controls could monitor the cross-border supply of services, such monitoring would provide only a partial picture of the value of the services at issue. The heterogeneous nature of services poses acute challenges for the statistical calculation of 'like' services.

In view of the differences discussed above, the challenge of feasibility is either to reconceptualise most of the aspects that are relevant for the application of a safeguards regime for goods or, alternatively, to devise an

[41] Its main features, however, such as the time spent in its delivery or its value can be recorded in the relevant accounts books.

[42] Services are usually customised responding in most instances to the specific requirements of the buyer.

[43] Hoekman and Kostecki, *The Political Economy of the World Trading System*, p. 239.

[44] P. Sauvé, 'Completing the GATS Framework: Addressing Uruguay Round Leftovers', *Aussenwirtschaft* 57 (2002), p. 319.

altogether different model. Although certain Members still believe that a goods-type framework could work in the services context,[45] others fail to see much merit in such an approach.[46]

This leads us to ask whether the goods-model safeguard could be adjusted to make it workable in the services context and, if not, which alternatives would address the policy interests of those interested in a GATS ESM.

2. General requirements of goods safeguards under Article XIX of the GATT and the Agreement on Safeguards

(a) Substantive requirements Attempts to reproduce the safeguards mechanism of GATT Article XIX and the Agreement on Safeguards in the services context have focused on the basic substantive requirements of these provisions in the context of goods trade, namely; that there must be (i) a surge in imports, (ii) that causes or threatens to cause, (iii) injury to the domestic industry of like products or directly competitive products.[47]

In addition to these requirements, the Appellate Body has clarified that a Member seeking to impose a safeguard measure must also demonstrate, as a matter of fact, that the surge in imports that causes or threatens to cause injury to the domestic industry has been the result of 'unforeseen developments' and of the 'effects of obligations incurred by a Member under [the GATT]'.[48]

(b) Procedures and standard of review The fulfilment of substantive requirements is determined through an investigative process during which the investigating authority has to make an objective assessment of the matter. This assessment consists of providing a 'reasoned and

[45] See, e.g., the Philippines' position, Working Party on GATS Rules, Report of the Meeting of 10 April 2006, Note by the Secretariat, S/WPGR/M/55, 4 May 2006, para. 15.

[46] See, e.g., US position, Working Party on GATS Rules, Report of the Meeting of 10 April 2006, Note by the Secretariat, S/WPGR/M/55, 4 May 2006, para. 12. This view is also shared by some commentators. See Sauvé, 'Completing the GATS Framework', pp. 311–313; Niscovolos, 'A Way Out of the Fruitless Debate on Services Safeguards?', p. 3.

[47] Article XIX:1(a) of the GATT 1994 and Article 2.1 of the Agreement on Safeguards.

[48] Korea – Definitive Safeguard Measure on Imports of Certain Dairy Products, Appellate Body Report, WT/DS98/AB/R, adopted 12 January 2000, paras. 83–85; Argentina – Safeguard Measures on Imports of Footwear, Appellate Body Report, WT/DS121/AB/R, adopted 12 January 2000, paras. 90–92; United States – Safeguard Measures on Imports of Fresh, Chilled or Frozen Lamb Meat from New Zealand and Australia, Appellate Body Report, WT/DS177/AB/R, WT/DS178/AB/R, adopted 16 May 2001, para. 68.

adequate' explanation, in its relevant determinations, of how it has established and evaluated all the relevant facts[49] and the manner in which it has interpreted the provisions of Article XIX of the GATT 1994 and of the Agreement on Safeguards in accordance with customary rules of interpretation of public international law, as contained in Articles 31 and 32 of the Vienna Convention on the Law of Treaties.[50]

(c) Necessity requirement and compensation If the substantive requirements are met in the course of the investigation process, the safeguard may apply only to the extent necessary to prevent or remedy the injury to the domestic industry, whether in the form of tariffs, quotas or tariff quotas.[51] In parallel to the imposition of the measure, both GATT Article XIX and the Agreement on Safeguards foresee a rebalancing mechanism through negotiations on compensation with the countries that may be affected by the safeguard measure.[52]

In practice, WTO adjudicating bodies have been very demanding about the fulfilment of these requirements. Thus far, no safeguard measure that has been challenged has withstood the scrutiny of a panel.

Given the greater uncertainty with respect to the application of an ESM for services, it is legitimate to wonder whether a goods-type safeguard would be feasible and desirable,[53] and therefore, whether a panel or the Appellate Body might be more deferential to domestic authorities than in the case of goods trade.

B. Specific considerations

There are two approaches to meeting the specific requirements for the imposition of a goods-type ESM: one approach favours a multilateral agreement on basic concepts such as the definition of the domestic industry,[54]

[49] United States – Safeguard Measures on Imports of Fresh, Chilled or Frozen Lamb Meat from New Zealand and Australia, Appellate Body Report, WT/DS177/AB/R, WT/DS178/AB/R, adopted 16 May 2001, para. 103.

[50] Articles 3.2 and 11 of the Understanding on Rules and Procedures Governing the Settlement of Disputes (DSU).

[51] Article XIX:1(a) of the GATT 1994 and Article 5 of the Agreement on Safeguards.

[52] Article XIX:2 of GATT 1994 and Articles 8.1 and 12.3 of the Agreement on Safeguards.

[53] See, e.g., Canada's position, S/WPGR/M/52, para. 22.

[54] See, e.g., Chile's position, S/WPGR/M/54, para. 10; European Communities' position, S/WPGR/M/54, para. 5.

whereas the other would favour a greater degree of deference to domestic legislation.[55]

While the first approach is generally accepted by the WTO membership, the latter approach raises major areas of debate. In the absence of multilateral regulation it would be incumbent on a Member to determine the best means of complying with WTO law and define the notions underlying the appropriate obligations accordingly. However, the explicit transfer of the clarification of such important concepts to national law may pose certain challenges. If national attempts to deal with general concepts in the context of trade in goods have proven unsuccessful (in the light of WTO jurisprudence), there is no reason to suppose that the same situation would not arise in the services context, especially if the language to be used would be vaguer than that applicable to the goods safeguards. This would militate in favour of a more rigorous standard of review than that applied by panels in goods-related safeguard cases. It would appear that the proponents of transferring the definition of certain concepts to domestic legislation are mindful of this requirement.[56]

1. Would the 'unforeseen developments' requirement apply?

Since the GATS must be seen as a contract consisting of rights and obligations between parties, a determination of 'unforeseen developments' should be required for permitting the imposition of an ESM. Under the logic of contract law, if at the time of making commitments, Members were mindful of all likely events that could lead to injury as a result of increased imports, they should not be able to renege on their liberalisation commitments because of the occurrence of these events. The general principle of *pacta sunt servanda* would apply in such a situation.

However, in reality, Members scheduling commitments cannot be expected to foresee all possible scenarios that could trigger an increase in imports. Attempting to predict all possible scenarios may significantly increase the negotiation costs for the Members and lead eventually to the failure of those negotiations. In certain circumstances, it may be

[55] See, e.g., The Philippines' position, Working Party on GATS Rules, Report of the Meeting of 24 March 2004, Note by the Secretariat, S/WPGR/M/47, 22 April 2004, para. 8.

[56] 'This might be done by ensuring appropriate transparency and by prohibiting arbitrariness on the part of national regulators.' See, e.g., the Philippines' position, Working Party on GATS Rules, Report of the Meeting of 10 April 2006, Note by the Secretariat, S/WPGR/M/55, 4 May 2006, para. 11.

more efficient to leave certain lacunae in a contract than to envisage all possible situations that may arise in the execution of that contract.[57] In this context, a safeguard clause may serve as a safety net, to regulate a Member's reactions in a certain situation unforeseen by the parties. Thus, allowing deviation from an original commitment because of 'unforeseen developments' can be argued to secure the most efficient result in negotiations, especially if the Member undertaking a commitment is risk-averse, heavily pressured by domestic constituents, or simply misinformed as to the situation and potential development of its domestic industries in the light of any future liberalisation process.

In the context of goods, the Appellate Body has defined unforeseen developments as developments occurring after the negotiation of the relevant tariff concession which it would not be reasonable to expect that the negotiators of the country making the concession could and should have foreseen at the time when the concession was negotiated.[58]

Unforeseen developments must refer to circumstances different from the expected adverse effects of liberalisation on domestic service suppliers. These circumstances could not have been predicted on the basis of the information and knowledge available when the commitment was made.[59]

In the context of services, it has been argued that a Member making a commitment might be able to foresee that 'structural adjustments' would be required in relation to specific sectors.[60] In the author's view, no particular category should be excluded from the definition of 'unforeseen developments' in this particular case. Given the Appellate Body's jurisprudence that a Member imposing a safeguard bears the burden of establishing the existence of the 'unforeseen developments',[61] it would be incumbent upon that Member to demonstrate that the resulting 'structural problems' in a particular sector were, in effect, unforeseen. However, it must be recognised that this raises a problem of 'moral

[57] R. Cooter and T. Ulen, Derecho y Economía, Fondo de Cultura Económica (1998), pp. 256–257.

[58] Argentina – Safeguard Measures on Imports of Footwear, Appellate Body Report, WT/DS121/AB/R, adopted 12 January 2000, para. 96.

[59] See Argentina – Safeguard Measures on Imports of Footwear, Appellate Body Report, WT/DS121/AB/R/, adopted 12 January 2000, para. 93.

[60] S/WPGR/M/47, para. 11.

[61] See, e.g., United States – Safeguard Measures on Imports of Fresh, Chilled or Frozen Lamb Meat from New Zealand and Australia, Appellate Body Report, WT/DS177/AB/R, WT/DS178/AB/R, adopted 16 May 2001, para. 76.

hazard' in that the Member would have the incentive not to reveal how much it knew of the possible 'development' when it made the commitment. Therefore, it has been argued that unforeseen developments cannot refer to developments that are dependent upon acts or conduct of the government or even the domestic industry involved.[62]

In this context, it would be necessary to determine the level of knowledge and information of the negotiators making the commitments and the circumstances prevailing at the time they were made. What level of knowledge and information would be required? For instance, if business forecasts predicted a boom of investments in a particular service sector, could negotiators be 'deemed' to know of such a potential development? Apparently, under certain circumstances, that could be a possibility.[63] However, if such a standard were accepted, developing and least-developed countries with limited human resources available for collecting and processing all the relevant information could be at a distinct disadvantage.

2. The determination of the 'imported' service and of the like domestic service

The determination of the service at issue and of the like domestic service poses more challenges than in the context of goods trade. The main reason for this is the different 'object' at issue. As noted above, there are unique characteristics that differentiate services from goods in international trade, particularly their intangibility, non-storability, heterogeneity, and typical simultaneity in production and consumption.[64] In addition, services cannot be clearly defined as specific 'objects' but rather as 'bundles' of activities, processes, transformations and often goods in which they are embedded.[65] These features make the definition of the service at issue a complex matter. Services provided from one foreign supplier to a particular customer may not be the same as those provided to a different customer because the services may be tailored to different

[62] Sykes, *The Safeguards Mess: A Critique of WTO Jurisprudence*, p. 30.

[63] In the context of Article 32 of the Vienna Convention, in determining the kind of knowledge that a WTO Member might have of the circumstances of the conclusion of a treaty, the Appellate Body described as 'constructive knowledge' the fact that 'parties have deemed notice of a particular event, act or instrument through publication'. European Communities – Customs Classification of Frozen Boneless Chicken Cuts, Complaint by Thailand, Appellate Body Report, WT/DS286/R, para. 295.

[64] Hoekman and Kostecki, *The Political Economy of the World Trading System*, p. 239.

[65] B. M. Hoekman, 'Safeguard Provisions and International Trade Agreements Involving Services', in *The World Economy* 16 (1993), p. 41.

customers' needs.[66] In principle, common sense would dictate that allowance should be made for the different characteristics of services. However, given the intangibility and non-storability of services, it might be hard to appreciate and measure those differences in determining a single 'imported' service. In addition, given that services are generally delivered in bundles, how should one distinguish between the different activities in the package?

Once an imported service has been defined, the next question is how to determine that it is like or directly competitive with the service provided by the domestic industry. The concept of 'likeness' as interpreted by the Appellate Body, evoking the notion of an 'accordion',[67] raises a host of questions when applied to services. Given the nature of services and the problem of monitoring them at the border, it appears that any agreed GATS ESM would have to involve recourse to domestic regulatory measures. In this case there should be no reason to distinguish between the notion of 'likeness' with respect to the national treatment principle and that of likeness for the purposes of an ESM. As the relevant notion in services involves not only a 'like service' but also a 'like service supplier', one issue that must be addressed is the impact of making distinctions between identical or similar services based on the characteristics of the suppliers.

Another relevant issue in the context of the determination of the imported service and the like domestic service relates to the various modes through which trade in services is conducted. In determining whether services are 'like', differences in the modes of supply may be relevant in making the appropriate comparisons, particularly if the unit of measurement is the value of the service rendered. The definition of the imported service and the like domestic service should therefore be made on a case-by-case basis.

3. What is the 'domestic industry'?

This is one of the core issues of the policy debate, as it ultimately relates to the issue of who is the ESM for and why it is needed in the first place.[68]

[66] G. Gauthier, E. O'Brien and S. Spencer, 'Déjà Vu, or New Beginning for Safeguards and Subsidies Rules in Services Trade?', in P. Sauvé and R. M. Stern (eds.), *GATS 2000, New Directions in Services and Trade Liberalization* (The Brookings Institution, 2000), p. 171.

[67] Japan – Taxes on Alcoholic Beverages, Appellate Body Report, WT/DS8/AB/R, WT/DS10/AB/R, WT/DS11/AB/R, adopted 1 November 1996, p. 23.

[68] See, e.g., Hong Kong's position, Working Party on GATS Rules, Report of the Meeting of 10 April 2006, Note by the Secretariat, S/WPGR/M/55, 4 May 2006, para. 9.

In trade remedy investigations relating to trade in goods, two issues that are different but interconnected are (i) the 'standing' of domestic producers to request the initiation of a trade remedies investigation and (ii) the definition of the 'domestic industry' for the purposes of examining the injury that the trade remedy is intended to redress – including a number of producers that may be larger than the petitioner.

(a) The industry at issue and related industries When considering the domestic industry, the first problem that arises in the context of services concerns the identification of domestic service suppliers, given that services are generally delivered in bundles. This means that a supplier of one service could also be a supplier of several related services and, for the purposes of the determination of standing, it would be relevant to make a clear distinction between its participation in the production of the service at issue and that in the production of other services. This may not be an easy task. The measurement of a supplier's participation may vary depending on how the data is collected: collecting data at the establishment level – i.e. at the precise 'locations' at which specific services are provided – may provide a more accurate description of the industry than data collection at the enterprise level – involving the multiple services that the company or 'producer' supplies.[69]

Another matter to be considered is the definition of domestic industry when the final 'product' is the result of multi-stage service processing, and when at least one of the services provided is supplied abroad (e.g. engineering consultancy, part of which is carried out in a different country). The question then arises of the application of rules of origin to determine whether or not the service is domestic.

(b) The 'domestic' industry and locally established foreign suppliers The second issue of relevance in the definition of the domestic industry relates to the situation of foreign suppliers that, by virtue of their commercial presence in the importing country under mode 3, become 'local' suppliers and form part of the domestic economy.[70] Should they be included as part of the domestic industry or should

[69] United Nations, Manual on Statistics in International Trade in Services, para. 4.27, p. 60.

[70] See P. Sauvé, *Trade Rules Behind Borders: Essays on Services, Investment and the New Trade Agenda* (Cameron May, 2003), p. 83; Gauthier, O'Brien and Spencer, 'Déjà Vu, or New Beginning for Safeguards and Subsidies Rules in Services Trade?', p. 170; M. Marconini, 'Emergency Safeguard Measures in the GATS: Beyond Feasible and Desirable', UNCTAD/DITC/TNDC/2005/4, 9 March 2005, p. 11.

they be excluded and therefore become subject to the ESM like any other foreign supplier under a different mode?

Two different approaches have been suggested to address this matter. The first[71] would be to contemplate a dual definition of domestic industry, one for modes 1, 2, and 4, and another for mode 3.[72] The other approach would consist of excluding established foreign suppliers of services from the definition of domestic industry altogether and to provide such suppliers with certain acquired rights to immunise them against the application of an ESM.[73] It would indeed seem unfair that investors and foreign service suppliers that have taken the risk of establishing a commercial presence in a foreign market may be subject to a contingency that may push them out of the market or diminish their expected returns on investment.[74] Some WTO Members and commentators have thus argued that if an ESM were to be adopted, there should be an exemption for established service suppliers from the definition of foreign suppliers.[75] Such an exemption would appear to make good economic sense. By contrast to a cross-border supplier, an investor with commercial presence is beneficial for the welfare of the host country since its presence typically generates jobs, favours technology transfers and linkages to distribution networks and raises tax revenue for the host government.

While the above exemption appears reasonable in principle, caution is required in weighing up the economic incentives it may generate; in particular, with respect to deterring other foreign competitors from entry into a market. The role of competition policies in this respect may need to be further explored.

Similarly, it could be argued that any adverse consequences suffered by domestic workers may be offset by the fact that a foreign service supplier established in that country also provides job opportunities. In this context, it is therefore not clear whether it would make sense to impose an ESM that would only have the effect of favouring certain (domestic) economic (producer) groups over others at the expense of consumers. In such instances, it might be more appropriate to address the preferential treatment that a government may wish to provide to

[71] See the Philippines' position, Working Party on GATS Rules, Report of the Meeting of 10 April 2006, Note by the Secretariat, S/WPGR/M/55, 4 May 2006, para. 11.

[72] *Ibid.* [73] *Ibid.*

[74] See, e.g., Canada, S/WPGR/M/55, para. 7; U.S., S/WPGR/M/55, para. 12.

[75] *Ibid.* See also S/WPGR/M/50, paras. 46, 49.

domestic suppliers through other means such as a domestic production subsidy.[76]

An exemption from the application of the ESM to all domestic service suppliers may create distortions in foreign investment policies.[77] Indeed, it may create an incentive to circumvent a potential safeguard measure by encouraging firms to set up an established presence in the importing country with a view to avoiding an ESM.[78] Such a situation would raise questions regarding the real *necessity* of an ESM because the injury could continue to occur through the services provided by mode 3 suppliers.

An important factor in this respect is whether the inclusion of mode 3 suppliers in an ESM investigation might entail the breach of a bilateral investment treaty (BIT) between the importing and exporting Members, notably in respect of indirect expropriation (so-called regulatory takings for which compensation may be requested by the aggrieved investor). One pertinent issue is whether one law could contradict another and whether there may be an overlap of jurisdictions between the WTO dispute settlement mechanism and the dispute settlement mechanism of the Convention for the Settlement of Investment Disputes between States and Nationals of other States (ICSID Convention) or other tribunals for investor-to-State disputes, such as those mentioned in BITs. Issues for consideration in this regard include the following: (i) the access of parties is different in the two mechanisms: private parties have direct standing before ICSID and similar tribunals but not before WTO panels or the Appellate Body, and; (ii) the remedies are quite different – under investor–State arbitration rules, the parties to the dispute can request compensatory damages as determined by the award, and such an award may be enforced and recognised in the territory of the losing party.[79] The WTO system on the other hand only provides prospective remedies and the possibility of retaliation against a WTO Member as a last resort to induce compliance.[80]

[76] While the exemption of domestic suppliers from certain taxes appears to be the most suitable alternative to offer to developing countries (in the light of resource constraints), this carries the risk that such government aid might be considered as a discriminatory tax measure that affects the conditions of competition between foreign and domestic service suppliers and could therefore be inconsistent with Article XVII of the GATS.

[77] Sauvé, 'Completing the GATS Framework', p. 319.

[78] Gauthier, O'Brien and Spencer, 'Déjà Vu, or New Beginning for Safeguards and Subsidies Rules in Services Trade?', p. 174.

[79] Article 54 of the ICSID Convention. [80] Article 3.7 of the DSU.

The choice between the WTO dispute settlement system and that of the ICSID Convention or any other investor-to-State jurisdiction may become relevant if, for instance, an ESM may eventually be justified under WTO law, but nonetheless be deemed illegal under the relevant BIT or investment treaty-obligation.

4. How to determine whether there is an import surge in services?

The issue of import surges raises numerous questions including the theoretical question as to the meaning of services 'imports'. As mentioned above, although one could argue that services transactions under mode 1 constitute 'imports' in the traditional sense of the term (analogous to trade in goods), things are less straightforward when it comes to the delivery of services under modes 2, 3, and 4.[81] Therefore, the notion of a surge in imports, as used for the imposition of a goods safeguard, should be adjusted to take into account the different modes of supply of services.

Accurate measurement requires the collection of suitable data. Certain Members and authors have highlighted the difficulties of gathering data in the context of ESM investigations in services.[82] Despite progress in measuring trade in services,[83] several important questions, concerning the collection of data and how best to determine the units for measurement, remain unanswered. Regarding the first question, the main issue is how to detect particular services transactions. The World Bank has identified various sources depending on the relevant modes. However, it also points out certain shortcomings.[84]

If the purpose of the exercise was to emulate a trade remedy investigation as in the case of goods, it would be incumbent on the domestic industry to submit the relevant data showing compliance with the requirements for initiation of the investigation. In such circumstances, it will be the petitioner's task to demonstrate that the data submitted is reliable and was obtained from a trustworthy source.[85] If the complainant fails to satisfy the investigating authority, then it cannot succeed with the imposition of the ESM.[86]

The second challenge relates to the units used for measurement purposes. These units may vary from sector to sector – for instance, for

[81] See Sauvé, 'Completing the GATS Framework', pp. 311–312.
[82] *Ibid*, pp. 311–312; see e.g., US position, S/WPGR/M/52, para. 14.
[83] United Nations, Manual on Statistics in International Trade in Services.
[84] WTO, Measuring Trade in Services, A Training Module for the World Bank, p. 11.
[85] S/WPGR/M/52, para. 35. [86] The Philippines' position, S/WPGR/M/51, para. 56.

certain telecommunication services it may be more relevant to measure increases of services supplied in terms of the volume of telecommunications services provided (in minutes) rather than its monetary value, whereas in sectors such as financial services it may be more relevant to measure increases in services in monetary value.

5. The determination of 'injury'

Several issues arising from the above discussion could have implications for the determination of injury. First, given the particular nature of services, some of the factors that are relevant for an injury determination in the context of goods may not apply to services (i.e. inventories). Given that production and consumption of services usually take place simultaneously, the level of sales may be the same as that of production, and capacity utilisation may be the same as employment.[87]

Once the domestic industry has been defined, the gathering of information becomes crucial. If domestic suppliers provide services in addition to those being investigated, it might be necessary for the investigating authority to establish guidelines for the gathering and processing of the relevant data. Compliance with these guidelines, in light of the character of services as 'bundles', seems onerous for everyone concerned – domestic industry, investigating authority and exporters/importers.

Another challenging issue relates to allegations of a threat of injury. In safeguard investigations relating to trade in goods, one of the issues examined is the export capacity of the exporting country. Given the numerous modes of supply in services trade, such an analysis would apparently require investigating authorities to undertake more research than in the goods context. For instance, how could the export capacity of a Member be determined for a particular sector under mode 3: availability of the foreign suppliers' capital or ability to invest in the importing Member? How could that export capacity be assessed with respect to mode 2 services, which are delivered in the exporting country? It appears that the classical notion of threat would have to be adjusted to exclude these two modes or would have to be eliminated from the injury assessment.

[87] The ASEAN proposal referred to a number of indicators either in absolute or relative terms. S/WPGR/M/51, para. 57.

6. The attribution of injury to causes other than the surge in imports (and the 'non-attribution' of injury to the surge in imports

Given the peculiar nature of services, it seems even more imperative to conduct a non-attribution analysis in the context of causation than in the context of goods trade.[88] A task that the unforeseen developments requirement would impose is the separation of the amount of injury that is being suffered due to the extraordinary and unexpected surge in 'imported' services from that which would have otherwise occurred in the ordinary course of events.

Another interesting issue is the situation that arises from a Member entering into an Economic Integration Agreement (EIA) and applying an ESM. Article V:1(b) of the GATS would apparently prohibit members of an EIA from applying an ESM among themselves.[89] If so, an EIA member imposing an ESM would also have to consider the domestic industry of its EIA partner as its own. If it decides to exclude its EIA partner's industry from its definition of domestic industry and likewise from the application of the ESM, it would have to exclude the EIA imports from the determination of injury to the domestic industry as well. This is mandated by the requirement of parallelism whereby the extent of the safeguard measure must be commensurate with the injury

[88] Pursuant to Article 4.2 (b) of the Agreement on Safeguards '[w]hen factors other than increased imports are causing injury to the domestic industry at the same time [as imports], such injury shall not be attributed to increased imports'. WTO jurisprudence has clarified that the 'non-attribution' obligation requires the identification of any factor that may be causing injury, other than the *investigated imports*, and that the injury caused by those other factors be separated from that caused by the *investigated imports*. See, e.g., *Argentina – Safeguard Measures on Imports of Footwear*, Panel Report, WT/DS121/R, adopted 12 January 2000, modified by Appellate Body Report, WT/DS121/AB/R, paras. 8.228–8.274; *United States – Definitive Safeguard Measures on Imports of Wheat Gluten from the European Communities*, Appellate Body Report, WT/DS166/AB/R, adopted 19 January 2001, paras. 60–92.

[89] Article V:1(b) of the GATS does not contemplate as an exception to the general obligation to eliminate barriers between the members of the EIA, the possibility of introducing any potential ESM under Article X:1 of the GATS. This provision states that an EIA must:

> provid[e] for the absence or elimination of substantially all discrimination, in the sense of Article XVII, between or among the parties, in the sectors covered under paragraph (a), through:
> (i) elimination of existing discriminatory measures, and/or
> (ii) prohibition of new or more discriminatory measures,

either at the entry into force of that agreement or on the basis of a reasonable time-frame, except for measures permitted under Articles XI, XII, XIV and XV *bis*.

that it is intended to address.[90] If this were a valid interpretation of GATS Article VI:1(b), when an investigation involved a sector covered by an EIA, the investigating authority would need to cooperate closely with the authority of its EIA partners to collect information for the determinations of injury and causation.

7. The determination of the form and level of the ESM in the light of the different modes of supply

As discussed above, the development of a GATS ESM must perforce deal with the various modes of supplying services bearing in mind the different natures of the four modes of service supply. Cross-border supply in services takes place in a manner analogous to that of goods trade. As Sauvé has pointed out, the limitation on trade can take the form of constraining sales by foreign service suppliers in the importing country.[91] However, this type of limitation may be difficult to enforce as it is difficult to monitor services trade. As noted earlier, services are often intangible and rarely cross borders in a physical sense (e.g. when they are supplied from a country to another through electronic means or by telephone). If they do cross physical borders, this is usually in a manner that cannot be easily monitored by customs authorities (e.g. medical advice or accounting work sent by private post or embedded in the people dispensing such services). Moreover, the approaches used to monitor 'imports' may raise concerns regarding fundamental rights, particularly privacy. An alternative may be to raise safeguards on the other side of the transaction, that is, on the payment of the service, for instance, through foreign exchange restrictions. However, such a measure might conflict with other provisions of the GATS that govern payments and transfers. There are also administrative problems that pose further challenges. For instance, when a transaction takes place through the Internet, how would it be possible to impede the delivery of the service or otherwise to tax the payment of the transaction? Given the non-territorial nature of cyberspace, there may be some issues of jurisdiction regarding the imposition of restrictions on e-commerce.

[90] See, e.g., Argentina – Safeguard Measures on Imports of Footwear, Appellate Body Report, WT/DS121/AB/R, adopted 12 January 2000, paras. 99–114; United States – Definitive Safeguard Measures on Imports of Wheat Gluten from the European Communities, Appellate Body Report, WT/DS166/AB/R, adopted 19 January 2001, paras. 93–100.

[91] Sauvé, 'Completing the GATS Framework', p. 311.

With respect to mode 2 (consumption abroad), the issue of enforcing an ESM poses other challenges. The first question is how a government can impose a safeguard preventing its consumers from going abroad to obtain a service. If such a restriction is imposed on consumers, it may restrict fundamental liberties in the importing Member. Even if it were legally possible, how could it work administratively: would it require travellers to declare the purpose of their trips? How could a Member monitor compliance with a traveller's declaration?

Moving on to mode 3 (commercial presence), a special regime for already-established service suppliers has been suggested[92] and if an ESM were to be accepted, such differential treatment appears to be the preference of the majority of Members. Paradoxically, this is perhaps the most effective way of controlling one of the modes of service supply. For instance, it is easier to impose limits on equity or capital shares than to monitor cross-border supply. A provision that is frequently referred to as an example of a safeguard under mode 3 is Annex 1413.6 Section B of the North American Free Trade Agreement (NAFTA), according to which Mexican authorities were granted the right to limit the granting of new licences in Mexico to financial institutions from other NAFTA partners should the aggregate share of financial assets under their control exceed a particular threshold. Although that threshold has been exceeded in reality, Mexico has never made use of this type of safeguard measure under the NAFTA.[93]

Finally, mode 4 on the presence of natural persons in the territory of other Members is also a mode of supply under which enforcement is relatively inexpensive as it can be controlled at the border through immigration policy and the issuance of work permits. However, in implementing these policies, there is a risk that Members may rely on the professional qualifications of natural persons to impose unnecessary barriers for people wishing to travel for reasons other than professional ones.

Another issue to be dealt with relates to the question of whether an ESM should apply to all modes of supply or only to some. In answering this question, one must bear in mind that what is at issue is a particular service irrespective of the modes in which it is supplied. Thus, even though the injury may have been caused only by one particular mode, it would be advisable to apply the ESM to all modes to avoid any possible circumvention.

92 See ASEAN's position, S/WPGR/M/47, para. 6.

93 P. Sauvé, 'Been There, Not Yet Done That: Lessons and Challenges in Services Trade', ch. 27 in this volume.

Following the architecture of the safeguards in goods, it is likely that an eventual GATS ESM would be required to apply 'only to the extent necessary to prevent or remedy the injury'. Given that this obligation has been construed as requiring that 'the right to apply a safeguard measure – even where it has been found to exist in a particular case and thus can be exercised – is not unlimited',[94] then the design of a multi-modal ESM becomes a more complex issue.

8. How to determine the gradual liberalisation of the ESM

The answer to this question appears to depend on the specific form of the ESM at issue. The quantitative nature of the possible forms of a safeguard in goods (a tariff, a quota or a tariff-rate quota) makes it possible to contemplate a gradual phase-out. However, such a gradual dismantling in services may only be possible if the ESM had a quantitative character. The imposition of taxes in certain services under mode 1, capital limits for mode 3 and quotas for mode 4 may in principle allow such a dismantling. The answer remains unknown with respect to mode 2 and for other types of trade- and investment-restrictive measures of a qualitative nature.

V. The way forward

The foregoing analysis suggests that the discussion on the desirability of a GATS ESM should be based in reality. Members (and more particularly, developing countries) should assess the repercussions of an ESM with respect to their position not only as 'importers' of services, but also as exporters.

The enforceability of an ESM under different modes may vary, and it is incumbent on each Member to assess whether or not the introduction of an ESM is likely to benefit it given the sectors and modes in which that Member is an importer and exporter of services. While an ESM may be a useful policy instrument to protect small and medium-sized businesses under certain circumstances, it may simultaneously hinder the movement of natural persons to a foreign market.

Given the current stalemate in negotiations, constructive negotiations will not take place unless the proponents are willing to reconsider their conceptual framework and to advance market opening offers that may

[94] United States – Definitive Safeguard Measures on Imports of Circular Welded Carbon Quality Line Pipe from Korea, Appellate Body Report, WT/DS202/AB/R, adopted 8 March 2002, para. 84.

induce other Members to discuss the issue with greater resolve. Such offers would have to consist of a substantial liberalisation package, and the linkage between the ESM discussions and liberalisation should be made clear in this respect.

It seems that basing a GATS ESM on a goods-type model raises numerous complications that may be insurmountable. It may thus be advisable to also consider other options. Members should favour alternatives that, for the Member seeking the measure, avoid the complications of trade remedy procedures and which, for those affected by the measure, provide guarantees of compensation.

A simplified GATS Article XXI-like procedure,[95] or an amendment to Article XXI, may be an alternative. Under the current procedure, a modification or withdrawal of a commitment pursuant to this provision can only take place after compensatory adjustments to affected Members have been made (either through arbitration or on a voluntary basis). Article XXI thus requires *ex ante* compensation.

A reformulated procedure, whereby a withdrawal or modification can be made without waiting until the compensatory adjustment has been determined, may be of interest to those pushing for the ESM. Thus, an ESM may be taken and upon request of any Member affected, compensation can be determined on an *ex post* basis through agreement of the parties or through binding and expedited arbitration. In order to avoid any unwarranted distortions, compensation could be applied retroactively to the date of introduction of the ESM, and might consist of commitments in other sectors and/or the award of monetary damages for any foreign service supplier affected. The ESM could also be combined with certain acquired rights exemptions for those foreign suppliers already established in the importing Member.

A second feature of an Article XXI-like procedure should be the temporary nature of the withdrawal or modification of commitments until the domestic industry resolves its problems or troubled firms exit the market in an orderly fashion. Once the ESM is implemented, such a timeframe may be determined by mutual agreement of the Members concerned or through binding and expedited arbitration that determines the level of compensation and/or damages.

[95] According to Article XXI of the GATS, a Member may modify or withdraw any commitment in its services schedule at any time, provided that it complies with the procedures and compensatory requirements (in favour of those other Members affected by the modification or withdrawal) as set out in that provision.

If the compensation and/or damages are not provided or the time-frame is exceeded, any affected Member should be able to withdraw substantially equivalent commitments as currently foreseen under Article XXI:4 (a) of GATS.

VI. Modalities for the introduction of a GATS ESM

This study suggests that there are no reasons to exclude a priori certain sectors from the scope of a GATS ESM. An ESM should be part of a legal instrument that applies across the board. The most suitable option appears to be to follow the path of the Reference Paper on Telecommunications Services and the Understanding on Commitments in Financial Services. These two instruments, while not binding per se, are, however, enforceable under WTO law by virtue of their incorporation through reference into the schedules of commitments of those Members who have accepted them.[96] Given that an ESM would apply as an internal measure – and therefore in a manner potentially inconsistent with the national treatment and market access obligations under Articles XVI and XVII of GATS – the question may arise as to whether the incorporation of an ESM through Members' schedules (for instance via Article XVIII on Additional Commitments) might also be WTO-inconsistent.[97] In this respect, it must be noted that the wording of Article X:1 of the GATS is broad. It does contemplate the possibility of introducing an ESM into the regulation of the GATS, which by definition would clearly be inconsistent with Articles XVI and XVII of the GATS. Consequently, it may be argued that Article X:1 itself constitutes an implicit *ab initio* exemption from Articles XVI and XVII of the GATS. Thus, the incorporation of an ESM into WTO law through the services schedules would be WTO-consistent.

VII. Concluding remarks

Negotiations on a GATS ESM are currently stalled because of the rigid stance of WTO Members both as proponents and opponents of the issue. While the proponents seem intent on replicating a GATT-type safeguard mechanism, with all its complications aggravated in the services context,

[96] Nottage and Sebastian 'Giving Legal Effect to the Results of the WTO Trade Negotiations' pp. 1012–1014.

[97] This question is posed in light of the debate that arose in European Communities – Regime for the Importation, Sale, and Distribution of Bananas, WT/DS27.

opponents systematically resist any kind of proposal on both desirability and feasibility grounds.

For the proponents, the main interests at stake are the need for a workable adjustment mechanism (if the economic circumstances change) and their desire to bring closure to an important outstanding rule-making issue left over since the Uruguay Round. For the opponents, the desire to protect their foreign service suppliers under mode 3 (or in other words, their investors) seems paramount.

To date, the negotiating process has been compartmentalised into the 'desirability' and 'feasibility' of an ESM. While the economic case for an ESM appears weak, there are political economy reasons that provide the basis for proponents to continue to argue in favour of an ESM, particularly the proposition that an ESM would encourage developing countries to take on deeper liberalisation commitments. However, when faced with the question of the new and improved commitments that the proponents might be willing to make in the presence of an ESM, the lack of clarity in the answer undermines the strength of their political argument.

On the issue of feasibility, the approach towards the adoption of a goods-type safeguard has led the discussions to an impasse. The opponents have focused on the weaknesses of the goods safeguards, and pointed out how these are likely to be magnified in a services context given the complexity of the concepts involved, such as the special nature of services, the different modes of supply and the challenge of data collection and injury determination. The proponents have taken a defensive approach without considering any alternative safeguard model that may allow them to get out of the corner.

There is little doubt that a goods-type safeguard model raises a series of intractable challenges in services trade. Such challenges relate to all the requirements of a goods-type safeguard, including the requirement of unforeseen developments, the notion of like services and services suppliers, the definition of the domestic industry, the determination of surge in imports, and the determination of injury and causation.

Given such complications, it would appear advisable for the proponents of a GATS ESM to start looking for an alternative approach. This chapter has advanced the idea of a mechanism similar to that found under Article XXI of the GATS that would simplify the modification or withdrawal of commitments and would clearly allow those modifications or withdrawals to occur on a temporary basis with provision being made for retroactive compensation subject to dispute settlement.

Bibliography

A. Books

Cooter, R., and T. Ulen, *Derecho y Economía*, (Fondo de Cultura Económica, 1998).

Hoekman, B. M., *The Uruguay Round of Multilateral Trade Negotiations: Investigating the Scope for Agreement on Safeguards, Services, and Agriculture* (The University of Michigan, 1988).

Hoekman, B. and M. Kostecki, *The Political Economy of the World Trading System, The WTO and Beyond*, 2nd edn (Oxford University Press, 2001).

Jackson, J. H., *The World Trading System*, (The MIT Press, 1997).

Lee, Y- S., *Safeguard Measures in World Trade, The Legal Analysis* (Kluwer Law International, 2003).

Macrory, P. F. J., A. E. Appleton and M. G. Plummer (eds.), *The World Trade Organization: Legal, Economic and Political Analysis*, volume I (Springer, 2005).

Sauvé, P. and R. M. Stern (eds.), *GATS 2000, New Directions in Services and Trade Liberalization* (The Brookings Institution, 2000).

Sauvé, P., *Trade Rules Behind Borders, Essays on Services, Investment and the New Trade Agenda* (Cameron May, 2003).

B. Articles and papers

Clogstoun, R., R. Trewin and M. Bosworth, 'Would Emergency Safeguard Measures Work for Services' in *Asian-Pacific Economic Literature* (Journal Compilation) (The Australian National University and Blackwell Publishing Asia Pty. Ltd).

Hoekman, B. M., 'Safeguard Provisions and International Trade Agreements Involving Services', *The World Economy* 16 (1993).

Jara, A. and C. Domínguez, 'Liberalization of Trade in Services and Trade Negotiations', *Journal of World Trade* 40(1) (2006).

Marconini, M., 'Emergency Safeguard Measures in the GATS: Beyond Feasible and Desirable', UNCTAD/DITC/TNDC/2005/4, 9 March 2005.

Niscovolos, L. P., 'A Way Out of the Fruitless Debate on Services Safeguards?', *Bridges* 10(6) (September–October 2006).

Nottage, H., 'Trade and Competition in the WTO, Pondering the Applicability of Special and Differential Treatment', *Journal of International Economic Law* 6(1) (2003).

Nottage, H. and T. Sebastian, 'Giving Legal Effect to the Results of the WTO Trade Negotiations: An Analysis of the Methods of Changing WTO Law', *Journal of International Economic Law* 9(4) (2006).

Piérola, F. and G. Horlick, 'WTO Dispute Settlement and Dispute Settlement in the North-South Agreements of the Americas: Considerations for Choice of Forum', *Journal of World Trade* 41(5) (2007).

Sauvé, P., 'Completing the GATS Framework: Addressing Uruguay Round Leftovers', *Aussenwirtschaft* 57 (2002).

Sauvé, P., 'Been There Not Yet Done That: Lessons and Challenges in Services Trade' (2007) (Chapter 27 in this volume).

Sykes, A. O., 'The Safeguards Mess: A Critique of WTO Jurisprudence', John M. Olin Law & Economics Working Paper No. 87 (The University of Chicago, 2003).

United Nations, Manual on Statistics in International Trade in Services, Statistical Papers, Series M No. 86 (2002).

C. *WTO negotiation-related documents*

(i) *Council for Trade in Services*

Council for Trade in Services, Decision on Negotiations on Emergency Safeguard Measures, Adopted by the Council for Trade in Services on 26 November 1997, S/L/43, 2 December 1997.

Council for Trade in Services, Second Decision on Negotiations on Emergency Safeguard Measures, Adopted by the Council for Trade in Services on 24 June 1999, S/L/73, 5 July 1999.

Council for Trade in Services, Third Decision on Negotiations on Emergency Safeguard Measures, Adopted by the Council for Trade in Services on 1 December 2000, S/L/90, 8 December 2000.

Council for Trade in Services, Fourth Decision on Negotiations on Emergency Safeguard Measures, Adopted by the Council for Trade in Services on 15 March 2002, S/L/102, 27 March 2002.

Council for Trade in Services, Fifth Decision on Negotiations on Emergency Safeguard Measures, Adopted by the Council for Trade in Services on 15 March 2004, S/L/159, 17 March 2004.

Council for Trade in Services (Special Session), Special Session of the Council for Trade in Services, Report by the Chairman to the Trade Negotiations Committee, TN/S/25, 21 March 2006.

Council for Trade in Services, TN/S/O/MYS/Rev. 1, 31 January 2006.

(ii) *Working Party on GATS Rules*

Working Party on GATS Rules, Emergency Safeguard Measures under Article X of GATS, Note by the Secretariat, S/WPGR/W/1, 6 July 1995.

Working Party on GATS Rules, Activities of the Working Party on GATS Rules, Report to the Council for Trade in Services, S/WPGR/1, 23 October 1996.

Working Party on GATS Rules, Report of Meeting of 24 March 2004, Note by the Secretariat, S/WPGR/M/47, 22 April 2004.

Working Party on GATS Rules, Report of the Meeting of 20 September 2004, Note by the Secretariat, S/WPGR/M/49, 27 October 2004.

Working Party on GATS Rules, Report of the Meeting of 24 November 2004, Note by the Secretariat, S/WPGR/M/50, 17 January 2005.

Working Party on GATS Rules, Report of the Meeting of 20 June 2005, Note by the Secretariat, S/WPGR/M/52, 7 September 2005.

Working Party on GATS Rules, Report of the Meeting of 10 February 2006, Note by the Secretariat, S/WPGR/M/54, 22 February 2006.

Working Party on GATS Rules, Report of the Meeting of 10 April 2006, Note by the Secretariat, S/WPGR/M/55, 4 May 2006.

Annual Report of the Working Party on GATS Rules to the Council for Trade in Services, S/WPGR/16, 23 November 2006.

D. WTO dispute-related reports

Japan – Taxes on Alcoholic Beverages, Appellate Body Report, WT/DS8/AB/R, WT/DS10/AB/R, WT/DS11/AB/R, adopted 1 November 1996.

Argentina – Safeguard Measures on Imports of Footwear, Appellate Body Report, WT/DS121/AB/R, adopted 12 January 2000.

Argentina – Safeguard Measures on Imports of Footwear, Panel Report, WT/DS121/R, adopted 12 January 2000, modified by Appellate Body Report, WT/DS121/AB/R, adopted 12 January 2000.

Korea – Definitive Safeguard Measure on Imports of Certain Dairy Products, Appellate Body Report WT/DS98/AB/R, adopted 12 January 2000.

United States – Definitive Safeguard Measures on Imports of Wheat Gluten from the European Communities, Appellate Body Report, WT/DS166/AB/R, adopted 19 January 2001.

United States – Safeguard Measures on Imports of Fresh, Chilled or Frozen Lamb Meat from New Zealand and Australia, Appellate Body Report, WT/DS177/AB/R, WT/DS178/AB/R, adopted 16 May 2001.

United States – Definitive Safeguard Measures on Imports of Circular Welded Carbon Quality Line Pipe from Korea, Appellate Body Report, WT/DS202/AB/R, adopted 8 March 2002.

European Communities – Customs Classification of Frozen Boneless Chicken Cuts, Complaint by Thailand, Appellate Body Report, WT/DS286/R, adopted 27 September 2005.

20

Waiting for Godot: Subsidy disciplines in services trade

PIETRO PORETTI*

Introduction

Although it covers subsidies directed towards industrial and agricultural goods,[1] the WTO framework does not yet contain specific disciplines for services subsidies. Article XV of the General Agreement on Trade in Services (GATS) requires Members to develop the multilateral disciplines necessary to avoid the distortive effects subsidies may have on trade in services. However, these negotiations, which have been taking place in the Working Party on GATS Rules (WPGR), have not progressed significantly since they began in 1995. The challenge confronting WTO Members in this area is of considerable complexity. Services and trade in services differ significantly from goods and trade in goods. Their salient characteristics, such as invisibility, non-storability and intangibility, and the existence of multiple modes of supply, have a profound impact on the elaboration of possible disciplines.

The Negotiating mandate of Article XV

Limited negotiations on the possible introduction of disciplines on service subsidies took place during the Uruguay Round.[2] Having been unable to reach an agreement prior to the end of the Round,[3] negotiators agreed to defer the issue of subsidy disciplines in services to the

* The author would like to thank Sakaria Parak.

[1] See the Agreement on Subsidies and Countervailing Duties (ASCM) and the Agreement on Agriculture (AoA), respectively.

[2] GATT Document MTN.GNS/W/98 reports on the content of the debates.

[3] See e.g. GATT Document, MTN.GNS/W/95, 10.

then newborn WTO.[4] The negotiating mandate of GATS Article XV states that

> Members recognize that, in certain circumstances, subsidies may have distortive effects on trade in services. Members shall enter into negotiations with a view to developing the necessary multilateral disciplines to avoid such trade-distortive effects. The negotiations shall also address the appropriateness of countervailing procedures. Such negotiations shall recognize the role of subsidies in relation to the development programmes of developing countries and take into account the needs of Members, particularly developing country Members, for flexibility in this area. For the purpose of such negotiations, Members shall exchange information concerning all subsidies related to trade in services that they provide to their domestic service suppliers.[5]

Existing services subsidies disciplines

The current GATS framework contains no specific services subsidies discipline or remedy. At the same time, however, subsidies are not excluded from the field of application of any of the twenty-nine GATS articles.[6] Being 'measures by Members affecting trade in services' within the meaning of Article I:1, subsidies are fully covered by the provisions contained in the GATS. A number of these provisions exert a measure of discipline on the governments' ability to provide services subsidies or to offer a remedy to those Members harmed by their negative effects. These are Article II (MFN), Article III (transparency), Article VIII (monopolies and exclusive service suppliers), Article XV:2 (consultations), Article XVII (national treatment) and Article XXIII:3 (non-violation complaints). The analysis provided in the following paragraphs is limited to two of these GATS provisions, namely national treatment (Article XVII) and the non-violation complaints instrument (Article XXIII:3), which, on the basis of the limited discussions that have so far taken place, has

[4] In addition to the progressive achievement of increased market access, as requested by Art. XIX, the GATS 'built-in agenda' is completed by negotiating mandates on domestic regulation (Art. VI:4), emergency safeguard measures (Art. X) and government procurement (Art. XIII). See Pierre Sauvé, 'Completing the GATS Framework: Addressing Uruguay Round Leftovers', *Aussenwirtschaft* 57 (3) (2002), pp. 301–341.

[5] Original footnote omitted.

[6] Consider in this respect GATT Art. III:8 (b) explicitly excluding production subsidies from the scope of the national treatment provision. Other forms of governmental intervention that affect trade in services, such as government procurement, are only partially subject to the GATS obligations, as stated in GATS Art. XIII.

emerged as the most promising for the fulfilment of the mandate of Article XV.[7]

For the sake of completeness, it bears recalling how increased transparency would benefit the ongoing negotiations under Article XV by remedying the current opacity and acting as an ancillary instrument to those existing measures that exert a measure of discipline on services subsidies. Indeed, only when aware of the existence of a subsidy would Members be able to undertake the steps necessary to analyse its potentially harmful effects and, where deemed necessary, decide to make use of the available instruments. Further, forcing governments to make detailed information on subsidies publicly available is likely to foster domestic debate on the appropriateness of a given measure of support and on its economic costs.

GATS Article XVII (national treatment)

GATS Article XVII exerts a measure of discipline on subsidies. When subsidies are granted on a national treatment basis, both domestic and foreign operators are on an equal footing and there are therefore less likely to be trade distortive effects.[8] Furthermore, since having to grant a subsidy indistinctly to domestic and foreign suppliers would arguably rule out the possibility of providing a competitive advantage exclusively to domestic suppliers, and because a country's resources are finite, the non-discriminatory principle of national treatment can be expected to lead to an overall reduction in the magnitude of governmental support to services activities.[9]

Yet, the flexible character of the GATS significantly impairs the practical efficacy of Article XVII as a services subsidies discipline. First, the GATS national treatment is not a general (or horizontal) obligation, but a conditional one.[10] This means that it applies only to those sectors in which Member countries undertook specific commitments. In other words, in sectors where no commitments have been made, Members remain free to restrict subsidisation to domestic suppliers without violating the GATS national treatment obligation. A look at the Members'

[7] See WTO Document S/WPGR/W/9, pp. 7–9.

[8] See WTO Document S/WPGR/M/30, p. 7.

[9] See WTO Document S/WPGR/W/9, p. 11.

[10] Art. XVII belongs to part III of the GATS on 'Specific Commitments', whereas general or horizontal obligations and disciplines (such as MFN and transparency) are listed in part II of the Agreement.

schedules of specific commitments reveals that many of the sectors in which the level of subsidisation is deemed to be particularly high, such as education, health, transport and audiovisuals, rank among the less committed sectors.[11]

The simple inscription of a given service sector in a country's schedule of specific commitments does not yet lead to the conclusion that foreign competitors can expect to be treated like domestic ones, including being eligible for any public support offered to domestic suppliers. Article XVII allows Members to maintain measures that are incompatible with the national treatment obligation if they reserved the right to do so in their schedules of specific commitments. Members have made use of this option, and specific limitations on the eligibility for subsidies can be found in sectors such as entertainment services, audiovisuals, education, medical, dental and veterinary services, and telecommunication services.[12] It is equally possible to inscribe horizontal limitations through which Members can exclude the eligibility of foreign suppliers for subsidy programmes in all services in which commitments have been undertaken.[13] Finally, an additional element hindering GATS Article XVII from fully exerting its natural disciplinary effects on subsidies is paragraph 10 of the document 'Scheduling of Initial Commitments in Trade in Services: Explanatory Note' (Explanatory Note), which states: 'There is no obligation in the GATS which requires a Member to take measures outside its territorial jurisdiction. It therefore follows that the national treatment obligation in Article XVII does not require a Member to extend such treatment to a service provider located outside the territory of another Member.'[14] The practical effect of paragraph 10 of the Explanatory Note is to reduce the territorial applicability of the national treatment obligation to foreign suppliers operating through modes 3 and 4 only. Although subsidies granted exclusively to domestic suppliers

[11] For an analysis of the distribution of commitments across different groups of Members and in the different sectors, see Rudolf Adlung and Martin Roy, 'Turning Hills into Mountains? Current Commitments under the GATS and Prospects for Change', WTO, Economic Research and Statistics Division, 2005, Staff Working Paper ERSD-2005-01.

[12] See the information contained in the WTO Secretariat compilations of national treatment limitations concerning subsidies contained in the schedules of specific commitments, WTO Document S/WPGR/W/13, 22 May 1996, updated by S/WPGR/W/13/Add.1, 14 June 2000 and the last update contained in WTO Document S/WPGR/W/13/Add.2, 30 August 2004.

[13] *Ibid.*

[14] Scheduling of Initial Commitments in Trade in Services: Explanatory Note. MTN.GNS/W/164, 3 September 1993.

affect the conditions of competition to the detriment of foreign suppliers operating through all modes of supply, paragraph 10 of the Explanatory Note precludes foreign suppliers operating through modes 1 and 2 from benefiting from the protection offered by the non-discriminatory obligation of Article XVII.

In sum, the GATS flexibility resulting from the positive (or bottom-up) scheduling approach, the possibility of maintaining limitations on national treatment, and the territorial limitation of paragraph 10 of the Explanatory Note largely compensate for the absence of a provision comparable to GATT Article III:8 (b) in the GATS,[15] de facto leaving the decision of how incisively the current national treatment provision applies to subsidies in the hands of the individual Members.[16]

That being said, even in the best-case scenario (i.e. the insertion of a given sector into a Member's schedule of specific commitments, the absence of limitations and the hypothetical non-existence of the restricting provision of paragraph 10 of the Explanatory Note), the measure of discipline offered by the national treatment obligation is confined to distortive effects caused by import-displacing subsidies only. Article XVII remains toothless against the potential trade-distortive effects of export-enhancing (which cause trade distortion in the market of the importing country) and investment-diverting subsidies, the latter typically consisting in advantages granted to foreign investors. In the case of investment-diverting subsidies, subsidisation does not discriminate against foreign service suppliers which, on the contrary, may even benefit from particular advantages not available to domestic competitors. Discrimination resulting from investment incentives therefore often represents a constellation that is the opposite of the one contemplated by GATS Article XVII. With regard to export-enhancing subsidies, their trade-distortive effects arise in the market of the importing country. The victims of such negative effects are principally like services suppliers of the importing country, as well as like services suppliers from third-countries exporting to the same market.[17]

[15] GATT Art. III:8 (b) explicitly exempts production subsidies from the national treatment obligation by stating that 'The provisions of this Article shall not prevent the payment of subsidies exclusively to domestic producers, including payments to domestic producers derived from the proceeds of internal taxes or charges applied consistently with the provisions of this Article and subsidies effected through governmental purchases of domestic products.'

[16] See WTO Document S/WPGR/W/9, p. 8.

[17] See WTO Document S/WPGR/M/48, 20 July 2004, para. 8.

GATS Article XXIII: 3 (non-violation complaints)

Besides traditional violation complaints, the GATS offers a second cause of action in the form of non-violation complaints. Members can complain of nullification and impairment of benefits expected to accrue to them under the Agreement even if no actual violation of a GATS obligation has occurred.[18] The concept of non-violation complaints is rooted in the principles of good faith and legitimate expectations[19] and its scope is to protect the delicate balance of concessions exchanged by the Members during the negotiations (i.e. specific commitments relating to market access, national treatment, or additional commitments with respect to particular sectors and/or modes of supply subject to terms, limitations, conditions and qualifications undertaken by Members) from being undermined by lawful governmental interventions, including subsidisation.[20] Although the use of this instrument remains extremely limited – no GATS non-violation complaint has so far reached the panel stage[21] – it is worth recalling that during the GATT era Contracting Parties relied on non-violation complaints as a means to challenge indirect protection of domestic companies through subsidisation.[22] Also in favour of a more in-depth analysis of the non-violation complaint instrument as a

[18] See also GATT Art. XXIII:1 (b), Art. 64:2 of the WTO Trade Related Aspects of Intellectual Property Rights Agreement (TRIPS) and the procedural requirements to be fulfilled when bringing a non-violation complaint according to Art. 26 of the WTO Dispute Settlement Understanding (DSU).

[19] See Thomas Cottier and Krista Schefer, 'Good Faith and the Protection of Legitimate Expectations in the WTO', in Marco Bronckers and Raymond Quick (eds.), *New Directions in International Economic Law, Essays in Honour of John H. Jackson* (The Hague: Kluwer Law International, 2000), pp. 47–68, at 58.

[20] See GATT Document MTN.GNG/NG13/W/31.

[21] To date, non-violation claims under GATS Art. XXIII:3 have not gone beyond the request for consultations stage. See *United States – The Cuban Liberty and Democratic Solidarity Act* (DS 38), *Japan – Measures Affecting Distribution Services* (DS 45) and *Belgium – Measures Affecting Commercial Telephone Directory Services* (DS 80).

[22] In the context of subsidies, the non-violation, nullification and impairment of benefits was usually claimed on the basis of the introduction of product-specific subsidies alleged to undermine specific tariff concessions. See, e.g., *Australia – Subsidy*, The Australian Subsidy on Ammonium Sulphate, Working Party Report, adopted 3 April 1950, BISD II/188, para. 12, and and *EEC – Oilseeds I*, GATT Panel Report, European Economic Community-Payments and Subsidies Paid to Processors and Producers of Oilseeds and Related Animal-Feed Proteins, L/6627, adopted 25 January 1990, BISD 37S/86. See on this issue James P. Durling and Simon N. Lester, 'Original Meanings and the Film Dispute: The Drafting History, Textual Evaluation, and Application of the Non-Violation Nullification or Impairment Remedy', *George Washington Journal of International Law & Economics* 32 (1999), pp. 211–269, at 214.

possible remedy against harmful services subsidies, is the fact that many situations involving subsidies do not seem to violate any of the existing GATS obligations, thus foreclosing the recourse to standard violation complaints.

Even though the text of GATS Article XXIII:3 differs slightly from that of GATT Article XXIII:1 (b),[23] the 'non-violation complaints test' developed by the GATT and WTO jurisprudence provides a valuable point of departure for the application of the non-violation complaints instrument to services subsidies.[24] The complaining party has to cumulatively prove: (i) the application of a measure by a WTO Member (a law or regulation or other governmental actions); (ii) the existence of a benefit accruing under a relevant agreement; and (iii) nullification and impairment of such benefit as a result of the application of the measure referred to in (i).[25] These requirements, and the way in which they apply to services subsidies, are discussed below.

The key to analysing the efficacy of the non-violation complaints instrument as a discipline on services subsidies is the existence of a benefit accruing to WTO Members under the GATS. Benefits accrue to a Member on the basis of another Member's specific commitments, which represent all that the rest of the WTO Membership can and has to expect from it. By undertaking specific commitments, a country accepts a certain level of market access to its domestic market. This makes the non-violation complaints instrument useless against trade distortive effects caused by export-enhancing subsidies, where trade distortion occurs in third-country markets. Similar conclusions are reached after an examination of the potential trade distortive effects of investment-diverting subsidies.

[23] The most significant difference between the GATS and the GATT provisions on non-violation complaints consists in the remedies the party successfully challenging a Member's measure through the non-violation complaints instrument is entitled to request. Whereas under the GATT the losing party has no obligation to withdraw the non-violating measure, the remedies available under GATS Art. XXIII:3 are similar to those foreseen in the case of violation complaints, and therefore include the possibility for the successful complainant to request the removal of the non-violating measure as one of the possible ways to achieve mutually satisfactory adjustment.

[24] See Art. XVI:1 of the Agreement Establishing the World Trade Organization stating 'Except as otherwise provided under this Agreement or the Multilateral Trade Agreements, the WTO shall be guided by the decisions, procedures and customary practices followed by the Contracting Parties to the GATT 1947.'

[25] See *Japan – Film*, Panel Report, *Japan – Measures Affecting Consumer Photographic Film and Paper*, WT/DS44/R, adopted 22 April 1998, DSR 1998:IV, 1179, para. 10.35 and *Korea – Procurement*, Panel Report, *Korea – Measures Affecting Government Procurement*, WT/DS163/R, adopted 19 June 2000, DSR 2000:VIII, 3541, paras. 7.85–7.86.

'Stealing' potential inward FDI by offering particularly attractive conditions to foreign investors does not per se nullify or impair the benefits accruing to a Member under the GATS and protected by the provision of Article XXIII:3. Investment-diverting subsidies frustrate the benefits a Member can expect to accrue from its own commitments, such as the decision to refrain from maintaining foreign ownership ceilings or requirements of specific types of legal entities (e.g. compulsory joint ventures) for foreign services suppliers, but not those accruing from commitments undertaken by other Members. The efficacy of the non-violation complaints instrument is arguably concentrated on import-displacing subsidies, where the bulk of trade distortion occurs in the market of the subsidising Member itself, in the form of an impediment to market entry of new suppliers or to business expansion of already present suppliers.[26]

The burden of proving that the frustrated benefit could not have been 'legitimately' (or 'reasonably', in the words of GATS Article XXIII:3) expected at the time of negotiations remains with the complainant. This confers an essentially prospective nature to the non-violation complaints instrument. The Panel in *Japan – Film* concluded that, for measures introduced after conclusion of the tariff negotiations in question, a presumption is made that the complaining party should not have anticipated the introduction of these measures.[27] Transposing the Panel's reasoning to the services subsidies context means that in the case of subsidies introduced after the negotiations of a Member's specific commitments, the complainant would benefit from a presumption that it could not have anticipated the existence of such a subsidy. Doubts remain as to the usefulness of the non-violation complaints instrument against subsidies predating the negotiations that led to the adoption of the

[26] A similar scenario was behind *Oilseeds*, where a GATT Panel ruled that subsidies paid by the EC to producers of oilseeds impaired the benefits accruing to the US under a zero-tariff subsidy the EC had negotiated with the US in 1962. According to the Panel, the EC subsidies had the effect of offsetting the economic benefits accruing to the US from the negotiated tariff reduction. See *EEC – Oilseeds I*, note 22 above, paras. 77–78. The Panel based its ruling on a decision adopted by consensus by the GATT Contracting Parties in 1955 according to which 'it was agreed that a Contracting Party which has negotiated a tariff concession under Article II may be assumed, for the purposes of Article XXIII, to have a reasonable expectation, failing evidence to the contrary, that the value of the concession will not be nullified or impaired by the introduction or increase of a domestic subsidy on the product concerned'.

[27] *Japan – Film*, Panel Report, note 25 above, paras. 10.79–10.81. It is then for the defendant to rebut such a presumption.

schedules of specific commitments. In *Japan–Film*, the Panel introduced a second presumption, this time in favour of the party implementing the challenged measure, that the complaining party should have anticipated such a measure. It is then for the complaining party to rebut the presumption by clearly demonstrating 'why initially it could not have reasonably anticipated the effect of an existing measure [. . .] and when it did realize the effect'.[28] In the specific case of services, the opacity surrounding subsidies might be favourable to the complainant.

Finally, the complaining party has to prove a disruption of the competitive relationship between foreign and like domestic services or services suppliers.[29] This condition implies conducting an analysis of the more practical issue of how to prove the nullification and impairment of a given benefit by a subsidy. The complaining party would have to submit information on three main elements. First, the schedule of specific commitments of the Member against which the non-violation complaint has been filed has to contain a specific commitment covering the allegedly subsidised activity. As will be shown below, this dependence on specific commitments, in the light of the rather low level of bound market access liberalisation, significantly reduces the efficacy of GATS Article XXIII:3 as discipline on services subsidies. Second, the complaining party has to prove the existence of a measure taken by a Member. There is no need under the non-violation complaints procedure to prove the existence of a subsidy within the meaning of any definition whatsoever. Notwithstanding the lack of specification in GATS Article XXIII:3, the practical recourse to the non-violation complaints instrument would benefit from greater compliance with the information exchange requirement. The third requirement consists in demonstrating that 'a specific commitment is being nullified or impaired as a result of the application of any measure'. The lack of data on subsidies, and more generally on trade in services is likely to make the fulfillment of this requirement an arduous task. The complaining party would have to provide sufficient

[28] *Japan – Film*, note 25 above, paras. 10.79–10.81.

[29] For examples of practical application of the third element of the non-violation complaint test in relation to goods see *Japan–Film*, note 25 above, paras. 10.72–10.75. See also *Australia–Subsidy*, note 22 above, para.10, stating 'The Working Party then examined the question of whether the Australian Government had complied with the terms of Article XVI on subsidies. It noted that, although this Article is drafted in very general terms, the type of subsidy which it was intended to cover was the financial aid given by a government to support its domestic production and to improve its competitive position either on the domestic market or on foreign markets.'

evidence that the worsened conditions of competition for its like services and services suppliers were the result of the introduction of a subsidy and not, for instance, of fair (or unfair) competition of third countries' suppliers. Also, it might prove difficult to distinguish between the effect of a subsidy *stricto senso* and the effect of a domestic regulatory measure lawfully introduced after the end of the negotiations, based on the right to regulate that Members retain.[30] While GATS Article XXIII:3 contains no indication of the strength of the causal relationship to be proven, the WTO case law on non-violation complaints indicates a low standard of proof for the causation requirement. According to the Panel in *Japan – Film* 'the issue is whether such a measure has caused nullification or impairment, i.e., whether it has made more than a *de minimis* contribution to nullification or impairment'.[31] If maintained for the purpose of GATS Article XXIII:3, such a low standard of proof for the causation requirement could compensate for the current absence of precise information on services and services subsidies.

Overall efficacy of the existing GATS disciplines on services subsidies

Despite the lack of accurate data on subsidies in the services context, the disciplinary and remedial properties of the national treatment obligation and the non-violation complaints instrument appears limited. First, as discussed above, the two provisions only address trade distortive effects as a result of import-displacing subsidies. Their value as a response to the distortive effects subsidies may have on services trade therefore depends on the prevalence of domestic support over other types. Second, both provisions are weakened by the inherent flexibility of the GATS and the considerable leeway left to the Members regarding the extent of liberalisation they are willing to undertake. Setting apart these two provisions from the existence of specific commitments would dramatically increase their efficacy as disciplines against trade distortion caused by import-displacing subsidies.[32] Although this would be theoretically feasible in

[30] See para. 4 of the GATS Preamble. [31] *Japan – Film*, note 25 above, para. 10.84.

[32] Similar conclusions can be drawn on GATS Art. VIII (Monopolies and Exclusive Service Suppliers), a provision that exerts a certain discipline on situations involving intra-company cross-subsidisation from a reserved activity to one that is open to competition.

the case of the national treatment obligation,[33] it is a priori incompatible with the concept of nullification and impairment of benefits as grounds for the non-violation cause of action.

The current state of Article XV negotiations

The minutes of the Working Party on GATS Rules (WPGR)[34] reveal that most of the negotiators' attention has been captured by two closely intertwined issues: the lack of a definition of 'subsidy' in the negotiating mandate of Article XV and the non-fulfilment of the information exchange request. Concerning the latter aspect, comprehensive and reliable information is a *sine qua non* condition for every negotiation.[35] The current lack of data on services subsidies makes it impossible to answer with sufficient accuracy a number of questions of crucial importance for the progress of the negotiations, such as whether governmental support is prevalent in services and if so, in what form, whether it has distortive effects on services trade, and whether it is widespread or concentrated in certain services sectors. Combined with the absence of a generally agreed definition of subsidies in the services context, this lack of information creates a sort of chicken-and-egg dilemma that has hampered progress in the negotiations.[36] Various attempts to facilitate the exchange of information on services subsidies have been unsuccessful to date.[37] Whether

[33] As suggested by the Swiss Representative, the strengthening of national treatment for the purpose of subsidies could be limited to that which is necessary to tackle trade distortive subsidies while other measures of support would remain subject to the ordinary meaning of Art. XVII. See S/WPGR/M/31, para. 9.

[34] The minutes of the WPGR meetings have been classified under S/WPGR/M/-, followed by a sequential number. They can be accessed through the WTO official website at www.wto.org.

[35] Noting a lack of precise information on trade in services at the beginning of the Uruguay Round, Jackson asked 'Is it wise policy to embark upon negotiations on trade in services without more complete data?' See John H. Jackson and William J. Davey, *Legal Problems of International Economic Relations*, 2nd edn (St Paul, Minn.: West Publishing Co., 1986), p. 989.

[36] As aptly summarised by Chan 'it is difficult to trawl for information in the absence of definition, but difficult to formulate a meaningful definition without more information on subsidies out there'. See Chan Thomas, Speaking Points at ICTSD Round Table on Trade in Services and Sustainable Development, 'Towards Pro-Sustainable Development Rules for Subsidies in Trade in Services', International Centre for Trade and Sustainable Development (ICTSD), Geneva, 2003.

[37] In 1997, the WTO Secretariat circulated a document entitled 'Questions Relevant to the Information Exchange Required under the Subsidies Negotiating Mandate' modelled on the list of questions used for the notification of industrial subsidies under ASCM Art. 25. See

the non-fulfilment of the required[38] information exchange mandate is the result of genuine technical difficulties, due to a political unwillingness to disclose potentially sensitive information, and/or to the deliberate intention to prevent negotiations from progressing, is debatable.

On the question of how to define a subsidy in a services context, Members seem to favour the definition contained in Article 1 of the GATT Agreement on Subsidies and Countervailing Measures (ASCM) which states that a subsidy exists if there is a financial contribution from a government or public entity[39] which confers a benefit on its recipient.[40] While additional aspects might need to be considered, such as the subsidy-like effects of regulatory measures,[41] the basic constitutive elements of the

WTO Document S/WPGR/W/16. Only five WTO Members have so far replied to this questionnaire, namely Norway, New Zealand, Hong Kong China, Poland and Switzerland. See WTO Documents S/WPGR/W/16/Add.1, S/WPGR/W/16/Add.2, S/WPGR/W/16/Add.3, S/WPGR/W/16/Add.4, S/WPGR/W/16/Add.4 sup.1, and S/WPGR/W/16/Add.5.

[38] The use of the verb 'shall' in the text of GATS Art. XV leaves no doubt as to the mandatory nature of the information exchange. If GATS negotiators had intended a facultative request, they would have presumably made use of the verb 'should', or of the words 'in principle', thus conferring to the request the character of a best endeavour obligation. Consider in this respect para. 6 of Annex on Article II exemptions stating that 'In principle, such exemptions should not exceed a period of 10 years.'

[39] ASCM Art. 1:1 (a)(1) (i) to (iii) foresees three main forms of financial contribution, i.e. direct transfer of funds, tax breaks, government provision of goods or services other than general infrastructure and government purchase of goods and payments to funds. According to Art. 1:1 (a)(1)(iv) financial contributions by private bodies in the forms illustrated in Art. Art. 1:1 (a)(1) (i) to (iii) are also caught by the ASCM if such private bodies have been entrusted or directed to do so by governments.

[40] The concept of benefit enables legitimate commercial transactions occurring between governments and firms to be distinguished from those that involve elements of subsidisation. The case law developed on the base of ASCM Art. 1 clarified that' 'A benefit does not exist in the abstract, but must be received and enjoyed by a beneficiary or a recipient. Logically, a benefit can be said to arise only if a person, natural or legal, or a group of persons, has in fact received something. The term benefit, therefore, implies that there must be a recipient.' A benefit exists 'when a company is placed in a better position financially than it otherwise would be absent the financial contribution or price support', and that the marketplace of the subsidy's recipient is the benchmark against which existence of the benefit is assessed. See *Canada – Aircraft*, Appellate Body Report, *Canada – Measures Affecting the Export of Civilian Aircraft*, WT/DS70/AB/R, adopted 20 August 1999, DSR 1999:III, 1377, para. 157 and para. 154. Finally, a cost to the government does not need to be demonstrated in order to establish the existence of a subsidy within the meaning of the ASCM, the decisive factor being the conferral of a benefit on the recipient. See *Canada – Aircraft*, Appellate Body Report, *Canada – Measures Affecting the Export of Civilian Aircraft*, WT/DS70/AB/R, adopted 20 August 1999, DSR 1999:III, 1377, para. 155.

[41] The fact that regulatory measures do not involve any financial contribution automatically excludes them from the scope of a definition modelled on ASCM Art. 1. See, on the effects of implicit subsidisation and on its possible inclusion in the services subsidies

definition of Article 1 ASCM appear to be suitable to define a subsidy in the services context as well.

Is there a need for disciplines on service subsidies?

The limited data available means that answering this question manifestly implies a fair amount of guesswork. The basic economic justifications for regulatory intervention in the field of services subsidies do not differ from those underpinning the multilateral instruments constraining the use of agricultural and industrial goods subsidies. As with subsidies on industrial and agricultural goods, subsidies on services can divert resources by sending a distorted signal to a service supplier concerning its real production costs, thus leading to an artificial overproduction of the subsidised goods (or services) compared to what the supplier would have been likely to produce in a 'distortion free' environment. Besides causing a misallocation of resources, which per se remains a domestic problem, subsidies can be responsible for the misallocation of outputs between foreign and domestic markets resulting from the lower costs of subsidised products or services. In an increasingly globalised world, this matter can no longer be viewed as a merely domestic issue, hence the necessity to develop international regulatory frameworks.[42]

Disciplines on services subsidies could be expected to exert a beneficial effect on the ongoing market access negotiations by promoting a level playing field for all WTO Members.[43] Prohibiting the use of trade distortive subsidies, or introducing instruments allowing Members to respond effectively to harmful subsidies, would render markets more contestable, thus increasing the value of the negotiated market access

debate, Sauvé, as note 4 above, p. 328. A number of WTO Members have suggested that the issue of implicit subsidies resulting from regulatory measures should be addressed in the Working Party on Domestic Regulation (WPDR), in the context of the negotiations mandated under GATS Art. VI:4.

42 See Gary Clyde Hufbauer and Johanna Shelton Erb, *Subsidies in International Trade* (Washington, DC: Institute for International Economics (IIE), 1984), p. 5.

43 As noted by Benitah 'it seems that countries perceive subsidies to services as an ace hidden in the liberalization game played by many countries'. See Marc Benitah, ICTSD Roundtable on Trade in Services and Sustainable Development: 'Towards Pro-Sustainable Development Rules for Subsidies in Trade in Services', Roundtable, proposed structure for discussion, Geneva, 10 March 2003, p. 4. available at www.ictsd.org/dlogue/2003-03-10/Benitah_working%20paper_final.pdf.

commitments.[44] By the same token, disciplines on subsidies would help Members who are asked to undertake new commitments in sectors where they maintain public support, to clarify the WTO compatibility of such support measures. The prevailing uncertainty, which hinders Members from determining whether or not the use of subsidies will be regulated by specific rules, and if so, to what degree, might deter Members from undertaking commitments in subsidised sectors.[45] Moreover, dedicated attention to the special needs of developing economies in the context of the regulation of services subsidies could contribute to achieving a more balanced and sustainable liberalisation of services trade.[46]

The appropriateness of a countervailing duty mechanism in services

The WPGR negotiations have so far failed to provide a clear answer to the question of whether future disciplines on services subsidies should comprise a countervailing duty mechanism. Assessing the appropriateness of such a mechanism should start with its desirability. This aspect is inextricably linked to the unresolved debate on the nature of trade remedies (both countervailing and anti-dumping duties) either as legitimate instruments aimed at safeguarding domestic suppliers against unfair trade practices or as protectionist tools for shielding uncompetitive domestic industries, and the effects on the economies of the countries that rely on these instruments.

A case can be made that, in the light of the significant tariff cuts achieved since the entry into force of the GATT in 1948,[47] WTO Members would only accept undertaking substantial liberalisation in services, if unilateral

[44] Members underscored the importance of knowing the amount of subsidies in existence when undertaking commitments in the context of the request-offer negotiations. See e.g. WTO Document S/WPGR/M/55, 4 May 2006, para. 37. The reluctance of developing countries to include construction and engineering services in their Uruguay Round schedules of specific commitments was motivated by the fact that, due to the absence of disciplines on services subsidies and their lack of capacity to compete with developed countries on a level playing field, it would have been unwise on their part to enter into market access commitments. See Sunsonline.org, Services Subsidies Need Sector-Specific Approaches, 14 July 1994, available at www.sunsonline.org/trade/areas/services/07140094.htm.

[45] Sauvé, as note 4 above, p. 306. [46] See GATS Art. XIX:2.

[47] See e.g. Thomas R. Howell, 'The Trade Remedies: A US Perspective', in Geza Feketekuty and Bruce Stokes (eds.), *Trade Strategies for a New Era: Ensuring US Leadership in a Global Economy* (Council on Foreign Relations and the Monterey Institute of Foreign International Studies, 1988), pp. 299–323 at 299.

trade remedies targeting the most disruptive effects of market-distorting practices abroad (i.e. dumping and subsidies), or remedies reacting to increases in imports resulting from unforeseen developments (i.e. through the imposition of safeguard measures) were available.[48]

The economic rationale for trade remedies, including countervailing duties, has been the subject of numerous studies that show why responding to subsidised imports via countervailing duties is not economically desirable since it results in a welfare loss for the country imposing such duties.[49] Other aspects, such as the costs of cumbersome administration, the increased risk of rent-seeking behaviour on the part of domestic producer industries,[50] the overall limited efficacy of such instruments[51] and the markedly unbalanced recourse to such instruments by some WTO Members,[52] all raise serious questions as to the desirability of a countervailing duty mechanism in services trade.

The appropriateness of a countervailing duty mechanism in services also needs to be analysed from the perspective of its technical feasibility. The salient characteristics of services introduce complexities both at the investigation and the enforcement levels of countervailing duty procedures. A number of relevant issues were identified during the Uruguay Round, for instance how such terms as 'products imported in the

[48] Similar arguments have been advanced by those Members that support the introduction of an emergency safeguard mechanism in the services context. See S/WPGR/W/30.

[49] See Alan O. Sykes, 'The Economics of WTO Rules on Subsidies and Countervailing Measures', John M. Olin Program in Law & Economics Working Papers, No. 186, 2003, University of Chicago, at p. 2.

[50] Domestic industries might seek protection even when they are not subject to unfair competition, but simply find themselves placed in an unfavourable (but fair) situation vis-à-vis their foreign competitors. See Alan O. Sykes, 'Countervailing Duty Law: An Economic Critique', *Columbia Law Review* 89(2) (1989), pp. 199–263, at 215; and more generally on the question of the influence of groups of interest on decision-makers Mancur Olson, *The Logic of Collective Action, Public Goods and Theory of Groups* (Harvard University Press, 1965).

[51] Countervailing duties only offer a remedy in situations where country A subsidises its exports to country B, thus harming domestic producers of like products of country B. They are, however, toothless when country A subsidises its domestic production, putting exporters of country B at a disadvantage, or when country A subsidises exports to a third country, thus unfairly competing against B's exports to the same market.

[52] According to WTO data, of a total of 108 countervailing duties imposed between January 1995 and December 2004, 76 (or 70.73 per cent) have been put in place by developed countries: United States (45), European Union (22), Canada (8) and Australia (1). This led a commentator to question 'whether a weapon mostly used by developing countries' should have a place among the future disciplines on services subsidies. See Marc Benitah, 'Subsidies, Services and Sustainable Development', Issue Paper No. 1, ICTSD, 2004, p. 32.

territory of a contracting party', 'established domestic industry', 'amount of estimated bounty or subsidy' and 'material injury', could be defined in the services context, and the difficulties of identifying the origin of services.[53]

Some of these issues are more complex in the services than in the goods trade context because of the lack of detailed and comprehensive statistics on services trade flows. Other difficulties stem from the peculiarities of services, not least their intangible nature and the existence of the four different modes of supply. For instance, the determination of material injury requires an objective examination of the volume of subsidised imports, their effects on domestic prices in the importing country market and their consequent impact on the domestic industry.[54] Authorities in charge of conducting countervailing duty investigations are likely to face enormous difficulties in establishing the volume of subsidised imports with a sufficient degree of precision, likewise their increase in absolute or relative terms and their effects on prices in the domestic market for like services and the consequent impact of these imports on domestic suppliers of like services.[55] For the same reasons, proving the causal relationship between subsidisation and injury would be a complicated exercise.

Additional difficulties are likely to emerge at the enforcement level. Under the ASCM, after determining the existence of a subsidy, injury to the domestic industry and a causal relationship between the two, a country is allowed to impose countervailing measures in the form of additional duties on the imports of the subsidised product.[56] Additional duties are collected by the customs authorities operating at a country's borders. The effectiveness of this method lies in the fact that virtually all goods entering a country must go through customs procedures at its borders. In the case of international trade in services, such a 'filtering operation' does not necessarily take place. The invisible and intangible

[53] See GATT Document MTN.GNS/W/98. See also UN Conference on Trade and Development (UNCTAD), The Impact of Subsidies on Trade in Services, Background Note by the UNCTAD Secretariat, UNCTAD/SDD/SER/3, 4 October 1993, p. 11.

[54] See ASCM Art. 15:1. [55] See ASCM Art. 15:2.

[56] Alternatively, the ASCM offers the possibility of concluding price undertakings with the foreign producer, through which the government of the exporting country agrees to eliminate or limit the subsidy, or the exporter agrees to revise its prices. See ASCM Art. 18. The imposition of countervailing duties represents an exception to the otherwise absolute principle contained in GATT Art. II, i.e. the respect by all WTO Members of the bound level of tariffs inscribed in their schedules of concessions annexed to the General Agreement and to GATT Art. I (MFN), which prohibits countries from imposing measures discriminating against one or more WTO Members.

character of services and the existence of the four different modes of supply make the enforcement of border measures difficult, for the simple reason that customs agents will normally not be able to see the service as it 'passes the frontier'.[57] In the best-case scenario, they will merely register the suppliers (such as a business operator in the case of mode 4) or the consumer (for instance a tourist in the case of mode 2) as they gain access to the market of a given country. Customs authorities, however, will not be able to determine the value (or volume) of the service transactions until after the services have been rendered or consumed. As regards services supplied across borders, such as telecommunications and telecom-based transactions (e.g. e-banking), invisibility at the border is virtually absolute.[58]

Lastly, the enforcement of countervailing duties in the services context would have to take into account the duties' country- and product-specific character. This brings the question of rules of origin into the debate. Criteria such as where (and how much) value was added to a certain product are applied to determine the origin of a good; this is essential in deciding whether or not a particular import is subject to an extra duty. Little attention has so far been paid to the issue of rules of origin for services.[59] The absence of clear procedures for the determination of the

[57] See in this respect Thomas Cottier and Matthias Oesch, *International Trade Regulation: Law & Policy in the WTO, the EU and Switzerland* (London: Cameron May, 2005), pp. 1001 and 1027. The existence of legislation regulating the application of unilateral redressive measures to subsidised services, such as EEC Regulation 4057/86 and EC Regulation 868/2004 covering circumstances of subsidisation in the maritime and air transport sectors shows that border control for the purpose of countervailing duties is possible when activities which are per se invisible and intangible, 'materialise' at a certain point of their life cycle, for instance in the shape of transported goods, either at the initial (loading) or at the final (discharging) stage of supply, or in the form of passengers and airplanes landing and taking off from an airport within the territory of the country willing to impose the extra duty. See Council Regulation (EEC) 4057/86, 1986 on Unfair Prices Practices in Maritime Transport, OJ L 378, p. 14–20 and Regulation (EC) 868/2004 of the European Parliament and of the Council of 21 April 2004 concerning protection against subsidisation and unfair pricing practices causing injury to Community air carriers in the supply of air services from countries not Members of the European Union, OJ L 162 of 30.04.2004, pp. 1–7.

[58] Where, absent physical cross-border transit, taxing the service itself is not technically feasible, imposing visa fees on the entry of the services suppliers themselves (mode 4) and exit taxes on those citizens leaving their own country in order to consume the subsidised service abroad (mode 2), and levying extra duties on a subsidised commercial presence represent technically feasible but questionable options.

[59] Zampetti and Sauvé identify a number of characteristics of services and of trade in services that are likely to make the substantial transformation and value-added tests difficult to apply in the services context. These include the intangible nature of various

origin of services carries a twofold risk: that of arbitrary application of countervailing duties by importing countries, and of quasi-infinite possibilities of circumvention for exporters.

Public services and Article XV negotiations

In compliance with the mandate of GATS Art. XV, discussions on possible disciplines on services subsidies have so far primarily focused on the potential distortive effects subsidies may have on trade in services. Limiting the analysis to the concept of trade distortion, however, does not provide a full picture of the universe of services subsidies. Unlike export subsidies, which are clearly imposed with the aim of achieving trade-oriented objectives, domestic subsidies comprise numerous government policies whose legitimacy is unanimously accepted.[60] Subsidies may be used by governments to remedy market failures and internalise positive externalities. Among other reasons, subsidies are granted to encourage firms to relocate to a disadvantaged region; to guarantee the provision of services such as telecommunications, transport and postal services in a country's most remote areas, to foster research, development or culture, or to ensure affordable access to education or health services for the entire population. The common denominator of these activities is the fact that they are expected to generate positive spillover effects for the society as a whole. In order to remedy situations where market forces alone might not serve the public interest, governments may decide to intervene in various ways, including through the use of subsidies.

The existing multilateral disciplines on subsidies (contained in the Agreement on Agriculture (AoA) and ASCM), as well the European State Aid regime, foresee preferential legal treatment for certain categories of subsidies.[61] The rationale behind the existence of a double standard lies in two main aspects. First, it has been recognised that certain subsidies do

transactions and the associated difficulty of measuring them; the importance of network-based service delivery and the difficulty of assigning added value along various parts of the supply chain; and the strong growth in services traded remotely over electronic networks. See Americo Beviglia Zampetti and Pierre Sauvé, 'Rules of Origin for Services: A Review of Current Practice', in Oliver Cadot *et al.* (eds.), *The Origin of Trade in Goods: Rules of Origin in Regional Trade Agreements* (Oxford University Press, 2006), pp. 114–145, at 117.

60 See John H. Jackson, *The World Trading System, Law and Policy of International Economic Relations*, 2nd edn (Cambridge, Mass.: The MIT Press, 1997), p. 280.

61 See ASCM Art. 8, Annex 2 of the AoA and Art. 87.2 and 87.3 of the Treaty Establishing the European Community.

not have the primary objective of interfering with trade by increasing the export competitiveness of domestic industries or by making market access harder for foreign competitors. The trade-distortive effects they might cause are therefore considered as minimal. Second, in conformity with the concept of positive externalities discussed above, subsidies may be imposed in pursuit of legitimate policies that governments should be allowed to implement without particular restrictions.

The negotiating mandate falls short, however, of mentioning the essential role of subsidies in the provision of public services, nor does it call for flexibility in relation to environmental protection subsidies. The discussions that took place in the WPGR meetings nevertheless underscored the willingness of the WTO Members to retain sufficient latitude to implement support programmes in these areas.

An issue that captured particular attention in the debates on possible disciplines on services subsidies, and also caught the public eye, relates to the impact possible rules might have on the ability of governments to subsidise public services. The term 'public services' is rather vague, and no definition can be found in the GATS. In the WPGR debates, public services have often been linked to the provision of Article I:3 (b). This provision reduces the otherwise extremely wide coverage of the GATS[62] by excluding services supplied in the exercise of governmental authority and would therefore operate as a built-in exclusion of such services from the scope of possible disciplines on services subsidies as well.[63] Clarifying the scope of the GATS in relation to public services would also have beneficial effects on the ongoing negotiations under GATS Article XIX (negotiations on specific commitments) by allowing a less contentious exchange of requests and offers in sectors in which there are rising levels of international trade, such as education and health. It would also help to counteract many unwarranted concerns by those who view the GATS as

[62] See GATS Art. I:1 and I:3 (a).

[63] According to a publication of the WTO Secretariat that appeared in 2001 'The GATS has no implications for the public funding of services provided in the exercise of governmental authority. Whatever disciplines are developed [on the basis of Art. XV] will not apply to governmental services, because these are simply outside the scope of the GATS'. See WTO Secretariat, GATS Facts and Fiction, 2001, p. 8. A second blanket exclusion relates to air traffic rights and directly related services. See Annex on Air Transport Services. Governmental support provided to air transport companies in activities excluded from the scope of the GATS, typically in the form of rescue and restructuring interventions, therefore remains unaffected by the existing GATS disciplines on subsidies.

a threat to democracy and a danger to governments' autonomy to supply public services.[64]

Although the rationale behind Article I:3 (b) is quite straightforward (it would be nonsensical to assume trade obligations in areas that are closed to any form of commercial activity), the practical meaning of this self imposed-limitation remains unclear. To date, no case law has interpreted the scope of GATS Article I:3 (b), and a number of papers published by the WTO Secretariat have given a rather confusing and sometimes contradictory impression of the issue.[65] Article I:3 (c) elaborates on the provision of Article I:3 (b) by stating that 'a service supplied in the exercise of governmental authority means any service which is supplied neither on a commercial basis, nor in competition with one or more service suppliers'. The breadth of the exclusion of public services from the scope of the GATS largely depends on the interpretation given to the terms 'commercial basis' and 'in competition'. Studies on this issue have concluded that the exclusion of Article I:3 (b) is narrowly construed and that most services are therefore captured by the GATS.[66] The progressive withdrawal of the state as service provider that has occurred through privatisation or through the emergence of public–private partnerships, further contributes to enlarging the scope of the GATS in the public services domain.[67]

The impact of existing disciplines on services subsidies, such as that of Article XVII and Article XXIII:3, on the governmental latitude to financially support the provision of public services, is arguably minimal. As argued above, their efficacy is significantly impaired by the lack of specific commitments in relevant sectors, such as health and education, combined, in the case of national treatment, with the existence of specific or horizontal limitations. Fears of excessive intrusiveness of multilateral rules on the freedom of governments to support public services therefore seem unwarranted. In view of the sensitivity surrounding this issue, it would nevertheless appear particularly important to provide an official

[64] See, e.g., www.attac.org/indexfla.htm, http://www.gatswatch.org/.

[65] See WTO Document S/C/W/39, p. 2; S/C/W/50, p. 10–11; WTO Secretariat, as note 63 above, 8, and WTO, 'Market Access: Unfinished Business, Post Uruguay-Round Inventory and Issues', Special Study No. 6, Geneva, 2001, pp. 122–123.

[66] See Marcus Krajewski, 'Public Services and Trade Liberalization: Mapping the Legal Framework', *Journal of International Economic Law* 6(2) (2003), pp. 341–367; and Rudolf Adlung, 'Public Services and the GATS, WTO, Economic Research and Statistic Division', 2005, Working Paper ERSD - 2005 - 03.

[67] See Werner Zdouc, 'WTO Dispute Settlement Practice in the Relation to GATS', *Journal of International Economic Law*, 2(2) (1999), pp. 295–346, at 321.

clarification of the scope of the GATS in relation to public services, which might otherwise become a major stumbling block to progress in the negotiations under Article XV.

Conclusion

The paucity of data on services subsidies does not yet allow definitive conclusions to be drawn on the question of whether and how any regulatory framework would be necessary to address the potentially distortive effects subsidies may have on services trade. If further information were to confirm that export subsidies play only a marginal role in the services context and that the bulk of subsidisation takes the form of import-displacing subsidies,[68] the existing GATS framework might already feature instruments capable of disciplining the potentially distorting effects of such subsidies via the national treatment obligation and non-violation complaints. This would imply strengthening these two provisions by granting them an unconditional character, thus delinked from the existence of specific commitments.

The question of whether distortive subsidies are widespread or else concentrated in a few services sectors also remains largely unanswered. The data emerging from the Trade Policy Review reports suggests that subsidisation is common in areas such as transport, financial, audiovisual and tourism services. If confirmed, such information might well be used to argue in favour of elaborating a limited number of ad hoc instruments, rather than horizontally applicable disciplines. Such an approach might also be preferable in addressing the sector-specific characteristics and sensitivities that arise in sectors such as audiovisual (e.g. cultural diversity) or financial services (e.g. financial institution bail-outs). On the question of the appropriateness of introducing a countervailing duty mechanism in the services context, this chapter suggests that such a policy response would be neither desirable nor likely to be feasible. In this respect, negotiations on Article XV might represent an appealing venue for ground-breaking steps in the direction of a general 'multilateral

[68] Feketekuty concludes that 'there are few, if any, instances of direct export subsidies in services'. See Geza Feketekuty, 'Trade in Services – Bringing Service into the Multilateral Trading System', in Jagdish Bhagwati and Mathias Hirsch, *The Uruguay Round and Beyond, Essays in Honor of Arthur Dunkel* (Ann Arbor: The University of Michigan Press, 1998), pp. 79–100, at 89.

remedies only' approach in the context of subsidies.[69] The increased capacity of the multilateral framework to resolve contentious issues among its Members that emerged from the Uruguay Round with the creation of a permanent interstate adjudicatory body, whose decisions are automatically adopted unless there is consensus to the contrary among all Member States, strongly encourages this option.[70]

Bibliography

Adlung, Rudolf and Martin Roy, 'Turning Hills into Mountains? Current Commitments under the GATS and Prospects for Change', WTO, Economic Research and Statistics Division, 2005, Staff Working Paper ERSD-2005-01.

Adlung, Rudolf, 'Public Services and the GATS', WTO, Economic Research and Statistic Division, 2005, Working Paper ERSD-2005-03.

APEC, Guide to Investment Regimes of the APEC Member Economies, Fifth edition, APEC Committee on Trade and Investment, 2003, available at www.apec.org/apec/apec_groups/committees/committee_on_trade/investment_experts.html.

Benitah, Marc, ICTSD Roundtable on Trade in Services and Sustainable Development: 'Towards Pro-Sustainable Development Rules for Subsidies in Trade in Services', Roundtable, proposed structure for discussion, Geneva, 10 March 2003, available at www.ictsd.org/dlogue/2003-03-10/Benitah_working%20paper_final.pdf.

Beviglia Zampetti, Americo and Pierre Sauvé, 'Rules of Origin for Services: A Review of Current Practice', in Oliver Cadot *et al.* (eds.), *The Origin of Trade in Goods: Rules of Origin in Regional Trade Agreements* (Oxford University Press, 2006), pp. 114–145.

Cottier, Thomas and Matthias Oesch, *International Trade Regulation: Law and Policy in the WTO, the EU and Switzerland* (London: Cameron May, 2005).

Cottier, Thomas and Krista Schefer, 'Good Faith and the Protection of Legitimate Expectations in the WTO', in Marco Bronckers and Raymond Quick (eds.), *New Directions in International Economic Law, Essays in Honour of John H. Jackson* (The Hague: Kluwer Law International, 2000), pp. 47–68.

Durling, James P. and Simon N. Lester, 'Original Meanings and the Film Dispute: The Drafting History, Textual Evaluation, and Application of the Non-Violation Nullification or Impairment Remedy', *George Washington Journal of International Law & Economics* 32 (1999), pp. 211–269.

[69] See in this respect ASCM Art. 4 and 7 and WTO Document S/WPGR/W/31, 16 March 2000, p. 5.

[70] See DSU Art. 16:4.

Feketekuty, Geza, 'Trade in Services-Bringing Service into the Multilateral Trading System', in Jagdish Bhagwati and Mathias Hirsch, *The Uruguay Round and Beyond, Essays in Honor of Arthur Dunkel* (Ann Arbor: The University of Michigan Press, 1998), pp. 79–100.

Howell, Thomas R., 'The Trade Remedies: A US Perspective', in Geza Feketekuty and Bruce Stokes (eds.), *Trade Strategies for a New Era: Ensuring US Leadership in a Global Economy* (Council on Foreign Relations and the Monterey Institute of Foreign International Studies, 1988), pp. 299–323.

Hufbauer, Gary Clyde and Johanna Shelton Erb, Subsidies in *International Trade* (Washington, DC: Institute for International Economics (IIE), 1984).

Jackson, John H. and William J. Davey, *Legal Problems of International Economic Relations*, 2nd edn (St Paul, Minn.: West Publishing Co., 1986).

Jackson, John H., *The World Trading System, Law and Policy of International Economic Relations*, 2nd edn (Cambridge, Mass.: The MIT Press, 1997).

Krajewski, Marcus, 'Public Services and Trade Liberalization: Mapping the Legal Framework', *Journal of International Economic Law* 6(2) (2003), pp. 341–367.

Olson, Mancur, *The Logic of Collective Action, Public Goods and Theory of Groups* (Harvard University Press, 1965).

Sauvé, Pierre, 'Completing the GATS Framework: Addressing Uruguay Round Leftovers', *Aussenwirtschaft* 57 (3) (2002), pp. 301–341.

Sunsonline.org, 'Services Subsidies Need Sector-Specific Approaches', 14 July 1994, available at www.sunsonline.org/trade/areas/services/07140094.htm.

Sykes, Alan O., 'Countervailing Duty Law: An Economic Critique', *Columbia Law Review* 89(2) (1989), pp. 199–263.

——'The Economics of WTO Rules on Subsidies and Countervailing Measures', John M. Olin Program in Law & Economics Working Papers, No. 186, 2003, University of Chicago.

Thomas, Chan, Speaking Points at ICTSD Round Table on Trade in Services and Sustainable Development, 'Towards Pro-Sustainable Development Rules for Subsidies in Trade in Services', ICTSD, Geneva, 2003.

UNCTAD, Regulation and Trade Liberalization in the Construction Services Sector and its Contribution to the Development of Developing Countries, TD/B/COM.1/EM.12/2, 2000.

WTO Secretariat, 'Market Access: Unfinished Business, Post Uruguay-Round Inventory and Issues', Special Study No. 6, 2001, available online at www.wto.org.

WTO Secretariat, GATS Facts and Fiction, 2001, available online at www.wto.org.

21

Comment: One set of rules for fair and unfair trade in services: A possible merger?

KANITHA KUNGSAWANICH

Godot will not come today, but surely tomorrow.

In chapter 20 Pietro Poretti subjects subsidies to very close analysis. His chapter is a painstaking enquiry into important aspects of subsidies rule-making, namely: (1) the categorisation of subsidies; (2) the possible scope of future disciplines as defined by and in relation to other GATS provisions; (3) the inadequacy of the conditional national treatment obligation and non-violation complaint provisions in disciplining subsidies; and (4) the impracticality of a retaliatory mechanism in the services context.

I do not disagree with the arguments put forward in the chapter.

Subsidies continue to be an active policy tool which a government uses to redistribute wealth for specific social, political or economic gains.

An important fact remains however, that subsidies alter the conditions of competition and interfere with price signals. Subsidies can become problematic in any liberalised services market as their effects can hardly be contained within borders. The degree of 'distortiveness' nevertheless depends on the form of subsidy, the duration, the market structure, the regulatory framework, the eligibility conditions and the way in which the subsidy scheme in question interacts with other policies.

From a negotiating perspective, trade officials need comprehensive information about Members' existing subsidy schemes before determining distortive effects and subsequently the scope and application of future disciplines. As it happens, procrastination, despite explicit mandate under Article 15:1,[1] in favour of the status quo has effectively deterred information sharing.

[1] Article 15:1 of GATS provides that 'Members recognise that, in certain circumstances, subsidies may have distortive effects on trade in services. Members shall enter into negotiations with a view to developing the necessary multilateral disciplines to avoid such trade-distortive effects . . . For the purpose of such negotiations, Members *shall exchange information* concerning *all* subsidies related to trade in services that they provide to their domestic service supplier.' (emphasis added)

There are several reasons for inaction; the recent confessionals conducted by the Chair of the Working Party on GATS Rules in December 2006 have confirmed some of the author's findings.

First, a sense of urgency is lacking. The absence of complaints, if not proven injuries on the part of the domestic industry, has led the authorities concerned to believe that there is no pressing need for multilateral disciplines on subsidies.

In fact Article 15:2 provides that if a Member considers itself adversely affected by a subsidy of another Member, it may request consultations. So far, no Member has ever invoked this provision.

It is worth noting that the audiovisual sector, one of the most heavily subsidised sectors[2] and, perhaps, most vulnerable to a challenge under Article 15:2, is de facto carved out by the recent adoption of the UNESCO Convention on Protection and Promotion of the Diversity of Cultural Expressions in 2005.[3] The immediate value of having disciplines on subsidies at the horizontal level (cutting across all sectors) is undermined if not undercut by this development.

Second, Members, having simultaneously offensive and defensive interests in subsidies, are being extremely cautious as it is unclear how the shared information will be used in creating future disciplines. To alleviate this state of ambivalence, some Members suggested that subsidies considered as 'green' be identified upfront to ascertain some policy space. There is a likelihood that this type of subsidy would be subject to looser disciplines.

Third, there is also the persistent problem of lack of resources and coordination amongst domestic agencies to come up with relevant and consistent data, especially where subsidisation does not distinguish between goods and services.

Last but not least, a consensus is yet to emerge on the term 'subsidies' in the context of services as understood by Members. Some Members proposed the idea of having a provisional definition so as to make the information exercise more manageable.[4] Such a definition can be

[2] The EC, for example, will spend 755 million euros over the next seven years to subsidise European movies. An increase of two-thirds of its budget for supporting the film industry. *International Herald Tribune*, 13 February 2007, p. 11.

[3] The operative provisions of the Convention seem to provide the Parties with broad authorisation to impose a broad range of trade restrictive/anticompetitive measures to 'protect' cultural diversity. Article 6, for example, states that 'each Party may adopt measures aimed at protecting and promoting the diversity of cultural expressions within its territory'.

[4] JOB(04)127 Communication from Hong Kong, China, 'Some Thoughts on the Way Forward for Subsidies Negotiations', 15 Sept. 2004.

modified as the exercise progresses. A few Members feel that the definition contained in the Agreement on Subsidies and Countervailing Measures (ASCM) could be a useful point of reference.[5]

The definition is in fact is closely related to the way in which subsidies are categorised.

Precisely because many services industries are inseparable from social and economic development – education, health, energy,[6] financial services to name a few – one can always find a well-reasoned argument to support government intervention on development grounds.[7] Poretti points out this challenge also when he delves into 'import-displacing subsidies' – the basket into which most subsidy schemes are likely to fall.

In many instances, innovative and productive activities resulted from government subsidies and could never have happened if left to market forces.[8]

The time when a government intervenes in the utilities sector to correct market failures such as natural monopoly and externalities is perhaps, as Poretti reflects under the section on 'Public services and Article 15 negotiations', the time when subsidies are deemed to be legitimate,

[5] JOB(05)/5 Communication from the United States, 'Working Toward a Productive Information Exchange', 31 Jan. 05. JOB(05)/96 Communication from Chile; Hong Kong China; Mexico; Peru and Switzerland. 'Proposal for a Provisional Definition of Subsidies in Services', 9 Jun. 2005. According to Article 1 of the ASCM, subsidies can take the form of monetary payment, other transfers or the relief of an opportunity cost. There are doubts on the part of some Members whether the definition should include revenue foregone in the strictest sense or also encompass certain government regulatory intervention. See also JOB(05)/4 'Synthesis of Views Expressed on the Definition of Subsidy', Informal Note by the Secretariat, p. 3, para. 12.

[6] Subsidies that favour renewable energy sources of electricity generation, for example, where renewable energy obligations are being imposed on grid operators or retailers. Providers of services that are inputs in the production, distribution, transmission and sale would be the targeted beneficiaries. 'World Trade Law and Renewable Energy: The Case of Non-Tariff Measures', by the Renewable Energy and International Law Project, prepared for UNCTAD (Feb. 2005) and the International Trade Commission Hearing for the USTR (April 2005).

[7] Under mode 4, for example, government assistance such as a direct grant to vocational training would be regarded as human resources development, a legitimate role of the state although it could target certain professions. The increased employability at home and abroad would seem to be a by-product.

[8] The example of public R&D funding is often cited to support this argument. Subsidies are provided as an incentive for firms to innovate and recoup heavy fixed costs associated with R&D activities, leading to a reduction of private costs and more investment in R&D. Microeconomic literature seems to confirm that R&D is associated with productivity gains both at the firm and industry levels.

particularly if it could be demonstrated that they assist the firms in question to the extent that such firms can operate along average cost lines.

The legitimacy is less clear when a government in the most traditional sense of investment promotion provides incentives in order to encourage inward FDI or to establish (re)export capacity in certain services sectors.[9] This type of subsidy ('import diverting subsidies' as termed by Poretti), is often provided in a non-discriminatory fashion. This makes the situation in services distinct from goods as, oddly, subsidies can be given by the government of the importing country (through import diverting subsidies) along with the exporting countries (through export enhancing subsidies) at the same time and in the same services sector.

Again the legitimacy seems less clear when a government maintains its control over industries related to national security and infrastructure such as power transmission, civil aviation,[10] postal and courier, and shipping, while nurturing those state-owned enterprises to become internationally competitive companies. The role of the state as a funder (through subsidies and state aids) and as an investor (golden shares kept by the state in privatised firms) can intersect. Therefore the interplay between Articles 1:3 and 15 will continue to be grey, given the nature and workings of different political systems in the world.

Poretti's contribution does not elaborate to what extent further clarification of public services would help the practical interpretation of 'commercial basis' and 'in competition with one or more services suppliers'. For the moment, some WTO Members attempt to make better use of GATS Article 18 (Additional Commitments) by means of a Reference Paper (e.g., telecoms and postal and courier including express delivery) to come to terms with cross-subsidisation and potential predatory pricing by some state enterprises.

When a government uses subsidies to foster the growth of some home-grown industries with their own intellectual property rights and brands,[11] it is unequivocal that this type of subsidy, 'export-enhancing

[9] *Ibid.*, pp. 2, 4, 7. [10] *Ibid.*, p. 3.

[11] S/WPGR/W/13/Add. 2, pp. 5, 8. See also 'Wind Shifting Against Corporate Tax Breaks', *International Herald Tribune*, 13 Feb. 2007, p. 12. GE has benefited from a 1997 law that allowed its international financial services business, General Electric Capital Services, to defer US taxes on its foreign profit. Switzerland allows its cantonal governments to completely or partially exempt profits generated abroad by domestic companies from local company taxes. The system, which according to the EU, discriminates between domestic and foreign companies. 'EU Urges Swiss to Alter "Unfair" Tax Policies', *International Herald Tribune*, 14 Feb. 2007, p. 12.

subsidies' as Poretti terms it, must be disciplined, arguably with flexibilities available only for developing countries and LDCs (such as *de minimis* of market share) as they strive to make their national economy more diversified.

For the time being, the current scheduling method, focusing solely on the import side of trade, addresses only the eligibility aspect of subsidies, i.e. access to subsidies by foreign suppliers, through restrictions or lack of such under the national treatment column.

Limitation entries in Members' schedules, while not providing much information on definition, reveal certain policy intentions. For example, in mode 3, only those companies that are present in the territory are eligible for subsidies, and in mode 4, only citizens and/or residents are eligible.

Apart from schedules of specific commitments, Members also rely on limited information on subsidies from other sources such as documents of the Trade Policy Review Body.[12]

This state of imperfect information, specifically on the level of real subsidy spending and objectives that a subsidy scheme serves, leads to an unclear picture of competition and an intuitive need to level the playing field through some form of restraint.

When it comes to disciplining those subsidies, in the goods context, there must be a financial contribution by the government and a competitive advantage conferred on the recipient. The subsidy must also be specific and have caused certain defined adverse effects. Domestic content-based subsidies and export subsidies are prohibited entirely.

In the services context, it is less straightforward, as Poretti elucidates, Members are basically free to reserve their rights to subsidies in their own terms by way of inscribing limitations on national treatment in their schedules of specific commitments.

In the attempt to establish trade-distortive effects and later injuries, we can hardly escape from the concepts of 'like services', 'like services suppliers' and 'like circumstances'.[13]

The attempt becomes even more challenging when a subsidised service is used as an input through a seamless chain of production and communication networks across different services sectors across the globe.

The difficulties of determining trade distortive effects of and injuries caused by subsidies effectively render the application of Article 23:3 (non-violation complaints) limited.

[12] S/WPGR/W/25 and addenda.

[13] See Mireille Cossy, 'Determining "Likeness" under the GATS: Squaring the Circle?', WTO, Staff Working Paper ERSD-2006-08, September 2006.

With regard to the question of appropriate remedies, one possible option is to establish soft disciplines encouraging subsidising Members to exercise voluntary self- restraints. Another possible option that Poretti suggests in his paper but does not elaborate in detail is the idea of creating horizontal disciplines independent of market access and national treatment commitments. This second option in my opinion may well work for prohibited subsidies (export-enhancing subsidies).

As WTO Members seek to find innovative ways to handle the information exchange obligation, emergency safeguard measures (ESMs), which in crude terms allow Members to suspend commitments on market access (Article 16), national treatment (Article 17), and additional commitments (Article 18), may have a role to play in helping Members, particularly developing countries, which most of the time are market followers, cope with the adverse effects of liberalisation including the inability to compete with subsidised services.

There is perhaps a tacit understanding that ESMs are to be invoked under a normal/fair trade circumstance. The problem is we may not know if the situation in which we find ourselves is one where trade is fair as long as Members have not fulfilled the mandate of Article 15 on subsidies regarding the information exchange.

The dynamics of the negotiations on subsidies and ESMs can change significantly were we to decide that having two separate remedies, one for fair trade and the other for unfair trade circumstances, may not be necessary as in the case of goods. After all, the two disciplines will have to borrow from each other technical concepts such as domestic industry, like services and determination of injuries.

Surely, ESMs cannot provide permanent solutions to all kinds of setbacks caused by the liberalisation process. But it could be a useful stop-gap and passive instrument available when there has not yet been discipline on subsidies to ensure fair trade.

To conclude, subsidies achieve trade-offs between competition, efficiencies and other policy concerns. In order to better understand the working of subsidies and their impact on trade in services, WTO Members have joint responsibility to complete the information exchange exercise. The very least this exercise could do is to enhance transparency in a broad sense of GATS negotiations, if not to lay a necessary groundwork for further subsidy disciplines. Not doing anything can only make a case for ESMs stronger.

It starts with subsidies but it can end with ESMs.

PART 7

Challenges to the scope of GATS and cosmopolitan governance in services trade

22

Trade rules for the digital age

SACHA WUNSCH-VINCENT*

The rapid development of the Internet and other information communication technologies (ICTs) has led to the growing electronic cross-border delivery of services and digital products such as software.[1] While regional trade agreements increasingly innovate as regards the cross-border delivery of services and the incorporation of chapters on e-commerce, on the multilateral level, the General Agreement on Trade in Services (GATS) has not evolved since the end of the Uruguay Round.

This chapter reviews the progress in bilateral and multilateral trade agreements in securing liberal digital trade, i.e. electronic cross-border trade flows of data, services and digital products. The chapter's purpose is to start thinking about what digital trade rules may be needed today and in fifteen years from now. It focuses on the role of the multilateral trading system as regards digital trade flows actually taking place over information networks.

The first and the second parts of this chapter analyse developments with respect to electronically delivered products and services at the multilateral and bilateral trade levels. The third part raises the question of what digital trade rules are needed today and in 2015–2020.

1. Digital trade and the WTO: Maintaining relevance in the information age

Ten years ago it was recognised that the Internet offers unseen possibilities for digital trade and that offline trade barriers should not be

* The views expressed in this chapter are those of the author, and shall neither be attributed to the Organisation for Economic Co-Operation and Development (OECD) nor its member countries.

[1] The term 'e-commerce' is used within the WTO as the 'production, distribution, marketing, sale, or delivery of goods and services by electronic means' (see General Council (GC), Work Programme on Electronic Commerce, WT/L/274 (30 September 1998). With the term digital content the author refers to products which are digitally encoded and transmitted electronically over networks (e.g. movies, music, software, computer games).

replicated online. Consequently, in 1998 WTO Members issued a declaration on global e-commerce.[2]

The ten years following the rapid development of ICTs have seen the growth of the electronic cross-border delivery of services and digital products such as software. After *Mexico – Measures Affecting Telecommunications Services (Mexico – Telecoms)*[3] and *United States – Measures Affecting the Cross-Border Supply of Gambling and Betting Services* (*US – Gambling*),[4] it is becoming clear that cross-border electronic service transmissions and the Internet are leading cases of GATS trade disputes.

Part 1.A provides an overview of the achievements within the WTO Work Programme on E-commerce, while Part 1.B assesses digital trade-related progress in the Doha Development Agenda (DDA).

A. Rewind on the WTO Work Programme on E-Commerce: 'much ado about nothing' or 'much to do about something'?

In May 1998, the WTO Members issued a declaration on global e-commerce that established a comprehensive WTO Work Programme on E-Commerce to examine all trade-related issues connected with global e-commerce. This Declaration included a political statement calling upon Members to 'continue their current practice of not imposing customs duties on electronic transmissions' (the WTO Duty-free Moratorium on Electronic Transmissions).[5] As part of the work programme, the Council for Trade in Services (CTS) raised core questions which have to be settled.

The first column of Table 28 presents nine of the most relevant CTS questions and supplements the list with one core issue relating to technical barriers to trade in e-commerce which comes from the work mandate of the Council for Trade in Goods (CTG). Table 28 also summarises the progress achieved on these questions in the WTO Work Programme on E-commerce and in related GATS dispute settlement. The last column serves as a prelude to the results of bilateral trade negotiations discussed in Part 2 of this chapter.

[2] WTO, Ministerial Declaration on Global E-Commerce, WT/MIN(98)/DEC/2 (20 May 1998).

[3] *Mexico – Telecoms*, Mexico – Measures Affecting Telecommunications Services, Panel Report, WT/DS204/R, adopted 2 April 2004.

[4] *US – Gambling*, US – Measures Affecting the Cross-border Supply of Gambling and Betting Services, Panel Report, WT/DS285/R, adopted 10 November 2004, as modified by *US – Gambling*, US – Measures Affecting the Cross-Border Supply of Gambling and Betting Services , Appellate Body Report, AB-2005-1, WT/DS285/AB/R, adopted 7 April 2005.

[5] WT/MIN(98)/DEC/2 at fn. 2.

Table 28 *Performance of the WTO versus preferential trade deals on digital trade issues as raised in the WTO Work Programme on e-commerce*

Issues as suggested by WTO Work Programme on E-commerce	Dealt with by WTO Work Programme on E-commerce/ negotiations	Dealt with by Dispute Settlement	Overall WTO Results	Preferential Trade Agreements Results[a]
1) Instauration and applicability of a clear, permanent duty-free moratorium on electronic transmissions and their content	No binding decision	Not subject to dispute	Pending	Dealt with
2) Applicability of general GATS obligations (e.g. MFN, transparency) to the electronic delivery of services	No binding decision	Not subject to dispute	Pending	Dealt with
3) Applicability of specific commitments to the electronic delivery of services	No binding decision	YES	Dealt with	Dealt with
4) Classification of electronically traded services as mode 1 or mode 2	No binding decision	Potentially: classify as Mode 1	Pending? / Dealt with?	Dealt with as negative list approach
5) Classification and scheduling of new services arising in the context of electronic commerce	No binding decision	Not subject to dispute	Pending	Dealt with when no limitations

Table 28 (*cont.*)

Issues as suggested by WTO Work Programme on E-commerce	Dealt with by WTO Work Programme on E-commerce/ negotiations	Dealt with by Dispute Settlement	Overall WTO Results	Preferential Trade Agreements Results[a]
6) Classification of digital products	No binding decision	Not subject to dispute	Pending	Classification issue is pending but E-commerce Chapters provide for non-discriminatory trade treatment for digital products
7) Determining 'likeness' for application of MFN obligations and national treatment commitments	No binding decision	NO, despite significant opportunity to rule on matter	Pending	Pending but less necessary in the negative list context
8) Application of GATS Art. VI regarding domestic regulations relevant to digital trade	YES, but only in principle	Confirmed that it applies to electronic transaction	Dealt with in theory. To be determined in practice.	Pending, especially in the light of more specific provisions on domestic regulation
9) Application of GATS Art. XIV regarding general exceptions for e-commerce	YES, but only in principle	Confirmed that it applies to electronic transaction	Dealt with in theory and practice.	Same as in WTO but sometimes supplemented by additional provisions
10) GATT Council: Standards and e-commerce (Agreement on Technical Barriers to Trade)	YES, on the principle of full applicability but no detailed discussion	Not subject to dispute	Dealt with in theory. To be elaborated further and determined in practice	Same or weaker than in WTO?

[a] refers to PTAs discussed in Part 2.

Details about the GATS-related questions elaborated on in the above WTO Work Programme are beyond the scope of this paper.[6] Suffice it to say that WTO negotiators have done a forward-looking job in 'mapping the WTO e-commerce issues'. Nevertheless, the progress achieved in terms of converting thinking into actions has been a failure: i.e. even on simple issues such as confirming the applicability of WTO rules and commitments to electronically-traded services no results have been achieved. This is well reflected in the Hong Kong Ministerial Declaration of December 2005 (para. 46), in which WTO Members adopted the following minimalist stance:

> We take note that the examination of issues under the [Work Programme on E-Commerce] is not yet complete. We agree to reinvigorate that work . . . We declare that Members will maintain their current practice of not imposing customs duties on electronic transmissions until our next Session.

Meanwhile, *US – Gambling*, the second GATS case, filled this void and has provided a set of answers to the unresolved questions of the Work Programme on E-Commerce, mainly confirming the applicability of GATS commitments to electronically supplied services but leaving many other issues undecided (e.g. the trade treatment of digital products).[7]

- **Agreement on a clear, permanent duty-free moratorium on electronic transmissions and their content**: Hitherto, it has not been possible to agree on such a moratorium in the WTO. At the Hong Kong Ministerial, WTO Members only prolonged the temporary duty-free moratorium on electronic transmissions which does not clearly apply to the content of the transmissions themselves.[8]
- **Applicability of general GATS rules and specific commitments to the electronic delivery of services**: To date, the situation prevails that no clear affirmation concerning the applicability of WTO rules to

[6] For a discussion of these GATS-related questions, see W. Drake and K. Nicolaidis, 'Global Electronic Commerce and the GATS: The "Millennium Round" and Beyond', in P. Sauvé and R. M. Stern (eds.), *GATS 2000: New Directions in Services Trade Liberalisation* (Washington DC: The Brookings Institution, 2000), pp. 399–437.

[7] See S. Wunsch-Vincent 'The Internet, Cross-Border Trade in Services, and the GATS: Lessons from US–Gambling', *World Trade Review* 3 (2006), pp. 1–37.

[8] There is no clear understanding of what the moratorium covers when it refers to 'electronic transmissions'. It is uncertain whether it bans the imposition of customs duties on the content of the transmissions itself, namely on digital products or electronically delivered services.

cross-border electronic services has been forthcoming from WTO Members. The greatest progress made in *US – Gambling* is the confirmation that WTO rules are indeed applicable to e-commerce and to electronically supplied services. The Panel and the Appellate Body report apply the GATS framework to the electronic cross-border delivery of services without hesitation.

- **Classification of electronically traded services as mode 1 or mode 2:** So far, WTO Members have found it difficult to determine whether the electronic cross-border delivery of a service is a service supplied through GATS mode 1 or mode 2.[9] In *US – Gambling*, it is noteworthy that the statements of the concerned parties, Antigua and the US, as well as the rulings of the Panel and the Appellate Body imply that GATS mode 1 commitments are indeed applicable to cross-border delivery of electronic services.[10] But neither the Panel nor the Appellate Body formally examined the difference between GATS mode 1 and mode 2.
- **Classification and scheduling of new services arising in the context of e-commerce**: Since the conclusion of the first GATS round in 1994, many new services that can be delivered across borders have appeared, which cannot be clearly captured by existing specific GATS commitments. In fact, the Central Product Classification (CPC) was updated twice to reflect the rapidly changing economic activities and technologies since the end of the Uruguay Round. Moreover, a complete draft of the third revision – i.e. the CPC 2007 – containing many updates as regards IT-related services is now ready for adoption. However, the ongoing services negotiations are still based on the W/120 and the provisional CPC of 1991.[11]
- **Classification of digital products**: The lack of a decision on the correct classification of digital products has been the 'hottest potato' in the ongoing Work Programme, stalling progress on other matters.[12] WTO Members cannot agree on whether digital products traded electronically are goods governed by GATT, services governed

[9] CTS, The Work Programme on Electronic Commerce, S/C/W/68 (16 Nov. 1998), paras. 6 ff.

[10] *US – Gambling*, Panel Report, paras. 3.29 and 215.

[11] The GATS Services Sectoral Classification List (called W/120) can be found at www.wto.org/english/tratop_e/serv_e/mtn_gns_w_120_e.doc.

[12] See S. Wunsch-Vincent, *The WTO, the Internet and Digital Products: EC and US Perspectives* (Oxford: Hart Publishing, 2006).

by GATS or some unique category deserving its own set of trade rules. If GATS commitments are pertinent, it also remains to be decided which specific GATS commitments apply (those on audiovisual, telecommunication or computer services?). Interestingly, the trade liberalisation of digital products is, however, a cornerstone of preferential trade agreements.

- **Determining 'likeness' for application of MFN obligations and national treatment commitments**: The CTS expressed the need for more work on the concepts of technological neutrality and the likeness of electronic versus non-electronically supplied services.[13] Two variations on this problem and two interpretations of the technological neutrality concept were discussed:
  - Intra-modal technological neutrality: In the context of GATS market access and national treatment obligations, the question was raised whether specific commitments for GATS mode 1 encompass the delivery of services through electronic means.[14] In *US – Gambling* the Panel confirmed this view when it assessed that 'a market access commitment ... implies the right ... to supply a service through all means of delivery ... unless otherwise specified in a Member's Schedule'[15] and that '[a] prohibition on one, several or all of the means of delivery included in mode 1 thus constitutes a limitation on the total number of service operations ... within the meaning of Article XVI:2(c)'.[16]
  - Likeness between electronic and non-electronic services: In the context of GATS MFN (Article III) and national treatment obligations, the question is whether electronically delivered services and those delivered by more traditional methods should be considered 'like services'. In the WTO Work Programme on E-Commerce, some delegations argued that, on the basis of technological neutrality, services provided electronically and services provided non-electronically were like services. In an explanatory note without binding character, the WTO Secretariat also emphasised that 'likeness in the national treatment context ... depends in principle

[13] CTS, Work Programme on E-Commerce, Interim Report to the General Council, S/C/8 (31 March 1999).

[14] General Council (GC), Work Programme on E-Commerce, Submission by the United States, WT/GC/16 (12 Feb. 1999).

[15] *US – Gambling*, Panel Report, para. 6.285. See also paras. 6.355 and 7.2(b).

[16] *US – Gambling*, Panel Report (note 4 above), paras. 6.355 and 7.2(b). Cf. S/C/8 (31 March 1999) (note 13 above), p. 1.

on attributes of the product or supplier *per se* rather than on the means by which the product is delivered'.[17] However, no consensus could be reached on this matter.

Likewise, in *US – Gambling* the question of when electronically-delivered services can be considered 'unlike' their non-electronic counterparts has yet to be answered.[18] Moreover, the rulings did not directly address the thorniest question, i.e. how the likeness of domestic versus foreign service providers should be assessed.

- **Application of GATS Article VI regarding domestic regulations**: In the light of increasing cross-border trade in services, the ensuing juxtaposition of domestic regulations and standards and the rise of domestic regulations applicable to digital transactions will become an ever-important trade issue. During debates in the WTO Work Programme there was agreement that the GATS discipline on domestic regulation – i.e. the one to be elaborated under GATS Article VI – applies to e-commerce.

  But Members disagreed on how to treat e-commerce under GATS Article VI. Some Members favoured an e-commerce-specific discipline that would distinguish the types of regulatory restriction which a Member could impose on digital trade-related activities in order to protect consumers, public morals, privacy and other values with a view to minimising unnecessary barriers to trade.[19] Others thought that a general purpose GATS regulatory discipline would adequately address e-commerce considerations and that a safe harbour for digital trade regulations would only justify potentially unnecessary regulations. Furthermore, it is important to reiterate that the GATS discipline on domestic regulation has not been concluded, despite more than ten years of negotiations.
- **Application of Article XIV regarding general exceptions for e-commerce**: Online content regulation as well as measures applied to the protection of privacy and public morals and the prevention of fraud were identified as regulations likely to be permissible under GATS Article XIV.[20] But it was also stressed that measures should be

[17] See S/C/W/68 (note 9 above), para. 33 (concerning GATS Article XVII).
[18] *US – Gambling*, Panel Report (note 4 above), paras. 6.18–6.25 and 6.425–6.426.
[19] See CTS, Communication from the European Communities and their Member States, S/C/W/98 (23 February 1999).
[20] Drake and Nicolaidis (note 6 above). See S/C/W/98 (note 19 above), para. 26 and CTS, Work Programme on Electronic Commerce – Progress Report to the General Council, S/L/74 (27 July 1999), para. 8.

subject to a necessity test and should not constitute a means of arbitrary or unjustifiable discrimination nor a disguised restriction on trade in services.[21] While some WTO Members and academics were concerned that the exemptions were not flexible enough,[22] others argued that Article XIV had to be interpreted narrowly and its scope should not be expanded to cover regulatory objectives other than those listed in the Article.[23]

US – Gambling tackled this thorny issue and produced two noteworthy findings of great relevance to other digital trade flows. First, the Appellate Body ultimately found the US gambling laws in question to fall under the public morals exception of GATS Article XIV and to be compatible with its *chapeau*. It was thus shown that WTO Members can – despite full specific GATS commitments – rely on this provision when trying to achieve certain public policy objectives. Second, the Panel ruled that these measures aimed at consumers contain limitations which do not fall within the scope of GATS Articles XVI:2(a) and/or XVI:2(c) and that they are thus not inconsistent with the specific commitments made by the US under the GATS.[24] This ruling seems to imply that measures aimed at consumers do not come under the realm of specific GATS market access commitments.[25]

B. Cross-border trade in services in the Doha Development Agenda: Getting the job done without talking digital trade?

In the run-up to the DDA, many GATS 2000 negotiation proposals had addressed the potential for the Internet to expand services trade.[26] Many WTO Members called for new or improved services commitments that

[21] S/C/8, pp. 9–10. CTS, Communication from Australia, S/C/W/108 (18 May 1999).

[22] Drake and Nicolaidis (note 6 above). [23] S/L/74 (note 20 above).

[24] *US – Gambling*, Panel Report (note 4 above), paras. 6.382–6.383, 6.397–6.398, 6.401–6.402, and 6.405–6.406.

[25] The Appellate Body decided that it need not rule on the above findings of the Panel because it had ruled out consideration of any of the state laws under GATS Article XVI. *US – Gambling*, Appellate Body Report (note 4 above), para. 373 (ii).

[26] See UN ICT Task Force, *WTO, E-commerce and Information Technologies: From the Uruguay Round through the Doha Development Agenda* (New York: United Nations Information and Communication Technology Task Force, 2005), http://www.unicttaskforce.org/perl/documents.pl?id=1536, pp. 65 ff.

would facilitate digital trade, mostly asking for more liberal GATS commitments in mode 1.

A few submissions in the area of financial services ventured outside the scope of specific GATS commitments broaching the topic of delineating responsibilities between home and host countries in supervising and regulating cross-border electronic banking services,[27] shedding light on regulatory trade barriers impeding cross-border electronic financial transactions (e.g. prudential rules and limitations on the transfer of financial information) and even e-commerce issues such as mobile commerce, data privacy, cyber threats and electronic payments.[28]

Presaging Part 3 of this chapter on possible digital trade rules, certain submissions in the areas of aviation, tourism and logistics have raised interesting new types of emerging barriers to digital trade, namely the lack of access to technology distribution channels and information networks. The access on a commercial basis to information networks, subject to transparent, reasonable and objective criteria and the elimination of anti-competitive practices and unfair competition was seen as a major concern.[29]

Since the start of the DDA, Members have started to exchange liberalisation requests and offers. The final GATS draft schedules would have been due on 31 October 2006.[30] The majority of the proposals address the issue of facilitating cross-border trade in services (summarised in Table 30). A group of countries led by India also suggested a model schedule for securing full market access commitments on a range of business process outsourcing services which addressed certain classification problems (e.g. 'call centre services' are not unambiguously covered by the existing GATS commitments).[31]

The idea of preserving the 'de facto level of openness' on cross-border delivery of electronic and non-electronic services was the underlying philosophy of many related proposals. There have also been several calls for GATS negotiators to consider the elimination of discriminatory market access barriers across the board as a priority – rather than

[27] Committee on Trade in Financial Services, Communication from Switzerland, E-banking in Switzerland, S/FIN/W/26 (30 April 2003).

[28] Committee on Trade in Financial Services, S/FIN/M/40 (30 June 2003).

[29] See, for example, CTS, Communication by Hong Kong, China, Logistics and Related Services, S/CSS/W/68 (28 March 2001).

[30] Hong Kong Ministerial Declaration, Sixth Session, WT/MIN(05)/DEC (22 December 2005), paras. 25–27 and Annex C.

[31] Joint statement on the 'Liberalization of Mode 1 under GATS Negotiations' from Chile, India and Mexico contained in Job(04)/87.

focusing on the traditional specific commitments under market access and national treatment.[32]

The service section of the Hong Kong Ministerial Declaration builds on the above suggestions and demands: (i) GATS mode 1 commitments at existing levels of market access on a non-discriminatory basis across sectors of interest to Members; and (ii) the removal of existing requirements of commercial presence.[33] Besides, the Hong Kong Ministerial Declaration only suggests that commitments on GATS mode 2 should be made where commitments on mode 1 exist (which is usually already the case).[34]

So far few of the revised GATS offers available in June 2006 had achieved the required mode 1 market access level (e.g. via the pursuit of model schedules or the pursuit of non-discrimination) or identical commitment levels between GATS modes 1 and 2. Despite more than eight years of existence of the WTO Work Programme on E-Commerce and five years of the DDA, few of the horizontal questions regarding digital trade raised in Part 1. A have been conclusively addressed in the ongoing negotiations.

2. Digital trade in preferential trade deals: What is hot and what is not?

The last five years have seen a proliferation of preferential trade agreements (PTAs). These PTAs increasingly innovate as regards the cross-border delivery of services, cooperation on ICTs and Chapters on e-Commerce. The following subsections review and evaluate new trade rules and obligations which help secure free digital trade. While Table 30 contrasts the advances made in PTAs to the efforts at the multilateral level, Annex Tables 29 and 31 depict the state of the PTAs with respect to digital trade matters.

A. E-commerce Chapters: Securing the applicability of trade rules and deepening digital trade commitments

What started with the incorporation of a non-binding E-commerce Chapter in the US–Jordan PTA in 2000, has led since the conclusion of the first legally binding US e-commerce Chapter in bilateral trade agreements

[32] See the presentation at the WTO Symposium on Cross-Border Supply of Services, www.wto.org/english/tratop_e/serv_e/sym_april05_e/mattoo_wunschvincentII_e.ppt and Mattoo (2005).

[33] Hong Kong Ministerial Declaration (note 30 above), Annex C, para. 1(a).

[34] Hong Kong Ministerial Declaration (note 30 above), Annex C, para. 1(b)(ii).

Table 29 *Provisions of e-commerce Chapters in bilateral trade agreements*[a]

	US–Australia	US–Bahrain	US–CAFTA	US–Chile	US–Morocco	US–Oman	US–Peru	US–Singapore	Singapore–Australia	Thailand–Australia	Thailand–New Zealand	New Zealand–Singapore	India–Singapore	Republic of Korea–Singapore
Applicability of WTO rules to e-commerce	✓	✓	✓	No	✓	✓	✓	✓	✓	✓	✓		✓	✓
Applicability of trade rules to the digital service supply	✓	✓	✓	✓	✓	✓	✓	✓					✓	✓
Duty-free moratorium on digital products	✓	✓	✓	✓	✓	✓	✓	✓					✓	
Chapter on cross-border trade in services	✓	✓	✓	✓	✓	✓	✓	✓						✓
Negative list approach	✓	✓	✓	✓	✓	✓	✓	✓						
Non-discrimination for digital products	✓	✓	✓	✓	✓	✓	✓	✓						✓
Exceptions	YES	YES	YES	YES	YES			YES					YES	YES

CAFTA, Central American Free Trade Agreement.

[a] The table is not exhaustive and does not review all trade agreements.

Table 30 *Plurilateral requests and cross-border electronic service trade*

Theme	Requested actions
Specific GATS commitments	• full commitments in modes 1 and 2 and removal of unbound entries in mode 1 in specified sectors (model schedule: professional, business, other business services, computer and related, research and development, tourism, part of education services + singling out sectors such as telecoms, transport, postal and courier, distribution, and financial services) • similar levels of commitments in GATS modes 1 and 2 whenever possible – clarification of the distinction between modes 1 and 2 • lift commercial presence/citizen/residency requirements (including such requirements for licensing or certification, requirements for local participation in services production and discriminatory measures + quantitative limitations) • consideration of other restrictions such as horizontal limitations (especially subsidies) which would limit the cross-border delivery of services • use of plurilateral approaches, such as model schedules or checklists/understanding on scheduling at the 2-digit level • address MFN exemptions
Rules and qualification requirements	• improve the transparency of domestic regulations • how to avoid domestic regulations (including consumer protection, *e.g.* different national rules prohibiting certain forms of advertising) constituting an excessive trade barrier. • reciprocity conditions on professional qualifications • the lack of accreditation possibilities in areas such as online education services should be addressed
Advanced digital trade issues	• capture technological developments in the field of services, including through two-digit classification and specific model schedules of new activities • avoidance of trade barriers in the area of computer reservation systems access, elimination of anticompetitive practices and unfair competition in the area of technology distribution channels and information/reservation networks • Restrictions on the electronic transmission of certain materials (advertising, educational material and audiovisual content) and messages (advertising)

Sources: Plurilateral requests of WTO Members and CTS, Report by the Chairman to the Trade Negotiations Committee, TN/S/23 (28 November 2005).

Table 31 *Deep e-commerce regulatory issues in selected preferential trade agreements*[a]

	EU–Chile	EU–Algeria	US–Australia	US–Bahrain	US–CAFTA	US–Chile	US–Morocco	US–Peru	US–Singapore	Singapore–Australia	Thailand–Australia	Thailand–New Zealand	New Zealand–Singapore	India–Singapore	Japan–Singapore
Pledge for cooperation in the e-commerce and ICT area[b]	✓	✓			✓	✓					✓	✓		✓	
Pledge to avoid unnecessary regulatory barriers to e-commerce	✓		✓	✓	✓	✓	✓	✓	✓	✓including pledge to follow UNCITRAL Model law	✓including pledge to follow UNCITRAL Model Law	✓including pledge to follow UNCITRAL Model Law			
Transparency					✓			✓		✓				✓	
Consumer protection			✓					✓		✓	✓	✓			
Online personal data	✓	✓								✓	✓	✓			
Authentication, certification, electronic signatures			✓					✓		✓	✓				
Free flow of information and data	✓	✓													
Paperless trade administration and customs facilitation			✓					✓		✓	✓	✓	✓	✓	✓

CAFTA, Central American Free Trade Agreement.

[a] The table is not exhaustive and does not review all trade agreements.

[b] Such ICT Cooperation pledges are included in many more PTAs: India-Thailand, Maghreb Arab Union State, Japan-Mexico, Japan-ASEAN, India-ASEAN, etc.

in US–Singapore in 2003 to a flurry of bilateral PTAs that incorporate e-commerce Chapters, notably US PTAs with Australia, Central American Free Trade Agreement, Chile, Morocco, and Singapore. Interestingly, the trend has spread somewhat further with PTAs such as Singapore–Australia, Thailand–Australia, Thailand–New Zealand, New Zealand–Singapore, India–Singapore, Japan–Singapore, Korea–Singapore. Other PTAs (e.g. Maghreb Arab Union, India–Thailand, Japan–Mexico, Japan–ASEAN, India–ASEAN, China–ASEAN) and trade-related statements from APEC and cooperation agreements increasingly contain pledges and rules for ICT cooperation and digital trade.

Conclusion of e-commerce Chapters with a focus on digital products

The e-commerce Chapters bring about direct or indirect solutions to many of the questions raised earlier as they formalise a definition of digital products, confirm the applicability of WTO trade rules to e-commerce, assure a clear zero-duty rate on the content of digital trade and provide for non-discrimination and MFN treatment for digital products (See last column of Table 28 and Annex Table 29). Without actually taking the politically contentious classification decision, the e-commerce Chapters create a special trade discipline tailored to digital products.

- **Formulation of relevant digital trade definitions**: The bilateral e-commerce Chapters introduce the concept of 'digital products' and the concept of 'electronic delivery or transmission (and electronic means)'. Remarkably, it is often explicitly stated that these definitions are without prejudice to the ongoing WTO classification discussions. Because the 'digital product' definition refers to offline and online-delivered digital products, the treaties aim at the technologically neutral treatment of both delivery forms. Finally, the concept of 'authentication' is often defined.

Four steps have been taken that make reference to the multilateral level and that significantly advance the principles of free digital trade.

- **Recognition of the applicability of WTO rules to e-commerce**: Most e-commerce Chapters explicitly recognise the applicability of WTO rules to e-commerce.[35]

[35] E.g. US–Singapore FTA Article 14.1 and US–Australia FTA Article 16.1.

- **Recognition of the applicability of trade rules to the electronic supply of services**: The e-commerce Chapters also affirm that the supply of a service using electronic means falls within the scope of the obligations of the relevant provisions in the cross-border trade in services Chapter,[36] signifying that trade rules, obligations, non-conforming measures listed in Annexes I and II of PTAs and exceptions specified in the services Chapters are fully applicable to digitally delivered services; a problematic legal construct discussed later in detail.
- **Establishment of a clear and applicable duty-free moratorium**: Almost all e-commerce Chapters specify that the parties 'shall not impose customs duties or other duties, fees, or charges on or in connection with the importation or exportation of *digital products* by electronic transmission'.[37] It is clear that the zero duty obligation applies to the content of the digital transmission, namely digital products. Due to the national treatment obligations included in the e-commerce Chapters, the duty-free status has to be accorded to digital products that 'transit' via a third party to parties of the PTA as well.[38] However, the moratorium does not seem to instate a duty-free moratorium for digitally-delivered services.

At first glance, the e-commerce Chapters also bring about non-discriminatory treatment of digital products, thus addressing the trickiest issue encountered at the WTO.

- **Non-discriminatory treatment obligation for digital products**: The e-commerce Chapters specify a national treatment obligation for digital products. Specifically, a party shall not accord less favourable treatment to certain digital products than it accords to other like products, on the basis that these are: 'created, produced, published, stored, transmitted, contracted for, commissioned, or first made available on commercial terms' outside its territory; or 'whose author, performer, producer, developer, or distributor is a person of another party or a non-party'.[39] These obligations also constrain both parties

[36] E.g. US–Chile FTA Article 15.2 and US–Singapore FTA Article 14.2.

[37] E.g. US–Singapore FTA Article 14.3, para. 1. The US–Chile FTA Article 15.3 notes that neither party may apply customs duties on digital products of the other party.

[38] An exception applies in the US–CAFTA FTA Article 14.3. Fn. 1. Later FTAs between Australia–Singapore, Australia– Thailand and Thailand–New Zealand also specify that the moratorium only applies to 'electronic transmissions between the two parties'.

[39] E.g. US–Singapore FTA Article 14.3, para. 3 and US–Australia FTA Article 16.4, para. 1.

to accord the same treatment to 'like' physically and digitally delivered content products.

- **MFN treatment obligation for digital products**: The e-commerce Chapters use very similar wording to specify an MFN obligation for digital products.[40] Specifically, a party shall not accord less favourable treatment to a digital product 'created, produced, published, stored, transmitted, contracted for, commissioned, or first made available on commercial terms' in the territory of the other party than it accords to a like digital product 'created, produced, published', etc. in the territory of a non-party. In the same vein, a party shall not accord less favourable treatment to digital products whose 'author, performer, producer, developer, or distributor is a person of the other party' than it accords to like digital products whose 'author, performer, producer, developer, or distributor is a person of a non-party'. Interestingly, in many PTAs digital products must not be fully produced and exported via one of the contracting parties of the bilateral PTAs to benefit from these obligations that assure non-discrimination. The negotiating parties have partly given up on complex rules of origin, potentially setting a useful precedent for services trade negotiations as a whole. Judging from these principles alone, the e-commerce Chapters provide sound principles of non-discrimination and MFN obligations.

Limitations of the e-commerce Chapters: carve-in/carve-out?

The e-commerce Chapters appear next to the Chapter on trade in goods and the Chapter on cross-border trade in services without addressing the question of the classification of digital products.

As mentioned before, the e-commerce Chapters contain exceptions which indicate that the 'Chapter is subject to any other relevant provisions, exceptions, or nonconforming measures set forth in other Chapters or Annexes of this Agreement'. This means that in overlapping cases, it is the trade in service-obligations and the related nonconforming measures that override the principles of national treatment and MFN specified by the e-commerce Chapters. Furthermore, some US-led and Asian PTAs with e-commerce Chapters specify that the parties are 'not prevented from adopting or maintaining measures in the audio-visual and broadcasting sectors' and that the Article on non-discrimination does not apply to measures affecting the electronic transmission of so-called linear, point to multipoint traditional

[40] E.g. US–Singapore FTA Article 14.3, para. 4 and US–Australia FTA Article 16.4, para. 2.

broadcasting services.[41] The US–Australia FTA goes as far as stating that its e-commerce Chapter shall not prevent a party from adopting new or maintaining existing measures in the audiovisual and broadcasting sectors.[42]

Furthermore, in some cases, the value gained from having a special e-commerce Chapter is not obvious. In cases where no reservations are taken in pertinent sectors, many provisions of the e-commerce Chapter – e.g. its duty-free moratorium or its commitments for national treatment obligations for digital products – become superfluous. This holds true as the signatory parties are committed either to full market access, national treatment and MFN obligations through the cross-border trade in services Chapter or to duty-free treatment of ICT goods and non-discrimination through the Chapters on market access for goods.

Finally, the services Chapters contain elements that the e-commerce Chapters do not. For example, the former guarantee market access and they boast a solid framework of general obligations modelled after the GATS (e.g. on domestic regulation). All in all, the e-Commerce Chapters, which mainly deal with digital products, seem to be a second-best solution which must be viewed in the context of the lack of a classification decision as regards digital products.

B. Chapters to secure free cross-border (electronic) trade in services

The cross-border trade in services chapters of the newly agreed PTAs also innovate.

- **Use of a negative list approach**: The PTAs use the most liberal form, namely the negative list approach, to schedule service trade commitments.[43] This top-down approach guarantees that narrow or outdated classification schemes and uncertainties relating to the mode of delivery do not unnecessarily limit the applicability of commitments to existing and future digitally-delivered services.

[41] See, for instance, the e-commerce Chapters of PTAs between US–Singapore and Korea–Singapore.

[42] US–Australia FTA Article 16.4, para. 4.

[43] E.g. US–Singapore FTA Article 8.3 (national treatment), Article 8.4 (most-favoured nation treatment), Article 8.5 (market access) and Article 8.7 (non-conforming measures).

- **Dropping of local presence requirements**: The PTAs specify that '[n] either Party may require a service supplier of the other Party to establish or maintain a representative office or any form of enterprise, or to be resident, in its territory as a condition for the cross-border supply of a service' (see barriers as in Table 30).
- **Dropping of MFN exemptions**: The PTAs specify that '[e]ach Party shall accord to service suppliers of the other Party treatment no less favourable than that it accords, in like circumstances, to service suppliers of a non-Party'.

On the surface, these provisions deepening the specific commitments seem very comprehensive. But again the devil is in the detail as attention must be paid to specified non-conforming measures.

A comprehensive overview of all limitations is not possible here. Suffice it to say that in the case of many PTAs, the number of limitations seems rather small and that due to the negative list approach many current and future services are covered by free trade obligations. Hence the impression arises that a GATS-plus level of liberalisation is achieved. However, only a sector-specific examination can reveal how relevant the specified non-conforming measures really are.[44]

In the area of rule-making, the bilateral PTAs also bring to the table a few new elements which are particularly relevant to cross-border delivery of electronic services.

- **Strengthened transparency requirements**: Obligations to publish regulations are supplemented by obligations to afford other Members access to the development of the regulations (e.g. advance notice, opportunity to comment prior to the date they come into effect). The service-specific rules are strengthened by a fully-fledged transparency Chapter applicable across all trade agreements.
- **Domestic regulation**: Whereas GATS Article VI:4 only instructs Members to develop such a discipline on domestic regulations, the PTAs specify that 'each Party shall endeavour to ensure … that such measures are: (a) based on objective and transparent criteria, such as

[44] To pick out an extreme case, the US–Australia, the US–Morocco and most other US-led PTAs contain a limitation which specifies that all existing non-conforming measures of all US States are exempted from its specific free trade obligations. However, it is particularly the regulations at the US State level that often pose the most significant barriers to trade in professional, legal and financial services.

competence and the ability to supply the service; (b) not more burdensome than necessary to ensure the quality of the service; and (c) in the case of licensing procedures, not in themselves a restriction on the supply of the service'.[45]

C. E-commerce Chapters introducing cooperation pledges and 'deep' digital trade rules

Beyond the desire to secure the applicability of trade rules and obligations to digital trade, for roughly ten years there has also been a consistent aspiration to address regulations designed to govern the conduct of electronic supply which are outside the traditional scope of specific GATS commitments.

Non-binding Joint Understandings on e-commerce

Since 1997, trading nations have concluded a significant number of bilateral 'Understandings' or 'Joint Statements on e-Commerce'. These have also been agreed upon on the regional level[46] and political declarations have been issued in APEC, ASEAN and Asia-Europe forums.

These non-binding pledges call for liberal digital trade principles and have thus been seen in the context of related WTO discussions.[47] But they also deal with a number of digital trade rules which go beyond the usual market access issues while pursuing policy principles fostering access to ICTs, and achieving ground rules for the digital marketplace.

ICT cooperation pledges and 'deep' digital trade rules in PTAs

Pledges for cooperation in the area of ICTs and e-commerce which relate to the above Understandings have recently become very visible items throughout most new PTAs; not only in US-engendered bilateral agreements but also in EU bilateral trade agreements (e.g. EU–Chile), and in a wide range of Asian ones (e.g. India–Thailand, China–ASEAN, and other trade agreements).[48] Although they are more a declaration of

[45] E.g. US–Singapore FTA Article 8.8 2.

[46] 'Statement to Implement APEC Policies on Trade and the Digital Economy', X APEC Leaders Meeting Declaration, 27 October 2002, Los Cabos (Mexico), www.apec.org/apec/leaders_declarations/2002/statement_to_implement.html.

[47] Cf GC, Fourth Dedicated Discussion on E-Commerce on 27 February 2003, WT/GC/W/492 (8 April 2003), para. 3.

[48] See the following PTAs: Maghreb Arab Union, Japan–Mexico, Japan–ASEAN, India–ASEAN, New Zealand Singapore, etc.

intent than legally binding laws, the permutation of these digital trade elements into trade agreements is noteworthy.

These cooperation pledges range from short statements on the promotion of ICT and e-commerce to broader agreements. Whereas the simpler statements suggest cooperation on the market access and regulatory issues raised by e-commerce (as, e.g., in the EU–Chile PTA), the more comprehensive ones suggest cooperation on various aspects of the information society but in particular in the following areas: telecommunications policy, ICT research and standards, interoperability issues, cyber-security, electronic signatures and payments, the balance between privacy protection and the free cross-border flow of information, intellectual property rights, consumer confidence, the increased dissemination and use of ICTs, encouraging the development of self-regulation and exchanging e-government experiences.

Beyond the incorporation of language on ICT cooperation, the most novel phenomenon in new PTAs is the integration of deep e-commerce regulatory issues into trade agreements.[49] The point of departure for this development is the view that the potential for inadequate and incompatible national regulations can constrain the expansion of global e-commerce. Trading nations seem to feel a need to address deep digital trade issues in trade agreements; either due to a lack of alternative, international agreements or bodies for these e-commerce-specific rules or as PTAs are thought to spur developments on the national level or in other relevant international fora.

Table 32 gives an overview of 'deep' digital trade provisions integrated in new trade agreements: domestic regulation, transparency, consumer protection, data protection, authentication and digital signatures, and paperless trading (Annex Table 31 provides the details for specific PTAs).

Here some initial observations on these provisions are offered; also in light of Part 3 of this chapter:

[49] For a discussion of deep versus shallow e-commerce regulatory issues see C. L. Mann, S. E. Eckert, and S. C. Knight, *Global Electronic Commerce – A Policy Primer* (Washington DC: Institute for International Economics, 2000); S. Bach and G. Erber, 'Electronic Commerce: A Need for Regulation?', in K. G. Deutsch and B. Speyer (eds.), *The World Trade Organization Millennium Round* (London: Routledge, 2001), pp. 125–137. C. Primo Braga, 'E-commerce Regulation: New Game, New Rules?', *The Quarterly Review of Economics and Finance* 45 (2005), pp. 541–558 recently called for such deep digital trade rules.

Table 32 *Deep e-commerce integration rules in preferential trade agreements*

Theme	Rules
Domestic regulation	1. Each Party shall maintain domestic legal frameworks governing electronic transactions based on the UNCITRAL Model Law on Electronic Commerce. 2. Each Party shall: (a) minimise the regulatory burden on e-commerce; and (b) ensure that regulatory frameworks support industry-led development of e-commerce.
Transparency	Each Party shall publish or otherwise make publicly available its laws, regulations, and other measures of general application that pertain to e-commerce.
Consumer protection	*Variation 1* The Parties recognise the importance of maintaining and adopting transparent and effective measures to protect consumers from fraudulent and deceptive commercial practices when they engage in e-commerce. The Parties recognise the importance of cooperation between their respective national consumer protection agencies on activities related to cross-border e-commerce. *Variation 2* Each Party shall, to the extent possible and in a manner considered appropriate by each Party, provide protection for consumers using e-commerce that is at least equivalent to that provided for consumers of other forms of commerce under their respective laws, regulations and policies.
Data protection	*Variation 1* 1. Notwithstanding the differences in existing systems for personal data protection in the territories of the Parties, each Party shall take such measures as it considers appropriate and necessary to protect the personal data of users of e-commerce. 2. In the development of data protection standards, each Party shall, to the extent possible, take into account international standards and the criteria of relevant international organisations. *Variation 2* 1. The Parties agree to cooperate on the protection of personal data in order to improve the level of protection and avoid obstacles to trade that require transfers of personal data. 2. Cooperation on personal data protection may include technical assistance in the form of exchange of information and experts and the establishment of joint programmes.

Table 32 (*cont.*)

Theme	Rules
Authentication and Digital Signatures	*Variation 1* 1. Neither Party may adopt or maintain legislation for electronic authentication that would: (a) prohibit parties to an electronic transaction from mutually determining the appropriate authentication methods for that transaction; or (b) prevent parties from having the opportunity to prove in court that their electronic transaction complies with any legal requirements with respect to authentication. 2. Each Party shall work towards the recognition at the central level of government of digital certificates issued by the other Party or under authorisation of that Party. *Variation 2* 1. Each Party shall maintain domestic legislation for electronic authentication that: (a) permits parties to an electronic transaction to determine the appropriate authentication technologies and implementation models for their electronic transaction, without limiting the recognition of technologies and implementation models; and (b) permits parties to an electronic transaction to have the opportunity to prove in court that their electronic transaction complies with any legal requirements. 2. The Parties shall work towards mutual recognition of electronic signatures through a cross-recognition framework at government level based on internationally accepted standards. 3. The Parties shall encourage the interoperability of digital certificates in the business sector, including financial services.
Paperless trading	1. Each Party shall endeavour to make all trade administration documents available to the public in electronic form. 2. Each Party shall endeavour to accept trade administration documents submitted electronically as the legal equivalent of the paper version of such documents.

- It is noteworthy that many of the subjects of these digital trade provisions (such as the protection of privacy, the protection of consumers and security issues) are usually conceived under the GATS Article XIV exception provisions which 'tolerates' derogations from GATS rules and obligations in special circumstances.[50] Here, however, those digital trade provisions are not merely seen through the lens of an 'exception approach'. Rather, these digital trade policy objectives are displayed as necessary conditions for spurring international trade.
- While certain policy principles are encouraged, the e-commerce rules included in the PTAs do not mandate very detailed regulatory approaches which are to be adhered to by signatory parties. Often the digital trade provisions either: (i) suggest broadly formulated policy directions which can be filled with meaning at the national level (e.g. the mandate to minimise the regulatory burden on e-commerce); or (ii) they cross-refer to existing standards outside the trade agreement (e.g. the reference to the UNCITRAL Model Law on Electronic Commerce). Often the standards leave a lot of room for national regulatory preferences while making the policy objective unambiguously clear and demanding (e.g. rules on consumer protection that 'to the extent possible and in a manner considered appropriate by each Party, provide protection for consumers using e-commerce that is at least equivalent to that provided for consumers of other forms of commerce'). Some elements such as the requirement to 'minimise the regulatory burden on e-commerce' can – despite looking very innocent – have quite important implications in dispute settlement or bilateral negotiations; especially in the absence of fully-fledged regulatory disciplines on domestic service regulation. Often the requirements also mandate further work: 'The Parties recognize the importance of cooperation between their respective … consumer protection agencies on … cross-border e-commerce'.

The absence of very meticulous regulations seems reasonable as the WTO has never been considered the appropriate body for such regulation. Rather, 'policed decentralization'[51] via regulatory disciplines, which lie midway between harmonisation and regulatory heterogeneity, is the

[50] In the context of the WTO Work Programme on E-Commerce, for instance, these policy priorities were usually treated in the context of discussions on GATS Article XIV while pointing out that the latter Article would allow Members to derogate from their specific GATS commitments if the principles of its *chapeau* are respected.

[51] A term coined by A. O. Sykes, 'The (Limited) Role of Regulatory Harmonisation in International Goods and Services Markets', *Journal of International Economic Law* 2 (1999), pp. 49–70.

cornerstone of the WTO's influence on domestic regulation. Given that other bodies are often better at formulating detailed digital regulations, this form of policed decentralisation in the digital trade context is likely to make sense. However, external digital policy principles to which the WTO or its Dispute Settlement Body could refer in the case of trade litigation do not always exist. Hence the suggested policy areas must be considered closely and may demonstrate the need for more coordination on these information society regulations in other international organisations.

- While some digital trade principles are rather general, others are detailed and far-reaching. In particular the provisions on authentication which mandate certain technological and legal requirements, interoperability and non-discrimination, work on mutual recognition and international standards, are surprisingly powerful. Furthermore, certain broad provisions can sometimes be seen in the context of provisions in other parts of the agreement (for example in the case of the transparency and domestic regulatory disciplines which are evoked in detail in other parts of the bilateral treaties). In one case – the US–Australia PTA – the digital trade rules even refer to detailed additional obligations on cross-border consumer protection (including a reference to instruments developed by other international organisations such as the 2003 OECD Guidelines for Protecting Consumers from Fraudulent and Deceptive Commercial Practices across Borders).[52] This shows how special digital trade rules, horizontal trade obligations and external, non-trade instruments can function in conjunction with the external activities of other bodies.
- Some elements of the digital trade provisions, such as the transparency requirements, may be criticised for being redundant as other parts of the trade agreements sufficiently capture the need for transparency, consultation and publication; see Part 1.B of this chapter which shows that the cross-border trade in services Chapters of the PTAs and a special Chapter on transparency already mandate demanding transparency requirements which also apply to digital trade rules and the discussion in the WTO Work Programme on E-commerce that leant towards the interpretation that the GATS Article III on transparency is fully applicable and sufficient for digital trade. This is the beauty of having horizontal GATS rules which automatically apply to all GATS modes and new forms of delivery uniformly

[52] US–Australia FTA, Chapter 14 on Competition-related Matters, Article 2.

without the need to take extra steps. Similar areas of duplication could arise in the areas of market access and national treatment commitments, rules on domestic regulations, technical standards/interoperability, and topics which fall under the GATS Article XIV exceptions, i.e. most issues evoked in the form of 'deep' digital trade provisions.

- Avoiding duplication which could arise through the creation of unnecessary rules which single out digital trade seems particularly important, especially when it leads to disciplines which sit squarely between provisions on trade in goods and services without specifying which general rules and specific obligations apply (see the related criticism in Part 2.A). However, in some cases, special digital trade provisions will be necessary and useful to add political emphasis on certain policy issues. The identification of what is redundant and what is not will be key in determining which of these digital trade rules emanating from bilateral PTAs could become a building block for multilateral trade rules.
- It should be noted that only some of these digital trade provisions are subject to dispute settlement provisions. In fact, those bilateral trade agreements, such as Singapore–Australia, Thailand–Australia and Thailand–New Zealand which go furthest in detailed digital trade regulations in areas such as domestic regulation, electronic authentication and online consumer protection, specify that these digital trade rules are not subject to the dispute settlement provisions.[53] These provisions for non-application of dispute settlement provisions reflect the hesitancy to submit such sensitive domestic regulations to a supranational arbitration system, potentially leading to fines or trade disputes with implications for local laws and other trade flows. Nevertheless, these digital trade rules are an official part of the trade agreement and must thus be considered as binding international law.
- The e-commerce Chapters cover a broad range of topics pertinent to digital trade which are singled out as particularly relevant in fora such as the Understandings on e-Commerce. In addition, certain horizontal provisions such as those calling for a 'light' domestic regulatory

[53] E.g. Singapore–Australia FTA, Chapter 14, Article 10 specifies the non-applicability of dispute settlement provisions: 'Chapter 16 (Dispute Settlement) shall not apply to Articles 4 (Domestic Regulatory Framework), 5 (Electronic Authentication and Electronic Signature), 6 (Online Consumer Protection) and 7 (Online Personal Data Protection) of this Chapter.' See also Australia–Thailand FTA, Chapter 11, Article 1109.

framework for e-commerce affect all national digital trade regulations simultaneously. However, more areas come to mind that are currently not addressed in the digital trade provisions in PTAs (e.g. taxation, ICT network security, liability and Internet governance issues).

3. Digital trade rules for 2015–2020?

The last part of this chapter deals with the question of what digital trade rules may be needed now and in 10 or 15 years' time. The latter is a difficult and exploratory exercise.

A. Short-term: Building on what exists and putting the house in order

Looking back at the previous sections, it can be seen that the first priority is to ensure that existing GATS rules and obligations unambiguously apply to digital trade transactions. Furthermore, the existing and new specific GATS commitments must ensure that digital trade flows are covered by far-reaching free service trade commitments before trade barriers of a new sort arise. Finally, the conclusion of ongoing negotiations on GATS rules in the area of domestic regulations seems a particular priority.

Parts 1 and 2 of this chapter have shown that – in spite of some progress being made – all three conditions are far from being achieved, especially when it comes to the multilateral level. The most glaring examples are digital products and new services which are not clearly captured by existing GATS commitments. Moreover, relevant specific GATS commitments removing barriers to cross-border trade in services as indicated, for example, in Table 30 have to be pursued in earnest. This will include efforts to capture broad and new categories of services by means of negative list approaches, model schedules, liberalising at the two-digit CPC level and scheduling new types of services while drawing on the CPC 2007.

Despite shortcomings, the existing GATS rules and full specific GATS commitments are powerful instruments which have been shown to work in the Internet context (as demonstrated in *US – Gambling*). Once comprehensive specific GATS commitments are made, open questions such as the status of the WTO duty-free moratorium on electronic transmissions, the delineation between GATS modes 1 and 2, the rise of new services and the classification of digital products will be fully or partly resolved.

LLYFRGELL PRIFYSGOL BANGOR UNIVERSITY LIBRARY

Finally, it seems that not all open questions raised by the WTO Work Programme on E-commerce and this chapter – such as the applicability and interactions of GATS Article VI or XIV or possibly even proper classification decisions for certain services or digital products – have to be solved at the negotiation table. The exact interpretation of some GATS trade rules and specific commitments may eventually come through dispute settlement cases.

Nonetheless, it would be in the interests of legal certainty and of pre-empting digital trade barriers to seek clarity wherever possible without relying on disputes. At the multilateral level, WTO Members should study the provisions of the already concluded PTAs closely to ensure that the basic applicability of GATS rules and obligations is improved via additional agreements or clarifications.

To conclude, the PTAs themselves may also need to be revisited in the light of shortcomings such as those indicated in Parts 2 A and C of this chapter; especially if the PTAs continue to form the blueprint for further preferential or multilateral liberalisation of digital trade.

B. Medium- to long-term: Formulating 'deep' digital trade rules and anticipating new digital trade barriers

It is true that in the current context of the faltering Doha negotiations which mostly struggle with topics such as agriculture, asking for more in the area of digital trade seems like 'asking for the moon' at a very inappropriate time. The process of formulating new 'deep' digital trade rules and of anticipating new digital trade barriers will be a medium- to long-term exercise. Here two analytical steps are proposed that may help in meeting this challenge.

Step 1: Assessing the usefulness and trade relevance of 'deep' digital trade provisions in the PTAs

As a first, medium-term step, WTO Members, potential signatories of future e-commerce Chapters as part of upcoming PTAs and ICT experts may want to assess the usefulness and trade relevance of 'deep' provisions in existing PTAs while identifying lacunae.

One can expect that signatory parties to existing e-commerce Chapters have already undertaken the process of screening and selecting the 'deep' provisions which are most useful or which address the most pressing (and ideally most trade-relevant) matters. Moreover, the legal language provided in these bilateral exercises (see Table 32) provides a useful starting point for future agreements and related amendments or extensions.

This observation must be considered with the following in mind: there seem to be two types of 'deep' provision with two discrete but often overlapping goals: (i) rules bolstering certain policy objectives in the international context which should facilitate e-commerce transactions and ensure the trust of consumers and users at large (including measures relating to consumer and data protection); and (ii) rules or provisions which aim at the elimination of new barriers to digital trade which pursue non-discrimination and market access in the traditional sense (e.g. non-discrimination for digital products).

Moreover, with respect to the former type of 'deep' regulations, the question of trade-relevance of certain ICT policy objectives and related 'deep' digital trade rules seems crucial as there are mounting arguments that the role of the WTO is to focus narrowly on trade. Clearly, securing data protection in the cross-border Internet context is a policy objective worth pursuing, particularly if it can be achieved without the WTO having to formulate detailed regulations by itself. Nevertheless, it is necessary to ask whether the WTO can and should be involved in formulating measures such as appropriate framework conditions or regulations with the sole intent of stimulating trade flows: i.e. also in the context of having no alternative body other than the WTO equipped to guarantee the binding nature of agreements and a comprehensive geographical coverage.

Looking at the existing 'deep' provisions in Table 32 and keeping the associated observations in Part 2.C of this chapter in mind, the following questions may prove useful:

1. Are particular digital trade provisions redundant as potentially they are already covered by a horizontal discipline (as may be the case for the e-transparency provisions)?
2. Does it make sense to create such digital trade rules in a stand-alone e-commerce Chapter with specific application to digital trade? Or would its integration into the GATS as a stand-alone digital trade discipline or even as part of an existing or newly created horizontal GATS discipline make more sense (as is potentially the case for rules on e-domestic regulations, e-consumer and online data protection, or special rules on authentication and digital signatures, whereas the broader question of technical trade barriers is at issue for many more technologies)? In formulating an answer to this question, it

must be kept in mind that regulations and necessary digital trade provisions often cross the 'silo' boundaries of traditional GATT versus GATS approaches and may have to sit somewhere between the core WTO agreements.

3. Are the existing trade rules sufficiently detailed and understandable to be meaningful and effective in a cross-cultural context with its various styles of regulatory approach to the information society?[54]
4. Do enough WTO-external organisations and agreed international policy approaches exist concerning these principles to guarantee meaningfulness and to help trade partners and WTO or other courts to settle disputes? If not, should recognised international anchors such as the UNCITRAL Model Law on Electronic Commerce, ITU standards or OECD Recommendations/Guidelines be created in this area, with trade agreements potentially providing the momentum?
5. Finally: Should these digital trade rules be subject to the dispute settlement system of the WTO or PTAs? What are the merits and demerits? What is the political feasibility?

Step 2: Unlocking the true potential of digital trade: Anticipating existing and new digital trade barriers

As a second step with a longer-term ambit, new digital trade barriers have to be anticipated and preparations made to counter them with relevant innovations on the side of rule-making and specific GATS commitments.

Such a task will benefit from an approach inspired by deep technical, economic and legal knowledge of ICT market structures and digital transactions, one that goes beyond the usual GATS parlance and the 'offline' world as we know it. In this quest, unlocking the true potential of cross-border digital trade and preserving the contestability of electronic markets must be the guiding principle. The potential of digital trade is far from being met, as e-commerce continues to be a mainly national affair and e-business processes and ICT-based globalisation in the services sector are only just starting to take off. Undoubtedly, many (protectionist) efforts – within and between countries – are being or will be pursued

[54] E.g. the provisions on the domestic regulatory framework which state that '[e]ach Party shall: (a) minimise the regulatory burden on e-commerce and (b) ensure that regulatory frameworks support industry-led development of e-commerce'.

by incumbents to shield traditional revenue flows from potential online delivery forms and new competitors.

Ten years ago, the idea was that the Internet was impossible to regulate and that national borders would succumb to this global medium. OECD governments agreed that a non-regulatory approach to e-commerce would be the best guiding principle. Today, in some respects geographical borders have successfully been superimposed on the global Internet infrastructure.[55] In many countries the hands-off approach has often given way to instating regulations applicable to the Internet. The increased 'balkanisation' of e-commerce via domestic regulations threatens to disappoint the early hopes of a global trading environment free of any trade barriers.

In the following, some potential venues for existing or future digital barriers are suggested to stimulate the debate and help define a forward-looking research agenda on the matter. The following indicative list is only a start and complements the issues presented in Part 2.C. The first three points in particular must be seen in the context of the increasing prevalence of ubiquitous networks in society which rely on multiple distribution platforms and interoperability.

- Lack of access to technology distribution channels and information networks sometimes as a result of anticompetitive practices and unfair competition: The example given in Part 1.B was that of computer reservation/global distribution systems.
- Technical (sometimes national and proprietary) standards, interconnectivity, compatibility of protocols and hardware, and resulting interoperability problems.[56] The PTAs have started to address such issues via their provisions on authentication and digital signatures.
- Generally increased importance of pro-competitive telecom and network regulation and related trade principles.
- Competition-related matters: Securing the contestability of digital markets and promoting innovation taking into account new online market structures, the influence of 'infomediaries' such as search engines, software providers and aggregators, and the possible market

[55] J. R. Reidenberg 'Technology and Internet Jurisdiction', *Pennsylvania Law Review* 153 (2005), pp. 1951 ff and J. Goldsmith and T. Wu, *Who Controls the Internet? – Illusions of a Borderless World* (Oxford University Press, 2006).

[56] See Council for Trade in Goods, Work Programme on E-commerce, WT/GC/24 (12 April 1999).

dominance of a small number of companies. In this context, investigating the existing but largely unexplored GATS Article VIII on Monopolies and Exclusive Service Suppliers, GATS Article IX on Business Practices and the relevance of related provisions in the GATS telecom agreements may be useful.

- Issues relating to online content regulation including Internet filtering and blocking (e.g. the recent Yahoo and Google cases in China),[57] measures such as content or language quotas to preserve national identities, and online advertising restrictions.
- Territoriality of national law when transactions are global: the territorial and often heterogeneous nature of legal provisions affecting digital trade (e.g. consumer protection or copyrights) are barriers to electronic trade.
- Internet Governance and new broadband policies: the plethora of new issues raised by the Pandora's box of 'Internet governance' and the pursuit of broadband policy goals (see e.g. the issues addressed at the World Summit of the Information Society[58] or at the OECD[59]).

To conclude, although typical 'beyond the border' issues, most of the listed items will also be of concern at the purely national level and may not appear to be a WTO matter. This impression merits further debate. Nevertheless, the characteristic of the Internet as a borderless online medium with a concentrated set of industry players, ICT goods, software and services and with the juxtaposition of many domestic regulatory regimes due to the Internet and the inability to solve certain problems at the national level (e.g. lack of interoperability, spam, ICT network security) will have to be kept in mind when elaborating further.

The question remains as to whether these policy objectives are necessary to reap the benefits of digital trade and whether they really belong in trade agreements and especially in the WTO. Future research and a close eye on developments in digital trade and the rise of related trade barriers will provide answers to these queries.

[57] In this context, the CEO of Google has repeatedly mentioned that the Chinese limitations regarding free speech on the Internet should be seen as a trade policy and WTO settlement issue.

[58] World Summit of the Information Society, Tunis Agenda Outcome, 2005.

[59] E.g. OECD (2004), *Recommendation of the Council on Broadband Development*, www.oecd.org/dataoecd/31/38/29892925.pdf.

Bibliography

Bach, S. and G. Erber, 'Electronic Commerce: A Need for Regulation?', in K. G. Deutsch and B. Speyer (eds.), *The World Trade Organisation Millennium Round* (London: Routledge, 2001), pp. 125–137.

Drake, W. and K. Nicolaidis, 'Global Electronic Commerce and the GATS: The "Millennium Round" and Beyond', in P. Sauvé and R. M. Stern (eds.), *GATS 2000: New Directions in Services Trade Liberalisation* (Washington DC: The Brookings Institution, 2000), pp. 399–437.

Goldsmith, J. and T. Wu, *Who Controls the Internet? – Illusions of a Borderless World* (Oxford University Press, 2006).

Mann, C. L., S. E. Eckert, and S. C. Knight, *Global Electronic Commerce – A Policy Primer* (Washington DC: Institute for International Economics, 2000).

Mattoo, A., 'Services in a Development Round: Three Goals and Three Proposals', *Journal of World Trade* 6 (2005), pp. 1223–1238.

OECD, Information Technology Outlook 2006 (Paris: Organisation for Economic Co-Operation and Development, Working Party on the Information Economy, 2006).

Primo Braga, C., 'E-commerce Regulation: New Game, New Rules?', *The Quarterly Review of Economics and Finance* 45 (2005), pp. 541–558.

Reidenberg, J. R., 'Technology and Internet Jurisdiction', *Pennsylvania Law Review* 153 (2005), pp. 1951 ff.

Sykes, A. O., 'The (Limited) Role of Regulatory Harmonisation in International Goods and Services Markets', *Journal of International Economic Law* 2 (1999), pp. 49–70.

UN ICT Task Force, *WTO, E-commerce and Information Technologies: From the Uruguay Round through the Doha Development Agenda* (New York: United Nations ICT Task Force, 2005), www.unicttaskforce.org/perl/documents.pl?id=1536.

Wunsch-Vincent, S., *The WTO, the Internet and Digital Products: EC and US Perspectives* (Oxford: Hart Publishing, 2006).

——'The Internet, Cross-Border Trade in Services, and the GATS: Lessons from US–Gambling', *World Trade Review* 3 (2006), pp. 1–37.

23

Comment: Digital trade: Technology versus legislators

CHRISTIAN PAULETTO*

The previous chapter by Sacha Wunsch-Vincent carefully depicts the reasons for the growth of digital trade internationally and the evolving environment surrounding such trade. In particular, it presents the various attempts and motives for regulating digital trade – or for avoiding excessive specific regulation – at national and international level. In this field as in others, history is always a good starting point before contemplating the future.

In a sense, most past developments were conditioned by the rise and fall of different types of barriers. To start at the early days, international trade was always facing a natural barrier: the distance barrier. What new electronic technologies brought about was an erosion of this barrier. Distance mattered less and less for traders. This freed an immense potential for trade. Even more so because others were confronted with another type of barrier: lack of appropriate technological tools hindered regulators in their attempts to enforce specific (trade restrictive) rules on e-commerce. This is what Sacha Wunsch-Vincent calls the pristine state of e-commerce. With the advent of more sophisticated new technologies, regulators are now able to intervene. Interestingly, one main motive for enacting specific e-commerce rules is in order to reduce yet another barrier: namely the lack of confidence among market players, which is seen as hindering trade. With more stringent regulation, confidence in e-commerce would improve, which would allow trade to expand further. Nowadays though, technological development may prove more effective than legislators in this respect, and its potential should not in any way be underestimated. New generation firewalls, electronic certificates and fingerprints, secured sites and widespread use of cryptography

* The views expressed in this paper are those of the author, and shall not be attributed to the State Secretariat for Economic Affairs, Berne (SECO).

are devices that help the consumer to deem for himself whether a transaction will or will not be safe enough. Other devices are available on the supplier end (intrusion detection, central access lists, perimeter routers and inspection filters).

Against such a multi-faceted background it is no wonder that so many diverse multilateral and bilateral initiatives on e-commerce have emerged. The inventory made in Sacha Wunsch-Vincent's chapter is impressive indeed. Some e-commerce initiatives contain both pro-liberalisation elements and pro-regulation elements. E-commerce Chapters of PTAs are a case in point in this respect. Whatever the respective merits of trade liberalisation and regulation, the present state of affairs is regrettable at least in one respect, as Sacha Wunsch-Vincent points out. A number of sets of rules are being developed that are often overlapping, uncoordinated and sometimes difficult to reconcile. Looking back, it was perhaps an inevitable course of events. If it is just a transition towards a more coherent trade regime, it may be even a sound development. Testing several approaches is the main way to find optimal solutions. In the meantime, the institutional environment surrounding international e-commerce seems, ironically, in a similar degree of disorganisation as e-commerce markets were in the early days.

But, sooner or later, we will have to go back to basics. And in this case, the basics are to be found in the GATS, namely in the key principle of technological neutrality: in other words, the fact that trade disciplines apply equally whatever the means of a transaction. The fact is that many suppliers do offer their products and services both through traditional means and via electronic means, and which means is used in a particular transaction is more a matter of convenience than anything else. The same can be said regarding consumers. One can go to a bank counter and hand over a paper form to make a transfer. Or one can fill in and send an electronic form from a computer. Ultimately, one has transferred the same amount of the same currency to the same person in the same place at the same time. The difference between the two operations is slight.

Given that for both the suppliers and the consumers electronic and traditional commerce are just two alternative means for selling and buying essentially the same products or services, why should regulators and trade negotiators make a difference and be tempted to devise two sets of rules? To take one example from Sacha Wunsch-Vincent's chapter, why do some PTAs contain e-commerce provisions on prevention of deceptive and fraudulent trade practices or on confidentiality, which are overlapping with the corresponding exceptions applicable to trade in services and in goods (such as Article XIV of the GATS)? Maybe because national regulators showed the way by laying down specific e-commerce rules on essentially the same subject matter as that covered by generally applicable commercial rules?

The question is not only academic. The fact is that, in GATS, commitments undertaken by Members under cross-border modes (of which e-commerce of services is undoubtedly a part) are substantially below the level of the regimes that actually prevail nationally. There are numerous cases of entries in schedules that are unbound, while trade is not only allowed but is also taking place. In comparison, commitments on mode 3 reflect more closely the actual legal regime. One argument for refraining from undertaking new commitments is that it still remains to be seen whether trade through electronic means should or should not be treated like other forms of trade. This may lead the ongoing negotiations into a stalemate. Meanwhile, trade continues to grow and internet-based globalisation is deepening. What might occur is that this growing part of international trade will not be subject to appropriate market access and non-discrimination commitments. Allowing this situation to persist would cause a disservice to the market players and make the WTO less relevant. Turning to the issue of barriers, probably the ongoing confusing debate about concepts is standing as a barrier hampering the development of a stable, predictable and open trade regime. That is one reason why this debate needs to be clarified. Sacha Wunsch points out, among other questions, that of the definition of e-commerce and its relation to trade rules. Probably it should even first be checked whether some questions really still need to be answered. Some may actually have already been answered long ago. Some may not really matter that much for the purpose of undertaking commitments. For example, the question as to whether e-commerce is covered by the concept of trade in services, and is the subject of commitments undertaken, is undoubtedly settled – positively – by the principle of technological neutrality. Nothing within the GATS could suggest another interpretation. Another common debate is whether e-commerce is mode 1 or mode 2, or both. Whatever the technical answer, one should not forget that in the vast majority of sectors States have no restrictive measures on e-commerce in their legislation anyway (in terms of market access or national treatment). Thus whether e-commerce is mode 1 or 2 should not matter since, whatever the answer, a full commitment can be undertaken.

That said, for the sake of ending on a more pragmatic note, it will be recalled that trade in services was able to thrive and expand long before GATS arrived. It is perfectly possible that cross-border e-commerce in services, which is the most invisible of all invisibles, can continue to thrive even in the absence of the stable and predictable environment that GATS commitments are able to provide.

24

How human rights violations nullify and impair GATS commitments

MARION PANIZZON[1]

1. Introduction

Similarly to the United Nations, which considers gross human rights violations a threat to peace, the WTO should regard the effect of certain human rights violations as a restriction on multilateral trade liberalisation. Economic damage done to cross-border services trade by human rights restrictions results in the sending WTO Member no longer benefiting from the negotiated levels of the modal and sectoral commitments under GATS. Human rights violations may have a trade-restrictive effect when service suppliers, including investors, lose trading opportunities abroad. The DSU non-violation nullification and impairment instrument is the tool to redress the devaluation of a tariff reduction or of services market access commitment even in the absence of an outright violation of WTO treaty law. Thus, where a measure restricts human rights to the point that the violation affects and impairs mutually agreed GATS commitments, a non-violation type complaint offers a ground for legal action, not so much because non-WTO law has been violated, but because economic damage has been done. Some WTO Members may justify restricting the human rights of foreign service providers as being legitimate in terms of the security or public order exceptions to services liberalisation provided for in Article XIV GATS. In a twist on traditional human rights and trade doctrine, this chapter argues that protection of human rights is favourable to trade liberalisation.[2] A new perspective on the 'boundaries of

[1] This paper has benefited from the input of Benedict F. Christ, Nicolas Diebold, Henry Gao, Christoph Beat Graber, Martín Molinuevo, Jane Müller, Nicole Pohl and Simon Walker, as well as from style editing by Susan Kaplan. Thanks are due to Gabrielle Marceau for her valuable comments during the World Trade Forum 2006.

[2] GATS Preamble, para. 3. Traditional linkagists would criticise WTO jurisprudence for declaring human rights outside the scope of applicable law and thus for furthering the view that the laws of comparative advantage are irreconcilable with human rights.

the WTO' in relation to human rights[3] necessitates a look at the trade-effects human rights violations may have on the GATS commitments. When a WTO Member receiving services violates the human rights of the foreign service supplier, this may have the effect of nullifying or impairing existing trading opportunities because it offsets the value of the GATS commitment the sending country had relied upon when sending the service supplier abroad. For example, a governmental measure restricting human rights may result in a business-unfriendly climate of repression, terror and instability, preventing exporters and service suppliers from trading abroad and reaping the benefits of multilaterally negotiated trade. When a WTO Member has relied on such benefits in good faith to the point that this Member's legitimate expectation has been frustrated, the human rights violation may provide the grounds for a WTO non-violation nullification and impairment complaint. With the exception of *jus cogens*, which binds countries irrespective of their WTO membership, other human rights violations with trade-preventive effects will be relevant for WTO law once a WTO Panel examines them as questions of fact in a non-violation nullification and impairment complaint.

2. Sources and current status of human rights law in WTO norms

The legal authority of a particular human right depends on the quality of its source. Human rights vested with the authority of *jus cogens* prime those emerging from custom and these, in turn, take precedence over treaty-based human rights protection. These 'relationships of inferiority and superiority' also define the relationship between human rights and other norms of international law, including WTO trade obligations.[4] The question is which human rights have the hierarchical power to take precedence over the trade liberalisation obligations of the WTO Members and what are the effects of the normative hierarchy of human rights over WTO rules?

[3] See José, E. Alvarez, 'The WTO as a Linkage Machine', *American Journal of International Law* 96(1) (2002), p. 158.

[4] Martti Koskenniemi, 'Hierarchy in International Law, A Sketch', *European Journal of International Law* 8(4) (1997), p. 566.

1.1. Jus Cogens *norms*

Jus cogens as defined by Article 53 of the Vienna Convention on the Law of Treaties (VCLT) stands for a category of international legal norms that prevail in all circumstances over all other norms of international law. A norm of *jus cogens* is binding on all States, irrespective of whether or not a State has directly consented to be bound by it.[5] *Jus cogens* can only be violated as a matter of state policy. The content and the limits of *jus cogens* fluctuate and are subject to debate.[6]

Section 702 of the revised (third) Restatement of the American Law Institute lists the following prohibitory norms of international customary law as forming the body of *jus cogens*:[7] the right to life and the prohibition of genocide; the prohibition of slavery or slave trade, murder and causing disappearance of individuals; the prohibition of torture and other inhuman or degrading treatment or punishment; the prohibition of prolonged arbitrary detention; the prohibition of systematic racial discrimination (e.g. apartheid); the prohibition of consistent patterns of gross violations of internationally recognised human rights; and the prohibition of retroactive penal measures. The revised (third) Restatement of the American Law Institute takes a broad view by arguing that all customary human rights are *jus cogens* and that an international agreement violating them would be void.[8]

Under the narrower view, propagated by *Michael Domingues v. United States* (22 October 2002, a decision of the Inter-American Commission on Human Rights), a certain set of human rights play a more central role for the individual, while others are derogable and can thus be trumped by

[5] See Gordon. A. Christenson, 'The World Court and Jus Cogens', *American Journal of International Law* 81(1) (1987) fn. 20 to page 98.

[6] See Theodore Meron, 'On a Hierarchy of International Human Rights', *American Journal of International Law* 80(1) (1986), pp. 11, 15; see also Allain, Jean, 'The *jus cogens* Nature of Non-Refoulement', *International Journal of Refugee Law* 13(4) (2002), pp. 533–558. For example, Theodore Meron proposes counting due process as *jus cogens*, while others declare the right to food fundamental enough to qualify for *jus cogens*. Some, such as Jean Allain find non-refoulement (prohibition against returning refugees to places where their lives and freedoms are endangered) a principle serious enough to fall under *jus cogens*.

[7] See Restatement (Third) of Foreign Relations Law of the United States (Revised) § 702 comment l (1 Tent. Draft No. 6, 1985).

[8] Restatement (Third) of Foreign Relations Law, §102, and reporter's note 6 (1986), citing Report of the Proceedings of the Committee of the Whole, May 21, 1968, UN Doc.A/Conf. 39/11 at 471–472), 'customary international law of human rights are "pre-emptory norms" and an international agreement violating them would be void'; see also Gordon, A. Christenson, 'The World Court and Jus Cogens', *American Journal of International Law* 81(1) (1987), pp. 95–96.

treaty law. *Jus cogens* human rights are such pre-emptory norms, the violation of which is 'considered to shock the conscience of humankind and therefore bind the international community as a whole, irrespective of protest, recognition or acquiescence'.[9]

The *Barcelona Traction* Second Phase judgment[10] defines *jus cogens* with similar criteria: what makes a *jus cogens* human right more fundamental than a custom-based or treaty-founded human right is firstly, the *erga omnes* application of *jus cogens*, secondly, the inextricable link to the human being (subjective factor),[11] and thirdly, *jus cogens* being generally accepted as forming an inherent part of the body of international law (objective factor).[12]

Since *jus cogens* invalidates an inconsistent treaty obligation, it remains disputed to what theory on the content and limit of *jus cogens* WTO treaty law should subscribe.[13] The answer to this question will influence the scope of violation and non-violation-type complaints perhaps available in WTO law for responding to human rights violations.

Violations of *jus cogens* human rights pre-empt violations of other, non-*jus cogens* international obligations, because *jus cogens* stands hierarchically superior to international treaty law (e.g., WTO treaty obligations). Given that a *jus cogens* human right is non-derogable, it will rank higher in the hierarchy than the law of the WTO Agreements and bind all WTO Members. Consequently, WTO Members are responsible for violations of human rights vested with the identity of *jus cogens*, even if the violation was consistent with a GATS rule or necessary to fulfil a GATS-specific commitment.

1.2. Custom informs WTO treaty interpretation

The WTO jurisdiction extends its scope to sources of international law other than the WTO Agreements. According to the statement of the Panel in

9 Inter-American Commission on Human Rights, Report No. 62/02, Merits, Case 12.285, *Michael Domingues v. United States*, 22 October 2002, available at:www.cidh.org/annualrep/2002eng/USA.12285.htm, last accessed 2 November 2006.

10 *Barcelona Traction, Light & Power Co., Ltd. (New Application) (Belgium v. Spain)*, 1970 ICJ Rep. 4 (Second Phase Judgment of 5 February), para. 33.

11 Maurizio Ragazzi, *The Concept of International Obligations Erga Omnes* (Oxford University Press, 2000), p. 1.

12 See Theodore Meron, 'On a Hierarchy of International Human Rights', *American Journal of International Law* 80(1)(1986), p. 10.

13 See, e.g. Georg Schwarzenberger, 'International Jus Cogens?', *Texas Law Review* 43(4) (1965) for a critique of *jus cogens*.

Korea – Government Procurement, non-WTO law, specifically, *jus cogens* and other, non-pre-emptory customs apply to 'WTO treaties' as well as to the 'process of treaty formation'.[14] The *Korea – Government Procurement* Panel failed to explain whether or not (in addition to custom and *jus cogens*) non-WTO treaty law would apply to the interpretation of the WTO Agreements. However, the Appellate Body in *US – Shrimp* confirmed that international treaties other than the WTO Agreements could inform WTO treaty interpretation. This principle of effective treaty interpretation applies most obviously if such treaty law represents evolving international custom.[15] In *EC – Hormones* the Appellate Body established rules of conflict between customary law and the WTO treaties, when it found that emerging custom, such as the precautionary principle, conflicts with (but does not pre-empt) the SPS Agreement.[16] Thus, while it is unclear whether or not custom would trump a conflicting WTO treaty provision, *US – Shrimp* jurisprudence confirmed the *EC – Hormones* decision by implying that WTO treaty law does take precedence over non-WTO agreements failing to express a measure of customary law ('recent acknowledgment by the international community').[17]

The foundation in custom of human rights without the source-quality of *jus cogens* is vanishing, since most States have ratified human rights conventions. However, some human rights are applicable by force of custom. Such customary human rights may thus invalidate reservations by States to certain human rights guarantees.[18]

[14] *Korea – Measures Affecting Government Procurement*, Panel Report of 1 May 2000, WT/DS163/R, para. 7.98.

[15] This is so even where not all the parties to the dispute are parties to such a non-WTO international agreement. In the case of the Convention on Biological Diversity (CBD) called upon by the Appellate Body in *US – Shrimp* to interpret the meaning of Article XX(g) GATT, the US was not a member of the CBD, but the CBD was recognised as expressing a measure of customary international law; see *US – Import Prohibition of Certain Shrimp and Shrimp Products*, Appellate Body Report of 12 October 1998, WT/DS58/AB/R, paras. 168 and fn. 174 to para. 171.

[16] There is WTO jurisprudence on conflicts of customary law with the WTO treaties in the case of *EC – Hormones*, Appellate Body Report, paras. 123–124, where the precautionary principle was found to conflict with (but not to pre-empt) the SPS Agreement; see also Francesco Francionio, 'WTO Law in Context: The Integration of International Human Rights and Environmental Law in the Dispute Settlement Process', in Giorgio Sacerdoti, Alan Yanovich and Jan Bohanes (eds.), *The WTO at Ten* (Cambridge University Press, 2006), p. 149.

[17] *US – Import Prohibition of Certain Shrimp and Shrimp Products*, Appellate Body Report of 12 October 1998, WT/DS58/AB/R, para. 131,

[18] See Walter Kälin and Jörg Künzli, *Universeller Menschenrechtsschutz* (Basel: Helbing und Lichtenhahn, 2005), pp. 74–75.

Under the approach proposed by Pauwelyn, custom forms part of WTO applicable law. Thus, even if they do not form part of WTO jurisdiction, customary human rights may be applied to the examination of WTO claims,[19] and may inform GATS commitments, to the extent that Members are bound to respect the human rights of foreign service suppliers.[20]

To others, Article 3.2 DSU is clearly opposed to applying non-WTO rules to situations falling under the scope of WTO law, unless there is an express clause of *renvoi* in a WTO covered agreement.[21] However, this chapter agrees with Pauwelyn, Garcia-Rubio and many others that customary international law, including human rights, may be applied by the WTO judiciary in a case before the WTO dispute settlement body, even if the human rights do not fall under WTO jurisdiction.

1.3. Defensive human rights protection in WTO law and scholarship

Protecting human rights, as the classic trade and human rights scholar would say, comes at the cost of losing a comparative advantage, which trade liberalisation confers upon those countries that hold the costs of production or service delivery low by employing children, allowing forced labour or restricting the freedom of association of workers.

However, comparative advantage is not the only principle guiding WTO law. The fact that a WTO Member receiving foreign service suppliers violates human rights could diminish the chances of good faith negotiations succeeding in progressively submitting more service sectors to the multilateral disciplines. Thus, human rights violations impact negatively on the goals of the GATS Preamble, namely that services are being liberalised to achieve 'expansion of trade under conditions of transparency and progressive liberalization'.[22] If it can be shown that restrictions on human rights either impair the transparency principle of GATS commitments or impede progressive liberalisation, given that routine violations of human rights depress the climate for negotiating the elimination of barriers to services trade, the violation of human rights impairs at minimum the goals of the GATS Preamble.

[19] Joost Pauwelyn, *Conflict of Norms in Public International Law* (Cambridge University Press, 2003), p. 477.

[20] Mariano Garcia-Rubio, *On the Application of Customary Rules of State Responsibilty by the WTO Dispute Settlement Organs, A General International Law Perspective* (Geneva: Graduate Institute of International Studies, 2001), pp. 84–85.

[21] *Ibid.*, p. 83. [22] GATS Preamble, para. 2.

The principle of comparative advantage does not oppose trading in goods and services produced at the expense of human rights. Thus, the liberal trade and human rights scholars argue, free trade discourages protection of human rights. Given that the concept of likeness which functions as the backbone of the WTO principle of non-discrimination fails to take into account the process and methods of service delivery, two services may be considered 'like', but the assessment of likeness fails to take into account that the cheaper of the two services may have reduced costs because the workers have poor pay and working conditions and have been denied the opportunity to organise themselves to bargain for better conditions. The only way to protect human rights and other non-trade values,[23] is for a WTO Member to impose an import restriction and to invoke the general exception of GATT Article XX or GATS Article XIV in order to justify the barrier to trade.[24] Thus, under the classic liberal view, trade and human rights scholars consider human rights, even if not explicitly protected in WTO rules, as being implied in the substantive law of GATT Article XX and GATS Article XIV exceptions. They form part of the WTO applicable law, which the judiciary must take into account when interpreting,[25] but do not fall under the jurisdiction of the WTO.[26]

[23] The term 'non-trade' values is based in scholarship. Possibly, Joel Trachtman first used it in his article on 'Trade and ... Problems, Cost-Benefit Analysis and Subsidiarity', *European Journal of International Law* 9(1) (1998), pp. 32–85. WTO jurisprudence has addressed the protection of human, animal or plant life and health, the conservation of biological or cultural diversity and environmental sustainability and the protection of labour standards and human rights, but it has referred to these non-trade values as exceptions to the principles of free trade. The term is probably borrowed from 'non-trade' concerns which paragraph 5 of the Preamble to the WTO Agreement on Agriculture (AoA) uses to list, non-exclusively, the concerns other than trade liberalisation that the AoA should take into account: they include food security, environmental protection and special and differential treatment.

[24] Thus, governments may protect human rights at the expense of free trade; however, the restriction must be justified under the general exceptions of GATT (Article XX) or GATS (Article XIV). Thus, quantitative import restrictions or the imposition of new tariffs seeking to prevent services delivered in violation of human rights, even though inconsistent with the non-discrimination obligations of GATT or GATS, may be justified, if the restrictive measure is not imposed in a discriminatory or protectionist manner.

[25] See Gabrielle Marceau, 'The WTO Dispute Settlement and Human Rights', in Frederick M. Abbott, Christine Breining-Kaufmann and Thomas Cottier (eds.), *International Trade and Human Rights, Foundations and Conceptual Issues*, World Trade Forum, Volume 5 (Ann Arbor, Mich.: The University of Michigan Press, 2006), p. 201, who speaks of the use of the Article XX GATT exception as 'import restrictions imposed for human rights considerations'.

[26] See Pauwelyn, 2003, p. 477.

While human rights have often been perceived as exceptions to the principles of trade liberalisation, a novel view would suggest linking human rights violations to an impairment of the volume of trade between WTO Member countries. As long as human rights are viewed as exceptions to the principles of comparative advantage and multilateral liberalisation, it will be difficult to reconcile them with WTO law, because the trading system encourages lower production and delivery costs of goods and services and tolerates this price differentiation based upon the violation of human rights. However, from the protagonistic perspective proposed here, human rights should no longer be implied in exceptions to trading rules, but rather enabled to become promoters of free trade, because only human rights-compliant trade induces economic growth and raises standards of living.

Human rights could be relevant to all modes of services supply. For instance, under mode 4, a global news agency (like CNN or the BBC) of a WTO Member is entitled under the GATS commitments of a receiving WTO Member to research and to broadcast from that Member's territory to that Member's audience. If the human rights situation abroad renders it too dangerous and costly for either a self-employed journalist or for a media company, such as the BBC or CNN, to send its journalists abroad to provide that news service, the sending country will not have made use of the GATS market access commitments the receiving country had offered in mode 4. Thus, an economic operator faced with human rights violations in the receiving country will shift, for example, from supplying services through temporary movement of natural persons abroad (mode 4) to cross-border supply (mode 1) as in online research, video-conferencing for journalists, electronic banking, tele-education (e-learning) and tele-medicine, thus circumventing the need for the experts themselves to move abroad and risk their life or health or face serious impediments to the exercise of their profession. The consequence of shifting the mode of service supply is that the horizontal commitment to mode 4 is voided (since the service – due to human rights violations – is being supplied through mode 1 instead). This example demonstrates how violations of human rights law may constitute at the same time a violation of WTO obligations, thereby falling under the scope of GATS.

How human rights violations affect services delivery in mode 2 may be illustrated by the example of a health tourist who moves to another WTO Member for treatment. During this patient's stay abroad, his or her organs or tissues are used for medical experiments in the receiving

WTO Member and his or her personal data is disseminated for non-health treatment related reasons. Thus, his or her human right to personal integrity is being violated by the service-supplying country and this may lead the sending country to prohibit its citizens from seeking health treatment abroad, even if protectionist reasoning may also play a part. Another consequence of the human rights violations may be that the sending Member files a case for violation of human rights against the receiving Member. Such a legal action sheds a negative light on the receiving Member's health services, leading fewer health tourists to take advantage of the liberalised health services market.

Human rights violations are not usually GATS relevant. For instance, a government's restricted practice for the registration of NGOs falls outside the scope of GATS law, since it may be difficult to qualify NGO activity as a service. Also, when only nationals are the targets of human rights violations, the cross-border element, necessary for establishing a WTO and human rights case, is lacking.[27] However, those human rights violations exhibiting a sufficient relation to cross-border services trade, for instance by putting at risk the fulfilment of GATS commitments, as will be shown in the following sections, should be prosecuted with the multilateral rules for trade in services.

3. Offensive human rights protection in GATS law

1. Violation-type complaints

Some human rights violations are so remotely connected to trade that they will have no impact on the economic relations between two WTO Members. However, there may be instances where the human rights violation goes hand in hand with economic damage. Such human rights violations may directly lead to a decrease in volumes of services exported or may cancel out specific commitments within a certain mode of services supply.

By a violation complaint, the complainant claims that the respondent has violated a norm of the WTO covered agreement, which in the terms

[27] See Elizabeth, C. Economy, 'China's Environmental Movement', Testimony before the Congressional Executive Commission on China Roundtable on Environmental NGOs in China: Encouraging Action and Addressing Public Grievances, 7 February 2005, Rayburn House Office Building, Washington, DC, reprinted in: Council on Foreign Relations, Testimony, available at: www.cfr.org/publication.html?id=7770, last accessed 30 August 2006.

of Article XXIII:1(a) GATT 1994 translates as the respondent having 'failed to carry out its obligations' under any of the WTO covered agreements. To facilitate the use of redress for violations of the WTO covered agreements, Article 3.8 DSU establishes a legal presumption of nullification and impairment (only for violation-type complaints), if the complainant can show the respondent has violated a norm of WTO law (prima facie). The reversed burden of proof renders the presumption that there has been an impact on trade rebuttable. However, to date no case has been recorded in which the respondent was successful. If rebuttal fails, the respondent will try to show that its alleged non-compliance with the measure in question is justified under the general exceptions clause of the GATT or GATS.[28] Thus, according to Panel practice, the demonstration of an inconsistency with any of the WTO covered agreements quasi-automatically establishes the quasi-irrefutable presumption that the violation has had a negative impact on trade.[29]

Unless the respondent can claim otherwise, a legal inconsistency with a WTO-covered agreement results in a nullification or impairment of a benefit accruing to the complainant under these agreements and the complainant's claim will be successful.[30]

1.1. Human rights with *jus cogens* status

This section firstly explains why violations of human rights with *jus cogens* status form the basis of a violation-type complaint under GATS Article XXIII paragraph 1 in combination with the DSU, and thus fall within the jurisdiction of the GATS, even though the GATS does not explicitly require the WTO Members to recognise human rights.[31]

[28] See Veijo Heiskanen, 'The Regulatory Philosophy of International Trade Law', *Journal of World Trade* 38(1) (2004), p. 20.

[29] See WTO Secretariat, Legal Affairs Division and Appellate Body, *A Handbook on the WTO Dispute Settlement System* (Cambridge University Press, 2004), p. 32.

[30] See WTO Secretariat, 2004, pp. 30–31.

[31] See Robert Howse and Makau Mutua, 'Protecting Human Rights in a Global Economy: Challenges for the World Trade Organization', International Center for Human Rights and Democratic Development, Policy Paper, 2002, who argue that routine violations of human rights are inconsistent with adherence to and execution of WTO treaty obligations, since complying with WTO treaty law in good faith would conflict with systematically violating human rights; contra Gabrielle Marceau, 'WTO Dispute Settlement and Human Rights', *European Journal of International Law* 13(4) (2002), p. 814, who finds the view of Howse and Matua that 'violators of human rights should automatically be considered violators of WTO law' is giving too broad a scope of application to human rights in the WTO and that human rights only enter WTO rules for their interpretation

Secondly, the section will show that there are certain selective human rights-like obligations in the GATS treaty text (Articles III and VI), which may also provide the grounds for a violation-type complaint. Such individual rights-like norms guaranteeing due process rights of natural persons are the only human rights-related norms stated in the GATS text.

1.1.1. Receiving country's violations of *jus cogens* and impact on mode 4 Violations of (*jus cogens*) human rights vis-à-vis journalists may have an adverse effect upon the provision of services through mode 4. An example is the impact of Nepal's violation of journalists' human rights on the supply of print media services. In Nepal, which has been a WTO Member since 23 April 2004,[32] a civil war-type situation has led to human rights abuses, including death of and threats to the security of domestic and foreign journalists.[33]

Both Nepal's official government and the Maoist groups are responsible for committing such *jus cogens* violations.[34] While most violations are directed against Nepalese journalists, disappearances, illegal detention, torture and summary killings have targeted foreign-based journalists as well.[35] Journalism is a services sector operating through mode 4 and thus relies on the movement of natural persons. Suppliers of the print media services may be deterred from exercising their profession (from) abroad if there are (too many) human rights violations occuring, especially if they reach the degree of *jus cogens* violations, such as death or health threats. However, the situation of foreign journalists may only be analysed under the GATS to the extent that the GATS is applicable, which firstly requires a cross-border component. Secondly, the violating country would need to have made a specific or horizontal commitment on the services which it is impeding by restricting

or for factual determination: while WTO Members are liable for violations of non-WTO international law, such violations cannot form the ground for actions under WTO dispute settlement, since 'WTO adjudicating bodies cannot formally interpret other treaties and customs and thus cannot apply or enforce other treaties or customs or determine the legal consequences of rights and obligations that WTO Members may have under other treaties or by custom'.

[32] See WTO, 'Nepal and the WTO', www.wto.org/english/thewto_e/countries_e/nepal_e.htm

[33] See US Department of State, 'Nepal, Country Reports on Human Rights Practices', Released by the Bureau of Democracy, Human Rights, and Labor, 8 March 2006, www.state.gov/g/drl/rls/hrrpt/2005/61709.htm

[34] Human Rights News, 'Nepal: Human Rights Concerns for the 61st Session of the UN Commission on Human Rights', http://hrw.org/english/docs/2005/03/10/nepal10297.htm

[35] US Department of State, Nepal, 2006.

the human rights of the service supplier, i.e. the journalists. If no respective commitment is made, the GATS would remain entirely inapplicable and the State concerned would have to resort to diplomatic protection under the general principles of public international law.

But even if Nepal had made commitments on foreign news media, GATS would apply only to foreign journalists in Nepal and of those only to those service suppliers offering their news services to Nepalese people. Foreign journalists operating abroad in civil war zones, but providing news services exclusively to their audiences at home, would not fall under GATS mode 4 because they are not engaged in cross-border supply of news services.

However, if a foreign journalist is working for a news agency licensed to broadcast to the population of the receiving country, the reporting activity of the foreign journalist will fall under GATS mode 4, for which reason news reporting can be an example of a profession whose members are exposed to human rights violations when supplying services in a foreign country.

While journalists abroad are often faced with restrictions on their freedom of movement or freedom of expression, violations of these freedoms do not qualify as *jus cogens*, even if they are applied to the point of preventing the reasonable exercise of journalism. Against such restrictions no legal action could be taken under GATS/WTO violation-type complaints, but they could be addressed, as discussed below, with a WTO non-violation type complaint, if all other conditions (such as the existence of a mode 4 commitment for news services, etc.) were fulfilled.[36]

1.1.2. Violations of *jus cogens* and impact on Mode 3 Pursuant to a Presidential Decree on Land Acquisition (36/2005 amended in 2006) the Indonesian government violated the human right of protection against threats to health by forcibly evicting Indonesian citizens from their land in order to offer prime investment locations to foreign investors.[37]

[36] 'Building Union Capacity for Human Rights and Conflict Reporting', IFJ-FES Workshop Friedrich Ebert Stiftung background paper, available at: www.fesnepal.org, last accessed 9 August 2006.

[37] Fernando Cabrera, 'Human Rights Watch Warns Indonesia and Foreign Investors on Forced Evictions', Human Rights Watch's report 'Condemned Communities: Forced Evictions in Jakarta', available at: http://hrw.org/reports/2006/indonesia0906/, claims that Indonesia was expropriating and seizing land under 'excessive use of force – including beatings and destruction of homes and possessions' to prepare the land for 'major infrastructure projects' for attracting more foreign investment to the country. The Decree was issued after Indonesia had held an Infrastructure Summit with foreign investors in 2005 where it had pledged to to sort out unresolved land disputes in order to renew its effort to attract foreign investment which had often been stalled by such disputes.

Indonesia has undertaken commitments in GATS mode 3 for tourism and opened its market to '3, 4 or 5 starred hotels' in the 'eastern part of Indonesia, Kalimantan, Bengklu, Jambi and Sulawesi with capital share owned by 100% foreign investor'.[38] The commercial presence in Indonesia of foreign hotel chains will rely on land conflicts being resolved and a certain infrastructure being available to the foreign investor.

To fulfil its GATS commitments Indonesia may have committed human rights violations by evicting indigenous people. While the Indonesian government could have lawfully bought the land from the population, instead it chose to use force because the government wanted to make a profit by generating revenue out of its international obligations. If those human rights violations amount to *jus cogens* violations, Indonesia could be held accountable for them before the WTO DSU, as long as it can be shown that the restriction of human rights (prohibition against physical threat, prohibition of killings, etc.) has a causal link to the fulfilment of Indonesia's GATS commitment with respect to opening certain provinces to commercial presence in the tourism sector.

If it were shown that Indonesia's conduct failed to respect *jus cogens* human rights, its GATS commitments would be rendered void as regards both Indonesia and all other WTO Members. A new question for the WTO would be whether in such a situation the international community could bring a claim of responsibility vis-à-vis the WTO asking it to declare Indonesia's GATS commitments invalid or, a fortiori, rescind Indonesia's WTO Membership.

Another question would be whether, in such a case, any WTO Member could have the legal standing to bring a case against Indonesia before the WTO DSU. Such a case would be based on the fact that even if Indonesia did not infringe any express provision of WTO law, its conduct nevertheless amounts to a cross-border trade issue, firstly, because the violations having the degree of seriousness to fall under the scope of *jus cogens* are equivalent to violations of WTO law for the WTO DSU. Secondly, the WTO DSU must be the tribunal empowered to take legal action against Indonesia, because the *jus cogens* violations would have a link to trade insofar as it could be shown that Indonesia had restricted human rights – even those of its own nationals (as opposed to foreign service providers) – in order to avoid a conflict with its specific commitments under GATS.

[38] See GATS, Indonesia Schedule of Specific Commitments, WTO Document GATS/SC/43 of 15 April 1994, p. 27.

1.2. Due process 'rights' of GATS domestic regulation

International human rights protection typically admonishes States for violating the rights of individuals, including, for instance, restrictions on freedom of commerce. However, there are exceptions in WTO law, where certain covered agreements set up obligations that directly affect the individual. Because these obligations do not go so far as to protect the individual against the State, this chapter terms them 'individual rights-like' norms. Pertinent examples are the protection of intellectual property rights as private rights in Part II of the TRIPS Agreement and the obligations on WTO Members to install 'reasonable procedures for the acquisition of intellectual property rights' in Article 62 TRIPS. GATS includes the obligation for WTO Members to establish, vis-à-vis the natural or juridical person moving abroad to deliver services, judicial protection in matters relating to the domestic regulation of services pursuant to Article VI GATS.[39]

In summary, the consequence of the WTO covered agreements being a non-human rights treaty is that natural and juridical persons, even as services providers, are with few exceptions – such as the right to judicial review of work authorisation – excluded from the scope of WTO jurisdiction.

Where the GATS imposes limitations on government conduct, such as the transparency and domestic regulation requirements under Articles III and VI, with a view to improving the situation of the individual citizens vis-à-vis their government, the GATS has intervened in the relationship between the State and its nationals. The rule is that WTO/GATS obligations bind governments vis-à-vis other governments and not vis-à-vis individuals.[40] In Articles III and VI, the GATS limits the government's exercise of power over individuals; however, individuals will not have the legal standing to claim their rights. Therefore, these obligations remain due process requirements for the WTO Member, as opposed to obligations with direct effect. However, since their subject matter affects the individual, by improving the due process standards a country provides to its citizens, such due process minimal

[39] See Thomas Cottier, 'Governance, Trade and Human Rights', in Frederick M. Abbott, Christine Breining-Kaufmann and Thomas Cottier (eds.), *International Trade and Human Rights, Foundations and Conceptual Issues*, World Trade Forum, Volume 5 (Ann Arbor, Mich.: The University of Michigan Press, 2006), p. 103.

[40] See Article I para. 1 GATS: 'This Agreement applies to measures by Members affecting trade in services'; and Article I para. 2 (a–d) defines trade in services as being the cross-border supply of services between Members, through four different modes of supply.

standards, as expressed in Articles III and VI, can be described as individual 'rights-like' norms.

This section discusses the case of individual rights-like norms of GATS, where the 'failure of another Member to carry out its GATS obligations'[41] amounts to that Member violating either of GATS' two individual rights-like norms (Article III transparency or Article VI domestic regulation). In comparison to the *jus cogens* human rights violations described above, it is the violation of a GATS provision with an individual-rights impact, which engages WTO Members' responsibility, and not a non-WTO norm. The ground for the complaint is the positive treaty obligation, namely of Article VI or Article III GATS.

Articles VI and III call upon governments to comply with certain minimum standards vis-à-vis foreign service suppliers. Article VI imposes minimum requirements of due process on the domestic laws relating to the cross-border services trade.

While the transparency requirement in Article III GATS applies to all horizontal (modal) and sectoral commitments, the requirements for domestic regulation, including an objective and impartial judicial and administrative system, are only applicable to sectors in which WTO Members have undertaken specific commitments.[42]

Article VI posits the exceptions to the regulatory discretion of governments by imposing certain standardised rules of governmental conduct applicable to sectors in which WTO Members have undertaken specific commitments.

Such due process requirements of Articles III and VI GATS act as individual rights-like norms in Articles III and VI GATS and include firstly, a government's obligation to install enquiry points, secondly, its obligation to inform an applicant for work permits of the status of his/her application, thirdly, to provide for independent, impartial and objective judicial, arbitral or administrative tribunals and procedures, fourthly, to offer the possibility for review, and fifthly, to provide remedies for administrative decisions affecting trade in services.

Switzerland's horizontal commitment in mode 4 is conditioned on the foreign service provider obtaining authorisation in the form of both a residency and work permit from the Swiss government.[43] Pursuant to

[41] Cf. GATT Article XXIII:1(a). [42] See Article VI GATS, para. 1.

[43] See Switzerland – Schedule of Specific Commitments, Appendix 5 to Annex VIII, Horizontal Commitments, p. 3f., available at: http://secretariat.efta.int/Web/ExternalRelations/PartnerCountries/CL/CL_RUAP/annexes/CL_FTA_Annex_VIII_Appendix_V.pdf#search=%22specific%20commitments%20Switzerland%20%22, last accessed 24 August 2006.

Article VI GATS, Switzerland would have to take decisions on the authorisation of foreign service providers promptly, as well as providing information, without undue delay, on the status of the authorisation to the foreign service provider applying for a permit of stay and a work permit in Switzerland pursuant to Article VI:3 GATS. In addition, the Swiss government would have to ensure, under Article VI:2(a) GATS, that a judiciary, arbitral or administrative review of decisions on authorisation is possible. If Switzerland denies an authorisation to work to a foreign service provider and fails to provide for a review proceeding, the sending WTO Member could claim before the WTO DSU that Switzerland has violated Article VI GATS.

An example of a lack of transparent authorisation requirements and the failure to provide for the review of denied authorisations under Article VI GATS relates to the wording of China's market access commitments for education services. In addition to the right of foreign-majority owned schools to establish a commercial presence under mode 3, China also opens its education services to natural persons under mode 4, to so-called 'foreign individual education(s) service suppliers'. Unlike the Swiss horizontal commitments under mode 4, where an authorisation is required for any foreign natural person providing any type of service on Swiss territory, no such horizontal limitation on market access commitments exists in China. Instead, the threshold for the foreign professor or teacher is that he or she be 'invited' or 'employed' by a Chinese school(s) or educational institution.[44] The question is how transparent such invitations are and what the conditions are for receiving employment contracts. In the author's view, the invitation and employment requirement of China fails to fulfil the requirements of Article VI GATS relating to 'permits of stay' and 'work authorisation'.

The Chinese education services market is limited to those foreign teachers, professors and other education professionals who have been invited or employed by a Chinese institution. Such a restriction on a market access commitment may be a way to circumvent the due process requirements of GATS Article VI.

There is usually no possibility for a judicial, administrative or arbitral review for those who have been refused an invitation to teach at a

[44] See 'People's Republic of China, Schedule of Specfic Commitments on Services List of Article II MFN Exemptions', p. 28, in *WTO, Protocol on the Accession of China*, Doha, 10 November 2001, Volume 1 (Cambridge University Press, 2003), p. 922.

university or to be employed by a firm. The process of invitation is fraught with subjectivity, partiality and delay. It may also entail bribery and the renunciation by the foreign service supplier of certain of his or her human rights (such as freedom of expression or freedom of association). As such, an 'invitation' stands in contrast to an 'authorisation' as defined by GATS. Thus, in the view of this author, China's GATS mode 4-specific commitment on education services – that is, the limitation of market access to 'invited' and 'employed' foreign professors and teachers – is a violation of the GATS Article VI requirement for an objective, impartial and prompt authorisation process and review of such results.

The WTO Member whose service suppliers are moving abroad may claim under the WTO DSU that the receiving WTO Member is violating individual rights-like norms (Articles III or VI GATS). However, the GATS does not make any provision for a natural person who has been denied authorisation to supply the service to have the application submitted to review. Articles III and VI GATS nevertheless set up institutions and procedures for the protection of the individual as a service provider. Domestic regulation and transparency requirements form the basis for such individual rights-like norms in GATS, listed below, and their violation forms the basis of a violation-type complaint.

- To install judicial, arbitral or administrative tribunals for the review of administrative decisions affecting trade in services (Article VI para. 2(a) first sentence).
- Tribunals are to review administrative decisions affecting trade in services promptly (Article VI para. 2(a) first sentence).
- If the same agency taking the decision is also in charge of reviewing the decision, the review shall be objective and impartial (Article VI para. 2(a) second sentence).
- To inform the service provider applying for an authorisation to supply the service within a reasonable time:
  - of the decision concerning the application (Article VI para. 3 first sentence);
  - at the request of the applicant and without undue delay, of the status of the application (Article VI para. 3 second sentence).
- To provide adequate procedures for verifying the competence of professionals of another WTO Member (Article VI para. 6).
- To establish enquiry points (Article III, para. 4); but it is questioned in the present paper whether natural persons also have the right to gain

access to and be informed by the enquiry points, or whether this right is reserved to government officials of the other WTO Member).

Articles III and VI GATS are the only human rights-like provisions expressly codified under positive GATS/WTO treaty law. They do not codify human rights, since the individual service provider is not granted standing under WTO law. However, both the *jus cogens* violations of human rights and the violations of GATS human rights-like norms of Articles III and VI fall under GATS jurisdiction as questions of law and therefore form the basis of a GATS violation-type complaint.

2. *Non-violation type complaints*

The WTO Dispute Settlement Understanding has a tool for sanctioning measures or actions taken by its Members, which do not amount to a violation of WTO treaty law, including the GATS, but reduce the level of negotiated trade liberalisation when such non-violation frustrates the legitimate expectations of another WTO Member. This so-called non-violation type complaint codified under Article 26 DSU and Article XXIII para. 3 for GATS is especially useful for resolving conflicts in trade-related areas.[45]

2.1. Customary human rights

The failure to respect non-*jus cogens*, customary, human rights will not be considered as an issue of law under the WTO.[46] Where the violation of a human right is relevant enough to damage services trade, but falls short of constituting a *jus cogens* violation, the non-violation type complaint provides the procedural tool with which to sanction a WTO Member. A WTO Member affected by the human rights violations of another Member would claim that the value of the negotiated level of market access in a services sector had been nullified and impaired by the violation because it had been relying on this trade benefit. The burden of proof on the defendant is relatively high, since a WTO Member must show that its economic operators had been relying on outsourcing their services by moving natural persons abroad. Natural persons are now refusing to take

[45] Kyle Bagwell, Petros, C. Mavroidis and Robert. W. Staiger, 'It's a Question of Market Access', in *American Journal of International Law* 96 (2002), p. 74.

[46] There is no 'a priori hierarchy' of custom over treaty law, with the exception of the priority of *jus cogens* over treaty law, as described above.

advantage of a liberalised mode 3 or mode 4 commitment, because the non-*jus cogens* human rights violations pose too high a risk for either the natural or juridical person to supply such a service abroad.

2.2. The example of filtering Internet search engines

Restrictions on free speech by Internet filtering in China, Bahrain, Burma, Iran, Saudi Arabia, Singapore, Tunisia, Vietnam and Yemen provide an example of GATS-relevant human rights violations.[47] Even if China had agreed to undertake a radical reform of its services industry when it became a WTO Member on 11 December 2001, it still is among the world's more active Internet services filterers.[48]

The Internet filtering case that received the most attention from the media occured in January 2006, when the Chinese Government required foreign Internet search engines and blog sites to filter undesirable content.[49] While at first glance, such a restriction does not seem to fall within the scope of services liberalisation under the GATS and the relationship between free services trade and human rights is far less obvious, on closer consideration one realises that Internet filtering relates to human rights and impacts on trade.

In the example of China, regulations such as the Telecommunications Regulations of the People's Republic of China or the Measures for Managing the Internet Information Services curb the human right to free speech of the domestic and foreign Internet service providers.[50]

[47] Bahrain, Burma, Iran, Saudi Arabia, Singapore, Tunisia, Vietnam and Yemen are countries that have engaged in Internet filtering since 2004; see OpenNet Initiative,Case Studies, available at: www.opennetinitiative.net/modules.php?op=modload&name=Archive &file=index&req=viewarticle&artid=1, last accessed 25 August 2006.

[48] See WTO website, 'China and the WTO', available at: www.wto.org/English/thewto_e/countries_e/china_e.htm, last accessed 25 October, 2006.

[49] See, among others, BBC News, 'Google Censors Itself for China', 25 February 2006, available at: http://news.bbc.co.uk/2/hi/technology/4645596.stm, last accessed 25 October 2006; see also Jack Goldsmith and Tim Wu, *Who Controls the Internet: Illusions of a Borderless World* (Oxford University Press, 2006); see also Tim Wu, 'The World Trade Law of Internet Filtering' (May 3, 2006), available at SSRN: http://ssrn.com/abstract=882459, last accessed 25 October 2006, p. 1.

[50] 'Freedom of Expression and the Internet in China, A Human Rights Watch Backgrounder', Human Rights News, available at: www.hrw.org/backgrounder/asia/china-bck-0701.htm; last accessed 9 August 2006, Article 57 of the Telecommunications Regulations states that 'No organization or individual may use telecommunications networks to make, duplicate, issue, or disseminate information containing the following: … (2) Material that jeopardizes national security, reveals state secrets, subverts state power, or undermines national unity; … (6) Material that spreads rumours, disturbs social order, or undermines social stability; …

While it is China's sovereign right to restrict free speech, the potential effects of this piece of legislation on China's GATS commitments vis-à-vis its trading partners may be inconsistent with its membership of the WTO, because the economic damage caused could be in violation of GATS/WTO law. For a non-violation complaint against China under the GATS to be successful before the WTO judiciary, the trading partner would have to show that the Telecommunications Regulation and the Measures for Managing the Internet have led to a decline in the foreign direct investment in telecommunications and related services or to foreign Internet operators moving out of China. While there is no need to invoke a provision of the GATS prohibiting human rights violations, one must nevertheless demonstrate that China has made specific commitments under the GATS in the telecommunications sector, upon which the trading partner has relied. China would then be held accountable not for violating the human rights of foreign service suppliers per se, but for having violated GATS law by frustrating the legitimate expectations of its trading partners in the assurances of a free market it had given to foreign service suppliers in its GATS commitments.

Using the much publicised example of google.cn, the author will demonstrate how human rights violations may conflict with the supply of services and how the negative effect on the services economy can be eliminated via the WTO's non-violation-type complaint.

When google.cn, the US Internet search engine provider, was threatened with closure of the services it provided in China, unless it self-restricted the content its search machine offered, the filtering of the search engine's content could have formed the basis of a non-violation complaint under the WTO/GATS.[51] Even though google.cn has cooperated with the Chinese government,[52] it is argued here that the

(7) Material that spreads obscenities, pornography, gambling, violence, murder, terror, or instigates crime.' In addition, the Measures for Managing the Internet Information Services make service providers responsible for the content they display. Article 14 says that the service providers must record their subscribers' access to the Internet, their account numbers, the Web addresses they call up as well as the telephone numbers they use, and store this information for sixty days.

[51] See BBC News of 25 January 2006, 'Google Censors Itself for China'; interestingly, BBC News Online, which reported the story, among others, is also unavailable in China; see http://news.bbc.co.uk/1/hi/technology/4645596.stm, last accessed 25 August 2006.

[52] Many NGOs and the US Congressional Human Rights Caucus, have criticised google.com, yahoo and Microsoft which had agreed to self-censor their content and have thus cooperated with the Chinese Government to maintain restrictions on freedom of expression and information; see, e.g., remarks by Congressman Tom Lantos Co-Chairman, Congressional Human Rights Caucus, Caucus Members' Briefing,

restriction on freedom of expression and the threat of closure has had a negative impact on the depth and reach of foreign Internet search engines providing services in China.

China has undertaken GATS commitments in mode 1 on data-processing services, including their provision by the Internet.[53] Through mode 3, it has also liberalised value-added telecommunications services, but is unclear on the amount of foreign ownerhsip it allows for commercial presence in this sector.[54]

In its defence China could firstly state that it is up to the foreign Internet service provider wishing to take advantage of China's market access commitments to comply with national legislation on this issue.[55] Thus, google.cn would have to accept that China limits the content of its search services.

However, many human rights, including free speech have the validity of customary international law and are thus no longer a matter of national law, but have the authority of an international legal obligation binding upon China.

Also, the minimum requirements imposed upon domestic regulation under Article VI GATS may imply the prohibition of violations of human rights relating to the authorisation, technical standards and licencing requirements for foreign service providers.

One could argue that China has made a GATS commitment to open its market to foreign Internet service providers and that blocking certain content will have the effect of nullifying and impairing the value of that commitment to its trading partners and thus upset the level of concessions. Perhaps, in addititon to a claim of non-violation, a claim of violation would also be possible. It would be up to China to justify, for example by resorting to the GATS exception

Human Rights and the Internet – The People's Republic of China, stating: 'These massively successful high-tech companies which couldn't bring themselves to send their representatives to this meeting today, should be ashamed. With all their power and influence, wealth and high visibility, they neglected to commit to the kind of positive action that human rights activists in China take every day', available at: http://lantos.house.gov/HoR/CA12/Human+Rights+Caucus/Briefing+Testimonies/02-01-05+Opening+Remarks+for+Rep+Lantos+China+Google+Hearing.htm, last accessed 25 August 2006; see also Human Rights Watch, www.hrw.org/english/docs/2006/08/09/china13940.htm; Reporters sans frontières, www.rsf.org/article.php3?id_article=16262, last accessed 25 August 2006.

[53] Wu, 2006, pp. 23–28.

[54] *Ibid.*, p. 29 says that the CPC classification of Telecommunication services provides more of a sample than an exhaustive list of Internet services.

[55] *Ibid.*, 2006, pp. 23–28.

of Article XIV, its restriction on cross-border trade in services, which it operationalises through a restriction on free speech (Internet filtering).

To assess the economic damage it is necessary to examine the degree to which foreign Internet service providers, including google.cn were deterred by the restrictions on google.cn from delivering services to China and thus prevented from benefiting from China's market access commitments in mode 1 or mode 3.

In addition to having to demonstrate an impact on trade (there is no presumption of an impact on trade in non-violation complaints, unlike in violation-type cases), the defendant will have to show that it had relied on the benefit of trade liberalisation and that its legitimate expectations as to that benefit have been frustrated. Thus, the defending WTO Member will have to show both economic damage and a detrimental reliance.

Since it is the effect of the human rights violation which forms the grounds of a non-violation type complaint it is a non-legal, factual issue which causes the nullification and impairment of the benefits of trade. Therefore, the WTO Panel will consider the effect of a human right violation as a question of fact.

However, in the google.cn case, Google had chosen to self-censor its contents in order to avoid having to pull out of China altogether. Thus, while in the google.cn case the economic damage was slight, because Google could continue to operate in China with little loss due to censoring of searches (e.g. Tiananmen, Tibet, Falun Gong and other free churches cannot be found on google.cn), the human rights violations persisted.

Were China to justify its filtering and blocking of foreign Internet search services with the GATS general exception in Article XIV, it would argue that WTO Members are allowed to impose restrictions on their market access commitments for reasons of 'protection of public morals' or 'maintenance of public order' under paragraph (a) or it would find that the foreign Internet service provider compromises 'safety' under paragraph (c)(iii) Article XIV. However, it is questionable whether China can justify, under GATS Article XIV, a restriction of human rights. It is also questionable whether it is legitimate under WTO law for China to restrict google.cn's free speech by engaging in filtering practices in order to establish public order and safety, which it claims are at risk if its citizens are able to do research on Tiananmen, Falun Gong, Tibet etc. However, as Tim Wu writes, 'while WTO law leaves much room for exceptions, some of China's restrictions may not be easily justifiable under the GATS'.[56]

Since WTO law implicitly subscribes to the UN Charter and the protection of human rights included therein, it should not allow its exceptions to be used to violate such rights. Moreover, footnote 5 to Article XIV expressly prevents the abuse of the public order exception by stating that 'the public order exception may be invoked only where a genuine and sufficiently serious threat is posed to one of the fundamental interests of society'. Thus, a human rights-consistent interpretation of the public order/moral exception of GATS Article XIV would prohibit justifying restrictions on Internet search services for purposes of public order, if the restriction operates as a human rights violation, which cannot be in the 'fundamental interest of society'. WTO jurisprudence should insist that only a human rights-consistent interpretation of Article XIV will render public order and security considerations a justified exception to non-discriminatory market access and market conditions. As Tim Wu, an expert on China and Internet law goes on to say: 'In light of that language,' – limits on use of the public order exception are suggested in footnote 5 of Article XIV GATS – 'WTO panels and Appellate Bodies face the unappetizing prospect of trying to decide when a given part of China's system of information control represents a measure that combats "a genuine and sufficiently serious threat" that affects "one of the fundamental interests of society". That's a hard question when the content blocked may be more of a threat either to the Party or to a favored local company.'[57]

As yet, neither the google.cn case nor any similar cases have been challenged before the WTO, either by the US or by any other sending country. Most probably, the WTO judiciary would deny a justification by China under the GATS Article XIV, based on the fact that restricting the human right to Internet access cannot be in the interest of public order or morals.

4. Conclusions

The text of the WTO Agreements does not provide the legal basis for the WTO judiciary to prosecute human rights violations.[58] WTO Members are bound to respect *jus cogens* human rights, even if the WTO judiciary lacks the authority to adjucate *jus cogens* violations unrelated to

[56] Ibid., p. 2. [57] Ibid., p. 29. [58] See Marceau, 2002, pp. 753–814.

questions of WTO law. Similarly, human rights originating in customary international law, but without the status of *jus cogens* usually do not raise trade issues relevant enough to call into question their consistency with a provision of the WTO Agreements. Respect for human rights in WTO law, if at all, has traditionally been implied in Articles XX GATT and XIV GATS as justifying exceptions from otherwise unlawful restrictions to trade. Despite constituting a 'non-trade' issue, human rights are important to the stability and growth of the multilateral trading system.[59] Violations of human rights may have the effect of offsetting the mutually agreed benefits of trade liberalisation. Services trade liberalisation through mode 4, whereby the service supplier moves abroad to deliver a service, relies on the free movement of natural persons. This mode of service delivery renders GATS the WTO agreement with the closest affinity to the individual as a subject of international law and therefore, to human rights. Restricting the human rights of foreign service suppliers could therefore have the effect of nullifying and impairing the economic value and legal predictability of the GATS commitments. It is suggested that the non-violation nullification and impairment complaints may be used to redress the economic damage which occurs when human rights infringements negatively affect GATS commitments. If a human rights violation becomes so serious as to prevent the sending WTO Members from benefiting from the scheduled market opening in the receiving country and if that Member had relied on being able to benefit from sending service suppliers abroad, the human rights violations in the receiving country may form the basis of a non-violation type complaint under Article XXIII GATS in combination with Article 26 DSU. If the human right amounts to *jus cogens* or emanates from a human rights treaty to which both parties to a WTO dispute are signatories, the human right itself forms the ground of a WTO violation complaint. In all other cases, it is not the human rights violation itself, but its effect that represents the economic damage to the sending country's economy, which nullifies and impairs a trade benefit.

The human rights and trade-in-services linkage mostly plays out at the level of GATS commitments. The as yet unclarified legal nature and

[59] See, e.g., Kyle Bagwell and Robert W. Staiger, 'The WTO as a Mechanism for Securing Market Access Property Rights: Implications for Global Labour and Environmental Issues', *The Journal of Economic Perspectives* 15(3) (2001), pp. 69–88; Neil J. Mitchell and James M. McCormick, 'Economic and Political Explanations of Human Rights Violations', *World Politics* 40(4) (1988), pp. 476–498.

interpretation of such commitments adds to the uncertainty about how human rights violations against service suppliers could be addressed under GATS.[60]

A first impact of human righs violations occurs when a WTO Member restricts the human rights of foreign service providers and so deters the provider from making an investment in services by establishing a commercial presence abroad (mode 3) or from delivering the service by moving a natural person abroad (mode 4). This linkage of human rights violations and GATS law was discussed using the example of China's restriction on google.cn's right to free speech by filtering, even though China had made GATS mode 1 market access commitments for value-added telecommunications services.

A second nexus between human rights violations and GATS commitments appears to be relevant when the receiving country restricts the human rights of its citizens in order to implement its GATS commitments. The example used to illustrate this linkage is Indonesia's eviction of its citizens from areas of the country, for which it had offered commercial presence to foreign tourism service providers in accordance with its GATS mode 3 commitments. However, the causal link between the fulfilment of the GATS commitment and the human rights violation will be more difficult to show in this case.

A third nexus between human rights and GATS commitments is one inscribed in the GATS commitment itself. It exists where WTO Members have conditioned the access to their market or the national treatment to the foreign service supplier's obligation to respect the core labour standards and other human rights, which are part of the law and legal tradition of the receiving WTO Member. These could form a new category of 'human rights-contingent GATS commitments'. Usually, as the example of Switzerland shows, such human rights-contingent GATS commitments by the receiving WTO Member demand that the foreign services supplier complies with the wage and labour conditions prevalent in the receiving Member.

[60] See, e.g., Rudolf Adlung and Martin Roy, 'Turning Hills into Mountains? Current Commitments under the GATS and Prospects for Change', World Trade Organization Staff Working Paper ERSD-2005-01, Economic Research and Statistics Division, March, 2005, available at: www.wto.org/english/res_e/reser_e/ersd200501_e.doc, last accessed 23 August 2006, pp. 3, 28; see also William Davey, 'Specificities of WTO Dispute Settlement in Services Cases', ch. 12 in this volume; Eric Leroux, 'From Periodicals to Gambling: A Review of Systemic Issues Addressed by WTO Adjudicatory Bodies under the GATS', ch. 11 in this volume.

Bibliography

Adlung, Rudolf and Martin Roy, 'Turning Hills into Mountains? Current Commitments under the GATS and Prospects for Change', in World Trade Organization Staff Working Paper ERSD-2005-01, Economic Research and Statistics Division, March, 2005, available at: www.wto.org/english/res_e/reser_e/ersd200501_e.doc, last accessed 23 August 2006.

Allain, Jean, 'The *jus cogens* Nature of Non-Refoulement', *International Journal of Refugee Law* 13(4) (2002), pp. 533–558.

Alvarez, José E., 'The WTO as a Linkage Machine', *American Journal of International Law* 96(1) (2002), pp. 146–158.

Bagwell, Kyle, Petros C. Mavroidis and Robert. W. Staiger, 'It's a Question of Market Access', *American Journal of International Law* 96(1) (2002), pp. 56–76.

Bagwell, Kyle and Robert. W. Staiger, 'The WTO as a Mechanism for Securing Market Access Property Rights: Implications for Global Labour and Environmental Issues', *The Journal of Economic Perspectives* 15(3) (2001), pp. 69–88.

Bhagwati, Jagdish, 'Afterword: The Questions of Linkage', *American Journal of International Law* 96 (2002), pp. 118–125.

Christenson, Gordon, A., 'The World Court and Jus Cogens', *American Journal of International Law* 81(1) (1987), pp. 93–101.

Cottier, Thomas, 'Governance, Trade and Human Rights', in Frederick M. Abbott, Christine Breining-Kaufmann and Thomas Cottier (eds.), *International Trade and Human Rights, Foundations and Conceptual Issues*, World Trade Forum Volume 5 (Ann Arbor, Mich.: The University of Michigan Press, 2006), pp. 93–118.

Davey, William, 'Specificities of WTO Dispute Settlement in Services Cases', Ch. 12 in this volume, pp. 276–295.

Economy, Elizabeth, C., 'China's Environmental Movement', Testimony before the Congressional Executive Commission on China Roundtable on Environmental NGOs in China: Encouraging Action and Addressing Public Grievances, 7 February 2005, Rayburn House Office Building, Washington, DC, reprinted in: Council on Foreign Relations, Testimony, available at: www.cfr.org/publication.html?id=7770, last accessed 30 August 2006.

Francioni, Francesco, 'WTO Law in Context: The Integration of International Human Rights and Environmental Law in the Dispute Settlement Process', in Giorgio Sacerdoti, Alan Yanovich and Jan Bohanes (eds.), *The WTO at Ten* (Cambridge University Press, 2006), pp. 143–154.

Garcia-Rubio, Mariano, *On the Application of Customary Rules of State Responsibility by the WTO Dispute Settlement Organs, A General*

International Law Perspective (Geneva: Graduate Institute of International Studies, 2001).

Goldsmith, Jack and Tim Wu, *Who Controls the Internet: Illusions of a Borderless World* (Oxford University Press, 2006).

Heiskanen, Veijo, 'The Regulatory Philosophy of International Trade Law', *Journal of World Trade* 38(1) (2004), pp. 1–36.

Howse, Robert and Makau Mutua, 'Protecting Human Rights in a Global Economy: Challenges for the World Trade Organization', International Center for Human Rights and Democratic Development, Policy Paper, 2002.

Kälin, Walter and Jörg Künzli, *Universeller Menschenrechtsschutz* (Basel: Helbing und Lichtenhahn, 2005).

Koskenniemi, Martti, 'Hierarchy in International Law, A Sketch', *European Journal of International Law* 8(4) (1997), pp. 566–582.

Leroux, Eric, 'From Periodicals to Gambling: A Review of Systemic Issues Addressed by WTO Adjudicatory Bodies under the GATS', ch. 11 in this volume, pp. 236–275.

Marceau, Gabrielle, 'WTO Dispute Settlement and Human Rights', *European Journal of International Law* 13(4) (2002), pp. 753–814.

——'The WTO Dispute Settlement and Human Rights', in Frederick M. Abbott, Christine Breining-Kaufmann and Thomas Cottier (eds.), *International Trade and Human Rights, Foundations and Conceptual Issues*, World Trade Forum, Volume 5 (Ann Arbor, Mich.: The University of Michigan Press, 2006), pp. 181–260.

Meron, Theodore, 'On a Hierarchy of International Human Rights', *American Journal of International Law* 80(1) (1986), pp. 1–23.

Mitchell, Neil, J., and James M. McCormick, 'Economic and Political Explanations of Human Rights Violations', *World Politics* 40(4) (1988), pp. 476–498.

Pauwelyn, Joost, *Conflict of Norms in Public International Law, How WTO Law Relates to Other Rules of International Law* (Cambridge University Press, 2003).

Trachtman, Joel, 'Trade and ... Problems, Cost-Benefit Analysis and Subsidiarity', *European Journal of International Law* 9(1) (1998), pp. 32–85.

WTO Secretariat, Legal Affairs Division and Appellate Body, *A Handbook on the WTO Dispute Settlement System* (Cambridge University Press, 2004), pp. 30–31.

Wu, Tim, The World Trade Law of Internet Filtering (May 3, 2006), available at SSRN: http://ssrn.com/abstract=882459, last accessed 25 October 2006.

25

Comment: The instrumental rationale for protecting human rights in the context of trade services reform

SIMON WALKER[1]

Marion Panizzon's chapter presents a 'new perspective' on the human rights and trade debate through a consideration of the potential effects of human rights violations on GATS commitments. The article focuses in particular on commitments made by WTO Member States to liberalise the temporary movement of natural persons under GATS, mode 4. The chapter argues that violations of human rights in the country receiving migrant workers[2] might nullify or impair the sending country's legitimate expectations of commercial benefit arising from WTO commitments. Where that is the case, the chapter proposes that the WTO sending countries could bring claims against the receiving country to the WTO dispute settlement mechanism. Those claims could relate either to violations or non-violations of WTO law. Amongst other things, the chapter suggests that the WTO should consider the economic effects of human rights violations on trade commitments, while refraining from considering the altruistic reasons for protecting human rights, the latter being the domain of other intergovernmental organisations.

Marion Panizzon's focus on the economic effects of human rights violations is significant. It is an important reminder of the instrumental value of human rights – that respect for human rights can benefit trade and, conversely, that a failure to promote and protect human rights can have negative consequences for trade. The argument recalls the original discussions on the relationship between human rights and trade in goods that focused on the protection of workers' human rights and the recognition that poor protection of labour standards could distort fair

[1] The views expressed in this Comment are the author's own and do not necessarily reflect the views of the United Nations.

[2] The term 'migrant workers' is used here to refer to natural persons of a WTO Member State temporarily moving to offer services in another WTO Member State.

conditions of trade.[3] Marion Panizzon's chapter applies and extends the same argument to trade in services, namely that violations of human rights – not only workers' human rights but other human rights – can have negative implications for trade in services, specifically the temporary movement of migrant workers.

The argument is also timely. The UN reform programme launched by the UN Secretary-General in 2005 has sought to place human rights as a central pillar of the UN's work. In the former Secretary-General's words, 'We will not enjoy development without security, we will not enjoy security without development, and we will not enjoy either without respect for human rights.'[4] As momentum gathers to support human rights-based approaches to development, trade reform, security and other areas of international cooperation, it will be important for human rights practitioners to articulate more clearly the instrumental role of protecting human rights, demonstrating its application through concrete examples. In considering the economic and trade effects of human rights violations, Marion Panizzon's chapter can be seen as a contribution to this ongoing discussion.

Interestingly, recent research would appear to strengthen claims that protection of human rights can have beneficial implications for growth and development. The World Bank has noted, in its *World Development Report 2000/2001: Attacking Poverty*, 'lower inequality can increase efficiency and economic growth through a variety of channels'.[5] The World Bank reaffirmed this message more recently, noting that greater equity can, in the long term, underpin faster growth.[6] The Human Development Report 2005, focusing on international cooperation, analysed the link between equality and development and concluded that

[3] The Havana Charter (1948), Article 7 explicitly recognised 'that unfair labour conditions, particularly in production for export, create difficulties in international trade, and, accordingly, each Member shall take whatever action may be appropriate and feasible to eliminate such conditions within its territory'. While only two States ratified the Charter, the explicit recognition of the link between trade and workers' human rights indicates an early recognition of the instrumentalist rationale of human rights and an acknowledgment that the protection of human rights brings with it commercial benefits.

[4] 'In Larger Freedom: Towards Development, Security and Human Rights for All', Report of the Secretary-General, General Assembly, 21 March 2005, A/59/2005, para.17.

[5] World Bank, *World Development Report 2000/2001: Attacking Poverty* (Oxford University Press, 2001), p. 56.

[6] World Bank, *World Development Report 2006: Equity and Development* (The International Bank for Reconstruction and Development/World Bank, Washington DC, 2005), p. 17.

'extreme inequalities were rooted in power structures that deprived poor people of market opportunities, limited their access to services and denied them a political voice'. The Report clearly stated that 'pathologies of power were bad for market-based development as well as for political stability'.[7]

Research also suggests a positive link between the protection of the human rights of migrant workers and development. For example, in countries of origin, the impact of remittances sent by migrant workers can have a positive effect on poverty reduction and the enjoyment of economic and social rights – for example through the ongoing benefits of increased wealth to pay school fees, health costs and so on.[8] The Committee on the Rights of Migrant Workers has noted that temporary migration schemes enhance the contribution of migrants to the development of receiving countries as well as countries of origin.[9] Conversely, human rights violations can diminish the benefits of migration for development. Research suggests that disrespect for the human rights of migrant workers reduces migrants' ability to do decent work, support themselves and their families, live a life in which their personal rights are respected, and contribute generally to the development of their home and host societies.[10]

Of course, it is also important to note that challenges to the enjoyment of human rights might at times be linked to the liberalisation of the temporary movement of natural persons. The Special Rapporteur on the Right to Health, Mr Paul Hunt, considered the so-called 'brain-drain' effect resulting from the movement of health professionals from poorer to wealthier countries. This drain of health professionals can have serious effects on the provision of adequate health services and the enjoyment of the right to health in poorer countries. To the extent that GATS facilitates an environment conducive to the increased movement of health professionals, the Special Rapporteur has encouraged States to consider

[7] United Nations, *International Cooperation at a Crossroads: Aid, Trade and Security in an Unequal World*, Human Development Report 2005, United Nations Development Programme, New York, 2005, p. 7.

[8] Office of the High Commissioner for Human Rights, 'Migration and Development: a Human-Rights Approach', available on the website of OHCHR at www.ohchr.org accessed on 26 December 2006, p. 8.

[9] 'Protecting the Rights of All Migrant Workers as a Tool to Enhance Development', Contribution by the Committee on the Protection of the Rights of All Migrant Workers and Members of Their Families to the High-level Dialogue on Migration and Development of the General Assembly, 3 July 2006, A/61/120, para. 20.

[10] *Ibid*, p. 14.

the impact of commitments under mode 4 GATS on the enjoyment of the right to health.[11] A failure to do so might result in GATS exacerbating rather than facilitating the enjoyment of the right to health in poorer countries. Nonetheless, this should not detract from the broad message in Marion Panizzon's chapter that a failure to protect human rights could be bad for business.

In short, to the extent that addressing human rights violations through the stronger WTO enforcement mechanisms leads to improved enjoyment of human rights, the ideas raised in Marion Panizzon's chapter should be welcome. This in turn underlines the need for closer cooperation between human rights and trade bodies both at the expert and intergovernmental levels as well as the need for greater clarity on the role that human rights norms have as interpretative aids to trade treaties. Marion Panizzon alludes to this in her discussion of the International Convention on the Protection of the Rights of All Migrant Workers and Members of Their Families. However, I question her analysis that the Migrant Workers Convention might not have relevance to a dispute before the WTO Dispute Settlement Mechanism merely on the basis that 'no migration-related international intergovernmental organization ... has either applied or been granted observer status at the WTO'.

First, it is unclear why observer status should influence the WTO dispute bodies in promoting cohesion in the interpretation of international treaties. Second, assuming the criteria of observer status were critical to ensuring coherent interpretation and application of international rules, it is relevant to note that the United Nations,[12] as the secretariat of human rights treaties, has observer status with various councils of the WTO including the General Council and the Council for Trade in Services, thus suggesting that the requirement of observer status has been met. Moreover, a stronger basis for raising human rights norms in the WTO could be found through reliance on other more established human rights instruments than the Migrant Workers

[11] 'The Right of Everyone to the Enjoyment of the Highest Attainable Standard of Physical and Mental Health', Report of the Special Rapporteur, General Assembly, 12 September 2005, A/60/348, para. 63.

[12] The Office of the United Nations High Commissioner for Human Rights is the UN department with secretariat responsibilities for the UN human rights treaties and is part of the United Nations secretariat.

Convention with its low level of ratifications.[13] In any case, it is certainly clear that closer relationships must be forged between intergovernmental bodies, organisations and departments dealing with human rights and with trade, as the relationships between the two bodies of law and their potential for mutual reinforcement as well as conflict become clearer. This aspect of Marion Panizzon's work could be developed further.

[13] For a discussion on the various human rights and other instruments relevant to the rights of non-citizens, including migrant workers, see 'The Rights of Non-Citizens', Final report of the Special Rapporteur, Mr David Weissbrodt, Sub-Commission on the Promotion and Protection of Human Rights, May 2003, (E/CN.4/Sub.2/2003/23).

26

In pursuit of the cosmopolitan vocation for trade: GATS and aviation services

RICHARD JANDA AND MARK GLYNN*

The large question we want to reconnoitre here is how to situate the purpose behind enhancing the trade regime, and trade in services in particular, within the range of other goals pursued by the international community. We ask this question at a time when the trade regime itself is experiencing an identity crisis, lacking in commitment to its institutional development and lacking a sufficiently compelling account of the purpose it is seeking to achieve.[1] The question concerning its purpose nags away at the trade regime especially when it is being called to account for how it contributes to (or impedes) the advancement of the world's poorest countries, how it can be reconciled with the Marrakesh Agreement commitment to the objective of sustainable development, and how it relates to other overarching goals of international law. It is as if the trade regime is to the architecture of international law what a nondescript office tower is to architecture itself: it performs a purely economic function but is otherwise uninspiring and out of reach to the mass of people it looms over. Indeed, if trade law performs a purely economic function, the idea of moving the world toward further, ongoing economic integration, captured in the notion of progressive liberalisation, itself seems to have lost steam as doubts about the benefits of liberalised trade spread even to its erstwhile champions.

An example of this can be found in the recent debate between Paul Samuelson and his own students about the economic benefits of trade. Recall Samuelson's hand-wringing about outsourcing. He writes: 'High I.Q. secondary school graduates in South Dakota, who had been receiving

* The authors would like to thank Armand de Mestral, Paul Dempsey, Richard Lehun, Roderick Macdonald and Robert Wolfe for their comments and suggestions.

[1] On 1 July 2006, Pascal Lamy himself spoke of the 'crisis' in which the WTO found itself on the verge of the suspension of the Doha Round; see www.wto.org/english/news_e/sppl_e/sppl26_e.htm.

from my New York Bank wages one-and-a-half times the U.S. minimum wage for handling phone calls about my credit card, have been laid off since 1990 … [Offshore erosion of] the comparative advantage that had belonged to the United States can induce for the United States permanent *lost* per capita real income.'[2] Bhagwati, Panagariya and Srinivasan (2004) have answered that Samuelson is right about some shifts in comparative advantage but is not right about outsourcing in particular – something of specific significance to trade in services. Nevertheless, the overall impression the non-economist gets is that the economic case for trade is, from the standpoint of individual countries, remarkably murky. As Samuelson puts it, summarising a kind of consensus position:[3]

> If the past and the future bring both Type A inventions that *hurt* your country and Type B inventions that help – and when both *add* to real world net national product welfare – then free trade may turn out still to be pragmatically best for each region in comparison with lobbyist-induced tariffs and quotas which involve both perversion of democracy and non-subtle deadweight distortion losses.

Given this less than overwhelming statement in favour of free trade from a Nobel Prize-winning economist, are there in fact any supervening goals, beyond the pragmatic calculation that liberalised trade might enhance a Member State's economic welfare, to justify the trade regime? There is no doubt that if the trade regime were to decrease global economic welfare, it would lose its *raison d'être*. But if Samuelson is right that a WTO Member State's offer to lower trade barriers could in some circumstances produce national welfare losses – or at least losses to some actors and unevenly spread benefits – is there any principled reason nevertheless to opt for a liberalising agenda? After all, global environmental or health standards, for example, are strengthened even if this might impose costs so as to enable global public goods (Kaul *et al.*, 1999). Is there such an argument for strengthening the trade regime? (Mendoza, 2003).

In deference to economists, we will use another, older, economist, also drawn on by Samuelson, as our principal source of an answer to this question, namely John Stuart Mill. Mill develops what we will call a cosmopolitan argument for trade, positing that liberalised trade

[2] Paul Samuelson, 'Where Ricardo and Mill Rebut and Confirm Arguments of Mainstream Economists Supporting Globalization', *Journal of Economic Perspectives* 18 (2004), p. 135 at 137.

[3] *Ibid.* at pp. 142–143.

produces greater interdependency of peoples and thus tends to diminish conflict and build peace. Recently, Pascal Lamy, in his Herculean efforts to summon support for the Doha Round, made a version of this argument:[4]

> [The WTO is] a catalyst for international mutual respect towards international coherence and even for more global governance, which I believe is needed if we want the world we live in to become less violent, be it social, political, economic or environmental violence.

We will discuss the strengths and weaknesses of the cosmopolitan argument for trade, and gauge its specific applicability to trade in services. The lion's share of the paper is devoted to an exploration of the example of trade in aviation services as a possible candidate for principled extension of the current GATS regime on cosmopolitan grounds.

A selective intellectual history of the cosmopolitan argument for trade

In his *Principles of Political Economy*, Mill does of course begin his analysis of the benefits of trade with what he calls 'direct economic benefits'. These flow principally from the axiom that absent barriers to trade, inequalities of labour and capital will give rise to movement tending to level those inequalities. The direct benefits of trade are that such movements of labour and capital in line with the comparative advantage of nations will decrease costs of production and lead to a gain in consumer surplus. But Mill is alive to the possibility that part of this consumer surplus can be retained by oligopoly profits: hence the absence of constraints on market concentration will reduce the direct benefits of trade. We add in parenthesis that absence of significant competition safeguards is thus a gap in the trade regime.

Mill ties the gain in consumer surplus to two indirect economic benefits of trade, namely incentives to achieve economies of scale and the tendency to promote innovation. But these economic advantages, he claims, are eclipsed by non-economic advantages that he calls intellectual and moral. Let us quote a bit from Mill on this point, noting that contemporary economists tend to focus on what he says about

[4] Pascal Lamy, 'The Place and Role of the WTO (WTO Law) in the International Legal Order', Address before the European Society of International Law 19 May 2006, Sorbonne, Paris; available at: www.wto.org/English/news_e/sppl_e/sppl26_e.htm.

comparative advantage and to ignore this aspect of his argument, attributing to it a kind of pre-econometric fuzziness.

'It is hardly possible to overrate', Mill states, 'the value of placing human beings in contact with persons dissimilar to themselves, and with modes of thought and action unlike those with which they are familiar.'[5] Writing in 1848, Mill already concludes that '[c]ommerce is now, what war once was, the principal source of this contact'.[6] Such contact is to be privileged because '[to] human beings … it is indispensable to be perpetually comparing their own notions and customs with the experience and example of persons in different circumstances than themselves … [for] there is no notion that does not need to borrow from others'.[7] Notably, the expansion of trade can teach 'nations to view with good will the wealth and prosperity of one another'.[8] If we can come to see the wealth and advancement of others as contributing to our own, Mill envisages that we can gain a personal interest in preventing conflict with them. This leads Mill to claim that 'international trade [is] the principal guarantee of peace of the world, [and] is the great permanent security for the uninterrupted progress of the ideas, the institutions and the character of the human race'.[9] This set of claims constitutes what we mean by a cosmopolitan argument for trade, using the term 'cosmopolitan' in the sense employed by Ulrich Beck to denote 'shaping one's life and social relations under conditions of cultural mixture'.[10] Indeed Mill himself uses the term 'cosmopolitan' in connection with trade and capital,[11] and this is the first source of usage in the Oxford English Dictionary for the definition: 'Belonging to all parts of the world; not restricted to any one country or its inhabitants'.

Mill's cosmopolitan argument certainly has resonance in the contemporary experience of trade relations. Thus, for example, have we not learned through trade to welcome the growing prosperity of China and India, and was it not the initial appeal of the Doha 'Development Round' that it held out the promise of extending wealth and prosperity more broadly among nations?

Of course Mill was not alone in formulating a cosmopolitan argument in favour of trade. He had certainly been anticipated by Kant and Hegel.

[5] John Stuart Mill, *Principles of Political Economy* (London: Parker, 1848), at p. 122.
[6] *Ibid.* [7] *Ibid.* [8] *Ibid.* [9] *Ibid.*, at p. 123.
[10] Ulrich Beck, *The Cosmopolitan Vision* (London: Blackwell, 2006), at p. 3.
[11] *Principles of Political Economy*, at p. 113.

Kant for his part drew a clear connection between trade and the possibility of perpetual peace in his essay of that title:[12]

> Just as nature wisely separates peoples that the will of every nation, based on principles of international right, would gladly unite through cunning or force, so also by virtue of their mutual interest does nature unite peoples against violence or war, for the [mere] concept of cosmopolitan right does not protect them from it. The *spirit of trade* cannot coexist with war, and sooner or later this spirit dominates every people. For among all those powers (or means) that belong to a nation, financial power may be the most reliable in forcing nations to pursue the noble cause of peace (though not from moral motives) … In this fashion nature guarantees perpetual peace by virtue of all the mechanisms of man's inclinations themselves; to be sure it does not do so with a certainty sufficient to *prophesy* it from a theoretical point of view, but we can do so from a practical one, which makes it our duty to work toward bringing about this goal (which is not a chimerical one).

Here already is the idea that trade is ultimately incompatible with war because it creates mutual dependency and thus makes allies out of otherwise disparate nations.

Hegel, in the *Elements of the Philosophy of Right*, makes a similar point, tying it to the elements of risk, communication and education:[13]

> Just as the earth, the firm and solid ground, is a precondition of the principle of family life, so is the sea the natural element for industry, whose relations to the external world it enlivens. By exposing the pursuit of gain to danger, industry simultaneously rises above it; and for the ties of the soil and the limited circles of civil life with its pleasures and desires, it substitutes the element of fluidity, danger and destruction. Through this supreme medium of communication, it also creates trading links between distant countries, a legal [*rechtlichen*] relationship which gives rise to contracts; and at the same time, such trade [*Verkehr*] is the greatest educational asset [*Bildungsmittel*] and the source from which commerce derives its world-historical significance.

Hegel sees trade and commerce as propelling world – as opposed to national – history. He is perhaps less sanguine about trade than is Mill

[12] Immanuel Kant, 'Idea for a Universal History from a Cosmopolitan Point of View' (1784), translated by Lewis White Beck. From Immanuel Kant, *On History* (New York: Bobbs-Merrill, 1963), at p. 25.

[13] G. W. F. Hegel, *Elements of the Philosophy of Right* (1820), edited by Allen Wood, translated by H. B. Nisbet (Cambridge University Press, 1991), at p. 268.

since he sees the movement out from 'the limited circles of civil life' that it entails as involving dangers and even the possibility of destruction inherent in any transition from the known to the unknown. Yet, like Mill, he sees it principally as a source of contact and communication, and in calling it an educational asset, also seems to see it as a way to learn about and from encounters among the peoples of the world.

Not surprisingly, Marx radicalises Hegel's insight. In *The German Ideology*, he too sees a cosmopolitan vocation for trade, but insists even more on its destructive quality:[14]

> Big industry universalised competition in spite of [duties] (it is practical free trade, the protective duty is only a palliative, a measure of defence within free trade), established means of communication and the modern world market, subordinated trade to itself, transformed all capital into industrial capital, and thus produced the rapid circulation (development of the financial system) and the centralisation of capital. By universal competition it forced all individuals to strain their energy to the utmost. It destroyed as far as possible ideology, religion, morality, etc. and where it could not do this, made them into a palpable lie. It produced world history for the first time, insofar as it made all civilised nations and every individual member of them dependent for the satisfaction of their wants on the whole world, thus destroying the former natural exclusiveness of separate nations.

Anticipating Schumpeter's idea of 'creative destruction' (Schumpeter, 1942), Marx understood the emergence of a world market as already having had revolutionary consequences for national identities and as having created a form of global inter-dependency. Yet of course he and Engels were even less optimistic than was Hegel about whether trade would ultimately contribute to emancipation. In *Capital* (vol. 3, Chapter 14), Marx develops the theme of the relation between international trade and labour exploitation:[15]

> Although the total quantity of additional living labour contained in the commodities decreases, the unpaid portion increases in relation to the paid portion, either by an absolute or a relative shrinking of the paid portion; for the same mode of production which reduces the total quantity of additional living labour in a commodity is accompanied by a rise in the

[14] Karl Marx, *The German Ideology* (1846) (London: Lawrence and Wishart, 1965), reproduced by Electronic Book, at pp. 110–111.

[15] Karl Marx, *Capital* Volume III (1894), volume 37 of the *Marx–Engels Collected Works* (1932); available at www.econlib.org/library/YPDBooks/Marx/mrxCpC14.html.

> absolute and relative surplus-value. The tendency of the rate of profit to fall is bound up with a tendency of the rate of surplus-value to rise, hence with a tendency for the rate of labour exploitation to rise.

Thus, despite its cosmopolitan potential, Marx sees in trade an ineluctable tendency to exploit workers. Although this leads him to conclusions that have now been discredited, nevertheless, his critique remains powerful even today and must be weighed and considered if a principled argument for trade is to be made out. A recent US National Bureau of Economic Research working paper by Ian Dew-Becker and Robert J. Gordon (2005) points to the role of trade growth in contributing to increasing income inequality, at least in the United States. On the other hand, Piketty and Saez (2006) observe that although the U.S. pattern of an increasing share of income for the top 0.1 per cent has been reproduced in Canada and the United Kingdom, in France and Japan it has not. Although they do not purport to give a formal explanation for these differences, one factor to which they give attention is the presence or absence of effective progressive taxation. The interaction of trade with taxation serves to remind us that the trade regime alone cannot purport to address all of the externalities it contributes to generating. Other externalities include notably those concerning the environment, a subject we will address when considering the example of aviation services.

Cosmopolitanism and trade in services

Having set out the intellectual pedigree of the cosmopolitan argument as well as a significant critique emerging from it, we want to make the suggestion that trade in services should have pride of place in promoting the cosmopolitan potential of trade. This is so not only because of the rapid expansion of the services sector in the global economy, but also because of a special feature of trade in services as opposed to goods. Recall the following famous story about the origins of trade:[16]

> The Carthaginians also tell us that they trade with a race of men who live in a part of Libya beyond the Pillars of Heracles [i.e. the straits of Gibraltar]. On reaching this country, they unload their goods, arrange

[16] Herodotus, *The Histories*, translated by A. de Sélincourt, revised by J. M. Marincola (Harmondsworth: Penguin, 1996), at p. 196.

> them tidily along the beach, and then, returning to their boats, raise a smoke. Seeing the smoke, the natives come down to the beach, place on the ground a certain quantity of gold in exchange for the goods, and go off again to a distance. The Carthaginians then come ashore and take a look at the gold; and if they think it represents a fair price for their wares, they collect it and go away; if, on the other hand, it seems too little, they go back on board and wait, and the natives come and add to the gold until they are satisfied. There is perfect honesty on both sides; the Carthaginians never touch the gold until it equals in value what they have offered for sale, and the natives never touch the goods until the gold has been taken away.

This story reveals the point that trade in goods can be conducted without developing substantial relationships and indeed without substantial communication. Thus it need not contribute significantly to what Mill saw as the moral virtue of trade: placing nations into contact with each other. Trade in services, on the other hand, cannot be conducted without interpersonal contact. It requires communication or sign production so as to ascribe some shared meaning to the service to be provided (Harper 2004, 30–36). Furthermore, whereas even the silent trade in goods reported by Herodotus relied on 'perfect honesty' and thus on a degree of trust that neither would exploit the vulnerability of the other, trade in services requires placing oneself more directly at the other's mercy. If we are served food, lodging, transport, finance or the means to communicate, for example, or if we provide such services, we are entering into a relationship of mutual dependency absent in the 'take-it-or-leave-it' scheme of goods exchange. Indeed, as trade in goods becomes overlaid with trade in services, we add forms of dependency to trade in goods. Trade in services is thus a principal pathway of mutual learning and confidence building between peoples. One might say that absent deeper relationships of friendship, we tend to form our positive impressions of others through the services they provide. What we tend to mean by a service-oriented society is that it has invested in the capacity to build trust and facilitate relationships when meeting other people's commercial needs.

The cosmopolitan argument asserts that promoting international trade becomes a goal for the international community not simply for its own sake but as a way of helping to create the preconditions for peace derived from the interdependency of peoples that trade engenders. This is of course quite consistent with standard statements, like that of Robert Wolfe (2006), that the purpose of the trade regime is 'to promote international order and global prosperity' – note that in Canadian fashion he puts order first.[17] But the cosmopolitan argument that liberalised trade is a path to peace is not really being advanced today – at least not with great urgency. Certainly in North America one gets the sense that security concerns are in no way connected to the trade agenda and that indeed the notion of fostering mutual comparison, exchange of ideas and common understanding has given way in public discourse centred on gaining intelligence about foreign threats.

In order to renew its purpose and vigour, the trade agenda needs to regain pride of place in relation to the security agenda in a way that can best be described by analogy. Enhanced trade links should trump enhanced security in the same way as enhanced preventive medicine trumps improved cures for disease. It is not that preventive medicine puts an end to the need to cure disease. But we know that curing a disease is second best to fostering the conditions that prevent it. Liberalised trade in general, and liberalised trade in services in particular, fosters the conditions that can prevent conflict. Trade enhancement, unlike political reform, has precisely the virtue of being possible against a relatively broad diversity of political and cultural contexts.

An illustration: Trade in aviation services

We will now seek to apply the cosmopolitan argument to the example of aviation services. In so doing, we will emphasise the positive externalities generated by liberalised aviation trade but acknowledge as well that negative externalities must be anticipated. This chapter does not address how to design the international regime as a whole so as to ensure that the negative externalities of trade are confronted at the same time as trade is liberalised. Nevertheless, we note in passing that sustainability impact assessment of trade agreements can help to identify the adjustments to domestic and international regulation that should accompany liberalisation.[18] In particular, it should be acknowledged that air transport is having a growing impact on global warming and according to the recent

[17] Robert Wolfe, 'The WTO in Suspense: Is Institutional Reform Needed?' Unpublished Working Paper for Princeton Workshop (23–25 August 2006) of the Centre for International Governance Innovation project on Global Institutional Reform, p. 16; available at http://post.queensu.ca/~wolfer/Papers/DohaSuspense.pdf.

[18] See, for example, the work of the Institute for Development Policy and Management of the University of Manchester on sustainability impact assessment of WTO trade negotiations: www.sia-trade.org/wto/index.htm.

Stern Review is projected to account 'for around 5% of the total warming effect (radiative forcing) in 2050'.[19]

We seek to use the cosmopolitan argument in a narrow, balance-tilting manner. We do not deny that where there is compelling evidence of negative economic externalities for which the costs of adjustment clearly outweigh any increase in global economic welfare attributable to trade liberalisation, liberalisation cannot be the preferred option. But in the absence of such evidence, cosmopolitan benefits, that will be difficult to quantify, ought to weigh heavily in favour of liberalisation. We believe that the liberalisation of aviation services is an instance in which the cosmopolitan argument ought to weigh heavily.

We chose aviation for three reasons. First, it is a key infrastructure service sector that is all but excluded from the GATS, with no short term prospect of inclusion. This is despite the fact that some 90 GATS members have in their various bilateral arrangements been prepared to accept some degree of trade liberalisation as regards pricing, capacity, routes and designation of carriers. Second, the security agenda, informed to some degree by the outsourcing debate, has indeed come to trump the trade enhancement agenda in the case of aviation services. Finally, air transport is nevertheless the best example of a service that promotes cross-cultural contact as well as international interaction and understanding. Indeed, every element of international air transportation incorporates exposure to foreign cultures. In his 1820 discussion of the cosmopolitan benefit of trade, quoted above, Hegel gave pride of place to transport by sea. Today it is surely transport by air.

There is no international consensus on the ideal model for the exchange of aviation rights. The globe is currently a patchwork. Some developed countries continue to regulate the exchange of air transport rights in defence of domestic carriers and markets, while others opt for a liberalised environment. A similar dichotomy exists amongst least developed countries, some of which have entered into liberalised air service agreements, while others prefer to remain strictly regulated. The existence of regulation intrinsically signifies that the market is not determined by pure comparative advantage. We seek to sketch out how aviation may nevertheless be an appropriate target for GATS expansion – if not in the near term at least in the medium term. We acknowledge that

[19] Nicholas Stern, *The Economics of Climate Change: Stern Review* (Cambridge University Press, 2006), at p. 342 (Annex 7.c, Emissions from the Transport Sector); available at www.hm-treasury.gov.uk/media/3DD/5D/Transport_annex.pdf.

the argument that aviation contributes to cosmopolitanism cannot in itself overcome ingrained patterns of protectionism. Rather, we seek to show that there is something like a critical mass of countries that already operate within liberalised bilateral trade agreements, and thus that the cosmopolitan argument should serve to provide a further push towards rendering this reality multilateral.

A brief history of international air transport regulation

International air transport is exceptional in many ways, not least in its governance and regulation. Before discussing how the cosmopolitan argument could give impetus to the liberalisation of trade in aviation services under the GATS, a preliminary note is in order concerning the origins of the status quo. Two main tendencies can be detected, and they continue to interact. The first, an anti-cosmopolitan tendency, involves the assertion of national sovereignty over airspace with attendant restrictions on trade in aviation services. The second, a cosmopolitan tendency, involves the emergence of 'open skies' and open aviation area regimes. The first tendency was dominant roughly until the end of the 1970s, until deregulation of domestic civil aviation in the United States. The second tendency has gained momentum since that time although it had earlier manifestations even during the Chicago Conference of 1944. We divide our discussion in two to reflect these two tendencies.

The assertion of sovereignty over air space

War has proven to be a motor for development of air transport regulation, and it is not surprising that in the wake of war, a preoccupation with protecting national sovereignty predominates. In Paris, after World War 1, and in Chicago, in the dying days of World War II, major conferences were held leading to treaties framing international aviation policy. The Chicago Conference succeeded in producing agreement on many technical aspects of aviation regulation. Indeed, the Preamble to the Chicago Convention contains a promising statement of the cosmopolitan argument: 'The future development of international civil aviation can greatly help to create and preserve the friendship and understanding among the nations and peoples of the world.'[20] Nonetheless these words are

[20] Convention on International Civil Aviation, Signed at Chicago on 7 December 1944, Preamble; available at www.icao.int/cgi/goto_m.pl?icaonet/dcs/7300.html.

followed by a phrase redolent with the events of 1944: 'yet its abuse can become a threat to the general security'. In essence, the latter sentiment came to constrain the former at least as regards trade in aviation services. Attempts to achieve a global understanding on exchange of traffic rights led nowhere. Instead the delegates at the Conference insisted on a clear statement of national sovereignty over airspace as the founding principle for aviation relations. Thus, Article 1 of the Chicago Convention proclaims:

> **Sovereignty**
> The contracting States recognize that every State has complete and exclusive sovereignty over the airspace above its territory.

At Chicago, the United States had pushed for liberalised trade in air transport services in a Transport Agreement, but other nations, notably the United Kingdom, had deep reservations, fearful in particular of allowing the United States to become the dominant commercial aviation power. Critically, in the absence of support for the proposed Transport Agreement, even its proponent, the United States, never ratified it. It became necessary to find alternative means to exchange air traffic rights bilaterally between States.[21]

The earliest registered bilateral agreement is between the United States and Ireland, dated 3 February 1945.[22] However, the most significant bilateral exchange of traffic rights was concluded between the United Kingdom and the United States in Bermuda on 11 February 1946. The US–UK market today remains the most important in the global network with over 14 million people travelling between the two countries by scheduled air services every year.[23] The two parties entered into negotiations having opposing ideologies. The US sought a liberal bilateral agreement and the UK preferred a restrictive one. The focus of the negotiations was on reciprocal economic advantages, not cosmopolitan benefits. The United States, having a strong fleet of aircraft that it had built to fly to Europe during the war, wished to exploit this advantage by

[21] Paul S. Dempsey, *Public International Air Law* (forthcoming).

[22] There were no pre-war aviation agreements between States: see Manle Hudson, 'Aviation and international Law', *Air Law Review* I (1930) #2.

[23] Data based on ICAO OFOD 2005 data set which ranks Canada–US as the second largest market. N.B. that there is no single internationally accepted method for producing traffic figures and other sets, including IATA BSP rank Canada–US ahead of US–UK. However, even in such cases, when expressed in terms of revenue-passenger kilometres (RPKs), UK–US is, by a considerable margin, the largest international aviation market.

allowing open competition. The UK sought a division of the market owing to the fact that almost all of its aircraft had been decimated during the war. The result was a compromise of interests. Tariffs were to be strictly regulated, with approval from both aeronautical authorities required. However, multiple carriers could operate between the two countries, and capacity could be freely determined, subject only to ex post facto review. A wave of bilateral agreements followed in the wake of Bermuda, many adopting the same or similar terms.

The bilateral regime is a hindrance to cosmopolitanism both in its spirit and in its effects. Bilateral economic regulation confines air traffic by limiting capacity, imposing supra-competitive prices, restricting the number of carriers, and controlling the number of destinations both between the parties and beyond. This cannot but reduce the opportunities for trade and intercultural exchange. The results of bilateralism can also be anti-cosmopolitan in that an asymmetric structure develops benefiting those with the strongest bargaining power. The bilateral system has no way to foster special and differential treatment for developing countries. Some of the alternative suggestions made in Chicago for the organisation of international traffic rights could have avoided these problems. In particular, the Transport Agreement with its principle of multilateral exchange of rights could have developed an ethos of cooperation between governments, facilitated the expansion of global markets, and generated equality of treatment with respect to traffic rights. The other suggestion made in Chicago by the Australia and New Zealand States would have been radically cosmopolitan. They proposed the creation of a single global airline that would operate all routes worldwide. The idea was to have people from around the world working together toward the same goal of linking the world. However, not surprisingly, the idea of a global monopoly was almost unanimously rejected.

In the forty years that followed the failure of the Chicago Conference to agree upon a model for the multilateral exchange of traffic rights, and the consequent emergence of the bilateral negotiation process, no truly global initiative to liberalise the aviation sector has emerged. Indeed, rather than maintaining the status quo of modest Bermuda liberalisation, there was even a tendency for more restrictions to appear. As shown in Box 1, bilateral agreements between 1958 and 1978 became less generous, restricting flights beyond the partner countries (known as fifth freedom), disallowing multiple foreign carriers to operate on routes, and often imposing fixed capacity quotas rather than allowing free determination of capacity. Indeed, the United States and the United

Box 1: Bilateral agreements with liberalised features: 1945–1957 contrasted with 1958–1977

	Fifth freedom rights	Multiple designation	Bermuda 1 capacity
1945–1957 (299 agreement sample)	94%	74%	32%
1958–1977 (819 agreement sample)	79%	47%	22%

Kingdom, which had set the Bermuda I standard, renegotiated their bilateral on 23 July 1977, and the subsequent agreement, known as Bermuda II, is an example of the 1960s and 70s tendency toward restricting access.

The incentive for governments to adopt restrictive air services agreements during this period was purely economic and not based on invoking 'a threat to the general security'. Governments could curtail supply, thus allowing the national, and often government-owned, airlines to extract monopoly or duopoly rents on predetermined routes. While promoting profit, such a model flew in the face of cosmopolitanism, for it favoured restrictions on economic grounds without consideration of indirect non-economic advantages of increased service. It corresponded to a period in which air travel was a luxury.

Yet even with the onset of domestic liberalisation in the 1980s, protection of sovereignty over airspace is dying hard. The latest manifestation of the assertion of sovereignty was the rejection in 1995 of general inclusion of trade in air transport services under the GATS. An Annex to the Agreement specifically excludes GATS commitments from affecting traffic rights. Article 2 of the Annex states that the Agreement does not apply to air traffic rights or services linked to air traffic rights. Paragraph 3 of the Annex only renders the Agreement applicable to ancillary services in the aviation sector, namely computer reservation systems, selling and marketing and repair and maintenance. Indeed, during the 1993 Uruguay Round GATS negotiations, only Singapore, New Zealand and Australia favoured inclusion of air transport within the scope of the GATS.[24]

[24] Information courtesy of WTO Secretariat, Trade in Services Division.

The emergence of 'open skies' agreements

In 1978, at precisely the same time as the United States was undertaking its radical experiment in domestic aviation deregulation, the Governments of the US and Belgium expressed a common desire to 'promote an international aviation system based on competition among airlines in the market place with minimum governmental regulation'.[25] The parties agreed that the United States would have unrestricted fifth freedom rights with points behind or beyond Belgium. Belgium was granted extensive fifth freedom rights behind and beyond the United States, although it was limited in the airports it could use for these rights. Capacity constraints were eliminated from the agreement, and tariffs could only be blocked if the aeronautical authorities in both countries agreed to oppose the suggested fare.

Soon after, similarly liberal agreements were concluded with numerous States including South Korea, Singapore, Thailand, Finland and New Zealand. The United States renewed its interest in liberalising the world's skies in the beginning of the 1990s, and on 14 October 1992, the first of a new generation of 'open skies' agreements was concluded with the Netherlands. This form of agreement has now become a model for US bilateral agreements, and provides that an unlimited number of carriers can operate, routes between the partner countries are unrestricted, as is fifth freedom traffic, pricing is left to the carriers, and capacity is left to their free determination. Since 1992, the United States has entered into a total of 78 such open skies agreements.[26] These have been concluded with States from all geographic regions and States with all levels of development. Recently, Canada has announced that it too will pursue a policy of concluding open skies agreements with all of its partners.[27] Chart 1 shows the pace of conclusion of open skies agreements by the United States, whilst Box 2 shows the number of agreements concluded with partners from all regions of the world.

Although open skies agreements may not have been concluded with a cosmopolitan intention, they do have cosmopolitan advantages. Deregulating or liberalising pricing and capacity regimes disperses the benefits of travel by

[25] Preamble to the Protocol between the Government of the United States of America and the Government of Belgium Relating to Air Transport 14 December 1978 amending the Agreement of 5 April 1946, available in *Annals of Air & Space Law* XXX (2005), at p. 269.

[26] A full list of these open skies agreements with their date of conclusion can be found at www.state.gov/e/eb/rls/othr/2006/22281.htm.

[27] See Blue Sky: Canada's New International Air Policy (November, 2006) www.tc.gc.ca/pol/en/ace/consultations/blueSkyPolicy.htm.

Box 2: US open skies agreements by geographical region of the Contracting Party

Destination region	Number of open skies agreements
Africa	19
Americas	16
Asia & Pacific	14
Europe	22
Middle East	7

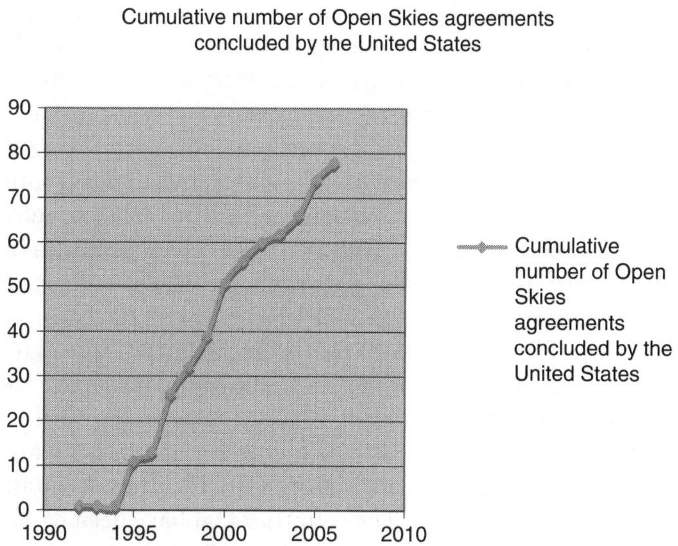

Chart 1 The progression of conclusion of open skies bilateral agreements by the United States

air, transforming it from an elite to a mass phenomenon. Fifth freedom routes allow service to markets which would otherwise not be sustainable under direct service and thus connects more parts of the world together. There are also some agreements that liberalise ownership and control restrictions on airlines. Ordinarily, bilateral agreements specify that only airlines that are owned and controlled by nationals of the other country can be designated by that country to benefit from traffic rights. Box 2 shows that open skies agreements have been concluded with states from all regions of the world representing all levels of development and prosperity.

Box 3: WASA database bilateral agreements containing liberalised features

	Capacity	Pricing	Ownership
Total agreements with feature	86	160	112
Agreements not involving US with feature	21	92	109
Number of countries accepting feature	75	103	63
Number of countries with feature and partners other than US	25	74	61

Liberalisation of bilateral arrangements has become a growing tendency over the last decade. The World Air Service Agreements database of bilateral agreements, produced by the International Civil Aviation Organization (ICAO), which is a compendium of all registered air service agreements, shows that the tendency is becoming widespread. However, the database is limited in two important ways and is thus under-reporting the phenomenon. First, not all States reliably register their bilateral agreements with ICAO.[28] Second, there is a registration lag which results in it taking three to four years for agreements to appear in the database. For example in the 2006 database, only 42 of the then 77 US Open Skies agreements appear.

Despite these limitations, Box 3 shows the significant spread of agreements with highly liberalised terms on traditionally restrictive elements of bilateral agreements.

In total there are 257 bilateral agreements that include at least one of these examples of advanced liberalisation, and 117 different countries are parties to at least one of them. The countries that have been party to one of the above forms of liberalisation include all of the leading aviation markets in the world: notably Australia, Brazil, Canada, China, France, Germany, Hong Kong, India, Japan, Mexico, Netherlands, Portugal, Russian Federation, Singapore, South Africa, Spain, UAE, UK and US. The States involved represent the origin or destination of a vast preponderance of international air traffic.

There is then evidence that the bulk of international traffic is carried between States that have been willing – with at least one partner – to enter into advanced liberalisation of the air transport sector. However, the cosmopolitan benefit of this development has been significantly

[28] See Michael Milde, 'The Chicago Convention – Are Major Amendments Necessary or Desirable 50 Years Later?', *Annals of Air & Space Law* XIX (1994).

diminished by the absence of a most favoured nation approach. While a few countries are prepared to enter into liberalised arrangements with all other States, most continue to seek a balance of commercial benefits. Thus, while it can be said that the bulk of international traffic is carried between States that have been willing to enter into at least one liberalised bilateral agreement, it cannot yet be said that the bulk of international traffic is governed by liberalised, let alone open skies, bilateral agreements.

Although bilateral agreements remain the norm, liberalised regional agreements have also emerged. Propelled by the development of the Common Aviation Area in Europe, there has been a recent proliferation of plurilateral agreements. We will first address the EU developments and then sketch out the plurilateral arrangements that have emerged elsewhere.

As the result of three increasingly liberalised packages, the EU has, since April 1997, operated its internal aviation market as a domestic market. For intra-EU service, all community carriers are subject to the same treatment. This includes the practice of cabotage – i.e allowing non-national carriers to provide a service within a country. For example, EasyJet, a British airline, operates between Paris and Nice in France. EU carriers are free to merge and engage in cross ownership without any consequence for their traffic rights within the EU. This is a radical development, the implications of which extend far beyond those of bilateral open skies agreements. It can fairly be asserted that the Open Aviation Area of the EU has had a dramatic cosmopolitan effect for Europe, even spawning a new generation of commuters who live in one country and work in another.[29]

In addition to creating a domestic regime over the skies of Europe, the EU has recently gone further in pursuit of deregulation and liberalisation. The impetus for this movement came with a set of decisions of the European Court of Justice in 2002, which concluded that Member States could not negotiate bilateral arrangements without reference to Community Law.[30] In particular, bilateral agreements that precluded the possibility of designating any EU-owned airline (i.e. through the

[29] Sean Coughlan, 'The New Commuter Belt', BBC News Magazine 18 July 2005; available at http://news.bbc.co.uk/2/hi/uk_news/magazine/5187096.stm.

[30] *E.C.J. Commission v. United Kingdom*, C-466/98 [2002] E.C.R. I-9427; *E.C.J. Commission v. Denmark*, C-467/98 [2002] E.C.R. I-9519; *E.C.J. Commission v. Sweden*, C-468/98 [2002] E.C.R. I-9575; *E.C.J. Commission v. Finland*, C-469/98 [2002] E.C.R. I-9627; *E.C.J. Commission v. Belgium*, C-471/98 [2002] E.C.R. I-9681; *E.C.J. Commission v. Luxembourg*, C-472/98 [2002] E.C.R. I-9741; E.C.J. *Commission v. Austria*, C-475/98 [2002] E.C.R. I-9797; E.C.J. *Commission v. Germany*, C-476/98 [2002] E.C.R. I-9855.

requirement that the airline be substantially owned and effectively controlled by nationals of the contracting party) were declared inconsistent with Community law.

This set of decisions prompted a flurry of activity. Negotiations between the United States and the European Commission in search of what the Commission has called an Open Aviation Area were taken up in earnest. In order to correct for the inconsistencies with European law, in June 2003 the Council, Commission and Member States agreed that Member States should renegotiate their bilateral agreements and insert into them a community ownership clause. However, more radically, the Commission was also granted the power to negotiate with third parties to replace the national ownership clause with a Community ownership clause. The obligations of Member States were promulgated as Community legislation by Regulation 847/2004. Sixty-three non-EU States have since accepted Community designation, and 23 of these directly renegotiated all of their EU bilateral agreements with the Commission (Geil). In December 2004, the Council also issued a mandate to the Commission to proceed to establish a European Common Aviation Area (ECAA) by integrating neighbouring European countries, including eight Balkan States, which will be future candidates to join the Union, as well as Norway and Iceland. Upon implementation of the text, which was agreed to in December 2005, the unified ECAA will encompass 35 States. The EU also aspires to have the ECAA benefit from liberal joint bilateral agreements with third party countries. An agreement that will all but integrate Morocco into the ECAA, extending all rights but cabotage, was signed on 12 December 2006.[31] It incorporates a broad set of EU rules into the agreement, including on safety, competition laws, air traffic management, consumer protection, and environmental standards. The Commission is undertaking negotiations with the Ukraine and Russia, and hopes to add further States in the Mediterranean region before extending east towards the Eurasia region. The Commission is also negotiating air service agreements with more distant like-minded States interested in liberalisation of the sector, including Australia, Canada, Chile and New Zealand, and with the critical emerging commercial powers of India and China.[32]

[31] See http://ec.europa.eu/transport/air_portal/international/pillars/common_aviation_area/morocco_en.htm.

[32] Information from the EU Air Transport portal: http://ec.europa.eu/transport/air_portal/.

However, plurilateralism has not been limited to the European context. At the 2006 Dubai Symposium of Global Liberalisation, held by ICAO, 15 regional or plurilateral agreements were noted.[33] These are:

1) the single aviation market within the European Union;
2) the Decision on Integration of Air Transport amongst the five Andean Pact States in 1991 (Andean 'open skies' policy);
3) the Caribbean Community (CARICOM) Air Service Agreement amongst 15 States in the Caribbean (1996, entry into force in 1998 for nine States);
4) the Fortaleza Agreement amongst six MERCOSUR States in South America (1997);
5) the Banjul Accord amongst six States in Western Africa (1997, a separate more liberal multilateral agreement was signed among seven States in 2004);
6) the CLMV Agreement by Cambodia, Lao People's Democratic Republic, Myanmar and Vietnam (1998, a formal multilateral agreement was signed in 2003);
7) the Intra-Arab Freedoms of the Air Programme amongst 16 States of the Arab Civil Aviation Commission (ACAC) in the Middle East and Northern Africa (1999);
8) an agreement amongst the six States of the Economic and Monetary Community of Central Africa (CEMAC) (1999);
9) the Air Transport Liberalisation Programme amongst 20 States of the Common Market for Eastern and Southern Africa (COMESA) (1999);
10) the Yamoussoukro II Ministerial Decision amongst 52 African Union States (1999, entry into force in 2000);
11) the agreement covering the IMT Growth Triangle region by Indonesia, Malaysia and Thailand (1999);
12) the BIMP East ASEAN Growth Area region by Brunei, Indonesia, Malaysia and Philippines (1999);
13) the Multilateral Agreement on the Liberalisation of International Air Transportation (MALIAT) also known as the 'Kona' open skies agreement was signed in 2001 by five like-minded members of the Asia Pacific Economic Cooperation (APEC) (i.e. Brunei, Chile, New Zealand, Singapore and the United States). It is open for adherence by other members of APEC as well as non-member States. Cook

[33] See www.icao.int/icao/en/atb/ecp/dubai2006/RegulatoryIndustryOverview.pdf.

Islands, Peru, Samoa and Tonga subsequently joined the agreement (Peru withdrew in 2005);

14) the 2004, Brunei, Singapore and Thailand Multilateral Agreements on the Full Liberalisation of All Cargo Services; and
15) a parallel 2004 agreement among those countries on the Liberalisation of Passenger Air Services – both are open to other member States of the Association of South East Asian Nations (ASEAN).

There are also a number of agreements in the midst of being negotiated:

1) a Common Air Transport Programme amongst eight States of the Economic and Monetary Union of West Africa (WAEMU, 2002);
2) a Pacific Islands Air Services Agreement (PIASA) amongst 16 States of the Pacific Islands Forum (2003);
3) a road map to liberalise air cargo and passenger services as well as to build a common ASEAN aviation market (2005); and
4) an Air Transport Agreement for a Common Aviation Area, which is open to 25 member States and three associate members of the Association of Caribbean States (ACS, 2004).

These agreements suggest that the open skies tendency is indeed counter-balancing the tendency toward assertion of national sovereignty and add weight to the conclusion that a critical mass of countries could contemplate multilateral liberalisation of air transport. Yet even this nexus of liberal bilateral, regional and plurilateral arrangements, the current alternative to the GATS, produces an example of the Sutherland Report's spaghetti bowl problem.[34] The cosmopolitan potential of air transport is significantly diminished by the patchwork of bilateral and regional air transport agreements since, for example, the restrictions between countries A and B can constrain connecting access to country C.

Toward a cosmopolitan aviation regime

Of the plurilateral agreements just listed, only MALIAT could in principle counter the current spaghetti bowl effect and become a truly cosmopolitan aviation framework since it is open to ratification by any other State. However, MALIAT is to say the least a very thin multilateral agreement since it has only attracted eight signatories and seems to have little

[34] Report of the WTO Director General's Consultative Board *The Future of the WTO – Addressing Institutional Challenges in the New Millennium* (2005).

prospect of attracting many others. Were the EU successful in extending its Open Aviation Area gradually to the entire world, that of course would also counter the spaghetti bowl problem. But the US-sponsored MALIAT and EU-sponsored Open Aviation Area reflect efforts to extend the regulatory frameworks of the respective sponsors. A truly cosmopolitan multilateral regime would not serve to entrench the policies of one sponsor but would rather reflect the interests and needs of all countries.

There are two pillars upon which a cosmopolitan aviation regime could be based: the most-favoured nation concept and phasing out of ownership and control restrictions. Both of these pillars are best fitted within the architecture of the GATS rather than outside it in some separate regime. We discuss each in turn.

MFN and trade in aviation services

The most-favoured nation concept is inherently cosmopolitan in the sense that it extends hospitality to all states on the same basis, but allows each state to determine what offer to make to the others trading with it. In the case of air transport, one of us has argued in a previous article that the GATS MFN concept would have to be adapted to the fact that the four modes of services supply (cross-border, consumption abroad, commercial presence, and movement of natural persons) do not fit easily with passenger service, the relevant market for which is a city-pair with one city in each Member.[35] As regards passengers, the service is not really a cross-border service supplied from country A to country B, but is rather a service between the two countries. In particular, it would thus not make sense for market access commitments to be made on the basis of in-bound traffic alone. If country A grants open skies access to all its own airports and country B takes a more restrictive approach to granting access, it would make no sense for country B's airlines to have unrestricted access to the A–B market while country A's airlines were restricted. Rather, it would make sense to schedule GATS commitments under a new reciprocal access mode of supply. Thus, Members would undertake to allow reciprocal access no less favourable than reciprocal access granted to any other country. Cargo service, on the other hand, could be scheduled as a cross-border service.

[35] Richard Janda, 'Passing the Torch: Why ICAO should Leave Economic Regulation to the WTO', *Annals of Air and Space Law* (1994), pp. 409–430.

The main advantage of this MFN approach over the status quo is that country A's most liberal bilateral reciprocal access agreement would automatically be available reciprocally to any other Member. Access would no longer be premised upon balance of commercial benefit. All countries, large and small, would have equal opportunity to gain enhanced aviation market access to their partners. Thus, for example, India had a change of heart and finally agreed to an open skies agreement with the US in 2005. Application of an MFN approach would entail that all Members could now enter into parallel open skies agreements with India. For this system to work, Members could no longer have recourse to confidential Memoranda of Understanding detailing special arrangements undisclosed to others. They would schedule market access commitments according to the key economic elements of bilateral agreements (rights, designation, revocation of authorisation, commercial opportunities, customs duties and charges, user charges, competition and pricing). As in the case of the Telecommunications Reference Paper, it might be possible to have a draft of agreed model commitments that the Members could adopt or adapt. At the same time, the ICAO registry of bilateral agreements would be maintained and indeed would have to be rendered more transparent and truly obligatory. Thus the GATS would not simply eliminate the bilateral system, but rather would provide some discipline to it and a mechanism to extend the cosmopolitan benefits of the liberalisation tendency. Members would remain free to address safety, security and environmental goods separately. This is where ICAO's role, which includes a mandate to develop environmental standards under the Kyoto Protocol, would remain preeminent.

Ownership rules and trade in aviation services

The other key area in which important cosmopolitan advantages can be extracted by liberalisation relates to foreign ownership rules. In order for an airline to be able to provide services between two countries it has to overcome a double regulatory hurdle. First, in order to be certified and licensed, it must respect legislation in its home country that stipulates a minimum level of national ownership. Second, it must respect the terms of the bilateral agreement between countries A and B, which typically will stipulate that if an airline of country B flies to country A, that airline must be owned and controlled by nationals of country B in order for it to qualify for designation under the agreement.

There are instances of ownership requirements being implicitly waived. For example, ABSA, a Brazilian international airline, is substantially owned by LAN, a Chilean company. Aerolineas Argentinas was 85 per cent owned by Iberia and another Spanish company, Marsens Group now owns 92 per cent of the company. Bilateral provisions have not been invoked to oppose these ownership structures. On the other hand, LAN Ecuador was 70 per cent owned by LAN of Chile, but when the US threatened to revoke traffic rights, this was reduced to a 45 per cent interest.[36] TAP Portugal was also prevented from further assisting Varig, the Brazilian flag carrier, in its bankruptcy refinancing due to restrictions in Brazilian law limiting foreign investment in an airline to 20 per cent.[37]

The EU has vigorously promoted the relaxation of ownership restrictions. The concept of the State-neutral airline has been adopted by Star Alliance which requires members to paint a small number of its aircraft in the design of Star Alliance and to bear the flags of all of the member carriers. Nonetheless, according to the WASA database, 95 per cent of bilateral agreements registered at ICAO contain the traditional substantive ownership and effective control criteria for withholding traffic rights. Even the five per cent of liberalised terms is to an extent misleading in that it is entirely accounted for by the renegotiated principal place of business terms that were inserted into Hong Kong and Macau bilateral agreements upon their being handed over to China. This was done because Hong Kong and Macau airlines were owned by nationals of the previous regime, i.e. UK and Portugal respectively.

The cosmopolitan benefits of air transport could be greatly advanced and accelerated by relaxed rules on foreign ownership allowing airlines to become truly transnational enterprises responding to global demand. This is already occurring in the air cargo domain. However, the EU has become a voice crying in the wilderness on this issue. Recently, the US Congress adopted a Bill blocking an Administration proposal to provide a more flexible interpretation as to when investments within existing 25 per cent voting share ownership limits could give rise to 'actual control' – this after a more ambitious proposal to raise ownership limits from 25 per cent to 49 per cent had been torpedoed in 2003.[38] In December

[36] See US Department of Transportation dockets OST-2002-13661 and OST 2003-14291.

[37] See Tom Murphy, 'Brazil's Varig Airline Reorganization Faces Debt Dilemma', 6 June 2005; available at www.skyscrapercity.com/showthread.php?t=143328&page=4.

[38] Department of Transportation, Notice of Proposed Rulemaking, 'Actual Control of U.S. Carriers' 70 Fed. Reg. 214; available at http://a257.g.akamaitech.net/7/257/2422/01jan20051800/edocket.access.gpo.gov/2005/05-22056.htm. See ALPA Fact Sheet, 'Timeline

2006, after intense lobbying, plans to change the interpretation of the control criteria were shelved.[39] This will surely further delay any chance of an agreement on transatlantic liberalisation. The extremely modest effort to adjust the ownership and control rule mobilised sustained opposition in the US, based in significant part on concerns about whether safety and security might somehow be prejudiced. This should give us pause. It testifies to the staying power, even in the usually pro-aviation trade US, of the sovereignty argument lurking behind the existing restrictive ownership and control rule.

Another instance of opposition to liberalisation of the provision of service involved US carrier Northwest Airlines, which planned to use a local flight attendant on an intra-Asian flight in 2005. The immediate response of the flight attendants' union was to lobby Congress against the threat to jobs posed by 'outsourcing' and to argue that foreign flight attendants would not be subject to the same degree of scrutiny in background checks as US flight attendants.[40]

These arguments should be placed into perspective in order to try to discern what in fact animates them. It is not clear why US safety would be compromised by hiring local staff, competent in both English and local languages, on intra-Asian routes. Furthermore, US nationals always have the opportunity to fly on foreign carriers, which may not have identical safety standards. Nor are staff on foreign carriers entering United States airspace subject to the same verifications as those on US carriers.

The Civil Reserve Air Fleet (CRAF) of the US gives rise to what is arguably a more significant reason to resist liberalisation.[41] Thirty-nine United States airlines contract with the government, promising to pledge

of Opposition to Foreign Control of U.S. Airlines'; available at www.alpa.org/DesktopModules/ALPA_Documents/ALPA_DocumentsView.aspx?itemid=4505&ModuleId=1316&Tabid=256.

[39] DOT News Release, 'U.S. Department of Transportation Withdraws International Investment Rule – Commits to Working on Open Skies Agreement', December 5, 2006; available at www.dot.gov/affairs/dot11006.htm.

[40] AFA-CWA News Release, 'Flight Attendants Join Together To Lobby Against Outsourcing', November 2, 2005; available at www.afanet.org/default.asp?id=692.

[41] See Allan Mendelsohn, 'Myths of International Aviation', *Journal of Air Law and Commerce* 68 (2003), p. 519, at pp. 532–534 (arguing that foreign-owned carriers could join CRAF); see *contra* Angela Edwards, Notes and Comments, 'Foreign Investment in the U.S. Airline Industry: Friend or Foe?', *Emory International Law Review* 9 (1995), p. 595, at p. 640 and Jacob Warden, '"Open Skies" at a Crossroads: How the United States and European Union Should Use the ECJ Transport Cases to Reconstruct the Transatlantic Aviation Regime', *Northwestern Journal of International Law and Business* 24 (2003) p. 227, at pp. 249–251 (arguing that dependence upon

up to 1,379 aircraft for military purposes, should this be necessary. In peacetime, CRAF participants have exclusive access to the Department of Defense airlift business. In the case of an emergency, carriers have to deliver aircraft to the Department of Defense in under 48 hours. This programme substantially lessens the burden on the air force to invest in aircraft.

CRAF is optional. United States airlines enter into it by contract for remuneration and there are conditions for participation, including United States registration and a minimum commitment of 15 per cent of cargo capacity and 30 per cent of passenger capacity. The nature of CRAF gives rise to concerns that foreign ownership of airlines could deter or render impossible partaking in the scheme, thereby threatening the United States' defence infrastructure. This argument has been invoked as a ground to oppose liberalisation, including by the pilots and flight attendants unions. Such concerns could be met, if necessary, by legislation requiring continued participation in the programme by foreign-owned US carriers as well as the continued registration of their aircraft in the United States.

Conclusion

We began this investigation of a cosmopolitan argument for liberalised trade in services, and air transport in particular, with reference to Paul Samuelson's misgivings about outsourcing. It turns out that precisely this sort of misgiving is at the root of what blocks the emergence of a truly global aviation market. Two US unions, the Air Line Pilots Association (ALPA), and the Association of Flight Attendants (AFA) led the fight against a proposed loosening of the actual control rule that had been negotiated between the US Administration and the EU. Although their arguments were sometimes cast as concerning the protection of safety and security, their principal concern was that such a change, coupled with liberalised traffic rights, could lead to a loss of US jobs.[42]

Yet even if multilateral aviation liberalisation might give rise to concerns about the impacts of crew outsourcing, with the kind of result Samuelson contemplated, the clear cosmopolitan benefit of liberalised

foreign-owned carriers for CRAF would pose and unacceptable risk for the US). For the US Air Force description of CRAF, see www.af.mil/factsheets/factsheet.asp?fsID=173.

42 ALPA New Release, 'ALPA Commends DOT Decision to Withdraw Proposal to Allow Foreign Control of U.S. Airlines', December 5, 2006; available at www.alpa.org/DesktopModules/ALPA_Documents/ALPA_DocumentsView.aspx?itemid=5936&ModuleId=2618&Tabid=73; and AFA-CWA News Release, 'Transportation Labor Applauds DOT Decision to Withdraw Airline Foreign Control Rule', December 5, 2006; available at www.afalax.org/default.asp?nc=6869&id=134.

global air transport should tilt us away from vague fears. Furthermore, as suggested earlier, the true response to any downward pressure on wages should be to address labour standards globally and income skews domestically through the tax regime rather than to contort the trade regime.

We suggest that a cosmopolitan approach to trade in air transport services would in fact best serve the aims of reinforcing safety and security in the long term. More complete globalisation of the industry could see increased cooperation between airlines from less developed countries and their more developed counterparts. This can improve safety in the same way that Air France's significant investment helped Korean Airlines to improve its safety programme and thus facilitated its entry into the SkyTeam alliance. Furthermore, a cosmopolitan approach encourages international cooperation and integration. This is an alternative, and ultimately sounder, approach to protecting national security than relying exclusively on force and a myriad of restrictive regulations. Indeed, liberalised ownership rules could remove the intrinsic tie between a State's flag and aviation services. A global carrier with a name not linked to a particular country might thus face a reduced risk of its airplanes being used as aerial targets against national policies. Is it coincidental or insignificant that United and American aircraft, rather than those of JetBlue or Frontier, were commandeered on 9/11?

In short, we have sought to argue that the trade regime has a cosmopolitan vocation, especially as concerns trade in services. As Mill insists, trade is ultimately our greatest guarantee of peace. This argument should be conjoined unabashedly with the usual economic arguments about trade benefits. In particular we have endeavoured to illustrate the importance of taking the argument into account in the aviation sector, a sector that is already producing important cosmopolitan gains for the world and could produce yet more.

Bibliography

Beck, Ulrich, *The Cosmopolitan Vision* (London: Blackwell, 2006).

Bhagwati, Jagdish, Arvind Panagariya and T. N. Srinivasan, 'The Muddles over Outsourcing', *Journal of Economic Perspectives* 18(4) (2004), pp. 93–114.

——'Reshaping the WTO'. *Far Eastern Economic Review* 168(2) (Jan/Feb 2005), ABI/INFORM global, p. 25.

Curtin, Philip, *Cross-Cultural Trade in World History* (Cambridge University Press, 1984).

Dew-Becker, Ian and Robert Gordon, 'Where Did the Productivity Growth Go? Inflation Dynamics and the Distribution of Income', National Bureau of Economic Research Working Paper, No. 11842, December 2005.

Dempsey, Paul, *Public International Air Law* (forthcoming).

Edwards, Angela, Notes and Comments, 'Foreign Investment in the U.S. Airline Industry: Friend or Foe?', *Emory International Law Review* 9 (1995) 595.

Geil, Klaus, 'The EU's Experience of Liberalization and its Internal and External Implications', ICAO Dubai Symposium on Global Liberalization, available online at www.icao.int/cgi/goto_m_atb.pl?icao/en/atb/ecp/dubai2006/Docs.htm.

Harper, David, 'Trade, Language and Communication' (2004), manuscript available online at www.econ.nyu.edu/dept/austrian/Trade&Comm.pdf.

Hegel, G. W. F., *Elements of the Philosophy of Right* (1820), edited by Allen Wood, translated by H. B. Nisbet (Cambridge University Press, 1991).

Herodotus, *The Histories*, translated by A. de Sélincourt, revised by J. M. Marincola (Harmondsworth: Penguin, 1996).

Hudson, Manle, 'Aviation and International Law', *Air Law Review* I (1930) #2.

Janda, Richard, 'Passing the Torch: Why ICAO should Leave Economic Regulation of International Air Transport to the WTO', *Annals of Air Space Law* XXI (1995).

Kant, Immanuel, 'Idea for a Universal History from a Cosmopolitan Point of View' (1784), translated by Lewis White Beck. From Immanuel Kant, *On History* (New York: Bobbs-Merrill, 1963).

——*To Perpetual Peace: A Philosophical Sketch* (1795), translated by Ted Humphrey (Indianapolis: Hackett, 2003).

Kaul, Inge, Isabelle Grunberg and Marc Stern (eds.), *Global Public Goods: International Cooperation in the 21st Century* (Oxford University Press, 1999).

Marx, Karl, *The German Ideology* (1846) (London: Lawrence and Wishart, 1965), reproduced by Electronic Book.

——*Capital Volume III* (1894), volume 37 of the *Marx–Engels Collected Works* (1932).

Mendelsohn, Allan. 'Myths of International Aviation', *Journal of Air Law and Commerce* 68 (2003) 519.

Mendoza, Ronald, 'The Multilateral Trade Regime: A Global Public Good For All?', in Inge Kaul, Pedro Conceicao, Katell Le Goulven, and Ronald U. Mendoza (eds.), *Providing Global Public Goods: Managing Globalization* (Oxford University Press, 2003).

Milde, Michael, 'The Chicago Convention – Are Major Amendments Necessary or Desirable 50 Years Later?', *Annals of Air & Space Law* XIX (1994).

Mill, John Stuart, *Principles of Political Economy* (London: Parker, 1848).

Piketty, Thomas and Emmanuel Saes, 'The Evolution of Top Incomes: A Historical and International Perspective', NBER Working Paper no. 11955, January 2006.

Samuelson, Paul A., 'Where Ricardo and Mill Rebut and Confirm Arguments of Mainstream Economists Supporting Globalization', *Journal of Economic Perspectives*, 18(3) (Summer 2004), p. 135.

Schumpeter, Joseph, *Capitalism, Socialism and Democracy* (1942).

Stern, Nicholas, *The Economics of Climate Change: Stern Review* (Cambridge University Press, 2006), at p. 342.

Warden, Jacob, '"Open Skies" at a Crossroads: How the United States and European Union Should Use the ECJ Transport Cases to Reconstruct the Transatlantic Aviation Regime', *Northwestern Journal of International Law and Business* 24 (2003), 227.

Wolfe, Robert, 'The WTO in Suspense: Is Institutional Reform Needed?', Unpublished Working Paper for Princeton Workshop (23–25 August 2006) of the Centre for International Governance Innovation project on Global Institutional Reform.

Annex

List of all countries that are currently part of some liberal aviation agreement

Albania	Egypt	Madagascar	Russian Federation
American Samoa	El Salvador	Malaysia	Rwanda
Armenia	Fiji	Maldives	Saint Lucia
Australia	Finland	Malta	Saudi Arabia
Austria	Gabon	Marshall Islands	Senegal
Azerbaijan	Gambia	Mauritius	Singapore
Bahrain	Germany	Mexico	Slovakia
Bangladesh	Ghana	Mongolia	South Africa
Barbados	Greece	Morocco	Spain
Belarus	Grenada	Myanmar	Sri Lanka
Benin	Guatemala	Namibia	Sweden
Bolivia	Honduras	Nauru	Switzerland
Botswana	Hungary	Nepal	Syrian Arab Republic
Brazil	Iceland	Netherlands	TFYR Macedonia
Brunei Darussalam	India	Netherlands Antilles	Thailand
Bulgaria	Indonesia	New Zealand	Turkey
Cambodia	Iran (Islamic Republic of)	Nicaragua	Uganda
Canada	Ireland	Nigeria	Ukraine
Cape Verde	Israel	Norway	United Arab Emirates
Chile	Italy	Oman	United Kingdom
China	Jamaica	Pakistan	United Republic of Tanzania
China, Hong Kong SAR	Japan	Panama	United States
China, Macao SAR	Jordan	Peru	Uzbekistan
Cook Islands	Kazakhstan	Philippines	Vanuatu
Costa Rica	Kyrgyzstan	Poland	Vietnam
Croatia	Lao People's Democratic Republic	Portugal	Yemen
Czech Republic	Latvia	Qatar	Zimbabwe
Democratic People's Republic of Korea	Lebanon	Republic of Korea	
Denmark	Lithuania	Republic of Moldova	
Dominican Republic	Luxembourg	Romania	

PART 8

Conclusion

27

Been there, not yet done that: Lessons and challenges in services trade

PIERRE SAUVÉ*

1. Background considerations

Judged against almost any qualitative or quantitative benchmark, the negotiated opening of services markets has proven fiendishly difficult, leading almost invariably to disappointing outcomes. These stand in stark contrast to the remarkable – and typically unilateral – opening that has otherwise characterised services markets across the globe over the past two decades.

The tendency for negotiated outcomes in services to fall short of expectations appears to hold regardless of the negotiating setting. The challenge of prying open services markets and of advancing unfinished rule-making challenges is indeed almost as intractable at the centre – i.e. under World Trade Organization's (WTO) General Agreement on Trade in Services (GATS) as it is at the burgeoning periphery of preferential trade agreements (PTAs) featuring Chapters on services and investment, despite the observed tendency for PTAs to achieve WTO+ outcomes in market-opening terms in a range of sectors.[1]

For a while, in identifying the various forces that conspired to produce such results, one could credibly invoke the regulatory and negotiating precaution that novelty typically induces among risk-averse bureaucratic

* The author is grateful to Americo Beviglia-Zampetti, Marion Panizzon and Nicole Pohl and to participants at the World Trade Institute's 10th World Trade Forum held in Berne, Switzerland on 8–9 September 2006 for helpful comments and discussions.

[1] The fact that the most recent wave of PTAs has achieved significant levels of (WTO+) market opening in a number of sectors is hardly surprising given the extent of autonomous liberalisation implemented since the end of the Uruguay Round and the proliferating set of PTAs that have been negotiated around the world during this period. Negotiating advances on the unfinished rule-making agenda of the GATS have, however, been significantly fewer. See Sauvé (2002; 2006); Marchetti and Mavroidis (2004); and Roy, Marchetti and Lim (2006).

constituencies. Nothing, indeed, is scarier than a blank page, and that is essentially what the early pioneers in services confronted at the negotiating table.

The trade policy community has been grappling with services for just over two decades now. The jury is still out as to whether this is a long enough period from which to expect some measure of policy- and rule-making maturity to take root. In all likelihood, it is not, and so collective judgements, including those of the author, may simply be too harsh.[2]

Though services negotiations continue to this day to be characterised by significant doses of learning by doing, much has been learned, studied, comparatively assessed and negotiated since the mid-1980s. Trade officials have been in perpetual negotiating motion on services since the launch of the Uruguay Round, owing to the 'overtime' negotiations that took place in a number of sectors after the Round's conclusion, to the fact that the GATS framework of rules has yet to be fully agreed and in light of the proliferating web of PTAs featuring disciplines on trade in services.

Relative to the situation prevailing at the time of the Uruguay Round's launch, there is today an incomparably better (and more solidly documented) grasp both of the potential returns to sound, pro-competitive, service sector reforms as well as a finer – and more realistic – appreciation of the regulatory challenges such reforms can pose and the consequent need for prior regulatory strengthening and sequencing in their enactment.

Services rules have also become largely commoditised over the past two decades. They come today in two main shapes, from which only minor deviations tend to be made in the multiplicity of negotiating settings in which they are used. These are: (i) the 'hybrid' approach practised in GATS and in a number of PTAs and (ii) the negative list approach pioneered in the ANZCERTA and NAFTA and replicated in the vast majority of subsequent PTAs.[3]

[2] Like all areas of trade policy, the services field has in recent years witnessed the emerging influence of non-governmental actors whose main preoccupations in services have centered on the defence of public services and the preservation of regulatory autonomy. Accordingly, the NGO community, particularly in the developed world, has generally been highly critical of the pursuit of market opening and rule-making initiatives in services trade at the WTO and regional levels. For a fuller discussion, see OECD (2002) and WTO (2001).

[3] The GATS, or so-called 'hybrid', approach to market opening operates on the basis of the positive selection of sectors, sub-sectors and modes of supply in which countries voluntarily choose to schedule liberalisation commitments, subject to the negative listing of non-conforming measures maintained in scheduled areas. *A contrario*, a negative list approach is one in which all measures affecting services trade are deemed to be fully

Policy officials today thus need to advance more sophisticated reasons than novelty in justifying what remains generally paltry negotiating results. This chapter explores some of the political economy forces behind such observed difficulties. It seeks answers to one overriding question: why is it seemingly so difficult to pry open services markets through the process of trade negotiations?

The chapter starts with a discussion of the nature of services markets in examining the exigencies of opening services markets. Such a discussion draws attention to the inherent tensions between generic (i.e. 'horizontal') and sector-specific (i.e. 'vertical') approaches to rule-design and market opening in services trade. The chapter recalls some of the reasons for the heightened regulatory precaution present in services agreements. It also discusses why the need has arisen to shift gears from bilateral to collective requests and offers on market opening, an important topic to which this publication devotes deserved attention.[4]

The chapter then turns its attention to the likely liberalising attributes of what remains to date a largely elusive quest for an operational emergency safeguard mechanism for services. It then tackles the difficulty of 'fitting' temporary labour mobility in a multilateral trade policy setting and the systemic implications deriving therefrom, particularly from a development perspective. The chapter closes with a few concluding thoughts.

2. Defining characteristics of services: Negotiating implications

The novelty, considerable sectoral diversity and greater overall regulatory complexity of services trade resulted in a limited initial harvest of liberalisation commitments in the Uruguay Round. Most attention during the Round was indeed focused on the development of a (yet unfinished) framework of rules governing the progressive liberalisation of services markets.[5] With the notable exception of newly-acceding

liberalised unless they are described in reservations lists annexed to the agreements opting for such an approach. While both approaches can achieve similar levels of market opening, negative listing tends to generate greater transparency on existing regulatory restrictions since it produces comprehensive lists of non-conforming measures, and not only those arising in sectors, sub-sectors or modes of supply that have been positively scheduled under hybrid approaches.

[4] See in particular the contributions by Türk, Kelly and Gao in this volume.

[5] Outstanding rule-making negotiations under GATS are proceeding in four areas: emergency safeguards; non-discriminatory domestic regulation; subsidies; and government procurement of services.

countries, whose often coerced level of initial commitments is higher in some instances than that which a number of OECD member countries undertook in the Uruguay Round,[6] the limited liberalisation commitments made by original WTO Members under the GATS recalls that the latter enjoy considerable policy flexibility. This belies the largely fictitious depiction of the GATS as a market-opening, sovereignty depriving, juggernaut that one hears about from time to time in academic and NGO circles.

While an increasing body of empirical evidence has come to show that the potential benefits of services trade reform can be considerable,[7] there is no escaping the reality that progress in services negotiations at the WTO has been disappointing.[8] One problem, of course, is guilt by association: services talks have been part of – and partly hostage to – a stagnant process of multilateral negotiations under the Doha Development Agenda (DDA). However, the problem is far from unique to the WTO process, as very similar difficulties can also be detected in the context of preferential liberalisation initiatives.

To be sure, the political geometry of the currently stalled WTO round has been such that progress in other areas of the DDA, and notably agriculture, appears to have become a necessary precondition for progress in services (and on other DDA issues). But it is not, nor should it be, a sufficient condition. As one informed observer aptly noted: 'the GATS negotiations have fallen into a low-level equilibrium trap: little is expected and even less offered'.[9]

Looking back on two decades of learning by doing in services trade, a number of reasons can be adduced to explain why services negotiations continue to be problematic even as the purpose and likely net benefits of them – the question of why – is largely seen as being positive and supportive of the development process.

If answers to the question of why seem clear enough to most (but not all) observers, things are decidedly murkier when answers are sought to the questions of who, what, how and where: who does the negotiating? Who are the constituents? What are services negotiations about? How are services negotiations conducted? And where is services liberalisation

[6] See Adlung and Roy (2005).

[7] See Mattoo, Rathindran and Subramanian (2001); OECD (2002; 2003; 2005); Robinson, Wang and Martin (1999); and World Bank (2001).

[8] See Adlung (2004) and Adlung and Roy (2005) for a comprehensive analysis of the level of market opening achieved to date under the GATS.

[9] See Mattoo (2006).

best pursued – at the centre or at the periphery? We turn our attention to the first four questions in what follows before taking up the question of where in a later section of the paper.

2.1. Who negotiates?

One of the hallmarks of the modern trade policy process is its near monopolisation by representatives of the legal community. This is perhaps not surprising given that trade agreements are, after all, primarily about the making and enforcement of legally binding rules. Services, of course, are no exception to this trend. The regulatory intensity of services trade and the wide range of sectoral interests, regimes and institutions they bring together actually imply an even greater predominance of lawyers at the negotiating table.

While all trade negotiators tend to be risk-averse bureaucrats subject to inevitable pressures of regulatory and political capture, experience suggests that lawyers and economists do not always go about their negotiating in quite the same way.

Lawyers, by their very training, tend to be more respectful, and perhaps more protective of the law. This arguably makes them more proficient captives. They are also less prone, unless they have been educated in the law and economics tradition, to question the policy rationale behind the kinds of measures – particularly home country measures – that may otherwise display trade- and investment-inhibiting effects. They may also be less prone to questioning the efficiency of the policy response to the market failure that created the need for a specific law or regulatory measure in the first place. Such an approach arguably lessens the scope for bargaining that may be needed in negotiations centred on the multi-sectoral elimination or progressive dismantling of trade-inhibiting laws and regulations of a non-tariff nature.

Such aspersions aside, lawyers are *sans égal* in their ability to translate the need for policy ambiguity into robust legal provisions. Coming in a policy area that was largely uncharted until very recently, such a skill set has been much in demand in services. A prime example can be found in the drafting of Article 1.3b of the GATS dealing with the decidedly elastic carve-out of services supplied in the exercise of government authority from the Agreement's scope of coverage.

Economists, for their part, often tend to look first at the nature of the market failure underlying a regulatory measure and to raise questions about its efficacy and its continued need in light of evolving market circumstances. The ubiquity of market failures in services, which run the gamut from information asymmetries in financial and professional services to monopolies and oligopolies in network-based industries and to externalities and universal service provision imperatives in sectors such as tourism, transport, education, health or culture, means that economists are much in need in the design of appropriate policy responses in services markets.[10] Their training is particularly useful in considering the cross-border implications of responses to domestic market failures. They may thus display greater interest and intellectual curiosity in seeking lesser or least-trade or investment-restrictive policy alternatives. Such differences, however subtle, can matter at the negotiating table to the extent that a readiness to contemplate a departure from the regulatory status quo may open up new bargaining possibilities.

Economists may also come in handy in prescribing policy choices, particularly in the market access phase of negotiations, that may yield greater development dividends to the home country than the preservation of the regulatory status quo to which lawyers may be more wedded.

It is impossible of course to generalise such arguments, all the more so as the author is himself a dismal scientist, but his repeated observance of the trends described above appear worthy of further analytical scrutiny.

The diversity of sectoral challenges and the differing sources of market failures to which regulation responds across service sectors represents a daunting challenge for services negotiators. The latter are all at once compelled to be steeped in several regulatory 'languages', to master the regulatory intricacies of sectors prone to market failures with highly divergent market access–inhibiting effects and to highly differentiated market structures. Rule-making in services typically confronts sectors of economic activity characterised by highly concentrated and powerful firms who derive their market power either from network attributes, as in telecommunications, energy, environmental or transportation services, or, somewhat paradoxically, from the merger and acquisition frenzy that has come in globalisation's wake and which has resulted, in some sectors, in greater market concentration.

Confronting such challenges is without doubt more complex for developing country negotiators, who do not typically enjoy the legion of sectoral specialists available to their developed country brethren. In OECD countries, it is not rare for services negotiators hailing from trade or foreign

[10] See Mattoo and Sauvé (2003) and Krajewski (2003) for a fuller discussion of the interface between domestic regulation and services liberalisation.

ministries to outsource much of the sectoral negotiating challenge to officials from line ministries and regulatory agencies. More often than not, the latter will be all too happy – turf protection *oblige* – to fill the gap.

Such deference to the expertise of sectoral regulators – which has been most pronounced in the field of financial services and is vividly reflected in the drafting of the GATS Annex on Financial Services[11] – may yet offer a further explanation of the tendency for services negotiations to be characterised by strong doses of regulatory precaution. Sectoral regulators, after all, tend to be closer to – and often subject to significant pressures of regulatory capture by – the industries they regulate. Accordingly, they are likely to be offensive in the pursuit of market access opportunities abroad but more rigidly defensive in protecting prevailing domestic regulation. That sectoral regulators are often drawn from the legal community may well heighten the above tendencies.

Deference to sectoral expertise invariably imparts greater verticality to rule-design, feeding tensions between generic (i.e. horizontally applicable) rules, towards which trade or foreign ministry officials are typically more attracted, and sector-specific rules that are commonly found in services agreements and which are generally favoured by line ministries and sectoral regulatory agencies.

Rule-making and market-opening efforts in services are typically led by sectoral officials and regulators that are often closer to the industries they regulate than to the foreign or trade ministries responsible for securing overall intersectoral bargains. This can lead to negotiated outcomes that are more narrowly drawn and self-contained for fear that sectoral interests and the complex domestic regulatory equilibrium they embody may be 'traded off' by bargain-hunting trade policy generalists, be they lawyers or economists.

A further remark on the question of who negotiates services agreements concerns the much greater involvement of developing country officials in services talks today. The Uruguay Round saw only a handful of developing countries actively involved in the design of the GATS, the great majority of developing country GATT members behaving as

[11] The Annex on Financial Services is unique in mandating the presence of financial expertise in the handling of possible trade disputes in the sector. It is also unique in its provision of a prudential carve-out for which financial officials had initially sought – but ultimately failed to secure – full immunity from WTO dispute settlement procedures in regard to prudential measures.

rule-takers in an area where expertise was in limited supply and where most felt they had negligible negotiating (i.e. exporting) interests.

A fuller appreciation of the contribution of services reforms to the development process, including on the import side, and a growing recognition of the fact that many developing countries have distinct exporting interests in services trade, coupled with the rising assertiveness of developing country coalitions in the WTO's implicit governance structure and cumulative investments in trade-related capacity building in services (much of it also dispensed in the context of PTAs as well) have given a strong voice to developing countries in the conduct of services negotiations.

At the same time, there can be no escaping the reality that a large number of developing countries continue to face acute capacity constraints in participating meaningfully in services discussions and in implementing resulting outcomes. The full extent of such shortcomings has become much clearer in the context of a multilateral negotiating round branded as centrally preoccupied with development matters.

In a DDA context that has witnessed a tangible reassertion of North-South tensions on many issues and where many developing countries harbour genuine concerns over the inequity of Uruguay Round outcomes (though not so much in services), this has produced a paradoxical tendency for defensive posturing – for instance on the treatment of investment as a Singapore Issue or on the desirability of moving from bilateral to collective requests and offers – in an area where the collective negotiating interests of developing countries would appear to call for more resolute engagement. In so doing, developing countries, including those least developing countries for whom the signalling and investment climate-enhancing benefits of international rule-making are arguably most evident, may well have underplayed their card on services and made the quest for acceptable cross-sectoral bargains harder.

Any belief that developing countries may fare better under PTAs entered into with developed countries, to which the stalled DDA will now give renewed impetus, appears highly misguided. Not only are such agreements fully commoditised in their content, offering little scope for developing countries to influence the substantive nature of the rules being adopted, many of them display substantive elements that can be characterised as WTO minus in areas where developing countries have strong export interests. This is notably the case for the movement of service providers, which has for instance been excluded from the scope of recent PTAs entered into by the United States.

A final remark on the question of who negotiates services agreements relates to the consequences of staff turnover in Geneva and in capitals. Anyone with experience of international negotiations will readily admit that such processes can be heavily influenced by the personalities, leadership, networking qualities and knowledge of precious few individuals. This has been very much the case in services negotiations, particularly at the WTO, given its leading role as an incubator of rule-making in what remains a relatively novel policy area. While staff turnover is inevitable in diplomatic circles, it nonetheless results in the loss of the institutional memory and substantive knowledge embodied in the departing experts. Such a loss may exert significant effects on negotiating dynamics. Moreover, such losses can never be fully tempered by the otherwise high degree of competence and professionalism of international secretariats. This is all the more so in a member-driven organisation like the WTO where the secretariat has limited scope for advancing its own ideas on issues under negotiation, particularly newer issues that may be more controversial simply because of their novel character.

2.2. In whose interest? Shifting constituent dynamics

Who do services negotiators work for? For their governments of course. However, governments rarely have a fully objective sense of where the national interest lies and even when they do, political constraints often stand in the way of its pursuit. Negotiating interests are thus dictated by the needs and policy preferences – offensive and defensive – of key constituents. Services negotiations are far from immune from the producer bias that characterises the political economy of trade negotiations in the goods area.

The political economy of constituent involvement in services negotiations has undergone considerable change in recent years. The Uruguay Round saw significant private sector engagement, including at the CEO level in a number of sectors, most visibly in the financial services industry. More than any other industry, the financial community invested the time, money and efforts required to give policy prominence to the development of a trade regime for services.

Beyond its own quest for enhanced access to world markets, the financial sector was also unique in the leadership it assumed in building and sustaining a coalition of business users in favour of liberalised telecommunications markets.

Notwithstanding the telecommunications example, whose success was due in no small measure to the industry's own (technologically induced) conversion to market liberalisation over the course of the Uruguay Round, user coalitions have proven fiendishly difficult to assemble in the services field. Consumers, patients, passengers and shippers have thus far proven no match for the vocal and entrenched interests of industry associations, professional licensing bodies or dominant firms in key sectors. For instance, the aviation and maritime industries, two sectors that symbolise more than any other the very conduct of world trade, are almost wholly excluded from the scope of trade agreements in services – explicitly in the case of most air transport services, indirectly in the case of the maritime transport industry owing to the refusal of the United States to engage in the sector, whether at the bilateral, regional or multilateral level.

The DDA landscape is much changed, with significantly lesser (and less vocal) engagement from the private sector[12] and the mass arrival on the services scene of civil society organisations concerned by the potential risks that services liberalisation might pose to the sovereign right of WTO Members to regulate in the public interest and by alleged pressures, stemming primarily from multinational firms, to promote market competition in a range of industries displaying public goods characteristics, such as education, health, water distribution or cultural industries.[13]

Governments, particularly those of developed countries, have responded in a predictable manner to this new landscape. Prodded on more forcibly by NGOs than by private sector interests, WTO Members have tended to exhibit greater regulatory prudence in precisely those sectors deemed sensitive by civil society organisations. This is notable for instance from the fact that not a single OECD country has advanced a market access commitment in health services at a time when such trade is booming and where a case for

[12] Part of the reason for the lessened involvement of private actors in services negotiations owes to the perception that trade agreements in services cannot deliver tangible benefits in real time and have not been able to do much beyond locking in the regulatory status quo. Such behaviour may also reflect the fact that private sector operators are less concerned today with trade and investment impediments in light of the continued wave of unilateral dismantling of protective measures and the limited evidence of backsliding given the intensity of competitive pressures that apply in key services markets in a globalising world economy. The absence of legally binding commitments under GATS or PTAs does not imply that access to emerging country markets is denied.

[13] For a fuller discussion of the GATS critique, see Sinclair (2000) and Sinclair and Grieshaber-Otto (2002). For a rebuttal of such criticisms, see WTO (2001) and OECD (2002).

collective action would seem highly desirable.[14] It is also reflected in the decision of a number of WTO Members, such as Canada and the members of the European Union, to renounce making market-opening requests to their trading partners in the educational sector at a time when home country institutions have been expanding abroad at an unprecedented rate.[15] The result offers a strange spectacle of rapid internationalisation conducted at arm's length from the very framework designed to provide disciplines and rules on how best to manage such market opening in the interests of home and host countries alike under conditions of transparency and orderly adjustment.

2.3. *What are services negotiations about?*

The very subject matter of services negotiations – the elimination and/or progressive dismantling of discriminatory and non-discriminatory regulatory measures that may directly or indirectly impede access to markets – goes a long way in explaining why progress at the negotiating table is so ponderous. Apart from the movement of service providers, whose tortuous political economy is taken up separately below, the border as a physical locus of trade regulation matters little in services given the irrelevance of tariffs as instruments of protection. A few heroic attempts have been made, most comprehensively in Australia,[16] to derive tariff equivalent measures of protection in services. Such efforts have largely run into intractable measurement problems owing to the lack of sufficiently disaggregated data on services trade.

Services negotiations do not therefore lend themselves to the mathematical niceties of tariff negotiations. With domestic regulation as the *matière première* of services talks, negotiations in the sector can thus be likened to discussions of non-tariff measures in the goods area. As discussions have shown since the Tokyo Round, negotiating on NTBs and on NTB-like measures is considerably more taxing and typically proceeds at a snail's pace.

The sheer diversity of the service economy and the powerful interests that lie behind domestic regulatory regimes and institutions obviously

[14] For a comprehensive analysis of the challenges of internationalisation in health services, see Blouin, Drager and Smith (2005).

[15] For a fuller discussion of the reasons for such regulatory precaution in higher education services, see Sauvé (2002a).

[16] See in particular the work by Dee (2003) and by McGuire and Schuele (2000).

add to the complexity of effecting regulatory change at the negotiating table. Doing so is all the more difficult as it is predicated upon modifying, at the behest of foreign trading partners, domestic legislation in what are often sensitive policy domains and where a multiplicity of policy objectives are pursued (equity, access, income redistribution, cultural diversity, consumer protection, regional development, infant industry protection, etc.).

Apart from the context-specific case of the WTO accession process and of governments who may occasionally find it convenient to invoke foreign pressures to unblock stalled domestic reform efforts (e.g. Japan and China), it is most unlikely that significant liberalisation requiring changed or *de novo* domestic legislative measures will be driven at the trade negotiating table.

Just as developing countries have shown considerable reluctance towards binding market-opening measures that were mandated by the Bretton Woods institutions, so too are most WTO Members unlikely to heed external calls for regulatory reform, however desirable these may be on efficiency or developmental grounds.

Reforming service industries, especially in mature economies where participatory democracy is vibrant, is a long-haul process requiring maturation for change to take hold. It is rare indeed that the time cycle of domestic regulatory reform in major WTO Members coincides with the trade negotiating cycle. Admittedly, WTO Members can make use of Article 18 of GATS (Additional Commitments) to do tomorrow what political conditions will not allow today. And precedents do exist where both cycles have come together. This was the case notably in the area of basic telecommunications in the immediate aftermath of the Uruguay Round, but such instances tend to be exceptions, not the rule.

Not surprisingly, trade agreements in services are far likelier to periodically harvest ongoing reforms, i.e. serve as agents of status quo lock-in, than to initiate significant doses of market opening. This tendency is reinforced by the very architecture of services agreements, which provide ample space for governments either: (i) not to make commitments in any given sector; (ii) to schedule commitments below the status quo, or, (iii) in agreements operating on the basis of negative listing, to allow for 'unbound' or open-ended reservations to be lodged, thereby preserving the right for governments to introduce new non-conforming regulatory measures in future.

Given the mercantilistic mindset that pervades the trade negotiating process, services negotiations are made no easier by the statistical reality that developed countries continue to account for roughly four-fifths of world services trade. Such a trend inevitably fuels lingering perceptions of developed county dominance in the benefits to be reaped from services trade, despite the weak underlying economic analysis such perceptions reveal. As a result, and despite the fact that services negotiations in the DDA have not so far proven particularly controversial at the intergovernmental level, negotiating bargains have proved hard to strike and offers have, with few exceptions, remained at a low, commercially meaningless, level.

Moreover, doubts arise as to whether the kinds of barriers restricting services markets within OECD countries (i.e. on a North-North basis) can be most efficiently tackled in the WTO. To be sure, trade relations in services among advanced industrial countries continue to confront an array of formal and informal barriers to trade and investment in areas such as professional licensing, government procurement, visa requirements, data privacy, economic patriotism, etc. Yet the will of OECD member countries to address these issues in the WTO, and the WTO's track record in delivering lasting solutions in these areas, remain far from convincing. More likely than not, the intra-OECD services agenda seems destined to be tackled in PTAs or, likelier still, within various regional (e.g. transatlantic) regulatory cooperation fora. Such a tendency, in turn, may well reinforce the North-South tensions and perceptions discussed above.

2.4. How are services negotiations conducted? Moving beyond bilateral request-offer negotiations

Several voices have been heard expressing alarm at the lack of engagement of WTO Members in the DDA's services negotiations. There are doubtless several reasons for this, starting with the generally desultory progress registered elsewhere in the negotiations, particularly in agriculture, which is by all accounts the defining issue of the Doha Round and that most likely to make or break the development dimension woven into it. The 'agriculture comes first' aspect of the DDA has unfortunately relegated services to a secondary role. It has seen many leading developing countries – those with arguably most at stake (i.e. emerging countries having much to offer by way of new or improved market access commitments) in services and the DDA more generally holding back until developed countries show their hands in farm trade.

Experience suggests, however, that it would be a mistake to read too much into such an account of the current state of play of DDA talks in services, as cross-sectoral considerations tend to weigh more heavily in negotiating bargains towards the very end of multilateral negotiations.

Faced with an outstanding rule-making agenda on services – the so-called 'unfinished agenda' on domestic regulation, emergency safeguards measures (see section 3 below), subsidies and government procurement in services – that has to date revealed few signs of DDA-induced progress, a number of proposals have been made to impart greater momentum to the market access dimension of negotiations under the GATS.

2.4.1. Inoperative, and now seen as such: The bilateral request-offer process

One major reason for such a push is the growing realisation that the current bilateral request-offer approach is largely inoperative. For lack of any credible alternative,[17] and drawing on mercantilistic reflexes long honed in goods (i.e. tariff) negotiations, the bilateral request-offer approach was adopted in the Uruguay Round as the dominant negotiating method for services.

Discussions at the December 2005 WTO Ministerial in Hong Kong on the idea of conducting,[18] where practicable, negotiations on a plurilateral basis revealed a paradoxical – if largely tactical on the part of some WTO Members – aversion of developing countries to considering alternatives to the current bilateral approach.

The paradox lies in the fact that such an approach is clearly much more taxing for developing countries than it is for developed countries. This is so given the considerable resources and time it consumes, the limited number of services experts available for bilateral discussions in Geneva missions and in capitals; the negotiating imbalances that flow from the limited ability of most developing countries to formulate their own requests; significant asymmetries of negotiating-relevant information available to policy officials; and the more limited extent of stakeholder consultations and private sector engagement – and presence abroad – of service suppliers from developing countries. All of the above factors tend not surprisingly to interact in ways that produce

[17] It bears recalling that the bulk of the Uruguay Round was spent on developing the framework of disciplines and rules for services trade. Considerably less time was spent on the market access dimension of the talks, and no specific attention was paid to the idea of alternative methods of conducting market access negotiations in services.

[18] See WTO (2005).

least common denominator, precaution-induced, outcomes at the negotiating table.

Such a stalemate, in turn, complicates attempts at marshalling corporate interest in multilateral negotiations, and tends to shift incentives towards bilateral or neighbourhood responses in the form of preferential trade agreements.

A strong case exists for complementing the current bilateral request-offer approach, which is still of relevance for countries with highly specific offensive or defensive interests, with collective approaches to negotiations. In a world of unequal bargaining power, plurilateral or multilateral approaches, which must be equitable and efficient if they are to produce agreement and must target areas of common interest in a flexible manner, are likely to yield a more desirable outcome than bilateral negotiations.

Collective (plurilateral) approaches are also likely to economise on the scarcest of commodities: time and human resources, and afford developing countries significant economies of scale in negotiating efforts. Avoiding sector-by-sector and country-by-country bartering of commitments can indeed substantially reduce the transaction costs of negotiations.[19]

2.4.2. Towards formula-based negotiating in services?

Most formula proposals advanced to date in the DDA centre on the idea of ratcheting up the overall level of bound commitments under GATS. The simplest approach would be horizontal in nature and consist of defining a percentage of service sectors to be covered by binding commitments and/or the number of sectors subject to full market opening (i.e. with no restrictions on national treatment and market access). While such an approach can be deemed attractive, one can easily see how it could translate into commitments in sectors that are less commercially meaningful – for instance in regard to mode 2 trade (movement of consumers) – for the sake of meeting a quantitative threshold.

Quantitative assessments of offers or numerical targets, which some WTO Members had espoused as one way forward in the market access negotiations under GATS, have thus quite sensibly been discarded as

[19] Use of such formulas may also represent the only feasible way to grant credit to unilateral liberalisers. In contrast, it is much more difficult to ensure compensation for the loss of negotiating coinage caused by unilateral liberalisation in a bilateral request-and-offer negotiation (Mattoo, 2006).

unhelpful distractions because even the best available methods of quantifying barriers to trade are widely viewed as inadequate. At best, it could be possible to measure differences in the sectoral coverage of commitments, possibly weighted by some measure of the level of openness.[20] Reaching agreement on any such target, however, would be extremely difficult and consume negotiating time and energy that are already in short supply.

The decision made by Trade Ministers at the December 2005 WTO Ministerial Meeting in Hong Kong to supplement bilateral request-offer discussions with plurilateral negotiations whose results would then be extended to all WTO Members on an MFN basis appears a more constructive alternative.[21] Such an approach primarily involves groups of members, akin to the numerous 'Friends' groups that already exist under GATS, to propose a set of negotiating objectives in a given sector or in a cluster of sectors.

Such objectives can be outlined in model schedules similar to the Understanding on Commitments in Financial Services agreed in 1997 or the Model Schedule for Maritime Transport advanced by a number of WTO Members in the DDA. They might also take the form of a set of additional regulatory disciplines, as was done successfully in the Telecommunications Reference Paper appended to the 1997 Agreement on Basic Telecommunications. The latter approach would likely be required should market opening discussions intensify in other network-based industries, such as energy services.[22] The building blocks of model schedules are relatively straightforward, and some have already been proposed for specific modes.[23]

2.4.3. The need for development-friendly clusters

Two clusters around which 'Friends' groups have emerged and which would appear to show significant promise from a development perspective are those relating to computer-related services and logistics. Both, as it happens, relate closely to – and usefully complement – recent or ongoing negotiating efforts in goods trade. In so doing, they recall the close linkages that exist between goods and services in a globalising

[20] Such an approach was first used in Hoekman (1995).

[21] See Annex C of WTO (2005).

[22] For a fuller description of pro-competitive regulatory disciplines in energy services, see Evans (2002).

[23] See in particular Mattoo, Chaudhuri and Self (2003); Mattoo and Wunsch-Vincent (2004); and Thompson (2000).

environment and the need to pursue negotiated strategies that relate more closely to the integrated manner in which firms operate in the global market-place.

The cluster on computer-related services could thus be crafted as the GATS complement to the highly successful 1997 Information Technology Agreement,[24] and would seek to address a range of policy challenges arising with greatest intensity at the interface of modes 1, 2 and 4. It would provide a vehicle for WTO Members to maintain the currently relatively open and benign trading environment governing remotely supplied services (e.g. e-commerce). It would also help pre-empt nascent forms of protectionism in regard to business process outsourcing while also facilitating the temporary business travel of a dedicated category of skilled professionals in the sector.

For its part, the cluster on trade logistics should be designed as the GATS complement to the ongoing DDA discussions on trade facilitation under the GATT. Services make up the bulk of what is ultimately involved in shipping goods across borders, from warehousing to customs brokering, freight-forwarding, port and airport management services, inspection services, express delivery and distribution services. This continuum provides a ready platform within which WTO Members can address key border infrastructure bottlenecks by engaging in selective, progressive liberalisation across a wide range of sectors. The scope for parallelism between the GATS and GATT negotiations is all the greater as talks on trade facilitation were the lone Singapore Issue survivor and appear to have generated significant policy interest among WTO Members in the course of the DDA.

A WTO Member's incentive to participate in a given negotiation, be it bilateral or plurilateral, will of essence depend on the willingness of its trading partners to make commitments in modes and sectors in which the member has an export interest, both within and outside services. A reformed negotiating method can help, especially if it chips away at the tendency for negotiating bargains to be sought along mutually exclusive sectoral lines, but ultimately members will need to make the hard political bargains necessary for a successful outcome.[25]

2.4.4. Binding the status quo?

Yet another, albeit potentially more controversial, complementary element, would be for WTO Members to strive to lock in the regulatory status quo in

[24] For a detailed analysis of the ITA, see Sauvé and Fliess (1998). [25] See Mattoo (2006).

sectors in which they voluntarily decide to schedule commitments. Without changing the way in which liberalisation commitments are scheduled under GATS (i.e. by preserving the Agreement's so-called 'hybrid' approach[26]), such an approach would aim to approximate the nature of commitments made in the vast majority of regional trade agreements that follow a negative list approach to market opening.

Doing so would reduce what in some instances are significant gaps between the actual level of market access afforded under domestic laws and regulations and the lower level of access provided under existing GATS commitments. Such an outcome could either proceed from an informal understanding among GATS members or be anchored in a more formal modification of the rules governing the scheduling of market access and national treatment commitments under the Agreement.[27]

2.4.5. Paying more than lip service: Towards a transparency undertaking?

Most developing countries appear unwilling to break with past practice in regard to the scheduling of GATS commitments. Accordingly, a softer variation to the proposal outlined above could be envisaged whereby WTO Members would continue to schedule commitments on a hybrid basis while agreeing to prepare non-binding lists of non-conforming measures affecting trade and investment in services for purposes of transparency.

Developing countries, and especially least developed countries, should be given more time and provided with needed technical assistance in preparing such lists. A growing number of WTO Members, it should be

[26] The hybrid approach to scheduling commitments under GATS entails the positive determination of sectors, sub-sectors and modes of supply which WTO Members voluntarily agree to inscribe in their schedules and the negative retention of any non-conforming measures maintained in such sectors, sub-sectors and modes of supply.

[27] The decision to allow WTO Members to schedule commitments below the regulatory status quo was taken in the Uruguay Round, replicating in services trade the mercantilistic instincts long practised for tariff negotiations in goods trade. In the Uruguay Round, only developing countries availed themselves of such flexibility, as the norm for OECD countries (and subsequently for acceding countries) was to lock in the prevailing level of market openness in their GATS commitments. Closing the gap between applied and bound regulation would arguably increase the predictability and transparency of host countries' services regimes, contributing in the process to enhancing their investment climates.

noted, have already assumed such an obligation under preferential trade and investment agreements operating on the basis of negative listing.

Such a Transparency Undertaking could serve several good-governance promoting purposes. It could help countries assess their regulatory regimes; benchmark them against best international or regional practice; identify policy objectives that may be achieved in a less trade- and/or investment-restrictive manner; identify sectors where the need for restrictions remains a national policy imperative; allow for the rank-ordering of impediments by sector, country, region and mode of supply for purposes of future negotiations; help in the formulation of possible new negotiating formulas; and provide the trade and investment community with a comprehensive reading of regulatory requirements and restrictions in foreign markets.

3. Needed: operational, sector-specific, emergency safeguard measures[28]

Few issues have proven more immune to rule-making advances than that of emergency safeguard measures (ESMs). The period since the end of the Uruguay Round has witnessed a depressing succession of missed deadlines on this issue. Efforts to advance a set of GATS provisions aimed at providing temporary import relief to domestic service providers that may suffer unanticipated injury or dislocation in the wake of market opening have indeed proven stillborn.

This is so for several reasons. First, because a number of WTO Members, especially developed countries, have professed outright scepticism on the very need for an ESM in services trade. This is so, they argue, in light of the flexibilities already embedded in the GATS, not least the freedom members enjoy not to schedule commitments, and the fact that the vast majority of commitments either preserve the regulatory status quo or actually bind less than prevailing market access conditions. Neither of these scenarios, it can be alleged, is likely to induce much dislocation in domestic markets.

Lack of progress can be traced, secondly, to the inability of the main (mostly developing country) proponents of a GATS ESM to identify the operational properties of such an instrument. This is so despite the generally acknowledged insurance policy attributes of a properly designed ESM and the likelihood that it could encourage developing

[28] This section draws on Sauvé (2006). For additional background on the issue of ESMs in services trade, see ch. 19 by Pierola in this volume.

countries to contemplate a higher overall level of bound commitments in services trade.

It is noteworthy that precious little progress has been made in tackling this issue in the context of preferential trade agreements. Tellingly, even the most ardent proponents of a GATS ESM – the member countries of ASEAN – have to date failed to embed an ESM within their own regional compact on services (e.g. the Asian Free Trade Agreement, or AFTA).

Still, there arguably remains much scope for useful experimentation on the issue of an ESM, perhaps more so at the regional level given that the negotiating stalemate on this issue seems deeply entrenched at the WTO level despite calls for a negotiated solution by the end of the Doha Round.

3.1. Requirements for forward movement

For forward movement to prove possible on the issue of a services ESM, it would be important that four elements be taken into account. First, it is important to acknowledge that service sectors differ significantly in the scope for – and forms of – potential liberalisation-induced dislocation. This then implies that an attempt be made to explore the scope for developing sector-specific ESMs rather than the generic, all-encompassing, instrument sought to date in GATS discussions. Tailor-made solutions may indeed be more fruitfully developed and deployed on a country, sector- and mode-specific basis under Article 18 (Additional Commitments) than through a generic catch-all instrument. Sectors that come most readily to mind in this regard include financial and distribution (retail) services.

Second, an ESM need not (and ideally should not) apply to all modes of transacting services. *A contrario*, it should be tailored to the particularities of specific sectors. Experience suggests that the mode of supplying services that is most likely to generate significant, potentially injurious, dislocations in domestic services markets is that relating to commercial presence, or mode 3 of GATS.

The stringent regulation and limited mobility of mode 4 service suppliers (temporary movement of service suppliers) make it an unlikely source of serious unanticipated injury. Meanwhile, the generally weak (and typically status quo minus) level of market opening commitments on cross-border supply (mode 1) found in most agreements covering services trade would appear to minimise the scope for significant cross-border-induced dislocation. Finally, mode 2 – consumption abroad, does not seem particularly relevant to the discussion of a services ESM from an importing country perspective. This so given the sectors – education, health, tourism – that such trade chiefly involves and the difficulties countries face in curtailing it (should they be prone to do so).

The question remains, however, whether dislocation induced through the operations of an established foreign supplier can be likened to an 'import surge' triggering safeguard action. In turn, this raises what could be likened to an assignment problem that may have in part fuelled OECD member country scepticism towards the ESM issue: whether the most appropriate policy response to investment-induced dislocation may reside in the application of competition rather than trade policy remedies.

Third, a services ESM should only be allowed to be invoked in instances where actual, *de novo*, liberalisation has taken place, such that a causal link between new market opening and potential injury can be readily established. And fourth, it is essential that any operative safeguard be triggered through recourse to market outcomes that can be properly measured and for which statistical information is both available and robust.[29]

3.2. A useful precedent?

It is in a PTA context, notably the financial services chapter of the 1994 North American Free Trade Agreement (NAFTA), that one example of an operational ESM (or ESM-type) instrument can be found. Prior to negotiating the NAFTA, Mexico's financial sector had been characterised by a complete absence of foreign competition, the country's financial system having been nationalised in the wake of the debt crisis of the early 1980s. At the time of the NAFTA negotiations (1991–1993), only one US bank, Citigroup, maintained a representative office in Mexico, which it used not to engage in banking services but rather to provide consulting services to the Mexican government on matters relating to the management and rescheduling of its external debt.

Not surprisingly, and despite the fact that it had already decided to embark on far-reaching reforms and (domestic) liberalisation of its financial sector at the time of the NAFTA talks, Mexico harboured genuine fears over the potential impact of external liberalisation on its

[29] This in itself can represent a daunting task given the paucity of sufficiently disaggregated data on services trade.

domestic financial system, many of whose leading institutions were saddled with high levels of non-performing assets and lagged their North American competitors in terms of competitiveness and financial innovation.

Accordingly, the Mexican negotiators proposed that their country's seven-year transition towards free trade in financial services under NAFTA would be accompanied by a right to temporarily suspend the issuing of new bank, securities or insurance licences if the share of financial assets under foreign control exceeded 25 per cent of aggregate assets at any point during the transition. Once passed, this threshold allowed Mexico to suspend the issuance of new licences for a period of up to two years, allowing domestic players some space to pursue a consolidation strategy and address their competitiveness problems. Under the terms of the financial services chapter, Mexico reserved the right to invoke such a safeguard only once during the seven-year transition period.

3.3. Lessons from the NAFTA experience

The Mexican example under NAFTA is useful in at least three regards for the purposes of its replication in other PTAs and its possible adoption under GATS. First, and perhaps most importantly, is the fact that the safeguard mechanism was clearly instrumental in raising Mexico's comfort level and allowing it to agree to a full liberalisation of its hitherto closed financial system. The NAFTA experience clearly demonstrated the 'insurance policy' dimension of an ESM.

Secondly, it is notable that Mexico never invoked the NAFTA safeguard during its seven-year transition period. This is so even as the share of financial assets under foreign control rather quickly came to exceed the 25 per cent threshold as a result of foreign takeovers of Mexican financial institutions. The level of foreign ownership of the country's financial system is today more than three times higher than the NAFTA threshold.

A third element of importance was the fact that the safeguard could be made operational through reliance on a statistical measure that was credible, objective and could be readily supplied by the country's central bank.

When the DDA resumes, it is likely that, alongside the issue of domestic regulation (the so-called Article VI:4 work programme dealing with the trade impact of non-discriminatory domestic regulation), the issue of a GATS ESM will assume renewed significance in outstanding rule-making discussions.[30] Services negotiators would do well to use the current lull in WTO discussions to assess the case for experimenting with an ESM on a sectoral basis before seeking, if necessary, a generic, horizontal, solution in future negotiating rounds.

4. Squaring a difficult circle: Mode 4 trade

The Doha Work Programme for services usefully calls for a review to be undertaken prior to the conclusion of the DDA to assess the degree to which WTO Members have complied with their pledge to schedule commitments in sectors and modes of supply of priority interest to developing countries. Such a review will likely exert meaningful – and much needed – political pressure on developed countries to live up to their promise of placing development at the heart of the current negotiating round. While the Doha Round is already littered with a number of *rendez-vous manqués* on development-related issues, one question that is certain to come up in this regard concerns the treatment of labour mobility, so-called mode 4 of GATS.

The very basis for international trade, be it of goods or services (including factors of production), is to exploit differences in relative prices flowing from diverging factor endowments. The larger such differences, the greater the likely gains from opening up international trade. In the case of mode 4 trade, recent policy research has shown that significant returns could be reaped from liberalisation if medium- and less-skilled workers, who are relatively abundant in developing countries, were allowed to move and provide their services on a temporary basis in developed countries (or indeed in higher income developing countries, as has been the case most notably in South-East Asia and the Gulf States).[31] Studies show that the gains from even a modest liberalisation of mode 4 trade could exceed those expected to flow from a full elimination of barriers to merchandise trade.[32]

[30] The other two outstanding rule-making issues under GATS, dealing respectively with rules governing the multilateral procurement of services and subsidy disciplines for services trade have revealed a fairly broad collective preference for regulatory inaction on the part of WTO Members.

[31] See Winters (2003). [32] See Winters (2005).

4.1. *A limited Uruguay Round harvest*

Mode 4 of the GATS concerns the temporary movement of natural persons linked to the supply of services, from one Member of the WTO to another Member. Mode 4 is by far the smallest mode of service delivery in terms of both trade flows and the level of scheduled commitments made in the Uruguay Round. Similar patterns hold at the PTA level, where things have recently taken a turn for the worse with the decision of US negotiators to eschew commitments on the movement of service providers in its most recent set of PTAs.[33]

The limited commitments made to date under mode 4 refer almost exclusively to higher-level personnel, and especially to intracorporate transferees, whose mobility is essentially an adjunct of investment liberalisation. For the most part, existing commitments have had limited significance for the majority of developing countries since their comparative advantage lies primarily in low- and medium-skilled labour-intensive services or in the movement of independent (including contract-based) service providers in higher-skilled activities.

A key priority in services for many developing countries under the Doha Development Agenda is to see greater liberalisation of the right of workers to move temporarily to provide services abroad. Constraints on the cross-border movement of service suppliers rank among the most important existing asymmetries in commitments under the GATS. Multilateral liberalisation of trade in services through mode 4 constitutes a key unfinished development agenda of the Uruguay Round. It is also an essential element of any balanced and development-oriented outcome of the current multilateral trade negotiations.

4.2. *Avoiding confusion: Temporary mobility is not migration*

The temporary movement of workers that is under discussion in trade agreements must not be confused with migration since the workers it concerns will remain long-term residents in their home countries. But the ability to care for the elderly, design software, operate ships or engage in construction work at (or near) American, European or Japanese wages

[33] This trend commenced with the FTA entered into with Australia, which was completed in 2004 and came into force on 1 January 2005. The US–Chile FTA, which entered into force on 1 January 2004, was thus the last US PTA to feature a Chapter dedicated to the temporary admission of business people.

would immeasurably increase the incomes of mobile workers from developing countries.[34]

Sending service suppliers abroad on a temporary basis can help a developing country reduce pressure on domestic labour markets while increasing capital flows and helping build human capital. Remittances from abroad can be an important source of revenue. In the case of Bangladesh, for instance, worker remittances totalled US$ 3.86 billion in 2004–2005. This represented almost 4 per cent of GDP and one-third of gross export earnings.[35]

But there are also some risks. When skilled personnel go abroad, the sending country loses not just their skills but also the resources invested in their education and training. However, these risks may be lessened by the temporary nature of mode 4 movement if ways are found – and incentives deployed – to ensure the return of temporary workers to their home countries (so-called brain circulation).

Workers' repatriated earnings in the form of remittances transferred to their home countries are an important way of generating investment and savings and promoting accelerated development of the domestic economy. Remittances have in recent years emerged as one of the most stable, continuous, and counter-cyclical sources of development finance in developing countries. For many developing countries, particularly poorer ones, such flows dwarf FDI and aid as sources of external funding.[36] Furthermore, as workers return to their home countries after temporary employment abroad, the knowledge and experience acquired abroad can stimulate the growth of domestic service sectors and enhance sending countries' ability to assimilate and apply new technologies.

For receiving countries, bringing people in temporarily to provide services can help improve competitiveness and provide short-term relief for labour market shortages. However, care must be taken to ensure that the downward pressures that may be exerted on the wages of unskilled workers are properly mitigated and that the potential social consequences of a greater influx of foreign workers on housing markets and on access to public services such as health and education are properly addressed.

An important challenge in trade agreements is thus to separate mode 4 trade (of a temporary character) from immigration-related matters so as to mitigate the difficult and often highly emotive political and cultural

[34] See Winters (2003). [35] See World Bank (2006). [36] See World Bank (2003; 2006).

issues that can hamper realisation of the full benefits of facilitated temporary entry for home and host countries alike.

4.3. Tempering the temptation for irrational mode 4 expectations

While developing countries are pinning high hopes on mode 4 liberalisation in the DDA, it is essential that such expectations be kept rational. Mode 4 liberalisation faces three daunting challenges, all of which recall the difficulty of meeting developing country expectations at the trade negotiating table, especially at the multilateral level.

A first challenge stems from the inherently cyclical nature of labour markets (i.e. the demand for labour), and the corresponding reluctance of labour market and immigration officials in receiving countries to take on significant quasi-permanent legal commitments in a trade policy setting. Almost by definition, such concerns imply precaution-induced commitments that are typically scheduled at a significantly lower level than host economies' actual (or historical) needs for temporary labour.

A second challenge arising specifically at the WTO level stems from the obligation under GATS to extend liberalisation commitments on a most-favoured nation treatment basis. This is a privilege many WTO Members may be reluctant to bestow on foreign workers, particularly in lower- to medium-skilled worker categories. Recourse to bilateral guest-worker programmes and labour cooperation agreements remain important – and typically the preferred (and perhaps preferable) policy options in this regard.

A third challenge owes to the inherent bias in trade discussions towards the movement of highly-skilled personnel, much of it deployed in the context of foreign direct investment activity abroad. Such a bias clearly favours capital exporting countries, a small (if growing) minority of which consists of developing countries.

Much attention has been paid by developing country stakeholders in the DDA in trying to de-link modes 3 and 4 so as to focus on worker categories (medium-skilled) and types (independent contract-based workers) that more clearly match the comparative advantage of a greater number of developing countries.

Seeking to pigeon-hole temporary access to labour markets in a multilateral trade policy setting, and to address those worker categories whose enhanced temporary mobility would make the greatest impact on poverty reduction, is thus far from easy. Doing so has become harder still since the horrific events of 11 September 2001, and in light of the growing controversy that surrounds migration debates in most parts of the world.[37]

Forward progress on the issue of temporary labour mobility may thus be more feasible – and its potential downsides more easily contained – under bilateral (guest-worker) or plurilateral labour market agreements than in the WTO.

4.4. *Acknowledging the systemic consequences of multilateral blockage*

The systemic downsides that stem from the above considerations are clear enough. They are also alarming, as they point to a likely continued modal imbalance in commitments – the WTO secretariat estimates that commitments on mode 3 are twenty-five to fifty times more commercially significant than those on mode 4.

Such imbalances have arguably become worse for those middle-income countries that are blessed with the dual ability to supply skilled workers to world markets (via mode 4 trade) and to compete in the market for remotely supplied business services (via mode 1 trade).[38] Both forms of trade have come to elicit, for different reasons, growing disquiet in many OECD countries.[39]

Imbalances of this type are likely to provide ready ammunition to developing countries in arguing that demands for improved access conditions in sectors and modes of supply of primary interest to them continue to go unheeded. Such imbalances may thus well exert negative effects within GATS, leading to fewer developing country commitments on mode 3-related issues than sound development considerations would otherwise dictate. They could also spill over beyond the GATS to other negotiating areas where North-South divides are particularly pronounced, such as in discussions on non-agricultural market access (NAMA).

[37] A worrisome development in this regard is the refusal of the United States government, on orders from Congress, to address the issue of mode 4 trade in its preferential trade agreements. Indeed, since the 2004 FTA with Austalia, no US FTA has featured a Chapter on the temporary entry of business people such as was found in the NAFTA or the US–Chile or US–Singapore FTAs. The United States has, not surprisingly, shown an unwillingness to make significant improvements to its mode 4 commitments under GATS.

[38] See Chanda (2006). [39] See Mattoo and Wunsch-Vincent (2004).

4.5. *Exploring the scope for forward movement in the WTO*

While obstacles to a bigger bargain on mode 4 of GATS are significant, there remains undeniable scope for progress in the DDA and in subsequent WTO negotiating rounds, all the more so as the forces underlying possible bargains are not about to abate: population ageing and acute labour shortages in certain occupational categories in the labour markets of advanced industrial countries and even of some emerging economies (e.g. China); the need for globally active firms to deploy their most precious asset – human capital – in an effective manner around the world; and a rising supply of workers (in all skill categories) from developing countries.

A development-friendly outcome on mode 4 in the Doha Round should thus target a number of elements, among which: (i) a broader range of service providers eligible for temporary entry, so as to include independent workers and contractual service providers de-linked from mode 3 commitments; (ii) the elimination of economic needs tests or a progressive reduction of their incidence by making them more predictable through the establishment of common, transparent, criteria; (iii) simplification, streamlining and easing of the process of granting temporary entry visas, work permits and licensing requirements and procedures; and (iv) facilitating the recognition of professional qualifications, including through mutual recognition agreements and horizontal application of the GATS guidelines on accountancy to other regulated professions.

4.6. *Towards a coherent approach to human mobility*

The above disussion suggests that developing country expectations on labour mobility issues, particularly in regard to lower- and medium-skilled worker categories, cannot readily be met in a trade policy setting, especially so at the WTO level. For this very reason, it is essential, not least on coherence grounds, that when the DDA resumes, developing countries be sent clear signals that the international community will devote the resources and commit to building the collective action institutions required for a more comprehensive treatment of the manifold challenges – economic, social and cultural – arising from the rising incidence of cross-border migration, both legal and illegal.[40]

[40] See the summary report of the Global Commission on International Migration (2005).

A broad human mobility agenda cannot be tackled by trade policy alone, but there is a complementary role that trade agreements can usefully play so long as expectations remain rational and that determined efforts are made in non-trade policy settings to tackle the need in sending and receiving countries for comprehensive solutions to what are all at once pressing, highly complex and ever sensitive development, labour market and demographic challenges.

5. Concluding remarks

This chapter takes stock of what has arguably been two frustrating decades of attempts at prying open services markets and at developing and refining the trade disciplines required to do so.

Yet a glass half empty is always and everywhere a glass half full, and it is important to recall that significant forward movement has been achieved over the past two decades in our understanding of the economics of services trade and of the legal translation deriving therefrom.

Forward movement is notable in respect of a collective appreciation of both the large development dividends likely to be reaped from well conceived and implemented service sector reforms and of the considerable difficulty of getting such reforms right, given the innate complexity of services markets, the ubiquitous nature of market failures affecting their operation and the continued novelty of the subject matter. That services liberalisation has tended to proceed at a slow, ponderous, precaution-induced pace, particularly at the multilateral level, should hardly surprise. The services field, indeed, continues to be characterised by significant doses of learning by doing.

Yet it is precisely because the potential gains from market opening in services are so significant that special care must be given to identifying how best to secure them and to overcome some of the roadblocks standing in the way of development-friendly outcomes at the trade negotiating table. This chapter has directed attention to a number of those roadblocks and advanced ideas on how best to impart renewed impetus to services negotiations wherever these may be pursued.

The chapter suggests that political economy goes a long way towards providing answers to the questions of who negotiates, on whose behalf, in what manner, and on what issues. Such answers on the whole appear to substantiate the chapter's premise that collective attitudes towards services negotiations (as opposed to unilateral conduct) continue to be shaped by strong doses of regulatory and bureaucratic precaution.

For the trade negotiating process to play more of a leading role in service sector policy reforms, this chapter argues that officials will need to think outside the box on a number of issues. These include: (i) embracing collective, multi-sectoral approaches to market opening and focusing negotiating efforts on a limited subset of clusters that complement recent or ongoing advances in goods trade and whose development pay-off appears particularly important (i.e. logistics/trade facilitation services and ICT-related services); (ii) experimenting with sector-specific emergency safeguard measures as a means to raise comfort levels over enhanced liberalisation commitments; and (iii) tempering expectations on far-reaching multilateral advances in respect of mode 4 trade while advancing concerted collective action responses to the manifold (and mostly non-trade-centric) challenge of human mobility.

Bibliography

Adlung, Rudolf (2004), 'The GATS Turns Ten: A Preliminary Stocktaking', Staff Working Papers ERSD 2004–05 (Geneva: World Trade Organization).

Adlung, Rudolf and Martin Roy (2005), 'Turning Hills into Mountains? Current Commitments under the GATS and Prospects for Change', Staff Working Papers ERSD 2005–01 (Geneva: World Trade Organization).

Blouin, Chantal, Nick Drager and Richard Smith (eds.) (2005), *International Trade in Services and the GATS: Current Issues and Debates* (Washington, DC: The World Bank, 2005).

Chanda, Rupa (2006), 'Inter-Modal Linkages in Services Trade', OECD Trade Directorate Working Paper, No. 30, TD/TC/WP(2004)41/FINAL, Paris: Organization for Economic Co-operation and Development, (27 January).

Dee, Philippa (2003), 'Modelling the Policy Issues in Services Trade', *Economie Internationale* 94–95 (2003), pp. 283–300.

Evans, Peter C. (2002), *Liberalizing Global Trade in Energy Services*, AEI Studies on Services Trade Negotiations, American Enterprise Institute, Washington DC, available at: www.aei.org/books/bookID.154,filter.all/book_detail.asp

Gao, Henry (2006), 'Evaluating Alternative Approaches to GATS Negotiations', Paper prepared for the World Trade Forum, World Trade Institute, Berne, Switzerland (8–9 September) (ch. 8 in this volume).

Global Commission on International Migration (2005), 'Migration in an Interconnected World: New Directions for Action', Geneva: Global Commision on International Migration.

Hoekman, Bernard (1995), 'Assessing the General Agreement on Trade in Services', in Will Martin and L. Alan Winters (eds.), *The Uruguay Round and the Developing Countries* (Washington, DC: The World Bank, 1995).

Kelly, Clare (2006), 'Negotiating Approaches from a Member's Perspective', Paper prepared for the World Trade Forum, World Trade Institute, Berne, Switzerland (8–9 September) (ch. 7 in this volume).

Krajewski, Markus (2003), *National Regulation and Trade Liberalization in Services. The Legal Impact of the General Agreement on Trade in Services (GATS) on National Regulatory Autonomy* (The Hague, London, New York: Kluwer Law International, 2003).

Marchetti, Juan and Petros Mavroidis (2004), 'What are the Main Challenges for the GATS Framework? Don't Talk about Revolution', *European Business Organization Law Review* 5 (2004), pp. 511–562.

McGuire, C. and M. Schuele (2000), 'Restrictiveness of International Trade in Banking Services', in C. Findlay and T. Warren, (eds.), *Impediments to Trade in Services: Measurement and Policy Implications* (London and New York: Routledge, 2000), pp. 201–214.

Mattoo, Aaditya (2003), 'Services in a Development Round', in *The World Trade Brief* (London: Agenda Publishing, September 2003), pp. 61–62.

——(2006), 'Services in a Development Round: Proposals for Overcoming Inertia', in Richard Newfarmer (ed.), *Trade, Doha and Development: A Window on the Issues* (Washington, DC: The World Bank, 2006), pp. 161–174.

Mattoo, A., R. Rathindran and A. Subramanian (2001), 'Measuring Services Trade Liberalization and its Impact on Economic Growth: An Illustration', World Bank Policy Research Working Paper No. 2380, World Bank, Washington, DC

Mattoo, Aaditya, Sumanta Chaudhuri and Richard Self (2003), 'Liberalizing Mode 4: A Possible Approach', Paper presented at an OECD–World Bank–IOM Seminar on Trade and Migration, Geneva (12–14 November).

Mattoo, Aaditya and Pierre Sauvé (eds.) (2003), *Domestic Regulation and Services Trade Liberalization* (Washington, DC: Oxford University Press for the World Bank, 2003).

Mattoo, A. and S. Wunsch-Vincent (2004), 'Pre-Empting Protectionism in Services: The GATS and Outsourcing', *Journal of International Economic Law* 7 (2004), pp. 765–800.

OECD (2002), 'GATS: The Case for Open Services Markets', Paris, Organization for Economic Co-operation and Development.

OECD (2003), 'Services Liberalisation: Identifying Opportunities and Gains – Part II: Modelling the Benefits of Services Trade Liberalisation', TD/TC/WP (2003)23/Part2/Rev1, Paris: OECD (22 September).

OECD (2005), 'Opening Up Trade in Services: Crucial for Economic Growth', Policy Brief, Paris: OECD, (September).

Panizzon, Marion (2006), 'How Human Rights Violations Nullify and Impair GATS Commitments', Paper prepared for the World Trade Forum, World Trade Institute, Berne, Switzerland (8–9 September) (ch. 24 in this volume).

Piérola, Fernando (2006), 'A Safeguard Regime for GATS', Paper prepared for the World Trade Forum, World Trade Institute, Berne, Switzerland (8–9 September) (ch. 19 in this volume).

Robinson, S., Z. Wang and W. Martin (1999), 'Capturing the Implications of Services Trade Liberalization', Paper presented at the Second Annual Conference on Global Economic Analysis, Ebberup, Denmark (June 20–22).

Roy, Martin, Juan Marchetti and Aik Hoe Lim (2006), 'The Race towards Preferential Trade Agreements in Services: How much Market Access is Really Achieved?', Paper prepared for the World Trade Forum, World Trade Institute, Berne, Switzerland (8–9 September) (ch. 3 in this volume).

Sauvé, Pierre (2002), 'Completing the GATS Framework: Addressing Uruguay Round Leftovers', *Aussenwirtschaft*, 57(3) (2002), pp. 310–341.

——(2002a), 'Trade, Education and the GATS: What's In, What's Out, What's All the Fuss About?', *Higher Education Management and Policy* 14(3) (2002), pp. 48–80.

——(2006), 'Services and the Doha Development Agenda: Southern Perspectives', in P. Van Dyck and G. Faber (eds.), *Completing the Doha Round* (London: Routledge, 2006).

Sauvé, Pierre, and Barbara Fliess (1998), 'Of Chips, Floppy Disks and Great Timing: Assessing the WTO Information Technology Agreement', *Les Cahiers de l'IFRI*, No. 26, Paris: Institut Français des Relations Internationales.

Sauvé, Pierre, and Christopher Wilkie (2000), 'Investment Liberalization in GATS', in Pierre Sauvé and Robert M. Stern (eds.), *GATS 2000: New Directions in Services Trade Liberalization* (Washington, DC: Brookings Institution Press and Centre for Business and Government, Harvard University, 2000), pp. 331–363.

Sinclair, Scott (2000), 'GATS: How the WTO's New Services Negotiations Threaten Democracy', Reports and Studies, Ottawa: Canadian Center for Policy Alternatives.

Sinclair, Scott and Jim Grieshaber-Otto (2002), 'Facing the Facts: A Guide to the GATS Debates', Reports and Studies, Ottawa: Canadian Center for Policy Alternatives.

te Velde, Dirk Willem (2005), 'Revitalizing Services Negotiations at the WTO: Can Technical Assistance Help?', London: Overseas Development Institute, (December).

Thompson, Rachel (2000), 'Formula Approaches to Improving GATS Commitments', in Pierre Sauvé and Robert M. Stern (eds.), *GATS 2000: New Directions in Services Trade Liberalization* (Washington, DC: Brookings Institution Press and Centre for Business and Government, Harvard University, 2000), pp. 473–486.

Türk, Elisabeth (2006), 'Services post-Hong Kong – Initial Experiences with Plurilaterals', Paper prepared for the World Trade Forum, World Trade Institute, Berne, Switzerland (8–9 September) (ch. 6 in this volume).

United Nations (2005), 'Trade for Development', A Background Report prepared for the UN Millennium Project, New York: United Nations (see chapter 4 on services).

Winters, L. Alan (2003), 'The Economic Implications of Liberalizing Mode 4 Trade', in Aaditya Mattoo and Antonia Carzaniga (eds.), *Moving People to Deliver Services* (Washington, DC: Oxford University Press for the World Bank, 2003).

——(2005), 'Developing Country proposals for the Liberalization of Movements of Natural Service Providers', Development Research Centre on Migration, Globalisation and Development, University of Sussex (January).

World Bank (2001), 'Global Economic Prospects and the Developing Economies' 2002, Washington, DC.

World Bank (2003), 'Global Economic Prospects and the Developing Economies 2004', Washington, DC.

World Bank (2006), 'Global Economic Prospects 2006: Economic Implications of Remittances and Migration', Washington, D.C: The World Bank.

WTO (2001), 'GATS: Fact and Fiction', Geneva, World Trade Organization.

——(2005), *Doha Work Programme: Ministerial Declaration*, Adopted on 18 December 2005, WT/MIN(05)/DEC, Geneva: World Trade Organization (22 December).

——(2006), *Recommendations of the Task Force on Aid for Trade*, WT/AFT/1, Geneva: World Trade Organization (27 July).

INDEX